AF394384

Footprints from the Past

The south-eastern extramural settlement of Roman Alchester and rural occupation in its hinterland: the archaeology of East West Rail Phase 1

by Andrew Simmonds and Steve Lawrence

with contributions by
*Enid Allison, Edward Biddulph, Paul Booth, Loïc Boscher, Lee G Broderick,
Dana Challinor, Michael Donnelly, Lynne Keys, Lauren McIntyre,
Marcos Martinón-Torres, Julia Meen, Gwladys Monteil, Rebecca Nicholson,
Cynthia Poole, Alice Rose, Mairead Rutherford, Ian R Scott,
Ruth Shaffrey and Elizabeth Stafford*

Illustrated by
Gary Jones, Sophie Lamb, Conan Parsons, Charles Rousseaux, Magdalena Wachnik

Oxford Archaeology Monograph No. 28
2018

The publication of this volume was generously funded by Chiltern Railways and Network Rail
Published by Oxford Archaeology as part of the Oxford Archaeology Monograph series

Designed by Oxford Archaeology Graphics Office

Edited by Edward Biddulph

Thus book is part of a series of monographs that can be bought from all good bookshops
and internet bookshops. For more information visit www.oxfordarchaeology.com

Front cover: Footprint of a young child or toddler on a roof tile from Building 7640 at Langford Lane East,
within the south-eastern extramural settlement of Alchester
Back cover: Middle Iron Age crucible from South of Oddington Crossing

ISBN 978-0-904220-82-7

Typeset by Production Line, Oxford
Printed in Great Britain by Short Run Press Ltd, Exeter, England

Contents

List of Figures

Chapter 3

List of Tables

Chapter 4

Chapter 5

Summary

This volume presents the results of archaeological investigations undertaken by Oxford Archaeology in relation to a programme of improvements to the railway between Bicester and Oxford. The investigations were commissioned by Chiltern Railway Company Ltd (Chiltern Railways), who, assisted by Network Rail, undertook the East-West Rail Phase 1 Bicester to Oxford Improvements.

Following desk-based assessment and field evaluation, eight areas were selected for archaeological mitigation. The largest and most complex part of the project was located at Langford Lane, where a road diversion and overbridge were to be constructed around the southern edge of the scheduled monument of Alchester Roman town to replace the existing road, which hitherto extended across he north-eastern part of the scheduled area. Archaeological mitigation in this area comprised a detailed excavation of the footprint of two cable trenches that extended into the scheduled monument and evaluation of the alignment of the new road, followed by detailed excavation of two areas (Langford Lane East and Langford Lane South) and a watching brief during construction of part of the road alignment within an area of the scheduled monument.

Evidence for activity during the early part of the prehistoric period was scarce, reflecting the limited archaeologically detectable impact of populations of this date, although a notable find was a broken core tool that may date to the Palaeolithic or Mesolithic periods. Sedentary occupation may have begun during the middle Iron Age, and four excavations uncovered parts of settlements of this period. These may have included both open and enclosed settlements, and three were situated in close proximity to cropmark evidence for possibly contemporary ditched enclosures. An enclosure ditch at South of Oddington Crossing contained a dump of debris from copper and iron working that included fragments from at least two crucibles.

The investigations at Langford Lane uncovered parts of two successive Roman roads to Dorchester-on-Thames, *c* 25km south of Alchester. The earlier road by-passed the eastern side of Otmoor and was replaced by a more direct route across the middle of the moor at the end of the 1st century. Settlement beside the earlier road, excavated at Langford Lane East, may have been a successor to a pre-Roman settlement and appears from artefactual evidence to have been of relatively high status during the initial, military phase, although no contemporary structural evidence was found. Stone-founded buildings were constructed during the late 1st-early 2nd century, including a probable strip building and two single-celled structures of uncertain function that may represent a gatehouse or a pair of shrines. The buildings were demolished by *c* AD 200. There was little evidence for industrial activity and it is possible that the extramural settlement was partly rural in character, engaged in farming the surrounding land. An insight into the diverse lives of the inhabitants is provided by finds that include part of a priestly headdress, two pairs of slave shackles and a group of roof tiles bearing the footprints of a young child. The landscape around the town appears to have been intensively managed for agricultural production, being divided into a pattern of rectilinear fields or pastures that were bounded by drainage ditches, some of which were designed to channel the natural watercourses that crossed the area.

At Langford Lane South, features beside the later road may have been part of either a second extramural area that extended alongside the road that extended across Otmoor to Dorchester or a discrete farming establishment. Occupation here began later than at Langford Lane East but likewise ended around the start of the 3rd century, and comprised successive arrangements of enclosures that were most likely used for livestock management. No buildings were identified but two large pits contained domestic refuse and building material.

Parts of three contemporary rural settlements of differing forms were excavated at South of Merton, Holts Farm Crossing and North of Oxford Parkway Station. The character of the site at South of Merton was difficult to ascertain, although an alignment of substantial postholes may be part of a large building on the frontage of the road from Alchester to Dorchester-on-Thames. The farmstead at Holts Farm Crossing appears to have always been of low status but was the most long-lived settlement investigated, with continuous occupation that extended from the middle Iron Age to the middle-late Roman period. The area excavated at North of Oxford Parkway Station formed part of an extensive agricultural landscape that had been recorded from cropmark evidence; a group of rectilinear enclosures, possibly animal pens, was succeeded by an arrangement of fields focused on a trackway associated with a settlement 400-500m to the south-west. None of the rural settlements appear to have continued long into the 3rd century.

Acknowledgements

The authors would like to thank Chiltern Railways and Network Rail for funding the archaeological fieldwork, post-excavation programme and publication. Particular mention is warranted for Chris Brooks of Network Rail for facilitating and supporting the excavation programme. Thanks are also extended to Environmental Resources Management as the client's consultants overseeing the programme of works. The authors are also grateful to Richard Oram, the Planning Archaeologist for Cherwell District at Oxfordshire County Council, for his support throughout the project. The same gratitude is extended to Chris Welch, Inspector of Ancient Monuments, and David Wilkinson, Assistant Inspector of Ancient Monuments, at Historic England for their advice and support with regards to the scheduled monument works at Alchester.

The project was managed by Steve Lawrence. The fieldwork, at both evaluation and mitigation stages, was directed by Jim Mumford, except for the excavations at Langford Lane South and South of Merton, which were supervised respectively by Alex Latham and Conan Parsons. The post-excavation programme was managed by Andrew Simmonds. Support was provided by Leigh Allen (finds management), Matt Bradley (geomatics management), Louise Loe (burials management), Rebecca Nicholson (environmental management), Nicola Scott (archives management) and Magdalena Wachnik (graphics management).

The project could not have been completed without the hard work of the many other Oxford Archaeology staff who contributed to the project, both in the field and during the post-excavation analysis. Gary Jones plotted the cropmarks for Figures 2.50, 2.52-5 and 2.58 and prepared the site plans for Chapter 2; Charles Rousseaux drew the other Chapter 2 figures, as well as drawing the pottery, metal and glass finds, crucibles and worked flint. Magdalena Wachnik took the photographs of the finds and Sophie Lamb drew the ceramic building materials. Conan Parsons created the orthomosaic of Langford Lane East for Figure 2.10. Thanks are also due to Dana Goodburn-Brown of CSI: Sittingbourne for the cleaning and conservation of the Roman coins. The authors would also like to thank Charlotte Malone, who helped to locate the photographs reproduced in Figures 1.4, 1.5 and 1.6. The report was edited for publication by Edward Biddulph.

Gwladys Monteil would like thank Brenda Dickinson and Geoffrey Dannell for providing much help and open access to their archives.

The authors are especially grateful to Professor Michael Fulford for reading and commenting on the draft text. Any errors, however, remain the responsibility of the authors alone.

Chapter 1

Introduction

PROJECT BACKGROUND

This volume presents the results of archaeological investigations that were undertaken in relation to a programme of improvements to the railway between Bicester and Oxford known as East West Rail (EWR) Phase 1. Oxford Archaeology was commissioned to carry out these investigations by Chiltern Railway Company Ltd (Chiltern Railways), who, assisted by Network Rail, were responsible for East West Rail Phase 1 works as authorised by the Secretary of State through the Chiltern Railways (Bicester to Oxford Improvements) Order 2012. This Transport and Works Act Order authorised the construction and operation of an improved railway between Bicester and Oxford. The Order was accompanied by a planning direction (or 'deemed planning permission') granted by the Secretary of State, which was subject to a number of conditions. In particular, Condition 9 of the deemed planning permission required that 'development shall not commence in respect of any Individual Section until a Written Scheme of Investigation (WSI) of archaeological potential within that Section has been submitted to and approved in writing by the local planning authority and such elements of that WSI as the local planning authority considers necessary before commencement of development have been implemented.' Condition 9 further required that 'construction of the replacement road from Wendlebury Road to Langford Lane and the bridge over the railway (being Work No. 11) shall not commence until details of the measures to avoid … protect … and record archaeological remains have been submitted to and approved in writing by the local planning authority … and the approved field evaluation has been completed.'

The archaeological work was undertaken ahead of and alongside the rail improvements construction programme. Permanent and temporary impacts associated with the works upon potential archaeological remains along the route were discussed with the Planning Archaeologist for Cherwell District at Oxfordshire County Council (Richard Oram), following which a proposed scheme of investigation was devised and discussed that identified locations of archaeological potential and defined a variety of methods that would be employed to evaluate, investigate and record any archaeological remains present (OA 2013). It also identified parameters for the preservation *in situ* of remains where possible. This document was submitted to and approved by

Richard Oram and the Oxford City Archaeologist, David Radford. However, the document did not specify site-specific details beyond generic approaches, and consequently detailed WSIs were required to cover the methodology for the investigations at Merton (OA 2015a) and a series of documents was produced regarding the work at Langford Lane (OA 2014a-d; 2015b-d).

Following initial desk-based assessment produced as part of an environmental statement (ERM 2009a and b) and subsequent trial trench evaluation, a combination of detailed excavation and watching brief was undertaken at one site, 'strip, map and sample' excavation at five sites, and a watching brief at one further site. The area of detailed excavation, at Langford Lane, included the footprint of two cable trenches that extended into the scheduled monument of Alchester Roman town (list entry no. 1006365). An evaluation followed by a watching brief was also undertaken during construction of a road alignment that crossed the scheduled area. Each of these investigations was completed in accordance with Scheduled Monument Consent.

LOCATION, TOPOGRAPHY AND GEOLOGY

The rail improvements were undertaken between Bicester and Oxford, most of the route extending NE-SW across the arable and pasture farmland of north-east Oxfordshire, within Cherwell District, and the southern part extending through the northern outskirts of Oxford to Oxford Station (Fig. 1.1). The excavation areas all lay within Cherwell District. This landscape forms part of a broad clay vale that extends diagonally across the county and separates the limestone hills of the Cotswolds to the north-west from the chalk of the Chilterns to the south-east. The topography of this part of the vale is predominantly level at *c* 60-65m aOD, with only minor local variations, except where it rises to *c* 100m aOD at Peartree Hill and Cutteslowe on the northern outskirts of Oxford. The railway unsurprisingly avoids these heights, however, passing between them to maintain an almost level course.

The north-eastern half of the route crosses flat land situated on Middle Jurassic Kellaways Clay, running parallel to a low and intermittent ridge of outcropping cornbrash that forms a series of domed rises on which the villages of Ambrosden, Merton, Charlton-on-Otmoor and Oddington are sited and

1

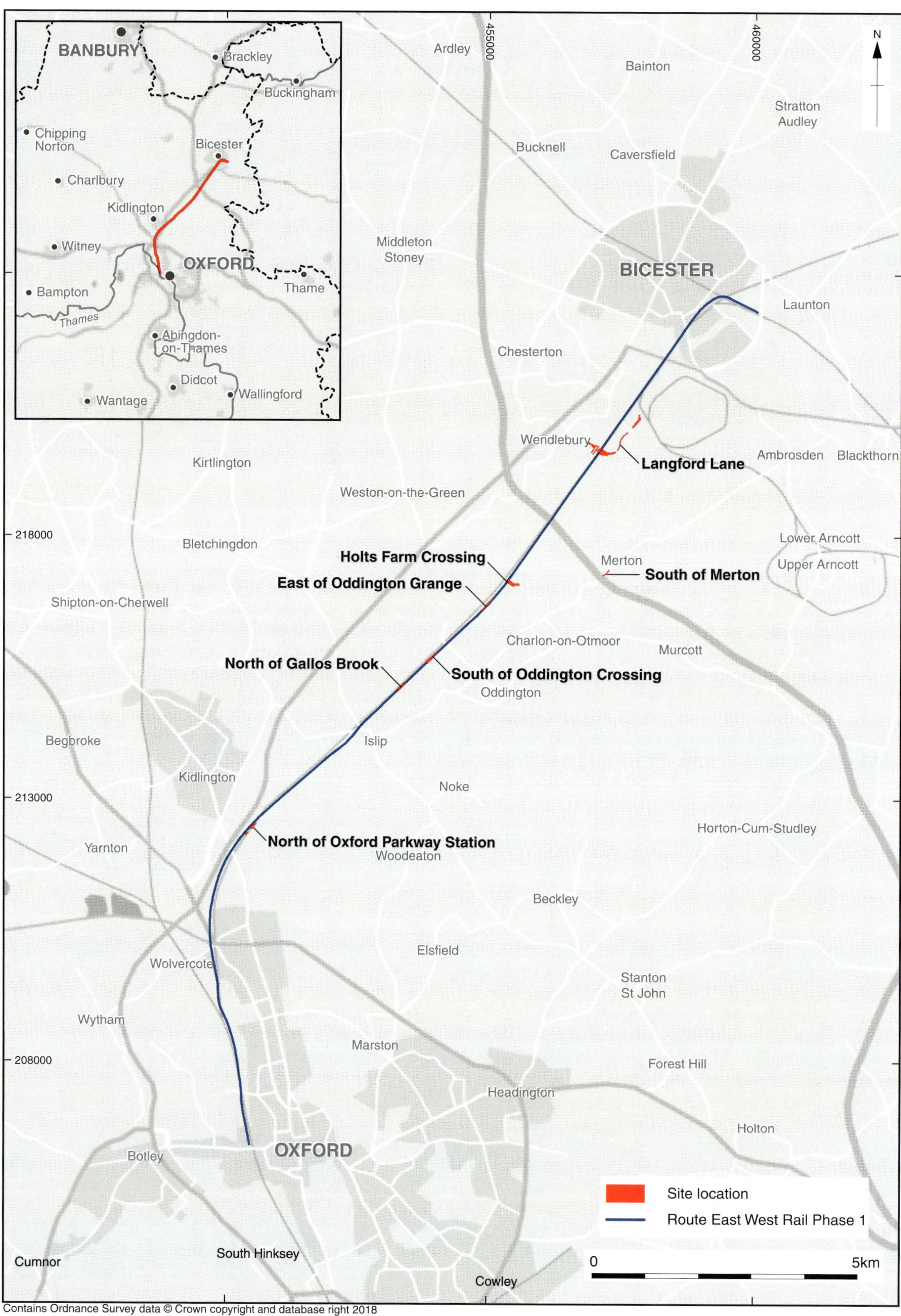

Fig. 1.1   Site location

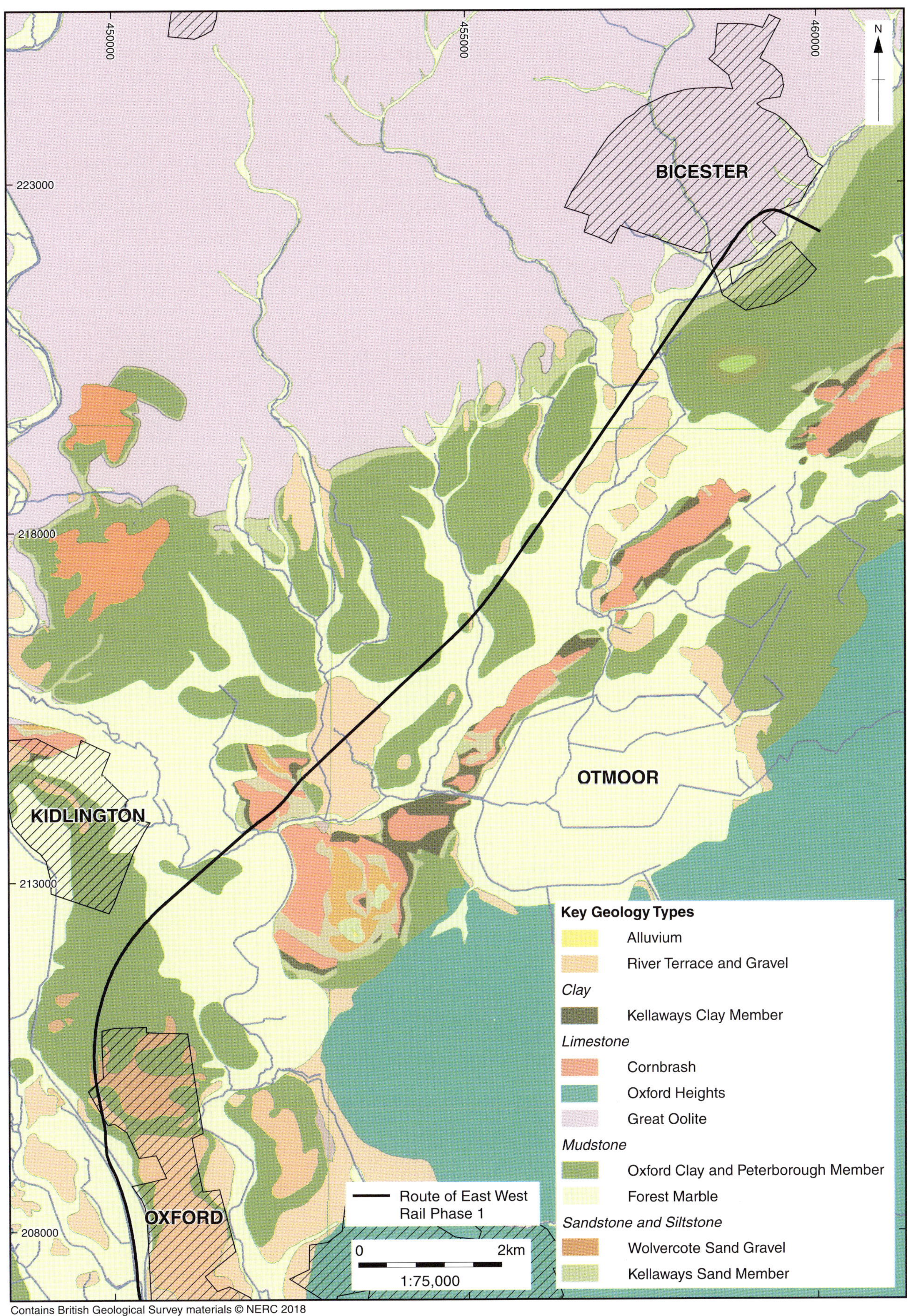

Fig. 1.2   Geology of East West Rail Phase 1

divides the main body of the clay vale from Otmoor to the south (Fig. 1.2). The impermeable character of the underlying geology has combined with the frequent flooding of the River Ray, which lies to the south of the railway, to produce a damp, poorly-drained landscape that was wetland until it was artificially drained during the early 18th century.

The uniformity of the clay is interrupted at a local level by the many minor watercourses that cross the route, predominantly draining north-south toward the River Ray, which have scoured shallow channels into the clay that are filled by alluvium and more occasional patches of gravel terrace. The most significant of these streams is the Langford Brook, which flows eastward between Bicester and Graven Hill before turning southward toward its ultimate confluence with the River Ray. Langford Brook is associated with some of the most extensive areas of gravel terrace in the project area, which encompass the site of the Roman town of Alchester and a considerable area to the south. At Alchester, the brook divides into two channels, which extend across the landscape south of the town, where the two largest excavation areas were situated. After crossing Langford Brook, the line of EWR Phase 1 crosses two of its tributary streams, the Gagle Brook, which flows west-east at Alchester, and the Wendlebury Brook, which it crosses between Wendlebury and Merton. South-west of this lie two further tributaries of the River Ray, an un-named stream west of Oddington and Gallos Brook, both of which are associated with alluvium-filled channels across the Kellaways Clay, the latter additionally flowing through an area of terrace gravel immediately east of Islip.

After Islip, the Kellaways Clay is not encountered at the surface as it is overlain by the alluvium of the Cherwell Valley, beyond which the alignment of EWR Phase 1 turns south along a tongue of Oxford Clay and gravel terrace between the Cherwell and the Thames, on which the historic core of Oxford is situated.

ARCHAEOLOGICAL BACKGROUND

The landscape through which EWR Phase 1 runs has seen relatively little previous archaeological investigation, with the exception of the extreme north-east end, where a number of excavations have taken place in relation to suburban development around the fringes of Bicester. Non-development-led investigations have been focused primarily on the Roman fort and small town at Alchester. Most of the route is rural in character and has consequently had little modern development that might result in archaeological investigations, and no significant work has been undertaken in the main, central part of the route.

Evidence for activity earlier than the middle Iron Age is relatively rare in the area, although small quantities of worked flints are not an uncommon find on excavated sites of later date. A pair of ring ditches has been excavated at Merton, both lacking a central burial but enclosing a scatter of cremation burials (Bradley *et al.* 1997). The date of the features is somewhat problematic but they are most likely early Bronze Age, although a Neolithic date has also been suggested. They are probably the remains of barrows whose mounds had been levelled by ploughing, although the internal arrangement suggests that the earthworks may have covered small cremation cemeteries rather than single burials. An apparently isolated cremation burial was excavated north of Alchester, while slightly further north a group of domestic Beaker sherds was also found, residual in a Roman pit (Booth *et al.* 2001, 423). A Beaker burial and an unurned early Bronze Age cremation burial were excavated at Whitelands Farm, further north again (Martin 2011, 185-7).

Sites of certain middle Iron Age date are limited to the north-eastern end of the EWR Phase 1 alignment, where settlements have been partly excavated at Chesterton Lane, immediately north of Alchester, and Slade Farm, within the northern part of Bicester. The site at Chesterton Lane was first identified during excavations in advance of the straightening of the A41 Oxford-Bicester road (then known as the A421), which revealed a number of Iron Age ditches overlain by Roman occupation (Harden 1937). The published report describes the Iron Age activity as 'beginning not long, if at all, before the Christian era and lasting to the middle of the first century' (ibid., 25), but re-assessment of the pottery showed that a little material was of the early Iron Age, with the majority of middle Iron Age date and a very few sherds that might be late Iron Age (Evans 2001a, 272). A larger area was examined in 1991, when the A41 was widened to form a dual carriageway and an overbridge inserted at the junction with Chesterton Lane (Booth *et al.* 2001). The excavation uncovered part of a settlement comprising at least three post-built roundhouses and a sequence of sub-rectangular enclosures. A linear boundary ditch of middle Iron Age date was recorded at Slade Farm, extending over a distance of more than 400m, alongside which lay a settlement composed of four (possibly five) ring gullies that represented roundhouses and associated animal pens (Ellis *et al.* 2000). Other sites of middle Iron Age date may be represented by undated cropmarks, including a banjo enclosure just outside the south-west corner of the Roman town at Alchester, a possible second such enclosure at East of Oddington Grange and a pair of enclosures in a field beside Gallos Brook.

The settlement at Chesterton Lane was replaced during the late Iron Age by a site 300m further north, where a group of curvilinear gullies that may have defined the locations of small buildings were replaced by a sequence of more linear boundaries (Booth *et al.* 2001, 29-36). Very little dating evidence was recovered, and none from the earliest phases, but the sequence of superimposed features suggests either a long period of occupation or a frequent reorganisation of the settlement. Further south-west, the earliest elements of a field system on the east bank of the Gagle Brook are likely to be of similar date (ibid., 424). Three late Iron Age settlements have been excavated further upstream within the floodplain of the Langford Brook, at Oxford Road, Bicester Fields Farm and Langford Park Farm (Mould 1996; Cromarty *et al.* 1999; Pine and Mundin forthcoming). The site at Oxford Road was situated in a low-lying location prone to flooding and comprised a complex of drainage and enclosure ditches and two hut circles. Closer to Alchester a site at Langford Park Farm originated as late Iron Age-early Roman enclosures close to the brook. Bicester Fields Farm was situated 300m from the confluence with the Pingle Stream and appears to have been largely pastoral in function, comprising a single roundhouse set within a rectilinear enclosure that was subsequently considerably enlarged. In contrast to the sites at Oxford Road and Langford Park Farm, occupation here did not continue into the Roman period. At the south-western end of EWR Phase 1, a penannular settlement enclosure that was excavated at Lock Crescent, Kidlington, on the terrace above the River Cherwell, was also interpreted as being pastoral in character (Booth 1997). Again, occupation does not appear to have continued long into the Roman period, if at all, and only two Roman sherds were recovered.

The Roman landscape was dominated by the fortress and subsequent town at Alchester, constructed on the west bank of the Langford Brook *c* 3.25km north of its confluence with the River Ray. The site has been recognised as a Roman settlement since at least the early 17th century, when it was noted by Camden (1607, 267), and in 1776 Stukeley produced an engraving depicting the site from the south, which clearly shows the line of the defences and the two main Roman roads meeting at a central crossroads (Fig. 1.3). The history of excavation at the site begins in 1776 with an investigation of an earthwork known as the 'Castle Mound', also visible on Stukeley's depiction, which proved to be a bathhouse with a tessellated floor and hypocaust. Further small-scale excavations during the early 20th centuries revealed details of the defences and parts of internal buildings (Hawkes 1927; Iliffe 1929; 1932). More recently, a plot of cropmarks compiled by the RCHME has provided a much clearer and more detailed understanding of the layout of the buildings within the town and the arrangement of the surrounding landscape. Details of the defences and important environmental evidence were recovered in 1975 when two trenches were excavated across the eastern rampart (Young 1975), and a research project conducted by Oxford, Leicester and Edinburgh Universities has involved a campaign of excavations in and around the town (Sauer 1998; 1999a; 1999b; 2000a; 2000b; 2001; 2002; 2003; 2004; 2005a; 2005b). The northern extramural area has been investigated in two episodes of excavation undertaken in relation to development of the A41

(Harden 1937; Booth *et al.* 2001) and an excavation at Faccenda Chicken Farm (Foreman and Rahtz 1984). A series of hand-dug trenches were excavated in 2002 at the locations of post settings for a new overhead powerline that extended across the south-eastern corner of the town and the adjacent areas (Wessex Archaeology 2002).

The earliest establishment at Alchester may have been a marching camp a short distance south-east of the main complex, although excavation was unable to establish a precise date for its construction (Sauer 1999a; 1999b). This was followed by the construction of what may have been a legionary vexillation fortress, with an unusual sub-rectangular annexe attached to its western side. Dendrochronological dating of the posts of the main gate of the annexe, which were preserved by the waterlogged ground conditions, gave dates of between October AD 44 and March AD 45, demonstrating the fortress's role as part of the immediate post-conquest deployment of Rome's British garrison (Sauer 2006, 13). The site occupied a key strategic location on the western edge of the territory of the Catuvellauni, close to the border with the Dobunni, which was probably defined by either the River Cherwell or the River Glyme. Little is known of the internal organisation of the fortress, since it is buried beneath the later town, but coin and pottery evidence suggests that it was abandoned shortly before *c* AD 70 (Sauer 2000b, 12). To the south-east of the main site lies a rectangular enclosure on the same alignment as the marching camp, accessed via a ditched trackway, that has been interpreted as a parade ground contemporary with the fortress, although excavation was unable to confirm its date (Sauer 1999a; 1999b). It is currently unclear how long an interval (if any) separated the departure of the military from the inception of civilian occupation, but buildings associated with the town were certainly in use by the late 1st century. Understanding of the character and arrangement of the buildings within the town is based predominantly on cropmark evidence, which is necessarily biased toward stone-founded structures and provides no chronological definition, potentially presenting an undifferentiated palimpsest of buildings of various date. Nevertheless, a few major buildings can be defined. A large courtyard set within the north-west angle of the central crossroads may be a public building or temple precinct, and more certain temples are represented by a concentric square building in the north-east quadrant and a circular building in the south-west (Foster 1989, 146-7). A rectangular building just inside the western wall may be a *mansio*. Most of the identifiable structures comprise the characteristic strip-buildings that proliferate in small towns, arranged end-on to the street frontage and containing shops or workshops with domestic accommodation to the rear or on an upper floor.

The extramural areas are currently only poorly understood and even their extent is uncertain. The

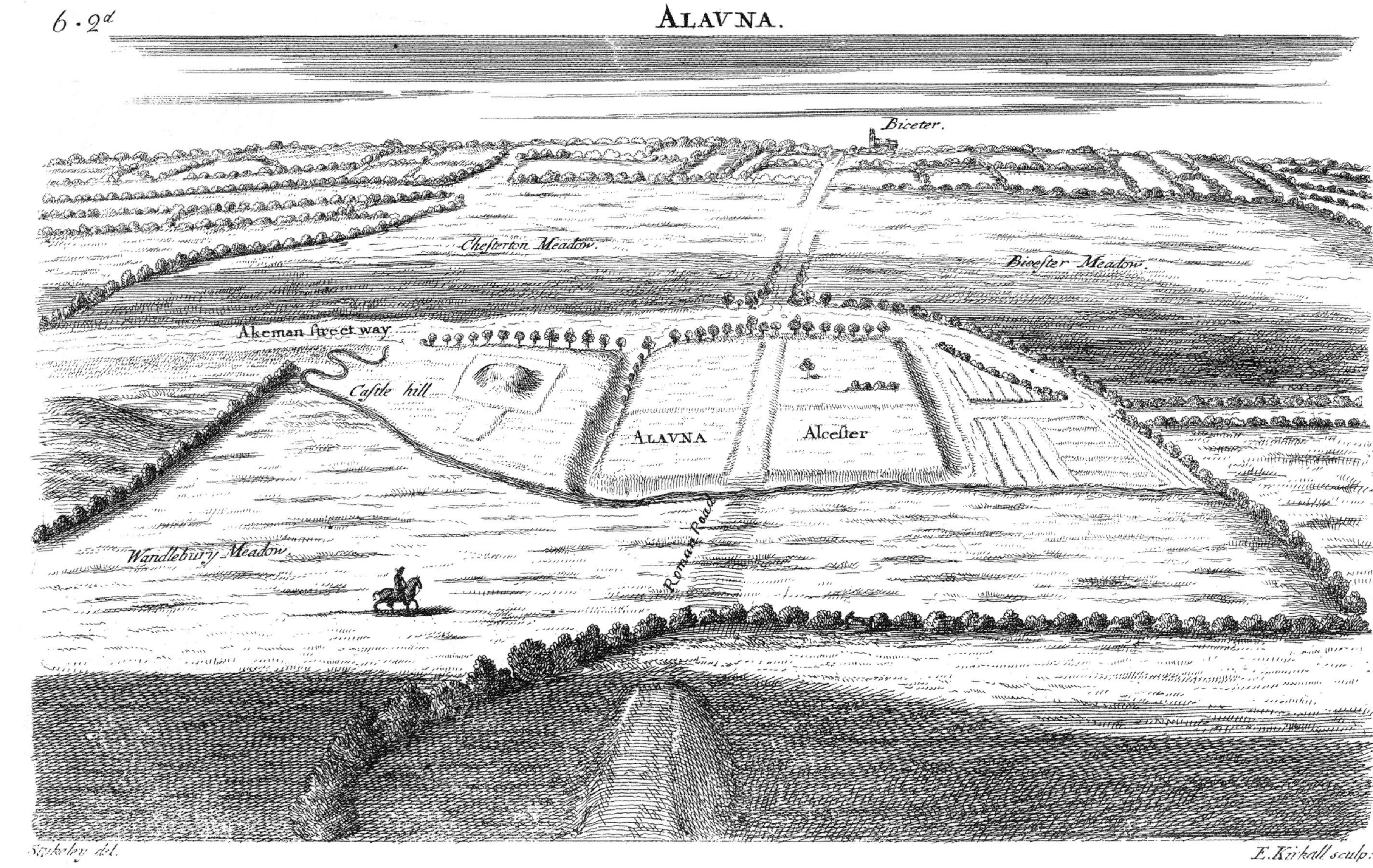

Fig. 1.3   *Stukeley's 1776 engraving of Alchester from the south*

northern extramural settlement appears to have been quite large, possibly comprising a secondary focus of settlement around the road junction 400m from the north gate of the walled town. Hand-dug trenches excavated at the locations of post settings for the 2002 overhead powerline encountered deposits that may have been associated with extramural occupation south of the south gate and to the east of the town. The town's cemeteries would have been located on the outskirts of the settlement but the only burials that are known are 28 inhumations that were uncovered outside the south-eastern corner of the town when the railway was constructed in 1848 (Harden 1939, 283) and some redeposited human bones that were found to the north of this in one of the trenches dug for the 2002 powerline (Wessex Archaeology 2002, 12). Thirty late Roman graves were associated with the northern extramural settlement (Booth *et al.* 2001, 152-61)

Alchester lies at the junction of two major early Roman routes: Akeman Street, which ran east-west from St Albans to Cirencester, and the south-north route that linked the south coast to Watling Street at Towcester. The direct line of Akeman Street passes just north of Alchester, and the relationship between the road and the military establishment and later town is discussed in Chapter 6. The road from the south gate of Alchester, which heads due south across Otmoor toward Dorchester-on-Thames, was crossed by the line of the Langford Lane replacement road and also by the new farm barn access track south of Merton. The road was sectioned a short distance south of the Langford Lane South excavation during 1967 (Chambers 1987) and the timbers of a bridge that carried it over the River Ray were exposed at Fencott as a result of dredging and a particularly low river level during September 1979 (Chambers 1986a). Part of a possible second southern route that branched off Akeman Street a short distance east of the town and followed the line of the modern Langford Lane to by-pass the eastern side of Otmoor was investigated by Oxford University Archaeological Society in 1998 (Sauer 1999b, 62-3). Cropmark evidence showed that both roads extended through a landscape that was divided into a patchwork of rectilinear fields (Fig. 2.1).

Evidence for settlement in the hinterland of the fortress and town has been recorded at a number of locations, although the known sites are again mostly located around Bicester. The late Iron Age field boundaries beside the Gagle Brook continued to be periodically recut until at least the 2nd century and the settlement at Oxford Road also continued in use into the Roman period, although it appears to have been increasingly affected by flooding and was eventually abandoned around AD 100-120. The enclosure at Bicester Fields Farm did not continue into the Roman period but was succeeded by a field system and may have been replaced by a settlement nearby at Bicester Park that was in use from the late 1st century AD until

the late 3rd/4th century (Westgarth and Carlyle 2008). This site exhibited greater evidence for spatial organisation than most in the vicinity, comprising a complex of rectangular enclosures with the northern area separated from a domestic area to the south by a trackway. A short distance east of Alchester, activity dating from the 2nd-3rd century and the line of Akeman Street were identified and investigated as part of an evaluation undertaken ahead of development at Graven Hill, to the east of Langford Brook (OA 2016a and 2016b). Activity most likely associated with the periphery of a rural settlement was recorded beside the Pingle Brook at the junction of Middleton Stoney Road and Oxford Road (Martin 2011), and extensive areas of occupation that were interpreted as possible villa complexes were identified at Kings End Farm and South Farm (Chambers 1979; 1989). These last two sites were developed with minimal archaeological investigation and now lie beneath housing estates on the west side of the town. Evidence from the rest of the alignment of EWR Phase 1 is less forthcoming, however, although surface evidence for occupation was noted at Merton during construction of the M40 in 1988-91 (Chambers 1992, 52) and cropmarks at Water Eaton and North of Gallos Brook probably represent Roman settlement (Fig. 1.4). The south-western part of the alignment passes within *c* 1km of a substantial villa that has been identified from cropmark evidence (eg Frere and St Joseph 1983, 195-6) on the north-facing slope of a hill overlooking Otmoor and a crossing of the River Ray at Islip. The nationally important temple complex at Woodeaton lies on the plateau at the top of the hill (Goodchild and Kirk 1954; Harding 1987).

Archaeological evidence for occupation after the Roman period is almost completely absent from the project area. Coins recovered from Alchester indicate that occupation continued into at least the early 5th century, but, in stark contrast to Dorchester-on-Thames in the south of the county, the town has produced almost no evidence for continued existence during the Anglo-Saxon period (Rowley 1975, 123). Early Anglo-Saxon pottery was found at two locations in the northern extramural area, in one case providing a *terminus post quem* for a group of ten burials immediately adjacent to the Roman cemetery at this site mentioned above (Booth *et al.* 2001, 201-7), while scattered early Anglo-Saxon features were also located a little further north at Whitelands Farm (Martin 2011, 198). The rural settlements that were occupied during the late Roman period similarly appear to have been abandoned, with no direct successors. The names of the villages of the medieval and modern landscape, however, indicate that they had Anglo-Saxon origins, presumably resulting from a dislocation in the settlement pattern during which settlement was moved to new locations, most of which were established on the few areas of slightly higher ground that punctuated the clay plain.

Assessment, evaluation and formation of the mitigation strategy

Research to inform an environmental impact assessment and environmental statement was undertaken in 2009 by Oxford Archaeology and comprised a detailed study of the known cultural and archaeological heritage resource within a 1km boundary to either side of the rail corridor (ERM 2009a and 2009b). This information provided the baseline for designing the strategy for evaluation and mitigation, as described in the scheme-wide written scheme of investigation (OA 2013). The WSI divided the route into 37 sites, although this included some retained structures, such as the existing bridges near Oxford, and demolition of the WWII grain silo at Water Eaton, where no negative impacts from the development were anticipated and archaeological mitigation was therefore unnecessary.

Three sites in the central part of the route, at East of Oddington Grange, South of Oddington Crossing and North of Gallos Brook, were identified for strip, map and sample excavation without recourse to an evaluation stage on account of their proximity to cropmark evidence for prehistoric or Roman features. The cropmark at East of Oddington Grange comprised a possible banjo enclosure situated immediately south of the railway, where works were proposed for the north side of the embankment (Fig. 1.5). The cropmark comprised a curvilinear enclosure from which a very straight ditched trackway extended to the south-east, where it joined a second enclosure. The north-western side of the main enclosure could not be plotted due to a change in the underlying geology from alluvium and terrace gravel to mudstone, but its projected alignment extended across the railway. At South of Oddington Crossing, embankment works on both sides of the railway and construction of a culvert were situated close to a cropmark of two conjoined or intersecting curvilinear enclosures on the north side of the railway. The southernmost of this group was North of Gallos Brook, where further embankment works were proposed for a location within a larger complex of cropmarks, comprising rectilinear enclosures and curvilinear ditched boundaries in the field to the north and a D-shaped enclosure and a more irregular enclosure with an annex in the field to the south (Fig. 1.6).

As their potential was uncertain, 16 sites were subject to trial trench evaluation in order to clarify the need for archaeological mitigation. In 13 instances the evaluations found no significant archaeological evidence, as a result of which no further work was required at these locations. Remains were found at three sites: South of Merton, Holts Farm Crossing and North of Oxford Parkway Station. At Merton Footbridge and South of Merton, a total of 19 trenches were excavated to investigate an area proposed for the construction of a

Fig. 1.4   Cropmarks of Roman trackways and settlement at Water Eaton, close to North of Oxford Parkway Station

Fig. 1.5   Cropmark of a possible banjo enclosure at East of Oddington Grange

footbridge over the railway, a replacement agricultural barn and a new access track to the barn. The alignment of the Roman road from Alchester to Dorchester-on-Thames was identified south-west of Merton village, as was evidence for occupation on the western road frontage, and this part of the evaluation area was consequently targeted for a combination of strip, map and sample and detailed excavation. The Holts Farm Crossing site was situated at the location of a possible rectilinear enclosure that had been identified as a low earthwork visible on a LIDAR survey of the site and confirmed during a walkover survey. An array of 30 trenches was excavated, representing an approximate 4% sample of the site by area and arranged to

provide the best coverage of the site and the associated construction impacts. A concentration of features dating to the late Iron Age and Roman period was recorded in trenches located on a ridge of higher ground that occupied much of the evaluation area. The earthwork was only clearly defined in one trench, where it was identified as a low bank and its date was not established. The features in the north-eastern part of the evaluation area were preserved *in situ*, in an area that was used as a compound with no intrusive groundworks, and strip, map and sample excavation was undertaken on an area of 0.9ha. Work at North of Oxford Parkway Station (referred to as Water Eaton Station during the assessment, evaluation and excavation

Fig. 1.6   Cropmarks of two enclosures at North of Gallos Brook

stages) comprised construction of a new aggregates depot and a newt pond habitat, and crossed the alignment of a trackway of probable Roman date that had been identified from cropmark evidence (Fig. 1.4). The trackway linked to a junction *c* 450m to the south-east that appears to have been a focus of settlement. Evaluation trenching confirmed the date of the trackway and identified further ditches of similar date, as a result of which a strip, map and sample excavation was undertaken.

The most complex part of the project was at Langford Lane, where a road replacement and over-bridge were constructed around the southern edge of Alchester Roman town scheduled monument to replace the existing road, which hitherto extended across the north-eastern part of the scheduled area. The existing lane, including the level crossing, was closed at the junction with Wendlebury Road, with no public access beyond toward the railway line, and the road to the south of the railway ended in a turning head. The replacement road runs from

Wendlebury Road at the western end of the new road alignment to a junction with the existing Langford Lane at Langford Brook at the eastern end, with overbridges crossing the railway line, the western channel of the Langford Brook and the Gagle Brook. The new alignment removes the road from the area of the scheduled monument but nevertheless extended across important remains of field systems associated with the town, which were known from cropmark evidence, as well as crossing the line of the road from Alchester to Dorchester-on-Thames. Magnetometer and resistivity surveys produced results that were consistent with the cropmark evidence but provided little new information, and the accuracy of the cropmark and geophysical data was confirmed by a 48-trench evaluation of the proposed route. The evaluation successfully identified each of the large enclosures fronting onto the road from Alchester to Dorchester-on-Thames, which had been indicated by the non-intrusive surveys, and found only natural features in the south-eastern part of the route, where the results of the surveys had been similarly blank. The mitigation strategy was presented in a series of separate WSIs (OA 2014a; 2014b; 2014c; 2014d; 2015b; 2015c; 2015d). The original mitigation strategy comprised preservation *in situ* of the footprints of the bridge abutments on the west side of the existing railway and on the west side of the Langford Brook, where the evaluation had identified well-preserved remains beneath a shallow topsoil, with the area west of the bridge over the railway, the bridge abutment on the eastern side of the railway and a small area west of the Langford Brook proposed for detailed excavation. In the event, however, it was decided that bridging the Langford Brook required a much more substantial structure than had initially been envisaged, with earth embankments, retaining walls and abutments, resulting in a substantially greater impact on the buried remains. Additionally, the proposed structure would have a much greater visual impact on the scheduled monument. As a result, the Cherwell District Planning Archaeologist agreed to a detailed excavation to be undertaken ahead of the construction programme. Prior to and alongside the detailed excavation, the possibility of realignment of the route to within the scheduled monument boundary to completely avoid the Langford Brook crossing was investigated with the landowners. Evaluation of this new alignment indicated that archaeological remains were sparse and were sealed beneath a considerable depth of alluvium, which enabled the area within the scheduled monument to be preserved *in situ*, with limited removal of turf and tree roots completed under the terms of an archaeological watching brief. Both the evaluation and watching brief were undertaken in accordance with separate Scheduled Monument Consents.

The excavation at Langford Lane South also encompassed the footprint of a pair of cable trenches and terminal poles that were necessary in order to bury two overhead power lines and which extended into the area of the scheduled monument. In addition to this, a watching brief was undertaken during construction of a turning head where the road that formerly crossed the railway by means of a level crossing was stopped up. Both these pieces of work were undertaken in accordance with Scheduled Monument Consent.

FIELDWORK AND ANALYSIS METHODOLOGY

Fieldwork methodologies

Open area excavation

The excavation area was stripped of topsoil and subsoil using a mechanical excavator with a flat-bladed bucket under close archaeological supervision. Mechanical excavation ceased at either undisturbed natural deposits or when archaeolog-

ical features were identified. The archaeological features that were exposed by the machine stripping were cleaned by hand where necessary and digitally mapped using a combination of EDM and GPS. Hand excavation then followed.

All archaeological features were investigated and recorded in order to establish their character, date and morphology and to investigate stratigraphic relationships between features. All pits and postholes were half-sectioned and hand excavated segments, each measuring at least 1m long, were spaced regularly along the visible length of each linear feature. Artefacts were recovered by context. Bulk soil samples were collected from undisturbed, securely dated deposits for the recovery of charred plant macrofossils, molluscs, and animal and human bone. Samples were of 40 litres where possible, or 100% of the deposit if the volume of the deposit amounted to less than this.

All features and deposits were issued with unique context numbers, and were recorded by measured drawing at an appropriate scale, usually 1:20. Spot heights and levels of individual features were recorded relative to Ordnance Datum (OD). Features were photographed using colour slide and black and white print film. Digital images were also recorded. All recording was carried out in accordance with established OA practice (Wilkinson 1992).

Strip, map and sample excavation

The sites selected for strip, map and sample excavation were chosen on the basis of their specific archaeological potential, identified from cropmark evidence, and the relatively localised and well-defined construction impacts at these sites, comprising embankment widening and associated temporary works such as haul road access. The excavation area was stripped of topsoil and subsoil in the same manner as for detailed excavation. The excavation methodology followed a two-stage approach, with the initial sample investigation being limited to characterisation of features and deposits and a plan of the archaeology exposed. The second phase, comprising more detailed excavation, was undertaken following definition and agreement of research aims that were appropriate and proportionate to the potential significance of the exposed archaeology, developed by OA in agreement with the Planning Archaeologist. Hand excavation and recording were carried out in accordance with the methodology outlined for detailed excavation.

Watching brief

Watching briefs were generally avoided in favour of detailed excavation, strip, map and sample or evaluation and were only undertaken on the turning head at Langford Lane and the part of Langford Lane replacement road that extended across the Alchester Roman town scheduled

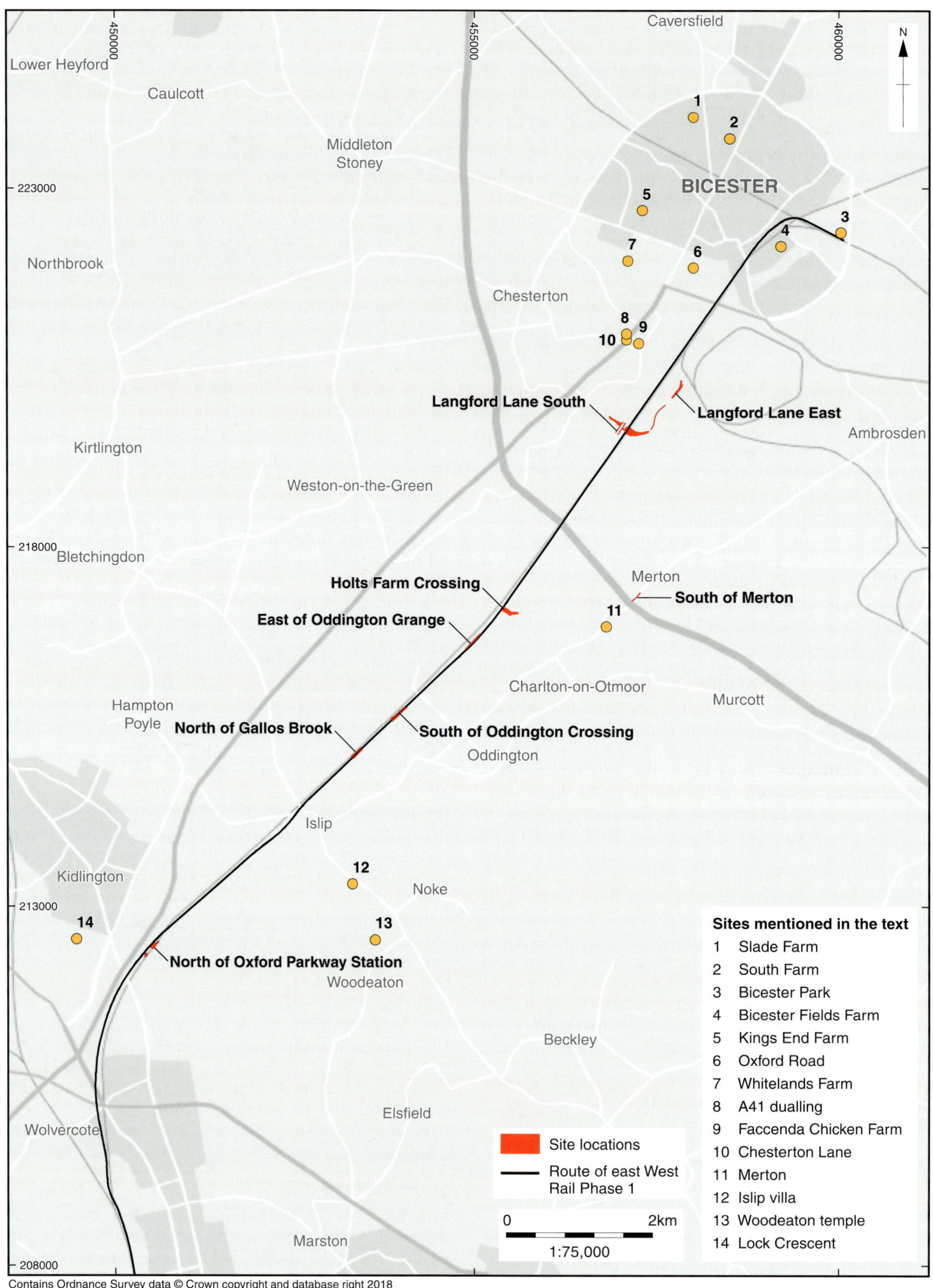

Contains Ordnance Survey data © Crown copyright and database right 2018

Fig. 1.7   Locations of excavations

monument, where the construction impact was not expected to be deep enough to reach archaeological levels. At both sites, an archaeologist was present during all activities impacting on sub-surface horizons to monitor the areas as they were stripped and to record as appropriate. No archaeological features were exposed at the turning head, but a very small area of the metalling of Akeman Street was exposed at the junction of the east end of Langford Lane replacement road with the existing road. The archaeological deposits were recorded according to the methodology outlined for detailed excavation.

Post-excavation methodology and phasing scheme

The understanding of each site sequence was based on the stratigraphic relationships recorded between cut features and on spatial associations between features. The resulting sequence was correlated with dating evidence provided principally by the pottery, supplemented by numismatic evidence at the two Langford Lane sites and by radiocarbon determinations at Langford Lane East and South of Oddington Crossing, which enabled the phasing to be established and approximate date ranges attributed. In order to facilitate correlation and comparison between the various sites, a project-wide phasing scheme was adopted that attributed the remains to nine phases. Not every phase is present on each site, and indeed Phase 4 was only distinguished from Phase 5 at Langford Lane East. At South of Merton and North of Oxford Parkway Station, Phase 6 was sub-divided into two subsidiary phases (6.1 and 6.2) in order to accommodate significant changes to the arrangement of the site that occurred during this phase but which could not be distinguished ceramically due to the similarity of the pottery assemblages. The phases were defined primarily as described in the following sections.

Phase 1: Early prehistory

Activity before the middle Iron Age was mostly represented by pieces of worked flint that were recovered from later features and from the subsoil and topsoil. Flintwork was found at Langford Lane East, Langford Lane South, South of Merton, Holts Farm Crossing, East of Oddington Grange, North of Gallos Brook and North of Oxford Parkway Station.

Phase 2: Middle Iron Age

This phase was defined by the presence of later prehistoric pottery in local handmade traditions occurring in a wide range of fabrics paralleled on other sites in the area. Some of the fabric traditions could be of longer duration, but there were no vessel forms that were necessarily earlier than the middle Iron Age. A date range from *c* 300 BC to the end of the 1st century BC is likely. Features attributed to this phase were identified at Holts Farm Crossing, East of Oddington Grange, South of Oddington Crossing and North of Gallos Brook.

Phase 3: Late Iron Age/early Roman

Phase 3 was defined ceramically by the presence of fabrics in the south-eastern 'Belgic type' tradition (ware group E, see Booth, Chapter 3), although these involved a variety of inclusion types other than just the archetypal grog, and not all the vessels were necessarily wheel-thrown. The date of the introduction of this pottery tradition in the region has been debated (eg Booth 2011a), with a date around the turn of the millennium suggested. A slightly earlier date is possible, however, for the eastern part of the Oxford region. In any case, it is clear that there was some overlap with the preceding 'middle Iron Age' potting traditions of Phase 2. Whatever the date of the introduction of 'Belgic type' wares, however, their production and use spanned the conquest period, and some use continued at least as late as the early Flavian period, though production (except for large storage vessels) may have ceased earlier. On this basis AD 70 is a convenient, if slightly arbitrary, end date for this phase at rural sites with a continuous occupation sequence. There may therefore be some overlap between the latter part of this phase and the subsequent Phase 4 and with Phase 5, although features that contained pottery of 'Romanised', clearly post-conquest, form were excluded from Phase 3. Features were attributed to Phase 3 at Langford Lane East, Holts Farm Crossing, East of Oddington Grange and North of Gallos Brook.

Phase 4: Roman military phase (c AD 43-70)

Phase 4 was defined specifically to isolate a phase of activity at Langford Lane East that may have been contemporary with the important phase of conquest-period military occupation at the adjacent fort at Alchester. At the other sites, features of this period will have been subsumed into the broader early Roman Phase 5. No specifically military deposits were identified and the pottery of this phase consisted largely of 'E wares' of Phase 3 character, but was distinguished from the preceding phase by the presence of small quantities of early post-conquest material. Amphorae and samian ware were present, and while the former are not chronologically specific, the latter included South Gaulish pre-Flavian material, supporting a notional date range of *c* AD 40-70. This phase is also marked by the appearance of white wares and 'Romanised' oxidised and reduced fabrics, though their character (and associated vessel forms) are rarely sufficiently well-defined to indicate an *a priori* Phase 4 date, and the overall quantities were quite small.

Phase 5: Early Roman (late 1st-early 2nd century)

This phase was defined by the supplementing and ultimate replacement of the native Phase 3 E wares by 'Romanised' oxidised and reduced fabrics. Flavian South Gaulish samian ware is the principal fine ware marker. Early examples of Oxford white ware mortaria should date after *c* AD 100. Phase 5 was present at Langford Lane East, Langford Lane South, South of Oddington Crossing and North of Oxford Parkway Station.

Phase 6: Middle Roman (2nd-early 3rd century)

The classic defining features of Phase 6 are the appearance of Central Gaulish (Lezoux) samian ware and Dorset black-burnished ware. The range of Oxford products was also quite wide and from about the middle of the 2nd century included the early colour-coated fabric F59, supplemented by the end of the century with occasional sherds of Nene Valley colour-coated ware. This phase was recorded at Langford Lane East, Langford Lane South, South of Merton, Holts Farm Crossing and North of Oxford Parkway Station.

Phase 7: Late Roman (mid 3rd-4th century)

Phase 7 is characterised by the appearance of standard Oxford colour-coated ware and the new range of white mortaria and other vessels that accompanied the major expansion of the Oxford industry. Late Roman activity was not widely represented but was found at Langford Lane East, Holts Farm Crossing and North of Oxford Parkway Station.

Phase 8: Medieval period

Medieval activity was represented only by evidence for ridge and furrow cultivation at South of Merton, Holts Farm Crossing, South of Oddington Crossing and North of Gallos Brook

Phase 9: Modern period

This phase encompassed features that were clearly of recent origin from their appearance and dark, humic fills, although only the field boundary ditch at North of Gallos Brook produced artefactual evidence to confirm its date. Stratigraphic relationships provided additional evidence that the ditches at Langford Lane East and North of Oxford Parkway Station and the pond at South of Oddington Crossing were more recent than the archaeological features.

STRUCTURE OF THE REPORT

Following this introductory chapter, the volume is divided between a description of the data recovered during the investigations in Chapters 2-5 and a synthetic discussion in Chapter 6.

In Chapter 2, the stratigraphic sequence at each site is described. The sites are presented in geographical order, progressing from Bicester to Oxford, that is, from north-east to south-west, beginning with Langford Lane East and ending with North of Oxford Parkway Station. Each site description proceeds chronologically. The site descriptions are illustrated by phase plans, as well as more detailed plans and sections, and photographs.

The subsequent chapters present the artefactual evidence (Chapter 3), palaeoenvironmental evidence and radiocarbon dating (Chapter 4), and human remains (Chapter 5). Within the report on each category of evidence a consistent structure has been adopted, with the material being described by site, in the order in which the sites appear in Chapter 2, followed by a combined discussion in those instances where inter-site comparison or consideration of the assemblage as a whole helps to elucidate the material. The various strands of stratigraphic, artefactual, environmental and dating evidence are brought together in the overall discussion in Chapter 6.

LOCATION OF THE ARCHIVE

The finds, paper record and digital archive are to be deposited with Oxfordshire Museum Service under accession codes assigned to the individual sites: OXCMS: 2013.119, OXCMS: 2014.15, OXCMS: 2014.90, OXCMS: 2014.155, OXCMS: 2014.177, OXCMS: 2014.182 and OXCMS: 2014.208. Owing to the increasing inaccessibility of microfilm services the basic digital archive will take the form of a pdfA scan of the hard copy records. These pdfA scans will be preserved on the OA South archive server and a copy on disc will accompany the hard copy with the archive. Digital data such as jpeg digital images and databases or geomatics data, which are not suitable for hard copy, will also be stored in this way. In time it is hoped that these digital archives will be made publicly available through the internet but in the interim anyone unable to access the hard copy or museum disc copy may approach OA South for access.

Chapter 2

The excavations

LANGFORD LANE EAST: THE EASTERN ROAD AND ASSOCIATED OCCUPATION

The Langford Lane replacement road snaked around the south and south-eastern sides of the scheduled monument of Alchester Roman town before crossing into the scheduled area on its eastern side. Investigations along its route provided the largest of the set-piece excavations in advance of the construction works. During the fieldwork this was treated as a single site divided into four excavation areas, but for the purposes of this report it has been decided that the distribution and character of the archaeological remains are best presented as two sites, dubbed Langford Lane East and Langford Lane South (Fig. 2.1). Langford Lane East comprised the south-western approach and abutment footprint of a proposed bridge over the Langford Brook (which in the event was not constructed) and a realignment of the route within the scheduled monument of Alchester Roman town. Langford Lane South encompassed the abutments for a bridge over the railway line and adjacent parts of the road. A long, sinuous trench was also excavated linking the two areas and confirmed the evidence from the evaluation that only natural features were located in this zone. No excavation was undertaken on the part of the replacement road between Langford Lane South and Wendlebury Road, where the clay geology of the shallow valley side offered little archaeological potential and the evaluation had produced only negative results. Similarly, the evaluation identified no archaeological features in the area between Langford Lane East and Wendlebury Gate Stables, on the east side of the Langford Brook.

Langford Land East comprised a linear excavation area extending south-west from Langford Brook, at NGR 4578 2203. It was 230m long and 20m wide and encompassed a total area of 0.49ha. Gagle Brook divided the south-western end of the site from the main part. The site was situated within an area of low-lying pasture fields at *c* 62.5-63m aOD. The underlying geology is mapped as alluvial clay, sand and gravel over Peterborough Member mudstone. The site lay east of the Roman town of Alchester and evidence from cropmarks and geophysical survey indicated that it crossed the alignments of a road that branched south-east off Akeman Street and a trackway that led to an enclosure interpreted as a parade ground associated with the fort that preceded the town, as well as boundaries interpreted as fields or enclosures forming the surrounding agricultural landscape. The evaluation confirmed the presence of these features and identified cobbled surfaces and possible occupation layers west of the branch road.

The initial machine stripping revealed that the archaeological deposits were buried beneath a topsoil whose shallow depth suggested that the site had not been ploughed during the medieval or modern periods and the features were consequently well preserved with little evidence for post-occupation truncation. Much of the area west of the road comprised a spread of undifferentiated soil. Excavation revealed that this comprised both inter-cutting features and a soil layer, which presumably formed the ground surface during the late Iron Age and Roman periods (Figs 2.2 to 2.5). With the exception of a few features whose fills were darker due to enhancement by the incorporation of charred remains or an organic component from the topsoil, the soil layer and feature fills comprised very similar grey silty clays with reddish brown mottling. Consequently it was very difficult to define features in plan or to establish stratigraphic relationships. Most features could therefore be phased only on the basis of pottery from their fills, and features lacking pottery could not be dated. Following excavation of the features that were visible in plan and of a series of sondages that confirmed the presence of further pits and ditches within the soil spread, the area was re-stripped, removing a further 0.15m of material. This successfully defined the features with greater clarity. A shallow and undated, but clearly post-Roman palaeochannel (6736) extended along the north-western edge of the excavation area and had truncated any archaeological features in this area (Fig. 2.4). Similarly, palaeochannels associated with the Gagle Brook were situated on either side of its current channel (Fig. 2.5). The palaeochannel on the south side of the current channel was cut by one of the ditches of the trackway that led to the parade ground, indicating that the palaeochannels were of earlier date and the brook has flowed on approximately its current alignment since before the 2nd century AD. A small amount of prehistoric flintwork was recovered, but most of the remains represented an unbroken period of occupation that started during the late Iron Age (Phase 3) and lasted until the 2nd century (Phase 6). Very little activity was indicated during the late Roman period (Phase 7).

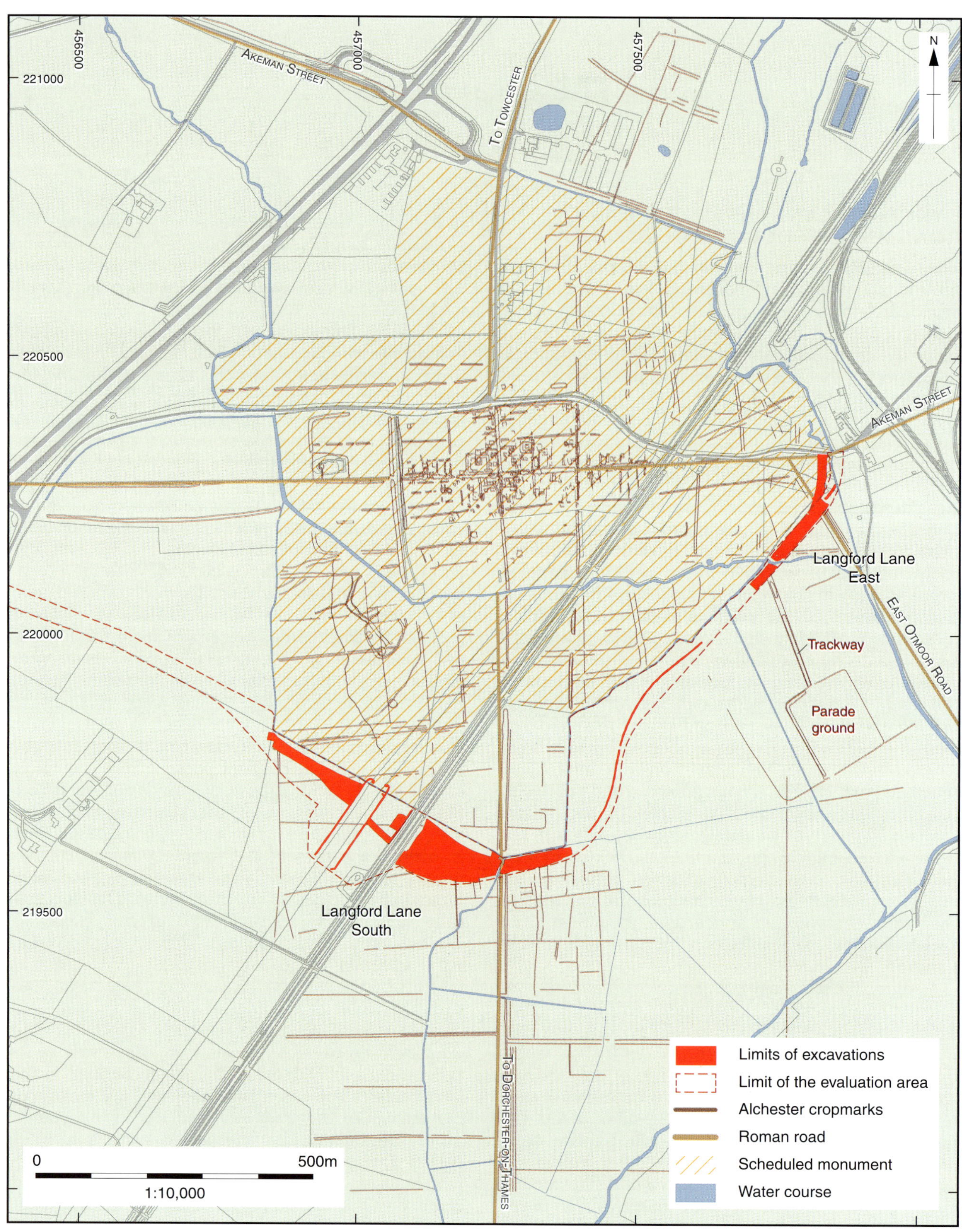

Fig. 2.1   Locations of Langford Lane East and Langford Lane South, showing Alchester Roman town and cropmark features

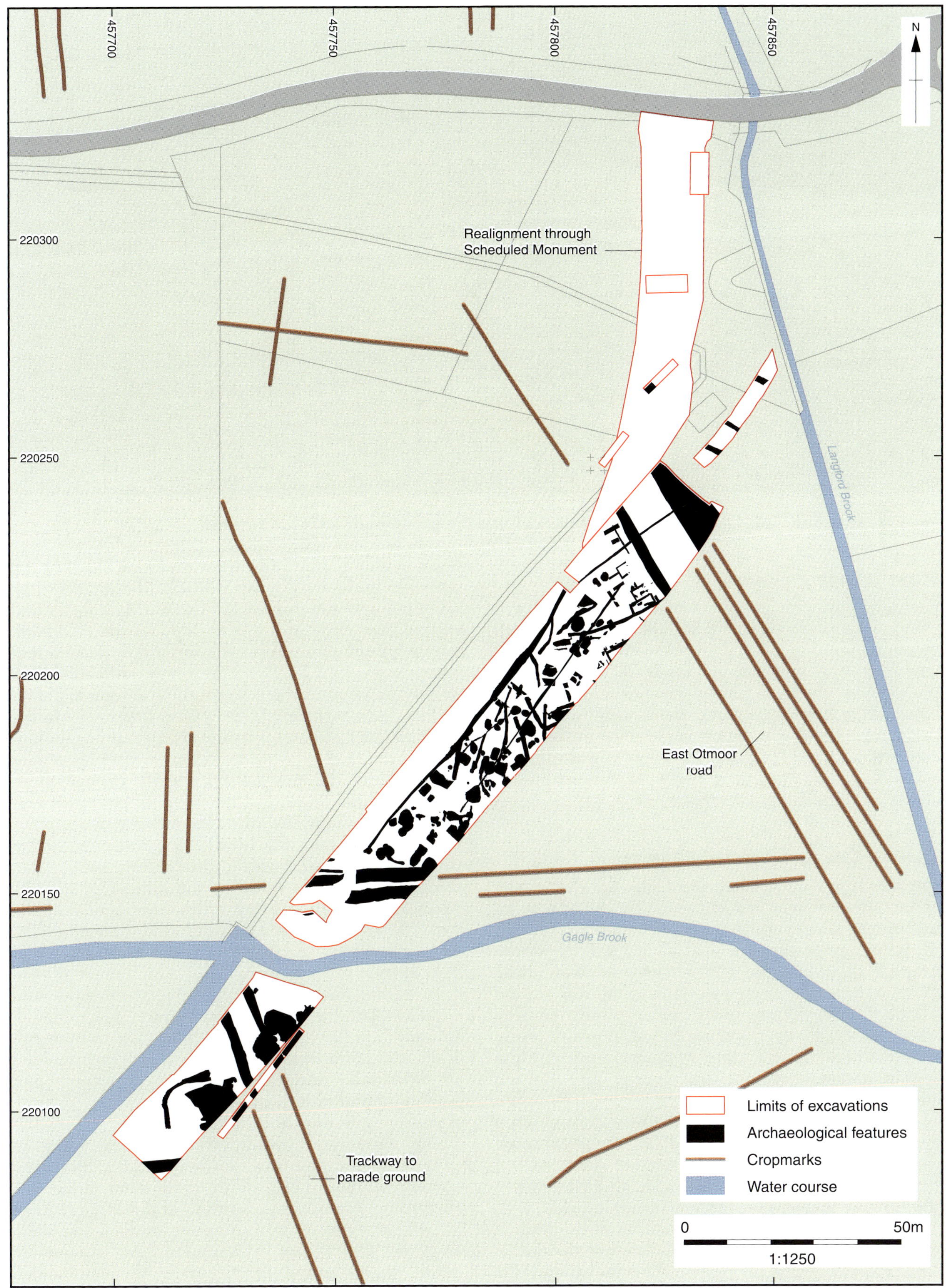

Fig. 2.2   Langford Lane East, plan of all features

Fig. 2.3   Langford Lane East, excavating features cut into the soil spread, looking north-east

Phase 1: Early prehistory

Early prehistoric activity was represented by a small assemblage of nine pieces of worked flint, all of which were recovered from residual contexts in late Iron Age and Roman features. None of the pieces was chronologically diagnostic. The hard-hammer technology of one flake suggests a later prehistoric date, although it was found in the same context as a quite long and early-looking blade. The assemblage also included two scrapers, including an atypical thumbnail scraper.

Phase 3: Late Iron Age/early Roman

The late Iron Age features were situated in the part of the site that was encompassed by the spread of undifferentiated soil. It was consequently difficult to define the features in plan or to establish stratigraphic relationships, and features of this phase may be under-represented owing to the reliance on pottery dating alone, since those without pottery have necessarily been left unphased. It is also likely that features of this date remained unidentified within areas where the soil spread and Roman surfaces were not fully removed.

The main concentration of features comprised a group of three ditches and 23 pits that were situated in the central part of the excavation area, with a further three pits that lay further north-east beneath the Roman features on the road frontage (Fig. 2.4). Three ditches were attributed to this phase, which may have defined three sides of a trapezoidal enclosure. However, it is far from certain that they were related, since they were not physically joined and were of rather different forms, ditches 8515 and 8518, which formed the west and east sides of the possible enclosure, being 0.3-0.5m deep, and ditch 6856 being a much slighter feature that measured only 0.24m wide and 0.06m deep. If the enclosure was a genuine feature, it encompassed an area that measured *c* 13m E-W and 20m N-S, with the south side lying beyond the edge of the excavation area.

Pits were situated both within and outside the possible enclosure, and where stratigraphic relationships existed they were both earlier and later than the ditches. The pits varied greatly in size, from small circular features 0.5m in diameter to a few large, sub-rectangular pits that measured up to 4 x 2m, but none was particularly deep, most measuring 0.2-0.4m deep and none measuring more than 0.65m. A group of three of the largest pits (7173, 7169, 7297) were situated within the centre of the possible enclosure and another such feature (7201) lay immediately outside its eastern limit. They had very similar brownish grey fills, which made it difficult to establish stratigraphic relationships, and typically produced only small finds assemblages, limited to pottery and animal bone. The only significant exception to this was pit 7184, which yielded an unusually large assemblage of pottery and animal bone. The pit was otherwise typical, comprising an oval hollow measuring 0.7 x 0.5m and 0.25m deep, but contained more than 3.4kg of pottery consisting almost entirely of grog-tempered sherds in fabric E80, with rims from three jars (including Fig. 3.3, nos 1 and 2) and a large storage jar (Fig. 3.3, no. 3) with a single small white ware fragment and 1kg of primary butchery waste from cattle, sheep and domestic fowl. The cattle bone included a skull and three vertebrae that may represent an articulated head and neck, as well as

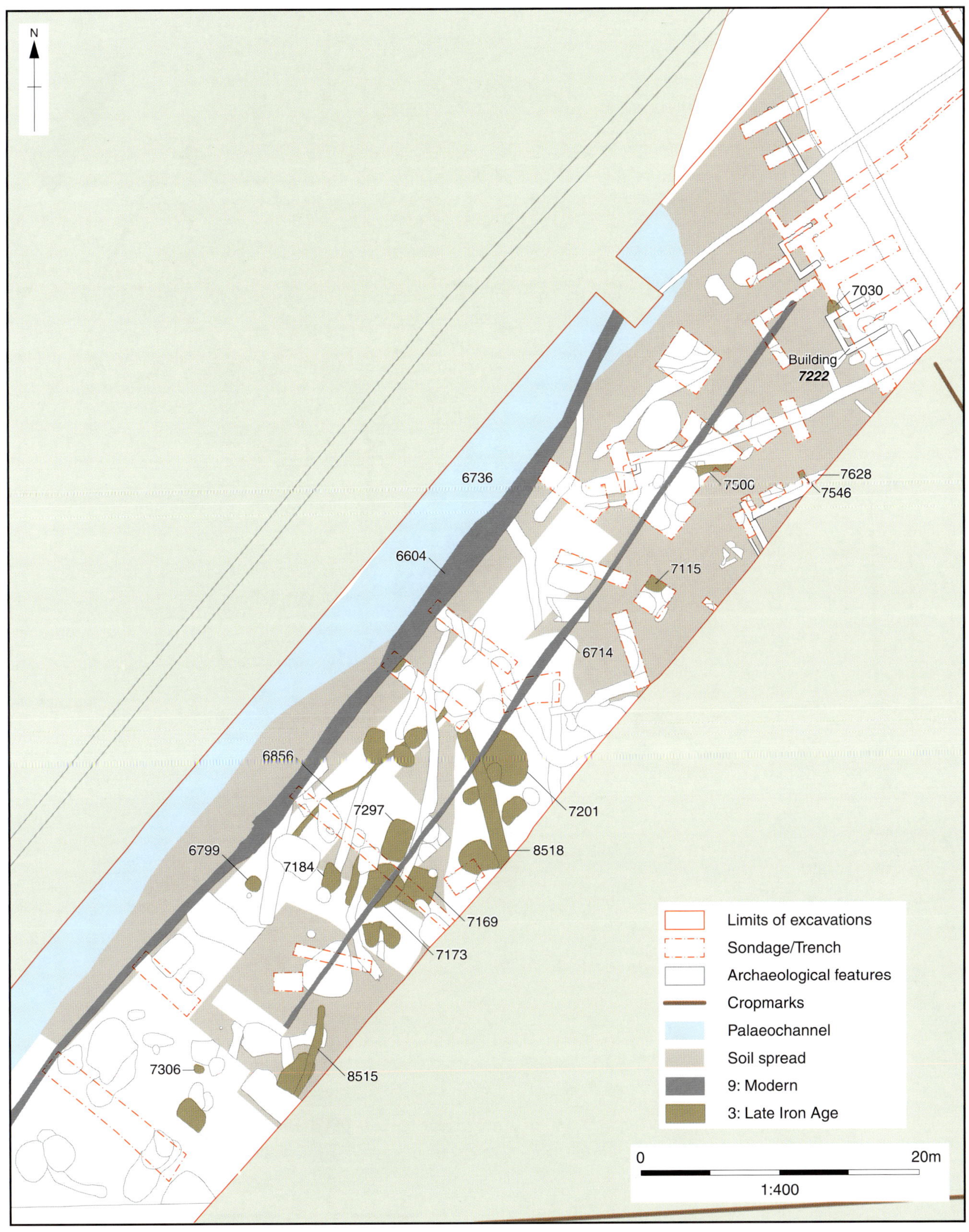

Fig. 2.4   Langford Lane East, plan of Phase 3 features

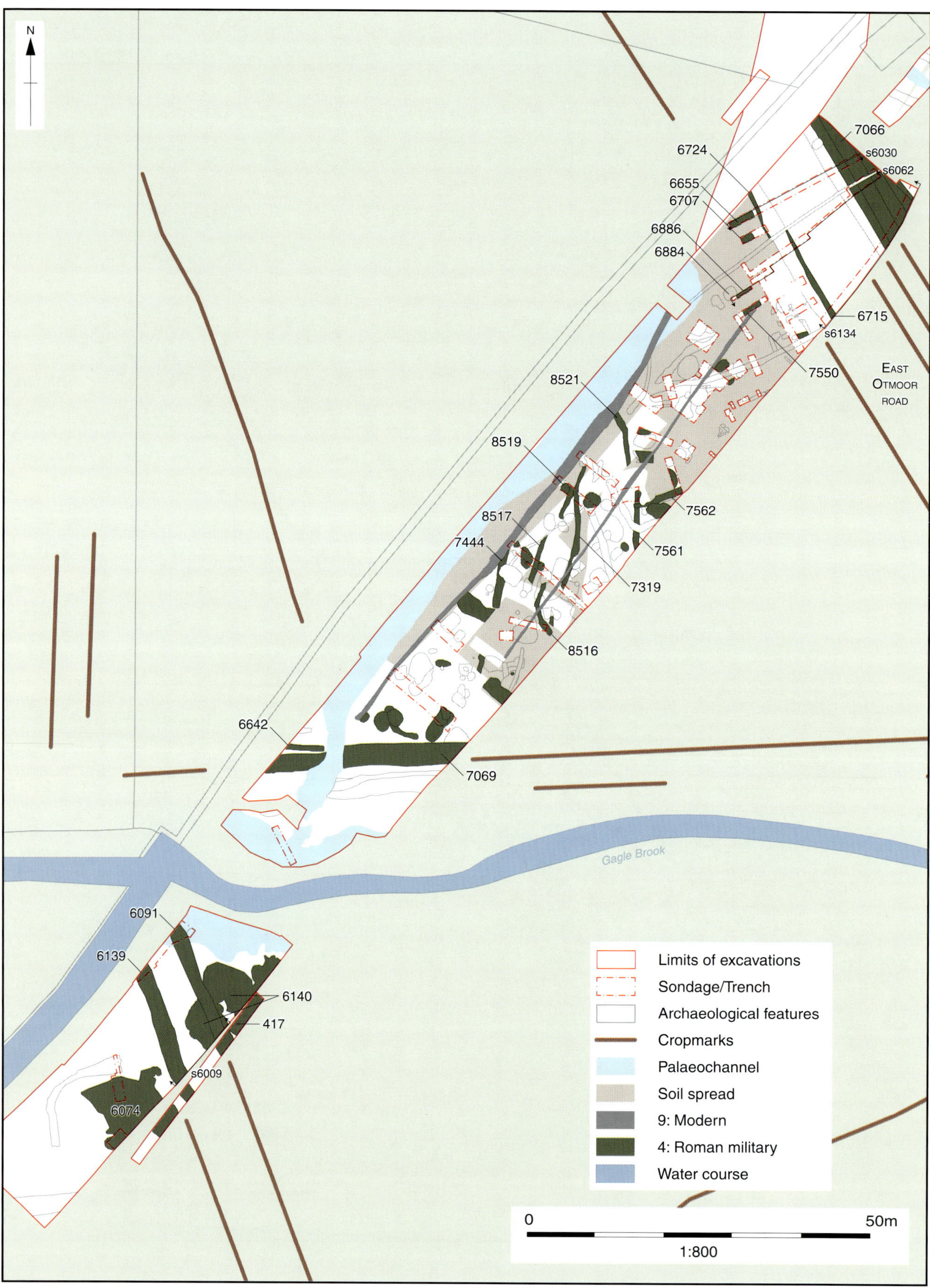

Fig. 2.5   *Langford Lane East, plan of Phase 4 features*

elements from the feet, and the sheep followed a similar pattern of head and feet elements. Two pits (6799 and 7306) produced significant assemblages of charcoal. Both were relatively insubstantial features, measuring less than 0.25m deep, but in both instances a lower fill similar to the fills of the other pits was overlain by a darker, gravelly upper fill.

Three pits, similar in form and contents to the main group, were uncovered beneath the Roman features on the frontage of the road. Pit 7030 was situated partly under Roman building 7222, which had truncated its southern half, pit 7546 was partly exposed in a sondage against the north wall of Building 7640, and pit 7628 was partly exposed beneath the foundation of the same building. Pit 7115 was exposed in a sondage dug through the soil layers mid-way between the main group of features and the pits beneath the Roman buildings, in an area where part of a fourth ditch (7506) was exposed within a sondage, where it was cut by later pits.

Phase 4: Roman military phase (*c* AD 43-70)

This phase was contemporary with the occupation of the fortress at Alchester and the initial development of the infrastructure of the Roman landscape in the surrounding area. The road was constructed during this phase, crossing the north-eastern part of the excavation area, and there was some evidence that plots may have been laid out fronting onto it,

while pits and insubstantial gullies similar to the late Iron Age features continued to be used (Fig. 2.5). Ditch 7069 appears to have defined a significant boundary that divided this roadside activity from the area to the south, which was apparently reserved for quarrying and a trackway that led to the parade ground. The features associated with the roadside plots lay within the area of undifferentiated soils that obscured understanding of the late Iron Age features and consequently were subject to some of the same difficulties of interpretation.

The road

The east Otmoor road extended across the northeastern end of the site on a straight NNW-SSE alignment and was exposed for a distance of 22m, although it could be traced beyond this as a cropmark. It comprised a metalled carriageway 9.5m wide flanked by ditches (Figs 2.2, 2.6 and 2.7). The road was flat with no evidence for an agger, although the topsoil had evidently been removed prior to construction. A layer of gravelly sand beneath the metalled surface may have been laid as a base layer, although this material could equally be trample associated with the construction activity (7070, Fig. 2.7, section 6062). The surface extended for the full width of the carriageway at the southern edge of the excavation area but became narrower to the north, presumably due to truncation, leaving

Fig. 2.6   *Langford Lane East, view across the east Otmoor road, looking north*

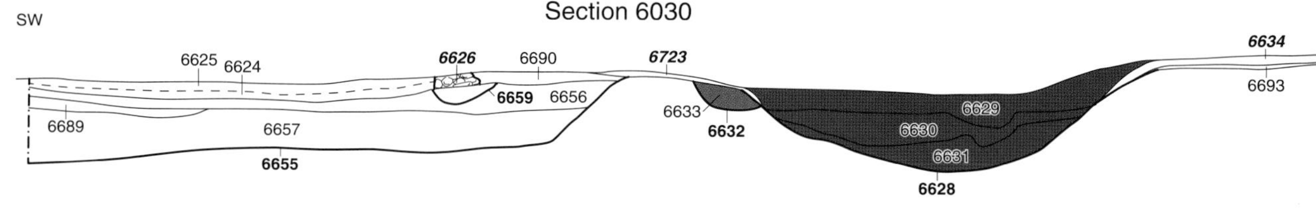

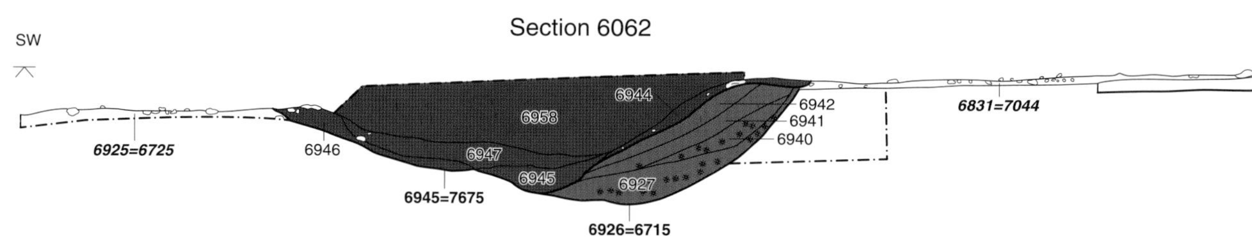

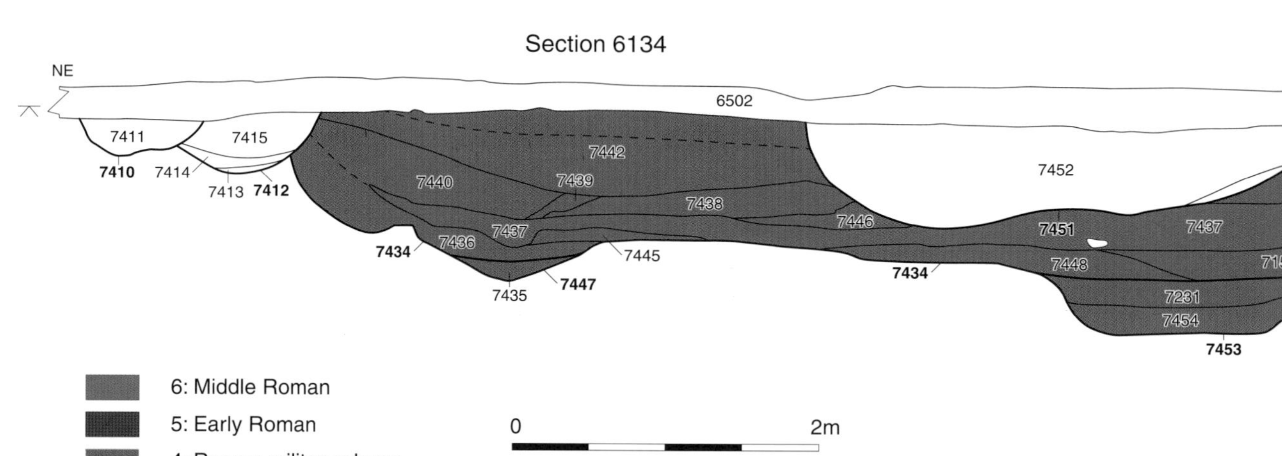

Fig. 2.7 (above and right) Langford Lane East, section through the east Otmoor road

the underlying layer exposed. The metalling (6634, 6831, 7462) comprised a compacted layer of worn limestone cobbles set in a sandy matrix, with wheel ruts clearly visible. Only a single layer of metalling was present and no artefactual material was recovered that might provide a date to indicate whether this was the original surface or a later re-surfacing, although a few sherds of 2nd-century pottery and an as of Claudius (SF 6513) were recovered from the silt layer overlying it (6503, Fig. 2.7, section 6030).

The flanking ditches were rather contrasting in character, the western feature (6715/6724) being a simple ditch, whereas the eastern one was a broader channel (7066). The western ditch (6715/6724) was 2m wide and 0.7m deep and had in places been completely removed by a recut attributed to Phase 5. The lower layers contained much pottery, a key group coming from fill 6927 (Fig. 2.7, section 6062), which comprised mostly of 'Belgic'-type wares but also

contained a substantial part of a South Gaulish samian bowl of form Ritterling 12, which is unlikely to date after the early Flavian period. The ditch on the east side of the road was a much larger feature, 5m across and 0.7m deep, which held flowing water and may represent deliberate channelling of the Langford Brook. The feature may have begun as a ditch similar to its western counterpart, represented by a deeper section immediately adjacent to the road (6985, Fig. 2.7, section 6062; 7453 section 6134), although it was not certain that this was a separate feature rather than an incidental variation in the feature's profile. This part of the feature was filled by deposits of black, humic clay (6999, 7000, Fig. 2.7, section 6062). One of these lower fills (7231, Fig. 2.7, section 6134)) contained a grey-ware 'cooking pot type' jar that contained the burnt remains of a domestic fowl (Fig. 3.6, no. 61 and Fig. 4.1). The subsequent fills comprised layers of light grey clay (7001-3 and 7611,

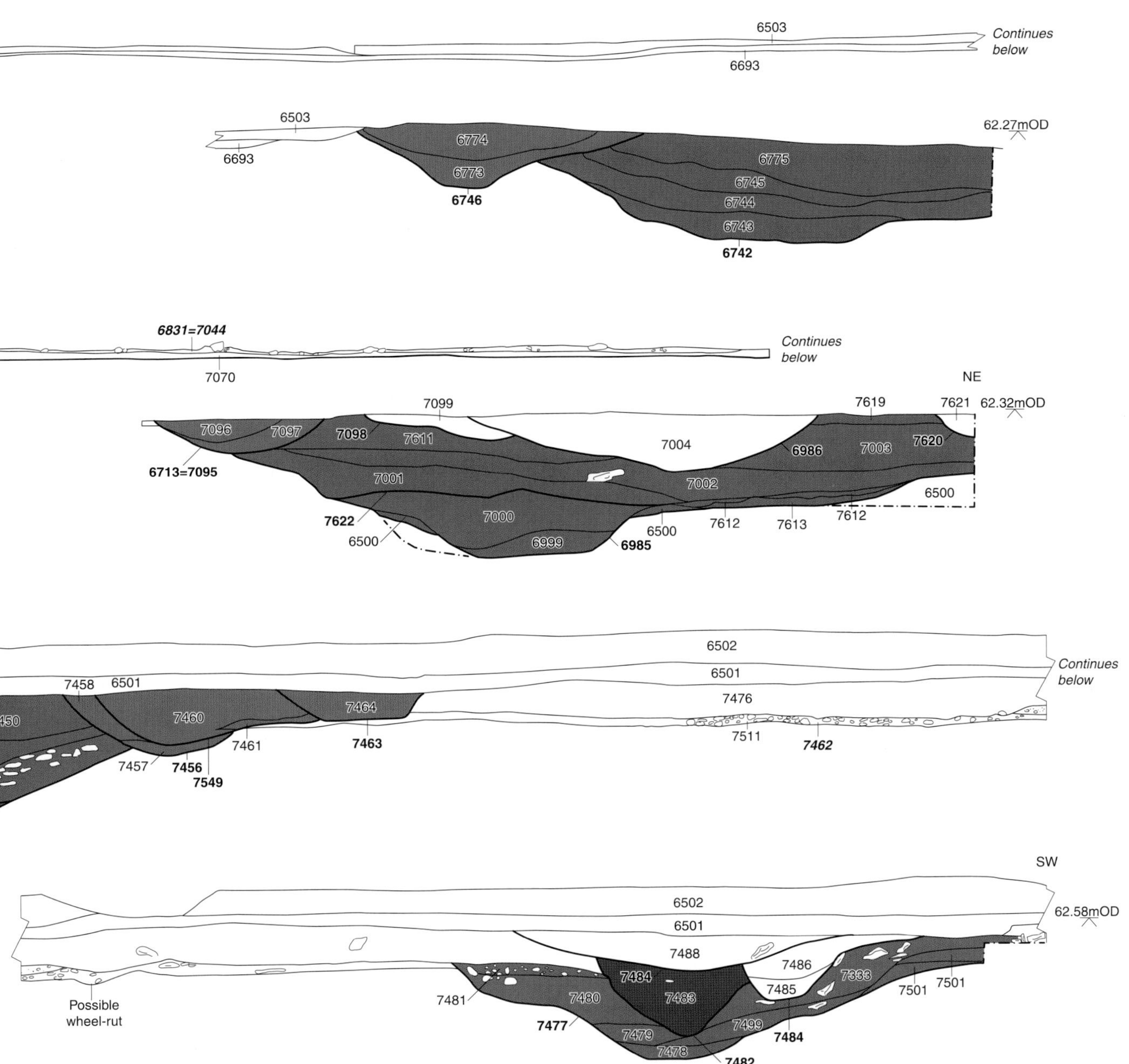

Fig. 2.7, section 6062). The molluscan assemblage from this feature contained a high proportion of species associated with deposition in flowing water. Dating evidence from this feature was very sparse, but it appeared to have silted up gradually over the course of the late 1st and 2nd centuries.

Roadside plots and associated features

A series of ditches in the central part of the excavation area lay on broadly N-S alignments and are likely to represent boundaries of plots beside the road. The precise arrangement of these features was difficult to resolve due to their limited exposure within the trench, obscuring of parts of the ditches by the soil spreads, truncation by later features, and the slight and in some instances curvilinear character of the ditches. Ditch 7561/8521 may have formed the rear boundary of plots fronting immediately onto the road, with ditch 7562 branching off it to divide two such plots. Ditch 7444 lay 18m west of ditch 7561/8521, on a roughly parallel alignment, and may have bounded a plot to the rear of the roadside plots. Although less than 0.2m deep, this feature contained a dump of pottery that amounted to more than 10kg, most of which derived from a single very large, though incomplete, storage jar (Fig. 3.4, no. 34). Ditches 7319, 8516, 8517 and 8519 lay between these boundaries and may have defined further subdivisions, but their functions were not well understood. The digging of so many ditches in this restricted area may indicate repeated attempts to address drainage problems associated with the low-lying location.

Pits were scattered throughout this part of the site and it is likely that further such features remained undetected beneath the later soil spreads and metalled surfaces, particularly close to the road frontage. They were generally similar to the corresponding features of the late Iron Age, with few being more than 0.4m deep. The fills typically contained small quantities of domestic refuse, mostly comprising pottery and animal bone, although the quantities were insufficient to suggest that they had been dug as rubbish pits and their original purpose was uncertain. Of particular note were features 6655 and 6707, which were exposed in adjacent sondages dug through the overlying later layers and are likely to be a single feature, broad and flat-based and measuring 0.7m deep and more than 3.8m wide. The feature's proximity to the road frontage suggests that it may have been a quarry for gravel used in constructing the road surface. A similar feature may have been represented by features 6886 and 7550, which were exposed in sondages a little further from the road.

Boundary ditch 7069 and features south of the Gagle Brook (Fig. 2.5)

Ditch 7069

The ditch represented the establishment of a significant and long-lived boundary, which was recut twice and subsequently replaced on a slightly different alignment by Phase 6 ditch 8514 and Phase 7 ditch 7443 (Figs 2.14 and 2.19). A total length of 30m was exposed within the excavation area but the feature could be traced as a cropmark for a total distance of 280m, extended on a very straight E-W alignment that branched off the road. The original ditch was a broad feature 3.4m wide and 0.6m deep, but the recuts were less substantial with depths of 0.25-0.35m. Four coins were recovered from the surface of the ditch, comprising a coin of Cunobelinus (SF 6550), a denarius of Tiberius (SF 6542) dated AD 36-7 and two 1st century issues that could not be assigned to a specific emperor (SF 6546 and SF 6563). A smaller ditch (6642) projected from the eastern baulk and ran alongside this feature for *c* 6m before terminating, presumably representing another phase of the boundary.

Quarry pits

Extensive, amorphous soil spreads (6074, 6140) were exposed south of ditch 7069, which on excavation were revealed to be complexes of irregular hollows up to 0.55m deep that were interpreted as quarry pits. The only artefactual material from the quarry pits was part of a fine oxidised jar of uncertain form but probable 1st century date (Fig. 3.5, no. 39) that was recovered from fill 6089 of pit 6086 (Fig. 2.8).

The trackway leading to the parade ground

The quarry pits were cut by the eastern ditch of a pair of ditches that defined a trackway that provided access to an enclosure to the south-east that has been interpreted as a parade ground contemporary with the occupation of the fortress at Alchester (Figs 2.5 and 2.8). The trackway has been traced for a distance of 230m as a cropmark of two parallel ditches that extends south from the Gagle Brook 330m east of the south-eastern corner of the Roman town. The excavation intersected it at the northern end, on the south bank of the brook. The ditches (6091, 6139) were 4.5-5.5m apart and the eastern ditch (6091) cut through a palaeochannel as well as quarry hollows (6140). Some very fragmented pottery was recorded as coming from a fill of the quarry pit , but since the interface between the ditch and the quarry was unclear at this point it is possible that the sherds in fact came from the ditch. The ditches were closely similar features, each measuring 1.5-2.5m wide and 0.5-0.8m deep, and had lower fills of bluish grey clay that are characteristic of deposition in standing water (6107, 6109, 6116, 6117). The small assemblage

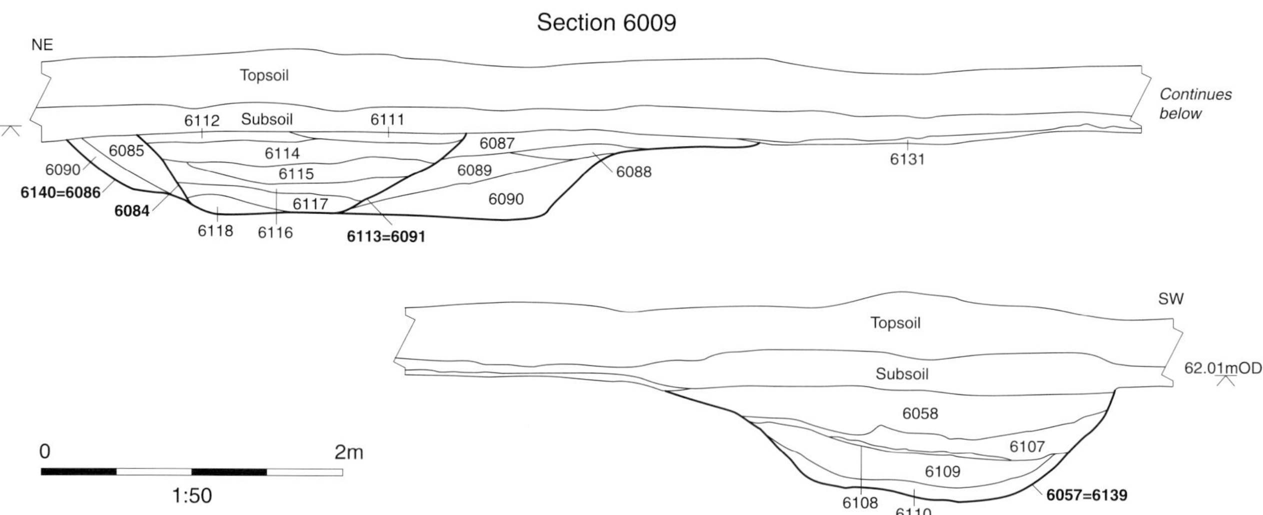

Fig. 2.8   Langford Lane East, section through the ditches of the trackway leading to the parade ground

of pottery that was recovered from the ditches dated entirely from the 2nd century, including sherds from the lowest fills, and was presumably associated with the backfilling of the features some time after they had gone out of use. A layer of sandy gravel (6131, Fig. 2.8) that was recorded between the ditches may represent the base of a plough-truncated surface. No other evidence for a metalled surface similar to that of the eastern road was present.

Cremation burials associated with the trackway to the parade ground

Two cremation burials (417 and 6084) were situated adjacent to the eastern ditch of the trackway (Fig. 2.5). Cremation burial 417 was recorded during the evaluation stage of the investigation and comprised a small, sub-circular pit that was cut into the top of the quarry backfill that the trackway also cut. The pit was only 0.12m deep and contained the partial remains of an adult mixed with substantial amounts of charcoal derived from the pyre (418). The bone amounted to 645g and a sample submitted for radiocarbon dating returned a date of cal AD 70-230. A total of 15 iron nails were recovered from the burial and their even spacing within the pit suggests that they were part of the construction of a small box or casket that either held the cremated remains or was buried with them. However, the cremated remains extended throughout the pit, so it is unlikely that they were held within a container and the latter interpretation is more likely. Analysis of the cremated remains also identified bones from a neonate pig and a possible domestic fowl, presumably representing animal offerings that were included within the cremation pyre.

Burial 6084 was cut by the trackway ditch (Fig. 2.8). The shape of the cremation pit was not certain, since it was only observed in section, but it measured at least 0.5m across and 0.4m deep. Cremated remains weighing 239.8g were recovered, representing a single adult of undetermined sex (6085). Only a small amount of charcoal was present, suggesting that the bone had been picked out of the pyre with some care for deposition within the pit. A sample from the femoral shaft was dated by radiocarbon to 60 cal BC-cal AD 70.

Phase 5: Early Roman (late 1st-early 2nd century)

During the late 1st-early 2nd century, activity associated with the road frontage became more coherent (Figs 2.9-2.11), with the construction of two stone-founded buildings (7062, 7222), a roadside wall (6718, 7602) and associated cobbled surfaces. The buildings comprised a matching pair of small square structures that were open (or at least lacking a stone foundation) on the north-eastern side, facing the road. They were 3.4m apart and corresponded with a break in the roadside wall, possibly indicating that the metalled surface between them represented an access from the road. The grave of a

child (7124) was inserted close to the buildings and a number of pits were dug to the rear, including three cremation burials (6711, 6720, 7408) situated at the western limit of the features associated with the roadside area from this phase. To the south, separated from the roadside activity by Phase 4 ditch 7069, the ditches of the trackway to the parade ground continued to silt and a small rectilinear enclosure was constructed beside it.

The road

Evidence for maintenance of the road was limited to recutting of the western ditch. The recut ditch (7675) was typically slightly shallower than the original Phase 4 feature, measuring 0.5-0.8m deep with a V-shaped profile (Figs 2.7 and 2.11). The evidence from pottery recovered from the fills of the eastern ditch (7066) indicated that the channel that had been dug during Phase 4 continued to be used during this phase. The road surface produced no artefactual dating material and it was therefore not possible to establish whether the recutting of the western ditch was accompanied by repairs or replacement of the metalling.

Structures on the road frontage

Boundary walls 6718 and 7602 (Fig. 2.11)

Walls 6718 and 7602 lay on the same alignment and appear to be elements of a wall that extended alongside the road, 1.5-2.0m from the edge of the adjacent roadside ditch. Wall 6718 represented the north-western part of the wall and comprised a pitched-stone foundation set in a vertical-sided foundation trench 7.5m long. It was sectioned at two locations, which revealed that it measured 0.6m wide and up to 0.36m deep, but was shallower near the north-western end, where it was only 0.12m deep. Wall 7602 extended into the site for a distance of 2.15m from the south-eastern edge of the excavation area, but had been truncated at the baulk by Phase 6 ditch 8522. Like wall 6718, it comprised a pitched-stone foundation 0.6m wide, but survived to a depth of only 0.1m. Between the surviving walls was a break of 11.3m, which corresponded with the position of buildings 7062 and 7222.

Building 7062

Building 7062 (Fig. 2.11) measured 3.1m wide and had an open side that fronted toward the road. The side walls were asymmetrical, the north-west wall extending for 2.8m and the south-east wall for 1.8m. The walls had a pitched-stone foundation of limestone pieces, which was cut into the underlying soil layers, but none of the above-ground part of the walls survived. Two courses of foundation stones survived in the south-west wall and the adjacent parts of the side walls, but the upper course petered out to the north-east, indicating that this part of the structure had been subject to some degree of trunca-

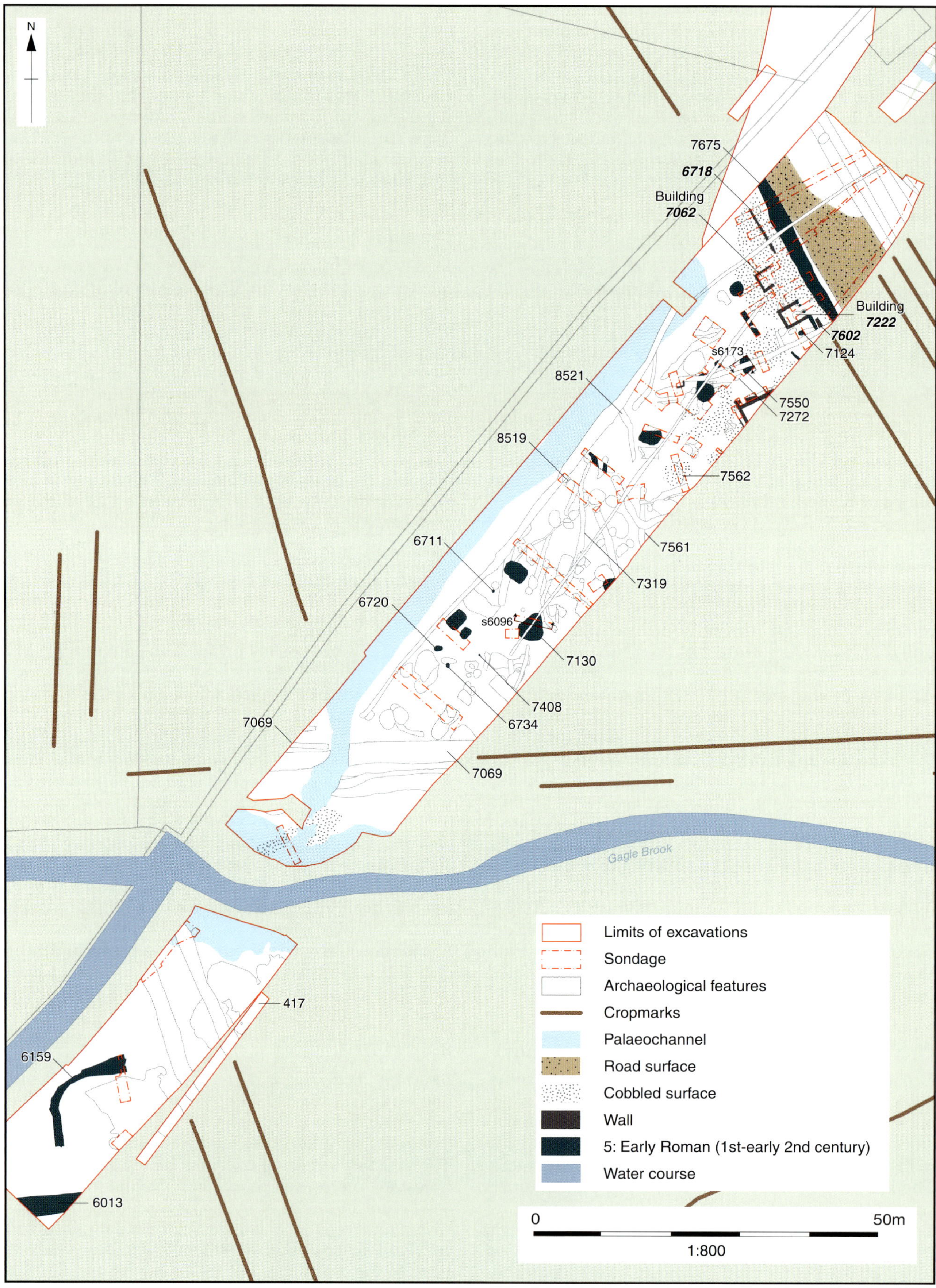

Fig. 2.9   *Langford Lane East, plan of Phase 5 features*

Fig. 2.10 Langford Lane East, orthomosaic of the north-eastern part of the site showing the east Otmoor road and adjacent structures

tion, which may have removed any north-east wall. A possible posthole (7057) 0.25m deep was situated just beyond the end of the south-east wall. Within the building was a layer of small pieces of limestone rubble with occasional fragments of ceramic building material (6826), which may have been a rough floor surface, although it could alternatively be demolition material. The walls and the possible surface were overlain by a layer of grey clay silt 0.05m thick (6829) that may be an occupation layer or post-abandonment accumulation, above which was a layer of limestone rubble (6828) presumably derived from the collapse or demolition of the

building. Dating evidence for the building was scarce. Floor surface 6826 yielded three small fragments of pottery, including one of South Gaulish samian, and silt layer 6829 produced a small fragment of Central Gaulish samian ware and a small piece of black burnished ware, which together suggest a date of at least AD 120. A coin of Victorinus dating to AD 268-70 was recovered from rubble layer 6828. In addition to this, cleaning before the building was excavated recovered nine sherds including a handle from a Dressel 7 or 11 amphora. Other artefacts were limited to a very small assemblage of animal bone and a nail fragment.

Limits of excavations
Sondage/Trench
Archaeological features
Cropmarks
Road surface
Cobbled surface
Wall
5: Early Roman (1st-early 2nd century)
N
6718
7675
Building 7062
7057
7379
7334
7316
7357
7602
Building 7222
7402
7572
7124
7644
0
5m
1:100

Fig. 2.12   Langford Lane East, Building 7222 and wall 7603, looking west

Building 7222

Building 7222 (Figs 2.11 and 2.12) was similar to Building 7062, comprising a three-sided structure that was open to the north-east and survived only at foundation level. The foundation was constructed using limestone set as pitched stone in a trench that was up to 0.4m deep, with three courses of stones surviving in the south-west wall and the adjacent parts of the side walls. The building was 2.15m wide internally and the north-west wall was 3.15m long. The stones of the south-east wall petered out after 2.65m, but the base of the construction cut could be traced beyond this, giving the wall a total length of 3.45m. A possible posthole (7357, 7379) was situated at the end of each wall and two further postholes (7316, 7334) lay between them and may have defined the north-east wall of the building, if they were contemporary features. A shallow feature (7402) that extended south-east from the east corner of the building, adjacent to roadside boundary wall 7602, had been backfilled with grey soil and small fragments of limestone rubble and may have been a robber trench, although whether it was associated with Building 7222 was uncertain. No internal layers survived within the building. Artefactual material was restricted to a small pottery assemblage and a few scraps of animal bone. Eleven sherds were recovered from the foundation, mostly residual late Iron Age sherds but including a small rim sherd from a South Gaulish samian dish of Dragendorff form 15/17, and posthole 7316 yielded sherds including a chip from a South Gaulish samian vessel, while cleaning of the building prior to excavation resulted in the recovery of 11 sherds, including two large body sherds from a Dressel 20 amphora.

Other features associated with the roadside occupation

Cobbled surfaces

The buildings were associated with an extensive area of cobbled surface (Figs 2.10 and 2.11). The surface varied in density and preservation and extended to the western lip of the roadside ditch, where it may have been intended to consolidate the ground surface at the edge of the ditch, as well as encompassing the area between and north and west of the buildings. A break to the rear of Building 7222 separated the main surface from a smaller spread that extended as far as Phase 6 Building 7640, although it is possible that they were originally continuous. The surface was constructed from limestone with occasional smaller quantities of tile, which occurred both as individual fragments and localised concentrations that may have been laid down as *ad hoc* repairs.

Burials

The burials comprised an inhumation grave (7124) close to the road frontage and three adult cremation burials (6711, 6720, 7408) that were clustered at the rear, south-western limit of the roadside occupation. Pit 6734, which was only 0.04m deep, may have been the base of a further cremation, but was almost

Fig. 2.11 (opposite)   Langford Lane East, plan of features on the road frontage

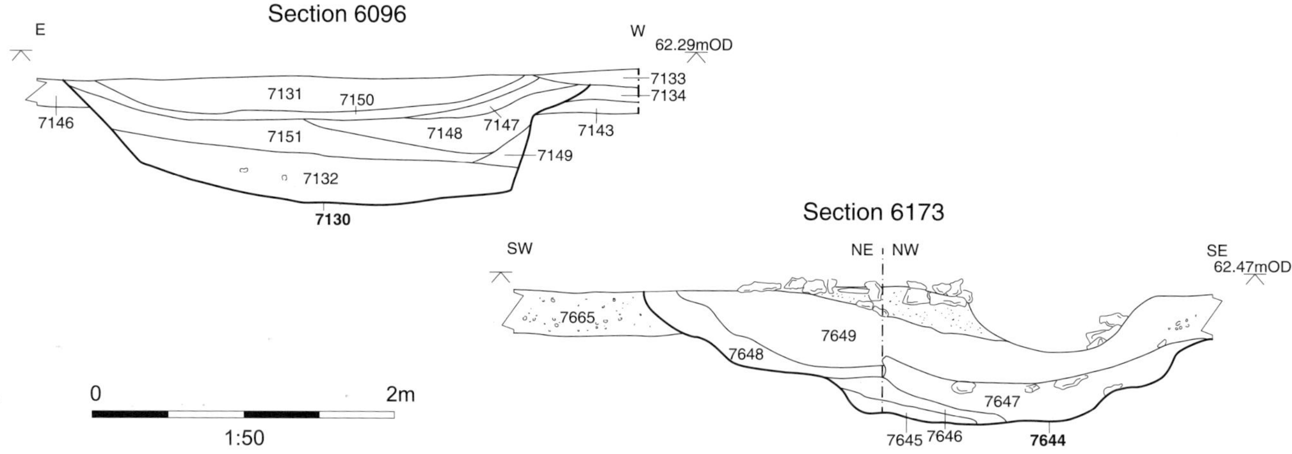

Fig. 2.13   Langford Lane East, sections of Phase 5 possible waterholes 7130 and 7644

completely truncated and no bone was identified. The inhumation burial contained the remains of a child (7125) aged approximately 5-7 years of age, who had been buried in a crouched position in a shallow oval pit (7124) 0.36m deep.

None of the cremation burials were urned, but burial 6720 contained pottery that may represent a vessel that had been deliberately buried with the remains. The burial was interred in a sub-rectangular pit that measured 1.26 x 0.7m and 0.33m deep and contained 335.8g of bone from two individuals. Most of the bone came from an adult aged 30-40 years at death, but a few juvenile bones were also present. The accompanying vessel was an oxidised flagon, which was represented by parts of the rim, neck and body but no base (Fig. 3.5, no. 46). Evidence for offerings placed on the pyre was provided by the inclusion of burnt animal bone, which included a possible rabbit tooth, a bird radius and elements from larger mammals that may have been cattle or sheep. Fragments of unburnt animal bone were also recovered but could not be identified to species and may have been residual. The charcoal assemblage from this burial was poor and did not contain sufficient material to justify detailed analysis, but the initial assessment identified ash and probable field maple in addition to oak.

Cremation burials 6711 and 7408 contained no pottery but were attributed to this phase on the basis of their proximity to the better-dated burial 6720. Both comprised simple small circular pits, into which the remains had been placed. Burial 6711 contained 140g of bone from an adult of undetermined sex, which was accompanied by fragments of burnt domestic fowl and a single fragment from an unidentified mammal, as well as two unburnt mammal bones. The individual in burial 7408 was represented by only 53.6g of bone from which the age and sex could not be established. As with burial 6720, the charcoal from these features was very sparse, suggesting that some care had been taken in picking the bones from the pyre.

Pits

A total of 17 pits were scattered between the road frontage and the area to the rear. The pits closest to the road (7572, 7644, Fig. 2.11) were exposed in sondages dug through the cobbled surfaces and soil layers and consequently their full extents could not be established. It is also possible that further such pits remain undiscovered beneath the unexcavated parts of the overlying surfaces. In general the pits were more substantial than those of the preceding phases, most measuring more than 1.5m in diameter and 0.4-0.6m deep, but artefactual assemblages were typically limited to small quantities of pottery and animal bone and provided no indication of the original function of the features. Calcined human bone was recovered from pit 7272, but the quantity (0.7g) was so small as to indicate incidental inclusion rather than a deliberate formal burial.

Two particularly large pits (7130, 7644, Figs 2.9 and 2.13) measured 0.8-0.85m deep and may have been dug as waterholes. Pit 7130 was situated near the south-western extent of the features and measured 4.2 x 3.8m and 0.8m deep, with steep sides and a flat base. The bottom fill was a layer of grey-blue clay (7132) 0.3m thick that may have resulted from silting in standing water. The middle layers (7148, 7151) were characterised by orange iron staining and were overlain by an upper fill (7131) that contained two sestertii of Trajan that were corroded together (SF 6556). Pit 7644 was exposed in a sondage dug through the cobbled surfaces close to the buildings (Fig. 2.11). It was not fully exposed and so its shape is unknown, but it measured 0.85m deep. The lowest fills were two deposits of grey clay (7645, 7646) that may have been deposited in standing water and were overlain by a backfill of redeposited mixed grey and yellow clay (7647) and an upper fill (7649) that was almost identical to the surrounding soil layers.

Features south of ditch 7069

The boundary defined in Phase 4 by ditch 7069 (Fig. 2.9) did not have an iteration that was attributed to this phase, but is likely to have continued to be of significance, since it was subsequently redefined during Phases 6 and 7. Ditch 6013 was constructed on an E-W alignment parallel to and *c* 60m south of ditch 7069. It was a substantial feature, 0.8m deep, that defined a boundary that probably branched off the trackway that led to the parade ground, although the junction of the ditch and the trackway lay a short distance beyond the limits of the construction corridor and thus beyond the excavation area. A small enclosure 17m square was constructed in the angle formed by the junction, enclosed on its north and west sides by a shallow, L-shaped gully (6159). No contemporary features were identified within the enclosure and its function is unknown.

Phase 6: Middle Roman (2nd-early 3rd century)

Features attributed to this phase were mostly located close to the road frontage (Fig. 2.14). The buildings that were constructed on the road frontage during Phase 5 continued in use into Phase 6 but were demolished before the end of the 2nd century, as indicated by the pottery from the associated demolition spreads. They were superseded by a rectangular enclosure (8520/8522) that contained a larger building (7640), although both the enclosure and the building extended beyond the limits of the excavation area and were only partly exposed. The enclosure was associated with a concentration of pits, and a further pit (7008) was situated towards the south-western end of the site, where Phase 4 ditch 7069 was replaced by ditch 8514. Evidence regarding the continued maintenance of the road itself was ambiguous, not least due to the absence of datable artefacts from the road surface.

The road

There was no certain evidence for continued maintenance of the road during this phase, although this may simply be due to the lack of dating evidence from the later phases of the roadside ditches. The latest recut of the western ditch (7484, Fig. 2.7, section 6134) could date from this phase but produced no artefactual material that might prove this. Small quantities of pottery dating from the 2nd century were recovered from the fills of the channel on the eastern side of the road, including an almost complete cooking pot-type jar (Fig. 3.6, no. 61), indicating that it continued to silt up during this phase. This feature also exhibited evidence for later recuts that were undated (Fig. 2.7) and it is possible that they dated from this phase.

Enclosure 8520/8522

The enclosure appeared to have been constructed around Building 7640, although this was not definite since a significant part of both lay beyond the edge of the excavation area. The ditch was clearly a later addition to this arrangement, however, as it cut through the cobbled surface and wall 7602. It was rectangular in form, aligned end-on to the road frontage, and measured *c* 35 x 15m. The north-western side was defined by ditch 8522 and the south-western and south-eastern sides were enclosed by the L-shaped ditch 8520. Ditch 8520 was up to 0.5m deep and ended in a definite terminus, indicating that an entrance had existed on the south-western side of the enclosure. Ditch 8522, which cut through Phase 5 wall 7602 and associated cobbled surfaces, was shallower and had apparently been truncated, resulting in the loss of the western part of the enclosure, including the corner. Almost half the enclosure lay beyond the edge of the excavation, including the whole of the north-eastern end, as a result of which its arrangement in relationship to the road frontage could not be established. Apart from Building 7640, the only contemporary features within the enclosure were a shallow hollow (7303) and a pit or ditch terminal (6737).

Building 7640

Only the western corner and parts of the north-west and south-west walls of Building 7640 extended into the excavation area (Figs 2.14-2.17). This was sufficient, however, to indicate that it was a rectilinear, stone-founded building. The exposed part measured 5.9 x 3.7m and the distance from the road frontage suggested a maximum possible length of 17-18m. All walls and foundations were constructed using limestone, with larger slab-like pieces being used for the walls. The north-west wall exhibited clear evidence for two phases of construction, lying on divergent alignments. The earlier phase was represented by a foundation of pitched stone (7535) 0.45m wide, set within a vertical-sided construction cut at least 0.25m deep. The foundation met that of the south-western wall at an oblique angle that could not be readily explained. The later phase of the wall (6574) lay at a squarer angle to the south-west wall and comprised a pitched-stone foundation of one course of stones, above which two courses of the wall survived. The two foundations converged to the north-east, where the later wall was built partly on the earlier foundation. The wall was 0.6m wide and was constructed from flat stones used for both faces and smaller, more irregular stones used as core infilling. The south-west wall survived only as a foundation, 0.5m wide and 0.35m deep, comprising two courses of pitched stone (7118). There was some indication that the north-western end of the foundation (7594), from the junction with wall 6574, utilised smaller stones, perhaps indicating that part of the wall had been rebuilt when wall 7535 was replaced by wall 6574. The foundation (7534) of a slightly-built wall lay immediately adjacent to the south-west wall and was presumably associated with the building,

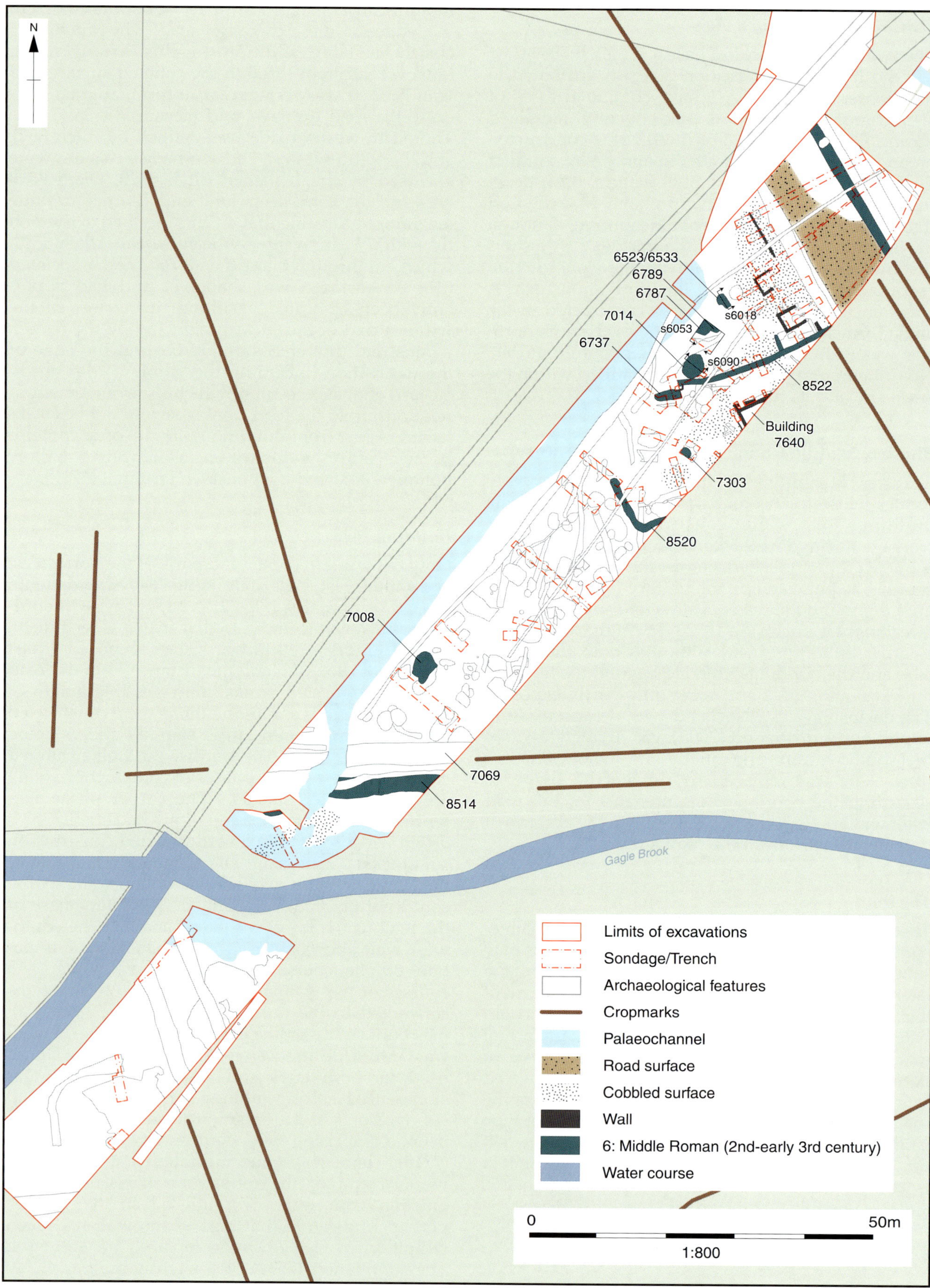

Fig. 2.14   Langford Lane East, plan of Phase 6 features

although its function was uncertain. It was 0.4m wide, constructed from a single line of pitched stones, and extended for at least 3.7m, continuing beyond the edge of the excavation area. No floor surfaces survived within the building, which was covered by a demolition layer (6548) that was 0.15m thick and contained three sherds of 1st century pottery as well as tegula/flat tile and imbrex, plus occasional brick. A large spread of material (6554) that extended for *c* 4m from the north-eastern wall comprised demolition debris from the building and included 90kg of tegula, flat tile and imbrex, together with a modest quantity of brick and a single small fragment of flue tile. This material included three that bore rare examples of human footprints, from a small child or toddler (Fig. 3.23). A substantial group of almost 1.8kg of pottery was recovered, including Central and (probably) East Gaulish samian ware and a range of grey wares. Key dating evidence was provided by an Oxford white ware mortarium of Young type M14, dated AD 180-240 (Fig. 3.6, no. 71). The earliest possible date for the deposit is therefore *c* AD 180, and a later date, almost certainly not before *c* AD 200, is more likely.

Pits north of enclosure 8520/8522

A cluster of pits was located immediately to the north of the enclosure. Closest to the enclosure was pit 7014, which was situated immediately adjacent to the enclosure ditch (Fig. 2.14). It was a circular pit 1.9m in diameter and 0.7m deep (Fig. 2.18, section 6090). The lower part contained two layers of black, peaty material (7016, 7018). A sample taken from fill 7018 contained abundant cereal grain, comprising both wheat and oat, some of which had sprouted. These deposits were overlain by a backfilling deposit (7015) from which two slave shackles were recovered (SF 6537 and SF 6584, Fig. 3.13, nos 2 and 3). Two inter-cutting pits (6787, 6789) were partly revealed in a sondage, where they cut several undated features (Fig. 2.18, section 6053). Neither feature contained any evidence regarding their original function, but the upper fills (6934, 6960) of pit 6789 contained pottery and fragments of limestone, as well as a bow brooch (SF 6516, Fig. 3.14, no. 6). The northernmost of this group of features was pit 6523/6533, a sub-rectangular feature that measured 2.95 x 0.8m and 0.3m deep, with steep sides and a flat base (Fig. 2.18,

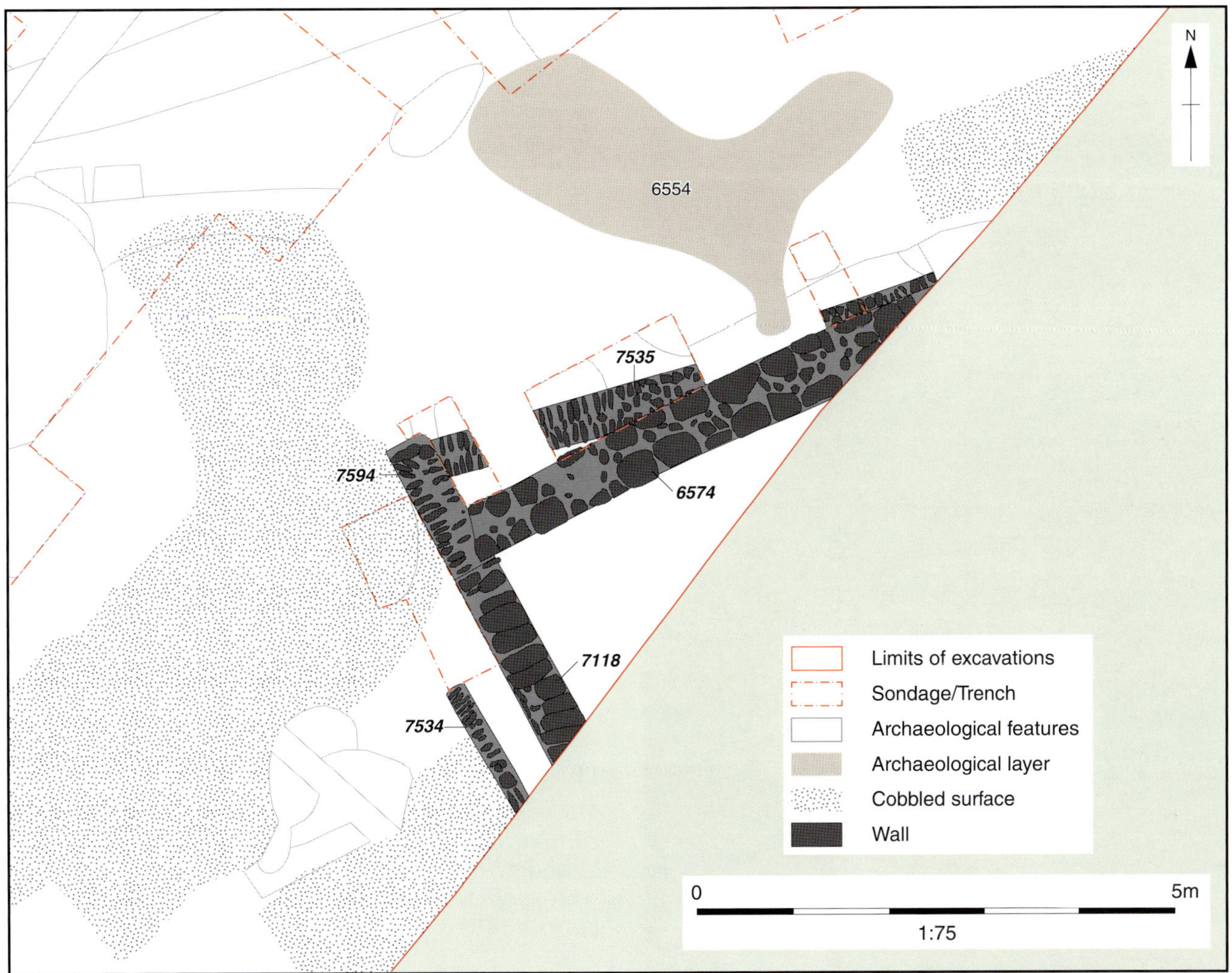

Fig. 2.15   Langford Lane East, plan of Building 7640

Fig. 2.16   Langford Lane East, Building 7640 from the south-west

section 6018). The bottom of the pit was filled by a deposit of stone rubble with some ceramic building material (6522). Two soil samples were collected from this layer, one of which was dominated by ash charcoal and the other by oak charcoal. The overlying backfill included numerous patches of grey silt, one of which (6524) yielded a plate brooch (SF 6503, Fig. 3.15, no. 17). A shallow hollow (7008) 35m south-west of the enclosure was also attributed to this phase.

Boundary ditch 8514

The boundary that had been marked during Phases 4 and 5 by ditch 7069, and which appeared to divide activity associated with the road from that to the south, was redefined by the digging of a new ditch (8514). The ditch lay on a parallel alignment to its predecessor, immediately adjacent on the south side, and like the original ditch it was a broad feature, measuring 2.6m wide and 0.55-0.75m deep. No contemporary activity was identified south of this boundary.

Phase 7: Late Roman (mid 3rd-4th century)

No evidence was found to indicate that the road continued in use beyond the early 3rd century, although the latest recuts of the roadside ditches were undated and could therefore date from this period. Occupation on the road frontage had

Fig. 2.17   Langford Lane East, Building 7640 from the north-west, showing the two phases of the west wall

certainly ceased and the only features that were definitely attributable to the late Roman period were situated further south-west, in the vicinity of the Gagle Brook (Fig. 2.19). The uppermost fill of Phase 6 boundary ditch 8514 contained a few sherds of late Roman pottery and the feature clearly continued to serve as a functioning boundary, since it was recut as a shallower ditch (7443). The recut was no more than 0.4m deep and produced no artefactual material. An amorphous cobble spread (6516) that lay on the south side of the ditch yielded a coin dated 260-96 (SF 6521). The proximity of the deposit to the Gagle Brook suggests that it may represent an area of hardstanding associated with a crossing. It may have been constructed from reused building material, since the rubble included a fragment from a socket stone. A shallow pit (7047) 25m north of the boundary ditch also contained late Roman material. The feature measured 0.75m in diameter but only 0.12m deep and had been backfilled with material that was probably domestic debris, including pottery, animal bone, a brooch and three coins. One of the

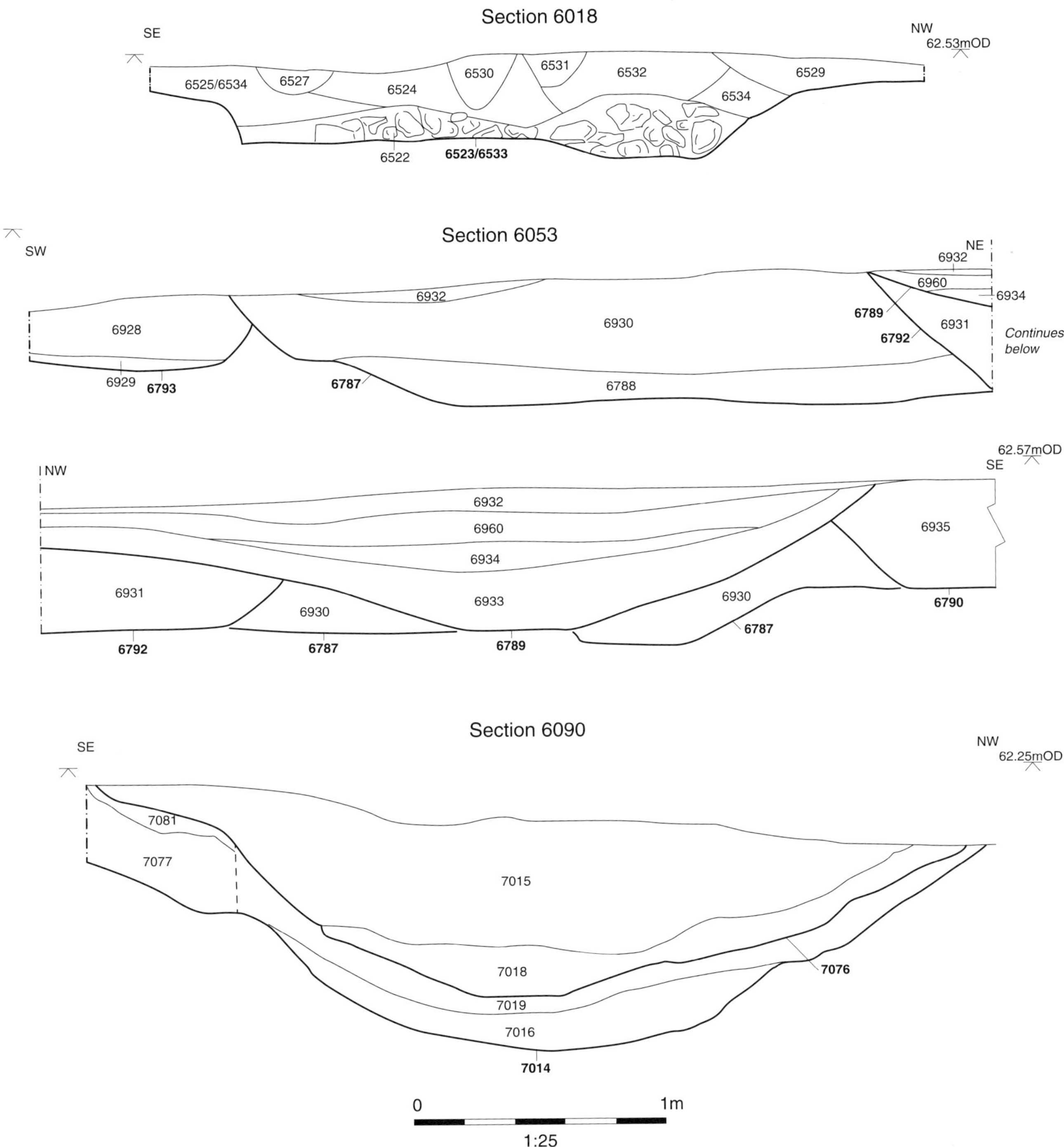

Fig. 2.18   Langford Lane East, sections through Phase 6 pits

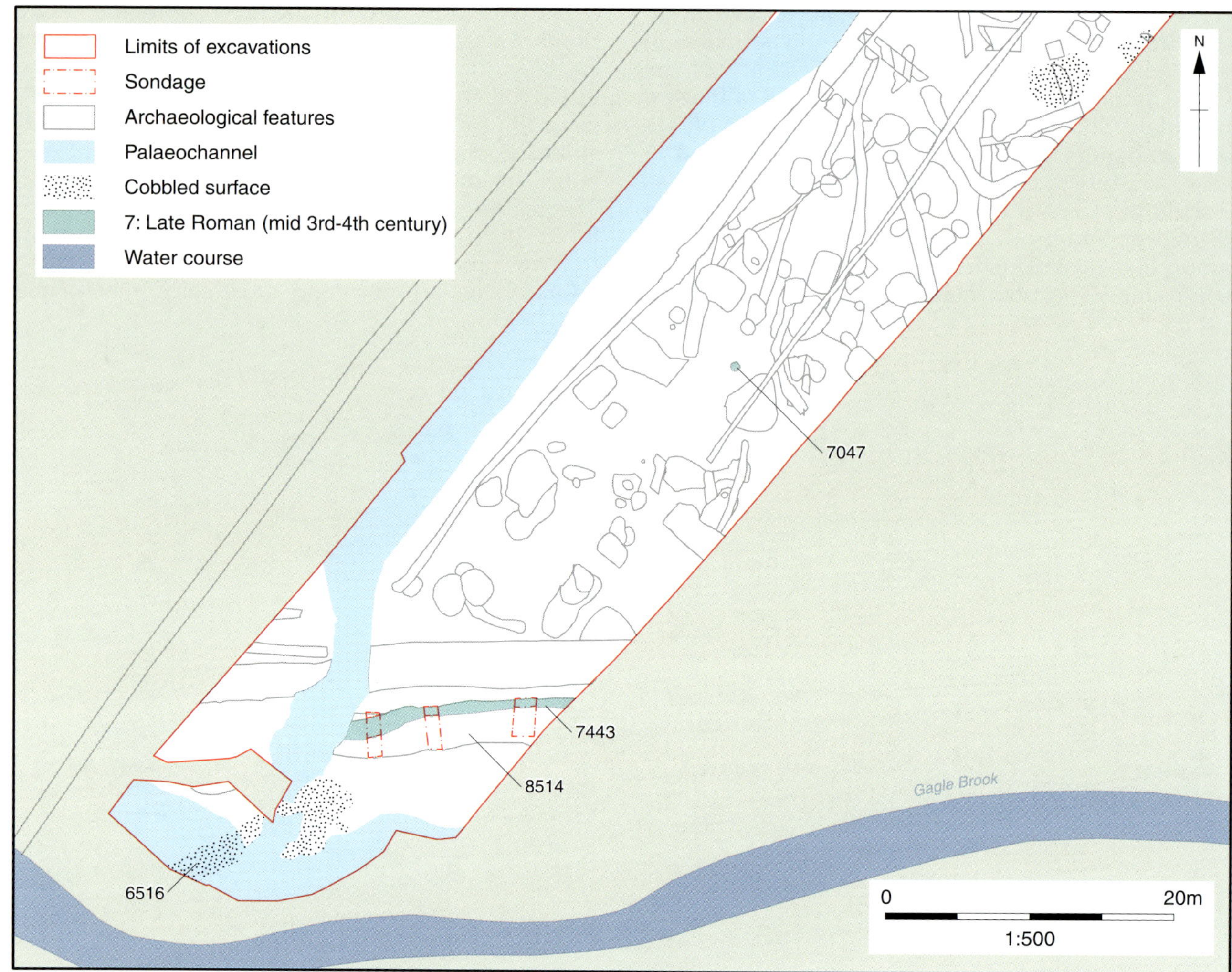

Fig. 2.19   Langford Lane East, plan of Phase 7 features

coins (SF 6572) was an *as* of Vespasian that would have been of some considerable age when deposited, but another (SF 6575) is an issue of Tetricus, dated 271-4, and the third (SF 6573), although eroded and possibly incomplete, may be 4th century.

Phase 9: Post-Roman features

Two ditches (6604 and 6714; Fig. 2.4) that extended along the site on NE-SW alignments and cut through any Roman features that they intersected are likely to be modern, although no dating evidence was forthcoming. Ditch 6604 also cut the palaeochannel (6736) that extended along the north-western edge of the site, which was itself post-Roman in date.

LANGFORD LANE EAST: THE SCHEDULED MONUMENT AREA

A more limited investigation was undertaken within the scheduled monument boundary between the main excavation area and the existing Langford Lane following a redesign of the replacement road to avoid the construction of the previously proposed

bridge crossing of the Langford Brook. This was limited to the initial excavation of four evaluation trenches to assess the presence and preservation of archaeological deposits, followed by a watching brief undertaken during subsequent topsoil stripping for the construction of the new road (Fig. 2.20).

Evaluation Trench 101 exposed part of the metalling of the Roman road that also passed through the adjacent excavation area, and the eastern roadside ditch was recorded in Trench 102 but no features were present in Trenches 103 and 104. The road surface in Trench 101 was constructed on a base of sand with gravel and small limestone pieces pressed in, which rested directly on the natural gravel. The metalling (8004) comprised small pebbles and limestone fragments and was only 2.5m wide, indicating that at this location it covered only a small part of the width of the carriageway. Part of the eastern roadside ditch was exposed in Trench 102, which exhibited a similar sequence of development to that recorded in the main excavation area. The feature began as a broad channel 3.2m wide and 0.3m deep with steep sloping sides and concave base with a step on the north-east side (8031). It was recut as a smaller channel, 1.9m wide and 0.4m deep (8029) and was subsequently recut again as a ditch with sloped sides and a humped base that measured 1.8m wide and 0.30m deep. The road and ditch were both overlain by a sequence of alluvial layers 0.5m thick, increasing to a maximum thickness of 0.8m in Trench 104, close to the Langford Brook. Fragments

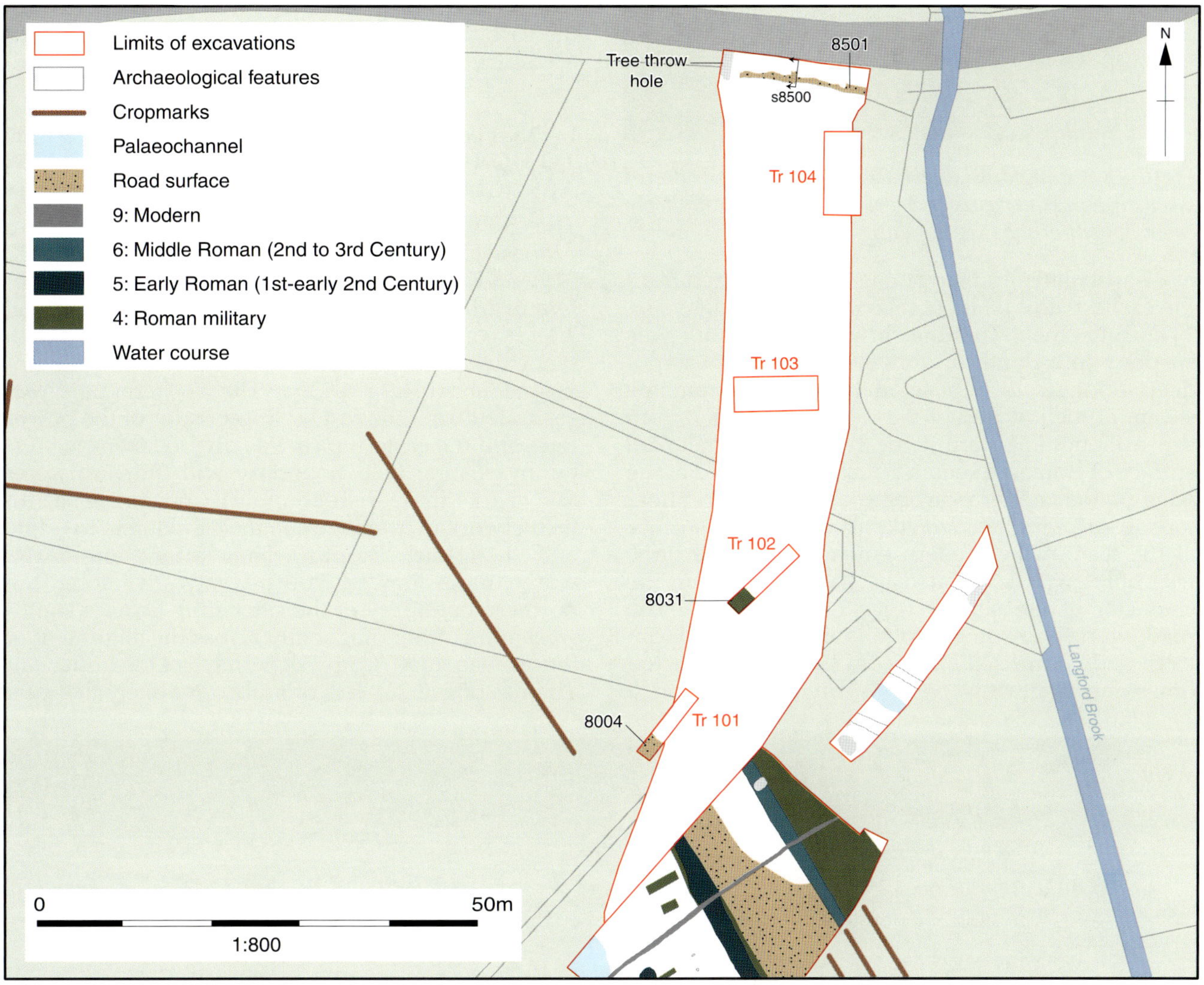

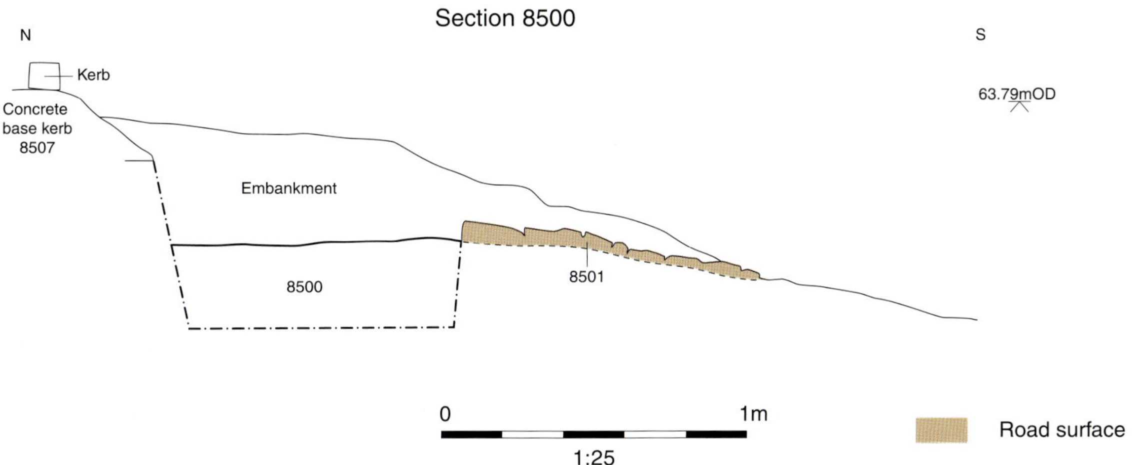

Fig. 2.20   *Langford Lane East, plan of the realignment through the scheduled monument*

Fig. 2.21   *Langford Lane East, section through the edge of Roman Akeman Street beneath the existing Langford Lane*

Fig. 2.22   Langford Lane East, the cobbled surface of Akeman Street exposed in a trial hole dug through the embankment of the existing Langford Lane

of disarticulated human bones were recovered from the earliest alluvial layer (8066) in Trench 104.

During the watching brief the topsoil was stripped to a depth of only 0.15m, which was not deep enough to expose archaeological remains except at the junction of the replacement road with the existing Langford Lane, where the metalled surface of Roman Akeman Street was exposed at the edge of the modern carriageway. At this location, topsoil stripping uncovered part of the road surface at the foot of the modern embankment and three trial holes were excavated by hand to confirm the character of the surface (Figs 2.21 and 2.22). The road overlay a sequence of alluvial deposits 0.65m thick and comprised a surface (8501) of compacted limestone fragments, very worn in places, on a

make-up layer of redeposited clay (8500). It had been entirely removed beneath the modern road and survived only where it was preserved beneath the clay embankment that had been built up against the edge of the carriageway, in a linear band no more than 1.45m wide. The surface sloped down to the east, perhaps indicating the approach to a ford across the Langford Brook a few metres to the east.

LANGFORD LANE SOUTH: THE ALCHESTER TO DORCHESTER-ON-THAMES ROAD AND ASSOCIATED SETTLEMENT

The site was located on either side of the site of a proposed bridge over the railway line at NGR 4572 2195 and also included the replacement of part of two overhead power lines with a buried cable (Fig. 2.1). It comprised a sinuous area of varying width that extended for a distance of *c* 580m and encompassed an area of 1.93ha. The western part was separated from the rest by the corridor of the power lines and the eastern part was divided from the rest by an existing field boundary with flowing water that marks the parish boundary and forms part of the network of drainage channels linking in to Gagle and Langford Brooks. The latter boundary/ watercourse flowed south-westward along the northern boundary of the site before turning south-west and cutting diagonally across the alignment of the Roman road from Alchester to Dorchester-on-Thames (Fig. 2.23). It is thought very likely that part

Fig. 2.23 Langford Lane South, the road from Alchester to Dorchester-on-Thames with the former western channel of the Langford Brook cutting diagonally across the carriageway, facing north

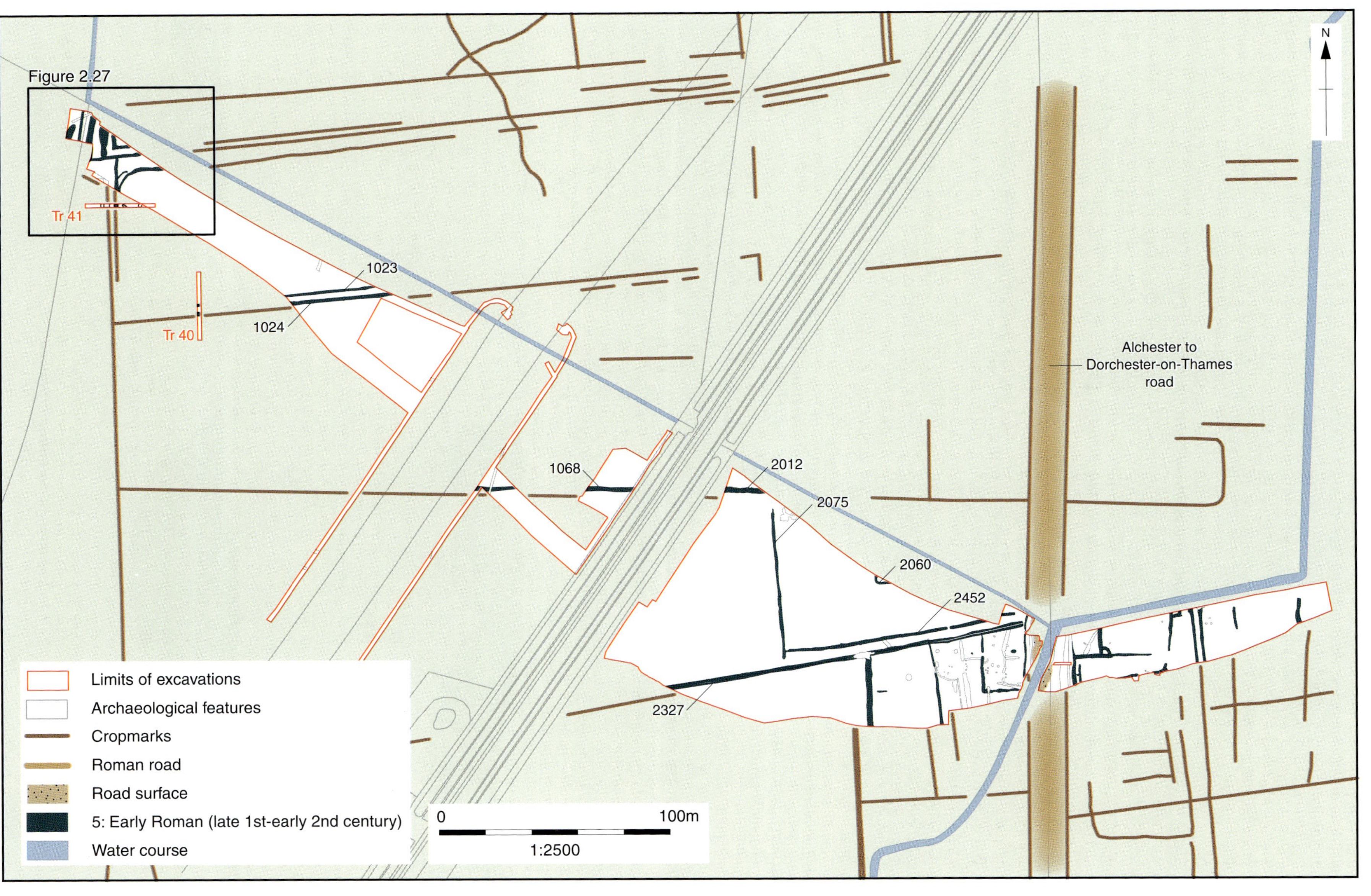

Fig. 2.24 Langford Lane South, plan of all Phase 5 features

of the feature preserves a Roman boundary, since its alignment corresponds with cropmarks representing Roman field boundaries. The site lay within pasture fields east of the railway line at *c* 61m aOD and within an arable field to the west on land rising from *c* 61-62.5m aOD from east to west on a geology of sand and gravel over Peterborough Member mudstone. The site lay *c* 475m south of the south gate of Alchester and extended across the line of the north-south road that linked the town to Dorchester-on-Thames. Cropmark evidence provided a clear arrangement of smaller enclosures fronting onto either side of the road with larger enclosures/fields to the rear, but the evaluation found little evidence for activity on the road frontage.

Activity began later on this site than at Langford Lane East, during the late 1st-early 2nd century (Phase 5), when the road was constructed and enclosures and fields laid out on either side. The road is likely to have continued in use throughout the Roman period and beyond, but there was no evidence for other activity later than the 2nd or early 3rd century (Phase 6).

Phase 1: Early prehistory

Two undiagnostic flint flakes were recovered, one from the topsoil and the other from an undated tree hole.

Phase 5: Early Roman (late 1st-early 2nd century)

Activity began during the late 1st century, when the road was laid out, flanked on both sides by ditched enclosures and fields (Fig. 2.24). The broad outline of these features had been recorded from cropmark evidence, with which the boundaries that were uncovered by the excavation corresponded closely, although the area exposed on the east side of the road was much smaller than that to the west and the arrangement here was consequently less well understood. The excavation uncovered parts of a series of major boundaries that divided the landscape on the west side of the road into fairly regular blocks and the northern part of a complex of smaller enclosures on the road frontage that were probably involved in the management of livestock.

Alchester to Dorchester-on-Thames road

The road was exposed in the eastern part of the excavation area, at a point where a modern field boundary and watercourse cut diagonally across it (Figs 2.23-2.26 and 2.28). The stream had destroyed part of the carriageway, as had a small modern boundary ditch along its eastern side, but both flanking ditches survived, and areas of the road surface were preserved on either side of the modern channel. The road lay in a low-lying part of the site and the eastern flanking ditches were cut into a series of localised alluvial layers (4184-6, 4191). The ditches had been recut on several occasions, as a result of which it was difficult to ascertain the precise original width of the carriageway, although it was in the region of 16-20m. The earliest ditches were an irregular pair, the eastern ditch (4473) being

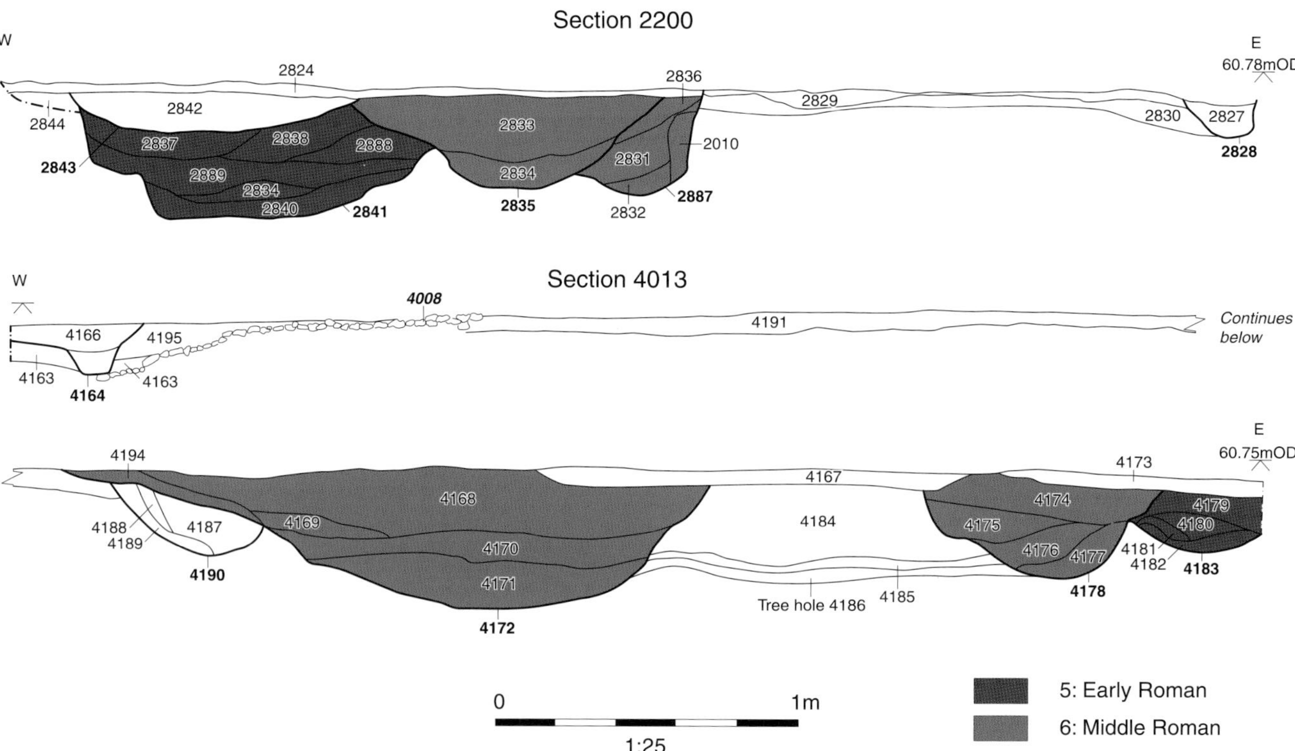

Fig. 2.25   Langford Lane South, sections through the road from Alchester to Dorchester-on-Thames

Fig. 2.26   Langford Lane South, the flanking ditches on the west side of the Alchester to Dorchester-on-Thames road, showing their distinctive alluvial fills, looking south-east

only 0.4m deep, its western counterpart (4479) measuring 0.6-1.05m deep (Fig. 2.25). The western ditch was a steep-sided feature with a flat base and its greater depth had resulted in the waterlogged preservation in its lower fill of a dark, organic layer with small fragments of preserved wood (2840, Fig. 2.25, section 2200). This was overlain by a sandy layer (2834) that may have been deposited by flowing water, above which the remaining fills were composed of blue and grey clays that are also likely to have been water-deposited (Fig. 2.26).

Parts of the road surface were exposed at the limits of the excavation area on either side of the stream. On the west side of the brook, the surface was exposed in the triangular area between the flanking ditches and the edge of the site and in a smaller area at the northern limit of the excavation. It was quite disturbed in these areas and comprised a patchy, discontinuous spread of limestone pieces (2754). The surface was better preserved on the east side of the brook, although it did not extend all the way to the eastern flanking ditch. It was not certain whether this was due to post-Roman truncation of the eastern part of the surface or whether this part of the carriageway had never been metalled. The road surface had been constructed directly on the surface of the natural gravelly sand substrate with no built up agger, and comprised a single layer of limestone gravel and cobbles (4008). It was observed that the larger stones were distributed toward the middle of the road, with the smaller gravel at the edge, perhaps representing episodes of construction and repair or resurfacing using different sized material. No artefactual material was recovered from the surface and it is therefore not certain whether the metalling was associated with the initial construction of the road or was added later.

Enclosures on the western side of the road

Cropmark evidence indicated that the boundaries on this side of the road comprised a regular, orthogonal arrangement dominated by a series of lateral boundary ditches that extended from the road to a terminal boundary 390-400m to the west (Fig. 2.24).

Four of these boundaries were partly exposed within the excavation area; three of them aligned approximately E-W while the southern boundary lay distinctly askew from the others on an alignment that was more approximately ENE-WSW. This boundary was defined, at least in part, by a trackway or livestock race, as may have been one of the others. The blocks of land defined by these boundaries were subdivided by subsidiary boundaries aligned N-S, which formed smaller enclosures close to the road. The southern boundary defined the northern extent of a complex of smaller enclosures, which were probably involved in the management of livestock. The artefactual assemblages from these features were sparse but much of the pottery, particularly from the upper fills, dated from the mid-2nd century, which indicates that the ditches silted up during Phase 6, although the boundaries may have continued to be used after this, defined by any associated above-ground features such as banks or hedgelines.

The main boundaries

The northern boundary was exposed at its junction with the western terminal boundary at the north-western end of the trench (Fig. 2.27). Cropmark evidence indicated that this was a complex junction, where the northern boundary was represented by at least four ditches and the terminal boundary by two ditches, and so it proved difficult to resolve during the excavation, since the excavation area did not expose the entire junction and few straightforward stratigraphic relationships between the two boundaries were identified. The western terminal boundary had been investigated by Evaluation Trench 41, which revealed three ditches on parallel N-S alignments (41002, 41004, 41021), none of which contained artefactual material. Ditch 41002 was 2.6m wide and more than 0.8m deep but could not be excavated to its full depth due to ingress of groundwater, while ditches 41004 and 41021 were 1.5-1.6m wide and measured 0.6m and 0.4m deep respectively. Ditches 41002 and 41021 were recorded within the excavation area as an unexcavated ditch and ditch 1066. The unexcavated ditch was only identified in a trench dug for a drain along the southern edge of the excavation area and was not found when the rest of the area was stripped, although it lay on the same alignment as ditch 1063 further north.

The northern boundary was also represented by three ditches (1064, 1065, 1067). They presumably represent successive phases of the junction, but they did not have a direct stratigraphic relationship that might indicate which was the earlier. The ditches were generally 0.4-0.5m deep, although ditch 1063 was up to 0.85m deep, and finds were generally rare with the exception of a localised dump of more than 2.5kg of pottery in the middle fill (137) of ditch 1063, which included a grey-ware jar and at least three shell-tempered jars, one of which contained the cremated remains of a domestic fowl. The pottery

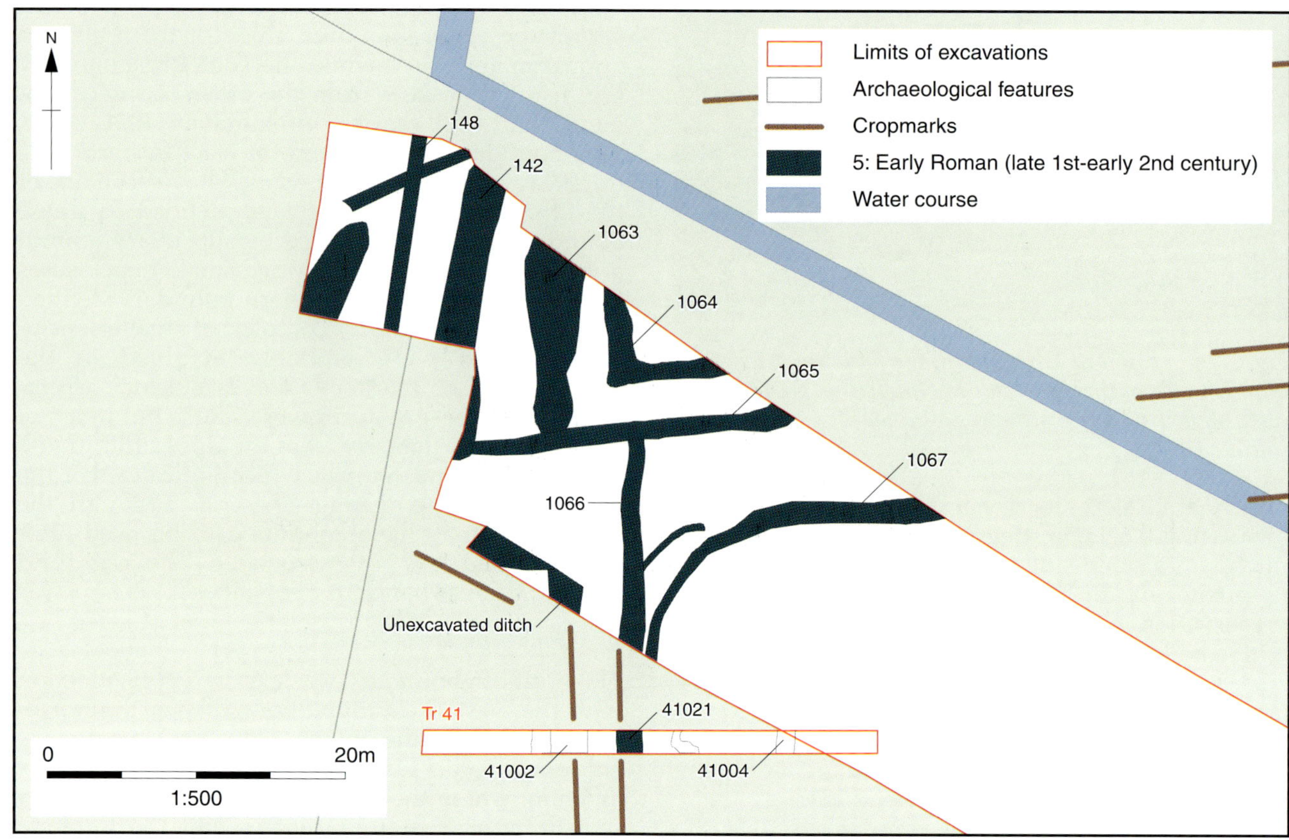

Fig. 2.27   Langford Lane South, detail of the complex junction of the northern boundary ditch and the terminal boundary

from the ditches was predominantly 2nd century in date, although some may have been as late as the early 3rd century, including the dump in ditch 1063. The western ends of the ditches did not end at the terminal boundary within the excavation area as anticipated from the cropmark evidence but exhibited different relationships. Ditch 1064 ended in a return to the north, ditch 1065 continued beyond the terminal boundary (1066), which branched off it, suggesting that in this instance the northern boundary may have been the earlier feature, and ditch 1067 represented a phase in which the two boundaries were defined by a single continuous ditch. In addition to this, four ditches (142, 148, 1063, 1064) appeared to represent continuations of the terminal boundary beyond the northern boundary. This had not been indicated by the cropmark evidence, but corresponded with the alignment of an existing field boundary that may therefore be a survival of an original Roman boundary.

Cropmark evidence indicated that the second boundary lay *c* 60m south of the northern boundary and was at least partly represented by a double-ditched feature (Fig. 2.24). This was confirmed by the excavation, which exposed two ditches 2.5m apart (1023 and 1024). They may have represented two successive phases of the boundary, but it is alternatively possible that they were contemporary and were dug together, either allowing the resultant

spoil to be used to form a bank between them or to create a narrow trackway or livestock race. They comprised a slightly mismatched pair, ditch 1023 being V-shaped and 0.4m deep, and ditch 1024 being somewhat steeper and 0.55-0.65m deep. The ditches were also exposed in Evaluation Trench 40, 36m west of the excavation area.

The third boundary lay *c* 85 further south and comprised a single ditch that was exposed by the excavation at three separate locations (1068, 2012, Fig. 2.24). It was quite a substantial, steep-sided feature that was more than 2m wide and up to 0.8m deep.

The southernmost boundary was exposed *c* 75m south of ditch 1068/2012 and comprised a double-ditched feature (2327, 2452) that was probably a minor trackway or livestock race (Fig. 2.24). This boundary lay on an ENE-WSW alignment that was somewhat askew to the alignments of the road and the other boundaries and was evidently a significant feature, since the arrangements to north and south differed. The trackway was *c* 4m wide and extended for 105m, beyond which ditch 2327 continued as a boundary ditch, extending beyond the limits of the excavation where it could be traced as a cropmark to the terminal boundary, and ditch 2452 turned northward to form a subsidiary boundary parallel to the road (2075). The trackway appeared to be intended to provide access from the

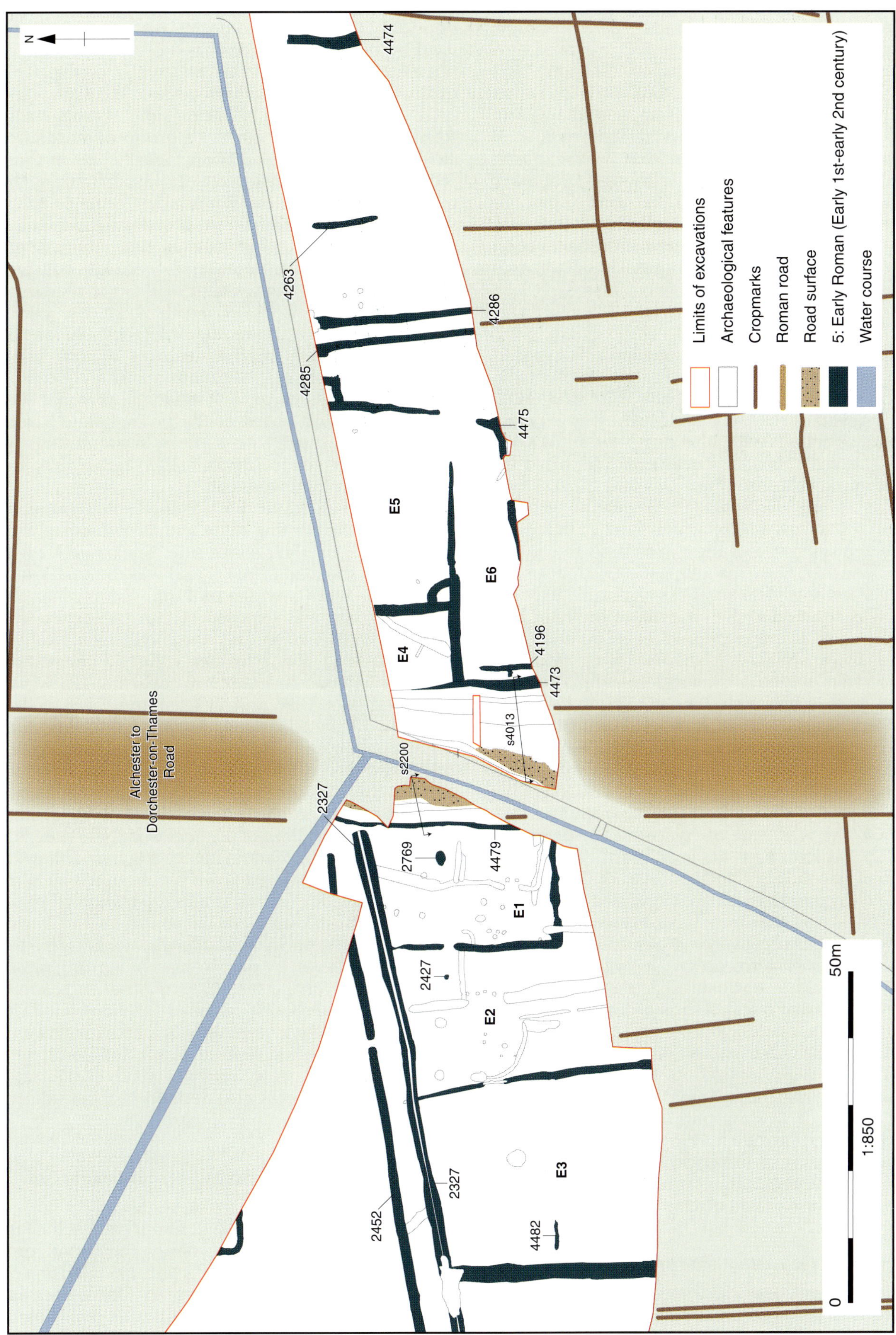

Fig. 2.28 Langford Lane South, plan of Phase 5 enclosures on the road frontage

road to the area west of ditch 2075 without passing through the enclosures on the road frontage, although access to the latter was also provided by a small break in ditch 2452. Ditches 2327 and 2452 were typically 0.4-0.65m deep, but ditch 2075 was less substantial, with a depth of no more than 0.3m, which presumably reflected its subsidiary role. It was the only lateral division that was exposed within these blocks of land, although cropmark evidence indicates features on the same alignment further north. An L-shaped ditch (2060) that was partly exposed at the eastern edge of the excavation area may have been the boundary of a small subsidiary enclosure.

Enclosures on the road frontage

The only part of the road frontage that was exposed by the excavation area was situated south of the trackway represented by ditches 2327 and 2452, where a group of roadside enclosures was exposed that corresponded with the northern limit of a concentration of smaller enclosures identified by the cropmark evidence (Figs 2.23 and 2.28). Three enclosures were identified (E1-3) and the absence of internal features and relatively small artefactual assemblage suggest that they were used to contain livestock rather than for domestic occupation or industrial activity. The smallest enclosure was E1, which was situated at the junction of the road and the trackway. It measured 25 x 17m and was defined by a shallow L-shaped ditch with an entrance 1.5m wide on the western side. The only internal feature was a shallow pit (2769) less than 0.2m deep, but the enclosure also defined the limits of a series of soil spreads (2699, 2796, 2849, 2998). The layers contained a small mixed assemblage of 1st- and 2nd-century pottery and are likely to represent part of the ground surface from Phases 5 and 6. On the west side of enclosure E1 lay enclosure E2, which was at least 18m wide and continued beyond the southern limit of the excavation area. Cropmark evidence suggested that it was a large enclosure that may have been up to *c* 70m long, with enclosure E1 being a subsidiary enclosure at its north-eastern corner. The only contemporary feature within enclosure E2 was a single pit (2747) that yielded a few sherds of late 1st-century pottery. The enclosure was bounded to the west by enclosure E3, which may also have been 70m long and was 28m wide. A shallow E-W aligned gully (4482) 4m long may have been part of a subdivision within the north-western part of the enclosure but this was not certain. Ditch 4196 may also have been an internal feature of the enclosure since, although it ran alongside the road, at 0.16m deep it was too shallow to be a roadside ditch.

Enclosures on the eastern side of the road

The arrangement of enclosures on the east side of the road was less well understood than that on the west, owing to the smaller excavation area and the relative paucity of cropmarks in this area. The boundary (2327) defined on the western side of the road by the trackway continued on the east side as the existing field boundary and water course. This extended along the northern edge of the excavation area, and, as on the western side, it apparently formed the northern limit of a group of enclosures close to the road (Figs 2.24 and 2.28). Parts of three rectilinear enclosures were exposed within the trench (E4-6), as well as boundaries to the east that were less well defined but probably represented further enclosures. The ditches that defined the enclosures and other boundaries were less substantial than those on the western side of the road, and rarely exceeded 0.3m in depth. Like the corresponding enclosures on the western side of the road, they lacked internal features or any other evidence for domestic occupation and are likely to have been livestock pens. Artefactual material was again sparse and much of the pottery dated from the middle and late 2nd century, representing the period over which the ditches silted rather than the date at which they were cut.

Enclosures E4 and E5 adjoined the boundary defined by the existing ditch and watercourse, with enclosure E6 on their south side. Enclosure E4 was situated on the road frontage and was the smallest of the group, with a width of 11m. The part of the enclosure that was exposed within the excavation area measured 11m N-S and the enclosure is likely to have extended for a further *c* 5m to the extant boundary. On its east side lay enclosure E5, which measured 30m E-W and at least 16m N-S, and is similarly likely to have extended to the existing watercourse boundary. Enclosure E6 measured 40m E-W but its N-S dimension was less certain, as it was not certain whether ditch 4475, which was partly exposed at the southern edge of the excavation area, was the southern limit of the enclosure or an internal sub-division. Cropmark evidence suggested that the enclosure may have extended for as much as 80m, with evidence for further internal partitions. Breaks in the enclosure ditches at the south-west of enclosure E2 and the north-west of enclosure E6 were the result of truncation by post-Roman ploughing rather than original entrances. East of the enclosures, ditches 4285 and 4286 defined a N-S boundary, although since they were only 2m apart it was not certain whether they represented a double-ditched boundary or a narrow trackway or livestock race. Ditches 4263 and 4474 also defined N-S boundaries that corresponded with cropmark features.

Phase 6: Middle Roman (2nd century–early 3rd century)

The landscape that had been laid out during the late 1st century continued in broadly the same form throughout the following century. Continued maintenance of the Alchester to Dorchester-on-Thames road was demonstrated by the recutting of the roadside ditches, which were redefined on at

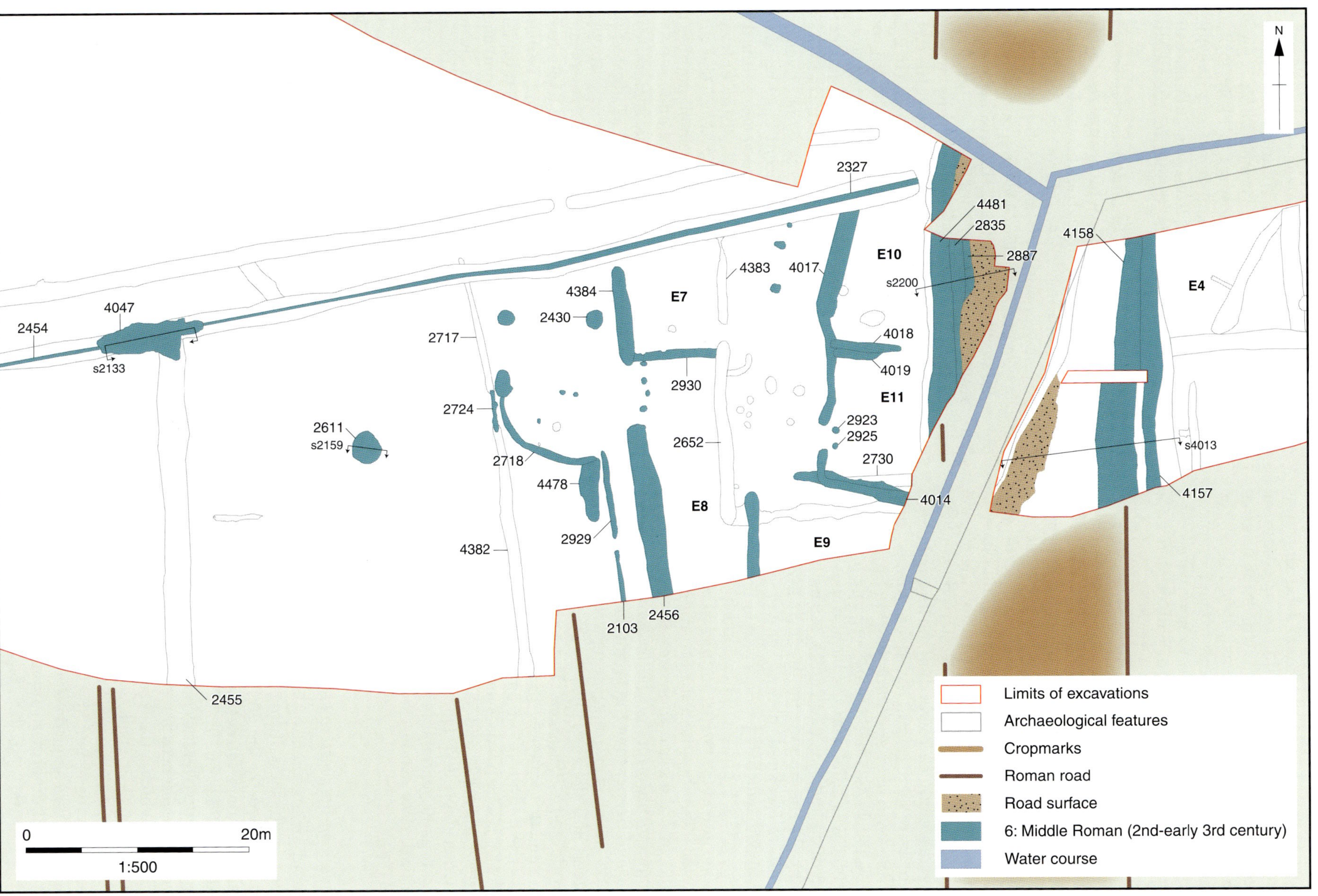

Fig. 2.29   Langford Lane South, plan of Phase 6 enclosures on the western road frontage

least two occasions during this century, and the pottery from the fills of the main land divisions indicated that most of their silting occurred during the 2nd century. The only area in which the original arrangement of boundaries was altered was the group of smaller enclosures that fronted onto the western side of the road, which were replaced by a new, more complex arrangement with evidence for occupation nearby.

Alchester to Dorchester-on-Thames road

The road continued in use throughout this period, during which both flanking ditches were recut at least twice (Figs. 2.25 and 2.29). Each recut was situated on the inner side of the preceding phase of the ditch, resulting in a slight narrowing of the carriageway. The recuts of the western ditch (2835, 4481) were slightly narrower than the original Phase 5 ditch but were similarly deep, ditch 2835 measuring 0.9m deep and ditch 4481 measuring up to 0.75m. Ditch 2835 had a dark, organic lower fill (2834) that was similar to the basal deposit in the Phase 5 ditch and was overlain by a pale blue clay sand (2833). The bottom fill of ditch 4481 was a slump of redeposited natural gravel and sand (2832), above which lay a layer of soft pale blue clayey sand (2831) and an upper deposit of blue clay with some gravel (2836). An additional recut (2887), which was cut by the latest recut 2835, only extended into the excavation area for 5.5m before terminating. The recuts of the eastern ditch were broader and deeper than the original Phase 5 ditch, the initial recut (4157) measuring 2.4m wide and 0.7m deep and the final ditch (4158) being up to 3.7m wide and 0.95m deep. These deeper ditches had a similar sequence of fills to the western ditches. The bottom fill of ditch 4157 was a gravel slump (4177), which was overlain by layers of blue and grey sandy silt and clay (4174-6) typical of being water-deposited. Ditch 4158 had a lower fill of dark, organic material (4171), above which were fills of dark grey sandy clay (4170) and light grey sand (4168).

Enclosures on the western side of the road

The broad arrangement of landscape division that had been established during Phase 5 was retained, as demonstrated by the 2nd-century pottery from the main boundary ditches, which were clearly still open during Phase 6. They appear to have been allowed to silt up over the course of the 2nd century, however, and evidence for recutting was only found in ditch 2327, which infilled some time after AD 120 and was recut as a shallow gully no more than 0.25m deep (2454), from which was recovered a coin of Antoninus Pius issued in AD 151-2. It is possible that this ditch was singled out for recutting because of its role as the northern limit of the complex of smaller enclosures on the road frontage, which continued to be an important focus for activity during Phase 6. Enclosures E1-3, which had been established on the road frontage during Phase 5, were superseded by a more complex arrangement of five enclosures (E7-11). Like their Phase 5 predecessors, this group of enclosures is likely to have been involved in management of livestock, although refuse recovered from pits 2611 and 4047 provided evidence for domestic occupation somewhere nearby.

The enclosures were bounded to the west by Phase 5 ditch 2717/4382, which appears to have been retained, since the entrance was blocked by the digging of ditch 2724. Ten metres east of this feature a new boundary was established with the construction of ditch 2456/4384, beyond which lay the main group of enclosures. The area between the two boundary ditches contained a group of features that may be associated with the management of livestock. A shallow ditch 2103/2929 extended on a parallel alignment to ditch 2456, defining a trackway or livestock race 2.0-2.3m wide that extended into the excavation area for a distance of 13m. The coincidence of its northern end with the entrance through ditch 2456/4384 suggests that it was designed to channel livestock in this direction, and the adjacent curving ditch (2718) was probably also associated with this process, either corralling livestock at the entrance or funnelling them into the trackway. The area enclosed by ditch 2718 contained a small number of postholes and pits, one of which (2430) was 0.85m deep but yielded no definite evidence regarding its function. To the south lay a ditch or elongated pit (4478) of uncertain purpose. The entrance through ditch 2456/4384 was 5.5m wide and was associated with a group of four postholes that are likely to be evidence for a gate structure of some sort, perhaps designed to facilitate management and handling of the livestock passing through. The entrance provided access to an area that contained a cluster of undated pits but no demonstrably contemporary features, from which enclosures opened off to the north, south and east.

The northern enclosure (E7), which was slightly trapezoidal in plan, adjoined boundary ditch 2454. It measured *c* 16m E-W and 8-12m N-S, although since the ditch that defined its southern side (2930) appeared to respect Phase 5 ditch 2652/4383 it is possible that the latter feature was retained and that the enclosure was thus subdivided into two. The only features within the enclosure were three shallow pits.

The southern enclosures (E8 and E9) both extended beyond the southern limit of the excavation area and so their full dimensions could not be established, except that enclosure E8 measured 7m E-W and enclosure E9 measured at least 13m and probably extended to the road frontage. Neither contained any internal features.

Enclosures E10 and E11 were situated on the road frontage, although no evidence was found to indicate whether they could be accessed from the road. They appear to have originated as a single enclosure, 25m long and 6-9m wide, defined by two ditches aligned at right angles (4014, 4017) with an entrance 4m wide at the south-western corner that provided access from the rest of the complex. The southern boundary was subsequently replaced by the L-shaped ditch 2730, which caused the width of the entrance to be reduced to 2.1m. A pair of postholes (2923, 2925) situated immediately inside the entrance are likely to be evidence for a gate structure. Possibly at the same time as this alteration, the enclosure was divided into two by the construction of ditch 4019 and its recut ditch 4018, which both ended 2.9-4.5m from the adjacent roadside ditch in order to allow access

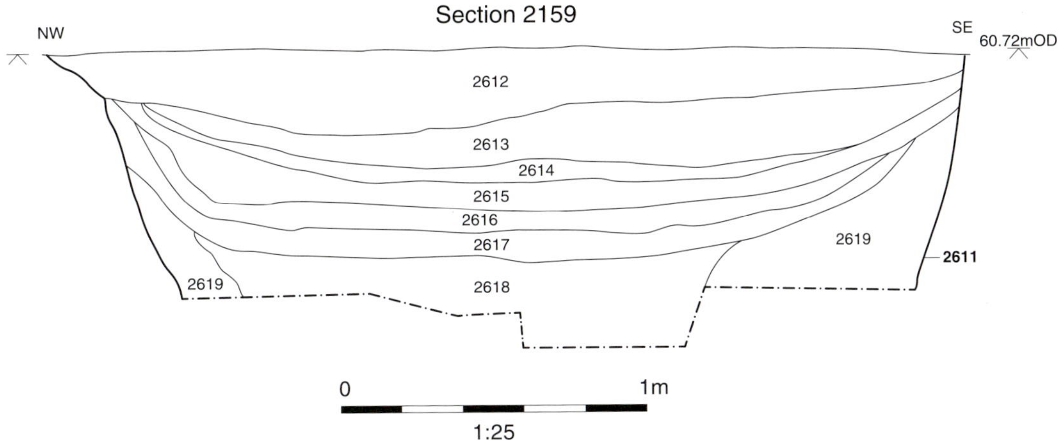

Fig. 2.30   Langford Lane South, section through Phase 6 waterhole 2611

Fig. 2.31   Langford Lane South, Phase 6 waterhole 2611 during excavation

Fig. 2.33   Langford Lane South, Phase 6 pit 4047 with its charcoal-rich fill, cutting Phase 5 ditch 2327, facing north-east

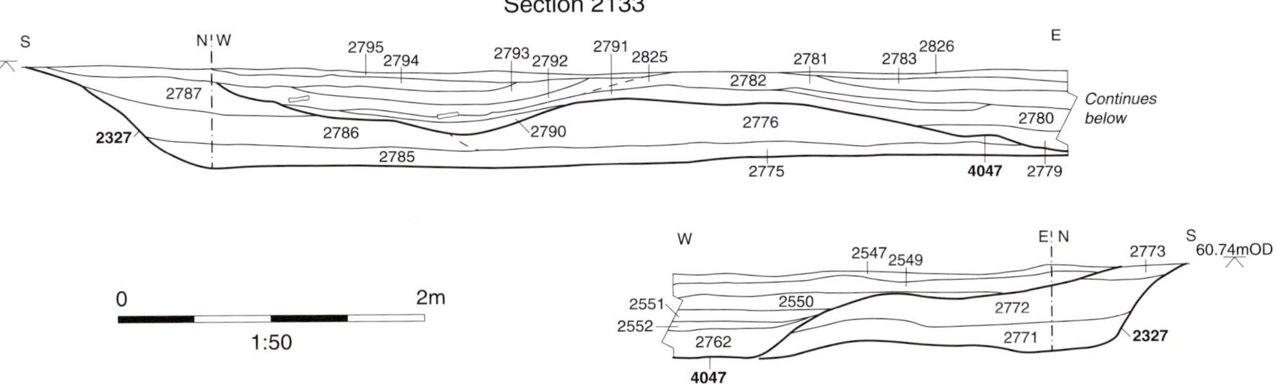

Fig. 2.32   Langford Lane South, section through pit 4047

between the enclosures. Neither enclosure contained any contemporary features associated with their function.

After the enclosure ditches had mostly silted, a thin gravel surface (2998, Fig. 2.29) was laid down across the southern part of the area. The surface had been truncated by post-Roman ploughing and did not survive *in situ*, but parts of it were preserved where it had sunk into the underlying ditches as the ditch fills settled. The small pottery assemblage from the surviving parts of the surface and from the tertiary ditch fills that overlay it within the ditches indicated that it dated from the 2nd century.

The only features west of the enclosure complex were two large pits (2611, 4047), both of which had been used for the disposal of domestic refuse, indicating that occupation was located somewhere nearby. Pit 2611 was a large, steep-sided pit whose depth suggested that it was dug as a waterhole

(Figs 2.30 and 2.31). The feature could only be hand excavated to a depth of 1m due to flooding by groundwater, but augering indicated that it was 1.3-1.4m deep in total. A large assemblage of domestic material was recovered, mostly from the middle fills (2615-2617), and indicated that the feature had been used as a rubbish pit after it ceased to be a source of water. The assemblage included more than 4kg of pottery, 1.2kg of animal bone, 14kg of ceramic building material, 6.6kg of oyster shell, and both window and vessel glass (Fig. 3.18), the pottery exhibiting a notably large proportion of samian ware and flagons. A layer of black, organic material (2618) at least 0.3m thick in the lower part of the feature contained water-logged plant remains indicative of wet or damp ground. Pit 4047 was a large, irregular feature at the junction of ditch 2454 and Phase 5 ditch 2455 (Figs 2.32 and 2.33). There was some uncertainty

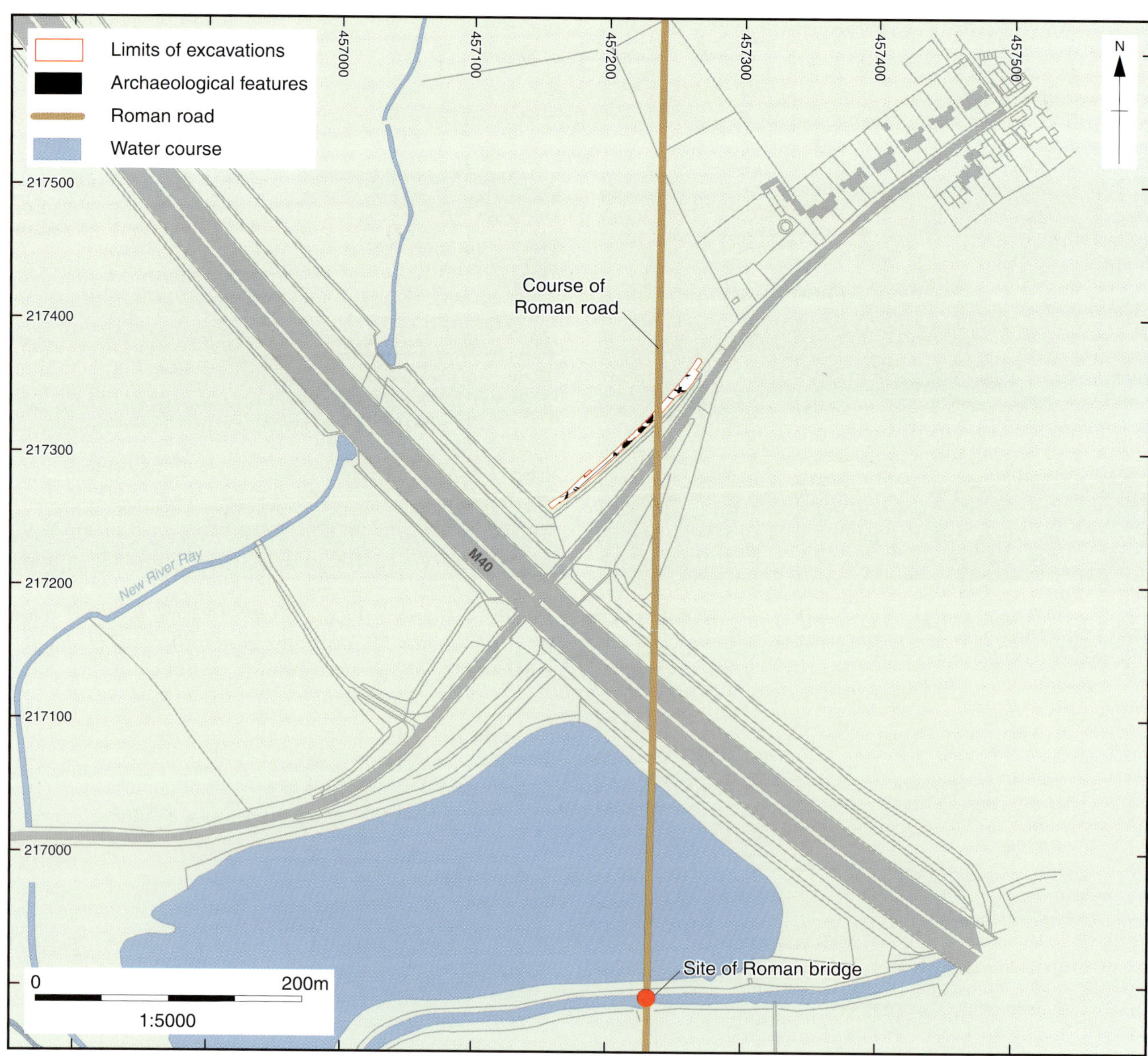

Fig. 2.34   Location of South of Merton

as to whether it represented a deliberate cut or simply localised deposition of burnt material within the ditch fills. It encompassed an area of 9.7 x 2.7m and was 0.4m deep and was filled by a sequence of charcoal-rich layers. The pit produced an assemblage of more than 3.5kg of pottery, 6.1kg of ceramic building material, 2.6kg of oyster shell, a turquoise melon bead (Fig. 3.17, no. 28), fragments of vessel glass and a fragment from a quernstone that had been reused as a hone. Like the assemblage from pit 2611, the pottery was characterised by a large quantity of samian ware and flagons. Substantial quantities of charred plant remains and charcoal were present throughout the fills and included much burnt crop-processing waste, some of which may have derived from malting.

Enclosures on the eastern side of the road

No new features were created on the east side of the road during this phase, but the pottery from the fills of the boundary ditches that had been established during Phase 5 indicated that most of their silting occurred during the 2nd century.

SOUTH OF MERTON

The investigations at South of Merton were undertaken in advance of the construction of an access track to a new barn for College Farm. The excavation area was located south-west of the village of Merton and adjacent to the M40 (Fig. 2.34). The site intersected the line of the Roman road from Alchester to Dorchester-on-Thames and an area of

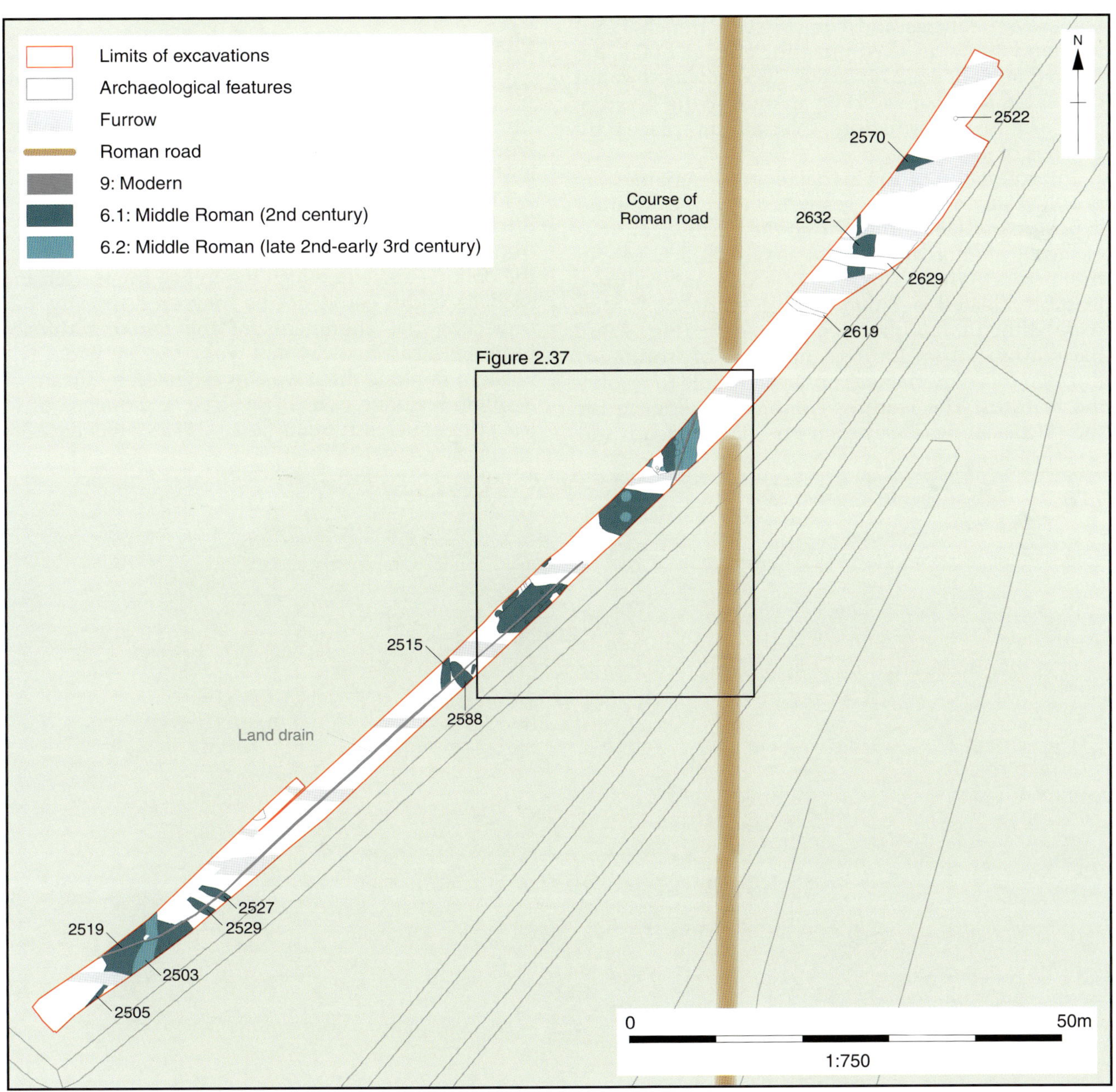

Fig. 2.35   South of Merton, plan of archaeological features

'dark earth and Romano-British occupation debris' had been noted nearby during construction of the M40 in 1988-91 (Chambers 1992, 52). The Roman road crossed the River Ray *c* 430m south of the site, where the remains of a timber bridge that was recorded in 1979 was dated by dendrochronology to shortly after AD 95 (Chambers 1986a). Evaluation Trenches 13 and 14 exposed ditches that may have been the flanking ditches of the road, but no road surface was found. Further associated boundaries were recorded, however. In the northern part of the evaluation area at Merton Footbridge, Trench 2 exposed two small pits, one of which yielded small sherds of late Iron Age-early Roman pottery, and in Trench 10 close to the new barn construction, a pit that was only 0.06m deep produced four small sherds of Roman date. The excavation area was targeted on the road and associated features and comprised a trench 155m long and 4m wide, encompassing an area of 0.07ha, located at NGR 4572 2173 (Fig. 2.35). It was situated on flat land at *c* 60m aOD on an underlying geology of Cornbrash Formation, overlain in places by patches of sandy clay.

Interpretation of the archaeological remains was problematic and was restricted by the limited exposure of the features within the narrow confines of the excavation area. This was particularly true in the central area, where numerous intercutting features created a broad spread of deposits that were difficult to differentiate in plan (Fig. 2.36). Excavation of a limited number of sondages through this material was only partly able to resolve the features. The features comprised evidence for the Alchester to Dorchester-on-Thames road and

roadside occupation, most of which was situated on the west side of the road. Two prehistoric flint blades (Phase 1) were recovered, but the most significant element of the remains comprised evidence for a continuous period of occupation spanning the 2nd century (Phase 6.1) and probably continuing into the early part of the 3rd century (Phase 6.2). The presence of a small quantity of late 1st century pottery provided some slight indication that occupation may have begun earlier, but no features could be attributed to this period.

Phase 1: Early prehistory

Two flint blades were recovered from residual contexts. Neither is chronologically diagnostic, although an early prehistoric date is likely.

Phase 6.1: Middle Roman (2nd century)

The Alchester to Dorchester-on-Thames road

The projected line of the road from Alchester to Dorchester-on-Thames extended through the eastern half of the excavation area on a N-S alignment. No evidence was found for a metalled surface, but ditches identified on this alignment are likely to be the road's flanking ditches (Figs 2.35–2.37). Due to the oblique angle at which the trench intersected the road its width could not be measured directly, but projecting the alignments of the flanking ditches indicates a carriageway that was *c* 18-23m wide. The western flanking ditch was investigated by means of a single sondage, which revealed a sequence of at least three successive cuts (2520, 2544, 2548; Figs 2.37-

Fig. 2.36   South of Merton, spread of features in the central part of the excavation area, looking east

8). The earliest ditch (2548) was attributed to this phase and the subsequent cuts to phase 6.2 on ceramic grounds. Ditch 2548 was 1.7m wide and 0.5m deep, with moderately sloped sides. A hollow that was 1.75m wide and 0.25m deep extended along the west side of the sequence of ditches, the purpose of which was unclear, although its relatively wide and shallow profile suggested that it was not an additional ditch phase. The stratigraphic relationship between the hollow and the roadside ditch was uncertain due to the similarity of their fills. Two irregularities in the base of the hollow were exposed that may have been postholes, possibly providing evidence for a fenceline alongside the ditch, but this interpretation was not certain.

The eastern flanking ditch (2632) was a wide but shallow feature that measured 2.4m wide and 0.25m deep (Fig. 2.35). A shallow ditch (2629) cut across it on a WNW-ESE alignment, and a similar ditch (2619) lay close by on a similar alignment, the latter within the carriageway of the road, but their date and significance are unknown.

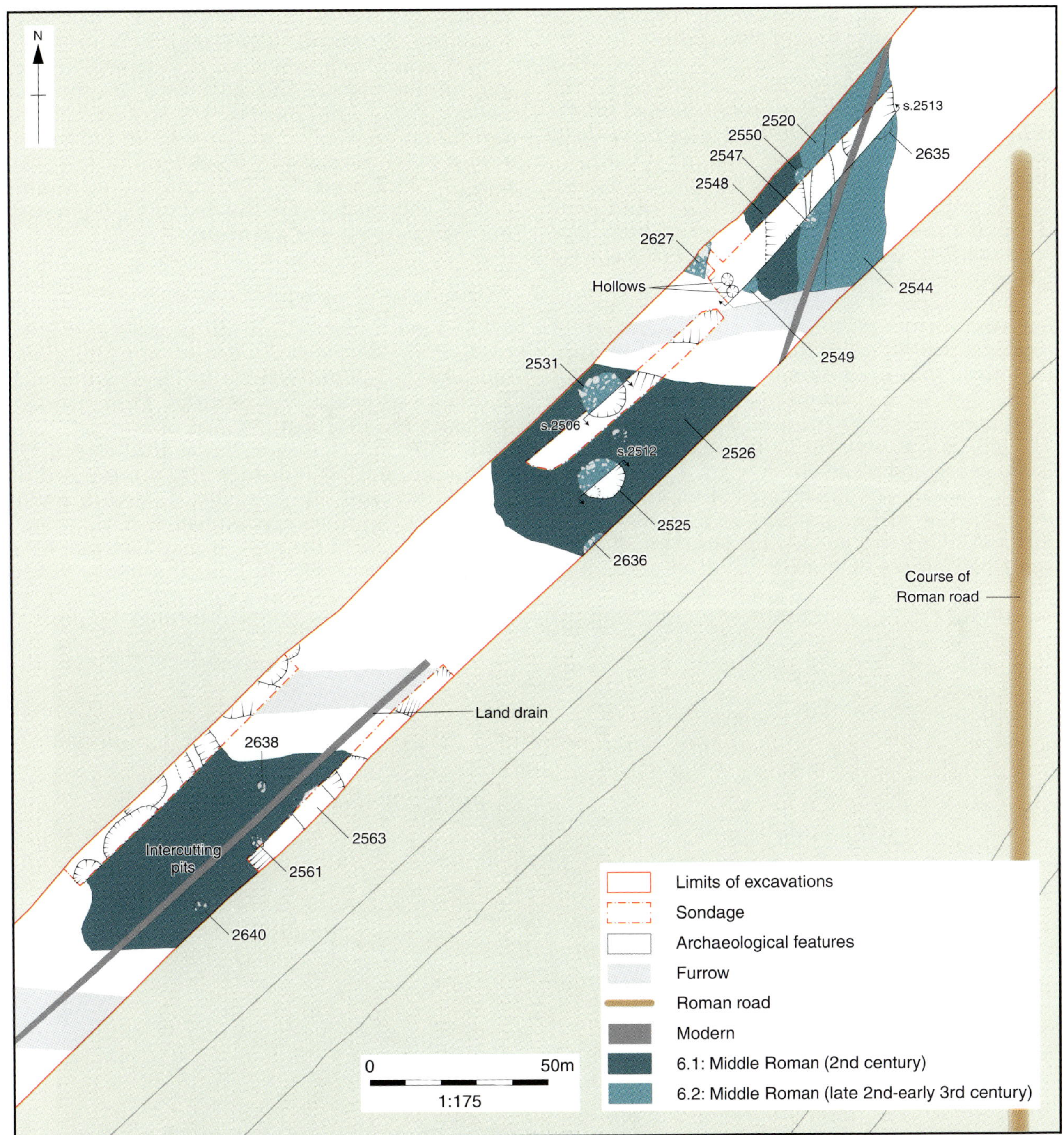

Fig. 2.37   South of Merton, plan of the roadside ditches on the west side of the Alchester to Dorchester-on-Thames road and features on the road frontage

Occupation west of the road

Evidence for occupation alongside the road lay exclusively on the western side, which may account for the greater emphasis on maintaining and redefining the western flanking ditch compared with the eastern one. The features attributed to this phase comprised spreads of deposits that, on excavation, were resolved into hollows and inter-cutting pits whose function was difficult to establish. It is possible that some of the features represent structures fronting onto the road, but this was not certain, in contrast to the definite evidence for buildings in this area during phase 6.2.

A large hollow (2526, Fig. 2.37) was situated immediately adjacent to the road frontage. The shape of the hollow could not be established since it extended beyond the trench, but it measured at least 4.2m across and was 0.36m deep with a flat base. The hollow was partly filled by a sterile clay deposit (2575), overlain by a darker layer (2574) with some charcoal and heat-reddened clay, which may have been domestic refuse that included spent fuel from a hearth. No finds were present.

Part of a second spread of material was exposed 8m south-west of hollow 2526. Excavation of sondages against either side of the trench resolved the spread into a complex of intercutting pits (Fig. 2.37). They were shallow, concave features up to 0.4m deep and may have been dug as quarry pits. The infilled pits were cut by three postholes (2561, 2638, 2640) and overlain by part of a possible cobbled surface (2563). The postholes were difficult to define due to the similarity of their fills to the material filling the underlying pits, but all three contained stones that may have been used as

packing. The cobbled surface extended for 1.25m from the south-east baulk and clearly continued beyond the edge of the trench. It comprised a single layer of stones, from which a mixed assemblage of 2nd-century pottery was recovered, as well as a small quantity of animal bone.

Two ditches (2503, 2515, Fig. 2.35) that extended on N-S alignments parallel to that of the road may have been the boundaries of roadside enclosures. Ditch 2515 lay *c* 25m from the edge of the road and was a very shallow feature that was truncated to the south by a modern field drain. An adjacent feature (2588) may have been an elongated pit or the end of a ditch on an oblique, NW-SE angle.

Soil layer 2519 was situated at the south-western end of the trench and contained 2nd-century pottery. Gully 2505 may have extended into the layer from the south, but the junction of the two features was truncated by a medieval furrow. Two shallow ditches (2527, 2529) that lay on parallel NW-SE alignments were situated to the north-east, but their purpose was unknown.

Features east of the road

While a much smaller area was exposed east of the road, it was clear that the density of features was much less compared with the area west of the road, and that occupation was restricted to the western frontage. The only features east of the road were ditch 2570 and cremation burial 2522 (Fig. 2.35). Only a very small part of ditch 2570 was exposed, as it was truncated by a medieval furrow, but it appeared to lie on an approximate E-W alignment, at a right angle to the road. It may therefore have defined a field or enclosure boundary that branched

Fig. 2.38   *South of Merton, the sequence of roadside ditches on the west side of the Alchester to Dorchester-on-Thames road*

off eastern roadside ditch 2632, but the junction of the two features lay a short distance beyond the edge of the excavation area. Ditch 2570 was quite substantial, measuring up to 2.1m wide and 0.5m deep. Cremation burial 2522 was located a short distance north of the ditch and comprised a small bowl-shaped pit 0.5m in diameter and 0.13m deep, into which the cremated remains of an adult of undetermined sex had been placed, mixed with charcoal from the pyre (2523). The calcined bone measured only 452.5g, suggesting that part of the deposit had been lost to truncation by later ploughing, while the charcoal indicated that the pyre consisted entirely of alder.

Phase 6.2: Middle Roman (late 2nd–early 3rd century)

The Alchester to Dorchester-on-Thames road

The second and third phases of the western flanking ditch were attributed to this phase (2520, 2544, Figs 2.37-2.39). They were very similar in form to the original phase of the ditch, measuring *c* 1.5-2m wide and 0.5-0.6m deep. The sequence of ditches progressed from west to east, resulting in a slight narrowing of the road with each redefinition. The middle fill (2521) of the second ditch in the sequence (2520) yielded by far the largest assemblage of pottery from the excavation, comprising nearly 1.8kg of sherds that included an almost complete mortarium of Young type M14, dated AD 180-240 (SF 2500; Fig. 3.9, no. 128), an unusual oxidised beaker (SF 2501, Fig. 3.9, no. 124), and a small grey-ware beaker (SF 2502, Fig. 3.9, no. 125), these last two being of similar date to the mortarium. The primary fill (2590) of the final phase of the ditch (2544) also contained pottery dating from the late 2nd or early 3rd century, namely sherds from a white ware flagon of Young type W6 and a base sherd from a vessel of probable East Gaulish samian.

Occupation west of the road

The evidence for buildings on the road frontage was provided by the identification of a number of postholes, but it was not possible to resolve them into coherent structures (Fig. 2.37). The most compelling evidence for a structure comprised an alignment of three large, stone-packed postholes (2525, 2531, 2636) cut into the fills of Phase 6.1 hollow 2526. The postholes formed a N-S alignment parallel to that of the road and were large, well-constructed features that were clearly intended to support a substantial structure, although the character of the structure is not known since no corresponding features were found that might represent the other side of the building. Postholes 2525 and 2531 were sub-circular in plan and measured 1.3-1.5m across (Figs 2.40 and 2.41). Neither posthole was bottomed but they were excavated to a depth of 0.6-0.7m and

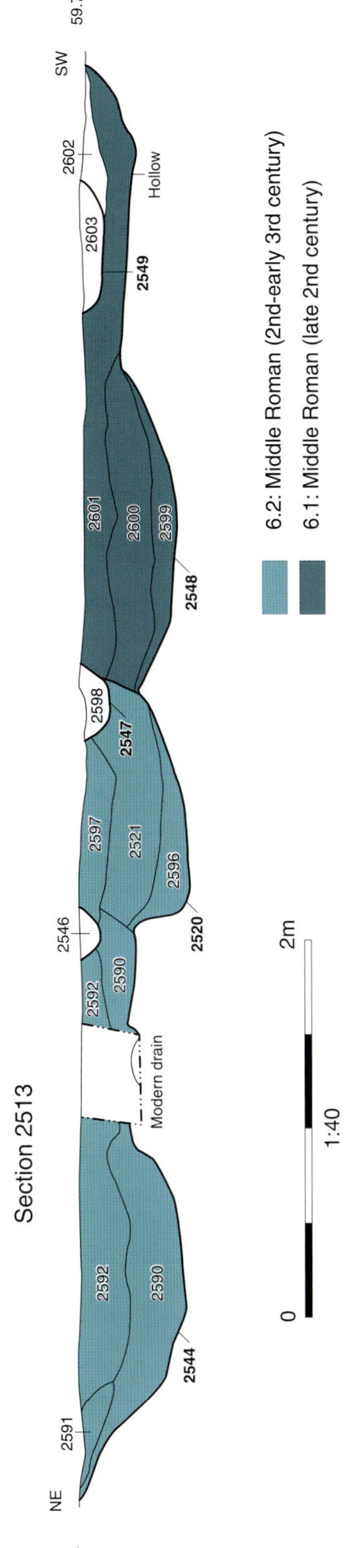

Fig. 2.39 South of Merton, section through the sequence of roadside ditches on the west side of the Alchester to Dorchester-on-Thames road

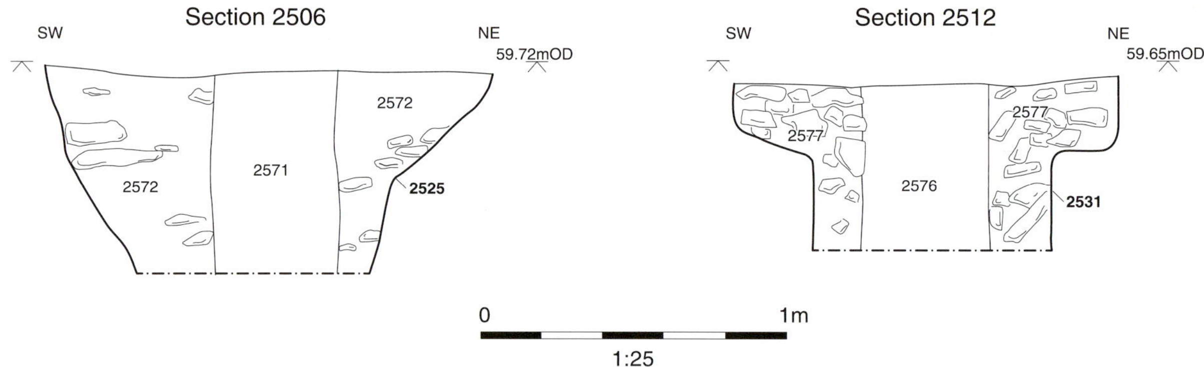

Fig. 2.40   South of Merton, sections through stone-packed postholes 2525 and 2531

Fig. 2.41   South of Merton, stone-packed postholes 2525 and 2531, looking north-west

had been dug through Phase 6.1 hollow 2526 and into the underlying geological substrate. Within each posthole a postpipe of dark grey silt 0.5m across was surrounded by a packing of limestone pieces. Posthole 2636 appeared to be similar, but was not excavated as only a very small part of it was exposed at the edge of the trench.

Four smaller postholes (2547, 2549, 2550, 2635) were cut into the fills of the roadside ditch, but formed no coherent pattern. Posthole 2550 was the most substantial, with a depth of 0.4m and a fill that included stones that may have been displaced packing material, but the others were very shallow.

A densely-packed deposit of limestone (2627) that was partly exposed at the north-western edge of the trench also appeared to be structural in nature. The feature extended beyond the limit of the excavation area, but the exposed part was triangular in shape and measured 1.05 x 0.60m and 0.30m deep. Its shape was suggestive of the corner of a rectangular structure but insufficient of the

feature was exposed within the excavation area to established whether it was a wall or a postpad.

Ditch 2503 (Fig. 2.35) was situated *c* 55-60m from the road and contained a pottery assemblage that included a piece from a white ware mortarium dated 180-240. It was a shallow feature, 0.3m deep, and presumably defined the rear of a field or enclosure beside the road.

Phase 8: Medieval period

Medieval and post-medieval ridge and furrow cultivation was represented by furrows that extended across the site on parallel E-W alignments.

HOLTS FARM CROSSING

The site was situated north-west of the village of Charlton-on-Otmoor and *c* 350m south of Holts Farm, where a new bridge over the railway was to be built, accessed by a new road from Mansmoor

Road, at NGR 4554 2171 (Fig. 2.42). It was situated on a low but distinct ridge of Lower Oxford Clay (Peterborough Member) that rose to a height of 2.5-3.0m above the surrounding fields and extended on an approximate N-S alignment. The plateau at the top of the ridge attained a maximum elevation of *c* 65m, north of the railway, and lay at *c* 64m aOD within the site. On all sides of the ridge, the ground sloped down to the River Ray and its tributary streams, at *c* 61-62m aOD. The evaluation identified a concentration of features dating from the late Iron Age and Roman period that were interpreted as the remains of a small farmstead on the plateau, situated mostly to the east of the railway but with outlying pits in Trenches 25 and 28 to the west (Fig. 2.43). The excavation area encompassed the footprint of the embankment on the east side of the proposed bridge and the adjacent part of the access road. The features to the north of the excavation area (Trenches 10-17) were preserved *in situ*, in an area that was used as a construction compound with no intrusive ground-works. Most of the features exposed in the trenches in this area comprised ditches that lay on NW-SE or NE-SW alignments that were consistent with the orientation of the trackway and enclosures within the excavation area, and clearly represented a continuation of the same complex of boundaries. With the exception of middle Iron Age features in Trenches 10 and 11, insufficient artefactual material was recovered from the evaluation to allow the features in the trenches to be fully incorporated into the phasing scheme of the excavation, not least because the ditches in Trenches 12, 14 and 15 contained no datable material at all.

The excavation encompassed a total area of 0.9ha and exposed a small group of prehistoric flints (Phase 1) and a long sequence of occupation that extended unbroken from the middle Iron Age to the late Roman period (Phases 2, 3, 5, 6 and 7) (Fig. 2.43). During the stripping of the site, three extensive baulks were left in place in order to provide standing sections through parts of a possible earthwork enclosure that had been identified during the initial walkover of the site but which proved to be a coincidental meeting of headlands.

Phase 1: Early prehistory

Prehistoric activity was attested by eight pieces of worked flint, although all were recovered from later features or from the subsoil and no features could be attributed to a period before the middle Iron Age. The most interesting piece was the butt-end of an axe/pick of probable Mesolithic or late Upper Palaeolithic date, and a blade core was probably also Mesolithic. The other pieces were not chronologically diagnostic.

Phase 2: Middle Iron Age

The earliest evidence for occupation dated to the middle Iron Age and comprised two penannular

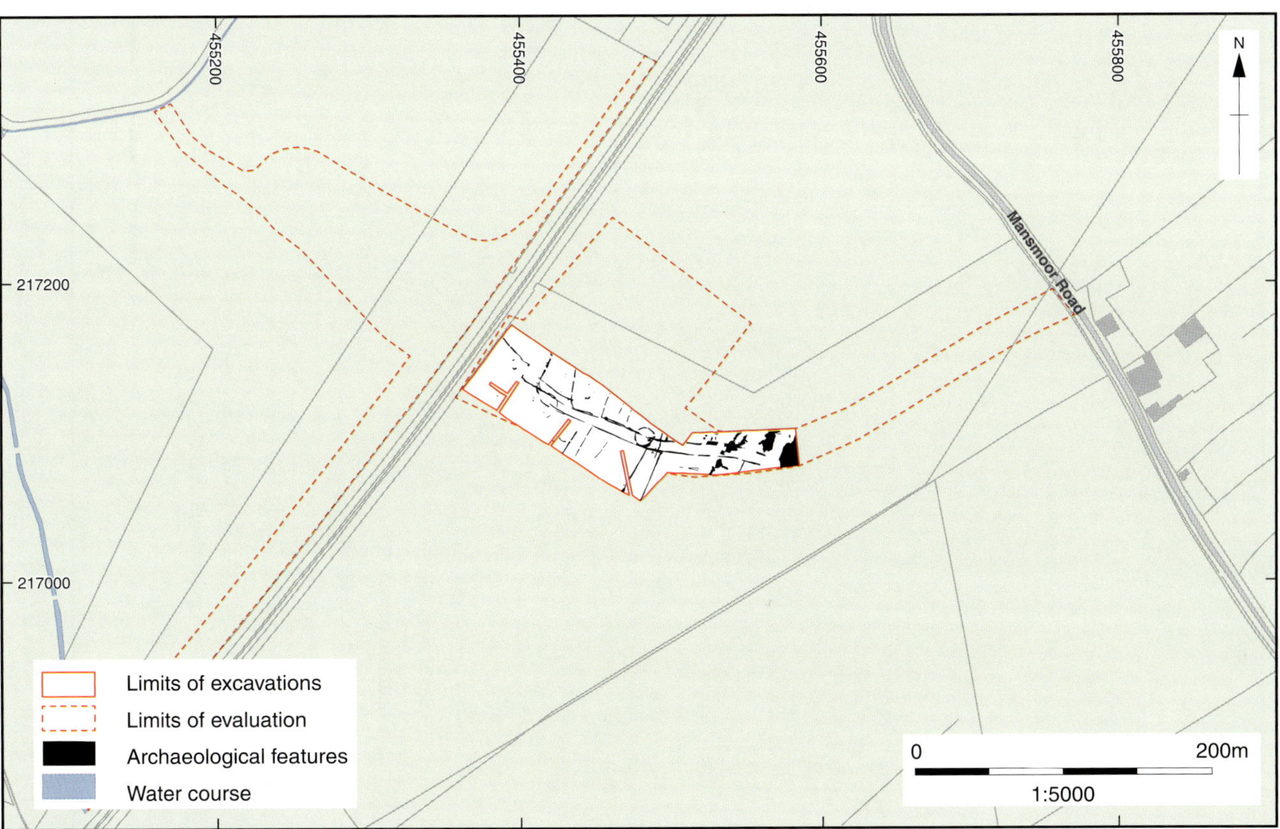

Fig. 2.42 Location of Holts Farm Crossing

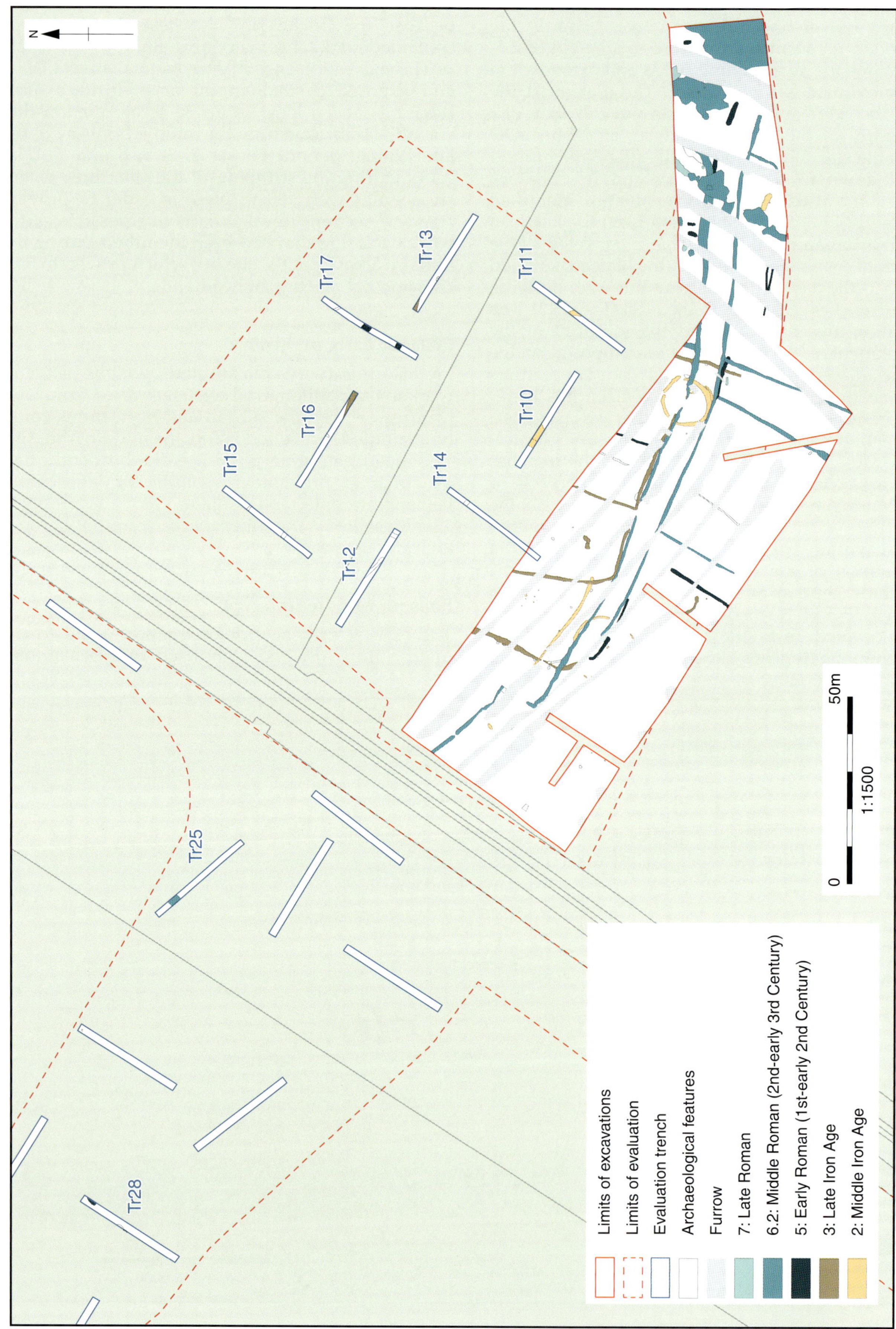

Fig. 2.43 Holts Farm Crossing, plan of all archaeological features

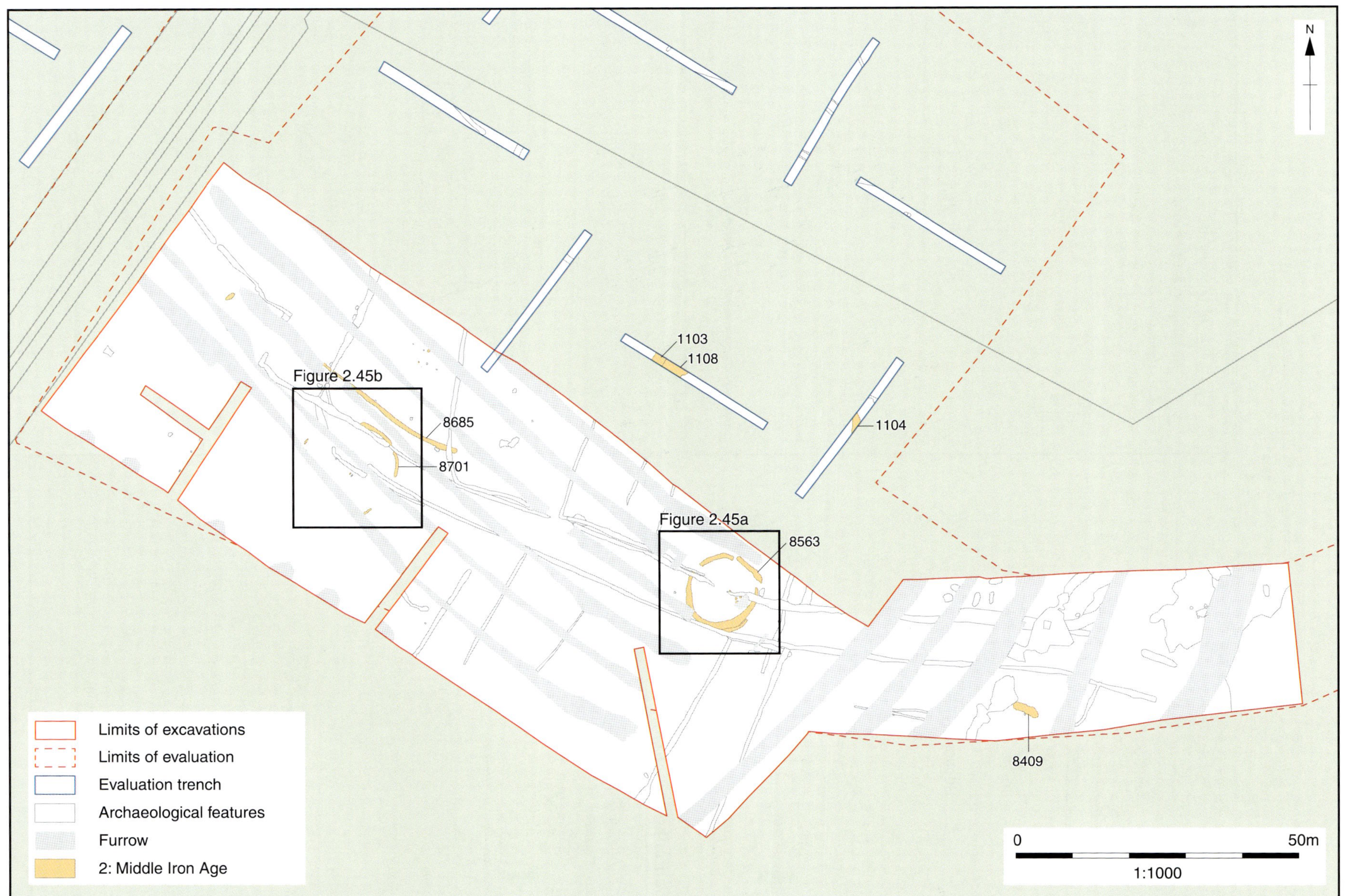

Fig. 2.44   Holts Farm Crossing, plan of middle Iron Age features

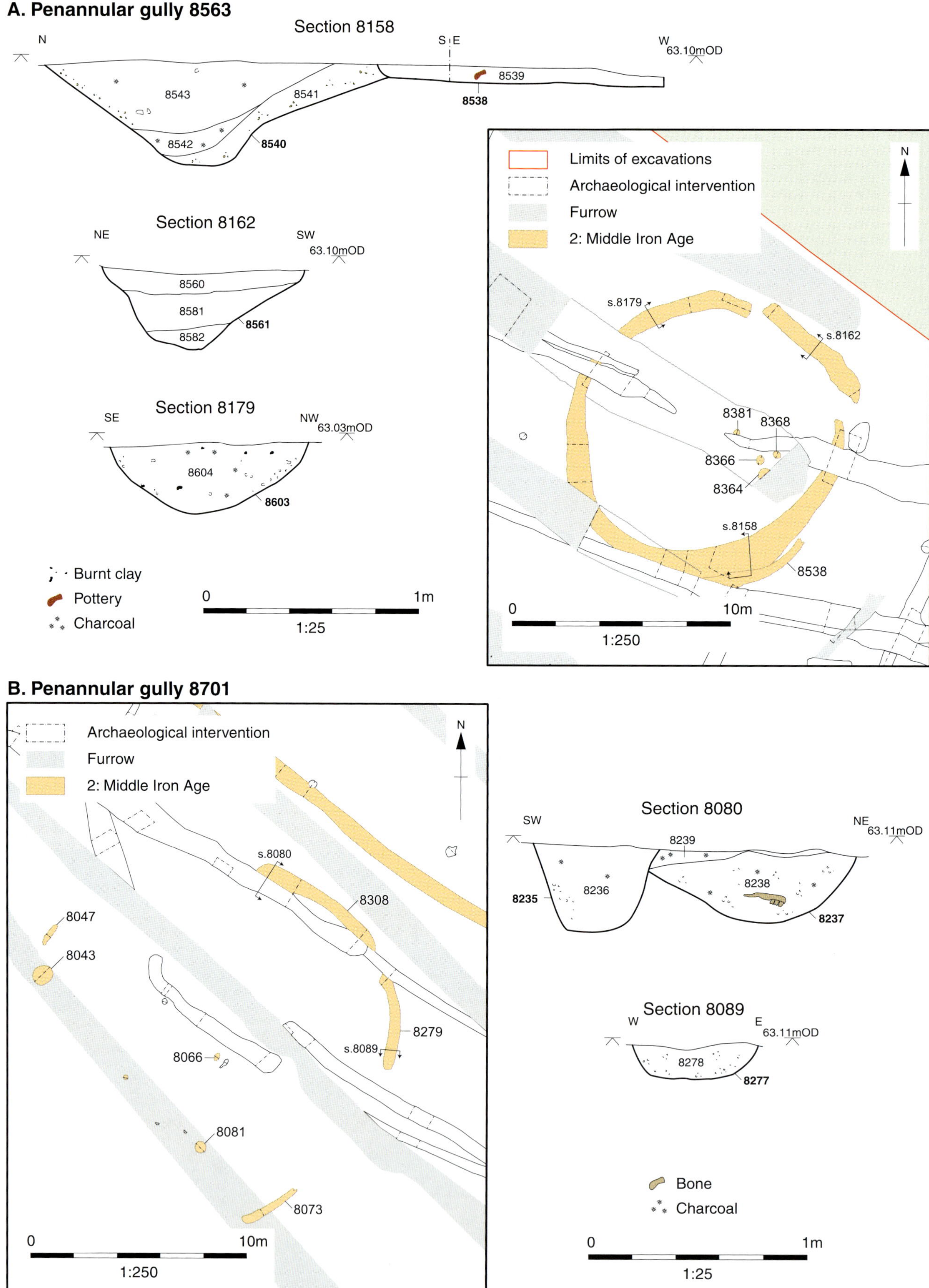

Fig. 2.45   *Holts Farm Crossing, detail of middle Iron Age penannular gullies 8563 and 8701*

gullies (8563 and 8701) and a possible third gully (1104), which are likely to represent the locations of roundhouses. A boundary ditch (8685) and a small number of pits were also recorded (Fig. 2.44). Most of the features were situated in the central and western parts of the excavation area but the pits were more widely dispersed, and north of the excavation area features of this date were recorded in Evaluation Trenches 10 and 11 within the area that was preserved *in situ*.

Penannular gully 8563

Penannular gully 8563 (Fig. 2.45a), which was located in the central part of the excavation area, was the more complete structure. Most of the circumference was enclosed by a single continuous gully, truncated on the west side by a medieval furrow, but the north-eastern part comprised a separate segment. The latter element was rather linear in form and did not align well with the main gully, perhaps suggesting that it was a later addition to a feature that was originally open on this side. These together formed a slightly elliptical feature with internal dimensions of 11.8m NE-SW and 10.7m NW-SE. The breaks between the main gully and the north-eastern segment measured only 0.6m and 1.05m and may have been too narrow to serve as entrances. The enclosing gully was V-shaped in profiled and measured 1.6m wide and 0.5m deep on the south-east side, where it was best preserved. Part of a curving feature (8538) was recorded on the outer edge of this part of the gully that may have been another phase of the structure, although it had a very shallow profile for a drip gully, measuring 1.5m wide but only 0.06m deep (Fig. 2.45, section 8158). The north-eastern segment was similar to the main gully, measuring 0.75m wide and 0.46m deep. Four shallow features that may have been postholes (8364, 8366, 8368, 8381) were recorded within the area enclosed by the gully and may have formed part of the structure, although they formed no coherent pattern.

Penannular gully 8701

Gully 8701 (Fig. 2.45b) was situated 55m west of penannular feature 8563. The feature had been severely affected by truncation from Roman ditches, medieval furrows and modern ploughing, as a result of which much of the circuit did not survive, the only substantial surviving part being the north-eastern quadrant, along with possible parts of the south-eastern and western sides. The north-eastern quadrant comprised two gully segments (8279 and 8308), which were separated by an interval of *c* 1.05m. Gully segment 8308 was the more substantial, measuring *c* 7m long and 0.2-0.3m deep, and appeared to end in a definite terminal at each end, although both had been truncated by a Roman ditch. Segment 8279 had a similar depth at its southern end, where it too ended in a deliberate

terminal, but was shallower at the northern end, where it appeared to peter out. The alignment and curvature of feature 8073 suggested that it may be part of the south-eastern quadrant, and a shallow feature (8047) to the west may have been a surviving part of this side of the gully. The curvature of the surviving elements suggested that the feature had an original diameter of *c* 16m. Two very shallow features (8043, 8081) within the footprint of the structure yielded middle Iron Age pottery and may be pits or postholes associated with it; a further six undated features may also be structural postholes, including feature 8066 which contained a small group of burnt animal bone and a charcoal assemblage comprising entirely of oak.

Possible penannular gully 1104

A third such feature may have been represented by ditch 1104, which was recorded in Evaluation Trench 11 *c* 30m north of penannular gully 8563. The feature may have been curvilinear in plan, although this is not certain due to the limited exposure within the evaluation trench, and it yielded a small group of middle Iron Age pottery. The ditch was 1.5m wide and 0.5m deep and its possible curvature may indicate that it was part of the eastern side of a penannular gully, although no corresponding western side was identified within the trench.

Boundary ditch 8685

Ditch 8685 was a shallow feature, only 0.2m deep, which defined a boundary that extended on a NW-SE alignment a short distance north of penannular gully 8279/8308. and was cut by two late Iron Age ditches. It extended for a distance of at least 28m, the south-eastern end finishing in a definite terminal and the north-western end being obscured by a medieval furrow, and was cut at either end by late Iron Age ditches.

Pits

A total of 11 pits scattered throughout the site were attributed to the middle Iron Age on the basis of small groups of pottery sherds. They were mostly shallow circular features, less than 0.25m deep, except pit 8409, near the south-eastern limit of the excavation, which was an elongated feature that measured 4.8 x 1.5m and 0.5m deep but similarly produced little artefactual material.

Features in Evaluation Trench 11

Part of a substantial feature measuring some 6m in extent was exposed in the western part of the trench. Characterisation of the feature was difficult, not least because it could not be fully excavated due to ingress of groundwater. However, the straightness of the north-western edge suggested that this part represented a ditch aligned NE-SW (1103);

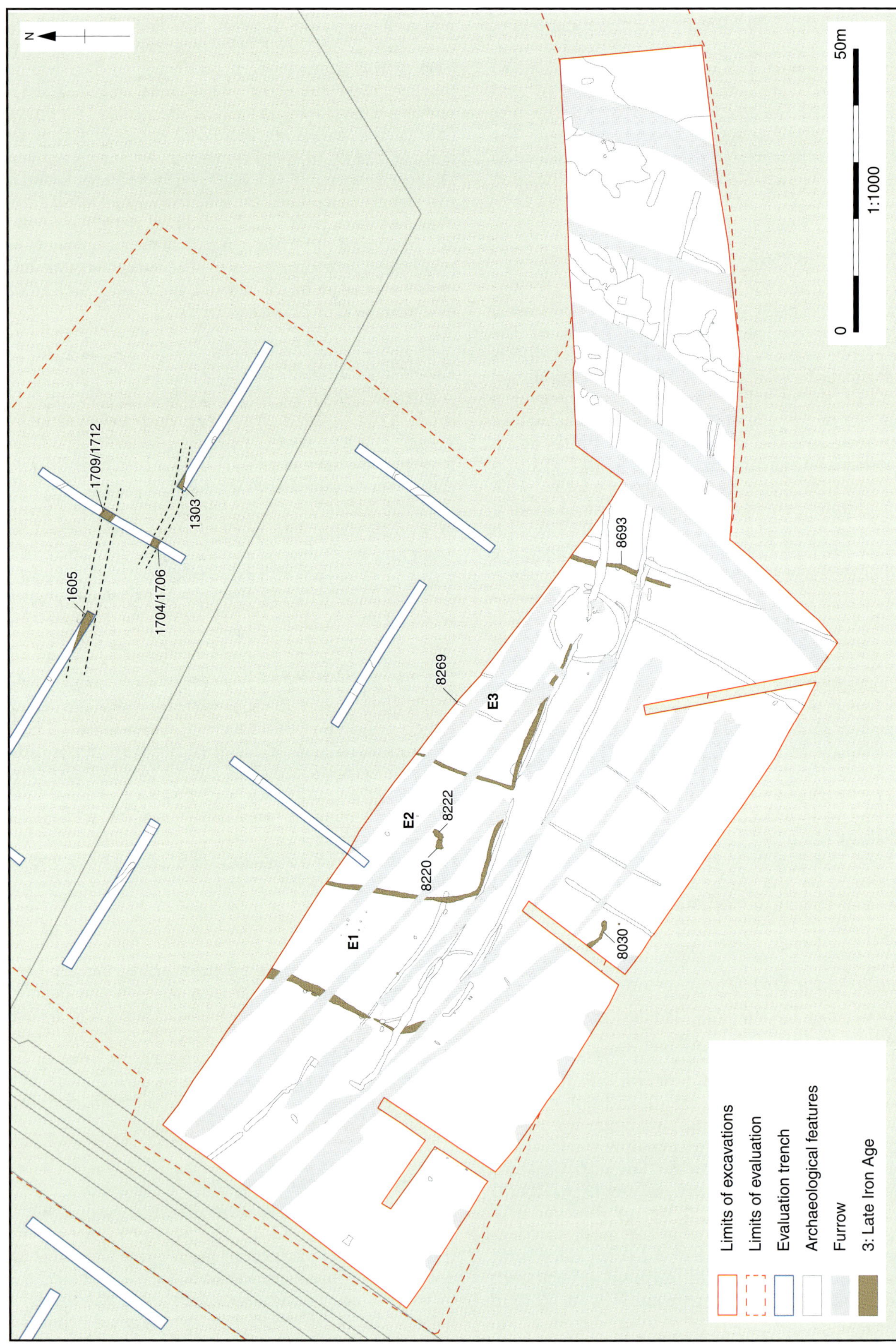

Fig. 2.46 *Holts Farm Crossing, plan of late Iron Age features*

Sherds from a jar of middle Iron Age date were recovered from the feature. The eastern side of the ditch was cut by a larger feature (1108), the precise form of which was uncertain. The feature measured 4.4m wide with a depth in excess of 0.6m, although it was not bottomed. The feature also contained a few sherds of middle Iron Age pottery. The features were overlain by a dark grey layer up to 0.35m deep, on the surface of which was an irregular area of burning approximately 0.8m in diameter.

Phase 3: Late Iron Age

Late Iron Age occupation was represented by a group of three conjoined enclosures (E1-3) that were constructed over the penannular gullies of the middle Iron Age settlement, with a small curvilinear gully (8030) of uncertain function to the south (Fig. 2.46). The enclosures had a common southern boundary and their arrangement clearly indicated that they continued to the north and are likely to represent the southern edge of a more extensive complex.

The enclosure complex

The enclosures were defined by ditches that typically measured 0.25-0.35m deep. The eastern limit of the complex appears to have been defined by a linear boundary represented by ditch 8693, which extended into the excavation area for a distance of 18m from the northern baulk before petering out, with the enclosures laid out to the west. The complex extended over a total distance of 90m from east to west, but the dimensions of the individual enclosures were varied, not least because the oblique alignments of the intervening ditches gave enclosures E1 and E2 trapezoidal rather than strictly rectangular shapes. The western enclosure, E1, measured 17.5-25m E-W and the adjoining middle enclosure E2 measured 20-26m. Enclosure E3, which adjoined boundary ditch 8693, was more regular in shape and was also considerably wider, measuring 42m. It is possible that this enclosure represented more than one enclosure, perhaps sub-divided by undated ditch 8269. The only discrete features within the complex were a pair of shallow intercutting pits in enclosure E2 (8220, 8222). The enclosure ditches yielded only small assemblages of artefacts, comprising pottery and animal bone.

Gully 8030 lay 20m south of the enclosures and comprised a curving gully 5.5m long and 0.25-0.35m deep. The eastern end may have been the feature's original terminal, but the western end continued under a baulk, although it did not extend far, since it did not emerge on the other side of the baulk.

Small quantities of late Iron Age-early Roman pottery were recovered from ditch 1303 in Evaluation Trench 13 and ditch 1605 in Trench 16, the latter feature containing quite large sherds of pottery. However, the alignment of ditch 1303 suggested that it may have been part of the same feature as ditch 1704/1706 in Trench 17, which yielded two post-conquest sherds, and ditch 1605 may similarly have been part of the same feature as ditch 1709/1712, which contained two chips from a South Spanish amphora.

Phase 5: Early Roman (late 1st-early 2nd century)

Features that could be attributed to the late 1st-early 2nd century were quite sparse but widely distributed (Fig. 2.47). The principal feature was a ditched trackway that extended across the site on an approximate E-W alignment, from which subsidiary boundary ditches extended to north and south. Three pits in the north-east part of the excavation area were also attributed to this phase, as well as an isolated pit to the north-west (8224) that cut a late Iron Age ditch.

The trackway

The trackway was represented by a pair of flanking ditches that were typically *c* 0.3m deep, with no evidence for a metalled surface. It was 6m wide and could be traced for a total distance of 155m. That the northern flanking ditch followed the alignment of the southern ditches of the late Iron Age enclosures suggested that the trackway's construction represented development of the existing landscape rather than the imposition of an entirely new scheme. Recutting during the 2nd century had removed most of the evidence for the original ditches, which consequently only survived at the eastern end of the northern ditch and at the western end and a short stretch of the central part of the southern ditch. The ends of the surviving part need not represent the original limits of the trackway, since the western end clearly petered out due to truncation by ploughing, and a large furrow beyond the eastern end may have masked any continuation. The truncation of the ditches made certainty impossible, but there was some evidence that they may have been dug in a segmented form. This was most apparent at the eastern end, where ditch segment 8696, which was up to 0.5m deep, appeared to have deliberate terminals at either end.

Boundaries associated with the trackway

The junction between the trackway and ditch 8688 had been truncated by a medieval furrow but it is likely that the ditch branched off the trackway and defined a boundary between adjoining enclosures. The ditch lay parallel to the ditches that divided late Iron Age enclosures E1-3, which may therefore have continued in use into this phase. To the south, ditch 8691 was aligned at right angles to the trackway and may similarly have divided adjoining enclosures, as may undated ditch 8062. It is possible that a pair of converging ditches (8480,

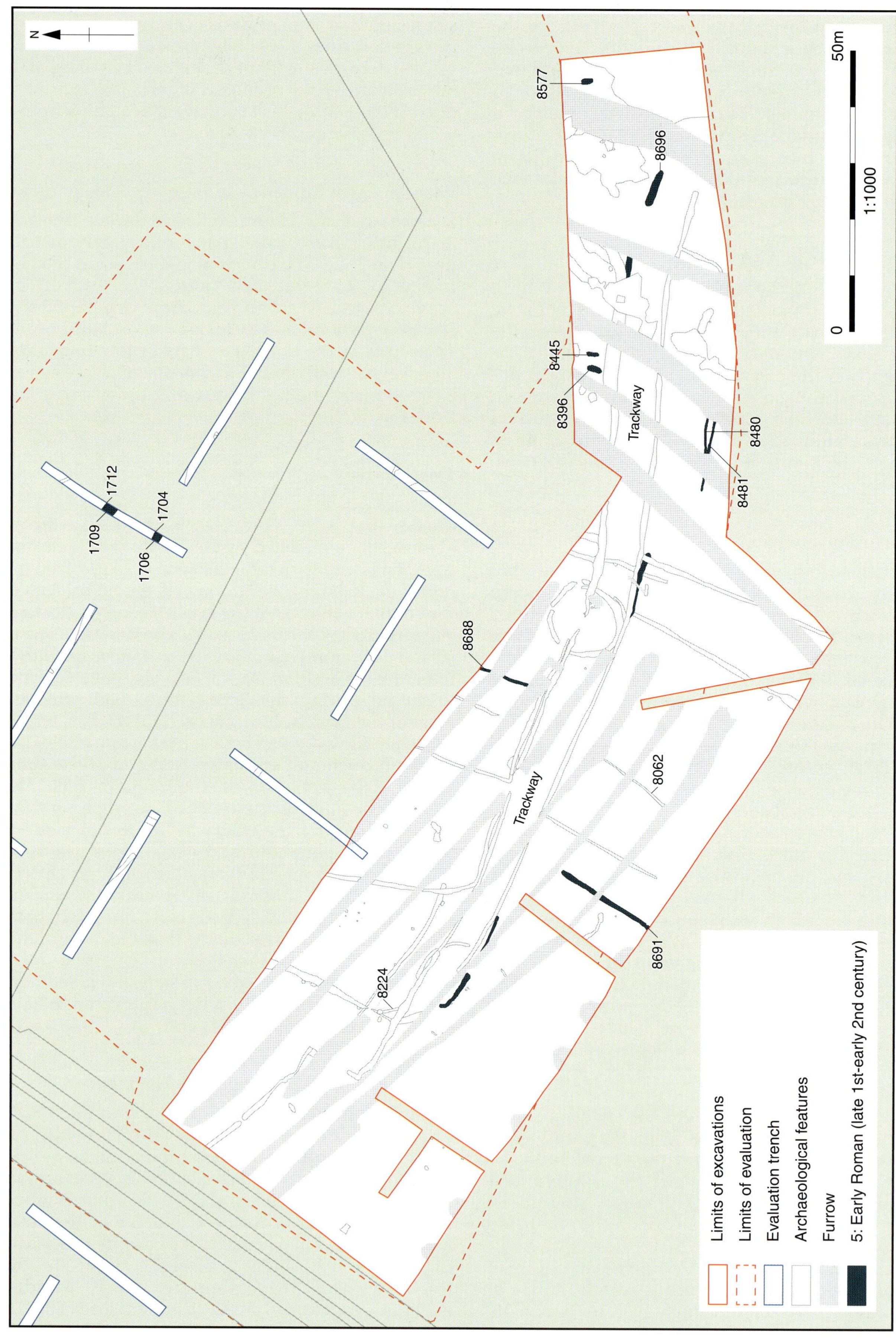

Fig. 2.47 Holts Farm Crossing, plan of early Roman features

8481) that lay on an alignment parallel to the trackway enclosed the rear of an enclosure that fronted onto it, but there was no surviving evidence for the enclosure's sides.

Two ditches that were recorded in Evaluation Trench 17 may belong to this phase (1704, 1709). Both lay on NW-SE alignments parallel to the trackway. Ditch 1704 contained two post-conquest sherds and was recut as ditch 1706, while ditch 1709 was recut as ditch 1712, each of which contained two chips from a South Spanish amphora.

Pits in the north-eastern part of the excavation area

Three pits (8396, 8445, 8577) were attributed to the early Roman period on the basis of pottery from their fills. Pits 8396 and 8445 were a pair of similar elongated features that lay side-by-side and measured 2-2.6m x 1m and 0.4-0.55m deep. Pit 8577 was situated 50m further east and was very similar, though only 0.14m deep. No evidence was found for their function and none produced more than a few sherds of pottery and animal bone.

Phase 6: Middle Roman (2nd-early 3rd century)

This phase saw the continuation of the arrangement that had been established during the early Roman period (Fig. 2.48). The trackway ditches were recut and the enclosure boundaries on either side were reorganised. Digging of pits in the north-eastern part of the site continued and a series of soil spreads were preserved towards the east end of the excavation area, which were cut by a cremation burial (8547).

The trackway

The ditches of the trackway established during the early Roman period were recut during the middle Roman period and consequently most of the surviving evidence for the feature dated from this phase. The trackway extended through the entire length of the excavation area and, possibly unlike the earlier phase, the flanking ditches were continuous except for several locations where they were truncated by medieval furrows. The southern ditch ended 50m from the western end of the site and the northern ditch initially did likewise but was subsequently extended by the addition of ditches 8311 and 8683. Ditch 8311 ended in a short northward return and the eastern end of ditch 8683 appeared to have a corresponding southward return, representing an abrupt and unexplained dog-leg in the alignment of the trackway at this point. At the eastern end, the northern ditch curved northward, unlike its early Roman predecessor. This part of the feature exhibited two cuts and continued beyond the limit of the excavation, although it was partly obscured here by a medieval furrow. The width of the trackway tapered somewhat from 6.8m at the east end to 4.3m towards the west. The south ditch

was up to 0.5m deep but the north ditch was only 0.25m for most of its length, increasing at the eastern end to a maximum depth of 0.7m.

Boundaries associated with the trackway

The only boundary on the north side of the trackway was ditch 8697, which branched off it in the central part of the site and was exposed for only 3m before it passed beyond the northern baulk. Four ditches on the south side were attributed to this phase (8050, 8331, 8692, 8700), and undated ditch 8062 may also have been of this date. The ditches were no more than 0.3m deep. Ditches 8331 and 8692 were exposed for a distance of 35m and continued beyond the southern edge of the excavation area and ditch 8050 may have done likewise had it not petered out a short distance from the southern baulk. Ditch 8700 extended for 8m and the southern end appeared to be curving to the west, perhaps to form the southern side of an enclosure adjoining the trackway, but was truncated by a medieval furrow.

Pits in the north-eastern part of the excavation area

Pits 8405 and 8407 were situated close to early Roman pits 8396 and 8445 and presumably represent the continuation of pit-digging in this part of the site, although they did not lie on the N-S alignment of the earlier features. Pit 8405 was subcircular and measured 1.7m in diameter and 0.36m deep and pit 8407 was an elongated feature that measured 2.3 x 1.1m and 0.12m deep. The artefactual assemblages were limited to a handful of sherds from each.

Soil spreads and cremation burial 8547

A series of amorphous soil spreads that were preserved in shallow hollows at the western end of the excavation area appeared to be Roman soil layers (Fig. 2.48). They comprised greyish brown silty clay soils, contained small groups of 2nd-century pottery, and in several instances were cut by medieval furrows. Excavation of these deposits was limited and was mainly aimed at clarifying their relationships with other features, but they appear to have had depths of 0.1-0.4m.

Cremation burial 8547 was cut into the soil spread and comprised a shallow hollow 0.5m in diameter and 0.1m deep, into which the cremated remains of a single individual of undetermined age and sex were deposited, commingled with charcoal from the pyre (8546). Four nail fragments were recovered but there was insufficient evidence to indicate whether they derived from the pyre structure or from an object placed as a grave or pyre good. The cremated remains weighed only 401g, possibly indicating that the feature had been truncated by later ploughing, and analysis of the charcoal found that the fuel for the pyre consisted entirely of oak.

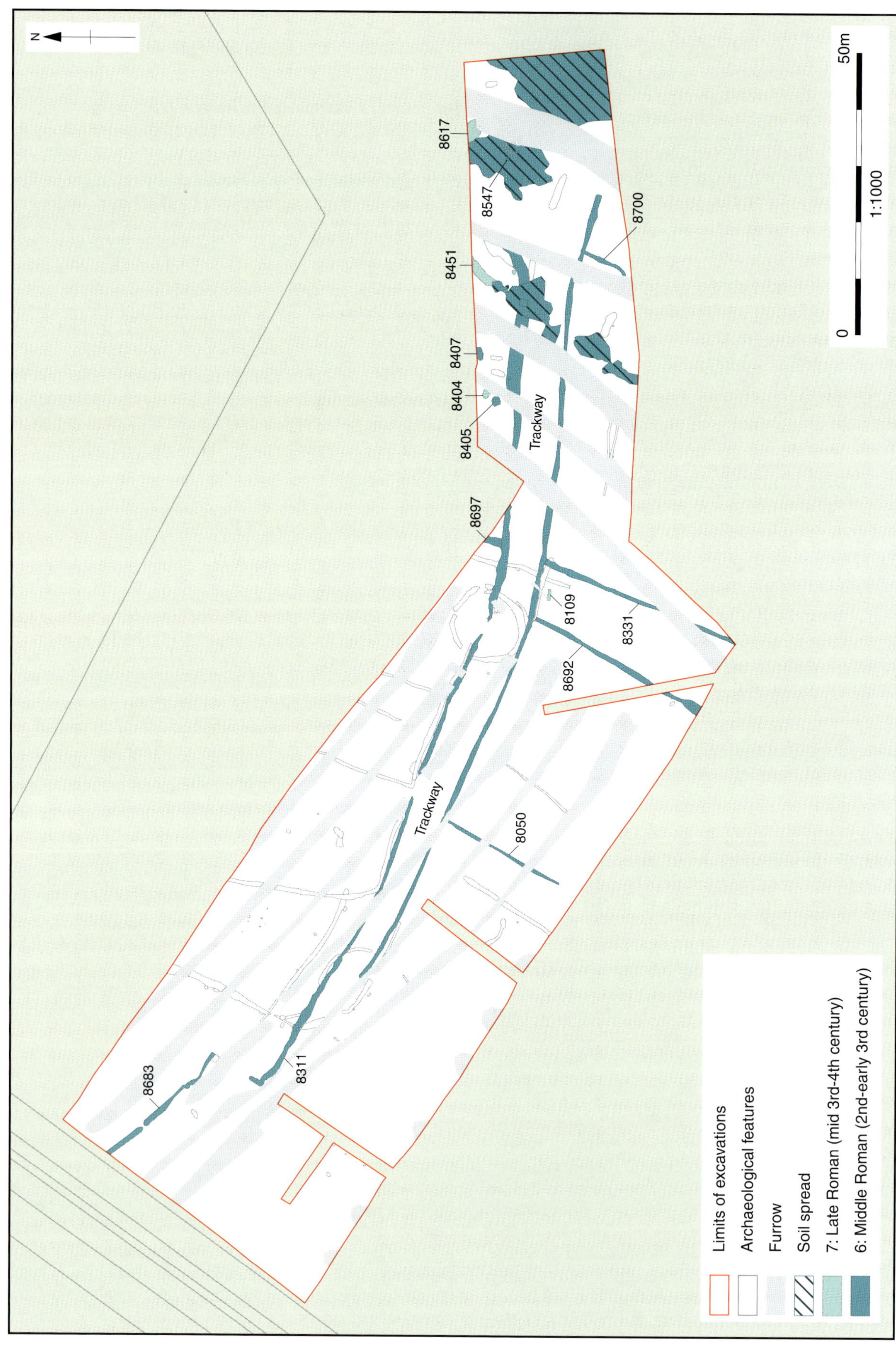

Fig. 2.48 Holts Farm Crossing, plan of middle and late Roman features

Phase 7: Late Roman (mid 3rd-4th century)

Evidence for late Roman activity was limited and was restricted to the eastern end of the site (Fig. 2.48). Continued use of the trackway was evidenced by recutting of the flanking ditches at this end and by the insertion of an inhumation burial (8109) beside it, and part of a large pit (8617) was also exposed.

The trackway

Two interventions in the northern flanking ditch and one in the southern ditch revealed evidence for recuts that contained late Roman pottery. In all three instances the recut was 0.3m deep and the northern ditch contained an almost complete jar-beaker dated to *c* 240-300 (SF 8006, Fig. 3.10, no. 163) that lay on the base of the recut feature. The relationship between the trackway and ditch 8451 was uncertain since the junction of the ditches was indistinct on account of being cut into a 2nd century soil layer. The ditch extended toward north-east, continuing beyond the edge of the excavation area, and may be a boundary ditch that branched off the trackway. Alternatively, it is possible that in its late Roman form the trackway turned toward north-east at this point and the ditch is the final phase of the northern flanking ditch.

Burial 8109

The burial of an adult, possibly male (8107), had been buried in a grave dug adjacent to the trackway (Fig. 2.49). The grave pit (8106) had been severely affected by truncation by later ploughing and survived to a depth of no more than 0.05m. As a result of the truncation, only the lower part of the skeleton survived, but the disposition of the legs was sufficiently clear to indicate that the individual had lain in an extended, supine posture. Furthermore, the head had been removed and placed to the right of the shins. No artefactual material was present.

Pits in the north-eastern part of the excavation area

Evidence for the continued digging of pits in this part of the site was provided by pit 8404. In contrast to the earlier pits, which had very sparse finds assemblages, this feature contained the burial of a ewe, as well as a small assemblage of 3rd century pottery.

Pit 8617 was situated against the northern baulk and extended slightly beyond the edge of the excavation area, but appeared to be oval in plan, measuring 3m wide and at least 3.9m long. Excavation of a slot across the middle of the feature revealed that it was 1.1m deep with vertical sides and a flat base. Following some initial silting of the lower corners, the feature was backfilled with a deposit (8618) that contained domestic refuse including a mixed assemblage of more than 3.8kg of pottery, as well as 1.6kg of animal bone. The depth of the feature, which is considerable compared to most other features on the site, may indicate a function as a waterhole, but there was no evidence to confirm this from the character of the fills and soil samples taken for waterlogged plant remains proved empty.

Phase 8: Medieval period

Medieval and post-medieval ridge and furrow cultivation was represented by furrows that comprised parts of three adjacent furlongs. A group of furrows extended across the western part of the excavation area on NW-SE alignments, terminating in the central part of the site. An interval of 30m, within which lay an associated headland that measured 7m wide and 0.3m high, separated them from a second furlong in the eastern part of the excavation area, comprising four furrows aligned NE-SW. The third furlong was represented by a group of furrow terminals at the southern edge of the site.

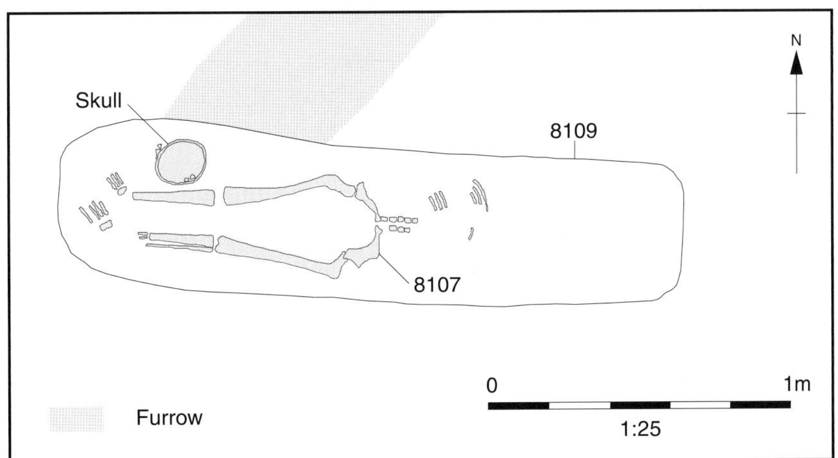

Fig. 2.49   Holts Farm Crossing, plan of late Roman inhumation burial 8109

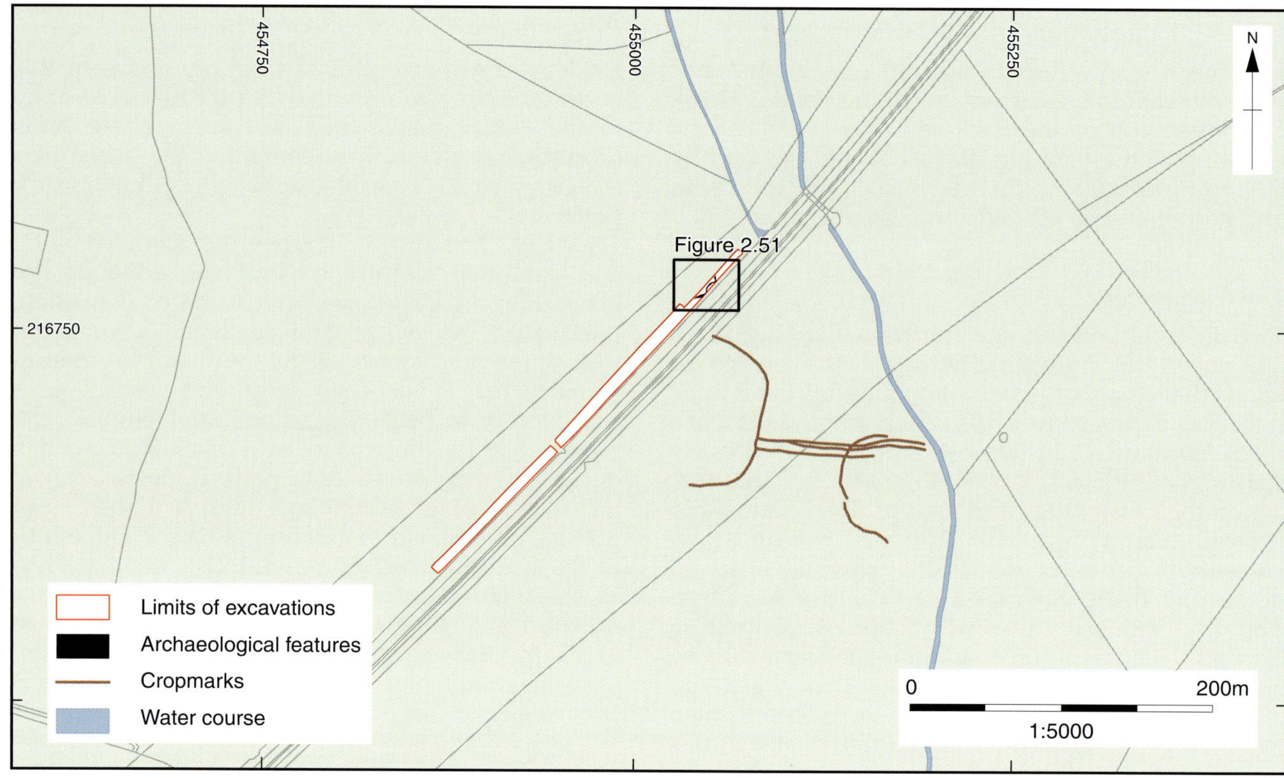

Fig. 2.50   Location of East of Oddington Grange

EAST OF ODDINGTON GRANGE

The site was situated 340m east of Oddington Grange and immediately adjacent to a tributary stream of the River Ray that forms the boundary between the parishes of Oddington and Charlton-on-Otmoor, at NGR 4549 2167 (Fig. 2.50). A cropmark of a possible banjo enclosure had been identified in the field to the south-east, comprising a curvilinear enclosure from which a very straight ditched trackway extended to the south-east, where it joined a second enclosure (Fig. 1.5). The north-western side of the main enclosure could not be plotted due to a change in the underlying geology from alluvium and terrace gravel to mudstone, but its projected alignment roughly coincided with the north-eastern part of the excavation area. The geology exposed within the trench comprised gravelly sand in the north-eastern half of the trench and mudstone to the south-west. The excavation area lay on the north-west side of the railway line and comprised a linear trench that was 295m long and 8m wide, except at the north-eastern end, where it was only 4m wide. This equated to an area of 0.2ha, and was bisected by a footpath. Archaeological features were restricted to the north-east end of the site and were attributed to the middle Iron Age (Phase 2) and late Iron Age (Phase 3). They were overlain by a subsoil that varied in thickness from 0.05-0.2m and a modern topsoil that was 0.25m thick.

Phase 1: Early prehistory

A single flint flake was recovered from the fill of late Iron Age ditch 45.

Phase 2: Middle Iron Age

The north-western side of curvilinear gully 29 was exposed within the trench, the remainder of the feature lying beyond the limits of the stripped area (Fig. 2.51). Its curvature suggests that the feature may be a penannular gully associated with the site of a roundhouse. The gully was fairly deep, at 0.62-0.68m, and had a steep-sided, V-shaped profile (Fig. 2.51, section 3).

Phase 3: Late Iron Age

The curvilinear gully was cut by a pair of late Iron Age ditches (44 and 45; Fig. 2.51). Ditch 44 extended obliquely across the trench on an E-W alignment that corresponded with the projected alignment of the cropmark of the possible banjo enclosure. It probably converged beyond the south-eastern edge of the excavation area with ditch 45, which was aligned N-S. Both ditches had steep-sided profiles similar to that of the middle Iron Age gully and measured 0.8-0.9m deep.

Undated

The only other archaeological feature was a very shallow undated pit (32) with a few charcoal flecks

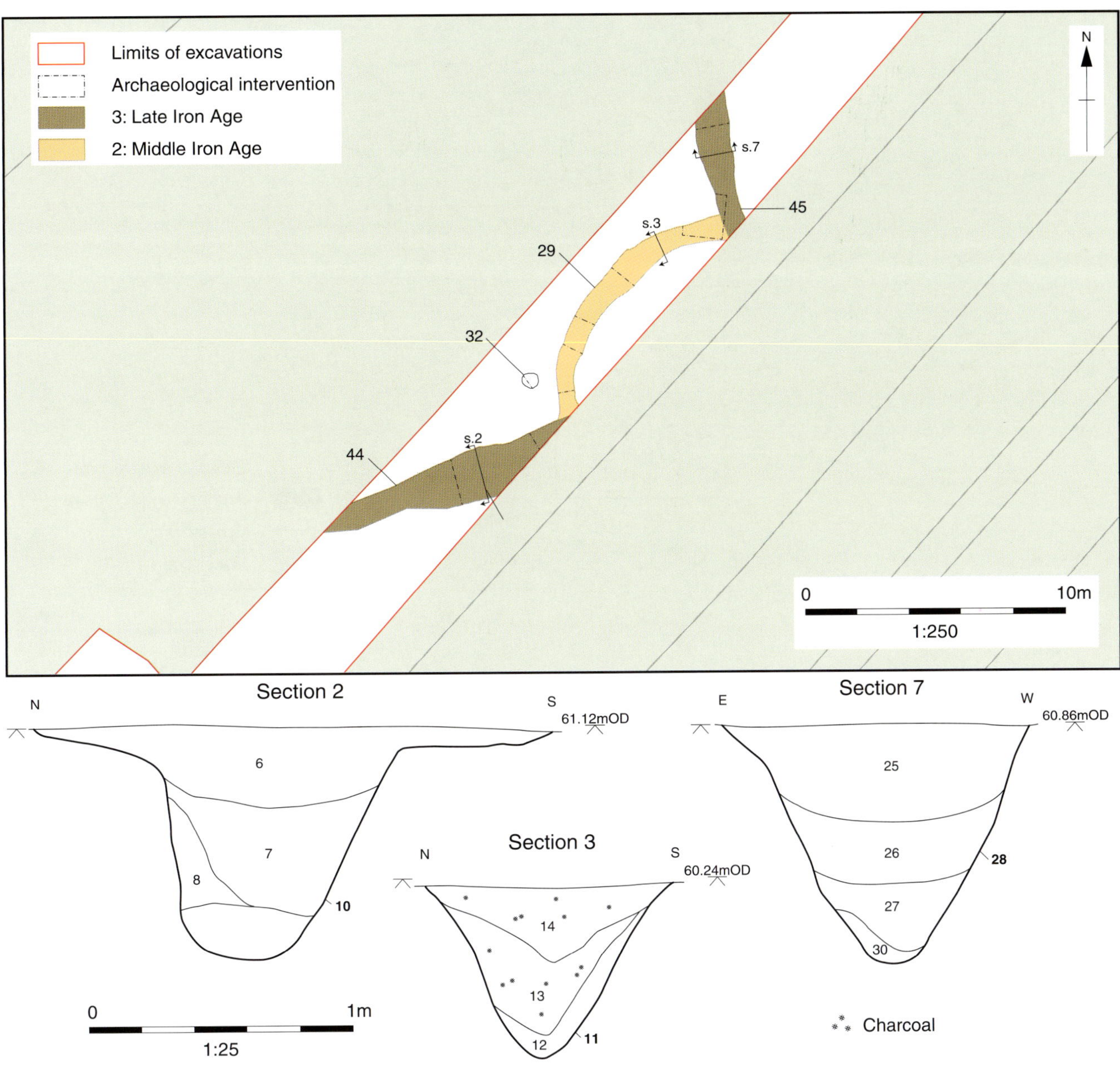

Fig. 2.51   Features at the north-eastern end of East of Oddington Grange

in its fill that was situated immediately west of gully 29.

SOUTH OF ODDINGTON CROSSING

The site lay in the central part of the parish of Oddington at NGR 4539 2156, 175m south-east of Oddington Crossing, where the railway is crossed by a road that provides access to Oddington Grange and Barndon Farm (Fig. 2.52). The site lay in flat terrain on a geology of alluvium. A cropmark of two conjoined or intersecting circular enclosures had been recorded on the north-western side of the railway. The site comprised a trench on either side of the railway line, extending for a distance of 280m and encompassing a total area of 0.24ha. The south-western end of the site was divided from the rest by a ditched field boundary and a footpath. Archaeological features were restricted to the south-western end of the site, with the exception of a single undated ditch at the north-eastern end, and were attributed to the middle Iron Age (Phase 2) and the late 1st-early 2nd century AD (Phase 5) (Fig. 2.53).

Phase 2: Middle Iron Age

Ditches 153 and 154 (Fig. 2.53) lay on alignments that suggested that they formed the west and north sides of a rectilinear enclosure. Ditch 154 was a shallow feature, no more than 0.21m deep, and it is uncertain whether the break between this and ditch 153 represents an original entrance into the enclosure or whether the ditch simply petered out at this

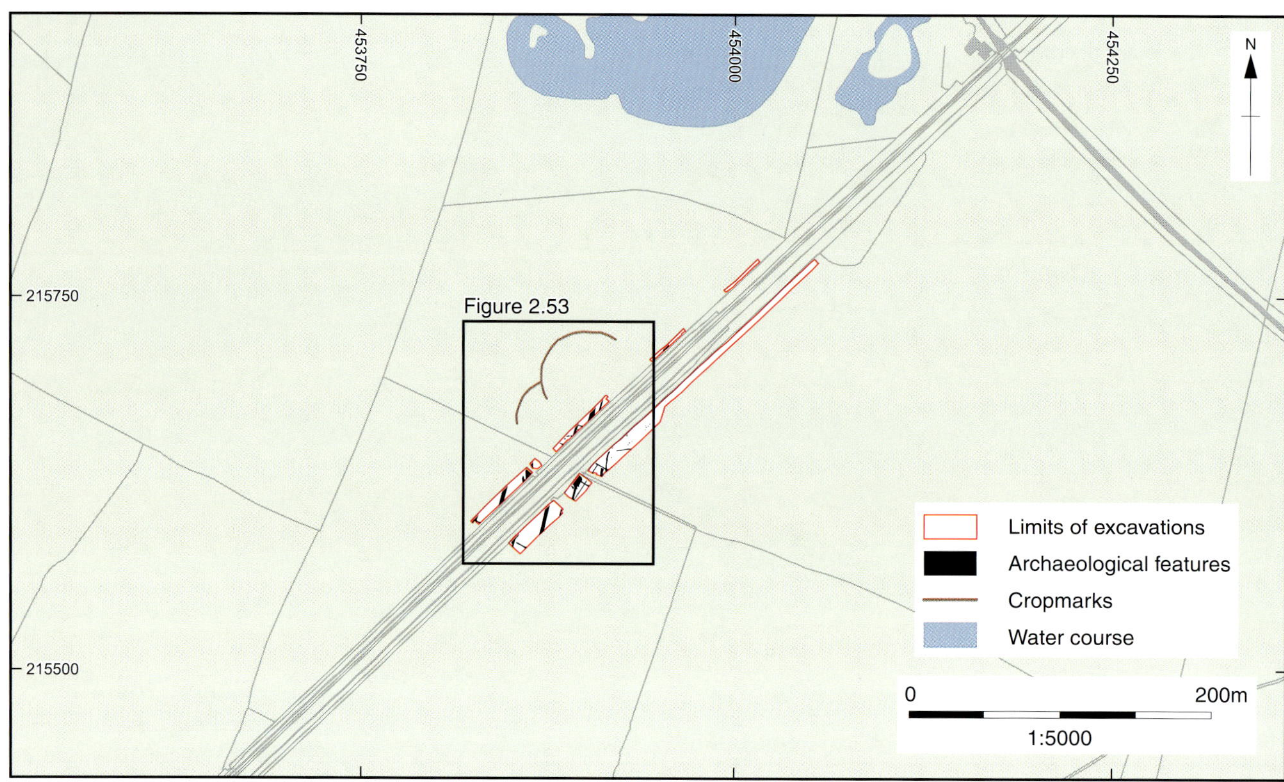

Fig. 2.52   Location of South of Oddington Crossing

point due to truncation by more recent ploughing. Ditch 153 was more substantial, comprising a V-shaped ditch up to 0.8m wide and 0.5m deep (Fig. 2.53, section 4). Most of the ditch was filled by a natural infilling of sterile clay (16), which was overlain by a darker layer with some charcoal inclusions (15). A localised deposit of metalworking debris (14), some 4.3m in extent, had been dumped into the top of the feature. This comprised a charcoal-rich layer that was completely excavated, yielding fragments from two ceramic crucibles (Fig. 3.19) and 5.2kg of slag, as well as a large quantity of fired clay from the demolished superstructure of a furnace. A further 964g of slag was recovered from the underlying part of fill 15. The slag derived entirely from ironworking and included smithing hearth bottoms, indicating that both iron and copper were worked nearby. A sample of charcoal from the deposit returned a radiocarbon date range of 200-40 cal BC (95.4% confidence, 2096 ± 30, SUERC 70734).

Only two shallow, undated pits (19, 50) were situated within the putative enclosure. Pit 50 had a burnt fill and may have been the base of a hearth, although no slag was recovered and it is therefore likely to have had a domestic rather than industrial function. Pit 109, which lay 35m west of the enclosure, yielded a single sherd of middle Iron Age pottery and a cluster of four pits (102, 119, 129, 130) nearby may also have been contemporary, although none produced any dating evidence. The pits were of similar form, with steep sides and

depths of 0.2-0.4m, and may have been the bases of small ovens or hearths, although there was no heat-discolouration of the pit edges. Pits 102, 109, 119, 129 and 130 all contained fragments of fired clay that may have derived from the superstructure of such features.

Phase 5: Early Roman (late 1st-early 2nd century)

An orthogonal arrangement of shallow boundary ditches was attributed to the early Roman period. The features were extremely slight, mostly measuring less than 0.2m deep, and the extremely sparse artefactual assemblage comprised mainly of small sherds of late prehistoric pottery, with the exception of a Roman sherd from ditch 54. Ditch 152, which extended on a NW-SE alignment and cut across the middle Iron Age features, appeared to form the north-eastern limit of the boundaries, and ditches 151 and 54/133 lay on parallel alignments to the south-west. Ditch 150 branched off ditch 152 and extended laterally across these boundaries, probably dividing the arrangement into rectilinear fields. A small quantity of iron slag that was recovered from ditch 152 may be residual from the middle Iron Age metalworking in the vicinity.

Phase 8: Medieval period

Medieval and post-medieval ridge and furrow cultivation was represented by furrows that extended across the site on parallel N-S alignments.

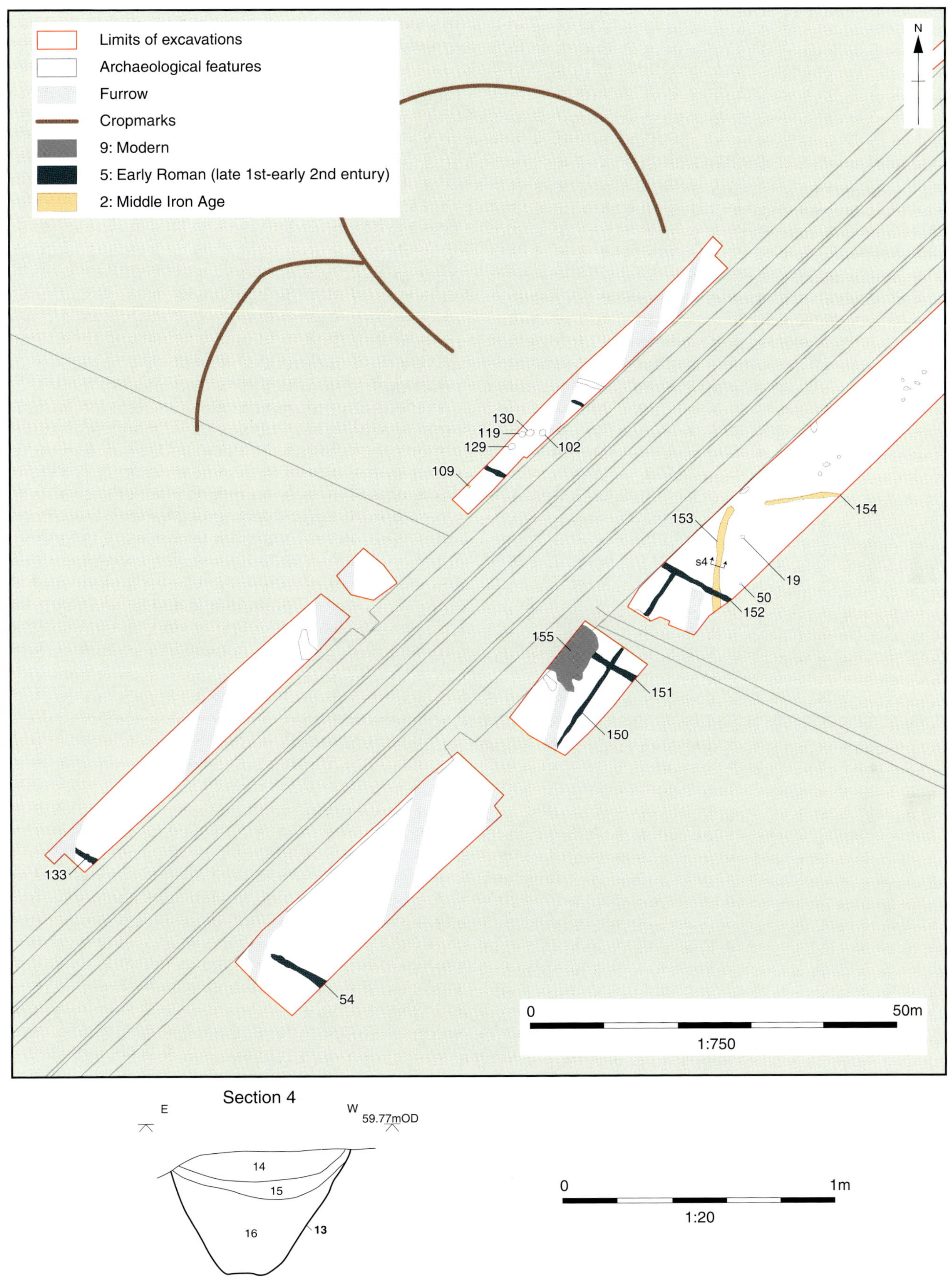

Fig. 2.53   Features at the south-western end of South of Oddington Crossing

Phase 9: Modern period

A large modern pond (155), 7.5m wide and 0.65m deep, was situated near the south-western end of the site, where it had cut early Roman ditch 151 and one of the furrows.

NORTH OF GALLOS BROOK

As its name suggests, the site was located on the north-east bank of Gallos Brook, which here forms the boundary between the parishes of Oddington and Bletchingdon, at NGR 4533 2151 (Fig. 2.54). The site was flat and lay on a geology of first terrace gravel. Cropmarks of possible prehistoric or Roman features had been recorded on both sides of the railway: a palimpsest of rectilinear enclosures and curvilinear ditched boundaries in the field to the north and a D-shaped enclosure and a more irregular enclosure with an annexe in the field to the south (Fig. 1.6). A strip, map and sample excavation was undertaken, comprising a trench on either side of the railway, each measuring 190m long. The northern trench measured 2.5-3.0m wide and the southern trench 5m wide, amounting to a combined area of 0.27ha. An intermittent subsoil layer (5) up to 0.1m thick was recorded but was absent from the south-western end of the site. The modern topsoil extended throughout the excavation area and was 0.3m thick. The archaeological features comprised part of a middle Iron Age (Phase 2) settlement at the south-western end of the trench and elements of a probable field system of late Iron Age or early Roman date (Phase 3-5; Fig. 2.55)

Phase 1: Early prehistory

A flint knife of late Neolithic/early Bronze Age date was recovered from a late Iron Age/Roman ditch fill.

Phase 2: Middle Iron Age

A middle Iron Age settlement was represented by parts of four penannular gullies (106, 107, 110/111 and 112) at the south-western end of the site, restricted to the trench on the south side of the railway line (Figs 2.56 and 2.57). Gullies 106, 107 and 110/111 intersected, providing a sequence in which gully 106 was the earliest and 110 the latest, and probably represent the locations of round-houses. Gully 112 comprised a more substantial barrier and may have been a ditched enclosure rather than a house site. A linear ditch (269) a short distance east of these features contained two sherds of middle Iron Age pottery and so may have been contemporary, although the pieces were extremely small and the attribution of the feature to this period is far from certain. The ditch also yielded two refitting fragments of fired clay that may be part of the rim of a metalworking hearth, although no slag or other evidence for metalworking was recovered from the site.

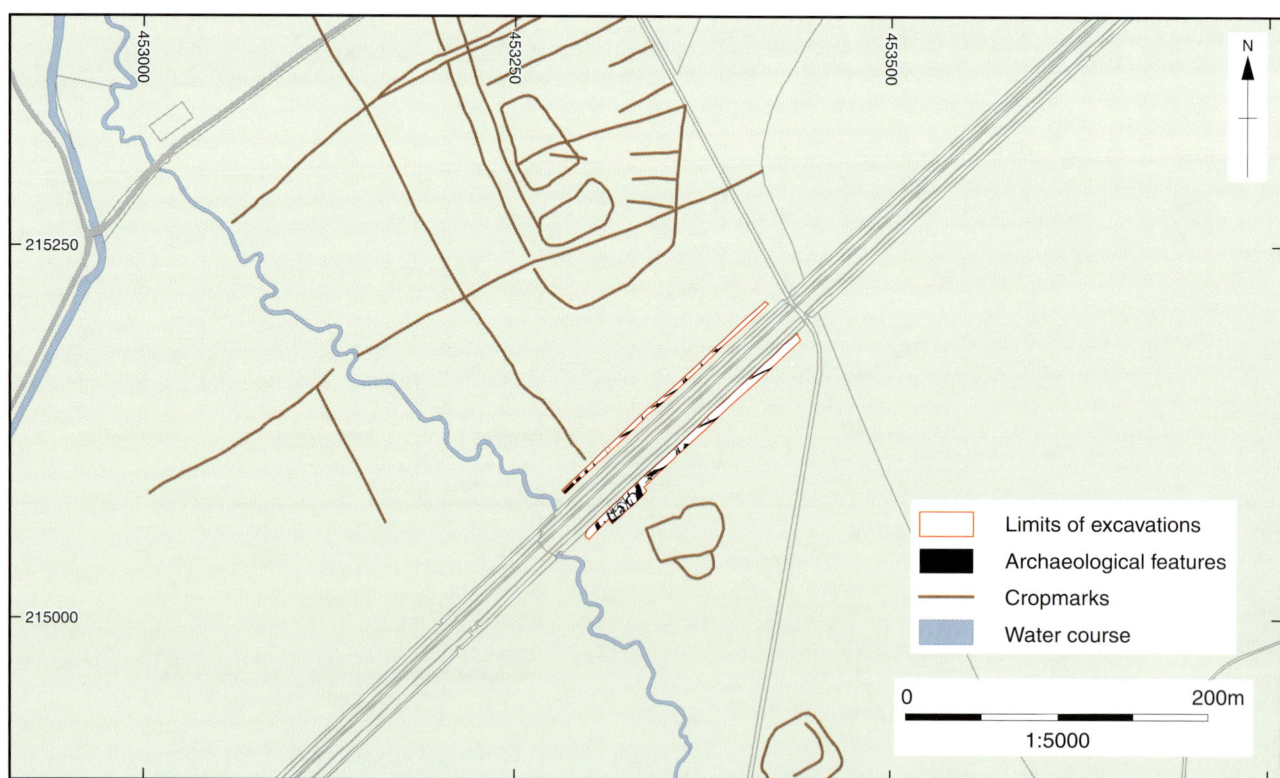

Fig. 2.54   Location of North of Gallos Brook

Gully 106 was a curving feature that probably represented the south and east sides of a penannular gully with a projected original diameter of *c* 8.5-9.0m (Fig. 2.56, section 20). A terminal at the north-eastern end may have formed one side of an entrance, although given the shallowness of the feature it could alternatively have resulted from truncation by more recent ploughing. The gully was *c* 0.2m deep and had a gravelly primary fill that was not present in all interventions, overlain by a main fill of homogeneous silt. The lower parts of two vessels (SF 1 and SF 2) were recovered from the east side of the feature and, although only a small proportion of each vessel survived, appeared to have been deposited upright. SF 1 was a coarse limestone-tempered jar of which very little survived, while SF 2 was a flat-based, sand-tempered vessel with burnishing that may indicate that the vessel was a globular bowl. Bulk samples were collected from the soil around the vessels, but only a single pig tooth

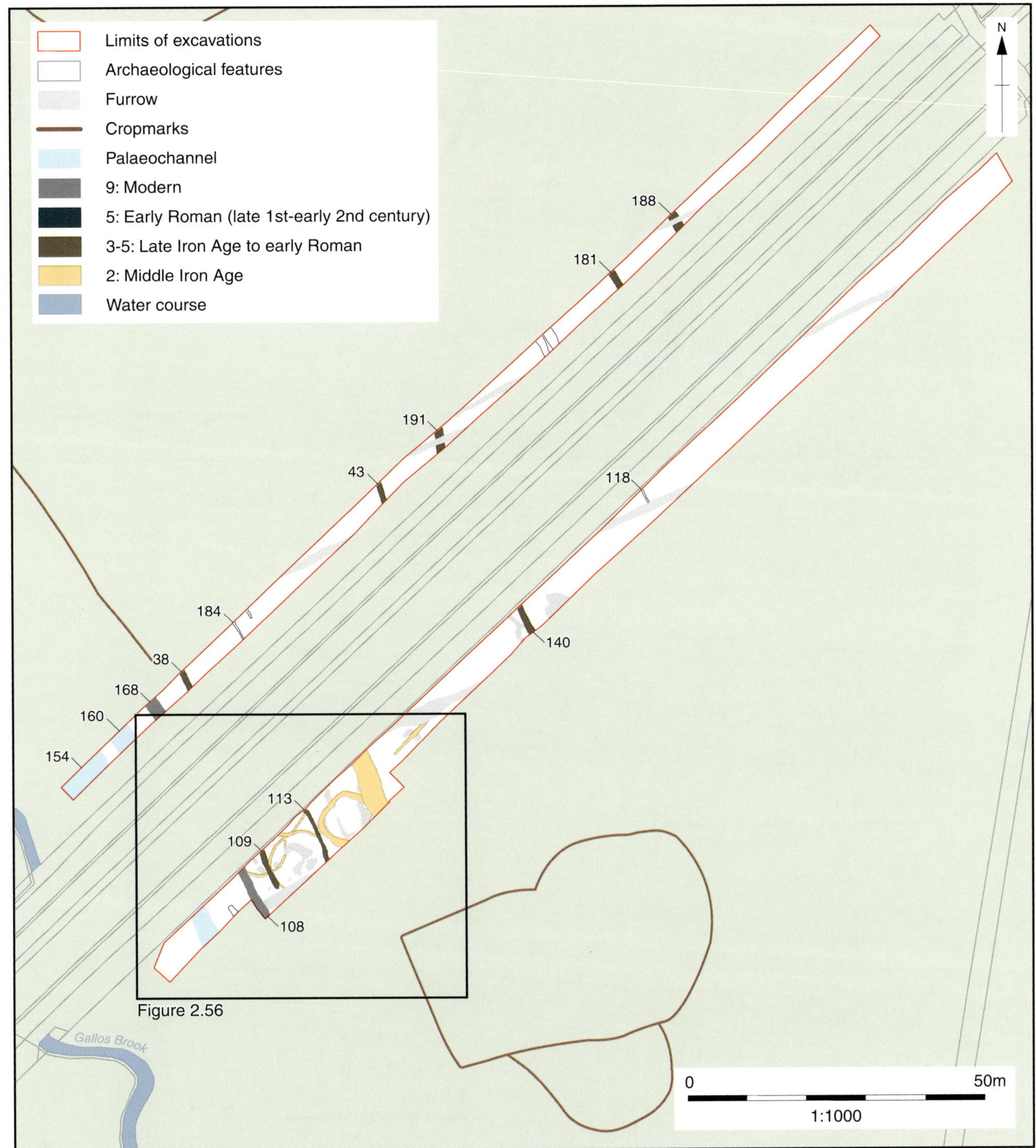

Fig. 2.55   North of Gallos Brook, plan of archaeological features

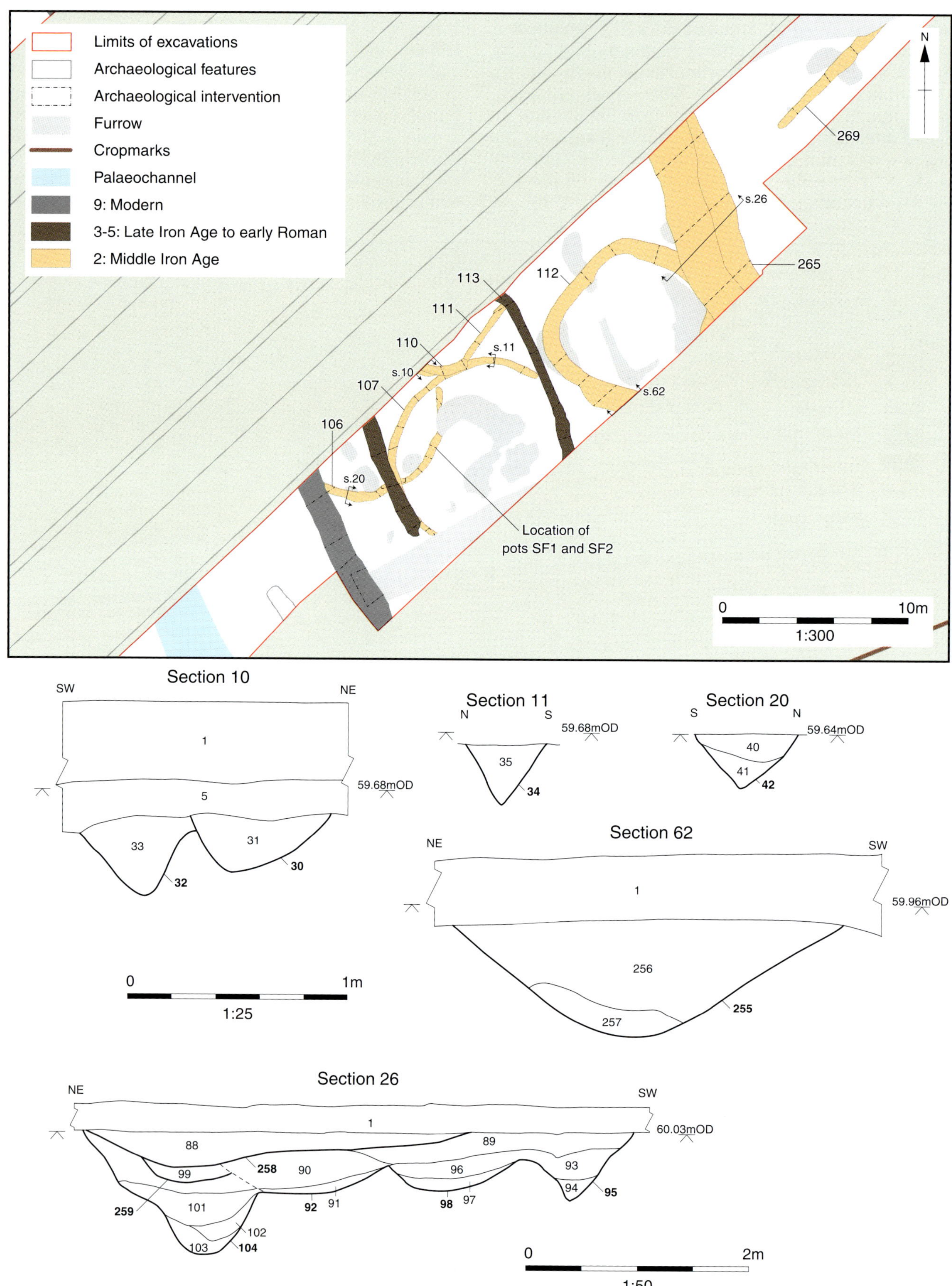

Fig. 2.56   North of Gallos Brook, plan of the middle Iron Age settlement at the south-western end of the excavation area

and a few unidentifiable crumbs of animal bone were recovered.

Gully 106 was cut by gully 107, which was the most complete of the three penannular features, with only the south-east quadrant missing due to truncation by Roman ditch 113 and a medieval furrow (Fig. 2.56, section 11). It measured 10m in diameter and a terminal on the east side may be evidence for an entrance. The gully had a V-shaped profile and was 0.20-0.26m deep with a single fill of homogeneous brown silt.

Only a small part of the third and final gully in the sequence was exposed within the limits of the excavation area (Fig. 2.56, section 10). It was the only one of this group of features that exhibited evidence for more than a single phase. In its initial iteration (111) it comprised a curvilinear gully that was somewhat more angular than the preceding gullies, with a less regular curve. It survived to a depth of 0.3m at the baulk but was only 0.1m deep elsewhere. The western part of the feature was recut as gully 110, which was 0.25-0.3m deep and ended at its east end in a definite terminal.

Gully 112 did not intersect with the other penannular features and had a somewhat different character, with relatively straight sides and curved corners hinting at a possible sub-rectangular shape, rather than the circular form of the other features. Certainty is difficult, however, since the south-eastern extent lay beyond the limits of the excavation area and the feature was truncated on the east side by ditch 265. The part of the feature that lay within the excavation area measured 7.25m NW-SE and at least 6.5m NE-SW, with no evidence for an entrance. The gully was up to 1.5m wide and 0.5m deep, with a V-shaped profile, and contained no artefactual material (Fig. 2.56, section 62).

The east side of enclosure gully 112 was cut by a substantial and long-lived boundary ditch (265) that extended on a NNW-SSE alignment across the trench on the south side of the railway. The ditch did not appear to the north of the railway and so must have terminated or turned at some point between the two trenches, but no return was exposed in the excavation. The ditch had been recut on at least three occasions (Fig. 2.56, section 26). The earliest phase was the deepest, comprising a steep-sided feature with a rounded base that was up to 0.9m deep and which yielded an assemblage of more than 2kg of pottery. The subsequent recuts were more shallow, with typical depths of 0.4-0.55m, and produced only a few sherds of pottery that included a few sherds of late Iron Age date in addition to middle Iron Age material. The final silting of the hollow (258) left by the feature contained a few sherds that dated from the late 1st century AD.

Phase 3-5: Late Iron Age or Roman features

A series of shallow ditches that extended across the site on roughly parallel NNW-SSE alignments may

Fig. 2.57   North of Gallos Brook, the complex of middle Iron Age penannular gullies, looking north

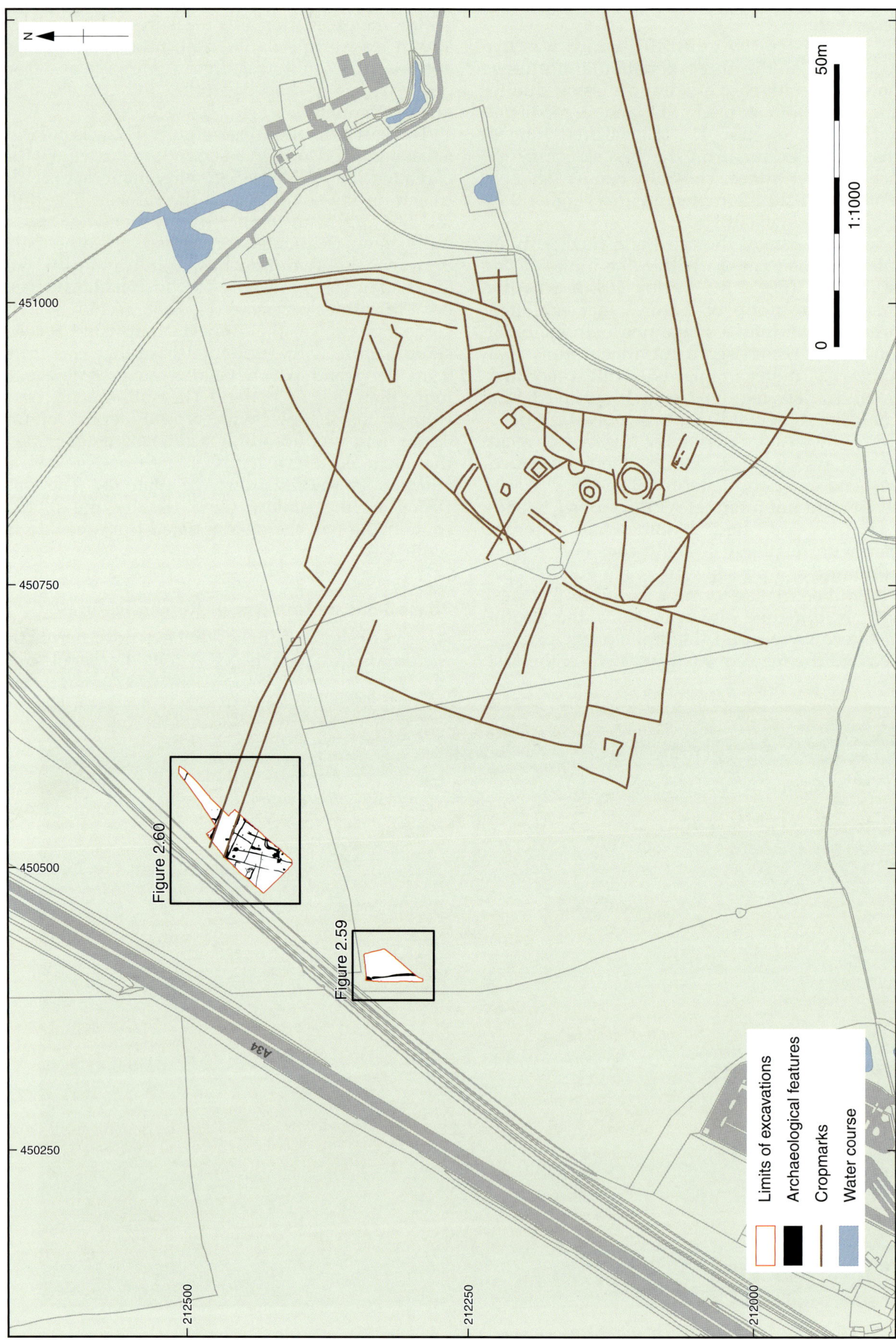

Fig. 2.58   Location of North of Oxford Parkway Station

have been late Iron Age or Roman in date, although there was little artefactual evidence for their date (38, 43, 109, 113, 118, 140, 181, 184, 188, 191; Fig. 2.55). They evidently post-dated the middle Iron Age settlement, since ditches 109 and 113 cut across the complex of penannular gullies, and a date before the medieval period was indicated by the furrows that cut across ditches 188 and 191. The artefactual evidence was limited to a small quantity of middle Iron Age pottery from ditch 113, which is presumably residual given its relationship with the settlement, and a single small sherd of late Iron Age or Roman pottery from ditch 188. Few of the ditches attained a depth of more than 0.3m but their common alignment suggests that they were the boundaries of a rectilinear field system.

Phase 8: Medieval period

Medieval and post-medieval ridge and furrow cultivation was represented by furrows that extended across the site on parallel E-W alignments (Fig. 2.55).

Phase 9: Modern period

Ditch 108/168, which crossed the south-eastern end of the site on a NW-SE alignment, contained a single post-medieval brick fragment. The ditch was distinguished from the undated ditches on a similar alignment by virtue of its greater depth, which amounted to 0.68m, and was cut into the subsoil that overlay the archaeological features.

Palaeochannels

Two palaeochannels (154 and 160) extended across the south-western end of the site on NNW-SSE alignments that were parallel to that of the current channel of the Gallos Brook. Both were shallow features, measuring no more than 0.3m deep and filled by homogeneous silting deposits, and no evidence was found for their date.

NORTH OF OXFORD PARKWAY STATION

The site was located 250m north-east of the site now occupied by Oxford Parkway Station, at NGR 4505 2124 (Fig. 2.58). It was situated on relatively flat land at *c* 60m aOD at the north-eastern extent of a low ridge between the River Thames and River Cherwell, on which Oxford is situated. The site lay at the foot of the ridge, which rises locally to *c* 75m aOD at North Oxford Golf Course, 1km to the south-west. The northern part of the ridge is composed of Oxford Clay, with alluvium associated with the River Cherwell beginning a short distance to the east of the site. The site was situated at the edge of an extensive complex of cropmarks comprising areas of settlement and associated trackways and field systems. One of the principal elements of the complex is a ditched trackway that

extended across the railway line. An evaluation confirmed that the trackway was Roman in date and also exposed several other contemporary features. Two excavation areas *c* 100m apart were opened up, comprising a western area encompassing 0.1ha, which was focused on a sequence of undated parallel ditches, and a larger eastern area of 0.3ha, which targeted the area of Roman features observed in the evaluation.

The only features uncovered in the western excavation area were a shallow field boundary ditch (3044) and a rough limestone cobbled surface (3043), both of which are probably of recent origin (Fig. 2.59). The ditch was aligned N-S, parallel to the existing field boundary 10-13m to the west. The boundary is shown on the 1st edition Ordnance Survey map of 1884 as a track that ran north from Water Eaton Lodge on the A4165 Oxford Road and crossed the railway line to converge with other tracks at Gosford Farm. Ditch 3044 may therefore have defined the eastern side of the track. The cobbled surface was associated with a break in the ditch and may have been laid as hardstanding at an entrance between fields.

The eastern excavation area recovered a small group of early prehistoric flint (Phase 1) and exposed part of a developing agricultural landscape dating from the late 1st century/early 2nd century to the late Roman period (Phases 5, 6 and 7, Fig. 2.60).

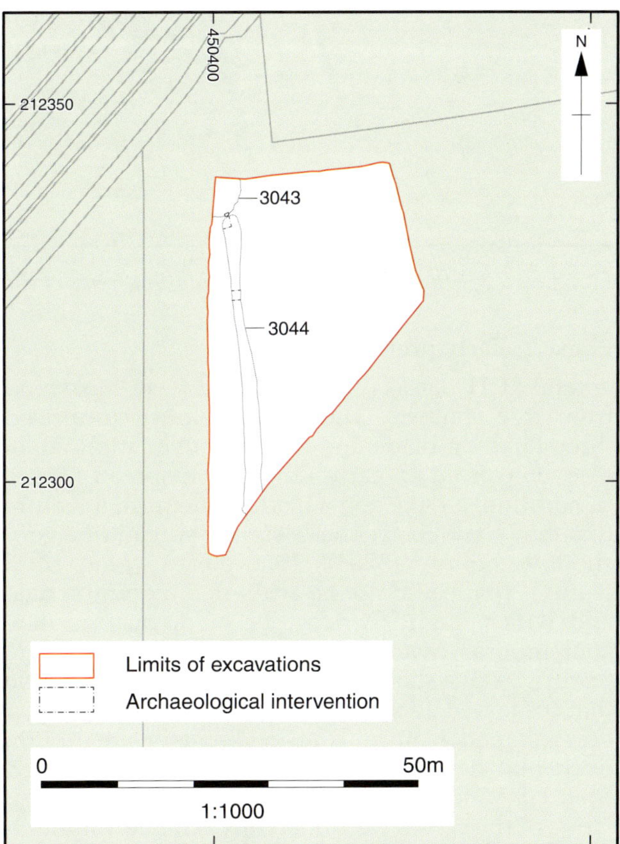

Fig. 2.59 North of Oxford Parkway Station, plan of the western excavation area

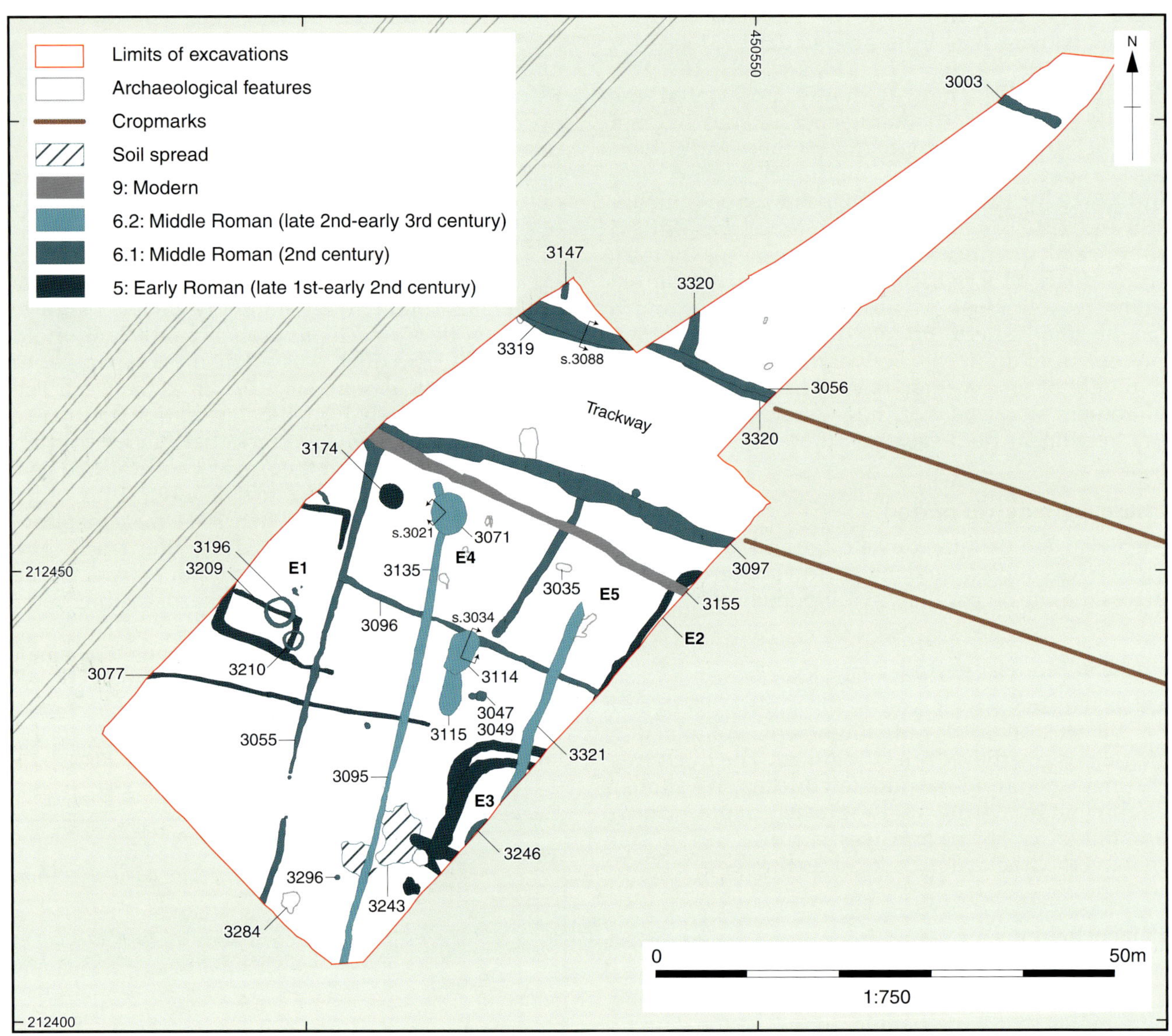

Fig. 2.60 North of Oxford Parkway Station, plan of the eastern excavation area

Phase 1: Early prehistory

A total of 11 pieces of worked flint were recovered from five contexts. The largest group comprised three flakes, a blade and a core rejuvenation tablet recovered from an early Roman soil spread (3243). In addition, a flake and a blade came from a feature that may have been either a similar spread or a very shallow hollow (3284). Two pieces came from features that could not be attributed a definite date and which might therefore be of prehistoric date contemporary with the associated flints. These were feature 3035, a shallow, irregularly-shaped tree hole that contained an undiagnostic flake, and pit 3296, a bowl-shaped feature 0.6m in diameter and 0.12m deep that had been filled with soil that included fired clay and charcoal flecks as well as a bladelet. None of the pieces was inherently datable, although the core tablet, the bladelet and several of the flakes display the soft-hammer bulbs usually associated with early prehistoric flintwork.

Phase 5: Early Roman (late 1st-early 2nd century)

Early Roman features were restricted to the southern part of the excavation area and comprised a group of rectilinear enclosures, defined by shallow ditches. At least three enclosures (E1-3, Fig. 2.60) were identified but none of them lay entirely within the exposed area and it was consequently uncertain whether they comprised discrete enclosures or were part of a larger conjoined complex, although the former seemed more likely. They evidently formed elements of a coherent landscape, since they shared a common orientation. The ditches that defined the enclosures consistently measured *c* 0.3m deep, with only occasional minor variations. The absence of internal features and the relatively small artefactual assemblage associated with the enclosures suggests that they were not domestic in character and are more likely to represent stock enclosures.

Enclosure E1 was the most northerly of the group and was also the enclosure whose plan was most fully exposed within the excavation area, although the north-western corner lay beyond the north-western edge of the site. It was defined by two L-shaped ditches and was rectangular in plan with dimensions of 15 x 10m. The east side of the structure was only partly enclosed, the enclosure ditch ending *c* 4m south of the north-east corner in a very definite terminal that, at 0.4m, was the deepest excavated part of the enclosure boundary. It is, of course, possible that the boundary was continued in another medium that has left no archaeologically detectable trace. Two rim sherds from samian bowls of Dragendorff form 38 from the fill of the southern part of the enclosure ditch indicated that it was still silting into at least the middle of the 2nd century.

A pair of small annular gullies (3196, 3210) were situated within the southern part of the enclosure. Gully 3196 was the larger of the two, with a diameter of 2.75m, and was defined by a gully 0.5m wide and 0.12-0.19m deep. Gully 3210 was only 1.75m in diameter and comprised a gully 0.3m wide and 0.07-0.14m deep. The small diameter of the gullies suggests that they are likely to represent stack rings rather than the wall lines or drip gullies of plough-truncated roundhouses. The gullies were subsequently replaced by a small rectangular sub-enclosure constructed against the southern side of the main enclosure, which was defined by ditch 3209 and measured 7.6 x 3.3m.

Part of a second possible enclosure (E2) was exposed at the eastern edge of the excavation area, 35m from enclosure E1. Its identification as an enclosure is very tentative, since it was represented only by a ditch that extended along the eastern edge of the site for a distance of 18m, although the presence of a return at its northern end is suggestive of an enclosure ditch rather than a simple linear boundary.

South of Enclosure E2 lay enclosure E3, which was similarly situated at the eastern edge of the site. The west side and parts of the north and south sides were exposed within the excavation area. The enclosure ditch appears to have comprised two separate elements, with an apparently linear south side that was abutted by an L-shaped ditch that enclosed the west and north sides, and which was subsequently recut.

Several large soil spreads at the southern end of the site contained pottery attributed to this phase and may represent an area of the contemporary soil layer that had been preserved within a shallow hollow. A more regularly-shaped hollow at the northern limit of the early Roman features (3174) was also attributed to this phase, although it was uncertain whether it was a deliberately dug feature.

Phase 6.1: Middle Roman (2nd century)

During the 2nd century, the ditched trackway identified as a cropmark on aerial photographs (Fig. 1.4) was constructed. It crossed the central part of the excavation area and appears to have been part of a wider reorganisation of the landscape during which the apparently discrete enclosures of the earlier period were replaced by an arrangement of more regular ditched enclosures and boundaries that branched off the trackway. The date of the samian sherds from the ditch of Phase 5 enclosure E1 would suggest that this phase did not begin until the second half of the century, since it post-dated that enclosure.

The trackway

The trackway extended across the excavation area on a WNW-ESE alignment and was recorded as a cropmark that continued on a curving alignment to a convergence with other trackways *c* 500m to the south-east. It was defined by a pair of flanking ditches but no evidence for a metalled surface was found, and its substantial width, which amounted to 15m, suggests that it was intended as a droveway for livestock in addition to serving the needs of human traffic. The ditch on the north side had been recut, but the southern ditch (3097) exhibited evidence for only a single phase. The south ditch and the original form of the northern ditch were both 0.45-0.8m deep, with moderately sloping sides. This phase of the northern ditch may have comprised two separate ditches on the same alignment (3319, 3320), although this was not certain as any relationship between them had been removed by the recut (3056). Ditch 3320 appeared to end to the west in a return that extended northward as an enclosure boundary and there may have been an entrance between this point and ditch 3319 that provided access onto the trackway. The recut was a substantial, steep-sided feature (3056) that was up to 2.2m wide and 0.9m deep. The lowest fills comprised a sequence of dark grey clay layers (3303, 3308, 3309, Fig. 2.61) that were characteristic of deposition in standing water. The fills contained plant and insect remains that had been preserved by waterlogging and the seed assemblage mostly comprised species that would be expected to grow around ditches (nettle, bramble, thistles etc), with some species indicating that the ditch may have been filled with water for part of the year. The presence of waterlogged twigs, a thorn of blackthorn/hawthorn and fruit stones may indicate that a hedge grew alongside the ditch. The upper fills were more typical of the minerogenic ditch fills that were found elsewhere on the site. The final fill of the intervention against the northern baulk (3183) contained a small quantity of pottery that dated from after *c* AD 240, indicating that the feature took a considerable period of time to fully silt up, during which the trackway may have continued in use.

Features north of the trackway

The arrangement of features north of the trackway was less well understood than that to the south because of the smaller area excavated. The northward return of ditch 3320 may have defined a

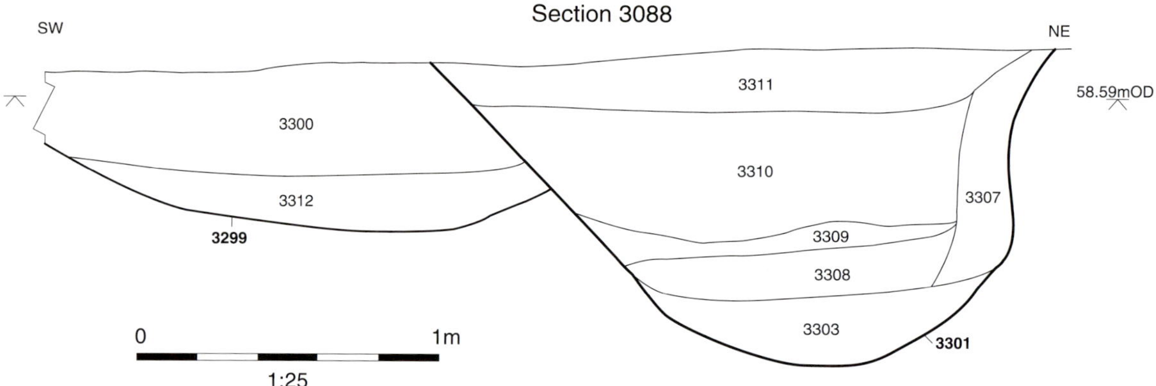

Fig. 2.61   North of Oxford Parkway Station, section through the north flanking ditch of the Roman trackway

boundary between adjacent enclosures adjoining the trackway and ditch 3003, which crossed the north-eastern end of the excavation area *c* 40m north of the trackway, may have formed the rear boundary. Ditch terminal 3147, which extended into the excavation area from the north and ended a short distance from the edge of the trackway ditch, may have represented another boundary, on an alignment roughly parallel to ditch 3320. This was quite a substantial feature, measuring 0.8m wide and 0.7m deep, and was the only feature other than the trackway ditch that produced late Roman pottery.

Features south of the trackway

The trackway was adjoined on the south side by a rectilinear arrangement of ditched enclosure boundaries that exhibited evidence for two phases. The ditches were typically shallow, rarely exceeding 0.3m in depth, and finds were limited to small quantities of pottery. The earliest feature appeared to be boundary ditch 3055, which branched off the trackway and extended towards the south. It was exposed for a total distance of 52m and continued south beyond the limits of the excavation area. A break mid-way along the ditch appeared to be the result of truncation of a particularly shallow part rather than a deliberate entrance.

Fig. 2.62   North of Oxford Parkway Station, oven/kiln 3047/3049

The area west of ditch 3055 appeared to have been left open, but the area to the east was subdivided when the northern end of the ditch was subsequently recut as ditch 3096, an L-shaped feature that turned east and defined the rear boundary of a pair of enclosures adjacent to the trackway. The western enclosure (E4) was slightly irregular in plan and measured 16-19m N-S and 17.5-22m E-W, and its neighbour (E5), which was not completely exposed within the limits of the excavation area, measured 19m N-S and at least 15.5m E-W. Neither enclosure contained any contemporary features, but pottery from the fill of ditch 3096 indicated that this arrangement remained in use until after *c* AD 180.

Discrete features were extremely sparse and were limited to an oven/kiln (3047/3049), a curving gully (3246) and a few very shallow pits of unknown function. Oven/kiln 3047/3049 comprised a circular pit (3047) that measured 0.7m in diameter and 0.26m deep, with a rake-out pit of slightly shallower depth on the east side (Fig. 2.62). The underlying clay geology around the pit had been discoloured to a reddish hue by the heat generated within, but the soil filling the feature contained only a few flecks of charcoal and must therefore represent soil from elsewhere that was used for backfilling rather than residue from its use. No evidence was found for a superstructure. Gully 3246 extended only slightly into the excavation area from the south-eastern baulk and its form is consequently uncertain, although its curvature may indicate that it was an annular feature similar to possible stack rings 3196 and 3210.

Phase 6.2: Middle Roman (late 2nd-3rd century)

Sometime after Phase 6.1 ditch 3096 filled in, after *c* AD 180, a new arrangement of boundaries was constructed that cut across this and several earlier features. This comprised a pair of ditches (3095, 3321) that lay on roughly parallel NNE-SSW alignments, perpendicular to the trackway, and a third ditch (3077) at a right angle to them. The ditches were shallow features, rarely more than 0.3m deep, and the very small pottery assemblage was not

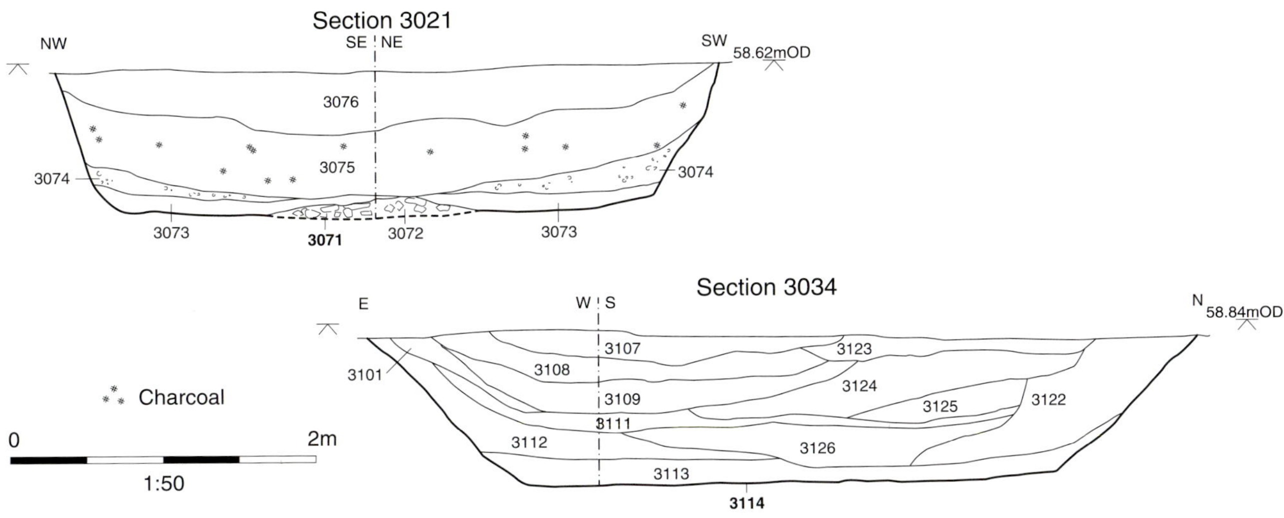

Fig. 2.63   North of Oxford Parkway Station, sections through pits 3071 and 3114

chronologically distinguishable from the material from the Phase 6.1 features and provided no indication of how long the features were in use, although ditch 3077 yielded the top of an Oxford ware flagon of Young's type W30, which dates from AD 180-240 (Fig. 3.12, no. 181). Ditch 3095 was cut by a large pit (3071), and two further substantial pits (3114 and 3115) were also attributed to this phase, since pit 3114 cut ditch 3096.

The size and depth of the large pits distinguished them from the rest of the features on the site and suggested a common function, although what this was is uncertain. Pit 3071 was almost circular and measured 4.2 x 4.1m and 0.75m deep, with near-vertical sides, while pits 3114 and 3115 were more oval in plan and respectively measured 5.2 x 3m and 0.8m deep and 4.7 x 2.25m and 0.6m deep. They may have been dug as quarry pits to extract clay or as waterholes, but there was no definite evidence. Pit 3071 (Fig. 2.63, section 3021) contained a thin basal layer of dark grey clay (3073). The layer was not substantial and so may not provide evidence for its primary function, but suggests that the feature was left open for some time, during which it held

standing water. The subsequent fills of this feature comprised homogeneous deposits of minerogenic clay that may have derived from either deliberate backfilling or natural silting. The fills of pit 3115 were similar, as were most of the fills of pit 3114, although the latest fills of the latter comprised dumps of grey material with charcoal inclusions (3107-9, Fig. 2.63, section 3034 and Fig. 2.64). Pit 3114 was the only one of the group that produced more than a handful of sherds of pottery, yielding an assemblage of more than 3.6kg of pottery that suggested that it had been used as a convenient receptacle in which to dispose of domestic refuse, although other categories of material were few. A soil sample from fill 3109 contained frequent charred cereal grains, mostly wheat with occasional barely and cultivated oat, as well as an unusually large representation of wild radish, presumably representing the disposal of waste plant material that had been used as fuel. The pits may have been among the latest features on the site, since they clearly post-dated some of the enclosures boundaries, pit 3071 cutting the northern end of ditch 3095 and pit 3114 cutting ditch 3096. The ceramic evidence, however, did not indicate a significantly later date than the enclosures.

Phase 7: Late Roman (mid 3rd-4th century)

No features were recorded that were created during the late Roman period but some evidence for continued activity in this period was indicated by the pottery from ditches 3056 and 3147.

Phase 9: Modern period

A modern ditch (3155) extended across the middle of the excavation area and cut across the southern ditch of the Roman trackway.

Fig. 2.64   North of Oxford Parkway Station, pit 3114

The finds

POTTERY *by Paul Booth*

Introduction

This report deals with the prehistoric and Roman pottery from the eight sites, with a total of some 10,913 sherds weighing *c* 154.4kg. There was no Anglo-Saxon pottery and overall quantities of medieval and post-medieval material were negligible. The material was scanned rapidly for purposes of assessment and preliminary dating, and was subsequently recorded in more detail. Recording was in line with the recent *A standard for pottery studies in archaeology* (PCRG *et al.* 2016) using codes set out in the OA later prehistoric and Roman recording system (Booth 2016). Quantification was by sherd count (note that sherd counts exclude new breaks where these were evident – as a result the overall sherd count presented here is some 20% less than the figure quoted in the assessment report, based on preliminary rough counts), weight and rim equivalents (REs), with an additional more subjective count of vessels based on individual rim sherds. Details of rim, base, handle, spout and decorative types and other characteristics were recorded where present. The full record of the pottery (on an Excel spreadsheet) is contained in the project archive.

For the purposes of the present report recording methodologies and general aspects of the assemblages are considered first. The assemblages are then treated on a site by site basis, particularly with regard to chronology, followed by an overall discus-sion. The quantities of pottery from each site are set out in Table 3.1.

The assemblages are very variable in size, with the two most substantial being those from the Langford Lane sites. The pottery was in very variable condition, both in terms of fragmentation (see Table 3.1) and surface condition, and regardless of period. For example, while the mean sherd weight (MSW) of the Langford Lane East assemblage was greater than those of the other sites, the physical condition of this material was otherwise no better, with numbers of somewhat abraded sherds present (probably a consequence of soil conditions rather than repeated redeposition). Even when the sherds are in apparently reasonable condition the scarcity of recorded instances of burnished zone decoration, which would usually be common, suggests that some surface erosion was widespread.

Later prehistoric

Fabrics

Later prehistoric pottery, probably (but not certainly) all of middle Iron Age and later date, was recovered from all the sites, but at Langford Lane East, Langford Lane South, South of Merton, and North of Oxford Parkway Station was present only as a small proportion of the assemblage, occurring solely in contexts of Roman date (Phase 4 or later). In total this material amounted to 689 sherds (6706g), thus constituting 6.4% of the total prehis-

Table 3.1 Quantities of late prehistoric and Roman pottery

Site	No. sherds	Wt (g)	MSW (g)	REs	Main chronological emphasis
Langford Lane East	4281	75,201	17.6	45.25	Late Iron Age/early Roman to 2nd century
Langford Lane South	3252	38,346	11.8	48.55	Mostly late 1st-late 2nd/early 3rd century
South of Merton	835	10,496	12.6	11.62	Late 1st to early 3rd century
Holts Farm Crossing	1595	16,188	10.2	16.38	Middle Iron Age-2nd century, a few late Roman groups
East of Oddington Grange	53	511	9.6	0.61	Middle Iron Age to late Iron Age/early Roman
South of Oddington Crossing	25	186	7.4	0.12	Middle to late Iron Age
North of Gallos Brook	279	3815	13.7	1.45	Almost all middle Iron Age
North of Oxford Parkway Station	593	9676	16.3	12.12	Mostly later 1st-2nd century
Total	10,913	154,419	14.2	136.10	

MSW = mean sherd weight

Table 3.2 Quantification of Iron Age pottery fabric groups from all sites by sherd count and weight (column %)

Fabric group	Component fabrics	Langford Lane East No. sh.	Wt (g)	Langford Lane South No. sh.	Wt (g)	South of Merton No. sh.	Wt (g)
A1	A, A3, AN2, AN2/3, AN3	6	8			3	13
A2	ACG3						
A3	AF3/4			1	22		
A4	AG, AG3, AGL3, AGS3/4, AGV3, AGV4, AGZ4						
A5	AI3, AIS3, AIV3, AP3/4, IA3						
A6	AL3, AL3/4, AL4, ALV3, ALV3/4						
A7	AQ4						
A8	AS, AS3, ASG3/4, ASGV4, ASGV5, ASV3/4	1	7				
A9	AV3, AV3/4, AV4, AVG3/4, AVI3, AVL, AVL3, AVL3/4, AVL4, AZ3	2	10				
A subt		*9*	*25*	*1*	*22*	*3*	*13*
F1	FA3/4, FA4	1	3				
F2	FG4, FGA3/4, FGA4	2	20				
F subt		*3*	*23*				
G1	G, GA3/4, GA4, GAS3/4, GAS4, GAV3/4, GAZ4/5	3	15				
G2	GLA4, GLV4, GS4, GSA3/4, GSA4						
G3	GV, GV4, GVA4, GZ, GZA3/4						
G subt		*3*	*15*				
L1	LN4, LN5						
L2	LA3/4, LA4, LAIZ4, LAV3/4, LAV4, LAV5						
L3	LC4, LCV4						
L4	LAG4, LGA3, LGA3/4, LGA4						
L5	LS4, LS4/5, LS5, LSA4, LSA4/5, LSA5, LSG4, LSV4, LSVA4						
L6	LV4, LVA, LVA4, LVA4/5, LZ4						
L subt							
S1	S, SN4	1	4				
S2	SA4, SA4/5, SA5, SAC5, SACV4, SAG4, SAV3, SAV4	1	3				
S3	SC4, CS4	1	20				
S4	SG, SG4, SG4/5, SGA3/4, SGA4, SGVA4						
S5	SI3, SIA4						
S6	SL4, SLA4, SLGA4, SLV3						
S7	SV4, SV5, SVA3, SVA4, SVGA4, SZ4						
S subt		*3*	*27*				
V1	VN4						
V2	VA, VA3, VA3/4, VA4, VA4/5, VA5, VAF4, VAL4, VAP4, VAS4						
V3	VGA4/5						
V4	VL5, VLA5						
V5	VSG4						
V subt							
Z1	Z4, ZN4, ZN5						
Z2	ZA4, ZA4/5, ZAI4						
Z subt							
Totals		18	90	1	22	3	13

Holts Farm Crossing		East of Oddington Grange		South of Oddington Crossing		North of Gallos Brook		North of Oxford Parkway Station		Total			
No. sh.	Wt (g)	No. sh.	Wt (g)	No. sh.	Wt (g)	No. sh.	Wt (g)	No. sh.	Wt (g)	No. sh.	No. sh.%	Wt (g)	Wt%
32	109			13	36	12	41			66	9.6	207	3.1
1	9									1	0.2	9	0.1
										1	0.2	22	0.3
19	133									19	2.8	133	2.0
6	22					10	23			16	2.3	45	0.7
7	39			1	7	50	669			58	8.4	715	10.7
1	7									1	0.2	7	0.1
9	64			1	40			1	7	12	1.7	118	1.8
13	65	2	39			12	108	1	14	30	4.4	236	3.5
88	*448*	*2*	*39*	*15*	*83*	*84*	*841*	*2*	*21*	*204*	*29.7*	*1492*	*22.3*
2	3									3	0.4	6	0.1
2	4									4	0.6	24	0.4
4	*7*									*7*	*1.0*	*30*	*0.4*
8	54	1	9							12	1.7	78	1.2
15	134									15	2.2	134	2.0
25	151									25	3.6	151	2.3
48	*339*	*1*	*9*							*52*	*7.6*	*363*	*5.4*
2	11					13	265			15	2.2	276	4.1
15	282	4	62	2	7	24	248			45	6.5	599	8.9
1	2					2	12			3	0.4	14	0.2
6	63									6	0.9	63	0.9
14	82			5	57	74	1021			93	13.5	1160	17.3
15	80	2	43			32	689			49	7.1	812	12.1
53	*520*	*6*	*105*	*7*	*64*	*145*	*2235*			*211*	*30.7*	*2924*	*43.6*
6	61									7	1.0	65	1.0
32	110					2	8			35	5.1	121	1.8
1	7									2	0.3	27	0.4
18	144									18	2.6	144	2.2
2	5									2	0.3	5	0.1
4	11					1	25			5	0.7	36	0.5
19	98									19	2.7	98	1.5
82	*436*					*3*	*33*			*88*	*12.8*	*496*	*7.4*
1	11									1	0.2	11	0.2
38	233	1	3			17	229	1	14	57	8.3	479	7.1
20	402									20	2.9	402	6.0
1	25					20	393			21	3.1	418	6.2
2	6									2	0.3	6	0.1
62	*677*	*1*	*3*			*37*	*622*	*1*	*14*	*101*	*14.7*	*1316*	*19.6*
1	4							18	49	19	2.8	53	0.8
		3	21					2	9	5	0.7	30	0.5
1	*4*	*3*	*21*					*20*	*58*	*24*	*3.5*	*83*	*1.2*
338	2431	13	177	22	147	269	3731	23	93	687		6704	

toric and Roman sherds from the project, and 4.4% of the weight, with the largest groups coming from Holts Farm Crossing (340 sherds, 2433g) and North of Gallos Brook (269 sherds, 3731g). These fabrics were recorded usually in terms of their two principal inclusion types (or more where present) and an indicator of their coarseness on a scale from 1 (very fine) to 5 (very coarse), with regular use of a binocular microscope at x10 or x20 magnification. The inclusion types identified are:

A	Quartz sand
C	Calcareous grit
F	Flint
G	Grog
I	Iron oxides
L	Limestone
N	None visible
Q	Quartzite?/large quartz grains
S	Shell
V	Vegetable/organic.
Z	Indeterminate voids

This approach has resulted in the identification of a very large number of differently coded fabrics, though many of the distinctions are quite subtle and in some cases likely to be of limited significance. The definition of fabrics using this system does not necessarily serve to identify production sources, since these are unknown for Iron Age material within the region. Nor does it automatically follow that identically coded sherds were necessarily from the same (unknown) source (although this is very likely), merely that their makers exploited very similar clay and tempering resources, indicating a uniformity of potting tradition. Quantification of the material by individual fabric is collated in the project archive. As it is highly unlikely that each of these represents a significant discrete production, an attempt to group the fabrics to reflect the output of more distinct potting traditions is presented in Table 3.2, which shows the component fabrics assigned to each of a smaller number of designated groups, quantified by site. Even so, some of these groups only contain small numbers of sherds.

The range of inclusion types encountered is consistent with possible or probable local production for almost all the Iron Age pottery. Geologies close by to the north would have been sources of limestone, calcareous grits and shell. At least some of the last was fossil material derived from crushed limestone (and the distinction between shell and limestone is therefore not always particularly meaningful), and the calcareous grit was also ultimately limestone-derived. The only fabric group that is less likely to have been very local in origin is the flint-tempered group (F1), and this was of minimal importance. The principal fabric groups, in order of numerical importance, were those tempered with limestone, quartz sand, organic material, and shell, for all of which relatively local sources can be

postulated. In many cases the principal inclusion type was combined with one or more of the other common inclusions. The only moderately common fabric group with no significant secondary inclusion type was the sand-tempered group A1, amounting to 9.6% of all later prehistoric sherds, but their representation in terms of weight was much less significant, for reasons which are not particularly clear. Limestone-tempered fabrics formed the single most important group and were particularly well-represented in terms of weight (43.6% of the total prehistoric assemblage). Absent from the small assemblages at the eastern end of the project route, these fabrics were particularly prominent at North of Gallos Brook, where they accounted for almost 54% of sherds (60% by weight). They were also proportionately significant in the other two (albeit very small) Oddington assemblages.

Unsurprisingly, variations in the representation of the major fabric groups are seen most clearly in the two largest later prehistoric assemblages, from Holts Farm Crossing and North of Gallos Brook. At the latter site, almost entirely of middle Iron Age date, the limestone-tempered fabric group was dominant, as already mentioned, and fabrics in sand-tempered and organic-tempered groups accounted for almost all the rest of the assemblage. At Holts Farm Crossing, by contrast, there was a much more uniform spread of material across the sand-, grog-, limestone-, shell-, and organic-tempered groups, with almost all the grog-tempered sherds, for example, coming from this particular site. This is likely to reflect a rather different chronological emphasis in this assemblage compared to North of Gallos Brook – at Holts Farm Crossing the later prehistoric material, though comprising the largest individual site assemblage of this date by sherd count (almost exactly half of all the later prehistoric sherds from the project), only amounted to about 21% of the total sherds from the site (and only 15% by weight). It is likely that the later prehistoric pottery here derives from activity on the site that was continuous from this period into the 2nd century AD, if not later, and therefore includes a component which reflects the very latest developments in the handmade middle Iron Age potting traditions of the area, trends which may have been absent at North of Gallos Brook. The relative importance of grog-tempering at Holts Farm Crossing reflects this – it is a characteristic seen in other late prehistoric assemblages in the Bicester area, but not further west in the region.

Evidence for surface treatment and decoration was scarce. The surfaces of most fabrics seem to have been at best partly smoothed, a characteristic that could not be recorded systematically. Burnished surfaces were only recorded on 32 sherds – 4.6% of the total – 25 of which were in sand-tempered fabrics (groups A1, A6 (18 sherds) and A8), with single examples of overall burnished sherds in fabric groups L1, L2, L5, L6 and S4 and partial burnishing on two more L2 sherds. Other miscellaneous decorative treatments were very rare, with single examples on a total of eight sherds: horizontal rilling (fabric A4), 'scratch marking' (G3), oblique incised lines (G1, L4, L6), geometric incised lines (G1), more complex incised lines (A8) and notching of a rim in fabric L2.

Vessel types

Forty-nine vessels were represented by rim sherds, with a total estimated RE value of 2.84 – estimation of rim percentages was particularly difficult given the fragmented nature of the assemblage overall. With the exception of a decorated globular bowl in fabric AS3 (fabric group A8) from South of Oddington Crossing, all the rims were from certain or probable examples of jar forms, many of rather indeterminate character, typically with fairly simple upright or slightly in- or out-sloping rims, either even-sided or slightly thickened. Thirteen rims were from vessels assigned to a 'barrel-shaped' jar type and these sherds, of which eight came from North of Gallos Brook, tended to be slightly more substantial than those from vessels only assigned to the generic jar category. Six rims were defined as being from type CH bead rim jars (for vessel type codes see Table 3.7), a form that would be expected to date to the later part of the middle Iron Age (and into the late Iron Age/early Roman period). These occurred in fabric groups A4, A9, L2, L5, V2 and Z2, indicating that this type was a component of the repertoire of most of the principal later prehistoric ceramic traditions in the area, rather than being a speciality of one. Four of these vessels came from North of Gallos Brook.

Late Iron Age-Roman

Fabrics

The excavation produced a wide range of late Iron Age and Roman fabrics. These are listed in Table 3.3 in order within the series of major ware groups defined by the OA system on the basis of significant common characteristics. The ware groups can be combined to constitute two main classes of material, fine and specialist wares on the one hand, and on the other the rest of the coarse wares (cf. Booth 2004). The fine and specialist ware groups (identi-fied by the initial letter of the fabric/ware code) are: samian ware (S); fine wares – colour-coated, lead glazed, mica coated etc – (F); amphorae (A); mortaria (M); white wares – other than mortaria – (W); and white-slipped wares (Q). The remaining ware groups are: 'Belgic type' (broadly in the sense of Thompson 1982, 4-5), usually grog-tempered, fabrics (E); 'Romanised' oxidised coarse wares (O); 'Romanised' reduced coarse wares (R); black-burnished ware (B); and calcareous (particularly shell-tempered) and other wares (C).

Within these classes there are hierarchically arranged subgroups, usually defined on the basis of inclusion type, and individual fabrics/wares are then indicated at a third level of precision, both levels of subdivision being expressed by numeric codes. Thus R10 is a general code for fine, slightly sandy reduced wares, while R11 is a specific distinc-tive reduced Oxford industry product (note that 'Oxford' is used as a convenient abbreviation for the major industry studied by Young (1977), since 'Oxfordshire' could refer to other productions in the area which are not part of this industry. References to 'Young' without further qualification are to the 1977 publication). For the bulk of the present assem-blage fabric identification was at the intermediate level of precision. Much of the material was in fabrics the sources of which are unknown or uncer-tain, and detailed assignment to specific fabric codes did not seem to be warranted. A particular example is the R30 group of medium sandy reduced coarse wares, which is likely to have included products of a number of different local and regional centres, including the Oxford industry, none of which is sufficiently distinctive to allow confident attribution on the basis of relatively superficial examination of fabric. Attribution of sherds to ware groups or to individual fabrics was on the basis of macroscopic inspection, with frequent but not universal use of the binocular microscope at x10 or x20 magnification.

Relatively summary fabric descriptions or labels are given in Table 3.3, although some fabrics recently added to the OA series (but mostly of minor significance) and others added specifically from the present assemblage are described in more detail. More comprehensive descriptions can be found in the project archive and/or in the handbook to the National Roman Pottery Fabric Reference Collection (Tomber and Dore 1998). Fabric codes from the latter are cross-referenced in the table in bold.

In addition to fabric codes and descriptions, Table 3.3 also gives an estimate of the distance of the source area of a particular fabric from the project area, taking Holts Farm Crossing as an arbitrary reference point for all the sites. The categories used are I (Continental import), ER (British, extra-regional), R (regional – in a radius of roughly 10-45km from the site) and L (local – up to c 10km distant). The 10km figure for the 'local' range includes the Oxford industry, though not all of the component production sites of this industry were within the 10km radius. Distances are 'as the crow flies' rather than involving calculations of how far a particular product might have had to move to reach the site depending on its mode of distribution. Despite the somewhat arbitrary nature of these definitions they do seem to result in a fairly coherent pattern of data. Some wares cannot be assigned confidently to one source category or another, and an L/R group is therefore used. This is particularly the case with the R30 (medium sandy reduced wares) group. This will have included products of the Oxford industry but also other

Table 3.3 Late Iron Age and Roman pottery fabric codes and descriptions

Ware code	Description	NRFRC code/reference	Source area
Samian ware			
S	Samian ware unspecified		
S20	South Gaulish samian ware (general).	incl **LGF SA**	I
S25	?Montans South Gaulish samian ware	**MON SA**	I
S30	Central Gaulish samian ware (general)	incl **LEZ SA 2**	I
S32	Les Martres-de-Veyre Central Gaulish samian ware	**LMV SA**	I
S40	East Gaulish samian ware (general)		I
S41	Rheinzabern samian ware	**RHZ SA**	I
Fine wares			
F43	Central Gaulish 'Rhenish'	**CNG BS**	I
F50	Major British colour-coated wares, but usually red-brown colour-coated wares (general). F50 mainly used for probable Oxford wares and related fabrics		R?
F51	Oxford colour-coated ware	**OXF RS**	L
OF	Oxidised probable Oxford fabric (F51) but with no surviving colour coat	cf **OXF RS**	L
F52	Nene Valley colour-coated ware	**LNV CC**	ER
F55	Fine oxidised fabric with brown colour-coat. ?Colchester	**COL CC2**	ER
F59	Oxford early colour-coated ware. A fine, moderately hard oxidised fabric with red-brown colour coat	Booth *et al.* 1993, 140	L
Amphorae			
A10	Buff amphora fabrics (general)		I
A11	Dressel 20 Baetican amphorae (Peacock and Williams 1986, 140)	**BAT AM 1** and **BAT AM 2**	I
A13	Gauloise South Gaulish amphorae (Peacock and Williams 1986, 143)	**GAL AM 1**	I
A18	Buff, fairly fine, hard fabric with common subangular-subrounded quartz up to 1mm but most <0.3mm. Sparse-moderate subrounded (occasionally elongate) black glassy inclusions, typically up to *c* 0.5mm. Unattributed		I
A26	Reddish brown, fairly hard and fine, with sparse sand <0.2mm, mica, ?rounded limestone and occasional other fine inclusions, all sparse-rare. Coarser sand (up to 1-2mm) on rim exterior	cf **GAL AM 2?**	I
A30	Coarse oxidised amphora fabrics		I
Mortaria			
M12	N Gaul/SE England (Hartley group 2)	**NOG WH 4**	I/ER?
M21	Verulamium region mortaria	**VER WH**	ER
M22	Oxford white ware mortaria (Young 1977, 56).	**OXF WH**	L
M33	Fairly hard, orange, with red/orange core, smooth fracture. Moderate subrounded black Fe or ferruginous grog inclusions >0.25mm, and very sparse subrounded quartz <0.25mm, both inclusions ill-sorted. Cream slip. Possibly a Minety product		ER?
White wares			
W10	Fairly fine white fabrics (general)		L/R/ER?
W20	Coarse sandy white fabrics (general)		L/R
W21	Verulamium white ware	**VER WH**	ER
W29	Buff white, fairly hard but with powdery surfaces. Rough, with sparse-moderate surrounded-subangular quartz sand up to 0.5mm and sparse-moderate angular quartz lumps, 1-2mm, exceptionally up to 4mm. Sparse black ?iron oxides and small linear voids		?
W30	Fine white fabrics (generally thin-walled and few/no obvious inclusions)		?
W36	Fine white/creamy-buff, abundant subrounded quartz <0.2mm but typically <0.1mm, occasional larger quartz grains. A little less fine and hard than W35 (cf W12)		L/R
W41	Fine pink-buff, south-east England/Kent?	Cf eg **COL WH**	ER
W42	Fine buff-white, cf M12	**NOG WH 4?**	I/ER?
W52	White ware with white core, margins and surfaces, common angular white grog 1mm, some fine sand 0.1-0.3mm and some red ironstone 1-4mm	Evans 2001a	?

Table 3.3 (continued)

Ware code	Description	NRFRC code/reference	Source area
White-slipped wares (except mortaria)			
Q20	Fine-moderately sandy oxidised white-slipped fabrics (general)		R?
Q21	Oxford (Young 1977) fabric WC– except mortaria (see fabric M31, above).	**OXF WS**	L
Q28	Oxidised throughout, some sand and ironstone	Evans 2001a	?
Q46	Orange, fairly hard, with moderate-common rounded-subrounded quartz sand inclusions up to 0.8mm but mostly 0.2-0.5mm. Occasional black ?iron oxides. Thick pale cream slip		?
'Belgic type' wares			
E10	Organic tempered 'Belgic type' fabrics		L/R
E20	Fine sand-tempered 'Belgic type' fabrics		L/R
E30	Medium to coarse sand-tempered 'Belgic type' fabrics		L/R
E40	Shell-tempered 'Belgic type' fabrics		L/R
E50	Limestone-tempered 'Belgic type' fabrics		L/R
E60	Flint-tempered 'Belgic type' fabrics		L/R
E80	Grog-tempered 'Belgic type' fabrics	**SOB GT**	L/R
E86	Oxidised hand-made fabric with orange-brown core, margins and surfaces, abundant sub-angular buff, orange and brown grog temper 0.5-4 mm.	Evans 2001a, 450	L/R
Oxidised 'coarse' wares			
O10	Fine oxidised coarse ware fabrics (general)		L/R?
O11	Oxford fine oxidised ware	Booth *et al.* 1993, 146; Young 1977, 185, fabric 1	L
O20	Sandy oxidised coarse ware fabrics (general)		L/R?
O30	Fine/medium sandy oxidised fabrics, includes North Wiltshire and related		R
O37	Fairly soft, moderate/abundant fine-medium quartz sand. Cf R37. O37F is a fine variant	Booth 1997, 114	R
O50	Miscellaneous oxidised coarse ware fabrics		?
O55	Fairly fine, common clay pellets/grog		L?
O60	Calcareous-tempered oxidised fabrics		R?
O80	Coarse tempered (usually grog) oxidised fabrics, equivalent to R90		L/R
O81	Pink grogged ware (Booth and Green 1989)	**PNK GT**	R
Reduced 'coarse' wares			
R10	Fine reduced 'coarse ware' fabrics (general)		L/R
R11	Oxford fine grey ware. Young (1977) reduced fabric 4	**OXF FR**	L
R20	Sandy reduced coarse ware fabrics (general)		L/R
R29	A very hard, sandy fabric, grey (5YR 6/1.5) with a reddish brown to strong brown core (5YR 5/3 to *c* 7.5YR 5/6). Contains abundant subrounded or rounded quartz, mainly in the range 0.2-0.4mm, with occasional grains from 1-2mm	Booth *et al.* 1993, 149; also Booth 2011b, 153	L/R
R30	Medium/fine sandy reduced coarse ware fabrics (general)		L/R
R37	Reduced fabric with distinctive light grey core and grey-to-black surfaces, generally grey, moderate-abundant fine quartz sand temper 0.2mm and occasional black ?iron ore and organic inclusions. The surface colour varies considerably, from light or mid grey to black. R37F is a fine variant	Booth 1997, 114	R
R38	As R37 with the addition of sparse-moderate clay pellet inclusions	Booth 1997, 114	R
R41	Fairly hard brownish-grey fabric. Moderate subrounded quartz up to 1mm, sparse angular grog, organic and black Fe inclusions. Moderate mica is prominent on surfaces in the type sherd, but not in the examples from Langford Lane South		L?
R50	A hard, slightly sandy fabric, usually black (*c* 5YR 2.5/1) to very dark grey (7.5YR 3/0), often with a reddish brown or reddish grey core (5YR 4/3, 4/4, 5/2). Inclusions are sparse to moderate rounded quartz usually in the range *c* 0.2-0.8mm	Booth *et al.* 1993, 151; cf Young 1977, 203 fabric 5	L?
R60	Reduced fabrics with significant organic inclusions (general)		L/R?
R61	A reduced fabric with mid grey core and paler grey margins and surfaces, with abundant organic temper voids 1-3mm, some rounded calcareous inclusions 0.3-1mm, occasional angular grey grog 2-4mm and sparse sand	Cf Evans 2001a, 451	L

Table 3.3 (continued)

Ware code	Description	NRFRC code/reference	Source area
R90	Coarse tempered (usually grog-tempered) reduced fabrics	eg Young 1977, 202 fabric 1	L/R
R94	Grey with moderate grog and occasional organic and rounded white ?limestone inclusions		L
R95	Savernake ware	**SAV GT**	ER
R96	Grey with moderate grog and occasional organic and rounded white ?limestone inclusions. Sparse quartz sand		R
Black-burnished wares			
B11	Dorset BB1	**DOR BB 1**	ER
Calcareous wares, etc			
C10	Shell-tempered fabrics (general)		L/R?

Source area codes: L = local; R = regional; ER = extra-regional; I = imported

similar vessels, some of which could have been produced at unknown sites, in some cases perhaps even more locally than the Oxford kilns to the south, but in others at more distant locations.

Quantification of the fabrics as percentages of each of the eight site assemblages is given in Tables 3.4 and 3.5, expressed in terms of sherd count and weight respectively. Inevitably, given the different chronological trajectories of the sites involved, there were significant differences in representation of ware groups or individual fabrics from site to site. The totals and percentages in the right hand columns of Tables 3.4 and 3.5 are therefore only broadly indicative, because they even out a complex picture of variation across the eight sites.

In overall terms the dominant ware groups were reduced coarse wares, E ('Belgic type') wares and oxidised coarse wares, in order of importance by percentage of sherd count, but the relative positions of the first two are reversed in terms of representation by weight. This pattern essentially reflects the emphasis of the Langford Lane East assemblage, in which E wares amount to almost 45% of sherds and 63.4% of the total weight. None of the other assemblages, except the tiny one from East of Oddington Grange, has remotely comparable figures. In general, reduced coarse wares are the most important element in site assemblages; they are substantially dominant at Langford Lane South, South of Merton and North of Oxford Parkway Station, but are less prominent at Holts Farm Crossing, where oxidised coarse wares were the dominant ware group, with identical percentages (26.7% of the assemblage) by both sherd count and weight.

Few fabrics in any of the site assemblages were intrinsically remarkable. As with the middle Iron Age pottery, most of the material can be attributed with varying degrees of certainty to fairly local sources. The local Oxford industry is likely to have been a supplier to the area from at least as early as the later 1st century, and it may well have

dominated supply in the 2nd century, a peak period of activity at a number of the EWR Phase 1 sites. Oxidised and reduced fabrics associated with this industry are typically not very diagnostic, however, and the relatively wide geographical spread of production sites means that there was considerable minor variation in these fabrics. This is likely to be reflected in the variation observed in sherds attributed to the fine oxidised and reduced ware groups O10 and R10, which together contributed 32.2% of all sherds (but only 16.9% by weight). As these figures suggest, these fabrics, sometimes used for fine, thin-walled vessels, were particularly prone to fragmentation, but their importance is underlined by the fact that they accounted for 30% of all late Iron Age and Roman vessels by REs. It is likely that a significant proportion, if not the great majority, of sherds in the O20, O30, R20 and R30 categories were also Oxford industry products, distinguished by coarse sandy textures (O20 and R20) and medium sandy ones (O30 and R30) – together amounting to 14.6% of sherds (11.2% by weight). It is probable, however, that these categories of pottery also included material from other, unknown local sources. This is perhaps particularly the case with the relatively small O30 group, but in general the scale of this problem is not considered to be large, and isolating such material does not seem realistic at present. Some fabrics within these broad groups were assigned with more confidence to a source to the west: fabrics O37, R37, R38, R96 and their variants are attributed to an unlocated 'West Oxfordshire' industry, thought to be focused near Akeman Street in the general vicinity of Asthall, roughly 25km west of the present sites. Together, these fabrics contributed just over 6% of all sherds and occurred in all the main assemblages, the chronology of which corresponded fairly closely with the late 1st-2nd century peak of production of this industry (for discussion see Booth 2018). Possible hints of

Table 3.4 Sherd count of Roman pottery fabrics by site (column % of late Iron Age and Roman total)

Fabric	Langford Lane East	Langford Lane South	South of Merton	Holts Farm Crossing	East of Oddington Grange	South of Oddington Crossing	North of Gallos Brook	North of Oxford Parkway Station	Total sherds	% excl. late prehistoric
S		+							1	+
S20 **LGF SA**	1.2	1.5		0.3				0.9	112	1.1
S25 **MON SA**	+								1	+
S30 **LEZ SA 2**	1.1	3.3	0.4	1.6			10.0	0.5	178	1.7
S32 **LMV SA**	0.3	0.9	0.2					0.4	45	0.4
S40		+							1	+
S41 **RHZ SA**		+						0.4	3	+
S subt	*2.6*	*5.8*	*0.6*	*1.9*	*-*	*-*	*10.0*	*2.2*	*341*	*3.3*
F43 **CNG BS**	+	0.1		0.1					6	0.1
FO	0.1	+		0.1				0.2	5	+
F50		0.1							4	+
F51 **OXF RS**	0.1			2.5					36	0.4
F52 **LNV CC**	+	0.1		0.1					6	0.1
F55 **COL CC2**		+							1	+
F59		0.2							7	0.1
F subt	*0.2*	*0.6*	*-*	*2.8*	*-*	*-*	*-*	*0.2*	*65*	*0.6*
A10	+								5	+
A11 **BAT AM 1&2**	1.3	0.4		0.4					74	0.7
A13 **GAL AM 1**		0.1							2	+
A18	+								1	+
A26 **GAL AM2?**	0.1								3	+
A30		0.1							2	+
A subt	*1.5*	*0.6*	*-*	*0.4*	*-*	*-*	*-*	*-*	*87*	*0.9*
M12 **NOG WH 4**		+							1	+
M21 **VER WH**		+							1	+
M22 **OXF WH**	0.7	0.6	1.7	1.4				0.2	81	0.8
M33	+								1	+
M subt	*0.8*	*0.6*	*1.7*	*1.4*	*-*	*-*	*-*	*0.2*	*84*	*0.8*
W10	0.6	2.4	2.5	1.8				0.5	146	1.4
W20	2.9	2.8	2.2	0.5				4.9	266	2.6
W21 **VER WH**		+	0.5	0.1				1.6	15	0.2
W29		+							1	+
W30	0.2								8	0.1
W36	0.1								5	+
W41 cf **COL WH**	+								1	+
W42 **NOG WH 4?**		+							1	+
W52		+							8	0.1
W subt	*3.8*	*5.5*	*5.2*	*2.4*	*-*	*-*	*-*	*7.0*	*451*	*4.4*
Q20	+								1	+
Q21 **OXF WS**	+	4.3	0.5	0.1				0.2	148	1.5
Q28		+							1	+
Q46		+							1	+
Q subt	*+*	*4.3*	*0.5*	*0.1*	*-*	*-*	*-*	*0.2*	*151*	*1.5*
F and S subtotal	**8.9**	**17.4**	**8.0**	**8.4**	**-**	**-**	**10.0**	**9.7**	**1179**	**11.5**
E10				0.3					4	+
E20	1.0	+		0.2				0.4	49	0.5
E30	2.6	1.2	0.1	1.5	5.3		10.0	1.9	182	1.8
E40	0.1	+	0.1	0.1					7	0.1
E50		0.1	0.1	0.2					6	0.1
E60	0.2								10	0.1
E80 **SOB GT**	40.9	4.1	1.0	15.9	94.7	66.7	20.0	6.3	2158	21.0
E86	+								2	+
E subt	*44.8*	*5.4*	*1.3*	*18.2*	*100.0*	*66.7*	*30.0*	*8.6*	*2418*	*23.7*

Table 3.4 (continued)

Fabric	Langford Lane East	Langford Lane South	South of Merton	Holts Farm Crossing	East of Oddington Grange	South of Oddington Crossing	North of Gallos Brook	North of Oxford Parkway Station	Total sherds	% excl. late prehistoric
O10	3.1	9.2	17.3	23.7			10.0	7.9	919	9.0
O11	+		1.1	0.2				0.5	15	0.2
O20	0.4	1.8	2.3	4.6				0.5	156	1.5
O30	1.1	1.8	2.1	1.5			10.0	1.1	149	1.5
O37		0.3							9	0.1
O37F								0.4	2	+
O50	0.1	0.1	0.1						5	+
O55		0.1		0.4					7	0.1
O60		+							1	+
O80	0.3	3.3	1.4	1.0				1.8	157	1.5
O81 **PNK GT**	+	0.5	0.1	2.5					49	0.5
O subt	*5.1*	*17.9*	*24.4*	*33.9*	*-*	*-*	*20.0*	*12.2*	*1469*	*14.3*
R10	19.5	28.6	40.0	16.1		33.3	10.0	12.8	2373	23.2
R11 **OXF FR**			0.2	0.2				1.2	11	0.1
R20	3.0	9.4	7.2	2.9			20.0	10.0	587	5.7
R29								0.4	2	+
R30	6.5	5.2	7.8	4.3			10.0	4.0	586	5.7
R37	6.4	5.3	0.5	2.6				4.6	506	4.9
R37F	+	0.2	0.5	0.6				13.2	92	0.9
R38	0.4	0.1	0.7					4.7	50	0.5
R38F		0.1		0.1				0.9	8	0.1
R41		0.1							2	+
R50	0.1	1.4	2.6	0.6				1.6	86	0.9
R60		0.4						1.1	19	0.2
R61	0.3	1.3							54	0.5
R90	0.1	0.8	1.8	1.2				3.9	82	0.8
R94								0.2	1	+
R95 **SAV GT**	0.1	0.1		0.2				0.4	12	0.1
R96			0.1					6.1	36	0.4
R subt	*36.2*	*53.0*	*61.4*	*28.8*	*-*	*33.3*	*40.0*	*65.1*	*4507*	*44.1*
B11 **DOR BB 1**	0.7	2.2	0.5	1.3	-	-	-	4.7	151	1.5
C10	4.2	5.3	4.2	8.9	-	-	-	-	500	4.9
Total excl. late prehistoric	4263	3251	832	1257	38	3	10	570	10,224	100%
Total sherds	4281	3252	835	1595	53	25	279	593	10,913	
LPreh % of total sherds	0.4	+	0.4	21.2	28.3	88.0	96.4	3.9	687	

Key: + = less than 0.1%

more local production are provided by the presence of two reduced ware jar rim sherds recorded as 'seconds' – distorted pieces. These were from a type CI vessel (see below) in fabric R10 at Langford Lane South and a type CC vessel in fabric R20 from South of Merton. In neither case, however, did the distortion appear sufficient to suggest that the vessel could only have derived from a very local source. Overall, therefore, direct evidence of production close to any of the railway sites is lacking. Questions remain, however, about the date of appearance and the sources of the earliest oxidised and reduced wares, particularly, but not exclusively, O10, R10 and R20. These occur in modest quantities at Langford Lane East in contexts of Phase 4, which should be of pre-Flavian date and are discussed further in the account of the pottery from that site below.

Few other coarse wares could be confidently assigned to known sources. Locally these included pink grogged ware (fabric O81), from the area around Stowe in Buckinghamshire, but this fabric, which is more common in the 3rd-4th centuries than earlier, was only a minor component of the assemblages in the sites closest to Alchester. A further minor element at these sites, and also at North of Oxford Parkway Station, was Savernake ware (R95), another product consistent with the primarily early

Table 3.5 Weight of Roman pottery fabrics by site (column % of late Iron Age and Roman total)

Fabric	Langford Lane East	Langford Lane South	South of Merton	Holts Farm Crossing	East of Oddington Grange	South of Oddington Crossing	North of Gallos Brook	North of Oxford Parkway Station	Total sherds	% excl. late prehistoric
S		+							1	+
S20 **LGF SA**	0.5	1.1		0.1				0.8	916	0.6
S25 **MON SA**	+								2	+
S30 **LEZ SA 2**	0.5	4.7	0.6	0.6			2.4	0.6	2356	1.6
S32 **LMV SA**	0.1	1.2	0.2					0.2	610	0.4
S40		+							1	+
S41 **RHZ SA**		+						0.8	77	0.1
S subt	*1.2*	*7.0*	*0.7*	*0.7*			*2.4*	*2.4*	*3963*	*2.7*
F43 **CNG BS**	+	0.1		0.1					36	+
FO	0.1	+		+				+	76	0.1
F50		+							13	+
F51 **OXF RS**	0.1			3.9					618	0.4
F52 **LNV CC**	0.1	0.1		+					80	0.1
F55 **COL CC2**		+							1	+
F59		0.1							32	+
F subt	*0.3*	*0.3*	*-*	*4.0*				*+*	*856*	*0.6*
A10	0.2								117	0.1
A11 **BAT AM 1&2**	6.2	3.7		1.0					6219	4.2
A13 **GAL AM 1**		0.1							34	+
A18	0.2								129	0.1
A26 **GAL AM2?**	0.2								116	0.1
A30		0.3							111	0.1
A subt	*6.8*	*4.1*	*-*	*1.0*					*6726*	*4.6*
M12 **NOG WH 4**		0.2							85	0.1
M21 **VER WH**		0.1							36	+
M22 **OXF WH**	2.1	2.0	21.7	6.4				0.2	5528	3.7
M33	0.2								154	0.1
M subt	*2.3*	*2.3*	*21.7*	*6.4*				*0.2*	*5803*	*3.9*
W10	0.3	1.8	1.4	1.7				0.6	1379	1.0
W20	1.5	2.6	1.8	0.4				6.3	2914	2.0
W21 **VER WH**		+	0.2	0.7				1.4	266	0.2
W29		0.1							28	+
W30	0.1								40	+
W36	0.1								41	+
W41 cf **COL WH**	+								3	+
W42		+							14	+
W52		0.2							74	0.1
W subt	*1.9*	*4.7*	*3.4*	*2.8*				*8.3*	*4759*	*3.2*
Q20	+								1	+
Q21 **OXF WS**	+	2.5	0.4	+				0.3	1030	0.7
Q28		+							5	+
Q46		0.1							26	+
Q subt	*+*	*2.5*	*0.4*	*+*				*0.3*	*1062*	*0.7*
F and S subtotal	**12.3**	**20.9**	**26.2**	**15.0**			**2.4**	**11.2**	**23,191**	**15.7**
E10				0.1					11	+
E20	1.4	+		0.2				0.1	1107	0.8
E30	1.8	1.1	0.1	1.2	3.9		20.2	1.3	2132	1.4
E40	0.1	+	0.1	+					115	0.1
E50		0.1	0.1	0.1					43	+
E60	0.3								219	0.2
E80 **SOB GT**	59.6	6.6	0.5	17.9	96.1	20.4	42.9	3.8	50,566	34.2
E86	0.1								72	0.1
E subt	*63.2*	*7.8*	*0.8*	*19.5*	*100.0*	*20.4*	*63.1*	*5.2*	*54,265*	*36.7*

Table 3.5 (continued)

Fabric	Langford Lane East	Langford Lane South	South of Merton	Holts Farm Crossing	East of Oddington Grange	South of Oddington Crossing	North of Gallos Brook	North of Oxford Parkway Station	Total sherds	% excl. late prehistoric
O10	0.7	4.7	9.3	15.7			2.4	4.3	5845	4.0
O11	0.1		2.5	+				0.1	312	0.2
O20	0.2	1.4	1.5	3.0				0.1	1275	0.9
O30	0.4	1.0	5.5	1.0			1.2	1.0	1510	1.0
O37		0.3							130	0.1
O37F								0.1	9	+
O50	+	0.1	0.1						45	+
O55		+		0.4					57	+
O60		+							8	+
O80	0.5	7.8	3.7	2.3				4.6	4512	3.1
O81	0.1	1.6	0.4	9.1					1943	1.3
O subt	*1.9*	*17.0*	*23.0*	*31.5*			*3.6*	*10.2*	*15,646*	*10.6*
R10	7.9	21.9	22.6	10.4		2.6	16.7	8.2	18,951	12.8
R11 **OXF FR**			0.5	0.7				0.9	246	0.2
R20	2.1	9.4	7.0	6.2			13.1	13.5	8077	5.5
R29								0.3	30	+
R30	3.0	5.2	6.3	3.4			1.2	2.0	5545	3.8
R37	4.3	6.6	0.6	2.2				6.3	6766	4.6
R37F	+	0.6	0.5	0.4				10.0	1303	0.9
R38	0.2	0.1	0.7					4.3	696	0.5
R38F		0.1		+				0.4	72	0.1
R41		+							16	+
R50	+	0.7	2.1	0.7				2.8	879	0.6
R60		0.8						0.7	370	0.3
R61	0.1	0.7							383	0.3
R90	0.4	1.3	5.7	2.2				7.4	2385	1.6
R94								0.1	6	+
R95 **SAV GT**	0.5	0.3		1.7				0.8	796	0.5
R96			+					13.5	1297	0.9
R subt	*18.6*	*47.7*	*46.0*	*27.9*		*2.6*	*31.0*	*71.2*	*47,818*	*32.4*
B11 **DOR BB 1**	0.2	2.0	0.2	0.7				2.3	1268	0.9
C10	3.5	4.6	3.8	5.3					5548	3.8
Total excl. late prehistoric	75,111	38,324	10,483	13,757	334	39	84	9583	147,714	100%
Total weight	75,201	38,343	10,496	16,190	511	186	3815	9676	154,418	
LPreh % of total weight	0.1	0.1	0.4	15.0	38.6	79.0	97.8	1.0	6704	
Mean sherd weight (g)	17.5	11.8	12.6	10.1	9.6	7.4	13.7	16.3	14.1	

Key: + = less than 0.1%

Roman date ranges of these sites. The only extra-regional coarse ware was Dorset black-burnished ware (BB1, here fabric B11), which amounted to 1.5% of the total sherds. It occurred at all sites except the small ones at East of Oddington Grange, South of Oddington Crossing and North of Gallos Brook, being best represented at North of Oxford Parkway Station, but overall quantities were always small and there is no clear evidence that it arrived at the railway sites before the generally accepted date for the commencement of large scale distribution, about AD 120.

Like the coarse wares, some of the categories in the broad 'fine and specialist wares' grouping were also dominated by Oxford products, which accounted for all but three of the 84 mortarium sherds, the majority if not all of the W10 and W20 white wares, and potentially all of the fine white-slipped oxidised ware flagon sherds recorded as fabric Q21. The sandy white ware W20 is sometimes disproportionately associated with jars and other 'coarse ware' forms at sites in the Oxford region, but that is certainly not the case here, where more than half the total REs in this fabric were of flagons, and a variety of beaker and bowl forms, *inter alia*, was also present. A large proportion of the few sherds in the fine ware category were also certain or probable Oxford products. The early Oxford (2nd-century) colour-coated ware tradition (Booth *et al.* 1993, 140) was represented by fabric F59, while certain examples of the standard late Roman colour-coated ware (fabric F51), with eroded possible examples of this fabric (recorded as fabrics OF and F50), together amounted to 72.7% of all fine ware sherds, despite the fact that contemporary (later 3rd-4th-century) activity was at best at a low level on most of the sites. Extra-regional fine wares were a single possible Colchester sherd and a handful of Nene Valley fragments, while the only imported fine ware was represented by six small sherds of Central Gaulish colour-coated ware (fabric F43).

Samian ware and amphorae were the significant imported contributors to the fine and specialist ware spectrum. Apart from five sherds of the common south Spanish Dressel 20 (etc) fabric A11 from Holts Farm Crossing, amphorae were confined to the two Langford Lane sites. In both cases the sherds were predominantly of fabric A11, one of only two represented by rim sherds – the sole A11 example (along with two sherds with handle stubs) being from Langford Lane South. From Langford Lane East came a larger portion of the neck of the same form, and a further handle fragment and scars. Other fabrics present included the south Gaulish fabric A13, used for Gauloise type wine containers. Fabric A18 is not certainly assigned to a source, but an oval-sectioned handle fragment, unfortunately unstratified, from Langford Lane East, is fairly certainly from a vessel in the range of Peacock and Williams (1986) classes 17-19 (see also Martin-Kilcher 2003), containers for fish products. A rim in fabric A26 (Fig. 3.5, no. 45) is probably of Gallic origin, perhaps from a London 555 type vessel (eg Peacock and Williams 1986, class 59; Sealey and Tyers 1989; Davies *et al.* 1994, 14-18; cf. Carreras Monfort 2004, 87). Fragments assigned to general fabric groups A10 and A30 (five and two sherds respectively) could not be assigned to source or vessel type.

Samian ware was quite widely distributed, occurring at all sites (including being one of the ten Roman sherds from North of Gallos Brook) except East of Oddington Grange and South of Oddington Crossing. It was best represented at the two Langford Lane sites, and was particularly prominent at Langford Lane South, where the various fabrics (principally Central Gaulish, but comprising a range of sources) amounted to 5.8% of all sherds and 7% of the assemblage by weight. South Gaulish samian ware was moderately well-represented by sherd count at the two Langford Lane sites, but tended to be quite fragmented. At Langford Lane East it was more common than Central Gaulish material by all measures. This site also produced a single fragment of possible Montans ware (fabric S25) alongside the La Graufesenque sherds. Les Martres-de-Veyre fabric was relatively prominent at Langford Lane South, but scarce elsewhere. There was almost no East Gaulish samian ware, the only identifiable form, in Rheinzabern fabric (S41) being a Dragendorff (Dr) 38 bowl from North of Oxford Parkway Station, found in the same context as another Dr 38 in Lezoux fabric.

Six samian ware vessels, one from Langford Lane East and the rest from Langford Lane South, were stamped (see Table 3.6), but only three of these stamps could be read with any confidence.

The most notable stamp, from Langford Lane East, was of Licinus, of pre-Flavian date, although the form on which it was used could not be identified.

A total of 35 samian ware sherds were decorated, amounting to 10.4% of the total sherds in all samian fabrics. With the exception of single fragments of Central Gaulish Dr 30 and 37, from North of Oxford Parkway Station and Holts Farm Crossing respectively, all these sherds were from Langford Lane East and Langford Lane South. Many of them were small fragments, but eight sherds were from the large part of a Central Gaulish Dr 37 bowl from Langford Lane South. Only four probable South Gaulish (La Graufesenque) ware sherds were decorated – sherds of Dr 29 and 37 from Langford Lane East and two sherds of Dr 37 from Langford Lane South – but none had distinctive features. The remaining decorated material is discussed in detail below. Most notable was the substantially complete vessel mentioned above, with a mould-maker's signature of Drusus ii.

Table 3.6 Samian ware stamps (die number after potter's name, Hartley and Dickinson 2008-2012)

Potter	Form	Stamp	Ware	Date	Context	Size	Phase	Context type	Comments
Licinus, 20a	Dish		S20	35-65	7271	Langford Lane East	4	pit	burnt
?	18/31		S20	90-110	2258	Langford Lane South	6	ditch	SF 2000, eroded. Date based on fabric/form
Burdo/Burdus 8b	31		S30	140-170	2615	Langford Lane South	6	pit	SF 2007
?	18/31-31		S30		2615	Langford Lane South	6	pit	eroded fragment
?	31	]?MANI	S30		2791	Langford Lane South	6	pit	as eg PRIMANI etc
Maritumus, 3a?	33	MARITV[	S30	155-200	2809	Langford Lane South	6	pit	incomplete

Decorated samian ware *by Gwladys Monteil*

Thirty-five fragments of decorated samian ware were recovered from four sites. Each sherd was examined, after taking a small fresh break, under a x20 binocular microscope as a first means to differentiate the fabric and production centre. The decorated fragments represent a maximum number of 18 vessels. Two fragments were too small for comment: a body sherd from a Dr 29 probably from Montans recovered at Langford Lane East and a Central Gaulish Dr 37 from Holts Farm Crossing.

The evidence provided by the decorated ware suggests a main phase of occupation from the Trajanic to the early Antonine period, with vessels from Les Martres-de-Veyre and Lezoux dominating the assemblage. Material from Les Martres-de-Veyre is particularly well-represented for an assemblage of this size, with four Trajanic bowls and a Hadrianic one in Langford Lane South (1030, joining sherds from 2572 and 2574, 2899, 2193 and 2863) and at least two, possibly three Hadrianic-early Antonine pieces in Langford Lane East (6553, 6554 and 7333). Hadrianic and Hadrianic-early Antonine bowls from Lezoux make up the rest of the group, with nine vessels for which comments are possible. Potters more characteristic of the mid to late Antonine period are completely absent from the group.

Catalogue of decorated samian (Figs 3.1 and 3.2)

The following catalogue lists the decorated pieces recovered from the sites that could be attributed to individual potters or groups of potters. The catalogue is organized in period order for each site, then by context; each entry gives the excavation context number, form type, production centre as evidenced by the fabric, details of the decoration and a date-range.

The letter and number codes used for the non-figured types on the Central Gaulish material – such as B223, C281, etc – are those created by Rogers (1974). The figured-types referred to as Os.000 are those illustrated by Felix Oswald in his index of figure-types on terra sigillata (1936-37).

The inventory numbers (Inv. No.) quoted are taken from the European intake of Roman samian ceramics (https://www1.rgzm.de/samian/home/frames.htm).

Langford Lane East

1. One body sherd, Dr 37, Les Martres-de-Veyre. Ovolo B263 and beaded border, Cettus. AD 130-160. Ctx 7333. Phase 5.
2. One body sherd, Dr 37, Lezoux. The small ovolo (B41), wavy border and the leaf tips recall the early work of Pugnus ii (Stanfield and Simpson 1990, pl. 153). The lion, perhaps Os.1402, is not known for him but is on stamped bowl by Tittius (Inv. No. 0012696b) with whom he had links (Hartley and Dickinson 2012, 65). Probably AD 130-160. Ctx 7116. Phase 6.
3. One body sherd, Dr 37, Lezoux. Partial scroll with possibly leaf H13 which is often used by Cinnamus ii (Inv. No. 0010805), Paullus iv (Inv. No. 0012365) but also Sissus ii (Inv. No. 0012659). AD 135-170. Ctx 7155. Phase 6.

4. One body sherd, Dr 37, Les Martres-de-Veyre. The surface is very abraded but the top of leaf J144 and part of Venus Os.281 are visible. Both are known for the potter Cettus (Romeuf 2001, pl. 79, nos M7 and M8). Possibly the same bowl as the one in 6554. AD 130-160. Ctx 6553. Unphased.
5. Three joining body sherds, Dr 37, Les Martres-de-Veyre. The surface is also very abraded but again leaf J144, typical of Cettus, is visible alongside Os.420 in a festoon. The double festoon and the leaf are on a bowl from Les Martres (Romeuf 2001, pl. 84, no. 41), as is the putto (ibid., no. 43). AD 130-160. Ctx 6554. Unphased.

Langford Lane South

6. One body sherd, Dr 37, Les Martres-de-Veyre. This is a very small fragment but it shows detail U105 and beaded borders as on a bowl attributed to Drusus i (Stanfield and Simpson 1990, pl. 15, no. 181). AD 100-125. Ctx 1030. Phase 5.
7. One body sherd, Dr 37, Les Martres-de-Veyre. The wreath of anchor motifs (G395) is typical of Drusus i (Stanfield and Simpson 1990, pl. 16, no. 205). The small leaf tips used as space fillers are also known for him (ibid., no. 184). AD 100-125. Ctx 2899. Phase 5.
8. One body sherd, Dr 37, Les Martres-de-Veyre. Partial vine-scroll, probably M2, known for anonymous potter X-12 (Stanfield and Simpson 1990, pl. 41, no. 477). AD 100-120. Ctx 2193. Phase 6.
9. One body sherd, Dr 37, Lezoux. Partial decoration with putto Os.426, beaded border and the foot of a figured type too partial for identification. The putto is known for a relatively small number of potters mostly at work in the Trajanic and Hadrianic period: Drusus ii (Inv. No. 0013052), Secundinus iii (style of – Rogers 1999, pl. 103, no. 28). Criciro v is the latest potter recorded for the putto (Inv. 0011376). Probably Hadrianic-early Antonine. Ctx 2228. Phase 6.
10. Almost complete Dr 37 with an infra-decorative signature. The fabric, finish and foot-ring suggest that the bowl was made at Les Martres-de-Veyre, the signature and style of the decoration point to a mould made by Drusus ii when he worked in Lezoux (Hartley and Dickinson 2008, 331-3). The decoration consists of three alternating panels separated by a very finely beaded border. The panels include Os.826, then Q6, then Os.401 under a festoon (F60?) with a blurred lion head, then Q6, then Os.826 and so on. Several of the motifs are known for Drusus ii and the overall style is close to his: the festoon is on a Dr 37 with one of his signatures (Inv. No.0013077), and the putto, victory and finely beaded borders on a Dr 37 with one of his signatures from Verulamium (Inv. No.0013050). The finely beaded borders used between the panels are indeed characteristic (Inv. No.0013056) and Q6 is on two fragments attributed to him by Rogers (1999, pl. 42, nos 4 and 5). The ovolo is perhaps B15 and is here associated with a wavy border. The various motifs listed above suggest that this piece fits with Drusus' stylistic phase called 'stage 2' by Hartley and Dickinson (2008, 333) which is broadly dated AD 125-135. This bowl is associated with a fabric and finish that suggest it was made in Les Martres-de-Veyre. Considering that Drusus' career started there, it is perhaps not surprising that one of his

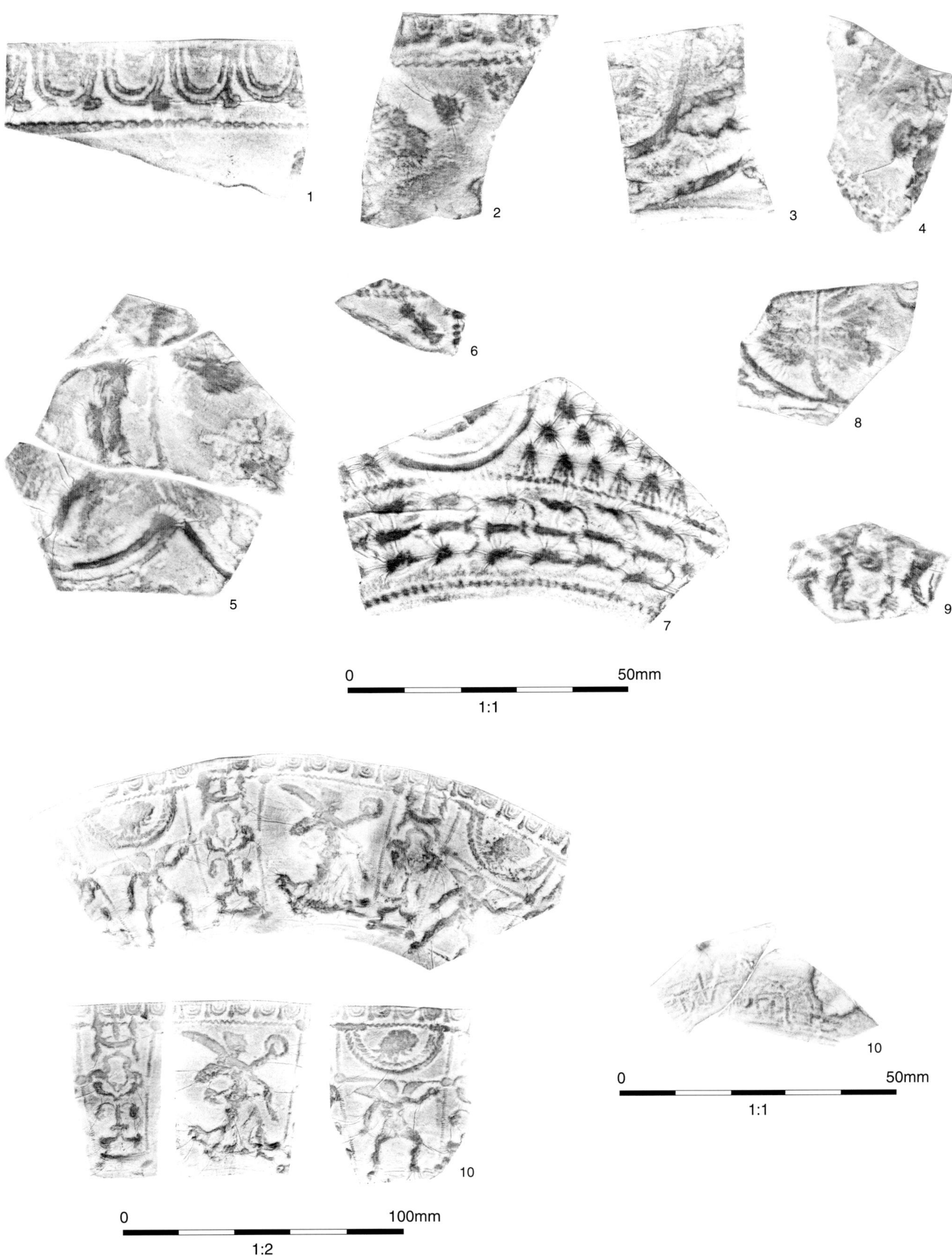

Fig. 3.1   Decorated samian, nos 1-10

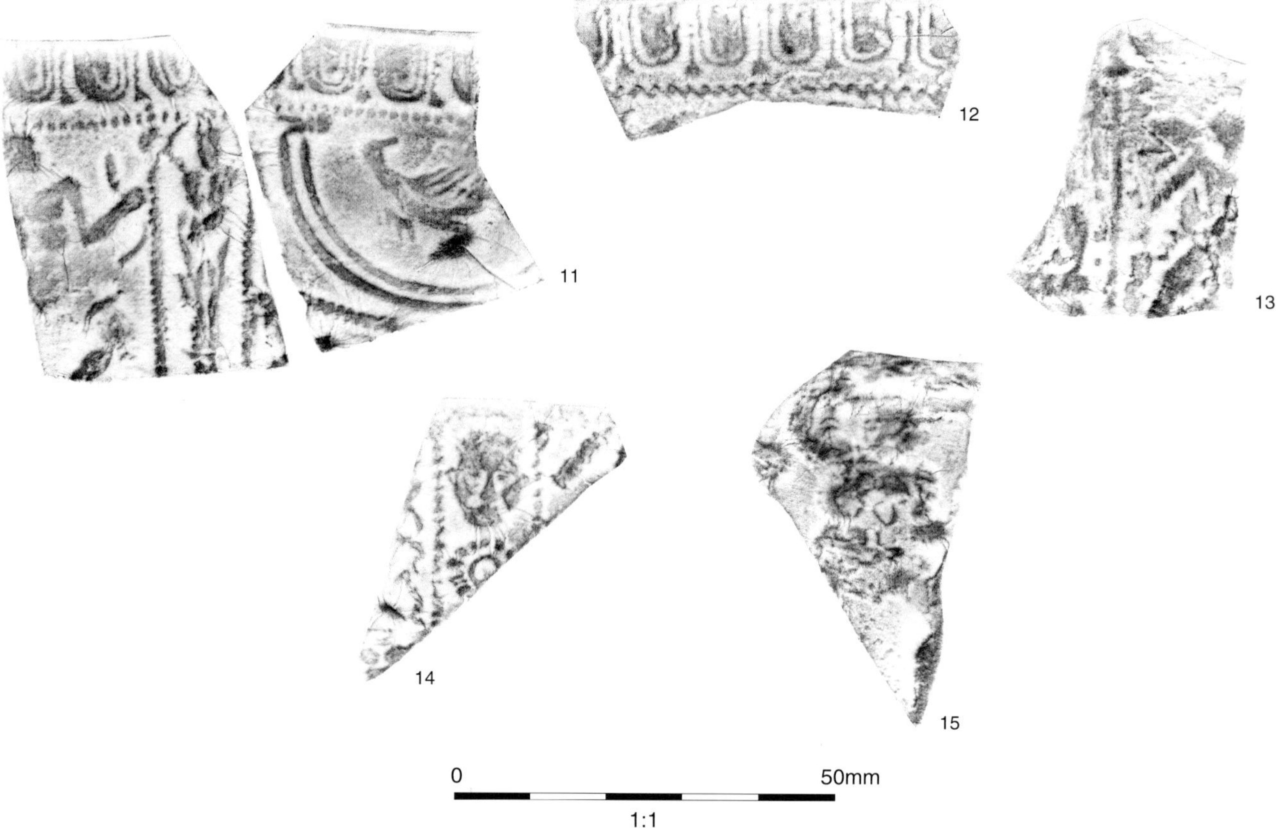

Fig. 3.2   Decorated samian, nos 11-15

moulds was used in Les Martres even when he moved to Lezoux. It was not unusual for moulds to travel from one centre to the other (see examples in the discarded shop group from Northgate House, London; Bird 2005, 32). Joining sherds from ctx 2572 and 2574. Phase 6. SF 2003 and 2004.

11. Two joining sherds, Dr 37, Lezoux. One rim with ovolo, Hercules with snakes Os.783 and caryatid Os.1201A(?), and a joining body sherd with the same ovolo and a bird (Os.2295A) in a festoon. All of the motifs are known on signed bowls by Criciro v (Inv. No. 0011340 for bird and festoon; Inv. No. 0011347 for bird, Hercules and caryatid). The ovolo with a beaded tongue and a lightly bent ending is possibly the same one as the ovolo on a bowl with a signature of Criciro v found in Budapest (Inv. No.0011362, B185?). AD 135-170. Ctx 2791. Phase 6.

12. One body sherd, Dr 37, Lezoux. Ovolo B28 and wavy border, both of which were used by the Quintilianus group (Stanfield and Simpson 1990, pl. 69, 70 and 72). Hadrianic. Ctx 2792. Phase 6.

13. One body sherd, Dr 37, Lezoux. The surface is excoriated and only a putto is visible, Os.401 used by a number of potters, Drusus ii (as on No. 10 above), Cinnamus ii (Inv. No.0010770), Catussa (Inv. No.0010614) and others. There is little else to indicate which one this vessel has links to. Hadrianic-Antonine. Ctx 4000. Phase 9.

14. One rim sherd, perhaps a Déchelette 64 or a very small Dr 37, Les Martres-de-Veyre. Three partial panels separated by beaded borders remain with

the edge of perhaps Q6 or a Q91 combination, a small mask (Os.1291A?) on top of a small beaded medallion (C296) and a small double astragalus in the third panel. The latter is on a bowl attributed to potter Me–ii by Rogers (1999, fig. 42, no. 45) as are the medallion (ibid., nos 3 and 6) and the mask (ibid., 177). Me–ii is a Lezoux potter who had links with Drusus i (Hartley and Dickinson 2010, 44; Rogers 1999, pl. 42) and here the piece is associated with a Les Martres-de-Veyre fabric. AD 100-120. Ctx 2863. Unphased.

North of Oxford Parkway Station
15. One body sherd, Dr 30, Lezoux. Abraded ovolo, beaded border and Os.167. The figured type is known for a very limited number of Lezoux potters, Drusus ii is the main one (Inv. No. 0013074). Hadrianic. Ctx 3032. Phase 6.

Vessel types

The late Iron Age and Roman vessels amounted to a total of 132.43 REs. A minimum figure of 1103 vessels based on a count of rim sherds is indicative, but less reliable, and these data are only used occasionally for comparative purposes. Vessels were recorded in terms of a series of major classes arranged approximately in a sequence from narrow mouthed to wide mouthed vessels, defined by letter codes. The classes/codes are amphorae (A), flagons/jugs (B), jars (C), uncertain jars/bowls (D), beakers (E), cups (F), bowls (H), uncertain bowls/dishes (I), dishes (J), mortaria (K), lids (L), miscellaneous forms (M) and unknown (Z). 'Intermediate' vessel classes (D and I) are used where insufficient of the rim survives to allow an estimate of the likely ratio of rim diameter to height, the key criterion for definition of the relevant types (Webster 1976, 17-19). Vessels of class G (tankards/ handled mugs etc) were not present in this assemblage. The class labels are conventional terms and are not necessarily indicative of specific functions. The vessel classes are divided into broad subgroups, usually with respect to key aspects of form (eg a simple division between straight-sided and curving-sided bowls (and dishes), and in some cases specific typologies were also used in the recording (for example for samian ware, for amphorae (where possible) and for Oxford fine wares and mortaria – Young's (1977) coarse ware typologies were used occasionally but not consistently. Further definition of each vessel is provided

by use of a fairly elaborate system of rim codes. This is essentially a descriptive tool, but serves as a useful guide to chronology in some cases, for example in distinguishing between the different types of flange on bowls and dishes, which can be of considerable significance for dating. As with the recording of fabrics, discussed above, the hierarchical approach to definition of vessel form is considered to provide an effective approach to the material, revealing broad patterns of assemblage composition very easily, while allowing for more detailed analysis if this appears to be useful. Vessel class and sub-class definitions and overall quantities are given in Table 3.7 and the quantities of each class by sites are given in Table 3.8.

In broad terms, jars were the dominant vessel class, amounting to just over half of the total vessels. This is as would be expected, but the figures show considerable site to site variation in the overall representation of jars, influenced by factors such as chronology and assemblage size

Table 3.7 Description and overall quantification of late Iron Age and Roman vessel classes by REs

Class	Description	REs	% of total REs
A	*Amphorae (not subdivided)*	*0.39*	*0.3*
B	Flagons/jugs (not specified)	7.79	5.9
BA	small flagons (up to 60mm rim diameter)	1.74	1.1
BB	larger flagons	1.31	1.0
BD	trefoil mouthed jugs/flagons	1.00	0.8
BE	two-handled flagons	*	
B total		*11.84*	*8.8*
C	Jars (not specified)	25.82	19.5
CC	narrow mouthed jars (rim diameter less than 2/3 girth)	5.98	4.5
CD	medium mouthed jars (general)	22.60	17.0
CE	squat, high shouldered (or `necked') jars	1.93	1.5
CF	carinated jars	*	
CH	bead rim jars	2.55	1.9
CI	angled everted rim jars	1.67	1.3
CJ	lid seated jars	0.38	0.3
CK	'cooking pot type' jars (eg black-burnished ware jar types)	4.50	3.4
CM	wide mouthed jars (rim diameter greater than girth)	1.34	1.0
CN	storage jars (large, generally thick walled)	3.07	2.3
CP	pedestal jars	*	
C total		*69.84*	*52.7*
D	*Uncertain jars/bowls*	*3.57*	*2.7*
E	Beakers (not specified)	3.96	3.0
EA	butt beakers	0.51	0.4
EC	bag shaped beakers	1.64	1.2
EE	indented beakers	*	
EF	poppyhead beakers	1.13	0.9
EG	carinated beakers	0.56	0.4
EH	'jar' beakers, usually small examples of angled everted rim types, cf CI, with small, fine rim	1.79	1.4
E total		*9.59*	*7.3*

Table 3.7 (continued)

Class	Description	REs	% of total REs
F	Cups (not specified)	0.14	0.2
FA	hemispherical cups	0.73	0.3
FB	campanulate cups (eg Drag 27)	1.74	1.2
FC	conical cups (eg Drag 33)	1.83	1.4
FD	carinated cups (eg Central Gaulish handled type)	*	
F total		*4.44*	*3.1*
H	Bowls (not specified) (diameter:height ratio from 1:1-3:1)	0.72	0.5
HA	carinated bowls	4.17	3.2
HB	straight sided (usually flat-based) bowls	1.75	1.3
HC	curving sided bowls	4.40	3.3
HG	spouted bowl	0.34	0.3
H total		*11.38*	*8.6*
I	Uncertain bowls/dishes	1.51	1.1
IA	straight sided bowls/dishes	3.70	2.8
IB	curving sided bowls/dishes	0.61	0.5
I total		*5.82*	*4.4*
J	Dishes (unspecified) (diameter:height ratio generally greater than 3:1)	0.28	0.2
JA	straight sided dishes	4.97	3.7
JB	curving sided dishes	7.16	5.6
J total		*12.41*	*9.5*
K	Mortaria (not specified)	0.11	0.1
KA	hook rimmed/bead and flange mortaria	0.62	0.5
KB	collared mortaria	0.32	0.2
KD	wall-sided mortaria	1.17	0.9
KE	tall bead/stubby or elongated flange mortaria (eg Young M17-M22)	0.86	0.6
K total		*3.08*	*2.3*
L	*Lids (not subdivided)*	*0.86*	*0.6*
M	Miscellaneous		
MF	triple vases	*	
MI	'Castor boxes'	*	
ML	tubular spouted bowls	*	
Z	*Uncertain/unidentified*	*0.10*	*0.1*
Total		133.35	

* Type present but not represented by rim sherd(s)

Table 3.8 Quantification of vessel classes by site (column % of REs)

Class	Langford Lane East	Langford Lane West	South of Merton	Holts Farm Crossing	East of Oddington Grange	South of Oddington Crossing	North of Gallos Brook	North of Oxford Parkway Station	Total REs	% of total REs
A	0.6	0.3							0.39	0.3
B	1.3	9.6	12.2	0.6				8.3	7.79	5.9
BA	1.6	2.1							1.74	1.1
BB	0.1	1.1		3.2				2.0	1.31	1.0
BD		2.1							1.00	0.8
BE	*								*	
B total	*3.0*	*14.9*	*12.2*	*3.8*				*10.3*	*11.84*	*8.8*

Table 3.8 (continued)

Class	Langford Lane East	Langford Lane West	South of Merton	Holts Farm Crossing	East of Oddington Grange	South of Oddington Crossing	North of Gallos Brook	North of Oxford Parkway Station	Total REs	% of total REs
C	19.7	16.6	25.7	25.9	66.7	100		13.9	25.82	19.5
CC	3.8	1.5	5.3	17.9			64.7		5.98	4.5
CD	17.3	18.6	6.5	13.9				30.1	22.60	17.0
CE	3.3	*		2.3	33.3			*	1.93	1.5
CF								*	*	
CH	4.5	0.5					35.3	1.7	2.55	1.9
CI	0.3	1.0		0.6				7.8	1.67	1.3
CJ	+	0.7							0.38	0.3
CK	2.2	4.6	0.1	5.9				2.9	4.50	3.4
CM	0.2	1.7		2.8					1.34	1.0
CN	5.3	0.5		0.5				2.8	3.07	2.3
CP	*								*	
C total	56.6	45.7	37.6	69.8	100	100	100	59.2	69.84	52.7
D	2.8	2.5	3.8	2.9				1.8	3.57	2.7
E	4.1	2.2	7.0	1.7				0.3	3.96	3.0
EA	1.1								0.51	0.4
EC	1.3	1.6	2.3						1.64	1.2
EE	*	*		*					*	
EF	1.7	0.4		0.5					1.13	0.9
EG	1.2								0.56	0.4
EH	1.8	0.6	1.5	1.9				2.7	1.79	1.4
E total	11.2	4.8	10.8	4.1				3.0	9.59	7.3
F	0.2	0.1	1.1					*	0.14	0.2
FA	0.3	1.0							0.73	0.3
FB	1.9	1.4						0.6	1.74	1.2
FC	0.6	2.8		1.3					1.83	1.4
FD								*	*	
F total	3.0	5.3	1.1	1.3				0.6	4.44	3.1
H	0.8	0.3	0.7	1.0				+	0.72	0.5
HA	1.3	4.6	4.4	0.3				6.7	4.17	3.2
HB	1.0	0.7	0.6	3.7				2.5	1.75	1.3
HC	2.4	4.0	0.7	1.1				9.4	4.40	3.3
HG		0.7							0.34	0.3
H total	5.5	10.3	6.4	6.1				18.6	11.38	8.6
I	0.9	1.1	2.3	1.1				1.1	1.51	1.1
IA	5.2	2.4	0.4	0.4				0.6	3.70	2.8
IB	0.2	0.9	0.4						0.61	0.5
I total	6.3	4.4	3.1	1.5				1.7	5.82	4.4
J	0.2	0.1	0.9	0.5				*	0.28	0.2
JA	5.8	2.3	6.1	1.3				3.0	4.97	3.7
JB	2.8	9.5	6.5	2.8				1.4	7.16	5.6
J total	8.8	11.9	13.5	4.6				4.4	12.41	9.5
K		0.2							0.11	0.1
KA	1.1	0.4							0.62	0.5
KB		0.2	2.1	*					0.32	0.2
KD	0.2		9.1	5.0					1.17	0.9
KE	+							0.5	0.86	0.6
K total	1.3	0.8	11.2	5.0				0.5	3.08	2.3
L	0.6	0.9		0.8					0.86	0.6
MF								*	*	
MI		*							*	
ML		*							*	
Z	0.2			0.1					0.10	0.1
Total	45.24	48.58	11.62	15.50	0.24	0.02	0.17	11.98	133.35	

* Type present but not represented by rim sherd(s); + less than 0.1%

(the small assemblages with an early Roman emphasis consisting solely of jars, for example), as well as by site specific character. No other vessel class contributed more than 10% of the total project assemblage: dishes, bowls, flagons and beakers (9.5%, 8.6%, 8.8% and 7.2% respectively) were all present in roughly similar quantities, while other classes were relatively insignificant overall, but again with occasional notable variations, such as the anomalously high representation of mortaria at South of Merton (9.9%), reflecting the presence of a complete rim in a fairly small assemblage.

A little over one third of all jar types were not defined beyond the general class level. Of the subclasses, medium mouthed (CD) types were the most important, though this was not the case at Holts Farm Crossing, where narrow mouthed (CC) jars were unusually well-represented. These types potentially had very long date ranges, with type CC, for example, well represented in Phases 4, 5 and 6, though apparently absent in Phase 7. Jar types usually with an early Roman chronological emphasis are CE, CF and CH, as well as the 'Belgic type' pedestal jar, only identified as a single base sherd at Langford Lane East, but none of these was particularly numerous. Jar types were produced in fabrics in most of the main ware groups, but were only a very minor component in white and white-slipped wares. Jars formed about 50% or more of vessels in all the coarse ware groups, and effectively dominated the E ware and C ware groups. Some 60% of all vessels in reduced coarse wares were jars, and these amounted to almost 55% of the total number of jars in the combined assemblage.

Vessel classes such as bowls and dishes occurred in a variety of both fine and specialist wares and coarse wares, but in both these cases, while the contribution of samian ware in respect of bowls and dishes, and of white wares for bowls, was quite important, the majority of vessels in these classes occurred in oxidised and reduced coarse wares, with smaller quantities in fabrics such as Dorset BB1. Oxidised and reduced coarse wares accounted for the great majority of beakers, including vessels of bag-shaped (EC), poppyhead (EF) and 'jar beaker' (EH) type. It is likely that many of the rims only assigned to the general beaker class were of bag-shaped type (EC), but with insufficient of the profile surviving for the form to be identified with certainty. A single small beaker occurred in samian ware, and only three fine ware beakers were represented by rims, one in fabric F51 and two in F59 (beakers were also present in fabrics F43, F52 and F55, but only as body sherds). Most of these vessels were of 2nd-century types. The only obvious 'early' beakers were type EA butt beakers. Single examples of these (based on rim sherds) occurred in white ware fabrics W30 and W36, in oxidised fabric O10 and reduced fabric R30, while there were two examples in fabric R10 and body sherds in fabric O30. Almost all the sherds in question were small, and none appeared to be particularly early (ie mid 1st century) in typological terms.

Apart from amphorae and mortaria, the two vessel classes produced principally in fine and specialist wares were flagons and cups. The former occurred in white and white-slipped fabrics, but also in fabrics O10, O20, O30, R10 and R20. Early flagon forms occurred in fabrics E20 and E30, but only the latter as

Table 3.9 Summary of ware group by vessel class REs (column %, except total column)

| | | | | | Ware group | | | | | | | | Total | |
	S	F	A	M	W	Q	Fine and spec total	E	O	R	B	C	REs	%
Type														
A Amphorae			100				100						0.39	0.3
B Flagons					52.4	94.4	70.8	0.3	14.4	1.5			11.84	8.8
C Jars					6.8	5.6	31.2	88.8	48.1	60.2	52.5	94.7	69.84	52.6
D Jars/bowls					0.1		+	1.3	3.8	4.2			3.57	2.7
E Beakers		42.2			13.9		16.7	0.4	14.8	8.4	5.6		9.59	7.2
F Cups	36.5						82.4			1.2			4.44	3.3
H Bowls	24.7	7.8			16.4		35.9	3.3	5.6	8.9	3.0		11.38	8.6
I Bowls/dishes	0.2				1.9		3.3	0.2	1.7	8.0	13.6		5.82	4.4
J Dishes	38.6	50.0			2.0		35.2	5.2	11.6	7.1	21.7	2.1	12.41	9.5
K Mortaria				100			100						3.11	2.3
L Lids					4.3		44.2	0.5		0.3	3.5	3.2	0.86	0.6
M Miscellaneous		*			*					*			*	
Z Uncertain								0.1	0.1	0.1			0.10	0.1
Total	10.02	0.64	0.39	3.11	8.88	3.95	26.29	19.99	17.24	62.84	1.98	4.31	133.35	
% of total	7.5	0.5	0.3	2.3	6.7	3.0	20.2	15.0	12.9	47.1	1.5	3.2		

* Type present but not represented by rim sherd(s); + less than 0.1%

a rim (Fig. 3.3, no. 7, but the form of this vessel is not certain), E20 contributing a large double handled vessel of a type comparable to the CAM 161-163 range (Hawkes and Hull 1947, plates LXIII-LXV), of which part of the neck and upper body was present. This type is considered to be of pre-conquest date (Bidwell 1999, 490). White ware flagons included a single Verulamium example and Oxford white ware types W2, W3, W5, W6 and the relatively rare jug type W30 (Fig. 3.12, no. 181). A further example of this last type occurred in the sandy oxidised fabric O20 (Fig. 3.7, no. 97). Although this type is paralleled in the Oxford reduced ware repertoire (Young type R7), hitherto it does not seem to have been noted in an oxidised fabric; this example presents a variation on the form with the handle attached to the top of the rim rather than being placed on the shoulder. Cups, which amounted to just over 3% of the assemblage, were more straightforwardly mainly in samian ware fabrics, with an estimated 34 vessels of various forms represented by rims. Non-samian ware cups amounted to only six vessels in reduced fabrics R10 (5) and R30 (1), five imitating Dr 27 (ie Young type R62) and one imitating Dr 33. The samian ware examples have been discussed above; in contrast to the reduced ware forms, Dr 33 was more common than Dr 27.

A notable characteristic of the assemblage overall is the scarcity of lids, which amounted to a mere 0.7% of the total vessels. This is, however, potentially consistent with Young's observation (1977, 226) that comparatively few are known from the Oxford kilns; only three reduced ware lid rims were noted. Amongst the lids in other fabrics a fragment from a very large item in fabric C10 was not certainly a vessel (as opposed, for example, to a piece of oven furniture), while two sherds in fabric W20 were possibly from the same small lid (Fig. 3.7, no. 94), reminiscent of vessels thought to be associated with amphorae (eg Symonds and Wade 1999, 137-8, 141, fig. 3.1).

Miscellaneous forms, none represented by a rim, consisted of part of a 'castor box' in Nene Valley colour-coated ware (fabric F52), a sherd from a spouted bowl in fabric W10, and the lower part of a 'cheese press' in fabric R10 from North of Oxford Parkway Station (Fig. 3.12, no. 190).

Chronology

Chronology is discussed in relation to the individual sites, but some broad characteristics are considered here. Quantification of late Iron Age and Roman fabrics in terms of the project-wide phasing scheme is presented in Table 3.10, which shows the overall phase totals as well as the occurrence of each fabric by phase. Almost half of all the late Iron Age and Roman sherds are from Phase 6, but this is of longer duration than other phases, being dated early/mid-2nd century to early/mid 3rd.

The main trends in pottery supply across all sites are fairly clear. The small number of Roman sherds

in contexts assigned to Phase 2 are presumably intrusive. The late Iron Age/early Roman Phase 3 assemblage is completely dominated by E wares, mostly grog-tempered (E80 fabrics). This dominance is reduced, but remains substantial, in the very early Roman Phase 4, when oxidised and reduced coarse wares in 'Romanised' fabrics both appear, and a range of fine and specialist wares, including samian ware, amphorae and white wares, is present. Shell-tempered (C10) fabrics make their highest phase contribution (8.5% of sherds) at this time. By the later 1st-early 2nd century (Phase 5) reduced coarse wares are the principal ware group, providing over 50% of all sherds, a dominance which is slightly enhanced in Phase 6. Oxidised wares also gradually increase in importance through time, while E wares would have been out of production by about AD 70 at the latest (although the tradition survived in the production of storage jars in fabrics classified as O80 and R90) and are probably completely residual in occurrence well before the end of Phase 5. Dorset BB1, always a minor component of the assemblage at best, is best represented in Phase 6.

The Phase 7 assemblage shows some changes from the earlier trends. The most notable feature is a significant reduction in the proportion of reduced wares and a corresponding increase in oxidised wares. The figures for sherd count, used as the basis for Table 3.10, are matched by those for weight, so this development is not simply a reflection of excessive fragmentation of oxidised wares in this phase. The reason for this trend is uncertain, however. Although the fine and specialist ware percentage only increases very slightly in comparison to Phase 6, its composition changes, as fine wares, essentially the Oxford colour-coated ware fabric F51, become significant for the first time. Other notable fabrics in Phase 7 include pink grogged ware (fabric O81) which, while present in very small quantities earlier, is always better represented in later Roman contexts in the region.

It is worth noting that mean sherd weights are very consistent across most of the phase groups, from the intrusive material in Phase 2 to that from post-Roman and unphased contexts. The Phase 3 and Phase 4 assemblages, however, had markedly higher mean sherd weights. This is a direct reflection of their dominance by fabrics in the E80 subgroup, which has an overall mean sherd weight of 22.4g. The relatively wide range of vessel types in E80 fabrics includes a number of thin walled vessels, but also large storage jars, of which one, (Fig. 3.4, no. 34), from a Phase 4 context at Langford Lane East, was represented by an estimated 151 sherds with a mean weight of 66.7g.

Aspects of vessel use and reuse

Evidence for these characteristics was relatively limited and difficult to categorise consistently. Use can be inferred from vessel form, but rarely demon-

Table 3.10 *Fabric by phase, percentage of sherd counts (column % excluding later prehistoric pottery)*

Fabric	Middle Iron Age		Late Iron Age-Roman				Post-Roman	Unphased	Total sherds	% excl. late prehistoric
	2	3	4	5	6	7	8-9	0		
No. L Preh sherds	458	85	10	30	97	3		6	689	
S					+				1	+
S20 **LGF SA**			1.9	1.7	0.9	0.3	0.6	0.9	112	1.1
S25 **MON SA**			0.1						1	+
S30 **LEZ SA 2**			0.2	0.4	2.5	2.3	3.0	3.2	178	1.7
S32 **LMV SA**				0.4	0.5	0.2	0.2	1.9	45	0.4
S40								0.2	1	+
S41 **RHZ SA**				0.2					3	+
S subt			2.2	2.7	3.9	2.8	3.8	6.2	340	3.3
F43 **CNG BS**					0.1	0.2			6	0.1
FO					+	0.2	0.6		5	+
F50					0.1				4	+
F51 **OXF RS**						5.2	0.9		36	0.4
F52 **LNV CC**					+	0.2	0.9		6	0.1
F55 **COL CC2**					+				1	+
F59				0.1	0.1				7	0.1
F subt				0.1	0.4	5.8	2.4		65	0.6
A10				0.3	+				5	+
A11 **BAT AM 1&2**			2.5	0.7	0.2	0.5	0.4	0.6	74	0.7
A13 **GAL AM 1**						0.2	0.4		2	+
A18								0.2	1	+
A26 **GAL AM2?**				0.2					3	
A30			0.1	0.1					2	+
A subt			2.6	1.3	0.3	0.7	0.8	0.8	87	0.9
M12 **NOG WH 4**					+				1	+
M21 **VER WH**				0.1					1	+
M22 **OXF WH**			0.1	0.4	0.9	2.1	1.3	2.1	81	0.8
M33			0.1						1	+
M subt			0.2	0.5	0.9	2.1	1.3	2.1	84	0.8
W10			0.1	0.7	2.1	2.6	2.4	0.6	146	1.4
W20		0.5	2.2	6.5	1.8	0.5	8.6	0.6	266	2.6
W21 **VER WH**				0.1	0.2		0.4		15	0.2
W29					+				1	+
W30			0.2	0.2	+				8	0.1
W36			0.3						5	+
W41 cf **COL WH**				0.1					1	+
W42					+				1	+
W52				0.5	+				8	0.1
W subt		0.5	2.8	8.1	4.2	3.1	11.4	1.2	451	4.4
Q20					+				1	+
Q21 **OXF WS**			0.1	0.1	2.8		0.6	0.4	148	1.5
Q28					+				1	+
Q46					+				1	+
Q subt			0.1	0.1	2.9		0.6	0.4	151	1.5
F and S subtotal		**0.5**	**7.6**	**12.7**	**12.5**	**13.8**	**20.3**	**10.5**	**1179**	**11.5**
E10	18.2								4	+
E20		0.7	1.6	0.4	0.2	0.3	0.2		49	0.5
E30		4.0	4.4	2.5	0.8	0.7	1.5	1.3	182	1.8
E40		0.5	0.1	0.1	+			0.2	7	0.1
E50		0.5		0.1	+	0.1			6	0.1
E60		0.2	0.4	0.1					10	0.1
E80 **SOB GT**	50.0	90.0	66.2	15.8	5.0	7.4	13.5	10.3	2158	21.0
E86			0.1						2	+
E subt	68.2	95.9	72.8	19.0	6.0	8.5	15.2	11.8	2418	23.6

Table 3.10 (continued)

	Middle Iron Age		Late Iron Age-Roman				Post-Roman	Unphased		
Fabric	2	3	4	5	6	7	8-9	0	*Total sherds*	*% excl. late prehistoric*
O10	4.5		4.3	4.4	11.0	25.4	9.6	4.9	919	9.0
O11				0.2	0.2				15	0.2
O20			0.6	1.4	1.1	7.2	3.6	1.9	156	1.5
O30			0.6	2.2	1.6	2.0	1.9	1.3	149	1.5
O37				0.1	0.1				9	0.1
O37F					+				2	+
O50			0.1	0.1			0.2		5	+
O55					+	0.8			7	0.1
O60							0.2		1	+
O80	4.5	0.2	0.1	2.0	1.5	1.3	4.3	4.7	157	1.5
O81 **PNK GT**				0.1	0.3	3.8	1.1	0.7	49	0.5
O subt	*9.0*	*0.2*	*5.7*	*10.5*	*15.8*	*40.5*	*20.9*	*13.5*	*1469*	*14.3*
R10		0.5	1.7	20.2	32.5	22.0	21.8	36.3	2373	23.2
R11 **OXF FR**					0.2	0.2		0.2	11	0.1
R20		0.2	2.8	10.3	6.6	2.8	6.0	3.2	587	5.7
R29					+				2	+
R30			0.6	8.1	6.7	5.1	7.1	12.0	586	5.7
R37			0.2	9.0	6.5	1.3	1.5	6.7	506	4.9
R37F				0.4	1.5		0.6	0.2	92	0.9
R38					0.9		0.9		50	0.5
R38F				0.2	0.1				8	0.1
R41					+				2	+
R50				0.4	1.3	1.5	0.9		86	0.9
R60				0.1	0.4				19	0.2
R61			0.2	2.6	0.2		0.6	0.2	54	0.5
R90				1.6	0.8	1.5	1.3	1.3	82	0.8
R94					+				1	+
R95 **SAV GT**			0.1	0.1	0.1	0.3	0.2		12	0.1
R96				0.2	0.6		0.2	0.2	36	0.4
R subt		*0.7*	*5.6*	*53.2*	*58.4*	*34.7*	*41.1*	*60.3*	*4507*	*44.1*
B11 **DOR BB 1**				0.2	2.4	1.8	0.9	2.2	151	1.5
C10	22.7	2.5	8.5	3.9	4.8	3.6	1.5	1.9	500	4.9
Total excl. late prehistoric	22	404	1782	1383	5021	610	467	535	10,224	100%
MSW per phase	12.5	21.0	25.2	11.5	11.7	11.8	12.2	11.7		
Phase total sherds	480	489	1792	1413	5118	613	467	541	10,913	

+ less than 0.1%

strated directly, and some vessel types, particularly jars, were potentially if not actually multifunctional. The commonest evidence of use is reflected in the occurrence of burning and sooting, summarised in Table 3.11. Burning itself is unspecific – simple burning was noted on 63 sherds in a variety of fabrics, but is much more easily detected on fabrics such as samian and white wares than on others, a fact reflected in the almost total absence of records of burning on reduced wares, for example. In many cases the burning is likely to have occurred post-breakage and will have been irrelevant to the use of vessels beforehand. A possible exception to this relates to white ware mortaria, as it has been suggested that the evidence of burning quite commonly observed on these vessels reflects a non-standard aspect of their use. Sixteen Oxford white ware mortarium sherds (almost 20% of the total of these sherds) were recorded as burnt, though it is difficult to be certain of the number of cases in which this occurred after breakage. At least five amphora (fabric A11) sherds were recorded as being burnt. This could have been accidental, but it is possible that sherds of such substantial vessels could have been incorporated in the structures of hearths or ovens.

Less equivocal is the evidence for external and internal sooting. This correlates much more closely with fabrics associated with vessels that might have been used for cooking. Particularly notable in this respect are fabrics E80, R20, R37 and C10. It is

Table 3.11 Quantification of burning and cooking-related evidence by fabric and sherd count

Fabric	General burning	Sooting	Internal burnt deposit	Limescale
S20	13			
S30	1			
S32	3			
F51	1			
A11	5			
M22	16			1?
W10	4			
W20	9			
Q21	2			
E30		1	2	
E40		1		
E80	1	25*	19*	
O10	6	5		1
O80		1		
R10	1	7	2	
R20		14	4	
R30	1	6		
R37/R37F		16		
R60		1		
R96		2	2	
B11		2	1	
C10		18	20	
Total	63	99	50	2

*internal and external sooting on same sherd in one case

notable, however, that by no means all these instances were on jars, sooting being recorded on three bowls, two dishes, three uncertain bowl/dishes and one beaker. While it is quite likely that many of these were used for cooking in some way, it is possible that in some cases soot deposits accumulated in post-breakage burial environments. Limescale, a result of heating water in a jar, was almost totally absent, however, and the significance of its association with a mortarium sherd in an early context at Langford Lane East is quite uncertain.

Vessel use indicated by wear was noted in only one case – a Dr 27 cup of South Gaulish samian ware had internal wear of a pattern noted by Biddulph (2008). In other cases, however, evidence of this sort might not have survived because of the variable surface condition of some of the pottery.

Repairs were noted in five cases, three of which were on samian ware. These took the form of rounded rivet holes in a South Gaulish form 37 from Langford Lane South and a Les Martres Dr 18/31 from Langford Lane East, and a sawn cleat groove on a Central Gaulish Dr 18/31 or 31 also from Langford Lane South. The other two repairs were on vessels in fabric E80. A storage jar (Fig. 3.3, no. 3) had a probable rivet hole in the shoulder, and a carinated bowl (Fig. 3.6, no. 68) had been repaired using a black adhesive. This was not analysed, but analogous material from Springhead has shown that birch bark tar was a primary ingredient (Seager Smith *et al.* 2011, 124-5), and the use of such a material here seems very likely. The practice may have been most common in the early Roman period, as noted at Springhead (ibid., 124) and elsewhere, for example in the large assemblage from Tiddington, Warwickshire (unpublished). More locally three examples of this use were recorded on sherds in fabric R90 at Gill Mill, near Witney (Booth 2018).

Two graffiti were recorded. One of these (Fig. 3.3, no. 4) appears to be part of a pre-firing graffito on the body of a Dressel 20 amphora from Langford Lane East. The second, more directly related to use,

Table 3.12: Quantification of late Iron Age and Roman pottery by broad context type (all sites and phases)

Context type	No.sh.	%	Weight (g)	%	MSW
0-2, 43 Uncertain/topsoil/cleaning layers etc	1003	9.8	9755	6.6	9.7
3 Layers – general	658	6.4	7147	4.8	10.9
6, 20 Layers – floors/surfaces	129	1.3	1505	1.0	11.7
4 Demolition layers	661	6.5	5344	3.6	8.1
8 Fills of cut features – type unspecified/uncertain	164	1.6	1645	1.1	10.0
9 Pit fills	2300	22.5	32,972	22.3	14.3
10 Posthole/stakehole fills	61	0.6	498	0.3	8.2
11 Well/waterhole fills	408	4.0	3989	2.7	9.8
12 Grave fills	28	0.3	242	0.2	8.6
13 Ditch fills	4194	41.0	75,947	51.4	18.1
14 Gully fills	24	0.2	271	0.2	11.3
15-16 Structural features – wall/beamslot etc	32	0.3	507	0.3	15.8
18, 23 30 'Natural' features including tree-throw holes	195	1.9	2194	1.5	11.3
28 Channel fill deposits	119	1.2	3108	2.1	26.1
29 Possible alluvial layers	248	2.4	2590	1.8	10.4
Total	10,224		147,714		14.4

*Context type only at this site

is an incised cross on the shoulder of a jar in fabric R10 from a late Roman deposit at Holts Farm Crossing (Fig. 3.10, no. 154).

The majority of the other examples of secondary use or reuse (ten in all) related to base sherds. There were four examples of jars in fabric E80 with holes drilled in the base (eg Fig. 3.3, nos 1 and 2) and a base in fabric R60 had a rather larger hole knocked in the bottom, while a further drilled hole in the shoulder of a jar in fabric R20 was of uncertain function, but not obviously for a rivet (cf. Bicester Fields Farm; Brown 1999, 186). Three sherds had been trimmed and pierced, presumably for use as spindle whorls. These comprised the base of a Central Gaulish samian ware Dr 33 cup, and a simple base and a body sherd in fabric R10, all from Phase 6 contexts at Langford Lane East, South of Merton and Langford Lane South respectively. All three were complete, but had distinctly different weights, respectively 15g, 21g and 8g. Finally, on a Dressel 20 sherd, from Langford Lane South, the handle had been neatly trimmed close to the shoulder of the vessel. This feature is relatively common and suggests preparation of the vessel for secondary use.

Context type

The breakdown of the overall late Iron Age and Roman assemblage in terms of broad context type is shown in Table 3.12. As is characteristic for the region, more pottery was retrieved from ditches than from other types of contexts, with pits the next best represented type. What is unusual, however, is that the representation of pottery in ditches is higher as a percentage of weight than of sherd count – it is much more normal for the weight of sherds from ditches to be below the site mean, and the weight of

---

Principal sites

Langford Lane East, Langford Lane South, South of Merton
Langford Lane East, South of Merton
South of Merton
Langford Lane East*
Langford Lane East, Langford Lane South, South of Merton
All main sites
South of Merton
Holts Farm Crossing
Langford Lane East*
All main sites
Langford Lane South
Langford Lane East*
Langford Lane South
Langford Lane East*
Langford Lane East, Langford Lane South

---

sherds from pits to be above the mean, because of the characteristic patterns of disturbance and redeposition of fills typically associated with these feature types. The relatively high sherd weight from ditches is found in a number of the EWR Phase 1 sites. At Langford Lane East it is explained in part by the presence of exceptional vessels such as Fig. 3.4, no. 34, mentioned above, which came from a ditch fill, but the situation also prevailed at South of Merton, where the MSW of pottery from ditches was 18.6g. At North of Oxford Parkway Station, the mean weight of sherds from ditches was 15.4g, above the overall project mean, but slightly less than the site-specific total MSW of 16.3g.

Langford Lane East produced pottery from a few context types not represented elsewhere in the project. These included stream channel deposits – a relatively modest number of sherds but with a particularly high mean weight – and demolition layers, where the associated material was particularly heavily fragmented (see further below).

The site assemblages

These are presented in geographical sequence from north-east to south-west. For the very small assemblages for which detailed presentation of data is not necessary here, the essential quantification in terms of Iron Age fabrics, Roman fabrics and vessel types can be found in Tables 3.2, 3.4, 3.5 and 3.8.

Langford Lane East

This site produced the largest pottery assemblage from the project, with a total of 4281 sherds weighing 75,201g sherds (MSW 17.6g), but with a slightly smaller quantity of vessels (45.24 REs) than that found at Langford Lane South. The pottery was recovered from 305 context groups. Occupation may have begun before the Roman conquest. Negligible quantities of middle Iron Age pottery (in total, 18 sherds weighing 90g) occurred in contexts of Phases 3, 4 and 5, but the extent to which the Phase 3 and 4 assemblages, and particularly the former, were dominated by E wares suggests pre-conquest settlement. The typically robust character of fabrics in the dominant E80 group, noted above, explains (at least in part) the particularly high MSW of pottery in these early phases, and thus for the Langford Lane East assemblage as a whole. The pottery indicates intensive activity on the site through the 1st century and much of the 2nd, but greatly reduced occupation thereafter. Such late Roman pottery as is present comes mainly from poorly-stratified contexts, most of which are assigned to the post-Roman period, although pottery of post-Roman date was lacking; in total 9.4% of sherds (7.4% by weight) were from post-Roman or unphased contexts. Quantification of the pottery by phase is given in Table 3.13.

The Phase 3 assemblage was small, comprising only 227 sherds from 29 context groups, but had a

Table 3.13 Quantification of pottery fabrics from Langford Lane East by phase

Fabric	Phase 3 No. sh.	Phase 3 Wt (g)	Phase 4 No. sh.	Phase 4 Wt (g)	Phase 5 No. sh.	Phase 5 Wt (g)	Phase 6 No. sh.	Phase 6 Wt (g)	Phase 7 No. sh.	Phase 7 Wt (g)	Post-Roman and unphased No. sh.	Post-Roman and unphased Wt (g)	Total No. sh.	Total Wt (g)
A1					6	8							6	8
A8			1	7									1	7
A9			2	10									2	10
F1			1	3									1	3
F2			2	20									2	20
G1	2	9	1	6									3	15
S1			1	4									1	4
S2			1	3									1	3
S3			1	20									1	20
S20 **LGF SA**			31	278	14	52	4	38			4	31	53	399
S25 **MON SA**			1	2									1	2
S30 **LEZ SA 2**			3	34	2	27	28	267			13	73	46	401
S32 **LMV SA**					1	21	2	7	1	4	5	29	12	81
F43 **CNG BS**							1	1					1	1
F51 **OXF RS**											4	81	4	81
FO											2	61	2	61
F52 **LNV CC**											1	60	1	60
A10					4	63	1	54					5	117
A11 **BAT AM 1&2**			43	3644	5	262	5	487			3	282	56	4675
A18											1	129	1	129
A26 **GAL AM 2?**					3	116							3	116
M22 **OXF WH**			1	14	3	111	19	612	1	69	7	768	31	1574
M33			1	154									1	154
W10			2	4	2	14	17	163			2	65	23	246
W20	1	3	38	461	77	590	6	24			1	9	123	1087
W30			4	14	3	20	1	6					8	40
W36			5	41									5	41
W41 cf **COL WH**					1	3							1	3

very high MSW of 27g. The assemblage was dominated by E wares, which accounted for all but seven sherds, with the huge majority being in E80 fabrics. The non-E ware material comprised two middle Iron Age sherds, four sherds of fabric C10, which was probably contemporary with the E wares, and a small fragment (3g) of sandy white ware W20. This fabric is common in Phases 4 and 5 and could have been intrusive here, though a pre-conquest date is also just possible.

The vessel repertoire in this phase (a single fabric E40 jar rim was the only example not in fabric E80) consisted almost entirely of jars, with medium mouthed (type CD) vessels prominent, but several large storage jars also present (eg Fig. 3.3, no. 3). The only certain examples of other types were two small rim sherds from dishes, totalling 3% of all REs in this phase, the remainder being from jars or probable jars.

A notable characteristic of this assemblage is that most of it came from pits, with only 11% by sherd count (7.4% by weight) from ditch fill contexts. The nature of the pit fills might help explain the very substantial MSW in this phase, but as is seen elsewhere in this project, in general terms the MSW of pottery from pits did not exceed that from ditches, despite the fact that this would usually be considered a typical pattern.

The Phase 4 assemblage was the most substantial at Langford Lane East, accounting for 39.2% of all sherds and 57% of the total weight, derived from 102 context groups. E wares remained dominant, and while this was not to the extent seen in Phase 3 their prominence largely accounts for the substantial MSW of 25.5g. By contrast with Phase 3, however, the majority of the pottery derived from ditch contexts rather than pits, although this is heavily influenced by the occurrence of sherds weighing just over 10kg from a single very large fabric E80 storage jar (Fig. 3.4, no. 34, mentioned above) in the fill of ditch 7444. On this basis, sherd count probably gives a better indication of the importance of E wares in this phase; by this measure they still amounted to 71.9%, while the figure for REs, 68.9%, might be more reliable still. Of the other constituents, fabric C10 was the most significant by all measures, amounting to just over 8% by sherd count and 9% of REs. A range of oxidised and reduced fabrics, most of which were probably of local origin (either very local or repre-

Table 3.13 (continued)

Fabric	Phase 3		Phase 4		Phase 5		Phase 6		Phase 7		Post-Roman and unphased		Total	
	No. sh.	Wt (g)	No. sh.	Wt (g)	No. sh.	Wt (g)	No. sh.	Wt (g)	No. sh.	Wt (g)	No. sh.	Wt (g)	No. sh.	Wt (g)
Q20							1	1					1	1
Q21 **OXF WS**			1	1			1	5					2	6
E20	3	47	28	925	6	53	6	35					43	1060
E30	5	50	71	1111	7	47	18	126			9	42	110	1376
E40	1	21	2	62							1	15	4	98
E60	1	17	8	191	1	11							10	219
E80 **SOB GT**	210	5941	1097	31,881	166	2890	168	2483	4	50	92	1469	1742	44,777
E86			1	36	1	36							2	72
O10			77	200	15	88	31	177			8	38	132	514
O11					1	36							1	36
O20			10	42	4	21	2	24			2	56	18	143
O30			10	63	19	141	14	63	1	3	3	34	47	304
O50			2	15									2	15
O80			1	30	3	108	5	100			6	128	15	366
O81 **PNK GT**									2	46			2	46
R10			31	253	115	1101	540	3600	2	9	133	949	832	5965
R20			47	827	17	164	45	369	2	12	12	178	125	1570
R30			10	96	74	696	137	1110	1	2	53	320	275	2224
R37			3	18	47	963	207	2102			14	181	271	3264
R37F							1	7					1	7
R38							15	184					15	184
R50							3	20					3	20
R61			3	30	2	14	4	23			2	33	11	100
R90					1	96	2	111			2	80	5	287
R95 **SAV GT**			2	46			2	117			1	221	5	384
B11 **DOR BB 1**							25	132			4	18	31	163
C10	4	38	136	2319	5	35	28	164			8	86	181	2642
Total	227	6126	1679	42,865	605	7787	1339	12,612	14	195	393	5436	4281	75,201

senting early productions of the Oxford industry) was present, though these were generally heavily fragmented. The question of the earliest appearance of Oxford oxidised and reduced fabrics was raised above. In this phase group the R10 fabric sherds included no rims at all, and the four base sherds were undiagnostic of form (all could, though need not necessarily, have been from jars). Sherds of fabric R20, the most numerous of these fabrics in this phase, included rims of two type CD jars and a high shouldered type CE jar (Fig. 3.4, no. 26) and two further similar rims from vessels of the indeterminate jar/bowl class D. Fabric R30 rims were from another type CD jar and two uncertain bowl/dish forms. Overall, there is nothing in these forms that is inconsistent with origin in the Oxford industry, though equally, none is sufficiently distinctive as to preclude the possibility of derivation from another relatively local source. The situation with regard to the oxidised fabrics (O10, O20 and O30) may, however, have been different. With one possible exception (a class D vessel) in sandy fabric O20 all the vessel types noted, whether as rims or (occasionally) body sherds, were from other types, including a flagon (Fig. 3.3, no. 6) in fabric O20, a

fine beaker (Fig. 3.5, no. 39) in fabric O10 and the base of a butt beaker in fabric O30. Other beaker sherds in fabric O10 included a fragment of an indented form. These vessels are not typical of the early Oxford oxidised ware range as currently understood, and though such an origin is possible, other sources, not necessarily local, may be involved, albeit that the character of the fabrics is closely similar to that of standard Oxford products. Definite non-local industries are represented by occasional sherds of fabrics R37 ('West Oxfordshire' grey ware) and R95 (Savernake ware) also occurred.

A range of fine and specialist wares accounted for 7.7% of sherds. The principal components by sherd count were southern Spanish amphorae, white wares (mostly the sandy fabric W20, whose status as a 'fine ware' is sometimes debatable) and samian ware. Amongst the latter a sherd of Montans ware is notable, but three sherds of Central Gaulish samian ware (two in pit fill 6704) must have been intrusive in this phase. The same should also be true of a mortarium sherd tentatively assigned to Oxford white fabric M22, which was atypical in a number of ways; it was burnt grey throughout and had an internal deposit of what appeared to be limescale.

The grits were consistent with those of some early Oxford mortaria, and on balance this seems the most likely identification, but in view of its unusual character it is perhaps possible that this piece pre-dated the inception of mainstream mortarium production in this industry, generally dated to about AD 100. A second mortarium sherd, extremely battered, was in fabric M33, possibly from the north Wiltshire kilns at Minety. Unfortunately, the rim is so poorly preserved that the form cannot be determined. Amongst the other material present in this phase the white wares contributed a jar-beaker and two butt beakers, one in fabric W30 and one in fabric W36. South Gaulish samian ware (S20) included cups of Dr 24, 27, and 27g, dishes 15/17 and 18 and a Dr 29 bowl, though this last, and some of the others, were only represented by body sherds. A base sherd from a dish had a stamp of Licinus, dated AD 35-65. The most substantial vessel in fabric S20 was a large part of a Ritterling 12 bowl, quite heavily burnt.

These examples notwithstanding, 73.8% of the Phase 4 assemblage consisted of jars. The dominance of these vessels is typical, but less comprehensive than is often seen, particularly when it is considered that the phase group is essentially of pre-Flavian date. The jars were of course primarily in E wares, but also in fabric C10. A broad range of jar types was present. Vessels not assigned to sub-classes, and those of the rather generic 'medium mouthed jar' category (type CD), were dominant, but distinctly early types such as CE (high shouldered jars) and CH (bead rim jars) were well represented, as well as large storage jars, of course including Fig. 3.4, no. 34. Apart from jars, beakers, bowls and dishes totalled 6.6%, 6.1% and 5.8% respectively of REs in this phase with other classes as minor components. Despite their relatively significant RE percentage only four beakers were represented by rim sherds, of which two were butt beakers and a third was a jar-beaker in fabric W20 (Fig. 3.5, no. 38).

The Phase 5 assemblage was much smaller than those of preceding and succeeding phases, for reasons which are not clear. It derived from 68 context groups with a MSW of 12.9g, half the weight of the previous phase, but part of a recognisable trend of decreasing MSW through successive phases. Exactly half of this material (by weight, 53.4% by sherd count) derived from pits, with the remaining pottery distributed across a variety of context types, including (amongst others) general layers, ditches, a stream channel and graves, although little of the pottery from the last clearly represented grave goods.

Reduced fabrics now formed the most important ware group, amounting to 42.3% of sherds, 39% by weight and a substantial 58.1% of REs. E wares remained a significant component, totalling 29.9% of sherds and 39% of the weight of the phase assemblage, but only 12.5% of REs. Oxidised wares only accounted for 6.9% of sherds, but 14.1% of REs, a figure partly boosted by a flagon (Fig. 3.5, no. 46) in fabric O30. Fine and specialist wares amounted to 19% of sherds, principally in sandy white ware W20, much consisting of sherds of a carinated bowl or beaker (Fig. 3.5, no. 50) from fill 7598 of pit 7597. South Gaulish samian ware, heavily fragmented, included rims of forms 27, 15/17 and 18, and a few amphora (fabric A11) and mortarium (fabric M22) body sherds were also present. More noteworthy were three sherds, including a rim, of amphora fabric A26 (Fig. 3.5, no. 45), probably from southern France.

The proportion of jars in this phase assemblage was greatly reduced, amounting to only 40% of REs. This was not obviously a consequence of skewing of the small phase total (only 7.52 REs) by a single vessel, and by rim count jars still amounted to less than half of all the vessels in this phase (35 out of 71 rims). The distinctive early jar types were now relatively scarce, but a notable presence was the base of a pedestal jar in fabric E80, the only example of this type recognised in the project (though it should be noted that rim and body sherds of this type are not of forms specific to it and are not readily identified without the distinctive base). As in Phase 4 the second most numerous vessel class consisted of beakers, but now these amounted to 21.1% of REs. While the carinated form (Fig. 3.5, no. 50) mentioned above was the most prominent, a further 11 vessels, including butt beakers, bag shaped and jar-beaker types, were represented by rims. Bowls and dishes now increased to 9.4% and 14.9% of the assemblage respectively. Bowls included the oxidised Oxford form O48 (Fig. 3.5, no. 52, in fabric O11) and reduced fabric R30 contributed both bowls and dishes (eg Fig. 3.5, no. 51).

The Phase 6 assemblage was relatively substantial, comprising 1339 sherds, but these had a mean weight of only 9.4g, indicating a well fragmented group, with only amphorae, mortaria and (to a lesser extent) fabric E80 retaining MSWs significantly above that for the phase as a whole. The figures reflect the fact that much of the material derived from layers, both of general character and also, more specifically, deposits defined as demolition layers. The latter contained almost half of the total sherds in this phase, with a MSW of only 8.1g. Pits and ditches produced 12.9% and 17.9% of the total phase sherds respectively.

Despite the problems suggested by the nature of the deposits from which much of the pottery derived, the material reflects at least some of the expected trends in assemblage evolution. E wares (essentially fabric E80) still contributed 14.3% of sherds, which must have been residual by this time, but reduced wares now dominated comprehensively, accounting for 71.4% of sherds and 76.8% of REs (though only 60.6% by weight). R10 was as usual the principal fabric, but showed a characteristic tendency to fragment more than most other fabrics (MSW 6.7g in this phase). Fabrics R30 and R37 were well represented, and R20 moderately so.

Oxidised wares were relatively unimportant, together amounting to only 3.9% of sherds, while Dorset BB1 appeared for the first time, but at a mere 1.9% of sherds. Fine and specialist wares together totalled only 6.4% of the assemblage (sherd count, 10.7% by REs), with samian ware (now mostly Central Gaulish) the main contributor by sherd count and REs. Quantities of white wares were much reduced compared to Phase 5, while mortaria (entirely in Oxford white ware) increased slightly in importance. There were single tiny fragments of fine ware (F43 – Central Gaulish), an unsourced white-slipped oxidised sherd (Q20) and a flagon rim in fabric Q21.

The percentage of the principal vessel class, jars, was slightly increased compared to the previous phase (45.7% of REs as opposed to 40% in Phase 5), but this may be partly accounted for by the presence of an almost complete type CK jar in fabric R10 (Fig. 3.6, no. 61) from fill 7231 of roadside ditch 7453; by rim count jars amount to 39.1% in this phase. The status of beakers as the second most important vessel class was maintained (13.3% of REs, including fine oxidised and reduced examples, Fig. 3.5, nos 54 and 55), while dishes amounted to 11.9% of REs. Bowls, however, were represented by a mere five rim sherds totalling 2.8% of REs, but by contrast the intermediate bowl/dish class was unusually numerous here, with examples amounting to 11.3% of REs. The combined representation of vessel classes H, I and J in Phases 5 and 6 was in fact very similar, amounting to 24.3% and 25.9% of REs respectively. Part of the explanation for the anomalous figures for bowl and indeterminate bowl/dish classes in Phase 6 is probably to do with the fragmented nature of the pottery, reducing the possibility of identification of bowl forms on the basis of their height to diameter ratio and correspondingly boosting the numbers of the indeterminate class.

Amongst the other vessel classes in this phase assemblage cups were quite well represented (4.9% of REs), consisting of Central Gaulish Dr 33s and, interestingly, copies of form Dr 27 in reduced fabrics, two in R10 and one (Fig. 3.5, no. 56) in R30. There were only two flagons, an Oxford type W3 in fabric W20 and an everted rim form in fine oxidised fabric O10. Oxford white ware mortaria included two of Young type M3 (one, Fig. 3.6, no. 59, with a very poorly preserved stamp) and a third of uncertain hook rimmed form. (Another stamped M3 mortarium (Fig. 3.6, no. 71) came from unphased context 6554 – it is just possible that these two pieces were from the same vessel, but their surface appearance was very different.)

The Phase 6 assemblage was examined briefly to see if there were any clearly discernible differences (apart from degree of fragmentation) between the material in the demolition layers (661 sherds, 5344g, 6.36 REs) and that in the other context groups. The main points seem to be that the demolition layer material was more heavily dominated by reduced wares than the phase group as a whole (84.4% of sherds, 69.8% of weight, 88.5% REs), that the importance of residual E wares was correspondingly reduced, and that the majority of the mortarium and Dorset BB1 sherds occurred in these deposits. The relative proportions of the principal vessel classes are broadly in line with those for the phase assemblage as a whole, with the percentage of jars similar, the overall numbers of classes H, I and J slightly reduced (21.4% rather than 25.9%) and those of beakers enhanced (18.1% rather than 13.3%). Overall, it is not clear that these figures represent a really significant difference between the pottery from the demolition layers and other Phase 6 contexts, whether in terms of relative chronology or of functional characteristics. There is no clear sense, for example, in which the demolition layer material can be seen as representing the latest stages of a Phase 6 assemblage (ie late 2nd-early 3rd century) distinct from the rest of the phase group, even though it is clear that there are no significant features or deposits later than these layers.

Three context groups, containing 14 sherds weighing 195g, were assigned to Phase 7. Chronological markers in this assemblage consisted of a burnt Oxford mortarium sherd of Young type M18 and (probably) two sherds of fabric O81. Conversely, sherds of fabric E80 and a rim of a South Gaulish form Dr 27 cup were clearly residual. Pottery from post-Roman and unphased contexts was very mixed in character, but contained a few vessels of intrinsic interest which have been illustrated.

Illustrated vessels (Figs 3.3-3.6)

Illustrated vessels are presented as site phase assemblages, in some cases focused on individual features. Within each phase group the vessels are in approximate typological order. Each entry commences with the fabric/ware code.

Phase 3
1. E80. Type CD jar. Ctx 7185, pit 7184.
2. E80. Type CD jar. Ctx 7185, pit 7184.
3. E80. Type CN 'storage' jar with groove on shoulder and ?rivet hole. Ctx 7185, pit 7184.

Phase 4
4. A11. Body sherd of ?Dressel 20 amphora with pre-firing graffito. Ctx 6636, ditch 7069.
5. W20. Flagon with stepped rim. Ctx 7273, pit 7272.
6. O20. Flagon with thickened everted rim. Ctx 7331, ditch 7330.
7. E30. Wide mouthed flagon or narrow mouthed jar with stepped, reeded rim. Ctx 7590, pit 7589.
8. E80. Type CC narrow-mouthed jar with grooves at base of neck and on shoulder. Ctx 6636 and 6641, ditch 7069.
9. E80. Type CC narrow-mouthed jar with cordon at base of neck and groove on shoulder. Ctx 6631, ditch 6715.
10. E80. Type CC narrow-mouthed jar with cordon on shoulder. Ctx 7227, ditch 7561.
11. E80. Type CD jar with groove on rim. Ctx 7290, ditch 7391.

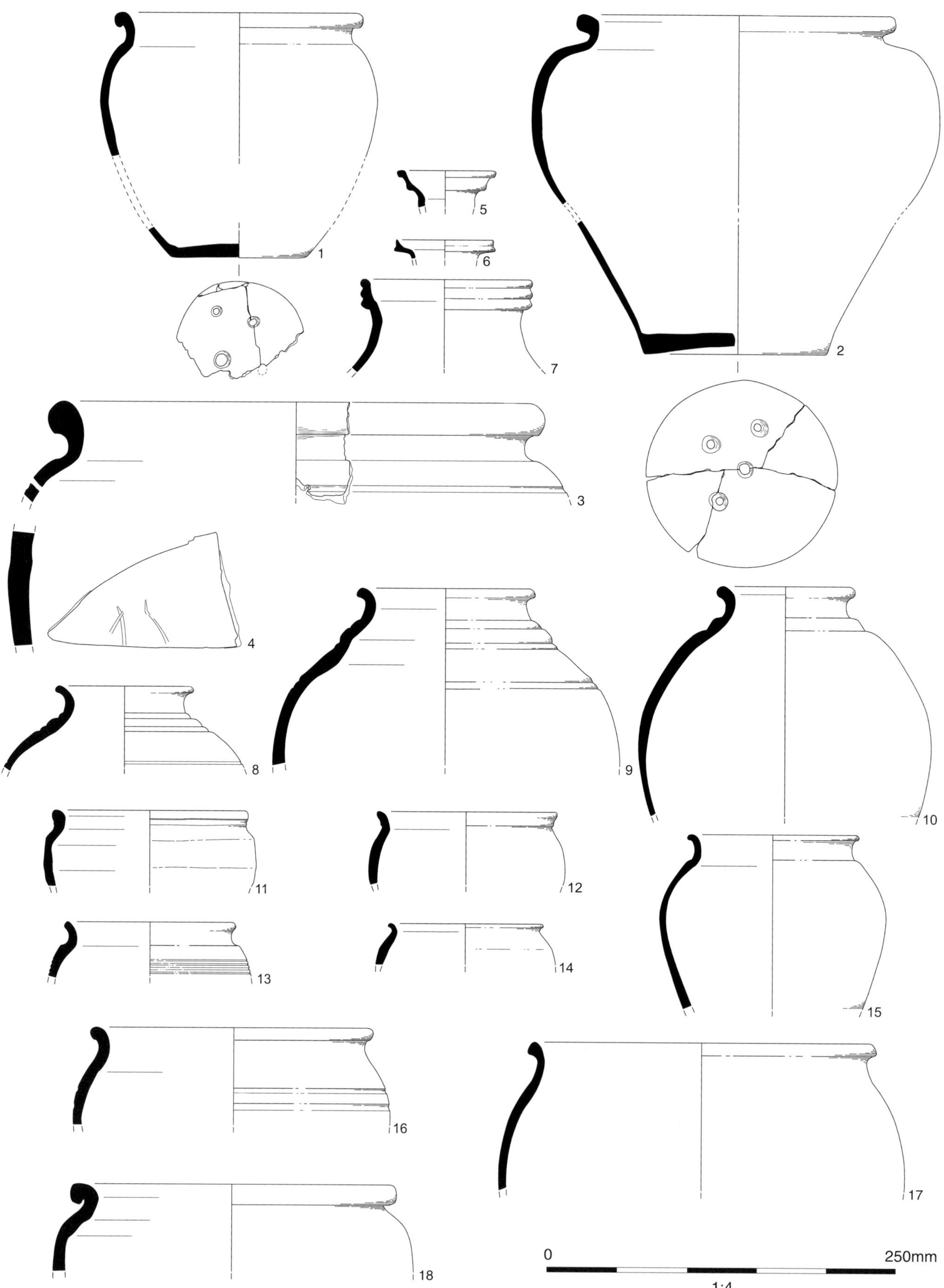

Fig. 3.3   Pottery from Langford Lane East, nos 1-18

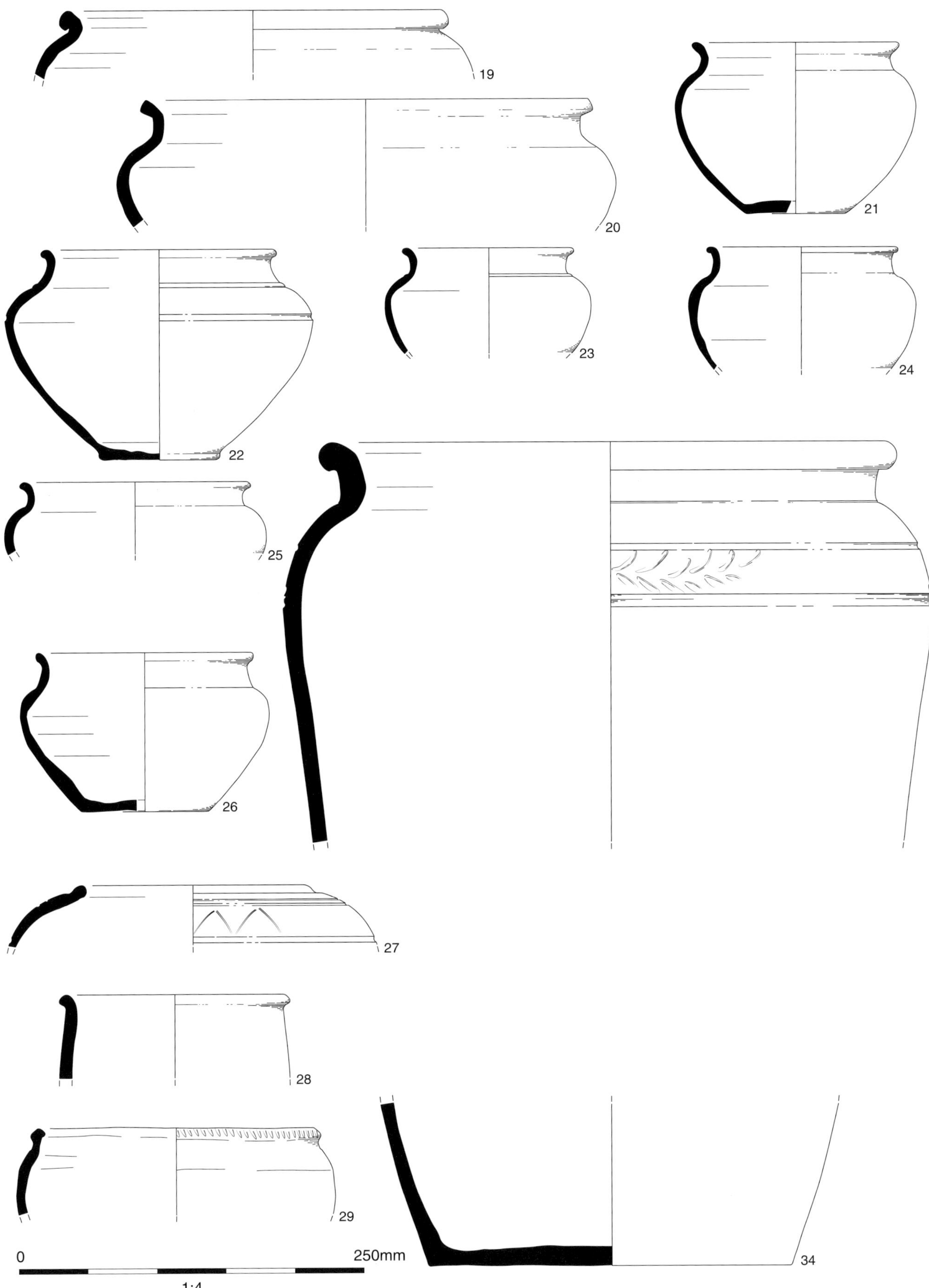

Fig. 3.4   Pottery from Langford Lane East, nos 19-29 and 34

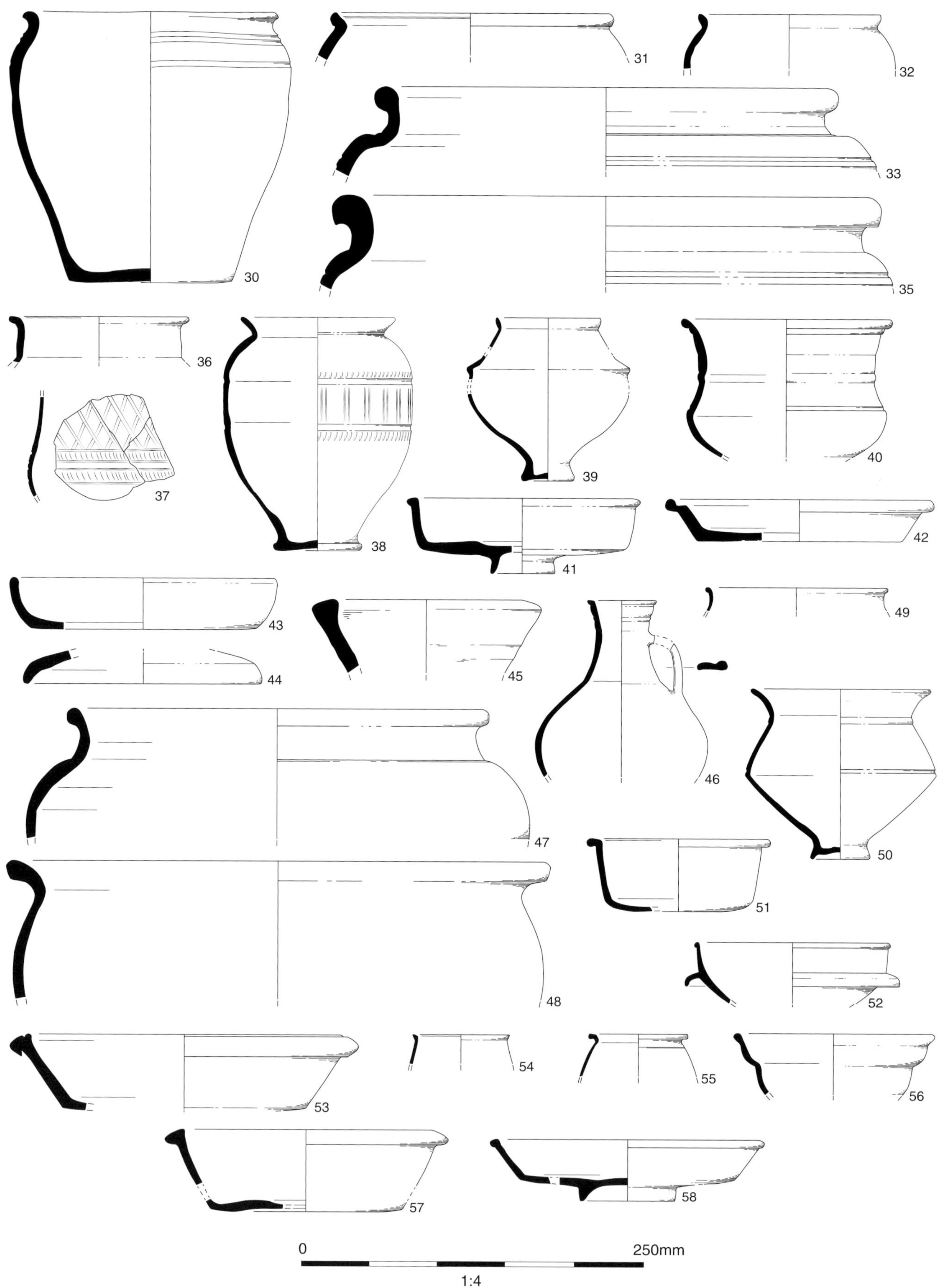

Fig. 3.5   Pottery from Langford Lane East, nos 30-3 and 35-58

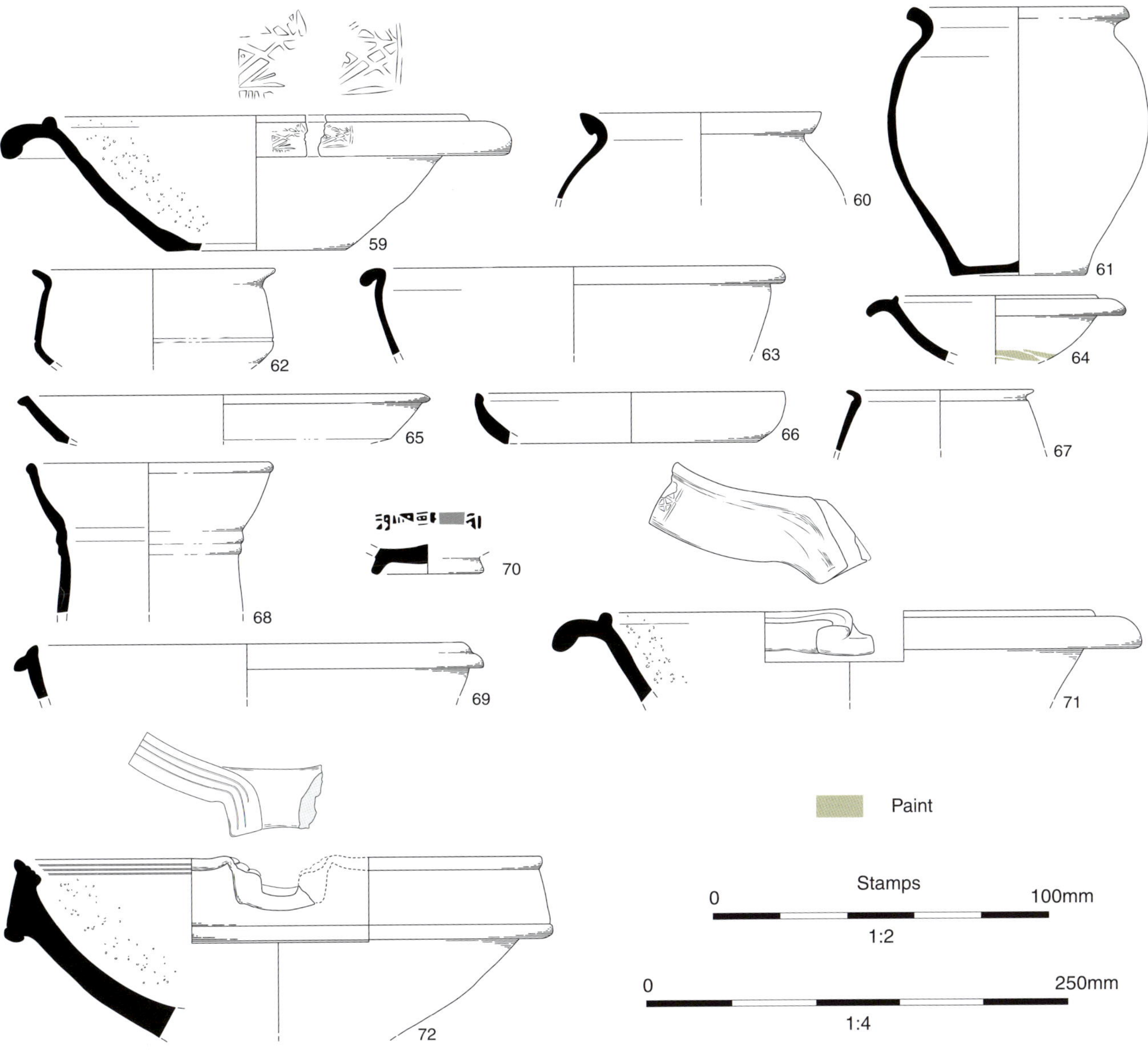

Fig. 3.6   Pottery from Langford Lane East, nos 59-72

12.   E80. Type CD jar with external sooting. Ctx 6817, pit 6816.
13.   E80. Type CD jar with groove on shoulder. Ctx 6636, ditch 7069.
14.   E80. Type CD jar. Ctx 7218, ditch 7157.
15.   E80. Type CD jar. Ctx 6638, ditch 7069.
16.   C10. Type CD jar with groove on shoulder. Ctx 7674, pit 7489.
17.   C10. Type CD jar. Ctx 7207, ditch 7561.
18.   E60. Type CD jar. Ctx 7643, ditch 8525.
19.   E60. Type CD jar. Ctx 7271, pit 7270.
20.   E30. Type CD jar. Ctx 6638, ditch 7069.
21.   E80. Type CE jar with groove and cordon at base of neck. Ctx 7207, ditch 7561.
22.   E80. Type CE jar with cordon at base of neck, girth groove, and overall burnish. Ctx 6927, ditch 6715.
23.   E80. Type CE jar with groove at base of neck and burnish on shoulder. Ctx 6927, ditch 6715.
24.   E80. Type CE jar. Ctx 6988, ditch 8521.
25.   E80. Type CE jar. Ctx 6854, pit 6853.
26.   E80. Type CE jar with groove at base of neck. Ctx 7467, ditch 7562.
27.   E30. Type CH jar with groove on shoulder and external sooting. Ctx 6927, ditch 6715.
28.   C10. Type CH jar with external sooting. Ctx 7391, ditch 7562.
29.   E80. Type CH jar with notched rim and external sooting. Ctx 6876, ditch 7444.
30.   E80. Type CH jar with grooves at base of neck, shoulder and girth, external sooting. Ctx 6630 and 6631, ditch 6715.
31.   C10. Type CI jar. Ctx 7520, ditch 7562.
32.   E80. Type CI jar. Ctx 6874, layer.
33.   E80. Type CN jar with cordon at base of neck and girth groove. Ctx 7518, ditch 7561.
34.   E80. Type CN jar with grooves on shoulder and band of leaf-like impressions between. Ctx 6876, ditch 7444.
35.   E80. Type CN jar with grooves at base of neck and on shoulder. Context 6940, ditch 6715.
36.   R37. Type D uncertain jar/bowl. Ctx 7221, ditch 7157.

37. W36. Body sherd of probable butt beaker (type EA) with grooves and incised lattice decoration between rows of rough 'rouletting'. Ctx 6636, ditch 7069.
38. W20. Type EH 'jar' beaker with groove, burnished shoulder and rows of large 'rouletted' decoration. Ctxs 7181 and 7182, ditch 8517.
39. O10. Small beaker. Ctx 6089, pit 6140.
40. E80. Type HA bowl with grooves at base of neck and girth. Ctx 7227, ditch 7561.
41. E80. Type JA dish. Ctx 7388, pit 7389.
42. E30. Type JA dish with offset rim. Ctx 6640, pit 6639.
43. E80. Type JB dish. Ctx 7013, ditch/pit 7010.
44. E80. Lid. Ctx 7044, pit 7041.

Phase 5
45. A26. Amphora of a form akin to Peacock and Williams (1986) type 59. Ctx 6826, surface.
46. O30. Flagon – the rim of a highly fragmented and only partially complete auxiliary vessel. Ctx 6722, cremation burial 6720.
47. E80. Type CD jar. Ctx 7383, layer.
48. R37. Type CM large wide-mouthed jar. Ctx 7333, ditch 6715.
49. O30. Small beaker of uncertain form. Ctx 6809, pit 6808.
50. W20. Type EG carinated beaker with cordon at base of neck and groove at carination. Ctx 7598, pit 7597.
51. R30. Type HB bowl. Ctx 7346, alluvial layer.
52. O11. Type HC bowl (Young type O48). Ctx 7346, alluvial layer.
53. R30. Type JA dish. Ctx 7333, ditch 6715.

Phase 6
54. O10. Small type EC beaker. Ctx 7116, demolition layer.
55. R10. Type EH jar-beaker with grooves at base of neck and shoulder. Ctx 7116, demolition layer.
56. R30. Type FB cup. Ctx 7116, demolition layer.
57. R30. Type JA dish (Young type R60) with eroded illiterate potter's stamp. Ctx 7116, demolition layer.
58. R10. Type JA dish. Ctx 7116, demolition layer.
59. M22. Mortarium (Young type M3) with eroded stamp. Burnt. Ctx 7116, demolition layer.
60. R30. Type CD jar. Ctx 6934, pit 6789.
61. R10. Type CK jar, almost complete. Ctx 7231, ditch 7453.
62. R30. Type HA bowl. Ctx 6919, ditch 8524.
63. R30. Type IA uncertain bowl/dish. Ctx 6096, hollow 6094.
64. W10. Type JB dish. Ctx 6524, pit 6523.

Table 3.14 Quantification of pottery fabrics from Langford Lane South by phase

Fabric	Phases 3 and 4		Phase 5		Phase 6		Phase 7		Post-Roman and unphased		Total	
	No. sh.	Wt (g)	No. sh.	Wt (g)	No. sh.	Wt (g)	No. sh.	Wt (g)	No. sh.	Wt (g)	No. sh.	Wt (g)
A3					1	22					1	22
S					1	1					1	1
S20 **LGF SA**	2	8	9	56	34	271			4	68	49	403
S30 **LEZ SA 2**			8	63	101	1682			16	235	106	1805
S32 **LMV SA**			5	60	21	364			3	53	29	477
S40									1	1	1	1
S41 **RHZ SA**			1	1							1	1
F43 **CNG BS**					4	27					4	27
F50					4	13					4	13
FO							1	9			1	9
F52 **LNV CC**					1	12			3	7	3	19
F55 **COL CC2**					1	1					1	1
F59			1	10	6	22					7	32
A11 **BAT AM 1&2**	1	23	3	137	7	1103			2	140	13	1403
A13 **GAL AM 1**									2	34	2	34
A30	1	105	1	6							2	111
M12 **NOG WH 4**					1	85					1	85
M21 **VER WH**			1	36							1	36
M22 **OXF WH**			2	88	8	550			8	137	18	775
W10			7	55	63	599	2	16	5	29	77	699
W20	1	3	9	121	46	537			35	328	91	976
W21 **VER WH**									1	5	1	5
W29					1	28					1	28
W42					1	14					1	14
W52			7	66	1	8					8	74
Q21 **OXF WS**			1	5	136	930			3	12	140	947
Q28					1	5					1	5
Q46					1	26					1	26
E20	1	12									1	12
E30	7	106	22	189	6	125			3	8	38	428

65. O10. Type JA dish with black interior coating. Ctx 6919, ditch 8524.
66. E80. Type JB dish. Ctx 7139, ditch 8520.

Phase 8-9, post-Roman
67. R10. Type EC beaker. Ctx 6598, tree hole.
68. E80. Type HA bowl. Ctx 6611, ditch 6604.
69. R20. Type HB bowl. Ctx 6603, ditch 6604.
70. FO (probably eroded F51). Base of dish with potter's stamp. Ctx 6581, palaeochannel 6736.

Unphased topsoil context 6554
71. M22. Mortarium (Young type M3) with incomplete, eroded potter's stamp. Cf. No. 59; it is just possible that these are the same vessel.
72. M22. Mortarium (Young type M14).

Langford Lane South

This assemblage comprised 3252 sherds weighing 38,346g (MSW 11.8g), with a total RE value of 48.55. This included material from evaluation trenches excavated in 2010 and derived from a total of 320 contexts. This is essentially an early-middle Roman assemblage. Only two sherds (23g) were assigned to Phase 3, but there is no certain pre-conquest material and the earliest groups are unlikely to date before about the middle of the 1st century. At the upper end of the date range only two small groups (contexts 2587 and 4168) were assigned to Phase 7. Overall the great majority of occupation at this site seems to fall in a range from late 1st to late 2nd/early 3rd century. Roughly 10% of the assemblage, by both sherd count and weight, was from unphased or post-Roman contexts. Quantification of fabrics by phase is given in Table 3.14.

The small Phase 4 assemblage (including two sherds of fabric E80 from Phase 3), derived entirely from the fills of ditches, which produced sherds with a significant MSW of 19.2g. The group was dominated by E wares (81.4% of sherd count, 81.2% of weight), mostly the grog-tempered E80 fabrics, supplemented by shell-tempered fabric C10. A jar in the latter fabric (Fig. 3.7, no. 73) was of a lid-seated type much more common to the east in Northamptonshire than in the Oxford region (cf. Friendship-Taylor 1999). South Gaulish samian ware and two amphora fabrics (A11 and A30) were also present. Identified vessel types were all jars except for a

Table 3.14 (continued)

Fabric	Phases 3 and 4		Phase 5		Phase 6		Phase 7		Post-Roman and unphased		Total	
	No. sh.	Wt (g)	No. sh.	Wt (g)	No. sh.	Wt (g)	No. sh.	Wt (g)	No. sh.	Wt (g)	No. sh.	Wt (g)
E40			1	3							1	3
E50			2	19							2	19
E80 **SOB GT**	84	1648	26	385	15	358			7	126	132	2517
O10			35	259	234	1194	11	283	19	51	299	1787
O20			14	72	33	376			11	104	58	552
O30			12	34	42	332			4	24	58	390
O37			2	34	7	96					9	130
O50			2	24							2	24
O55					2	5					2	5
O60									1	8	1	8
O80			22	428	49	1675	2	9	34	886	107	2998
O81 **PNK GT**			2	47	5	148			8	419	15	614
R10			141	976	722	7009	6	8	62	398	931	8391
R20	3	28	118	958	169	2288	3	31	13	298	306	3603
R30			28	366	118	1433	1	2	21	208	168	2009
R37			75	1018	74	1331			23	189	172	2538
R37F					4	222			1	13	5	235
R38					2	27					2	27
R38F			1	4	1	25					2	29
R41					2	16					2	16
R50					42	257	1	2	1	22	44	281
R60					13	300					13	300
R61			34	219	7	41			2	23	43	283
R90			19	154	10	262			5	68	25	484
R95 **SAV GT**			1	38	1	62					2	100
B11 **DOR BB 1**			3	18	64	690			6	50	73	758
C10	15	264	46	352	110	1159			1	1	172	1776
Total	115	2197	661	6301	2172	25,771	27	360	305	2945	3251	34,743

probable beaker in fabric E30 and a South Gaulish samian ware Dr 18 dish.

The Phase 5 assemblage was very different in character, though again derived very largely from ditch fill contexts. E wares, now only 7.9% of sherd count, were probably largely residual by this time, though fabric C10, which had supplemented them in Phase 4, was still in contemporary use. The sherds in this fabric and those in the numerically dominant oxidised and (particularly) reduced coarse wares were much more fragmented than previously, and the phase MSW was only 9.7g. The reduced wares amounted to 63.2% of the assemblage by sherd count (59.8% by weight) and 67.3% of REs, and included a significant proportion of 'West Oxfordshire' fabric R37. The date range of this phase is likely to have extended well into the first half of the 2nd century, as indicated by the presence of Central Gaulish samian ware, Oxford white mortaria, the probable early Oxford colour-coated fabric F59, and Dorset B11. Rare occurrences, in terms of the overall project, were a Verulamium region mortarium fragment, with an unfortunately badly damaged stamp, and sherds of the unsourced white ware fabric W52. The majority of sherds of a local coarse reduced fabric R61 were also from this site, many, present exclusively in jar forms, occurring in this phase group. The assemblage was dominated by jars (71% of REs), with dishes (10% of REs, mostly in fabric O10) and bowls (6.4% of REs) as relatively minor components and other vessel classes even less significant. Individual forms were typically unremarkable, the most notable vessel being a globular bowl in fabric R37 (Fig. 3.7, no. 81).

The relatively large Phase 6 assemblage – in fact the largest individual site/phase group of any in the project – contained 66.4% of the total sherds from the site (66.8% by weight), with a MSW of 11.9g. Here, however, fewer than half of the sherds (but 54.9% by weight) were from ditch fills. Pit fill deposits were, for this site, uniquely important in this phase, containing one third of all sherds. As also in the previous phase, however, more than 10% of sherds were from contexts described as 'finds references', not clearly associated with particular features. The range of fabrics was substantially that seen in Phase 5, with the addition of very small quantities of a few fine wares (still very scarce overall), and of the black-surfaced reduced fabric R50, while the early Roman fabric R61 declined in importance. Shell-tempered fabric C10 remained a significant minor component in the assemblage, and Dorset B11, never particularly important in these sites, now comprised 3% of sherds. The assemblage was still dominated by reduced coarse wares but their importance was slightly diminished compared with Phase 5 (54% of sherds; 51.8% of weight). The proportion of oxidised wares increased, particularly in terms of sherd count (to 17.2%). The most noticeable increase, however, related to fine and specialist wares, with both samian ware and the white-slipped fabric Q21, for

example, being quite well represented – these wares therefore totalled 19.7% of sherds and a substantial 35.4% of REs.

Vessels in the various samian ware fabrics contributed a remarkable 16.6% of all REs in this phase. Particularly notable amongst this material was a substantial part of a Central Gaulish Dr 37 bowl (with joining sherds from contexts 2572 and 2574, fills of ditches in the south-west corner of enclosure E7), but a wide range of forms was present, including Dr 27 (3), 37, 18 (6), 36, 42 and Curle 15 in South Gaulish samian, and Central Gaulish forms Dr 27 (3), 33 (10), 35 (3), 64, 37 (3 including the vessel already mentioned), 38, Curle 11, 18/31 (4?), 31 (2), 36 (2) and Curle 23, as well as a large number of less certain dishes of form 18/31 or 31. Overall, samian ware contributed over one third (by REs) of all the bowls, dishes and indeterminate bowl/dish forms present in this phase as well as providing almost the entirety of the cups (which amounted to 5.7% of the phase assemblage, against an overall project average of 3.1%, including coarse ware examples). Bowls and dishes in all fabrics amounted to 11.9% and 12.8% respectively, with the indeterminate (intermediate) forms another 4.7%, giving a combined total for 'open' forms of 29.3%, not far short of the overall figure for jars, which at 35.6% was notably low. The other unusually important component in the Phase 6 assemblage from Langford Lane South consisted of flagons, which amounted to a remarkable 18.9% of REs. As with some smaller phase groups, this figure was somewhat exaggerated by the presence of two complete rims (Fig. 3.7, nos. 103 and 97, respectively of Oxford white-ware type W2 in sandy fabric W20 and a version of Oxford white-ware type W30 (cf. Fig. 3.12, no. 181) in oxidised fabric O20), but by count of rim sherds the various flagons in this phase were more than twice as common as the overall project average. The majority of flagons occurred in fabric Q21, mirroring the relative importance of that fabric in this phase assemblage. Of the other vessel classes present, beakers amounted to 6% of REs, a moderate but not remarkable figure, but including two probable examples in the early Oxford colour-coated fabric F59 (Fig. 3.7, nos 88 and 99, the latter with roughcast decoration). Mortaria only totalled 0.6%, while lids, very poorly represented on the project sites overall, here amounted to 1.3% of the assemblage, the three examples amounting to more than half of the total RE value for lids across all the sites. In summary, the main characteristics of this phase assemblage are an unusually marked emphasis on table wares – open types amounting to 29.3% of REs, types associated with presentation and consumption of liquids totalling another 30.5% and jars only amounting to 35.6% (or 37.8% if it is assumed that vessels in the uncertain jar/bowl category (class D) were in fact jars). This group stands out amongst others from the project.

The most important component in the tiny Phase 7 assemblage was oxidised fabric O10, the principal

Fig. 3.7   Pottery from Langford Lane South, nos 73-104

vessel being a wide-mouthed jar, probably of Young type O38, a type usually dated after AD 240. The later Roman date for this group is supported by a single sherd of fabric FO, probably eroded Oxford colour-coated ware.

Illustrated vessels (Figs 3.7 and 3.8)

Phase 4
73. C10. Type CJ lid-seated jar. Ctx 3002, ditch 3004, Eval Tr 3.

Phase 5
74. O10. Type B ring-necked flagon. Ctx 2168, ditch 4382.

75. W20. Type B wide-necked flagon, or possibly a jar. Ctx 2972 and 2926, ditch 2652.
76. R20. Type CD jar with cordon at base of neck and girth groove. Ctx 2475, ditch 2327.
77. R37. Type CD jar with external sooting. Ctx 2055, ditch 2075.
78. C10. Type CJ lid-seated jar. Ctx 2750, posthole 2747.
79. O80. Type CN large 'storage' jar. Ctx 2007, ditch 2012.
80. W10. Type HA carinated bowl. Ctx 2369, ditch 2452.
81. R37. Type HG globular bowl with external sooting. Ctx 21003, ditch 21002, Eval Tr 21.
82. O10. Type JA dish (Young 1977, type O41). Ctx 2752, ditch 2651.

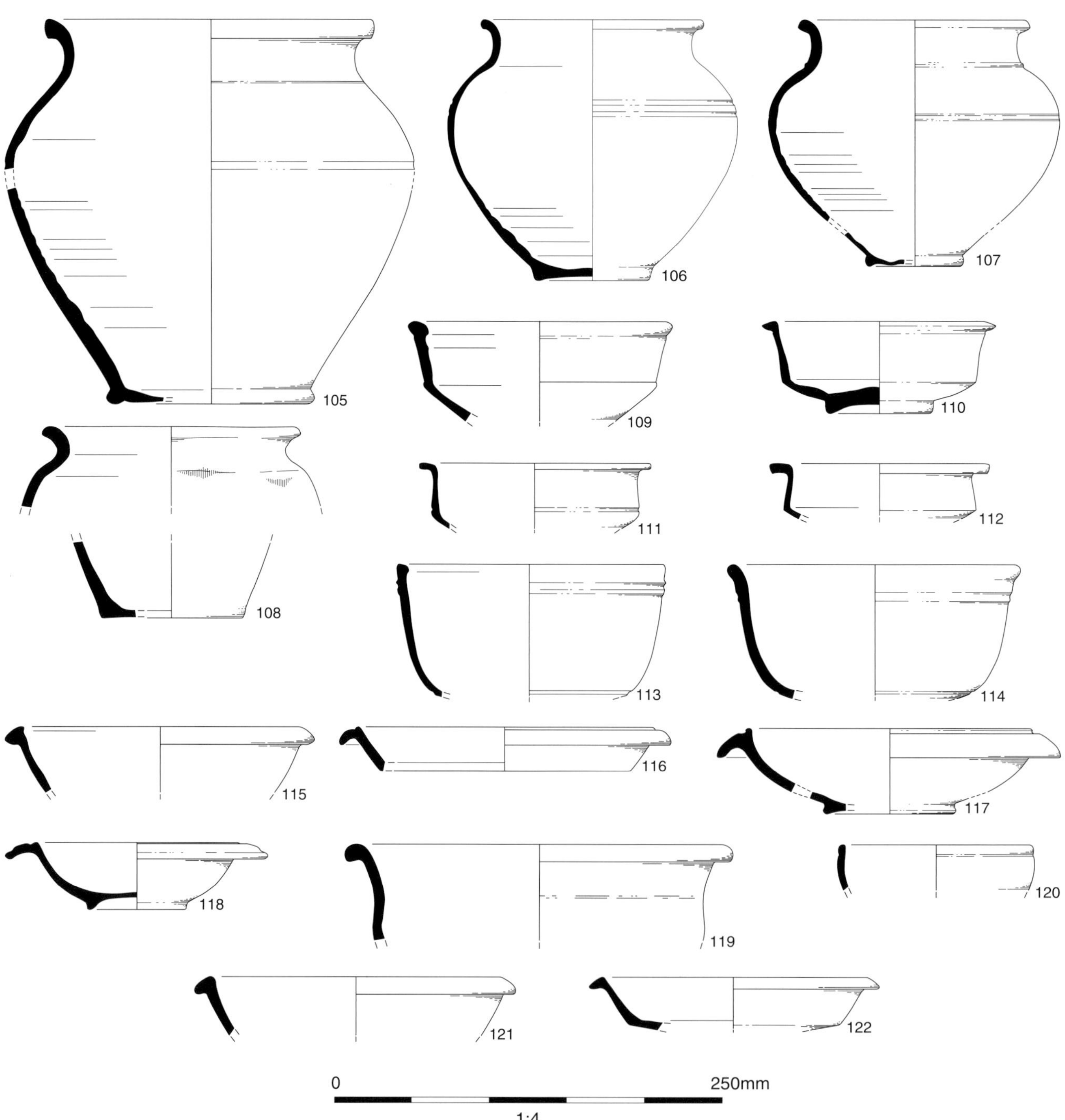

Fig. 3.8   Pottery from Langford Lane South, nos 105-21

83. O10. Type JB dish. Ctx 21003, ditch 21002, Eval Tr 21.
84. M22. Small mortarium, Young (1977) type M10, burnt. Ctx 4355, ditch 4368.

Phase 6

Pit 2611
85. Q21. Type B ring-necked flagon. Ctx 2808.
86. Q21. Type B ring-necked flagon. Ctx 2808.
87. Q46. Type CD jar. Ctx 2808.
88. F59. Type EC beaker with groove on shoulder. Ctx 2809.
89. F43. Incomplete applied face mask from a rounded beaker, probably of Déchelette form 74. The face is bearded, as Silenus or Pan. Cf. eg Simpson 1957 plate XIV nos 20, 21, 28 and 29; 1973, plate IX, nos 2 and 8, plate XI, no. 23 (all of Pan except plate IX no. 8), though none is clearly from the same mould as the present example. Ctx 2615.
90. W29. Type HB bowl with vestigial flange. Ctx 2808.
91. R30. Type HC rounded bowl with multiple grooves and bands of vertical comb decoration. Ctx 2809.
92. O10. Type JB dish. Ctx 2808.
93. M12. Mortarium. Rim form slightly uncertain (eroded). Ctx 2808.
94. W20. Small lid. Ctx 2615.

Pit 4047
95. W20. Type B ring-necked flagon. Ctx 2549.
96. Q21. Type B ring-necked flagon. Ctx 2792.
97. O20. Type BD flagon as Young (1977) type W30 (cf. no. 180 below). Ctx 2551.
98. R10. Type CD jar. Ctx 2792.
99. F59. Type EC beaker with roughcast decoration. Ctx 2791.
100. R30. Type HC rounded bowl. Ctx 2551.
101. R20. Type IB uncertain bowl/dish. Ctx 2793.
102. R20. Type JB dish. Ctx 2488.

Other Phase 6 contexts
103. W20. Type BA ring-necked flagon (Young 1977, type W2). Ctx 21025, ditch 21011, Eval Tr 21.
104. R20. Type BB large ring-necked flagon. Ctx 2903, ditch 4047.
105. R10. Type CD jar with grooves at base of neck and girth. Ctx 137, ditch 1063.
106. R10. Type CD jar with cordon at base of neck. Ctx 2571, ditch 4384.
107. R10. Type CD jar with cordon at base of neck, burnish on shoulder and girth groove. Ctx 2431 and 2432, pit 2430.
108. C10. Type CK jar with external sooting. Ctx 137, ditch 1063.
109. R20. Type HA carinated bowl with external sooting. Ctx 2572, ditch 4384.
110. R10. Type HA carinated bowl. Ctx 2572, ditch 4384.
111. R10. Type HA carinated bowl with groove at carination. Ctx 2737, alluvial layer.
112. R10. Type HA carinated bowl (Young type R57) with external sooting. Ctx 2990, ditch 4018.
113. W10. Type HC rounded bowl with grooves on upper and lower body. Ctx 2649, ditch 2929.
114. W10. Type HC rounded bowl with grooves on upper body. Ctx 2720, ditch 2718.
115. R10. Type IB bowl/dish. Ctx 2034, hollow 2032, Eval Tr 2.
116. R10. Type JA dish. Ctx 2596, ditch 2456.
117. R10. Type JB dish. Ctx 2432, pit 2430.
118. O10. Type JB dish, cf. Young type O44, burnt. Ctx 2644, ditch 4478.

Post-Roman and unphased tree-throw hole contexts
119. O81. Type CM wide-mouthed jar with groove at base of neck. Ctx 4002, alluvial layer.
120. O10. Type HC rounded bowl. Ctx 254, tree hole 253.
121. R30. Type JA dish. Ctx 4184, tree hole 4388.
122. O20. Type JA dish with chamfered base. Ctx 2027, tree hole.

South of Merton

The site produced 835 sherds weighing 10,496g (MSW 12.6g) and totalling 11.62 REs, from 51 context groups. The pottery falls almost entirely within a date range from the late 1st to the early 3rd century, and in terms of phasing within the Roman period this is essentially a single phase (Phase 6) site, so the quantification of pottery given in Tables 3.4, 3.5 and 3.8 is not re-expressed here. Residual middle Iron Age and late Iron Age/early Roman sherds amounted to a mere 1.8% of the total assemblage (0.8% of weight). There were no late Roman (post-AD 240) groups. Eight context groups containing Roman pottery, however, were phased as medieval or later, some containing a few medieval sherds. The mean sherd weight from this site is boosted by the presence of large parts of two Oxford white ware mortaria: an almost complete, though fragmented, Young type M14 (in context 2521), and part of an M10 (in context 1404). Together these eight sherds accounted for 21.9% of the weight of pottery in Phase 6 contexts (18.6% of the total site assemblage), and 10.7% of REs.

In terms of sherd count, reduced wares were dominant as usual, amounting to 60.6% (and 64% of the post-Roman Phase 8 total). Fine oxidised fabric O10 was common, and despite the very fragmented nature of the sherds (MSW 6.4g) contributed a variety of vessel types – jars, beakers, bowls and dishes – amounting to 10.7% of the phase RE total. A beaker (Fig. 3.9 no. 124) in the related fine oxidised fabric O11 was notable. The fabric is consistent with production in the Oxford kilns, but the form is unknown in the Oxford repertoire. It is, however, paralleled precisely by a colour-coated ware beaker in the Colchester kilns (Hull 1963, 170, fig. 96 no. 11). That vessel is subsumed under CAM 397 in the Colchester type series, dated late 2nd-3rd century, but is the only close parallel to the South of Merton example amongst the other vessels assigned to CAM 397 (eg Symonds and Wade 1999, 486). The origin of the present remarkable vessel remains uncertain. The Phase 6 fine and specialist ware percentage (7.7% of sherds) was close to that for the site overall, and was made up mainly of white wares, plus the Oxford mortarium sherds and a little samian ware. Fine wares and amphorae were totally absent from the site.

The RE figures for the site are skewed by the complete mortarium and a complete flagon rim (Young 1977, type W6; Fig. 3.9, no. 123).

Consequently, the RE value for jars, 37.7% of vessels, is much the lowest of any of the sites. However, the rim count data suggest that this figure is not completely unrepresentative; of exactly 100 vessels represented by rims, only 41 were jars, and even if the 8 uncertain jar/bowl rims are added to the jar total this is still less than 50% of the overall site figure. Vessels other than jars thus appear particularly important in this assemblage, despite the lack of the correlation that might have been anticipated between this characteristic and a relatively high representation of fine and specialist wares, the latter not being seen here. Dishes, second to jars in overall importance (13.6% of REs), contributed 17 of the 100 rim sherds, in a variety of forms.

Illustrated vessels (Fig. 3.9)

Phase 6 western roadside ditch contexts
123. W10. Flagon (Young 1977, type W6). Ctx 2590, ditch 2544.
124. O11. Beaker of unusual constricted girth form with overall 'rouletted' decoration. Ctx 2521, SF 2501.
125. R11. Type EC beaker. Ctx 2521, SF 2502 and Ctx 1309, ditch 1308, Eval Tr 13.
126. O10. Type EH beaker. Ctx 1310, ditch 1308, Eval Tr 13.
127. R10. Type HA carinated bowl (Young 1977, type R64) Ctxs 1309 and 1310, ditch 1308, Eval Tr 13.
128. M22. Mortarium (Young 1977, type M14). Ctx 2521, SF 2500.

Other Phase 6 contexts
129. R20. Type CD jar. Ctx 2504, ditch 2503.
130. R50. Type HA carinated bowl (Young 1977, type R57). Ctx 2543, layer.
131. W20. Type IA straight-sided bowl or dish. Ctx 2528, ditch 2527.
132. R20. Type JB curving sided dish. Ctx 2539, ditch 2538.
133. R10. Type JB curving-sided dish. Ctx 2543, layer.
134. M22. Mortarium (Young 1977, type M10). Ctx 1404, ditch 1403, Eval Tr 14.

Holts Farm Crossing

This site produced 1595 sherds weighing 16,188g (MSW 10.2g) and totalling 16.38 REs from some 192 context groups. The pottery suggests continuous activity from the middle Iron Age through late Iron

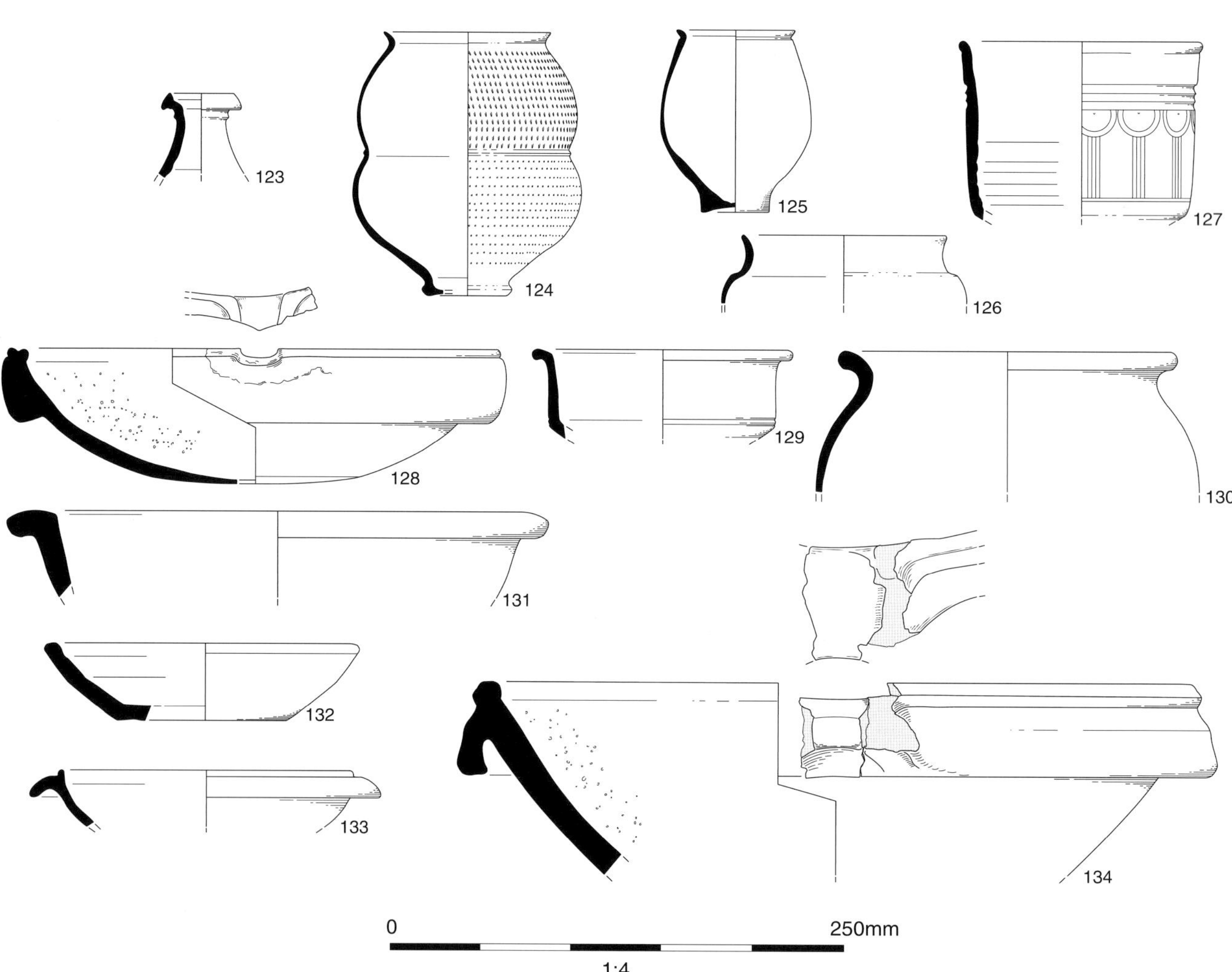

Fig. 3.9   Pottery from South of Merton, nos 122-34

Age/early Roman and into the middle Roman period, with reasonable amounts of material of 1st-2nd century date, but the Phase 5 assemblage is quite small. There is more limited evidence for later activity in the Roman period, but although only nine context groups were assigned to Phase 7, one of these (8618) is particularly large, and together they contain a third of the total site assemblage. The fabrics present are summarised by phase in Table 3.15.

This assemblage has the lowest mean sherd weight of all the larger groups from the project, and some fabric groups appeared to be particularly heavily fragmented – for example the mean sherd weight of the samian ware from the site was only 3.8g, and MSWs of three of the four fabrics with more than 100 sherds in the assemblage, O10, R10 and C10, were 7.2g, 7.1g and 6.5g respectively. A potentially related characteristic is the relatively high degree of mixing of some of the phase groups. In the case of the Phase 2 and Phase 3 assemblages this could reflect the continuous nature of activity between these two phases. This might support the idea, mentioned above, that some handmade pottery of middle Iron Age tradition continued in use alongside material in the 'Belgic' tradition (E wares), a situation perhaps seen most clearly in Phase 3, where E wares accounted for 67.7% of sherds (70.8% of weight) and handmade fabrics of middle Iron Age type, in a fairly wide range of fabrics, contributed 26.7% of sherds (26.3% by weight). Alternatively, a relatively high level of inter-cutting resulted in significant redeposition of earlier sherds in contexts of this date. Such an explanation seems unavoidable in Phase 6, when 14.8% of all sherds were still of middle Iron Age type, now with a MSW of only 4.5g.

This problem means that definition of meaningful trends in the development of the middle Iron Age assemblage is not possible. The fairly small Phase 2 assemblage contained sherds in most of the principal fabric groups of this period, with sand-tempered and shell-tempered fabrics the principal contributors, but the material was quite fragmented, with a MSW of 7.2g. This is partly explained in terms of the types of contexts from which the pottery derived. While much of the pottery came from ditches and pits, as usual, exactly one third of the Phase 2 sherds were from gullies, and this material was particularly fragmented, with a MSW of 4.7g. The nine vessels represented by rims in this phase group amounted to a mere 0.33 REs, all from jars or probable jars, with only a single notable vessel (Fig 3.10, no. 135) amongst them.

The Phase 3 assemblage was also small, but the MSW (14.5g) was twice that of the previous phase – as already indicated, this applied to the sherds of middle Iron Age tradition as well as those of the dominant E wares. Potentially contemporary 'Romanised' fabrics were negligible in this group. E wares provided 91.7% of REs in this phase, these consisting of a variety of jar forms and a single

(unusual) bowl (Fig. 3.10, no. 142), while one of the two sherds in fabric R10 was probably from the base of a small beaker. The majority of the pottery was again from ditches, with pit groups accounting for most of the rest. Only a single sherd was recorded as being sooted.

The Phase 5 assemblage had a rather wider range of fabrics, but was very small (only 80 sherds). Reduced coarse wares now formed the largest single ware group and fine and specialist wares were represented by white fabrics, including a large body sherd from a flagon attributed to the Verulamium region industry (fabric W21) and two small fragments of amphora fabric A11.

In the larger Phase 6 group, as already mentioned, residual middle and late Iron Age sherds were quite numerous, a characteristic which contributed to the relatively low MSW (8.3g) of this group. Reduced fabrics amounted to 22.8% of sherds (34.5% of weight), while oxidised ware sherds were more numerous but less significant as a proportion of weight. Oxidised sherds were mainly in the fine fabric O10, while the reduced ware group was more diverse, fabrics R10, R20, R30 and R37 all contributing. The finer fabrics, O10 and R10, however, accounted for the majority of REs in this phase group (62%), though this figure was boosted by a complete rim from a narrow mouthed jar in fabric O10 (Fig. 3.10, no. 146). Dorset fabric B11 appeared for the first time this phase, and amongst other coarse wares the shell-tempered fabric C10 was well represented, with rims from a number of jars, and one (Fig. 3.10, no. 150) perhaps from a very heavy lid, or possibly a ceramic disc (though the apparent angle of this piece suggests the former). Greater diversity is seen in the fine and specialist wares, with South and Central Gaulish samian ware, and Oxford mortaria and white-slipped fabric Q21 all appearing for the first time, albeit in modest quantities. The only mortarium rim sherd, in ditch fill 8678, is of Young (1977) type M17, dated after AD 240, and is presumably intrusive in this context. The greater diversity of fabrics is reflected in a wider range of forms. Flagons occurred in fabrics W10, Q21 and O10, and beakers, cups, bowls and dishes were all more numerous than previously.

The assemblage from Phase 7 was the most substantial from the site, despite deriving from only a few contexts. Of these, 8618, the uppermost fill of waterhole 8617, was the most important, the remaining material deriving, as usual, almost entirely from pits and ditches. The broad character of the group was not unlike that of the Phase 6 assemblage, but the importance of oxidised wares increased at the expense of reduced wares, particu-larly in terms of representation by REs, in which oxidised wares accounted for 48.6%, mostly consisting of a variety of jar forms. Fabric O81 was now a significant component amongst the oxidised wares, reflecting the growing regional importance of this product in the later Roman period. The most distinctive marker of the period was Oxford colour-

Table 3.15 Quantification of pottery fabrics from Holts Farm Crossing by phase

Fabric	Phase 2		Phase 3		Phase 5		Phase 6		Phase 7		Post-Roman and unphased		Total	
	No. sh.	Wt (g)	No. sh.	Wt (g)	No. sh.	Wt (g)	No. sh.	Wt (g)	No. sh.	Wt (g)	No. sh.	Wt (g)	No. sh.	Wt (g)
A1	26	98					5	10	1	1			32	109
A2			1	9									1	9
A4	7	59	3	15			9	59					19	133
A5	4	17	1	3			1	2					6	22
A6	2	4	1	1	1	2	3	32					7	39
A7					1	7							1	7
A8	5	49	2	13	1	1	1	1					9	64
A9	9	54			1	3	3	8					13	65
F1							2	3					2	3
F2			1	2			1	2					2	4
G1	3	22	2	12			3	20					8	54
G2	9	62	2	36			3	14	1	22			15	134
G3	12	98	1	19			12	34					25	151
L1	1	7					1	4					2	11
L2	9	229	2	23			3	22	1	8			15	282
L3	1	2											1	2
L4	2	11	2	26			2	26					6	63
L5	9	64	1	1	2	8	2	9					14	82
L6	4	42	1	11	5	16	5	11					15	80
S1	3	25	2	35			1	1					6	61
S2	31	122			2	6							33	128
S3	1	7											1	7
S4	9	75	1	48			8	21					18	144
S5	2	5											2	5
S6	1	1	2	8			1	2					4	11
S7	11	51	3	13	2	6	2	10					18	80
V1							1	11					1	11
V2	30	184	1	8	2	8	5	33					38	233
V3			20	402									20	402
V4			1	25									1	25
V5	1	1					1	5					2	6
Z1	1	4											1	4
S20 **LGF SA**							2	3	2	4			4	7
S30 **LEZ SA 2**							5	34	14	50	1	1	20	85
F43 **CNG BS**									1	8			1	8
F51 **OXF RS**									32	537			32	537

coated ware (F51), which provided the majority of the fine and specialist wares in this phase group, contributing to their total of 15.3% of sherds in this group (23.2% of REs), compared with 4.4% of sherds (9.6% of REs) in the Phase 6 assemblage (percentages of totals excluding the handmade middle Iron Age fabrics). Forms represented by rims in fabric F51 included a beaker, a bowl, and dishes (Young 1977 types C45 (2) and C47), while other beakers, including the indented form C29, were present as body sherds. Contemporary forms in the Oxford white ware mortarium fabric were an uncertain M17 or M18, M18 (4) and M22, together amounting to 11.7% of REs in this phase, an unusually high figure. Despite this, jars still formed the large majority of vessels in this phase assemblage (60.1% of REs), even though this figure was rather less than in the previous phase, when jars totalled 73.1% of REs.

Illustrated vessels (Fig. 3.10)

Phase 2

135. LAIZ4. Jar with simple upright rim. A small lead insert in the shoulder may be part of a repair, but this technique is usually only found in the Roman period. Ctx 1007, ditch 1003, Eval Tr 10.

Phase 3

136. LGA4. Simple jar with oblique incised line decoration. Ctx 8182, ditch 8684.
137. E80. Type CC jar with grooves at base of neck and on shoulder. Ctx 8213, ditch 8684.
138. E30. Type CD jar with girth groove. Ctx 8026, ditch 8030.
139. E80. Type CD jar with grooves at base of neck. Ctx 1304, ditch 1303, Eval Tr 13.
140. E80. Type CD jar with grooves at base of neck. Ctx 1603, ditch 1605, Eval Tr 16.
141. E80. Type CE jar. Ctx 8182, ditch 8684.

Table 3.15 (continued)

Fabric	Phase 2		Phase 3		Phase 5		Phase 6		Phase 7		Post Roman and unphased		Total	
	No. sh.	Wt (g)	No. sh.	Wt (g)	No. sh.	Wt (g)	No. sh.	Wt (g)	No. sh.	Wt (g)	No. sh.	Wt (g)	No. sh.	Wt (g)
FO											1	2	1	2
F52 **LNV CC**									1	1			1	1
A11 **BAT AM 1&2**					2	14			3	127			5	141
M22 **OXF WH**							6	184	11	702			17	886
W10					1	2	5	102	14	123	2	8	22	235
W20			1	6	1	24			3	18	1	7	6	55
W21 **VER WH**					1	102							1	102
Q21 **OXF WS**							1	6					1	6
E10	4	11											4	11
E20									2	23	1	5	3	28
E30			9	110	2	17	5	33	1	3	2	7	19	170
E40			1	3									1	3
E50			2	10					1	5			3	15
E80 **SOB GT**	9	117	114	1785	11	50	41	317	15	126	10	64	200	2459
O10	1	19			12	56	149	903	122	1083	14	96	298	2157
O11					2	6							2	6
O20					1	3	10	51	43	322	4	33	58	409
O30							1	8	10	84	8	49	19	141
O55									5	52			5	52
O80	1	80	1	36	2	27	1	7	6	126	2	43	13	319
O81 **PNK GT**							8	177	22	1061	1	8	31	1246
R10			2	9	12	123	52	385	123	703	13	203	202	1433
R11 **OXF FR**									1	5	1	97	2	102
R20					5	283	18	432	12	115	2	29	37	859
R30					6	53	15	151	29	300	4	59	54	463
R37					2	11	20	159	8	92	3	35	33	297
R37F							3	37	2	5	2	9	7	51
R38F							1	6					1	6
R50							2	6	6	86			8	92
R90							4	72	9	212	2	22	15	306
R95 **SAV GT**							1	193	2	43			3	236
B11 **DOR BB 1**							8	53	5	31	3	17	16	101
C10	5	21	6	26	3	8	75	534	22	133	1	8	112	730
Total	213	1541	186	2695	80	836	508	4203	530	6111	78	802	1595	16,188

142. E80. Type HC bowl with grooves and cordons on upper body. Ctx 8175, ditch 8684.

Phase 5
143. R20. Type CD jar. Ctx 8343, ditch 8688.

Phase 6
144. W10. Type BB wide-mouthed flagon. Ctx 8641, ditch 8643.
145. AGV3 (residual). Type CB jar with simple rim and horizontal combed decoration. Ctx 8294, ditch 8683.
146. O10. Type CC jar with cordon at base of neck. Ctx 8517, ditch 8310.
147. O10. Type EH beaker. Ctx 8673, ditch 8682.
148. W10. Type HA carinated bowl. Ctx 8521, ditch 8519.
149. R20. Type HB straight-sided bowl. Ctx 8566, ditch 8565.
150. C10. Possible large lid. Ctx 8677, ditch 8681.

Phase 7 ctx 8618 (upper fill of waterhole 8617)
151. W20. Type C jar, or possibly tazza, with notched angled everted rim.
152. O81. Type C jar.
153. O81. Type C jar with hooked rim.
154. R10. Shoulder of jar (Type C) with incised graffito (X).
155. O10. Type CM wide-mouthed jar.
156. O20. Type CM wide-mouthed jar.
157. O81. Type H bowl.
158. O10. Type HB bowl with bead and flanged rim.
159. R20. Type HB bowl with bead and flanged rim.
160. F51. Base of dish with worn, illiterate potter's stamp.
161. M22. Mortarium of Young form M18.

Phase 7 other contexts
162. O55. Type CD jar. Ctx 8668, pit 8669.
163. O10. Type CK jar. Ctx 8492, ditch 8694.
164. O10. Base of ?dish with worn, illiterate potter's stamp. Ctx 8455, ditch 8451.

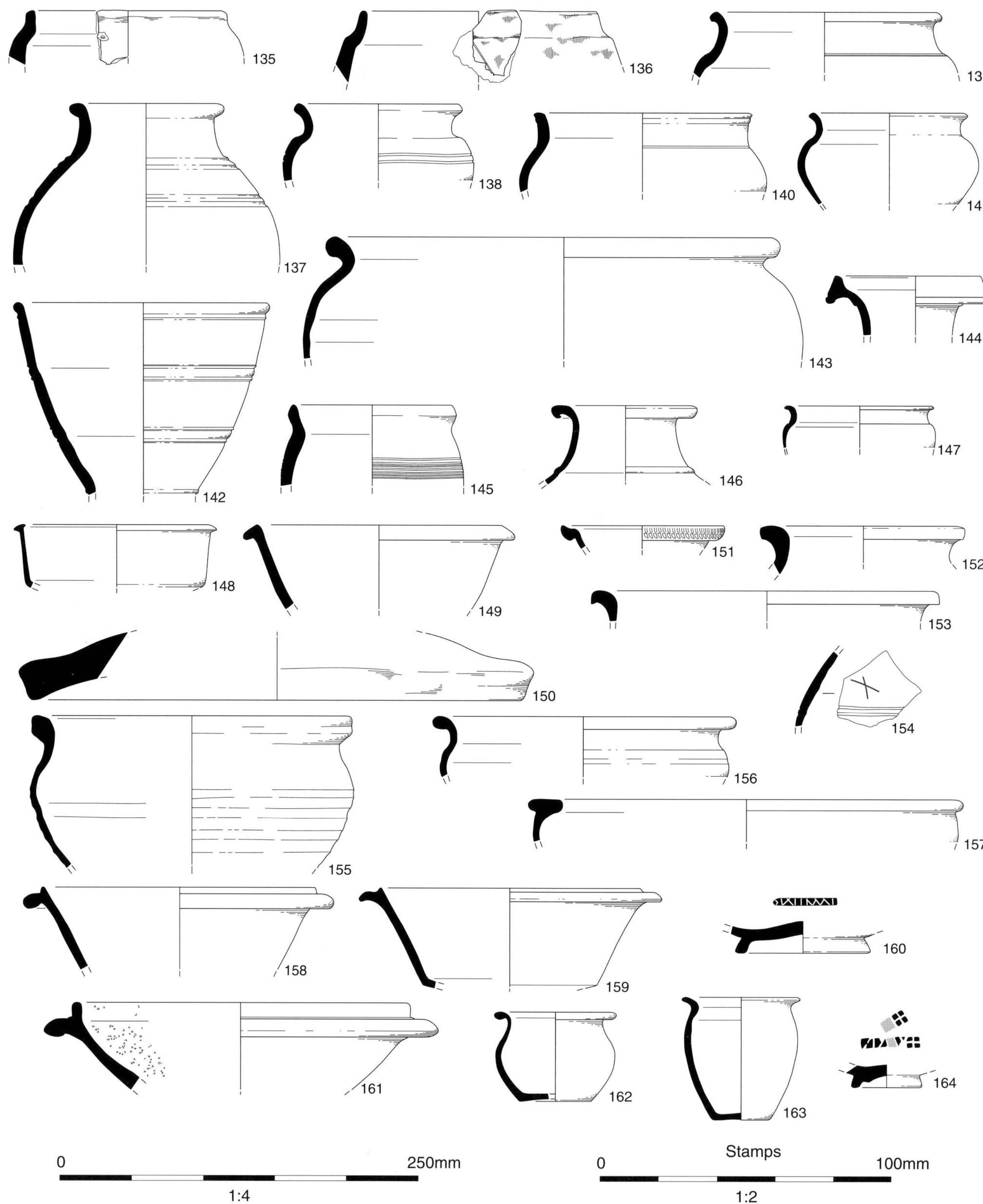

Fig. 3.10   Pottery from Holts Farm Crossing, nos 135-64

East of Oddington Grange

The site produced 53 sherds weighing 511g (MSW 9.6g) from nine context groups, all fills of ditches and gullies. The overall chronological range is from the middle Iron Age to the late Iron Age/early Roman period. The only possible exception to this was a crude slightly thickened and out-sloping rim sherd (not illustrated) which has possible notching on the top of the rim and perhaps fingertip impression just below the tip of the rim. This is perhaps of the earlier Iron Age, but rather uncertain. In terms

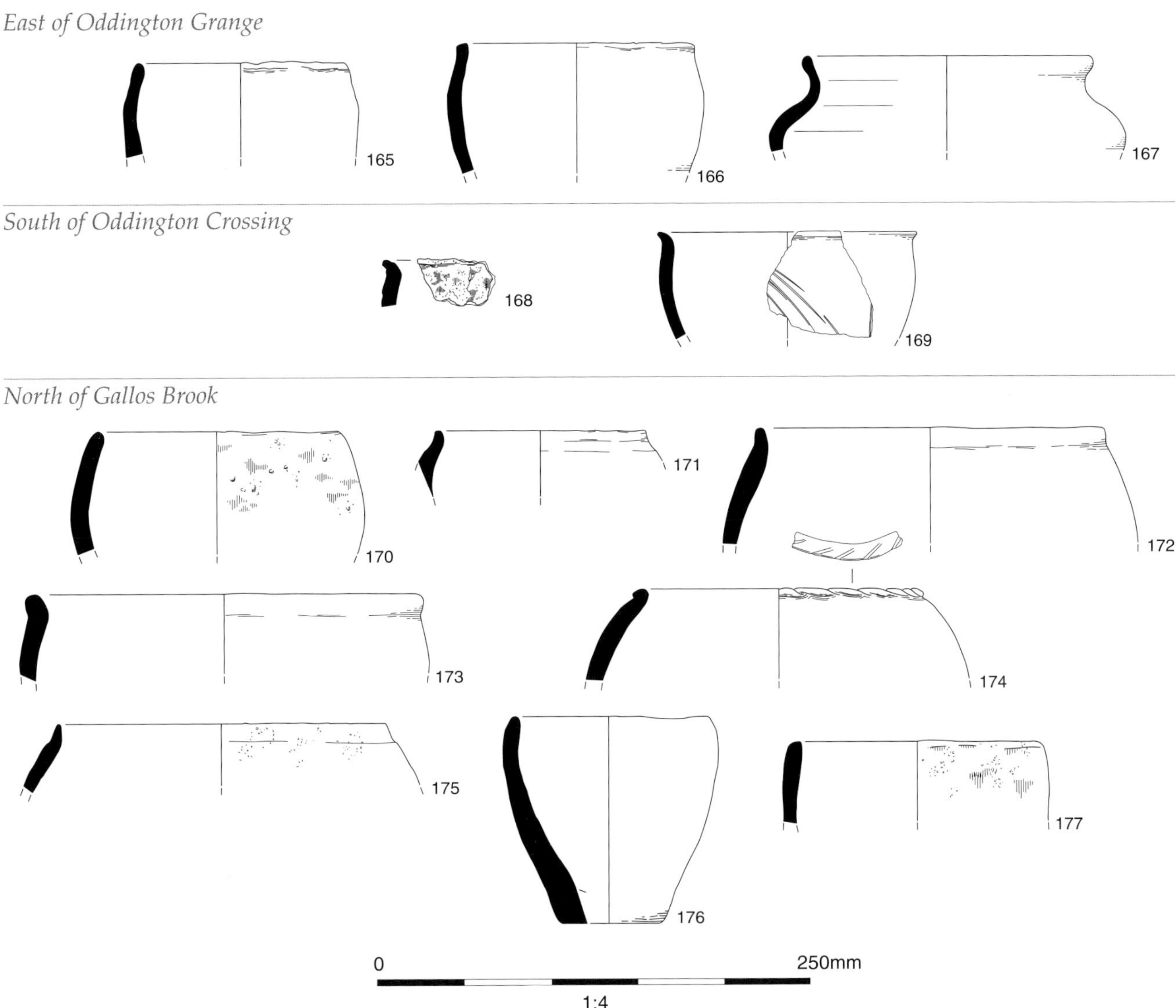

Fig. 3.11   Pottery from East of Oddington Grange, South of Oddington Crossing and North of Gallos Brook, nos 165-77

of fabric (LA4) it is entirely consistent with other material dated to the middle Iron Age. Its context (7) is in any case phased to the late Iron Age/early Roman period.

Four context groups from gullies (13, 14, 16 and 39) are assigned to the middle Iron Age phase. These produced eight sherds (132g) of pottery in sand-tempered, limestone-tempered and a fabric with undiagnostic voids and sand inclusions, as well as a small fragment (2g) of late Iron Age/early Roman fabric E80. Phase 3 context groups, all from ditches, produced a further seven Iron Age sherds (78g) and 37 (332g) late Iron Age/early Roman sherds, all but two in fabric E80. Overall, with the possible exception of the fabric LA4 sherd in context 7, the material suggests a fairly tight date range from the later part of the middle Iron Age up to about the middle of the 1st century AD. The physical overlap of 'middle' and 'late' Iron Age traditions might suggest their contemporaneous existence, but there is insufficient material to

demonstrate this conclusively. There is no 'Roman' pottery at all.

Illustrated vessels (Fig. 3.11)

165.   LVA4/5. Type CB barrel-shaped jar. Ctx 13, penannular gully 29, Phase 2.
166.   LA4. Type CB barrel-shaped jar with external sooting. Ctx 27, ditch 45, Phase 3.
167.   E80. Type CE high-shouldered jar with internal burnt residue. Ctx 6, ditch 44, Phase 3.

South of Oddington Crossing

The assemblage totalled 25 sherds weighing 186g (MSW 7.4g) from 7 context groups, of which two were phased to the middle Iron Age, four to the early Roman period (Phase 5) and one was unphased. The principal middle Iron Age group (ditch fill context 14) contained 18 sherds (125g) in sand-tempered and limestone-tempered fabrics, with two rims (Fig. 3.11, nos 168 and 169), while the other context assigned to the middle Iron Age (pit fill 108), produced a single late Iron Age/early Roman base sherd in fabric E80. A further rim sherd in this fabric, and four small middle Iron Age sherds (22g) came from ditch fills assigned to the early Roman period. The only later sherd, unphased, was a tiny fragment (1g) in fabric R10. Overall, the pottery suggests a later middle Iron Age to late Iron Age/early Roman date range, but beyond this the group is too small for meaningful comment.

Illustrated vessels (Fig. 3.11)

168. LS5. Jar. Ctx 14, ditch 153, Phase 2.
169. AS3. Globular bowl, burnished overall externally and with oblique and vertical fine incised line decoration. Ctx 14, ditch 153, Phase 2.

North of Gallos Brook

The assemblage comprises 279 sherds weighing 3,815g (MSW 13.7g) from 23 context groups. The pottery is almost entirely later prehistoric (middle Iron Age), despite the fact that six context groups are assigned to Phase 3 and a further three groups to Phase 5; late Iron Age and Roman fabrics together account for only 10 sherds (74g). Quantification of the pottery by phase is given in Table 3.16.

The later phase groups are too small to allow assessment of possible sequences in the currency of particular Iron Age fabric groups. Overall, 14 vessels in these fabrics were represented by rim sherds, with a total RE value of 1.28. All were from jars, but only two were from vessels assigned to the generic jar class, the majority being assigned to specific sub-classes, CB (barrel-shaped jars) and CH (bead rim jars), amounting to 0.78 and 0.33 REs respectively. The CH jar is generally thought of as a later Iron Age type, but that cannot be pressed too far here as the rims in question were not particularly pronounced. Nevertheless, both types appeared in contexts of Phase 2 as well as Phase 3, possibly, but not necessarily, suggesting a relatively condensed chronological span for the assemblage as a whole. A fabric E80 rim sherd from Phase 3 was also of type CH, and the only rim in Phase 5 was from a narrow-mouthed (type CC) jar in fabric R20.

Illustrated vessels (Fig. 3.11)

Phase 2
170. VAL4. Type CB jar with carbonised material on interior. Ctx 31, penannular gully 110.
171. LVA4. Type CB jar. Ctx 101, ditch 265.
172. LN4. Type CB jar, burnished on the upper body and top of rim. Ctx 220, ditch 265.
173. LS5. Type C jar. Ctx 102, ditch 265.
174. LAV4. Type CH jar with notched, slightly beaded rim. Ctx 31, penannular gully 110.

Phase 3
175. LAV4. Type CB jar, burnished on shoulder. Ctx 75, ditch 113.
176. LSVA4. Type CB jar. Ctx 75, ditch 113.
177. LS5. Type CB jar with carbonised material on interior. Ctx 199, ditch 113.

Table 3.16 Quantification of pottery fabrics from North of Gallos Brook by phase

Fabric	Phase 2 No. sh.	Phase 2 Wt (g)	Phase 3 No. sh.	Phase 3 Wt (g)	Phase 5 No. sh.	Phase 5 Wt (g)	Total No. sh.	Total Wt (g)
A1	12	41					12	41
A5	10	23					10	23
A6	47	661	3	8			50	669
A9	5	31	5	75	2	2	12	108
L1	12	262	1	3			13	265
L2	19	200	5	48			24	248
L3	2	12					2	12
L5	61	741	13	280			74	1021
L6	31	682	1	7			32	689
S2			2	8			2	8
S6			1	25			1	25
V2	16	213	1	16			17	229
V4	20	393					20	393
S30 **LEZ SA 2**					1	2	1	2
E30					1	17	1	17
E80 **SOB GT**			2	36			2	26
O10					1	2	1	2
O30			1	1			1	1
R10					1	14	1	14
R20			1	7	1	4	2	11
R30					1	1	1	1
Total	235	3259	36	514	8	42	279	3805

North of Oxford Parkway Station

This site produced 593 sherds weighing 9,676g (MSW 16.3g), with a total of 12.12 REs, from 73 context groups. The material is almost entirely of later 1st-2nd century date, with the majority of contexts and pottery assigned to Phase 6 and only three context groups assigned to Phase 7, after AD 240. Basic quantification of fabrics by site phase is given in Table 3.17.

Contexts assigned to Phase 5 included 3224, a fill of ditch 3223, which produced six sherds, of which three were samian ware representing two vessels of form Dr 38, one Central Gaulish and one East Gaulish. These, the only samian ware sherds in the phase assemblage, clearly post-date the Phase 5 range and this group must have accumulated in the fill of the ditch in the course of Phase 6. The two vessels contributed 0.48 of the phase RE total of 1.15, the remainder consisting of jars in a variety of fabrics and a single dish in fabric R10. Both this and the Phase 6 assemblage included a 'background noise' of redeposited middle Iron Age and late Iron Age/early Roman pottery. E wares amounted to

Table 3.17 Quantification of pottery fabrics from North of Oxford Parkway Station by phase

Fabric	Phase 5		Phase 6		Phase 7		Post-Roman and unphased		Total	
	No. sh.	Wt (g)	No. sh.	Wt (g)	No. sh.	Wt (g)	No. sh.	Wt (g)	No. sh.	Wt (g)
A8			1	7					1	7
A9	1	14							1	14
V2			1	14					1	14
Z1			12	33			6	16	18	49
Z2			2	9					2	9
S20 **LGF SA**			5	72					5	72
S30 **LEZ SA 2**	1	34	2	28					3	62
S32 **LMV SA**			2	15					2	15
S41 **RHZ SA**	2	76							2	76
FO			1	4					1	4
M22 **OXF WH**					1	22			1	22
W10			3	53					3	53
W20	3	36	25	569					28	605
W21 **VER WH**			9	139					9	139
Q21 **OXF WS**			1	29					1	29
E20			2	7					2	7
E30	3	71	8	52					11	123
E80 **SOB GT**	14	126	22	237					36	363
O10			22	220	22	191	1	1	45	412
O11			3	7					3	7
O20			1	5	1	4	1	2	3	11
O30			5	86	1	8			6	94
O37F			2	9					2	9
O80			10	437					10	437
R10	10	77	61	697	2	9			73	783
R11 **OXF FR**			7	90					7	90
R20	1	57	55	1232			1	8	57	1297
R29			2	30					2	30
R30	3	25	18	154			2	9	23	188
R37	1	63	25	536					26	599
R37F	6	61	62	739	7	155			67	848
R38			27	411					27	411
R38F	2	11	3	26					5	37
R50	6	138	1	13	2	119			9	270
R60	1	2	5	68					6	70
R90	11	255	11	458					22	713
R94			1	6					1	6
R95 **SAV GT**	1	41	1	35					2	76
R96	3	19	31	1270			1	4	35	1293
B11 **DOR BB 1**			21	158	6	67			27	225
Total	69	1106	470	7955	42	575	12	40	585	9569

8.3% of the total sherds from the site (including middle Iron Age material), but only 5.1% by weight. In view of the generally enhanced importance of these wares in contemporary contexts, particularly at Langford Lane East, these figures suggest that while there may have been occupation in the vicinity around the middle of the 1st century it was not located within the excavated area.

The Phase 6 assemblage was dominated by reduced coarse wares, amounting to 66% of sherds (72.5% of weight and 74.6% of REs). Amongst the reduced wares fabrics R10 and R20 are important, as usual, but collectively the contribution of fabrics assigned to the 'West Oxfordshire' industry (R37, R37F, R38, R38F and R96) is notable – all these fabrics except R37 being significantly better represented in percentage terms here than at other sites on EWR Phase 1. The reason for this is not clear; the fact that this site is marginally the closest of the sites to the probable source area of these fabrics does not seem an adequate explanation. The fine and specialist ware component in the Phase 6 assemblage, amounting to *c* 10% of the total sherds, consisted largely of white wares with a smaller quantity of samian ware. The white wares included a complete rim of the relatively uncommon Oxford flagon type W30 (Fig. 3.12, no. 181), which contributed to the enhanced representation of flagons in this phase (12.3% of REs, but only two out of 56 vessels counted by rim sherds). Jars, however, the principal vessel class, were almost identically represented by both measures, amounting to 62.9% of REs. Next most important were bowls, totalling 14.4% of REs, though the number of vessels involved was relatively small. They included carinated bowls (Young 1977, type R57) in reduced fabric R10 (Fig. 3.12, nos 186 and 187) and rounded bowls in fine and coarse sandy white wares (Fig. 3.12, nos 188 and 189 respectively).

The Phase 7 assemblage was very small. Its principal component in terms of sherd count was fabric O10, which also contributed four of the eight vessels represented by rim sherds (three jars and a jar/bowl), one of which (Fig. 3.12, no. 192) was of a form typical of the later Roman period. Other later Roman ceramic markers were an Oxford mortarium – the only such sherd from the site – of Young (1977)

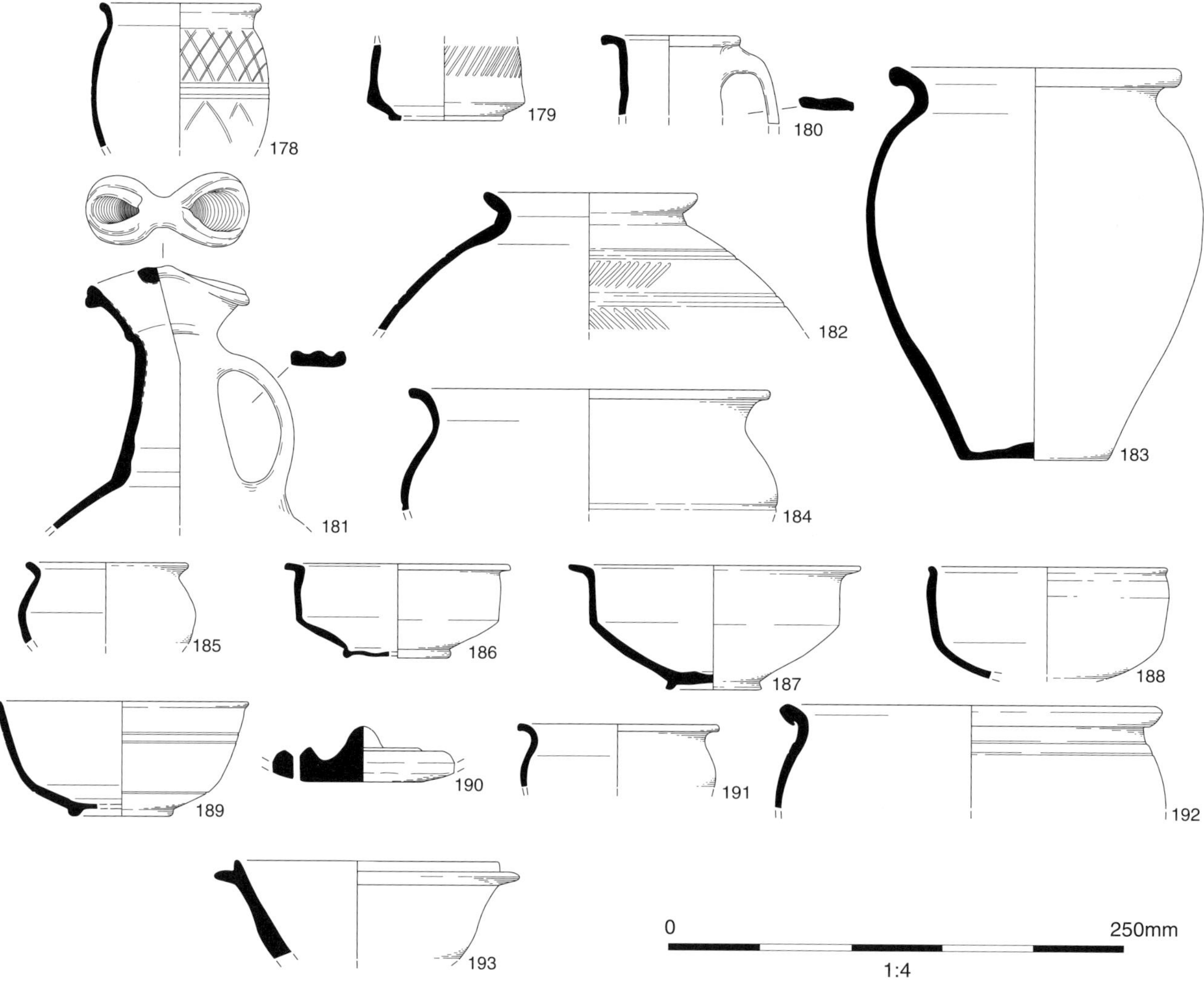

Fig. 3.12   Pottery from North of Oxford Parkway Station, nos 178-93

type M17, a bead and flanged bowl in fabric R50 (Fig. 3.12, no. 193) and a reasonable amount of Dorset fabric B11 including a straight-sided dish, a form not necessarily later than the end of the 2nd century, but particularly characteristic of the mid-3rd to 4th centuries.

A higher proportion of black-burnished ware (4.6% of sherds, but only half that by weight) was one characteristic of the site compared with others in this project. By contrast, shell-tempered (C10) fabrics were completely absent – this being the only one of the larger site assemblages where this was the case. In the middling fine and specialist ware assemblage, dominated by white wares, the total absence of amphora sherds is also notable, while only one of the 12 samian ware sherds (a body sherd of Dr 30) was decorated, and mortaria were also absent before the arrival of the single attested example in the mid-3rd century or later.

Illustrated vessels (Fig. 3.12)

Phase 5
178. R10. Type CK jar with girth groove and acute angled burnished lattice decoration. Ctx 3270, ditch 3322.
179. R30. Lower part of possible type FD carinated cup, with oblique burnished line decoration. Ctx 3277, ditch 3317.

Phase 6
180. R20. Flagon with flat flanged rim. Ctx 3111, pit 3114.
181. W20. Flagon with figure of eight mouth (Young 1977, type W30). Ctx 3106, ditch 3077.
182. R20. Type CC jar, with groove on shoulder and oblique burnished line decoration. Ctx 3113, pit 3114.
183. R96. Type CD jar. Ctx 3109, pit 3114.
184. R11. Type CD jar with girth groove. Ctx 3122, pit 3114.
185. R30. Type EH beaker (or small jar), worn and with external sooting. Ctx 3241, ditch 3095.
186. R10. Type HA carinated bowl (Young 1977, type R57). Ctx 3272, ditch 3096.
187. R10. Type HA carinated bowl (Young 1977, type R57), as above, but larger. Ctx 3164, ditch 3096.
188. W10. Type HC rounded bowl. Ctx 3220, gully 3210.
189. W20. Type HC rounded bowl with multiple grooves. Burnt. Ctx 3108 and 3109, pit 3114.
190. R10. Base of type MF, cheese press. Ctx 3111, pit 3114.

Phase 7
191. O30. Type CD small jar. Ctx 3149, ditch 3147.
192. O10. Type CD jar with groove and cordon at base of neck. Ctx 3183, ditch 3056.
193. R50. Type HB straight-sided bead and flange rimmed bowl. Ctx 3013, ditch 3056.

Discussion

The assemblages were very variable in size; only those from the two Langford Lane sites, that is, those closest to Alchester, were of sufficient size for detailed conclusions to have a chance of being statistically reliable. Even these assemblages were only of modest size compared to some reported from the region. For the other sites, broader assessments are possible, but in the case of the three Oddington assemblages, essentially of middle or middle to late Iron Age date, their very small size precludes discussion beyond questions of basic chronology. Late prehistoric and Roman pottery assemblage sizes from across the region have been listed recently (Booth 2018, table 7.29) and this is not repeated here, but some local assemblages are summarised for comparative purposes in Table 3.18, though not all have usable published data (eg Hughes 1984).

For the sites from the present project, quantification of the pottery by site phase as a percentage of each site total is summarised in Tables 3.19 and 3.20, using data for sherd count and weight respectively.

The assemblages show a variety of date ranges within the later prehistoric and Roman periods, the most striking overall characteristic being the significant lack of later Roman material (except, in relative terms, at Holts Farm Crossing). Significant prehistoric activity is not attested ceramically before the middle Iron Age, beginning perhaps *c* 350 BC. Middle and late Iron Age pottery dominates the three small assemblages from Oddington and is also a significant component at Holts Farm Crossing, the only site that appears to show a sequence of activity from the middle Iron Age through much of the Roman period, although it is not certain if this activity was continuous throughout that chronological range. A function of the phasing scheme adopted for the overall project is that Phase 4 was used specifically for those sites adjacent to the

Table 3.18 Quantities of reported later prehistoric and Roman pottery from Bicester sites

Site	Principal date range	No. sherds	Weight (g)	REs	Reference
Alchester, A421	MIA-EAS, most RB	36,807	546,074	570.13	Evans 2001a
Faccenda Chicken Farm	Late 1C-2C	2229			Hughes 1984
Bicester, Slade Farm	(EIA)-MIA-LIA	2480	16,192		Woodward and Marley 2000
Bicester, Oxford Road	LIA-ERB	1124	16,227	15.21	Booth 1996
Bicester, Fields Farm	(MIA)-LIA	3757	23,083	20.04	Brown 1999
Bicester Park	Late 1-3C	2081	19,185	21.33	Timby 2008
Bicester, Whitelands Farm	Late Pre-RB	3039	33,753	24.43	Brown 2011*

*The report deals with less than 40% of the pottery recovered

Table 3.19 Numbers of late prehistoric and Roman sherds from all sites by phase (row %)

| | Iron Age | | Late Iron Age-Roman | | | | | Post-Roman | Unphased | |
Site	2	3	4	5	6	7	Total IARB phased sherds	8-9	0	Total sherds
Langford Lane East		5.9	43.4	15.7	34.7	0.4	3864	94	323	4281
Langford Lane South		0.1	3.8	21.2	73.9	0.9	2947	131	174	3252
South of Merton					100.0		640	172	23	835
Holts Farm Crossing	14.0	12.3		5.3	33.5	34.9	1517	68	10	1595
East of Oddington Grange	17.0	83.0					53			53
South of Oddington Crossing	79.2			20.8			24		1	25
North of Gallos Brook	84.2	12.9		2.9			279			279
North of Oxford Parkway Station				11.9	80.9	7.2	581	2	10	593
Total							9905			10,913

Table 3.20 Weight of late prehistoric and Roman pottery from all sites by phase (row %)

| | Iron Age | | Late Iron Age-Roman | | | | | Post-Roman | Unphased | |
Site	2	3	4	5	6	7	Total IA and RB phased weight	8-9	0	Total sherds
Langford Lane East		8.8	61.6	10.4	16.6	0.3	69,585	1802	3814	75,201
Langford Lane South		0.1	6.3	17.8	74.8	1.0	34,414	1840	2092	38,346
South of Merton					100.0		8893	1415	188	10,496
Holts Farm Crossing	10.0	17.5		5.4	27.3	39.7	15,386	654	148	16,188
East of Oddington Grange	19.8	80.2					511			511
South of Oddington Crossing	80.5			19.5			185		1	186
North of Gallos Brook	85.4	13.5		1.1			3815			3815
North of Oxford Parkway Station				11.5	82.6	6.0	9636	3	37	9676
Total							142,425			154,419

known major focus of early Roman military activity at Alchester. The absence of material attributed to this phase in some of the other sites in this project does not necessarily mean that there was no activity in the period roughly from AD 40-70, though it is possible that this was the case in some instances. Holts Farm Crossing might in fact be one such case, where the quantity of pottery assigned to Phase 5 is so small, in relative terms, that it might indicate a discontinuity in the occupation sequence after Phase 3. Elsewhere the relevant quantities are so small that meaningful assessment of issues of continuity or discontinuity is not possible.

For the larger assemblages and for other sites in the vicinity of Alchester, however, the question is a very important one. To what extent and in what ways, if at all, were occupation sequences impacted or disrupted by the arrival of a substantial military force shortly after AD 43? The pottery, of course, is not capable of very precise chronological definition (and a hiatus of five or ten years in occupation sequences in the middle of the 1st century would not be detectable from pottery evidence, although

longer breaks could be) but it can provide pointers, particularly when it is considered that the regional trend, mainly based on evidence from the Upper Thames Valley, is for both site stratigraphic sequences and ceramics to indicate continuity of activity through the middle of the 1st century AD, that is to say through the equivalent of Phases 3-5 here. On this basis, the fact that in the Bicester area sites in the present project at East of Oddington Grange and North of Gallos Brook, and elsewhere at Slade Farm, have sequences that terminate in the (ceramic) late Iron Age, while at Holts Farm Crossing amongst the sites in the present project, and also at Bicester Fields Farm just to the east, the sequences indicate hiatus or (in the latter case) complete reconfiguration at this time, suggests a fairly major impact on these sites. Caution is necessary – it is not possible to demonstrate that these site sequence closures or interruptions were synchronous, much less to be able to attribute them to an individual event or events, or to link these directly with the presence of the Roman army, but the possibility of a connection must be considered and in the absence of other evidence must be one of the more likely causal factors.

Whatever the explanation of these developments in site occupation sequences, a useful side effect is to limit the problems of extensive cross-period redeposition and assemblage mixing found in long continuous occupation sequences. The middle Iron Age assemblages are therefore fairly clearly defined, though for the most part too small for detailed analysis and comparison with larger contemporary groups from the area, such as that from Slade Farm (Woodward and Marley 2000), or even that from the 1991 A421 excavations, which produced more middle Iron Age pottery than all the EWR Phase 1 sites combined (816 sherds; Evans and Booth 2001, 270).

While local provenance is likely for most if not all of the middle Iron Age pottery in the area, variation in the relative importance of different tempering traditions is observable from site to site. At Slade Farm and on the A421, for example, shelly lime-stone tempering was particularly prominent (cf. eg fabrics L1-L6 here), a pattern seen in the assemblage from North of Gallos Brook but less clearly elsewhere. Fabrics tempered principally with sand (also fairly prominent at North of Gallos Brook) or organic inclusions (again found at North of Gallos Brook but more important at Holts Farm Crossing) were rather less common a little further north in the A421 and Slade Farm assemblages. While sand-tempered fabrics were well represented at Bicester Fields Farm (where they were, however, less common than shell-tempered fabrics), organic-tempered fabrics were entirely absent at that site (Brown 1999, 184). This last characteristic might be a chronological indicator, given that the emphasis of the Bicester Fields Farm assemblage is very much on the late Iron Age, but this is not certain. Elsewhere it was suggested that chronological trends in use of particular fabric traditions were not discernible (eg Evans and Booth 2001, 271); for the most part the present assemblages are too small to allow identification of such trends.

It is clear that the late Iron Age assemblages of the area are very heavily dominated by grog-tempered fabrics. Vessels in these fabrics can be handmade or wheel thrown, though the latter is more common (eg Woodward and Marley 2000, 248). Antecedents of the classic 'Belgic type' grog-tempered wares seem to be present in the middle Iron Age assemblages of the area, as seen in the group of fabrics defined here as G1-G3. It is notable that these occurred almost exclusively at Holts Farm Crossing and were completely absent at North of Gallos Brook (see Table 3.2). This does seem likely to be a genuine indicator of a slight distinction between the date ranges of the two sites, contexts of the late Iron Age/early Roman Phase 3 providing only a small proportion of the total assemblage at Gallos Brook, while at Holts Farm Crossing quantities of pottery assigned to Phases 2 (middle Iron Age) and 3 (late Iron Age) were broadly similar

(leaving to one side the point that if this site had been occupied throughout the middle Iron Age the quantity of pottery being deposited at any one time would on average have been significantly less than in the later period).

The other site assemblages (Langford Lane East, Langford Lane South, South of Merton and North of Oxford Parkway Station) are all effectively of Roman date, except that the largest one, from Langford Lane East, also includes a late Iron Age component and is notable for a heavy emphasis (in terms of numbers of context groups assigned) on activity of the 1st century AD. It is in this site in Phase 4 that the impact of the arrival of the Roman army should be most clearly discernible, but from a ceramic point of view the picture is more one of evolution than of radical transformation. The fine and specialist wares, for example, included pre-Flavian samian ware and amphora sherds, neither of which would be typical of a rural settlement in the region at this time, but the quantities are not remarkable, and the other component of the fine and specialist ware group, white wares, is the one most commonly found across sites of all types in the region in the 1st century. While the Phase 4 assemblage (with a total fine and specialist ware component of 7.5% of sherds) is therefore clearly different from what would be expected in a contemporary rural context, it does not carry hallmarks which necessarily identify military rather than generally higher status associations, though the latter could have been a direct consequence of the former.

Full publication of Eberhard Sauer's excavations at Alchester is still awaited, so we do not have a clear view of what constitutes a fully 'military' early Roman pottery assemblage in this region. If his characterisation of the site as a legionary, or at least vexillation, fortress is accepted, something akin to the earliest, directly contemporary, assemblages from Colchester might be expected. Unfortunately, the presentation of the Colchester pottery (Symonds and Wade 1999) does not allow the compilation of precise figures on a broad phase basis. However, in the fortress levels it seems clear that a large proportion of pottery in the early military phases (up to AD 49/55) was of 'non-native' character – perhaps *c* 98% of the coarse wares were of oxidised and reduced wares, used for vessel types of which many 'were introduced by Continental potters following the conquest' (Bidwell 1999, 493). In combination with a range of imported fine and specialist wares these would have presented a very distinctive assemblage. What is seen at Langford Lane East in Phase 4 is of very different character. This could, of course, simply reflect the difference between pottery supply, consumption and discard within the fortress and that in a civilian context, however closely contemporary and adjacent. However, preliminary characterisation of the pottery from Sauer's excavations (Cooper 2000) suggests something rather similar to what is seen at Langford Lane East, although the extent of the dominance of the 'Belgic type' (E80) fabrics is not clear. The 'smaller proportion of imported fine and specialist wares' included 'amphorae, mortaria, South Gaulish samian and other colour-coats such as Lyon ware. The general character is therefore similar to other pre-Flavian military assemblages' (Cooper 2000, 57). Cooper's specific comparison, however, is with a Cirencester assemblage dated *c* AD 55-65, substantially dominated (67.5% of minimum number of vessels) by imported material (Cooper 1998, 325-327), a pattern that seems more like that suggested for Colchester than what is implied in the Alchester summary. Is it possible that an assemblage derived essentially from contexts in the fortress annexe at Alchester could have differed markedly from that to be expected within the fortress itself? Alternatively, was the pattern of pottery supply at Alchester radically different from that suggested for the early post-conquest period at Colchester (or in a marginally later chronological horizon in western England), or is it in fact the case that the character of the early military phase at Alchester was not as Sauer has suggested so far? Might an interpretation involving different types of military unit, for example, result in a rather different sort of pottery assemblage (though such differences are not clearly suggested by the Colchester and Cirencester comparison)? These questions cannot be resolved at present, but are directly relevant to understanding of the earliest phase of Roman activity at Langford Lane East. Even so, the Phase 4 pottery from that site does not suggest a very close connection with nearby military activity.

The much smaller Phase 4 assemblage from Langford Lane South is effectively a miniature version of the Langford Lane East group, and adds almost nothing to this discussion, though this site did produce the occasional vessel (eg Fig 3.7, no. 93) which would have been more readily at home in a military context than elsewhere at this time, albeit that it was found in a Phase 6 context. Activity at Langford Lane South, however, did not really get under way until the Flavian period, and a large majority of the pottery came from contexts assigned to Phase 6. This emphasis on 2nd-early 3rd century occupation is seen very clearly at North of Oxford Parkway Station and particularly at South of Merton, where Roman period activity was confined to this phase. Phase 6 also saw relatively intense activity at sites with longer overall occupation spans, Langford Lane East and Holts Farm Crossing. Overall, the character of activity in the preceding Phase 5 is less well defined and so a little difficult to judge from the pottery evidence. On the basis of the trajectories shown in Tables 3.19 and 3.20 it can be characterised as 'early stages of development' at Langford Lane South and North of Oxford Parkway Station, and perhaps 'reconfiguration and adjustment' as a consequence of interruptions related to the phase of military intervention at Langford Lane East and particularly at Holts Farm Crossing, where there may have been a hiatus in the occupation sequence, at least insofar as the latter was reflected in deposition of pottery.

With the possible exception of Phase 4 at Langford Lane East, Phase 6 then sees the peak of levels of activity at all the sites in this project that were occupied in the Roman period. This is unremarkable in itself, but a direct comparison of the Phase 6 assemblages from the five sites with occupation of this period is worthwhile. The summary data are presented in Tables 3.21 and 3.22

The data indicate considerable differences between the individual sites. While the cause of

Table 3.21 Summary quantification of fabrics from Phase 6 (middle Roman) assemblages (column % of total RB)

Fabric	Langford Lane East		Langford Lane South		South of Merton		Holts Farm Crossing		North of Oxford Parkway Station		Total			
	No. sh.	Wt (g)	No. sh.	Wt (g)	No. sh.	Wt (g)	No. sh.	Wt (g)	No. sh.	Wt (g)	No. sh.	%No. sh.	Wt (g)	%Wt
S subt	2.5	2.5	6.7	8.6	0.6	0.8	1.6	1.0	2.0	1.5	198	3.9	2741	4.7
F subt	0.1	+	0.7	0.3					0.2	0.1	18	0.4	80	0.1
A subt	0.4	4.3	0.3	4.3							13	0.3	1644	2.8
M subt	1.4	4.9	0.4	2.5	1.9	24.7	1.4	4.5			46	0.9	3625	6.2
W subt	1.8	1.5	5.2	4.6	4.4	2.8	1.2	2.6	8.1	9.6	209	4.2	2493	4.2
Q subt	0.1	+	6.4	3.8	0.3	0.3	0.2	0.2	0.2	0.4	144	2.9	1025	1.7
F and S subtotal	**6.4**	**13.2**	**19.7**	**24.1**	**7.2**	**28.6**	**4.4**	**8.5**	**10.6**	**11.5**	**628**	**12.5**	**11,608**	**19.7**
E subt	14.3	21.0	1.0	1.9	1.1	0.6	10.6	9.1	7.0	3.8	298	5.9	3829	6.5
O subt	3.9	2.9	17.2	14.9	25.4	22.2	39.0	29.7	9.5	9.7	798	15.9	8068	13.7
R subt	71.4	60.6	54.0	51.9	60.6	44.5	26.8	37.6	68.3	72.5	2935	58.5	32,081	54.5
B11	1.9	1.0	3.0	2.7	0.5	0.2	1.8	1.4	4.5	2.0	121	2.4	1052	1.8
C10	2.1	1.3	5.1	4.5	4.4	3.9	17.3	13.8			241	4.8	2204	3.7
Total RB	1339	12,612	2158	25,595	637	8880	433	3863	454	7892	5021		58,842	
Total including Iron Age	1339	12,612	2159	25,617	640	8893	508	4203	470	7955	5116		59,280	

+ less than 0.1%

Table 3.22 Summary quantification of vessel classes from Phase 6 (middle Roman) assemblages (column %)

Type	Langford Lane East	Langford Lane South	Site South of Merton	Holts Farm Crossing	North of Oxford Parkway Station	Total REs	%REs
A Amphorae		0.4				0.14	0.2
B Flagons	3.4	18.9	10.9	8.5	12.5	9.95	13.2
C Jars	45.7	35.7	39.5	71.5	62.6	33.19	44.1
D Jars/bowls	3.3	2.3	2.4	1.0	1.5	1.73	2.3
E Beakers	13.3	6.0	11.4	4.7	3.5	5.83	7.7
F Cups	4.9	6.2	1.3	1.0	0.7	3.30	4.4
H Bowls	2.8	11.9	7.3	3.7	14.6	6.99	9.3
I Bowls/dishes	11.3	4.7	1.4	2.2	1.0	3.68	4.9
J Dishes	11.9	12.3	13.6	3.7	3.5	7.93	10.5
K Mortaria	2.0	0.6	12.3	1.0		1.80	2.4
L Lids	0.8	1.3		2.6		0.70	0.9
M Miscellaneous		*			*		
Z Uncertain	0.6					0.09	0.1
Total	14.93	35.45	10.11	4.92	9.92	75.33	

* Type present but not represented by rim sherd(s)

some of these differences may lie in the small size of some of the phase groups this does not seem to be the only explanation. Some of the patterning is quite curious. For example, the Phase 6 assemblage at Holts Farm Crossing has the highest percentage of jars – a conservative characteristic, but a remarkably low percentage of the reduced fabrics in which jars would most typically occur. Except at this site reduced wares always form more than half of the assemblages by sherd count, the figures ranging from 54% at Langford Lane South to 71.4% at nearby Langford Lane East. With the exception, once again, of Holts Farm Crossing, it is notable that Langford Lane East has the lowest fine and specialist ware representation of all in this phase (by sherd count – fine and specialist ware representation by weight is generally rather higher, boosted by contributions from amphorae and mortaria), despite the presence of stone-founded structures in a roadside setting. In other respects, the Langford Lane East assemblage appears more 'mainstream', with affinities to Langford Lane South and South of Merton. Langford Lane South, however, does stand out from the other Phase 6 sites in a number of ways, and the fact that this is the largest assemblage of this phase encourages a degree of confidence in interpretation of its distinctive character. A relatively low percentage of reduced wares corresponds with much the highest representation of fine and specialist wares (19.7% by sherd count) of any of these sites (the anomalously high fine and specialist ware weight total at South of Merton being accounted for by a very small number of mortarium sherds). These characteristics are underlined by the data for vessel classes present. Langford Lane South has a distinctly low percentage of jars and correspondingly high percentages of what can loosely be termed table

wares (vessels associated with presentation and serving of liquids, and a range of bowl and dish types, see further below), which account for over 60% of the phase assemblage. Interestingly, these figures are most nearly approached in the assemblage from South of Merton (once the anomalous representation of mortaria is factored out), although in these terms Langford Lane East is not far behind. North of Oxford Parkway Station and Holts Farm Crossing have higher percentages of jars. Despite the curiously low percentage of reduced wares, noted above, Holts Farm Crossing is consistent in its correlation of low fine and specialist ware value and relatively low level of diversity in vessels present.

It is particularly noteworthy that only at Holts Farm Crossing does occupation continue on any scale into the later Roman period. This assessment is based on the relative frequency of Phase 7 pottery in this site, but (as noted above) the material derived from a very small number of contexts, and mostly from the uppermost fill of a single feature, waterhole 8617. The unusual prominence of oxidised wares, seen in Phase 6, was enhanced in this phase, but otherwise the progression from Phase 6 to Phase 7 assemblages followed established regional trends, with a significant increase in the level of fine and specialist wares reflecting the growth of the late Roman Oxford industry, particularly marked by the appearance of colour-coated fabric F51, and a decline in the percentage of jars, albeit that these still dominated the assemblage (and that the decline was fairly modest once the distorting effect of high mortarium RE values is factored out). The Oxford products provide the best (but imperfect) means of assessing the date of the end of occupation. The types present (listed in the site-specific discussion) do not include examples with a solely 4th-century or later 4th-century date range, but there are relatively few such forms in the Oxford repertoire so their absence in a small assemblage need not be significant. It is notable, however, that the mortaria are mostly of type M18 (or M17/M18), dated AD 240-300, with only one example of type M22 which, although dated from AD 240 onwards, becomes the principal white ware mortarium type in the 4th century. Amongst the coarse wares two bowls (eg Fig. 3.10, no. 158 in fabric R20) were of characteristic late Roman bead and flanged type. Overall the evidence suggests activity perhaps into the early 4th century, but not necessarily extending beyond that time (a complete absence of any coinage, including even the very common issues of the 330s onwards, might be significant here).

Overall, it is unfortunate that none of the sites has a sequence of phase assemblages that are large enough to allow development of assemblages to be traced throughout the Roman period. The character of the late Iron Age (Phase 3) assemblages is clear, while Phase 4 is effectively represented only at Langford Lane East, where proximity to and contemporaneity with large-scale early Roman military activity will have affected the composition of the assemblage, even if this was in ways that are not clear. The lack of a substantial Phase 5 assemblage across the sites is a major problem, though this very absence is probably significant in terms of the way that sites were developing subsequent to the military phase and coincident with the earliest development of the major civilian settlement at Alchester. It is presumably not coincidental that the clearest evidence for (relatively) intensive activity in the sites forming this project comes in Phase 6 at a time of (probable – given the lack of excavated evidence) equally intensive development within the town. The sites at Langford Lane East, Langford Lane South and South of Merton, all at least in part adjacent to Roman roads within a short distance of the town, show a broadly similar ceramic profile at this time that contrasts with that of the more distinctly rural settlements of Holts Farm Crossing and North of Oxford Parkway Station. Meanwhile, occupation at the three intervening Oddington sites had come to an end round about the time of the Roman conquest. Why later Roman settlement is only evident at Holts Farm Crossing, however, is an unresolved question.

The data from the EWR Phase 1 sites can be compared in various ways with evidence from elsewhere in the region, some of it from closely adjacent sites. An obvious chronological point is that at the 1991 A421 site (Booth *et al.* 2001), almost

Table 3.23 Proportions of fine and specialist wares in Upper Thames Valley sites by period: early Roman sites

Site	Site type	Date range	Total sherds	% Fine and spec
Old Shifford, early settlement	RS	1C	893	0.2
Hardwick/Yelford Smiths Field	RS	1C-early/mid 2C	3850	0.4
Thornhill Farm	RS	1C-early 2C	11,450	0.5
Gravelly Guy	RS	1C-early 2C	9444	0.6
Cotswold Community early Roman	RS	LIA-120/130	1577	c 1.5%
Bicester, Whitelands Farm	*RS*	*Most LIA-2C*	*2973*	*1.9*
Berinsfield Mount Farm	RS	1C-2C	2815	2.0
Watchfield Triangle	RS	Most1C-2C	1840	2.4
Hatford 1991	RS	1C-early/mid 2C	1756	2.5
Somerford Keynes Neigh Bridge	RS/shrine	1C-2C	10,174	2.5
Gill Mill all Period 3b	RS	70-120	2201	2.5
Yarnton LIR and ERB	RS	LIA-2C	4240	2.8
Gill Mill Area 13	RS	LIA-early/mid 2C	1906	3.3
Watchfield 1998	RS	Most 1C-2C	2954	3.5
Banbury Flood Alleviation Periods 3-4b	RS	1C-early/mid 2C	595	3.7
Gill Mill SLGM Area 6 Period 3a	RS	LIA-AD 70	526	3.8
Bicester, Oxford Road	*RS*	*1C-early 2C*	*1124*	*3.9*
Faringdon, Coxwell Road	RS	1C-2C	3144	4.1
Appleford Sidings	Proto-villa?	Mid 1C-early 2C	2862	4.2
Asthall Phases 2 and 3	MNS	Mid 1C-mid 2C	1049	6.5
Alchester (A421) Periods 1-4	*MNS*	*1C-early 2C*	*1673*	*7.5*
Ditches (Gloucestershire)	Villa	1C	3858	7.6
Didcot Great Western Park	RS	1C-early 2C	3001	8.2
Claydon Pike Phase 2	RS	1C-early 2C	4971	8.7
Langford Lane East Phases 3-5	**Military hinterland**	**LIA-early 2C**	**2511**	**9.8**
Combe	Villa	1-2C	3082	10.7

MNS - minor nucleated settlement; RS - rural settlement; EWR Phase 1 sites bold, other Bicester sites italicised exactly the same distance (*c* 550m) north of the walled town compared to Langford Lane South to the south. The occupation sequence involved a middle Iron Age phase, ditches related to the line of Akeman Street from roughly the middle of the 1st century AD onwards and then intensive occupation from the early/middle 2nd century right to the end of the Roman period (and perhaps beyond, though whether the early Saxon activity at this site was continuous with the late Roman sequence is a moot point). This site therefore presents a marked contrast with the EWR Phase 1 sites with regard to the later Roman period. Other sites in the area, however, may be more closely comparable in terms of an absence of late Roman activity. This is certainly the case at Oxford Road, where occupation probably ceased in the early 2nd century, while at Whitelands Farm activity was similarly mostly of the early Roman period. At Bicester Park, by contrast, the occupation sequence was essentially confined to the middle part of the Roman period.

These date ranges are reflected in the presentation of data in Tables 3.23-3.25 (derived in part from Booth 2018), showing fine and specialist ware values for a range of selected sites in the region (including local examples, where possible, shown in italics), to which the larger phase groups from the EWR Phase 1 sites (emphasised in bold) have been added and can be seen alongside contemporary groups. Issues of the correlation between quantities of fine and specialist wares and aspects of site status, related to perceptions of site character based on the excavated features, have been discussed elsewhere (eg Booth 2004; 2007b; 2018; see also Booth 2012a with specific reference to samian ware). These are not necessarily straightforward, and the nature of the perceived correlation seems to change over time. In the early Roman period, however, it appears to be most clearly defined in terms of social status. Had the Oddington sites (East of Oddington Grange, South of Oddington Crossing and North of Gallos Brook) been occupied into the early Roman period it can be speculated that they would have grouped with the rural settlements at the top of Table 3.23. The only site from this project for which the assemblage is sufficiently large to allow inclusion within this table (generally a minimum phase sherd total of about 500 is preferred, though not all the EWR Phase 1 sites quite match this) is Langford Lane East, the character of which is of course strongly influenced by external factors relating to the early military phase at Alchester. Unsurprisingly therefore, this site ranks highly amongst the broadly contemporary sites from the region, but is not outstanding. The Phase 6 assemblages discussed above are interestingly spread through the range of comparative sites. As anticipated, Holts Farm Crossing groups with sites towards the bottom end of the range of fine and specialist ware representation. Interestingly, Langford Lane East and South of Merton fall in the middle part of the range, in a group of sites mainly comprising (broadly lower status) rural settlements, despite being more distinctive in respect of their vessel class breakdown. In terms of fine and specialist ware representation, North of Oxford Parkway Station ranks rather above these two, though this small phase assemblage may have been skewed by an abnormally high percentage of white wares (in contrast with some of the other assemblages, the white wares here have not been discounted from the fine and specialist component of the assemblage because they are clearly associated with flagons and other forms rather than jars, as discussed above). By contrast, the Phase 6 assemblage from Langford Lane South stands out against the comparative groups. As already indicated, its size suggests that indications of unusual character can probably be taken at face value – and those based on the fine and specialist ware figure are supported by the vessel class analysis as well. The EWR Phase 1 sites only include one late Roman assemblage. As in the middle Roman period, the fine and specialist ware value for Holts Farm Crossing still groups with a cluster of sites in the lower half of the range of values, but not at the bottom of that range. It is apparent that these sites are a more diverse group than earlier and that fine and specialist ware repre-

Comment	Reference
	Timby 1995
	Booth 2004
	Timby 2004
	Green *et al.* 2004
	Biddulph 2010
Excludes 2.2% obvious late Roman fabrics	*Brown 2011*
	Brown 2010
	Biddulph 2004
Excludes F51 and 2.2% W20	Booth 2000b
	Brown 2007a
Excludes 3.3% W20	Booth and Simmonds 2018
	Booth 2011a
Excludes 1.6% W20	Booth and Simmonds 2018
	Laidlaw 2001
Excludes 2% coarse W50	Booth 2014
Excludes 1.7% W20	Booth and Simmonds 2018
	Booth 1996
	Bryan and Brown 2004
Excludes 3% W20	Booth 2009
	Booth 1997
	Evans 2001a
	Trow *et al.* 2009
Excludes 1.8% W20	Booth forthcoming c
	Green and Booth 2007
	Booth 2012b

Table 3.24 Proportions of fine and specialist wares in Upper Thames Valley sites by period: middle Roman sites

Site	Site type	Date range	Total sherds	% Fine and spec
Latton Lands	RS	Most 2C-early 3C	3716	2.8
Kempsford Stubbs Farm	RS	Most 2C	906	3.3
Cotswold Community middle Roman	RS	120/130-250/260	3777	c 4.0
Holts Farm Crossing Phase 6	**RS**	**Early 2C-early 3C**	**433**	**4.4**
Birdlip Quarry Period 1	MNS?	Late 2C-mid 3C	1098	5.1
Horcott Totterdown Lane Phases 4 and 5	RS	2C-3C	7230	5.1
Tubney Wood	RS	2C	2117	5.3
Langford Lane East Phase 6	**MNS**	**Early 2C-early 3C**	**1339**	**6.4**
Horcott Quarry	RS	Most 2C-3C	2825	6.7
Bicester, Bicester Park	*RS*	*Most mid/late 2C-3C*	*2081*	*6.9*
South of Merton Phase 6	**RS**	**Early 2C-early 3C**	**637**	**7.2**
Banbury Flood Alleviation Periods 4c-4d	RS	Early/mid 2C-early 3C	1131	7.3
Roughground Farm 1990	Villa	Early 2C-early 3C	517	7.5
Alchester (A421) Periods 5-6	MNS	Early 2C-mid 3C	8386	7.6
Kempsford Arkells Land	RS	2C-3C	10,141	8.7
Gill Mill all Period 4a	RS and MNS	120-250	10,661	9.3
North of Oxford Parkway Phase 6	**RS**	**Early 2C-early 3C**	**454**	**10.6**
Didcot Great Western Park	RS	120-250	1918	10.8
Wantage Mill Street Period 2	MNS	Most mid 2C-mid 3C	669	11.5
Whelford Bowmore	RS?	Most 2C	3364	11.5
Asthall Phases 3/5, 4, 4/5 and 5	MNS	Mid 2C-3C	4825	13.9
Claydon Pike Phase 3	Estate centre	Early 2C-early 4C	12,984	15.0
Langford Lane South	**MNS?**	**Early 2C-early 3C**	**2158**	**19.7**

MNS – minor nucleated settlement; RS – rural settlement; EWR Phase 1 sites bold, other Bicester sites italicised

Table 3.25 Proportions of fine and specialist wares in Upper Thames Valley sites by period: late Roman sites

Site	Site type	Date range	Total sherds	% Fine and spec
Yarnton LRB	RS	3C-4C	3090	7.2
Uffington Castle	RS	2C-4C	2658	9.5
Cotswold Community late Roman	RS	250/260-400	3326	c 10.0
Roughground Farm 1990	Villa	Mid 3C-4C	1641	11.0
Birdlip Quarry Periods 2 and 3	MNS	250-400	4165	14.4
Chilton	Villa	250-400	6319	15.3
Holts Farm Crossing Phase 7	**RS**	**Mid 3C-?early 4C**	**527**	**15.3**
Berinsfield Wally Corner	RS	Mid/late 2C-4C	2319	15.4
Asthall Phases 6 and 6/7	MNS	4C	4720	15.8
Old Shifford late settlement	RS	Most 4C	2686	17.5
Claydon Pike Phase 4	Villa	Early-late 4C	15,425	18.5
Gill Mill all Period 4b	MNS	250-370	44,784	19.0
Wantage Mill Street Period 3	MNS	Mid 3C-4C	494	19.4
Oxford, Mansfield College and New Chemistry Lab.	RS	Most late 2C-4C	2100	20.0
Alchester (A421) Periods 7-9	*MNS*	*Mid 3C-4C*	*20,175*	*20.8*
Roughground Farm East	RS/villa	Late 2C-4C	5599	24.6
Wantage, Denchworth Road Periods 3 and 4	MNS?	Mid 3C-4C	670	25.2
Didcot Great Western Park	RS/villa	Mid 3C-4C	9390	26.4
Dorchester Beech House	'Small town'	Mid 2C-4C	?	30.3+
Dorchester Allotments	'Small town'	Most late 3C-4C	38,410	31.1
Little Wittenham, Castle Hill	RS	Most 4C	2532	35.8

MNS – minor nucleated settlement; RS – rural settlement; EWR Phase 1 sites bold, other Bicester sites italicised

Comment	Reference
	Stansbie 2009
	Booth 2007a
	Biddulph 2010
	Timby 1999
	Timby and Harrison 2004
Excludes 10.3% W20	Booth 2011b
	Booth 2017a
11.5% if F51 sherds (mostly	*Timby 2008*
from 1 vessel) are included	
	Booth 2014
MIA sherds excluded	Green and Booth 1993
	Evans 2001a
	Booth 2017b
	Booth and Simmonds 2018
	Booth forthcoming
	Timby 1996
	Brown 2007b
High (fragmented) samian	Booth 1997
sherd count	
	Green and Booth 2007

Comment	Reference
'unphased' material would	Booth 2011a
boost F and S value	
	Brown 2003
	Biddulph 2010
	Green and Booth 1993
	Timby 1999b
	Timby 2015
	Booth and Simmonds 2018
	Booth 1995
	Booth 1997
	Timby 1995
	Green and Booth 2007
	Booth and Simmonds 2018
	Timby 1996
	Booth 2000a;
	Biddulph 2005a
	Evans 2001a
	Green and Booth 1993
Earlier period groups very	Timby 2001
small	
	Booth forthcoming
Report gives some	Rowley and Brown 1981
percentages (of sherd count)	
but no total. Samian and	
amphorae not included	
Provisional figures from	Unpublished OA data
ongoing excavation	
Small LIA-early Roman	Booth 2010
component	

sentation no longer correlates straightforwardly with a hierarchy of site statuses. The effectiveness of connection to pottery distribution networks, particularly for the products of the Oxford industry, seems to have become more important in this period, but other less easily identified factors may also have been involved.

Complementary comparative analyses focus on the breakdown of assemblages in terms of broad groupings of vessel classes (Table 3.26). As mentioned above, the tendency for lower status site assemblages to be more heavily dominated by jars than those from other sites, and for the percentage of jars to gradually decrease through time at sites of all types in southern Britain, has been well known for some time (eg Millett 1979). Work by Jeremy Evans (2001b) focused on the ratio of jars to 'table wares' (bowls and dishes) in an analysis that included some data from the Alchester 1991 (A421) excavations. In the present analysis a three-way distinction is made between vessels potentially associated with storage, serving and consumption of liquids (classes A, B, E and F), jars (classes C and the uncertain jar/bowls D) and bowls and dishes (classes H, I and J). Other vessel classes, mostly of minor significance, are excluded from the calculations. This approach is based on the broad premise that the more diverse (less 'jar-heavy') assemblages in any one phase are less likely to be from what Evans (2001b) terms 'basic rural sites'. The present analysis, using the same phase structure as that for the analysis of fine and specialist wares, gives a more complete view of general character of the assemblages considered. It relies, however, on quantification of assemblages by REs or estimated vessel equivalents (EVEs), a method which has not always been routinely applied in this region (or elsewhere); the number of assemblages that can be used in this analysis is therefore smaller than is available for comparisons based on sherd count. In addition, some of the phase assemblages from the EWR Phase 1 sites are very small and their interpretation in comparative terms should be treated with caution.

As with the fine and specialist ware comparisons, the anticipated correlation of assemblage character and site character based on non-ceramic criteria seems to be clearest in the early Roman period. As far as the present project is concerned, however, only one phase assemblage was large enough to be included here; being from Langford Lane East it is unsurprising that this is grouped with the sites showing the greatest typological diversity in the early Roman period, quite distinct from the individual or aggregated farmstead sites that form the majority at this time. The situation in the middle Roman period is much more varied, since here we have Phase 6 assemblages from five diverse EWR Phase 1 sites. That from Holts Farm Crossing is very small, but its position at the lower end of the spectrum of middle Roman sites in terms of the proportion of jars seems plausible (and is maintained in the late Roman period). What is

Table 3.26 Breakdown of regional pottery assemblages by major vessel class groupings

	Three way RE percentages			
	Liquid related	*Jars*	*Bowls/ dishes*	*Three way RE total*
Early Roman assemblages				
Gravelly Guy	1.8	93.0	5.2	115.57
Hatford	4.9	91.5	3.6	17.39
Cotswold Community Phase 7	4.0	88.5	7.5	11.83
Gill Mill Area 13	1.4	88.2	9.9	21.20
Thornhill Farm	6.7	87.1	6.2	72.73
Bicester Oxford Road	*5.4*	*85.2*	*9.4*	*15.05*
Yarnton	4.0	84.6	11.5	66.80
Banbury Flood Alleviation Periods 3 and 4b	6.3	83.7	10.0	7.68
Claydon Pike Phase 2 (LIA/ERB)	4.9	82.9	12.1	43.77
Asthall Phases 2 and 3	5.8	82.4	11.8	15.12
Gill Mill Period 3	13.2	75.4	11.4	50.29
Appleford Sidings	14.5	70.4	15.1	39.18
Didcot Great Western Park ERB	14.1	70.4	15.5	37.68
Langford Lane East Phases 3-5	**16.1**	**68.6**	**15.3**	**26.05**
Combe	16.8	66.7	16.5	42.09
Alchester Periods 1-4 (ERB)	*20.4*	*63.1*	*16.6*	*14.24*
Middle Roman assemblages				
Tubney Wood	8.7	77.4	13.9	32.07
Holts Farm Crossing Phase 6	**14.8**	**75.3**	**9.9**	**4.74**
Kempsford Stubbs Farm (mainly MRB)	13.0	73.7	13.3	8.40
Claydon Pike Phase 3 (ERB/MRB)	11.2	72.5	16.3	152.14
Latton Lands	13.5	72.3	14.1	37.35
Arkells Land (mainly MRB)	14.2	69.8	16.1	120.64
Asthall Phases 3/5, 4, 4/5 and 5 (MRB)	7.6	68.7	23.6	59.60
Cotswold Community Phase 8 (MRB)	11.5	67.6	20.9	40.86
Horcott Quarry (mainly MRB)	8.3	66.7	25.0	30.99
Whelford Bowmore (MRB)	12.3	66.3	21.4	26.25
Gill Mill Period 4a (MRB)	15.1	65.0	19.8	175.23
North of Oxford Parkway Phase 6	**16.7**	**64.1**	**19.1**	**9.92**
Didcot Great Western Park MRB	21.2	60.3	18.4	32.63
Banbury Flood Alleviation Periods 4c and 4d	18.0	52.6	29.4	15.54
Alchester Periods 5 and 6 (MRB)	*28.7*	*51.4*	*19.8*	*185.65*
Langford Lane East Phase 6	**22.4**	**50.8**	**26.8**	**14.42**
South of Merton Phase 6	**26.8**	**47.7**	**25.5**	**8.87**
Langford Lane South	**30.5**	**38.8**	**30.7**	**34.62**
Late Roman assemblages				
Yarnton	5.0	78.5	16.5	48.39
Holts Farm Crossing Phase 6	**6.3**	**74.7**	**19.0**	**5.53**
Claydon Pike Phases 3/4 and 4 (LRB)	11.7	68.1	20.2	164.44
Asthall Phases 6 and 6/7 (LRB)	10.3	68.0	21.7	56.15
Oxford, Mansfield College and New Chemistry Lab.	6.7	65.0	28.4	12.62
Cotswold Community Phase 9 (LRB)	7.7	64.1	28.1	36.32
Little Wittenham Castle Hill (LRB)	11.0	62.6	26.4	20.08
Chilton villa	16.0	58.1	25.9	65.65
Didcot Great Western Park LRB	13.4	57.0	29.5	163.92
Gill Mill Period 4b (LRB)	16.9	54.8	28.3	637.94
Alchester Periods 7-9 (LRB)	*24.2*	*43.4*	*32.4*	*361.92*

EWR Phase 1 sites bold, other Bicester sites italicised

really striking, however, is the grouping of the other Phase 6 EWR Phase 1 assemblages, which concentrate at the top end of the spectrum of assemblage diversity. North of Oxford Parkway Station, for example, has an overall assemblage breakdown closely comparable to that from the minor nucleated settlement at Gill Mill, while none of the contemporary assemblages with even lower percentages of jars are straightforward rural settlements (the site at Didcot Great Western Park, for example, is closely associated with a villa, while the Banbury Flood Alleviation site might, like Gill Mill, best be seen as a minor nucleated settlement at this time). At the very least the site at North of Oxford Parkway Station is a 'complex farm' in the terminology of the Roman Rural Settlement project (Smith *et al.* 2016, 155, 157). The other EWR Phase 1 sites are at the very top of the assemblage diversity range, and it is notable that in this respect they group with the much larger middle Roman assemblage from the A421 site immediately north of Alchester. Thus the four most distinctive sites in this period lie immediately adjacent to, and at most 2km from, the town of Alchester (though the contemporary Holts Farm Crossing assemblage, almost in the same radius, is markedly different, as noted above). This raises interesting questions. First, does the diversity of these assemblages simply reflect a more 'urban' pottery consumption pattern directly reflecting the character and the market capacity of Alchester? If this is so, why is the evidence from Asthall, the only other 'small town' assemblage in this dataset, so different? Were there status and market character distinctions between the unwalled and walled sites of this general type (given that the earthwork and stone wall defences of Alchester are thought to be contemporary and probably to belong to the later 2nd century)? Alternatively, are we seeing a distinct sub-regional pattern regarding the supply and use of vessel types? This might explain why the North of Oxford Parkway Station group is so relatively highly placed in terms of assemblage diversity in this period, but unfortunately there is a dearth of other data from this part of the region. Bicester Park might be another site that fits this pattern, with jars reported as comprising only 52.3% of REs (total 21.33) from this site (Timby 2008, 138). Unfortunately, this assemblage includes both early and, particularly, some late Roman material as well as pottery of primarily middle Roman date, so it is not possible to define the middle Roman group there with certainty.

As with the early Roman period, so with the late, there is only one phase group from the EWR Phase 1 sites. The small group from Holts Farm Crossing is consistent with the relatively conservative nature of some of the assemblages from farmstead sites in the region, maintaining the character of this site already seen there in the middle Roman Phase 6, when it contrasted completely with the contemporary EWR Phase 1 sites, and particularly the Langford Lane South assemblage. The latter group stands out remarkably against all of its contemporaries, both local and from the wider region, in terms of vessel composition, as it did also in terms of fine and specialist wares, and as noted above it is of sufficient size to allow confidence that this is not just a consequence of abnormal representation of one or two vessels. The excavated features, while indicating fairly intensive activity, do not suggest a specific character to the occupation here that might be readily reflected in the occurrence of a highly atypical collection of pottery. Two of the most prominent features in this phase at Langford Lane South were pits 2611 and 4047. Together these contained very roughly one third of the Phase 6 pottery from this site (31.5% of sherd count, 28.7% of weight and 36.5% of REs), but while they provided a very significant proportion of all the liquid containing/serving vessels from this site/phase assemblage (about two thirds), the converse was true in relation to bowls and dishes, so, although containing interesting groups, these features on their own do not account for all the distinguishing ceramic features of this assemblage. The location of the pits to the west of the roadside plots suggests, however, that while the source(s) of the material with which they were filled could have lain within the roadside plots (or ones adjacent to them outside the excavated area), it is less likely that the pottery and other material simply arrived as part of a process of roadside disposal of rubbish, derived for example from locations closer to Alchester to the north. The exact nature of those sources remains unclear: adjacent quite high-status domestic activity is one possibility, though conceivably provision of roadside eating and drinking facilities is another.

COINS *by Paul Booth*

The only coins from the project were recovered from Langford Lane (one from Langford Lane South (SF 2001) and the rest from Langford Lane East), where 22 coins, one of Iron Age date and the rest Roman, were found. These were scanned briefly for the purposes of assessment and 19 were submitted for cleaning by a conservator. Despite this, the condition of many of the coins precludes detailed identification. The coins are listed in Table 3.27 in approximate order of issue.

A number of the coins can be dated fairly closely, but the general character of those that cannot be is reasonably clear. The single late Iron Age silver unit is of Cunobelinus. Two thirds of the Roman coins are of 1st- or 2nd-century date. They range from a worn denarius of Tiberius to an issue of Antoninus Pius. The latter was the sole coin from Langford Lane South and contrasts with the early coins from Langford Lane East, none of which is certainly later than the reign of Trajan. Four of the undated early Roman coins have been assigned subjectively to the 1st century rather than to a broader 1st/2nd-century date range. This assessment is particularly likely in the case of the three coins in this group which come from ditches assigned on other criteria to Phase 4 in the site sequence, and it is possible that all three were of Neronian date. Five coins are radiates of the later 3rd century, but their condition makes it uncertain which, if any, are irregular issues. The three remaining coins are all broadly of later Roman date. Two are assigned, with varying degrees of confidence, to the 4th century, while the third can only be placed in a mid-3rd to 4th-century date bracket.

Despite the small size of the assemblage its composition is notable. The emphasis on the early Roman period is unusual in regional terms and contrasts markedly with the more typical late Roman focus of the much larger group from the northern extramural area of Alchester (Darwish 2001). This characteristic indicates a significant reduction in the level of activity at Langford Lane East by the early 4th century at the latest. More specifically it presumably reflects a closer association with early military activity in this part of Alchester as opposed to the northern extramural area which lay at some distance from that activity. The denarius of Tiberius could well have derived from an early military coin pool, as indeed might the Iron Age silver unit. Whether the certain and possible Neronian coins are also relevant in this context is less clear. Sauer (2000b, 50) suggests that military activity had ceased at Alchester by the mid-60s at the latest, based on a sample of 24 coins from the excavation of the military annexe area to the west (ibid., 66-67), but concludes that 'it may be safer to assume that military occupation came to an end no later than *c* AD 70' (ibid., 50). It is clear that the Flavian and Trajanic coins will have related to post-military occupation. The presence of at least five coins in this date range suggests that the occupation was relatively intensive at this time. The proportionately low representation of later coinage suggests either a significant reduction in activity levels, particularly after the later 3rd century, or at least a marked change in the character of activity.

METAL AND GLASS OBJECTS *by Ian R Scott*

Introduction and Methodology

There are finds from seven sites (Table 3.28). The majority of metal finds come from Langford Lane East and Langford Lane South, with only very limited assemblages from the other sites.

Langford Lane East

The metal finds assemblage from Langford Lane East comprises 109 objects (149 fragments), including 36 nails (72 fragments), 11 pieces of miscellaneous metalwork (11 fragments) and 15 items of uncertain identification (15 fragments). Most of the finds (n=75) are from Roman contexts (Phases 4-7).

Tools include a complete axe head (Fig. 3.13, no. 1) of Roman form from a cleaning layer, and a possible punch (SF 6611) from a middle Roman demolition layer (7234). There is also a strongly curved object with a socket at one end and pivot or tang at the opposite end (SF 6562). Its purpose is uncertain and it could be of more recent date although it was recovered from an alluvial deposit (6562) phased to the middle Roman period.

Table 3.27 Summary of coin assemblage

SF no.	Context	Phase	Context type	Date	Denomination	Obverse
6550	7067	4	ditch	early 1C	AG unit 12mm	bust r, CVNO
6542	7067	4	ditch	36-37	denarius	TI CAESAR DIVI AVG F AVGVSTVS
6513	6503	0	cleaning layer	37-38	dup/as 26mm	GERMANICVS] CAESAR [TI AVGUVST F DIVI AVG N
6578b	7004	5	roadside ditch	64-66	as 28mm	NERO CLAVD CAESAR AVG GERMANI[
6609	7002	5	roadside ditch	71-78	as 27mm	IMP CAES VESPASIAN AVG[
6572	7048	7	pit	71-78	as 27mm	IMP CAES VES]PASIAN AVG[
6578a	7004	5	roadside ditch	86	as 28mm	IMP CAES DOMIT AVG GERM COS XII CENS PER PP
6558	6851	4	ditch	1C	sestertius 34mm	]VS C[AE]SAR .A[
6563	7067	4	ditch	1C	dup/as 27mm	head l,]AVG GER[
6546	7067	4	ditch	1C	as? 24mm	head r
6567	6932	6	layer	1C?	sestertius? 30mm	head r
6556b	7131	5	pit	103-111	sestertius 31mm	]G GER DAC P M T [, Trajan
6556a	7131	5	pit	98-117	sestertius 35mm	head r, Trajan
2001	2425	6	gully	151-152	as 27mm	ANTONINVS AVG PIVS [
6604	6828	6	layer	268-270?	radiate 18mm	IMP C VICTORINVS PF AVG?
6575	7048	7	pit	271-274	radiate 17mm	..]TETRICVS P F AVG
6551b	7074	0	alluvium	271-274?	radiate 18mm	radiate head r (Tetricus?)
6521	6516	7	surface	260-296	radiate 19-22mm	radiate head r
6551a	7074	0	alluvium	260-296	radiate 19mm	radiate head r?
6632	6501	9	subsoil	4C?	AE3 16mm	head r?
6573	7048	7	pit	4C??	AE4 7mm	
6630	6501	9	subsoil	3-4C	AE3 14mm	

Table 3.28 Quantification of metal objects by site

Site	Object count	Fragment count
Langford Lane East	109	149
Langford Lane South	62	109
South of Merton	16	17
Holts Farm Crossing	14	31
South of Oddington Crossing	5	6
North of Gallos Brook	1	1
North of Oxford Parkway Station	4	4
Total	211	317

Two pairs of iron slave shackles (SF 6537 and SF 6584, Fig 3.13, nos 2 and 3) were found in a pit (7014) phased to the middle Roman period (Phase 6). The shackle form is widely paralleled and Thompson (1993, 117) has written that the type was widespread in Gaul and Britain, particularly in rural areas.

The cast copper alloy mount possibly from a priestly head-dress (Fig. 3.14, no. 4) is from a road surface (6051) dated to the middle Roman phase (Phase 6). The object is apparently pierced in at least two places at its edge for the attachment of rings, and brings to mind the fittings of Roman priestly head dresses identified at the Farley Heath (Bird 1996; 2007, 77, figs 17-18, nos 76-77) and Wanborough temples (Bird 1994, 93-106, figs 23-26, plates 12-3, 16-19).

The most striking aspect of the finds assemblage from Langford Lane East is the number of items of personal adornment and in particular brooches. There are 23 personal items including 17 brooches.

There are two brooches from late Iron Age (Phase 3) contexts. A one-piece Colchester brooch (Fig. 3.14, no. 8) from pit 7187 is appropriate for the phase, but the Hod Hill brooch (Fig. 3.14, no. 13) from pit 7041 would be more appropriate to the Roman military (Phase 4) or early Roman (Phase 5) period.

From the Roman military phase of occupation there are a simple bow brooch (Fig. 3.15, no. 15), a Hod Hill brooch (Fig. 3.15, no. 14), the eroded catch plate of a second Hod Hill brooch (7094, not ill.) and a well-preserved, broad, apparently undecorated penannular bracelet or armlet (Fig. 3.15, no. 18). The last came from ditch 7069, which also produced a plain circular headed stud or rivet and a small penannular collar or ferrule which had been secured by a tack or pin. In addition to items of personal adornment, this ditch also yielded part of spatula probe with an olivary head (Fig. 3.15, no. 20).

There were two brooches from early Roman (Phase 5) cobbled surfaces adjacent to building 7062: a Hod Hill brooch and part of the bow of a large Colchester brooch (Fig. 3.14, no. 9).

There are three brooches from 2nd-early 3rd century middle Roman (Phase 6) contexts. The bow brooches comprise a simple bow brooch (Fig. 3.14, no. 6) and a rear hook brooch (Fig. 3.14, no. 12) and

Reverse	Ref	Wear	Comment
winged sphinx l, TASCIO	Hobbs 1996, 1874-1878; Cottam *et al.* 2010, 2870	SW/SW	part encrusted
PONTIF MAXIM	RIC I^2 (Tiberius), 26	W/W	
S C in centre,	RIC I^2 (Gaius), 35	W/SW	obv encrusted
C CAESAR] AVG GERMANICVS PON M [TR POT around			
PON[ ] TR POT [Nero as Apollo S C	?RIC I^2, 414	SW/SW	encrusted
AEQVI[TAS AVGVSTI] S C	as RIC II^2, 1161	W/W	
eagle on globe S C		W/W	eroded
VIRTVTI AVGVSTI S C	RIC II^2, 499	SW/SW	eroded
figure standing l		W/W?	encrusted and illegible
figure standing?		W/EW	encrusted, rev almost flat
?Mars r		VW/EW	no legends, poss trimmed?
?		?	eroded and encrusted
large S C widely spaced in field, SPQR OPTIMO PRINCIPI around		SW/W	partly eroded. ?nothing between S C
?		W/?	encrusted and eroded
BONVS EVENTVS (stg l with altar), S C, COS IIII in exergue	RIC III, 899	W/W	
Pax standing l, V *	as RIC V, 116	VW/VW	
?Providentia standing l		SW/W	
Pietas Augg (etc), sacrificial implements		W/W?	encrusted and eroded
figure standing		VW/VW	encrusted
?		VW/EW	eroded and incomplete
		?	encrusted and illegible
		?	eroded, poss v incomplete
		VW/VW?	encrusted and broken

are arguably residual in these contexts, since both date to the mid-1st century. The symmetrical plate brooch (Fig. 3.15, no. 17) is a 2nd-century type and therefore contemporary with the pit from which it was recovered. In addition to these brooches there is a melon bead (Fig. 3.16, no. 19) from Phase 6 demolition layer 7065, a probable brooch pin fragment from ditch 6910 (fill 6919), and a small eroded copper alloy stud from alluvial deposit 7301.

Other personal items include a clearly residual fragment of a one-piece Colchester brooch in a late Roman (Phase 7) pit (7047), a Hod Hill brooch (Fig. 3.15, no. 15) from the subsoil and a small plate brooch in the form of a nailed shoe sole (Fig. 3.15, no. 16) from demolition layer 6554 (Building 7640).

Household items are very limited in number. There is a possibly casket or box stud from Phase 4 pit 7550, a long whittle tang knife (Fig. 3.16, no. 21) from modern ditch 6819 and a small whittle tang knife (Fig. 3.16, no. 22) from a deposit phased as post-Roman. Both knives could be Anglo-Saxon.

Illustrated finds (Figs 3.13-3.16)

Tools

1   **Axe** with back curved blade, oval eye flanked by lugs in front and behind. The poll or butt is rectangular in section and the blade is curved back. L: 210mm; Blade, edge or toe W: 75mm. Ctx 6503, alluvial layer, SF 6520.
Although this axe was not securely stratified, it is a good Roman form and conforms to Duvauchelle's Type 2a with rectangular lugs flanking the eye (Duvauchelle 1990, 14-17 and fig. 6; see also ibid., 52-3, 88-9, nos. 33-36).

Slave shackles

These fetters or shackles are similar to Thompson's 'Bavay type' (1993, 117) and were attached to the ankle. The individual shackle was closed by passing the elongated link through the opposed ring and secured either by passing a chain when used as part of gang chain, or individually by use of padlock (Thompson 1993, 117).

2   **Slave shackle**, comprising large incomplete loop with a rolled over loop at each end holding respectively a circular ring and elongated oval link curved though its length. The latter served to close the shackle and passed through the circular ring to be secured by a padlock. Fe. Overall L: 151mm; D of shackle: 117mm. Ctx 7015, pit 7014, SF 6537. Ph 6: middle Roman (2nd-early 3rd century).

3   **Slave shackle**, similar to no. 2, but slightly less well-preserved. Fe. Overall L: 151mm; D of shackle: 117mm. Ctx 7015, pit 7014, SF 6584. Ph 6: middle Roman (2nd-early 3rd century).

Votive – Priestly head-dress

4   **Cast mount** with outer flange pierced by holes with attached rings. The raised centre has a lipped socket, which is wedged with tiny copper alloy fragments. Possibly part of a priestly head dress. Cu alloy. D: 31mm; Ht: 14mm. Ctx 6051, road surface, SF

6001. Ph 6: middle Roman (2nd-early 3rd century). Cf the more elaborate mounts from the temples at Wanborough (Bird 1994, 93-106, figs 23-26, plates 12-3, 16-19) and Farley Heath, Surrey (Bird 1996; Bird 2007, 77, figs 17-18, nos 76-77.

Personal – Brooches

The simple bow brooches (nos 5-7) and one-piece Colchester brooch (no. 8) date to the early to mid 1st century. The fragment of Colchester brooch (probably a two-piece Colchester brooch) is of slightly later lst century date, as is the Durotrigian brooch. The Rosette brooch with hinged pin dates to the second half of the 1st century as does the Rear Hook. The Hod Hill brooches range in date from the Claudian conquest to the Flavian period, when they to go out of fashion. All the bow brooches are predominantly 1st century forms. The plate brooches date to the 2nd and even 3rd centuries.

5   **Simple bow brooch**, with sprung pin, now missing. Tapered bow of sub-rectangular section. Cu alloy. L: 41.5mm. Ctx 6847, ditch 8517, SF 6533. Ph 4: Roman military.

6   **Simple bow brooch**, sprung pin, somewhat eroded. Catchplate missing. L extant: 42mm. Cu alloy. Ctx 6960, pit 6789, SF 6516. Ph 6: middle Roman (2nd-early 3rd century).

7   **Simple bow brooch**, sprung pin. Four coils internal chord. Cu alloy. L: 42mm; W: 12mm. Ctx 7075, alluvial layer, SF 6554. Undated.

8   **One-piece Colchester brooch**, eroded. Has narrow probably eroded bow, with little of catchplate surviving. 8-coil spring(?) and vestigial wings. Cu alloy. L: 53mm; W: 22mm. Ctx 7190, pit 7187, SF 6596. Ph 3: late Iron Age.

9   **Colchester brooch**. Part of bow and pierced catchplate probably from a large brooch. Cu alloy. L extant: 40mm. Ctx 6827=7046, cobbled surface, SF 6603. Ph 5: early Roman (late 1st-early 2nd century).

10   **Durotrigian brooch**. Low flat section bow with grooves, tapering to catchplate. Deep catchplate. Hinged pin. Cu alloy. L: 57mm; W: 25mm. Ctx 6920, ditch 8520, SF 6535. Ph 6: middle Roman (2nd-early 3rd century).

11   **Rosette brooch**, hinged pin. Rosette missing. Cu alloy. L: 47mm; W: 27mm. Ctx 6964, natural feature 6963, SF 6553. Undated.

12   **Rear hook brooch**, small. Plain unpierced catchplate. Wings over spring, which is attached by means of a hook (or possibly a pierced lug). Cu alloy. L: 31mm; W: 23mm. Ctx 6813, alluvial layer, SF 6555. Ph 6: middle Roman (2nd-early 3rd century).

13   **Hod Hill brooch**, small, eroded. Hinged pin. Cu alloy. L: 33mm. Ctx 7043, pit 7041, SF 6557. Ph 3: late Iron Age.

14   **Hod Hill brooch**, hinged pin Cu alloy. L: 52mm; W: 18mm. Ctx 6898, ditch 7444, SF 6536. Ph 4: Roman military (*c* 43-70).

15   **Hod Hill brooch**, hinged pin. Cu alloy. L: 48mm; W: 17mm. Subsoil, SF 6600.

16   **Plate brooch** in the form of a nailed shoe sole. Inlaid with blue enamel with off-white dots representing nails. At the heel end is a small broken loop. Hinged pin. L: 39mm; W: 10mm. Ctx 6554, demolition layer, SF 6526. Cleaning.

17   **Symmetrical plate brooch**. Central lozenge panel has a central strip flanked by triangular panels.

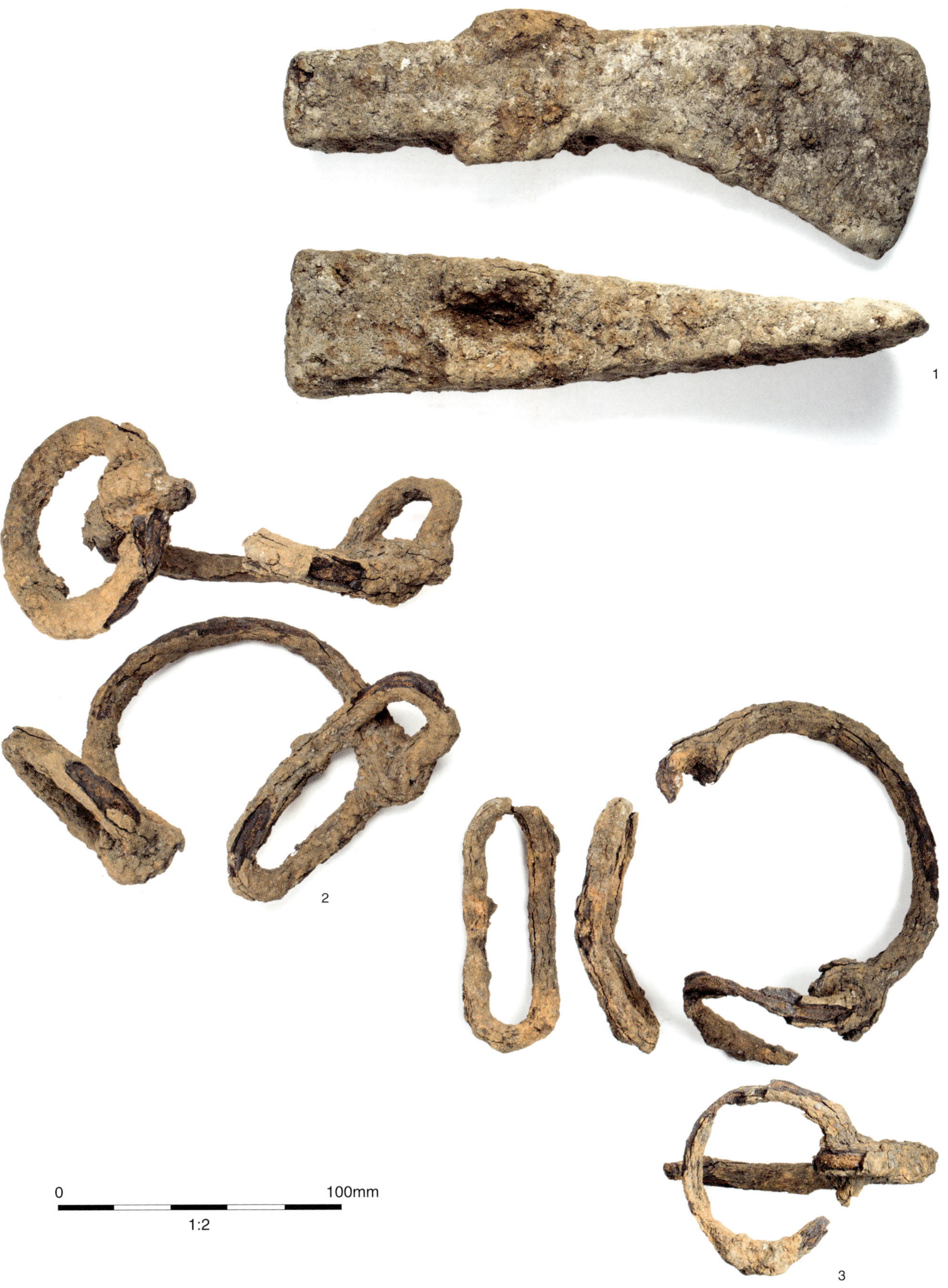

Fig. 3.13   Metal objects from Langford Lane East: tools, nos 1-3

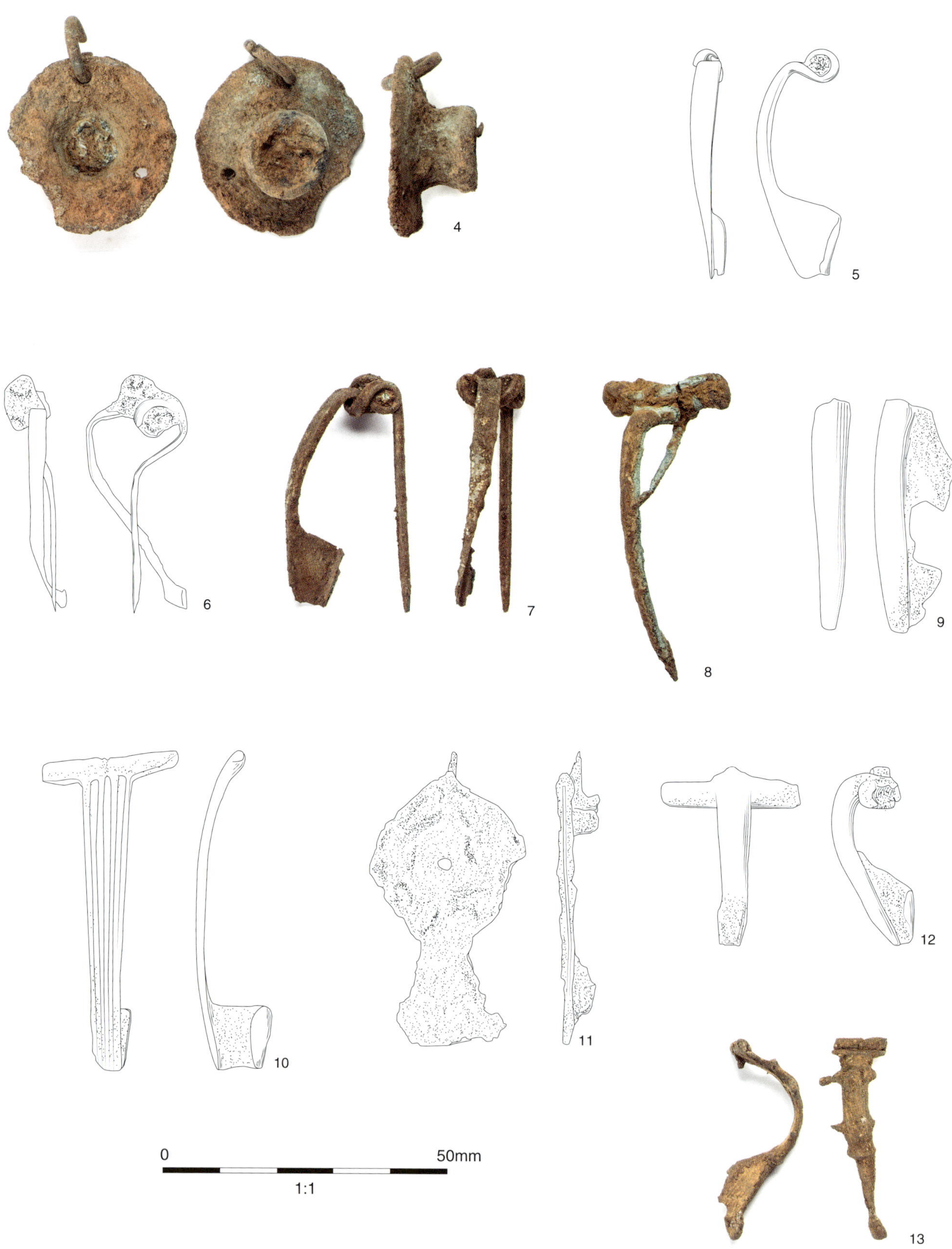

Fig. 3.14   *Metal objects from Langford Lane East: votive and personal items, nos 4-13*

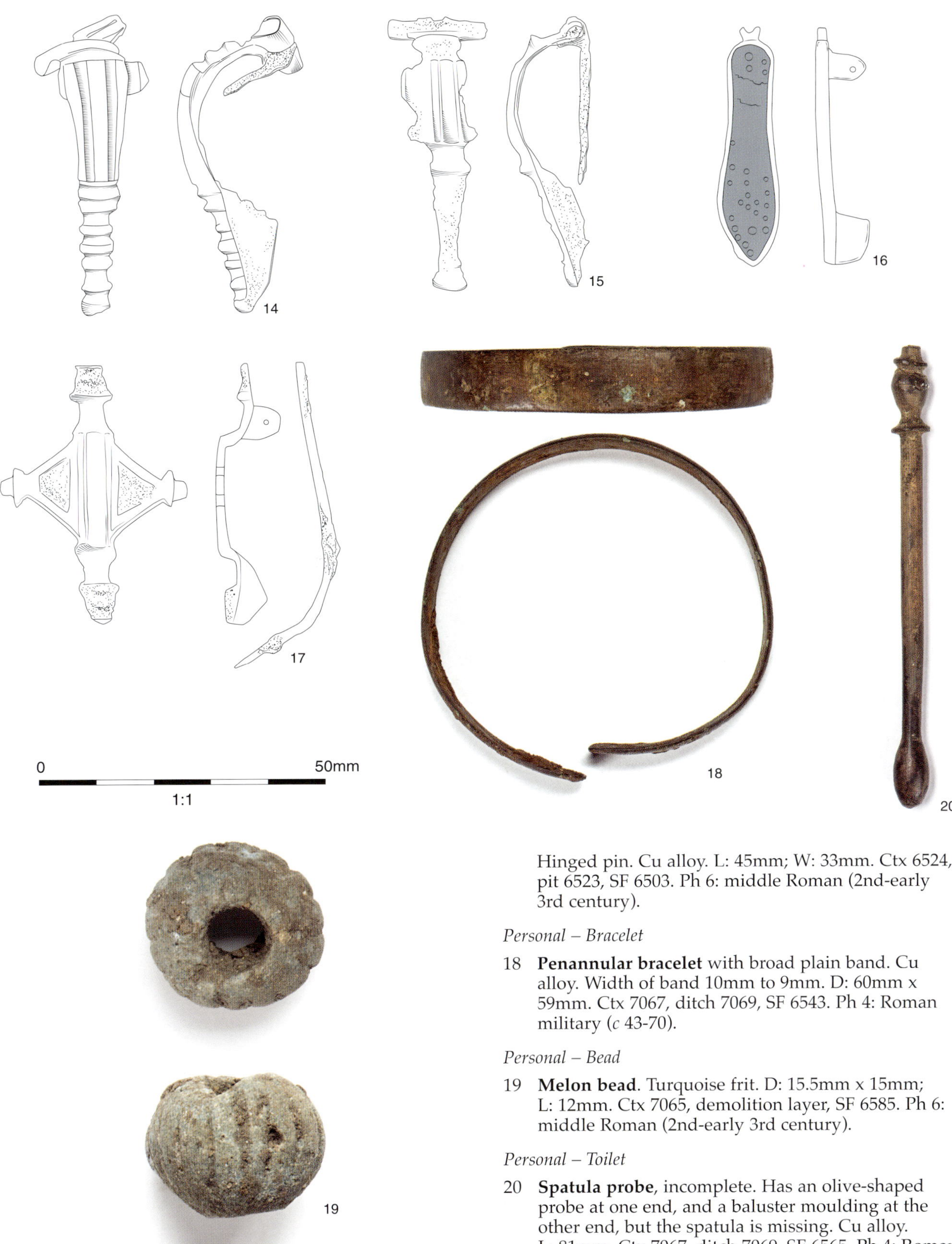

Fig. 3.15   *Metal and glass objects from Langford Lane East: personal items, nos 14-20*

Hinged pin. Cu alloy. L: 45mm; W: 33mm. Ctx 6524, pit 6523, SF 6503. Ph 6: middle Roman (2nd-early 3rd century).

Personal – Bracelet

18   **Penannular bracelet** with broad plain band. Cu alloy. Width of band 10mm to 9mm. D: 60mm x 59mm. Ctx 7067, ditch 7069, SF 6543. Ph 4: Roman military (*c* 43-70).

Personal – Bead

19   **Melon bead**. Turquoise frit. D: 15.5mm x 15mm; L: 12mm. Ctx 7065, demolition layer, SF 6585. Ph 6: middle Roman (2nd-early 3rd century).

Personal – Toilet

20   **Spatula probe**, incomplete. Has an olive-shaped probe at one end, and a baluster moulding at the other end, but the spatula is missing. Cu alloy. L: 81mm. Ctx 7067, ditch 7069, SF 6565. Ph 4: Roman military (*c* 43-70).

Household

21   **Long whittle tang knife** with blade of triangular section. Fe. L: 325mm. Ctx 6820, ditch 6558, SF 6532. Ph 9: modern.

145

22 **Small whittle tang knife** with slim blade with gently curved back. Fe. L; 122mm; blade L: *c* 95mm. Ctx 6681, alluvial layer, SF 6522. Post-Roman, possibly Saxon.

Miscellaneous

23 **Staple or clamp**, worked from copper alloy wire with flat broad central section. At one end the wire has been worked to a point rolled into a hook; at the other end the wire has still to be shaped and is at a right angle to the flat portion. Purpose uncertain. L: 36mm. W: 8mm. Ctx 6716, demolition layer, Building 7640, SF 6583. Ph 6: middle Roman (2nd-early 3rd century).

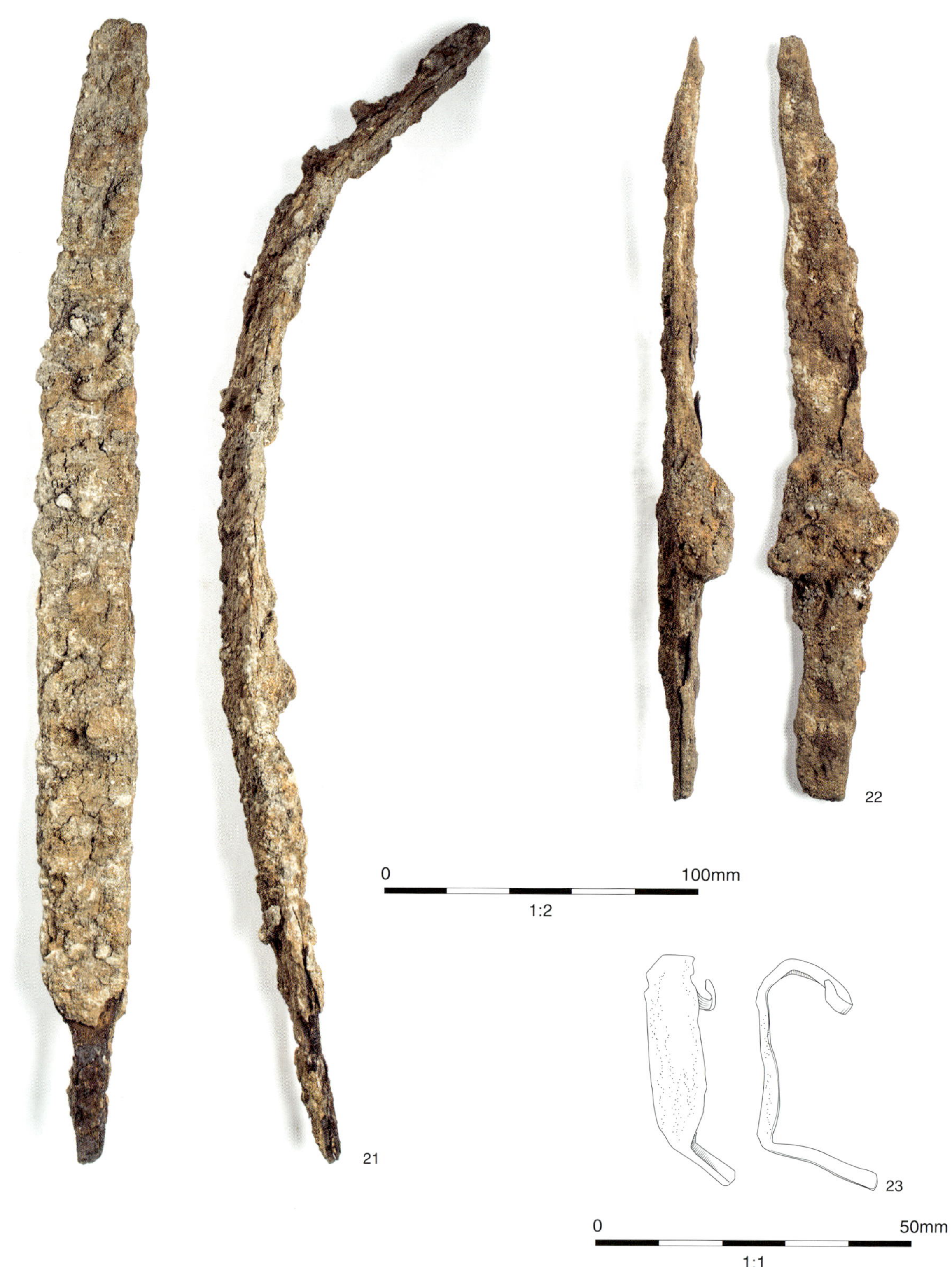

Fig. 3.16   Metal objects from Langford Lane East: toilet and household items, nos 21-3

146

Langford Lane South

The finds assemblage comprises 62 metal objects (109 fragments), including 34 nails (62 frags), nine pieces of miscellaneous metalwork (9 fragments) and four items of uncertain identification (4 fragments). There are also a broken annular glass bead and a melon bead. Most of the finds come from Roman phases and in particular from middle Roman contexts. Only small numbers of finds come from later or undated contexts.

There are no tools from this site and items of transport are limited to two horseshoes. One of these is complete but worn and of late medieval form and comes from post-Roman alluvial spread 4002, and the second is incomplete and comes from alluvial deposit 2737, which was dated to the middle Roman period. The latter is unlikely to be Roman and therefore possibly intrusive.

The only identifiable household item is a whittle tang knife (SF 4000; Fig. 3.17, no. 24) comes from an early Roman (Phase 5) silting layer (4163).

Personal items are limited to a simple sprung bow brooch (SF 2009; Fig. 3.17, no. 25) and a copper alloy hairpin with 'cotton reel' head (SF 2010; Fig. 3.17, no. 26), both from middle Roman alluvial deposit 2655, and two beads. A fragment of an annular glass bead in opaque pale green glass (Fig. 3.17, no. 27) came from Phase 6 pit 2271, which also contained a hobnail and hobnail stem, six nail stem fragments and ten tiny iron fragments. The finds suggest that this pit may have contained a pyre deposit. The second bead was a melon bead (Fig. 3.17, no. 28) from Phase 6 demolition layer 7065.

Overall the metal and other small finds are limited in number and range when compared to the finds from Langford Lane East. However, Langford Lane South produced more Roman glass than Langford Lane East.

Illustrated finds (Fig. 3.17)

24 **Whittle tang knife**, long and narrow, with gently curved back and slightly concave curved edge. Fe. L: 225mm; blade L: *c* 180mm. Ctx 4163, silting layer over road surface, SF 4000. Ph 5: early Roman (late 1st-early 2nd century).

25 **Small bow brooch** with sprung pin. The bow is thin and flat and widens in the middle, although now eroded. Cu alloy L: 31mm; W: 8mm. Ctx 2655, alluvial layer, SF 2009. Ph 6: middle Roman (2nd-early 3rd century).

26 **Hairpin** with cotton reel head and incomplete stem. Cu alloy. L extant: 41.5mm; D of head: 5mm. Ctx 2655, alluvial layer, SF 2010. Ph 6: middle Roman (2nd-early 3rd century).

27 **Annular glass bead**, fragment. Opaque pale green glass. D: 11mm. Ctx 2272, pit 2271, sample 2057. Ph 6: middle Roman (2nd-early 3rd century).

28 **Small melon bead**. Turquoise frit. L: 9mm; D: 11.5mm x 10mm. Ctx 2791, pit 2789, sample 2145. Ph 6: middle Roman (2nd-early 3rd century).

South of Merton

There are just 16 metal finds from the site, which

Fig. 3.17   Metal and glass objects from Langford Lane South, nos 24-8

include three personal items and two household items. Eleven of the objects were recovered from medieval furrows or more modern contexts and middle Roman contexts (Phases 6.1 and 6.2) produced just five metal objects. These include a fragment from a Roman bracelet from Phase 6.1 cremation 2522 (fill 2523, sample 2500). This appears to be part of a narrow plain penannular bracelet of lenticular cross section. Other finds from Phase 6 comprise two hobnails from Phase 6 hollow 1303 (fill 1304), a nail from Phase 6.1 ditch 2559 (fill 2556) and a plain iron ring (D: 50mm) from Phase 6.1 posthole 2640 (fill 2641). A single Roman hobnail was found in Phase 8 furrow 2509 (fill 2510). Other finds include personal objects comprising a fragment of a post-medieval shoe buckle from subsoil 2501 (Phase 9) and a post-medieval shank button from Phase 8 furrow 2507 (fill 2508). There are two household objects a post-medieval cast pewter spoon handle from and possible iron drop handle respectively from Phase 8 furrows 2507 (fill 2508) and 2509 (fill 2510). There is also a nail from furrow 2507 (fill 2508) and piece of melted lead from furrow 2611 (fill 2610). There is a plain copper alloy ring and a lump of lead from subsoil 2501.

Holts Farm Crossing

The metal assemblage from this site is small and comprises ten nails and a further nine nail stem fragments, including three nails from middle Roman cremation pit 8547 and a stem fragment, possibly intrusive, in middle Iron Age pit 8081. The only other finds from Roman contexts are a hobnail from hollow 8698 and a piece of iron strip from trackway ditch 8681. The only personal item is a fragment of a late 17th-century buckle from furrow 8115 (context 8114). There is a possible smith's punch or drift from furrow 8640 (context 8639). The latter could be Roman or later in date.

South of Oddington Crossing

There are just four pieces of miscellaneous metal-work from three contexts (14, 15 and 87). There are two pieces of iron rod (one consisting of two refitting fragments) (14) and a fragment of narrow iron strip (15) from fills of middle Iron Age ditch 153, none of which is diagnostic to function. There is a fragment of iron plate or strip from context 87 within modern waterhole 85.

North of Gallos Brook

The only metal object is a worn and broken heel iron, very probably of 19th- or early 20th-century date from the fill 170 of medieval furrow 172.

North of Oxford Parkway Station

There are just four metal objects from this site including three horseshoes from context 3192 in ditch 3091, which is dated to the middle Roman (2nd to early 3rd century). One of the horseshoes is of late medieval or early post-medieval type, and two are of post-medieval type. The horseshoes are clearly not Roman. The only other find is a nail from the subsoil.

VESSEL AND WINDOW GLASS *by Ian R Scott*

The glass assemblage included material from four sites, but the quantity of glass is very limited. Most of the glass comes from Langford Lane South. There are, additionally, three glass beads which are reported in the small finds report.

Langford Lane East

The vessel glass from this site is limited to five pieces and the only clearly identified sherd was the neck/shoulder junction of a square bottle from a Phase 5 fill of the eastern roadside ditch. There are just two sherds of possible window glass from contexts 6554 and 7078, part of the demolition spreads that extend to the north-west of building 7640.

Langford Lane South

Vessel glass

There are 18 pieces of vessel glass from the site, comprising body sherds and base sherds. Most came from Phase 6 features, as well as one from cleaning and one from an undated tree hole. The base of a hexagonal bottle (Fig. 3.18, no.1) came from the same pit (2611) as the window glass discussed below. Most of the remaining vessel sherds are small or very small and are not readily identified to vessel form. One tiny colourless vessel sherd from context 2792 (pit 4047, Phase 6) has wheel-cut grooves.

Window glass

Perhaps more interesting than the vessel glass is the evidence for Roman cast matt/glossy window glass, all from pit 2611. Four sherds from fill 2808 include two large sherds of cast glass, one an edge piece with a tool mark (Fig. 3.18, no. 2). The glass from fill 2612 consists of four pieces including one edge sherd. There are four sherds from fill 2615 and two sherds from fill 2616.

Other sites

The only pieces of Roman glass from the other sites were a single piece of thick blue-green window glass with crazed surfaces, very probably caused by heat, recovered from a furrow at South of Merton and a rim sherd in pale blue green glass from a collared bowl or jar dating from the 1st to early 2nd century that was found in a Phase 6 fill of the northern ditch of the trackway at Holts Farm Crossing.

Fig. 3.18   Vessel and window glass from Langford Lane South

Illustrated glass

1   **Hexagonal bottle**. Sherd from the base / heel of a Roman hexagonal bottle with concentric rings moulded on the base. Blue green glass. Langford Lane South. Fill 2616, pit 2611. Ph 6: middle Roman (2nd-early 3rd century).

2   **Window glass**. Large edge sherd of blue green matt glossy glass with trace of tool mark near the edge. 106mm x 96mm. Max Th: 6mm at edge of sheet. Min Th: 3mm. Langford Lane South. Fill 2808, pit 2611. Ph 6: middle Roman (2nd-early 3rd century.

METALWORKING DEBRIS FROM SOUTH OF ODDINGTON CROSSING

Crucibles *by Edward Biddulph*

The remains of two ceramic crucibles were recovered from the fills (14 and 15) of an intervention (13) through middle Iron Age ditch 153 at South of Oddington Crossing. A total of 30 fragments, weighing 263g, were recorded. Eight fragments (155g) were refitted to form a large portion of a single vessel (Fig. 3.19, no. 1). This had been made in a medium-coarse sand-tempered fabric, which additionally contained ferruginous, argillaceous (or possibly grog), and organic inclusions (the organic inclusions identified from elongated voids). The vessel is generally dark grey in colour, except the base, which is orange-brown on one side. The crucible is D-shaped in profile, albeit bowed along the rim, and triangular in plan. Two of the three pinched spouts are present. The wall of the vessel is *c* 11mm thick and survives to a height of *c* 60mm. The vessel measures *c* 120mm along the rim between spouts. The upper part of the interior surface is encrusted with a thick residue that includes green corrosion products, while the interior surface along the rim is vesicular. The residue and vesicular surface are concentrated in one corner of the vessel, suggesting that the spout there was preferentially used when casting the melted metal into moulds.

A further five fragments, weighing 56g, were refitted to form part of the rim and spout of a second crucible (Fig. 3.19, no. 2). The fabric is dark grey and sand-tempered, and is vesicular or pumice-like throughout as a result of the high-temperature working. The wall of the vessel is *c* 16mm at its thickest, and the surviving rim is 110mm long. A green and brown residue is present on the interior surface, while the top of the rim is discoloured black. The interior surface around the spout is vitrified and red-brown products are visible. Though only one spout survives, it is likely that this crucible is also of triangular type.

The remaining fragments do not join either vessel, though are likely to belong to one or the other. One small fragment is vitrified to the extent that it appears to have a green glaze. Neither crucible shows evidence for relining or the application of an external protective layer of clay. A middle Iron Age date for the material is confirmed by a radiocarbon date of 200-40 cal BC (95.4%; SUERC-70734) obtained from charcoal recovered from context 14.

In form, the vessels are typical of Iron Age crucibles in Southern Britain (Tylecote 1962, 131-3; Historic England 2015, fig. 36, no. 1), and parallels are known in Oxfordshire at Mingies Ditch (Salter 1993, fig. 36, no. 8) and at Thrupp, near Radley (Ainslie 1992, fig. 3).

Technical investigation of the crucibles
by Marcos Martinón-Torres and Loïc Boscher

The crucibles were subjected to technical analysis at the Wolfson Archaeological Science

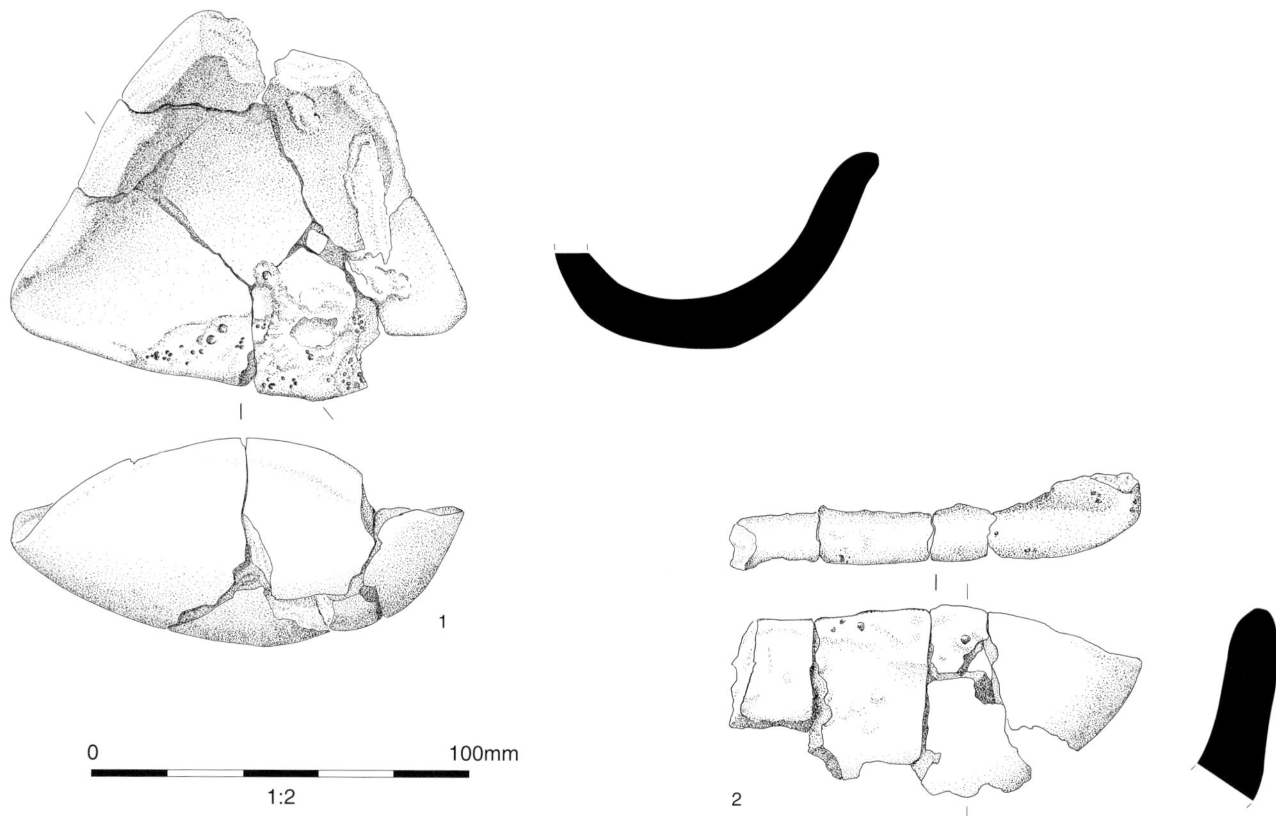

Fig. 3.19   Crucibles from South of Oddington Crossing

Laboratories at the UCL Institute of Archaeology to investigate their manufacture and use. Seven crucible sherds were analysed non-invasively by portable XRF, comparing spectra from inner and outer surfaces in each case, to obtain a qualitative indication of any heavy metal enrichment on the inner surfaces.

Strong signals of copper and tin were detected on all the inner surfaces, indicating that the crucibles would have been used for the processing of bronze. Low peaks of zinc, arsenic, silver, antimony and lead were also detected in spectra for those areas with thicker residues, but at very low levels that denote impurities in the metal rather than intentional alloying constituents. Of potential interest was the relatively high iron signal recorded on the inner surface of one of the sherds. The iron enrichment might denote a higher iron impurity in the metal, or perhaps the presence in the residue of iron-rich gangue that might suggest the addition of minerals to the charge (for example, to make bronze by cementation of metallic copper with mineral cassiterite). Alternatively, the iron could simply constitute surface contamination from the burial environment.

Seeking to clarify this issue and to characterise the metallurgical processes carried out in these crucibles, two sherds were sampled invasively and prepared as polished cross-sections. The sections were examined under optical microscope before further analysis on a Philips XL30 scanning electron microscope with an Oxford Instrument EDS detector operating at 20kV and at a working distance of 10mm. Elemental compositions were measured from the characteristic energy peaks using a ZAF correction procedure. Analysed certified reference basalt standards (BHVO-2, BIR-1, and BCR-2) confirmed that the instrument's accuracy and precision were within an acceptable range, with all elements in concentrations higher than 1% found well within 10% relative of the reference value.

The morphology and appearance of the crucibles indicate that they all derive from shallow, triangular vessels. The inner surfaces are dark and heavily vitrified, while the outer surfaces typically show an orange or buff colour, and a substantially lower heat impact. Analyses by SEM-EDS show the crucible fabrics as non-calcareous, with moderate alumina levels (17-21%) and relatively high iron oxide (8-11%), and hence not particularly refractory (Table 3.29). The fabric is rich in sub-rounded quartz grains of small size (<500μm in diameter), quite probably added deliberately as temper, which would improve toughness and thermal shock resistance. In both samples, a clear thermal gradient can be noted from the outer surface, which shows only initial vitrification, to the inner surface, which shows very large and abundant bloating pores as a result of exposure to higher temperatures; towards the inner surface, quartz grains are shattered as a result of thermal

Table 3.29 Average composition of the ceramic fabrics of the crucible samples

		NaO	MgO	Al_2O_3	SiO_2	P_2O_5	SO_3	Cl	K_2O	CaO	TiO_2	Fe	CuO
Crucible 1	mean (n=4)	0.4	0.9	17.2	66.7	0.5		0.2	1.4	3.2	0.9	8.0	0.4
	SD	0.3	0.1	1.9	3.0	0.2		0.1	0.2	0.2	0.2	0.5	0.2
Crucible 2	mean (n=4)	0.4	1.1	21.1	60.8	0.5	0.5	0.3	1.8	1.2	1.1	11.1	
	SD	0.1	0.2	1.9	2.3	0.2	0.2	0.1	0.4	0.1	0.2	0.3	

Values are averages of areas of approximately 1000 x 1200μm, which included some quartz grains, hence the results are indicative of the bulk ceramic composition rather than that of the ceramic matrix. Results are presented as stoichiometric oxides and normalised to 100% to account for the abundant porosity

stress, and other silicate minerals appear molten. This microstructure confirms that the crucibles would have been heated from within, that is, with the charcoal contained within the vessel and mixed with the charge, rather than beneath or outside. This arrangement is common for prehistoric crucibles, and it allowed metallurgists to melt metals using crucibles that were only moderately refractory, as the heat impact was constrained to the inner surface only (Bayley and Rehren 2007; Martinón-Torres and Rehren 2014).

The sample from crucible 1 had a particularly thick layer of residue situated directly opposite the vessel's spout. The inner surface of this sample was dominated by a relatively large bronze prill, several millimetres in diameter. SEM-EDS measurements of several areas of the uncorroded core yielded tin values typically ranging 5-7%, with occasional presence of lead, antimony and arsenic, always below 1% each, and no iron above detection limits (~0.1%). Small inclusions of copper sulphide (Cu_2S) and metallic lead (the latter occasionally with detectable silver) were present within the metal. In addition, there were relatively larger lumps of lead sulphate in corroded areas, probably resulting from lead redeposition during burial. Of especial interest is the inner structure of this prill, which showed numerous rhomboidal crystals of tin oxide (SnO_2), particularly abundant towards the outer surfaces of the metal. The morphology of these crystals was consistent with their formation during the burning of metallic tin, that is, the partial oxidation of the metal during melting. It is well-known that when a bronze is melted in insufficiently reducing conditions, tin will oxidise preferentially, forming a dross that is very rich in euhedral tin oxide crystals and resulting in a bronze of lower tin levels (Rademakers and Farci 2018). Clearly, this is the metallurgical process that explains the features documented within this crucible. Notably, no residual minerals were found in this sample.

The residue on the sample from crucible 2 was less substantial, consisting of a vitrification layer that included the thermally distorted ceramic fabric. This layer was dominated by interlocking needles of delafossite ($CuFeO_2$), interspersed with occasional tin oxide crystals (SnO_2) of diverse

morphology, but mostly euhedral and acicular, that is, resulting from the hot oxidation of metallic tin. The lime-rich glassy matrix was largely corroded but in a small region where it was preserved, fine dendrites of cuprite (Cu_2O) could be observed. Metallic prills were scarce and small, typically tens of μm or less in diameter. In all cases they were copper with around 1% iron, and variable contents of tin (0-2%), arsenic (0-1%) and antimony (0-1%). One of the prills also contained traces of bromine and sulphur, possibly resulting from post-depositional alteration. While it is of course possible that we have mixed signatures of successive processes carried out in the same crucible, the features observed were consistent with a process of metal melting in relatively oxidising conditions. The original metal would have been a bronze with relatively low tin levels (which would have been further reduced during the melting) but also with a considerable amount of iron as an impurity, much higher than that in crucible 1. The refining of copper containing iron is relatively easy, as the latter will oxidise preferentially during melting; however, in this crucible, tin and some copper were oxidised too. As in the previous case, there was no diagnostic feature that could be taken as an indication that alloying with fresh tin or cementation of metallic copper with cassiterite would have taken place. Having said this, it is worth noting the presence of a very small cluster of anhedral, nodular tin oxide crystals in the vitrified layer. Similar crystal assemblages have been interpreted elsewhere as pseudomorphs of cassiterite minerals added to a copper-bearing crucible in order to increase the tin content in the alloy (Farci *et al.* 2017; Rademakers *et al.* 2018); when they contain Nb, W or Ta, they can be confirmed as evidence of mineral addition (Rademakers and Farci 2018). However, with this being such a small and isolated occurrence here, and lacking any diagnostic chemical tracer, it would be premature to confirm the addition of tin minerals to the charge.

Overall, these crucibles are typical of Iron Age Britain and are consistent with those recovered from other sites, not only in their morphology but also in their manufacture with ordinary clays, and in their utilisation. The analyses confirm that the crucibles were heated from within and that the

Table 3.30 Slag types in assemblage and processes represented

Slag type	Wt (g)	Process
Cinder	107+	not diagnostic
Fuel ash slag	52+	not diagnostic
Smithing hearth bottom	2151	smithing
Iron-rich undiagnostic	979+	smithing or smelting
Undiagnostic	1819+	smithing or smelting

Table 3.31 Statistical data for the smithing hearth bottoms

	Range	Average	Standard deviation
Weight	135-516	195	131
Length	70-105	85	11
Breadth	65-90	70	8
Depth	20-45	30	9

metals processed were unleaded tin bronzes with relatively low traces of lead, arsenic, antimony and silver. In the case of crucible 2, the iron content in the metal would have been higher, and refined during remelting. While it is possible that active alloying of copper by the addition of cassiterite took place, this cannot be confirmed based on the sample analysed.

Iron slag and related high-temperature metal-working debris *by Lynne Keys*

Some 6.3kg of material, initially identified as slag, was recovered by hand on site and from soil samples processed after excavation. The assemblage appears to represent secondary smithing activity; no diagnostic smelting slags were present at all. No micro-slags from smithing (hammer-scale flakes and spheres) were present amongst the material (even from the samples) indicating the slag had been moved away from the focus or foci of smithing (Table 3.30). The smithing hearth bottoms were few and not large in size, indicating that the smithing activity was sporadic and limited in its duration (Table 3.31). Most of the material came from ditch 153, where it was associated with fragments from two crucibles; fill 14 contained the largest quantity of slag (5.2kg) and seven smithing hearth bottoms and fill 15 contained 964g of slag and two smithing hearth bottoms. A further 89g of material and no smithing hearth bottoms were recovered from early Roman ditch 152, which cut ditch 153, and this is likely to represent residual re-deposited slag from ditch 153. The assemblage is significant because it indicates that secondary smithing activity took place in the middle Iron Age, possibly within the enclosure of which ditch 153 forms part of the boundary, and because of its association with debris from copperworking.

CERAMIC BUILDING MATERIAL
by Cynthia Poole

Introduction

Ceramic building material (CBM) was recovered from seven sites, of which the largest quantity came from Langford Lane East, which produced 8097 fragments weighing 452.8kg, and to a lesser extent from Langford Lane South, which produced 895 fragments weighing 36.6kg. The vast majority of the tile was Roman in date but small quantities of post-Roman CBM were found on several sites, generally in post-medieval or modern contexts. At the Langford Lane sites this amounted to only seven fragments, mostly field drain, and is not described further though all pieces are fully recorded in the archive.

The tile from all areas was poorly preserved and no complete tiles were found. Only two objects were anywhere near complete – an imbrex and segmental brick, of which *c* 80% and 70% survived respectively. The only complete dimensions other than thickness came from these items and some additional incomplete imbrices from Langford Lane East. A very low mean fragment weight (MFW) pertained to all areas, although individual fragment size ranged from less than 1g to almost 3kg. The overall MFW for all sites combined is 55g and this varies very little in individual groups: Langford Lane South produced a MFW of 41g and Langford Lane East 56g, and the MFW for the combined small assemblages is 57g. Such a low mean fragment weight is surprising for Langford Lane East, where the tile is directly associated with buildings.

A high proportion of the tile from Langford Lane East was associated with the buildings fronting onto the road, although this material represented demolition or dumped debris rather than *in situ* structure. However, the assemblage was remarkably uniform, suggesting all was closely associated in origin. At Langford Lane South over half the assemblage came from just two pits (2611 and 4047) and the remainder from ditches, trackways, layers and a variety of other features. At the smaller sites the tile was recovered from a variety of features, but predominantly ditches and pits typical of rural settlements.

Methodology

The assemblage has been fully recorded in accordance with guidelines set out by the Archaeological Ceramic Building Materials Group (ACBMG 2007). The terminology follows Brodribb (1987). Coding for markings, tegula flanges, etc. follows that established by OA for the recording of CBM, and tegula cutaway types follow an OA typology linked to that established by Warry (2006). Fabrics were characterised with the aid of x20 hand lens or binocular microscope at x25. Material from both Langford Lane sites was discarded during the recording process: all indeterminate and flat tile was discarded as well as more poorly preserved identifiable forms; the better preserved diagnostic forms and tile with well-preserved markings was selected to ensure a characteristic sample was retained from the site as a whole, as well as from the large groups from individual contexts. Approximately two thirds (by weight) of the assemblage has been discarded. Where percentages are quoted in the text below, this is based on weight unless otherwise indicated.

Fabrics

The majority of the tile has been assigned to three broad fabric groups. Within each of these there are a number of sub-types, which can form a merging continuum. These are:

- Group A, a smooth argillaceous fabric,

- Group Q, a sandy fabric characterised by quartz sand inclusions and

- Group E, characterised by laminated clays and 'grog' inclusions.

There was also a small number of additional fabrics which fall outside these, usually represented by only a handful of fragments.

Fabric Group A

This group was essentially a smooth, fine, sandy-silty clay fabric, sometimes finely laminated, containing small white chalk-like pellets and dark red-black ferruginous pellets, usually present in low-moderate densities and less than 1mm in size, although occasionally larger up to *c* 9mm. Usually scattered small circular or oval voids were present, which may have resulted from leaching of calcareous material. Frequent fine cream flecking, possibly calcareous or from cream marl clays, was sometimes visible when viewed with a microscope. It is uncertain whether the white grits are in fact calcareous, but may in fact be leached white mudstone grits, as these were very similar to natural leached white mudstone nodules that had been collected as fired clay.

This group subdivided into four sub-types essentially on the basis of distinctive colour variations. These were:

- A-pp: a pink-cerise-mauve variety often with a purplish or mauve core;

- A-red: red-orange in colour;

- A-fe: reddish brown or brown, usually cracked throughout with black iron deposits on the

planes within the cracks (a similar effect was seen in a natural mudstone nodule from North Oxford Parkway Station);

- D: orange-red surface with a thick grey or bluish grey core.

Fine cream laminations and streaks were most commonly observed in the A-pp sub-type, but were also occasionally visible in the others. Intermediate versions between all these sub-types were observed, sometimes merging from one to the other in a single tile. It would seem that A-red, A-pp and A-fe represent variations in firing, with A-pp being the most heavily fired and including a significant number of overfired pieces, through A-red and D (probably the intended standard), to A-fe, which was underfired and very prone to shatter. A quantity of the discarded tile was deliberately dumped outside to weather and be subject to trample to establish whether the A-fe type was significantly inferior in quality. Over the course of a wet winter most of it had been reduced to unrecognisable shatter and mud in contrast to the relatively unscathed examples of A-red and A-pp.

Moulding sand found on the A group was predominantly fine, though on many pieces it appeared to have all rubbed off and no moulding sand was present. Sometimes the fine sand occurred in conjunction with coarser grits, frequently in the form of clay pellets. A greater size range was observed on the A-red sub-type, with medium and coarse quartz sand utilised as well as coarse grits of mudstone or clay pellets and limestone.

Fabric Group E

This fabric group utilised a low to moderately sandy clay, generally fired to shades of red and orange with streaks and laminations of cream marly clay (sub-type E1). The sand content consisted of medium to coarse quartz sand generally less than 1mm in size in moderate to dense quantities. This could also contain rounded cream marl pellets generally 1-4mm but up to 12mm (sub-type E2) together with red ferruginous clay pellets or red haematite, generally 1-3mm but ranging up to 8mm in size (sub-type E3). Occasionally flint grits were also present. This fabric may be compared to the laminated swirly marbled effect found in the products from the Minety kilns in north-west Wiltshire. On the other hand, it also has similarities to the medieval Oxford tile fabric IV, which is usually associated with the production site at Penn, Buckinghamshire. Evidence from the fired clay, which also included laminated clay fabrics, suggests it could have been a relatively local product. Moulding sand associated with E1 and E2 was generally medium-coarse, whilst fine moulding sand was observed on E1 and E3.

Table 3.32 Quantification of ceramic building material forms from Langford Lane East by phase

| | Phase 3: Late Iron Age | | Phase 4: Roman military | | Phase 5: Early Roman | | Phase 6: Middle Roman | |
	Nos	Wt (g)	Nos	Wt (g)	Nos	Wt (g)	Nos	Wt (g)
Roman								
Brick			7	2317	123	7572	152	33,286
Flat tile			134	6100	514	25,516	1455	77,213
Tegula			32	3391	217	25,144	708	74,011
Imbrex			39	1659	100	5594	986	45,269
Flue			3	109	2	43	5	302
Tessera								
Tile Disc							1	258
Indet	14	60	99	422	121	704	442	3859
Post-Roman								
Field drain								
Total	14	60	314	13,998	1077	64,573	3749	234,198

Table 3.33 Quantification of ceramic building material fabrics from Langford Lane East by phase

| | Phase 3: Late Iron Age | | Phase 4: Roman military | | Phase 5: Early Roman | | Phase 6: Middle Roman | |
	Nos	Wt (g)	Nos	Wt (g)	Nos	Wt (g)	Nos	Wt (g)
A					7	460	28	1127
A [A-cr]							1	38
A [A-fe]	13	57	131	3256	270	9082	1258	58,412
A [A-pp]			48	2423	225	18,355	820	66,853
A [A-red]	1	3	107	5952	449	27,154	1381	89,848
A [D]			19	1512	94	8736	229	16,490
E			2	596	30	567	10	517
Q			7	259	2	219	17	744
H							3	139
U							2	30
Mod								
Total	14	60	314	13,998	1077	64,573	3749	234,198

Fabric Group Q

This group was generally orange, red or brown in colour and is characterised by the presence of moderate to high densities of poorly-sorted fine-medium subangular-subrounded quartz sand, interspersed with scattered coarse sand. Red ferruginous grits and small argillaceous pellets could also be present, together with sparse coarser grits of quartzite, flint, limestone or grog. Fine cream flecks were occasionally observed through the clay matrix. This was subdivided into QF, where a high density of fine or very fine sand was present, generally less than 0.2mm although scattered coarser grains sometimes occurred. One example, categorised as QC, contained a high density of coarse quartz sand (0.5-1.5mm) and small black/grey sand-size inclusions. Sub-type C formed a significant proportion of this group, accounting for slightly under half. It was characterised by a moderate density of well-sorted medium quartz sand, *c* 0.4-0.6mm, evenly distributed throughout the clay matrix, which was red, orange,

pinkish or brownish red in colour, occasionally with cream streaks. Small cream marl or mudstone pellets and red ferruginous grits less than 2mm in size were occasionally present. The moulding sand associated with this group was generally medium-coarse quartz, except on the Q sub-type, where it was fine.

A distinctive sandy fabric only found at Langford Lane South was QL, which contained moderate densities of medium-coarse quartz sand combined with a distinct and consistent scatter of small white chalk or calcareous grits, mostly *c* 1-2mm but up to 6mm and rarely as large as 14mm. These grits also occurred pressed into the underside of the tiles mixed with the moulding sand.

Single occurrences of a highly micaceous sandy clay fabric (M) and another densely gritted with limestone 1-2mm and small brown grits (H) occurred at Langford Lane South and East respectively. Post-Roman tiles were either assigned to Oxford fabric groups OX III and IV, Fabric Group E or designated as modern. A noticeable absence is the Pink Grog tempered (PNKGT) fabric which was

| *Phase 7: Late Roman* | | *Phases 8 and 9: Post-Roman* | | *Unphased* | | *Total* | |
Nos	Wt (g)	Nos	Wt (g)	Nos	Wt (g)	Nos	Wt (g)
65	11,001	38	4514	8	1176	393	59,866
514	41,297	396	15,056	89	3262	3102	168,445
216	29,658	109	9984	32	2335	1314	144,523
120	5547	158	5396	81	1375	1484	64,840
2	76	5	328			17	858
		2	29	1	20	3	49
				1	36	2	294
811	5813	279	2972	15	69	1781	13,899
		1	40			1	40
1728	93,392	988	38,320	227	8273	8097	452,814

| *Phase 7: Late Roman* | | *Phases 8 and 9: Post-Roman* | | *Unphased* | | *Total* | |
Nos	Wt (g)	Nos	Wt (g)	Nos	Wt (g)	Nos	Wt (g)
6	121	8	457			49	2165
						1	38
1056	30,660	168	5486	101	1513	2997	108,465
180	21,548	201	11,379	30	2975	1504	123,533
458	39,400	323	13,396	74	2850	2793	178,603
20	1104	154	5953	21	920	537	34,715
8	559	2	183			52	2422
		131	1427			157	2649
						3	139
				1	15	3	45
		1	40			1	40
1728	93,392	988	38,320	227	8273	8097	452,814

found in the 1991 excavations (Fabric Group 6), only one very uncertain example of which has been identified from Holts Farm Crossing. The fabric sample retained from the earlier excavations is certainly PNKGT, but the quantity assigned to this fabric seems unrealistic in view of the small quantities identified at other sites in the Oxford area and it is likely that, apart from the large imbrices, much of the tile originally assigned to this fabric would prove to be of Group E if re-assessed.

Langford Lane East

The majority of the tile was associated with masonry buildings fronting onto the road. The assemblage was very uniform in character, being completely dominated by fabric A (Tables 3.32 and 3.33). Much of the tile was recovered from collapse or demolition deposits and robbing trenches, cobbled surfaces, roadside ditches and associated deposits. Half the tile was concentrated in contexts assigned to the middle Roman Phase 6. The assemblage was dominated by the standard range of roofing and brick, together with a small quantity of flue tile and possible tesserae. Indeterminate fragments account for a relatively small proportion of the assemblage by weight (3%), but rather larger based on fragment count (22%). Plain flat tile, which cannot be assigned definitively to a particular form, accounts for 37% (by weight) or 38% (by count) of the assemblage. Only 81 tiles had evidence of burning, indicating that only a small proportion had been reused in ovens or hearths in this area of the settlement. The greatest quantity of burnt material was plain flat tile, followed by brick and tegulae, with only a small number of imbrex. Just over 200 fragments had been overfired, resulting in a hard vesicular or vitrified fabric usually maroon, purple, blue-grey or black in colour; a few pieces were heavily distorted and blown. The quantity may indicate that tile production was carried out in the vicinity of the town either on a temporary or permanent basis.

Forms

Brick

Brick was identified on the basis of corner characteristics, when present, or thickness: any items of 40mm thickness or greater were classified as brick, except in a small number of cases where so little survived they could be confused with the outer edge of a tegula flange. Most of the brick was made in fabrics A-red, A-pp and A-fe with very few examples in D, C and E. Most brick had a smooth, flat upper surface and a flat, even, rough or irregular lower surface. The rougher bases also sometimes had evidence of knife or wire trimming. Edges could be rough or smooth, sometimes with evidence of one of each, which may indicate open-ended moulds were used. Some edges had evidence of knife trimming, rarely in their entirety, but more commonly along the lower section if present, to remove any lip of clay squeezed under the mould. In one case the lip had not been trimmed. The only complete dimension was thickness, which ranged from 25-63mm, and the bricks commonly thickened to the edge or corner creating a slightly dished top surface; the maximum surviving length/width was 240 and 255mm.

The surviving sizes suggest that a variety of brick types are represented and that at least *pedalis* or *lydion* sizes were in use. The number over 50mm thick suggests a few of the larger varieties such as *sesquipedalis* and *bipedalis* may also be present. Two bricks had a shallow vertical rectangular recess 20-23mm wide by 5mm deep made in the edge *c* 50mm from the corner. This may indicate the bricks were for use as wall tile, used in conjunction with a bobbin and T-clamp. However, no keying was present on the surfaces as might be expected, so the feature might relate to the type of moulds used to produce the bricks.

A total of 41 corners were present, representing a minimum number of 10 bricks. One brick has an indented border 20mm wide alongside the top edge, probably made by using the mould to flatten and neaten the edge. Finger- or thumb-prints from handling during manufacture were found on six bricks and on one a shallow groove extended from the print, suggestive of the brick sliding out of the tiler's grasp. Signature marks were identified on nine bricks, generally of the more common type 1 and 5 varieties when identifiable.

A common function for brick was in the construction of hypocausts, but there is no evidence for such structures in the excavation. In respect of the surviving buildings the brick is most likely to have been used as paving or in walls. A few pieces were found reused in the cobbled surfaces alongside the road ditch. The majority occurred in demolition deposits with some dumped in pits or ditches.

Tegulae and flat tile

Tegulae were rectangular roof tiles with a flange running along both sides with a cutaway at top and lower corners and were used in conjunction with

curved imbrices. They accounted for a third (32%) of the assemblage, whilst the flat tile forms slightly over a third (37%). The flat tile could derive from a range of forms, including tegula, brick, the plain sides of flue tiles and flatter, more angular-profiled imbrex. However, the similarity in finish and general character suggests a high proportion of the flat tile represents the central flat section of tegulae between the flanges, which is otherwise under-represented. The only complete dimension for tegulae was thickness, which ranged from 12mm up to 35mm; the bulk was concentrated between 18-30mm thick, although individual tiles could vary in their thickness, especially if knife-trimmed alongside the edge on the underside. The maximum surviving width of any tegula was 215mm and the maximum surviving length was 320mm.

The upper surfaces were smoothly finished in the majority of cases, although a very small number were rougher or lumpy or had fine striations from wiping. The bases were most commonly rough and flat or irregular and pitted, with a significant number being subsequently knife- or wire-trimmed across the whole base or alongside the edges. The coarse pitting in the base resulted from pellets of moulding sand or waste clay pellets pressing into the soft clay, though only a few adhered permanently. A small proportion had smooth, flat bases. Edges were rough-sanded or smoothed, with the characteristic knife trimming occurring along many edges, especially the lower half of the flange exterior. Top and lower ends were often trimmed along both upper and lower sections. Some edges were cut to a bevel in their entirety and on some the arris was cut to a narrow bevel. A total of 294 corner fragments survived, representing a gross minimum number of 74 tiles. When divided into the different corners this gives a minimum number of 91 tiles. The total weight is representative of approximately 18 tegulae (based on a weight of 8kg) and if the flat tile (a high proportion of which is likely to be tegula) is also included this adds the equivalent of a further 21 tegulae. Only three nail holes were found, two made pre-firing measuring 7mm and 10mm in diameter set 32mm from the top edge and one made post-firing, 4mm in diameter with a large flake scar encircling it.

Flange profiles (Fig. 3.20, Table 3.34) exhibited a wide range of sizes and forms, though more angular and rectangular forms (OA types A, A1-A3, B, C) were less common than curving types (OA types A4, D, D2, E, F, F2), which accounted for 88% of flanges. Nearly 500 flanges had a complete profile surviving and a further 46 were partial. Flange width ranged from 18-40mm and height from 26-66mm at a gross level. A taper was commonly noted on flanges where sufficient length survived: the flange was narrowest at the top, widening to the base, but there was usually little variation in the flange height. This feature becomes more frequent in later tiles, when the overall tile size decreases and the tiles taper to the base to form a slightly trapezoidal-shaped tile. The variations in width must in part reflect the taper of the flanges, but it is also clear that there was considerable variation in size across the range of flanges. Similarly, there was a lot of variation in flange profile with gradation between types and flattened facets or finger grooves running along the internal face creating atypical profiles (Fig. 3.20, no. 28) that cannot be readily assigned to the more standard forms. The lower internal angle could be rounded or fairly abrupt or angular, although a curved base angle tends to be more common on flanges with an overall curving profile. A single finger groove running along the inner base angle of the flange is a common feature on tegulae, but was only observed on about a fifth of examples. This may be accounted for by the large number of fragments that consisted of the flange alone; there appeared to be a disproportionate number of fragments of this type, which may

indicate that tegulae were deliberately being deflanged prior to re-use.

Cutaways at the corners of the tegulae were designed to enable tiles to be interlocked, and the changes of forms and sizes of lower cutaways has been demonstrated by Warry (2006) to be a chronological development reflecting overall changes in tile size and shape. Lower cutaways were identified on 159 pieces and upper cutaways on 116 tiles (Fig. 3.20). Upper cutaways were all of standard form (OA type A2), usually made by an inset in the mould creating a rectangular recess. It was not uncommon for this to be neatened or modified through knife trimming the surface or ends, resulting in some which had bases sloping to the outer edge or end or where the end of the flange had been cut to a bevel or at an angle. They measured 18-50mm long, apart from one that was 58-70mm long.

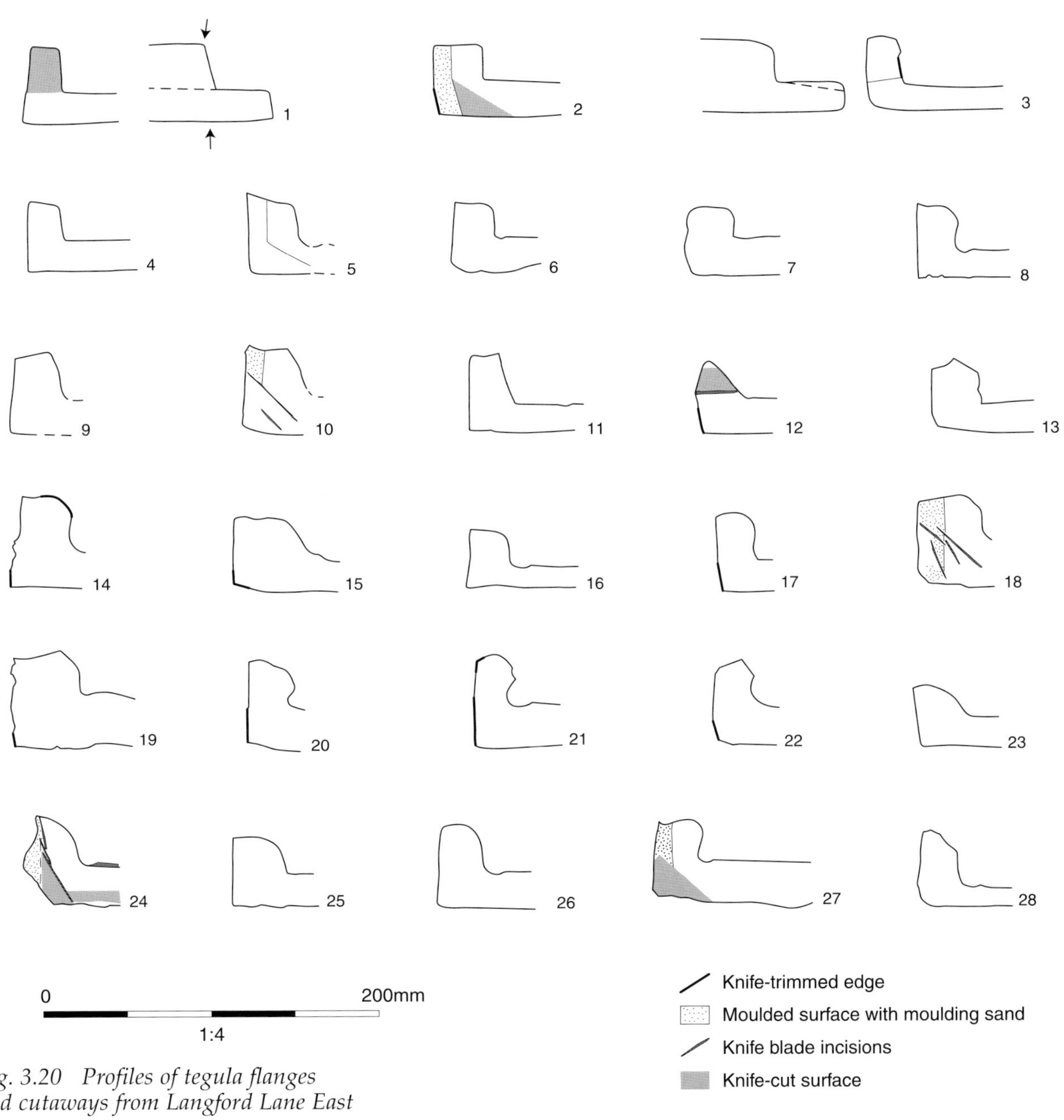

Fig. 3.20   Profiles of tegula flanges and cutaways from Langford Lane East

Table 3.34 Langford Lane East tegula flange types and sizes and associated features

Flange type	Number	Width mm	Height mm	Finger groove	Curved base angle	Angular base angle	Taper	Associated cutaway
A	21	18-32	38-58	3	0	11	5	C5
A2	4	23-27	42-47	1	2	1	-	-
A3	8	21-28	28-53	1	4	0	-	C4, C5
A4	103	18-42	26-58	17	43	22	24	B6, C5, D16
A5	11	22-35	40-49	3	4	2	-	C5
B	15	10-25t; 19-34b	32-54	1	7	0	-	C5
C	2	30-33	40-44	2	2	0	-	-
A4/D	27	17-37	38-61	7	10	3	9	C5, D16
D	180	18-40	32-63	28	68	22	21	B6, C4, C5, D16
D2	34	17-31	26-66	15	18	1	-	C5, D16
E	26	13-37	37-50	4	10	8	4	D16
F	33	20-36	34-56	4	9	8	5	B6, C4, C5
F2	17	21-33	38-58	3	11	2	2	C5
Total	481			89	188	80	70	

t = top and b = base widths for type B

Lower cutaways (Fig. 3.20, Table 3.35) ranged from 25-68mm long and fell into Warry's groups B, C and D (Warry 2006, 4). On some tiles where the flange is broken it has not always been possible to differentiate type B cutaways from the lower section of type C5. Complete measurements were not obtained for all cutaways, as they were often fragmentary and incomplete. The type B6 cutaways were made by cutting a wedge from the lower corner of the flange. The others were all initially produced by an inset in the mould producing a rectangular recess in the outer edge of the flange, which was usually left unmodified in C4 cutaways, although occasionally neatened with knife trimming, whilst the others were modified by cutting a further wedge from the lower angle in the case of C5 or a tall narrow wedge removing all or most of the side (OA types A3a and A3b), both of which have been assigned to Warry's D16 category. A modification noted on a quarter of the C5 category was a narrow bevel cut into the top end of the flange, usually measuring 5-15mm wide and 15-20mm deep. Tiles with this feature occur in all phases and it does not appear to reflect a chronological development. Warry has suggested broad dates for the cutaway types, which are compared with the site phasing in Table 3.36. None of Warry's early group A cutaways were found,

Table 3.35 Langford Lane East tegula lower cutaway types and sizes

Warry c/a type	Date	OA equivalent	Nos	Length (mm)	Width (mm, base of c/a)	Height (mm)	
B6	AD 100-180	C1	27	32-41 & >47	38, 40, >42	22	cut
C4	AD 160-260	A3	10	40	5-15	full ht	mould
C5	AD 160-260	A3/C1	81	25-58	7-15 / 23-58	full/20-45	mould/cut
C5	AD 160-260	A3/C1/B2	28	35-68	9-15/30-40	full ht/20-40, 53	mould/cut
D16	AD 240-380	A3a	8	32-55	25-42	full ht	mould/cut
D16	AD 240-380	A3b	5	40	17-35	30-44	mould/cut

Table 3.36 Langford Lane East tegula numbers of lower cutaway types in relation to phasing

Cutaway dating	AD 100-180	AD 160-260	AD 160-260	AD 240-380
Phase	B6	C4	C5	D16
4: Roman military phase (c 43-70)	-	-	4	-
5: Early Roman (late 1st-early 2nd century)	5	4	13	2
6: Middle Roman (2nd-early 3rd century)	13	4	62	10
7: Late Roman period (mid 3rd-4th century)	5	2	22	-
8: Post-Roman	4	-	8	1

which would be contemporary with the military phase. All the cutaways are of 2nd-century date or later. There is therefore something of a mismatch between the suggested dates of the cutaways in relation to phases 4 and 5, although the group B types could be contemporary with the latest years of Phase 5.

Imbrex and ridge tile

Imbrices accounted for 14% of the assemblage. Most imbrices were made in the group A fabrics, whilst only a handful were made in the sandy Fabric Q, a few in laminated fabric E and one in shelly fabric H. No complete examples survived, although width and height were estimated for some examples where the tile apex and edge survived. There was only one near-complete (80%) imbrex, reconstructed from 15 fragments (Fig. 3.21, no. 29). It measured 485mm long and 130mm wide at the top, increasing to 162mm at the lower end and 53mm high at the top end increasing to 88mm at the lower end. Thickness ranged from 11mm at the apex to 21mm

at the corner. A second imbrex from the same context had an incomplete length of 415mm and two others had complete widths of 150 and 155mm. Widths could be estimated on a number of fragments and ranged from 110 to 180mm, reflecting the variation in a single imbrex. Similarly, heights ranged from 60-90mm. Thickness ranged from 10-26mm, with individual tiles showing considerable variation, thickening from the apex area to the edges and corners. One exceptionally measured 19-31mm thick and could represent a ridge tile, though in general there was no suggestion of specialised ridge tiles and standard imbrex tiles may have served this purpose.

The outer surface was smooth and even, only rarely exhibiting fine striations from wiping or longitudinal shallow corrugations from shaping. The underside varied from smooth, through rough-sanded to irregular, often with rounded depressions left by clay pellets or lumps of moulding sand. Edges were a mix of rough and smooth, but both ends and sides were often concave.

Fig. 3.21   Imbrices from Langford Lane East

Flue tile

Flue tile represents less than 0.2% of the tile and was found as a sparse scatter with one or two examples occurring in all Roman and later phases. Most occurred in demolition and abandonment levels, although two were reused in cobbled surfaces. All were made in Group A fabrics, especially A-red, except for one in Fabric Q. Most were identified by keying, but a few were plain and only identified on the basis of an external corner. No vents were present. The flue tile is all *tubulus* or box flue, keyed with combing. The exclusive use of combing and absence of earlier keying techniques (scored or roller stamped) suggests the flue tile is of 2nd-century or later date.

The only complete dimension was thickness, which ranged from 12 to 25mm. The thickest fragment had few features to identify it as flue, but the convex exterior surface is similar to examples of thick flue tile with rounded angles at Cotswold Community, where this type occurred in middle-late Roman phased contexts (Poole 2010). Exterior surfaces were generally smooth and flat and the internal surface flat and even or slightly rough and sanded. Few edges survived but these were fairly even or smooth. No burning or heat discolouration was observed on the interior surface.

The combing took the form of straight and diagonal bands, sometimes with two bands crossing; on one piece the bands were slightly wavy (Fig. 3.21, no. 31). No complete keying designs survived, although crossing bands form a number of common designs, such as crosses, saltires or cross-hatch patterns. Few complete comb widths survived, although many were fairly coarse or with widely spaced teeth. There were several examples consisting of three (possibly more originally) thin teeth set 9-10mm apart. Only one complete comb width was found, measuring 41mm with five teeth, each 1.5-2.5mm wide and set 6-8mm apart.

Miscellaneous

Four possible tesserae, all in fabric A(D) measured 18-35mm and were trapezoidal or sub-square in shape. Only one had cream lime mortar attached to the edges and base. One was made from an imbrex; the others are pieces of flat tile probably from tegulae.

Two circular discs chipped from tile were found. One in fabric A-red was 160mm in diameter and

Table 3.37 Langford Lane East signature types in relation to form and phasing

Type	Total nos	Forms				Phasing			Fabric	Sizes/Comments
		Tegula	Brick	Flat	Mil	ER	MR	LR+		
1.1	16	5	2	9	0	3	8	5	A-red (5), A-pp (5), A-fe (6)	60mm w x 22mm h; 180mm w x *c* 90-100mm h
1.1b	4	1	0	3	0	0	4	0	A-red (2), A-fe (1), D (1),	230mm w x 60mm h
1.2	15	11	2	2	0	2	10	3	A-red (10), A-pp (2), D (2),	140mm w x 62mm h; *c* 150mm w x 70mm h; *c* 170-80mm w x *c* 90mm h
1.2b	2	0	0	2	0	0	2	0	A-fe	*c* 180mm w x 50mm h; 54mm h
1.3	1	1	0	0	0	0	0	1	A-red	
1.4	8	3	0	5	0	3	4	1	A-red (4), A-pp (2), A-fe (2)	*c* 230mm w x 90mm h; *c* 180mm w; 70mm h; 90mm h
2.1	5	2	0	3	0	1	2	2	A-red (2), A-pp (2), A-fe (1)	*c* 90mm w & h; *c* 85mm w x 71mm h
2.3	1	1	0	0	0	1	0	0	A-red	
4.1	12	7	0	5	1	2	1	8	A-red (4), A-pp (3), A-fe (4); D (1)	70mm dia, 90mm dia, 150mm dia, *c* 75mm dia, *c* 110mm dia; 70.5mm w x 87mm h; 65mm w x 72mm h; 65mm w x 85mm h
5.1	16	7	1	8	0	1	11	4	A-red (8), A-pp (6), A-fe (2)	55mm w x 95mm h; 48mm w x 40mm l; 40mm w x 100mm l; 46mm w x >85mm l; 67mm w x 94mm l; 70mm w x 85mm h; 60mm w
Curved	28	11	2	15	0	2	20	6	A-red (10), A-pp (7), A-fe (7), D (2)	
Straight	4	2	1	1	0	1	1	2	A-pp	Straight diagonal finger groove ?tail of type 5; short lengths could be larger curved types
Indet	10	3	1	6	1	2	5	2	A-red (5), A-pp (2), A-fe (1), D (2)	
Total	122	54	9	59	2	18	68	34		

neatly made. The other was made in fabric A-pp, roughly chipped to 145mm diameter, and had possibly broken and been left unfinished. The function of such discs is uncertain but they were possibly used as lids for amphorae or large storage jars.

Markings

Signatures

Signature marks (Fig. 3.22, Table 3.37) were the commonest form of marking, occurring on a total of 111 tiles – predominantly tegula and flat tile (most of which are likely to be tegula) and brick. Signatures relate to the production process and were possibly intended to indicate the tiler and their output. All were made by the fingers describing shapes in the soft clay after moulding and in one case had clearly been made before the tile edge was knife-trimmed (probably at the leather-hard stage). Four basic types were identified, classified as type 1: semi-circular or curved arc, type 2: horseshoe, type 4: circle or Q, and type 5: loop. Approximately a third could not be classi-

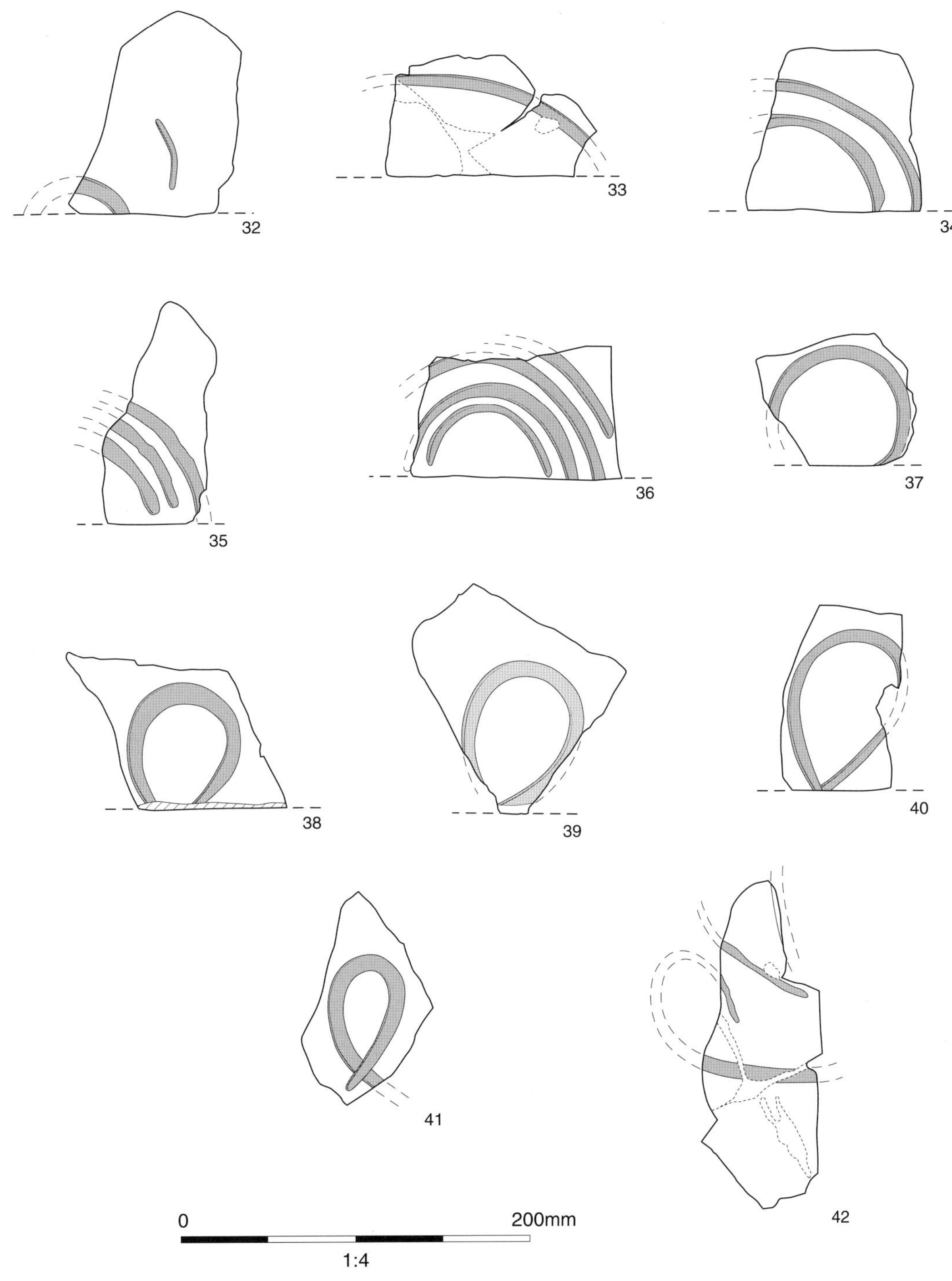

Fig. 3.22 Signature marks on tiles from Langford Lane East

fied but all are likely to derive from the types identified. Each type was subdivided by the number of finger-grooves present (1.1, 1.2 etc) and a sub-type was identified in group 1 as 1.1b, characterised by a shallow low arc. Most of the signatures started and finished close to or at the lower edge; only type 5 was sometimes set slightly above the edge. Type 5 occurred both perpendicular and at an angle to the tile edge and was found with and without tails (Fig. 3.22, nos 39-42). Type 1 could have been further subdivided based on the size as there is a considerable range from some very small examples to much larger. The signatures occur on all sub-types of fabric group A and there is no correlation between fabric types and particular signatures.

44

Fig. 3.23 Footprints on tiles from Langford Lane East

Imprints

A total of 33 imprints or impressions were found, all incidental and accidental, made during the production cycle except possibly for three lines of lightly impressed finger-marks on the apex of an imbrex, which may have been intended as some form of decoration, although unlikely to be visible once on a roof. The majority (20) were finger and thumb marks from the tilers when handling the tile while the clay was still soft. They occurred on tegula, imbrex, brick and flat tile in group A fabrics. A further five were occasional impressions of grass or straw stems, usually in the surface but occasionally caught in the tile core. These occurred on tegula, imbrex and flat tile in group A fabrics. The remainder were footprints, both human and animal. One large paw print consisting of two pads measuring 44mm wide is probably dog. A smaller print measuring 34 x 27mm with four pads visible is probably a cat paw print. Another partial imprint is probably an ovicaprid hoof mark. Human prints included one with two small circular depressions possibly from hobnails (ctx 7019). However, of greater interest are three examples of a young child or toddler's foot. The best preserved imprint (Fig. 3.23, no. 43) came from context 7063 and comprises the right foot with all five toes and the ball of the foot clearly impressed, but not the heel. The maximum width (across toes) is 59mm, the foot width 40mm, and length from top of big toe to instep 53mm; the big toe measured 24mm long x 19mm wide. This is similar to the partial imprint (ctx 6554) of a left foot consisting of a big toe, which measures 24 x19mm, and part of the ball. Further partial imprints on a tile from ctx 7116 appeared to consist of two (or possibly three) overlapping prints, probably of a toddler's toes (Fig. 3.23, no. 44). It is difficult to tell which feet are represented (left, right or both): there are a total of eight toe marks, two of which are overlapping. The largest toe measures 17.5 x 11.5mm and the possible widths of the feet are (a) 3 toes 31mm, (b) 4 toes 44mm. All occur on fragments of flat tile, probably tegula, made in fabric A-red/D in early and middle Roman and abandonment deposits.

Graffiti

Possible graffiti occurred on two tiles. On an imbrex (ctx 6503) were two scored lines diverging slightly, made post-firing. A flat tile (ctx 6554) had a thick line marked in the form of a V but extending beyond the broken edge. It is uncertain whether either is deliberate or what they might denote. The second could possibly be a tally mark or an odd type of signature mark.

Langford Lane South

A moderate-sized assemblage of CBM consisting of 894 fragments (36,584g) was recovered from

Langford Lane South, predominantly from ditch and pit fills, in particular pits 2611 and 4047 with lesser amounts from tree hollows and superficial layers (Tables 3.38 and 3.39). Nearly three quarters of the tile (two thirds of fragments) was concentrated in contexts assigned to the middle Roman Phase 6. The assemblage was dominated by the standard range of roofing and brick, together with a small quantity of flue tile and tesserae. Indeterminate fragments account for a small proportion of the assemblage by weight (2%) but rather larger based on fragment count (22%). Plain flat tile, which cannot be assigned definitively to a particular form, accounts for 30% (by weight) or 50% (by count) of

the assemblage. Only 25 tiles had evidence of burning, indicating that reuse of tile in ovens or hearths was very limited in this area of the settlement. The most frequently burnt was plain flat tile, together with two brick, five tegulae, an imbrex and two tesserae. Only 18 fragments had evidence of over-firing, resulting in a hard fabric with vitrified sheen and usually maroon or blue-grey in colour; there were no heavily distorted or vesicular-vitrified pieces present. Most of the overfired pieces were imbrex but also include a tegula and brick. Although the quantity is not as large as at Langford Lane East, the fabrics are more varied and include Groups Q and E as well as Group A.

Table 3.38 Quantification of ceramic building material forms from Langford Lane South by phase

	Phase 5: Early Roman		Phase 6: Middle Roman		Phase 7: Late Roman		Phases 8 and 9: Post-Roman		Unphased		Total	
	Nos	Wt (g)	Nos	Wt (g)	Nos	Wt (g)	Nos	Wt (g)	Nos	Wt (g)	Nos	Wt (g)
Roman												
Brick			19	5511			2	235			21	5746
Flat tile	85	956	283	7621	1	6	31	1118	46	1355	446	11,056
Tegula	15	1272	57	4859	1	92	5	412	16	1916	94	8551
Imbrex	9	343	75	7166			10	667	17	764	111	8940
Flue			7	532			1	150			8	682
Tessera	1	10	7	143			1	23	3	37	12	213
Tile disc							1	86			1	86
Indet	9	76	148	556			17	97	20	70	194	799
Post-Roman												
Roof							2	95			2	95
Field drain							4	159			4	159
Concrete			1	257							1	257
Total	119	2657	597	26,645	2	98	74	3042	102	4142	894	36,584

Table 3.39 Quantification of ceramic building material fabrics from Langford Lane South by phase

	Phase 5: Early Roman		Phase 6: Middle Roman		Phase 7: Late Roman		Phases 8 and 9: Post-Roman		Unphased		Total	
	Nos	Wt (g)	Nos	Wt (g)	Nos	Wt (g)	Nos	Wt (g)	Nos	Wt (g)	Nos	Wt (g)
Roman												
A	2	81									2	81
A [A-cr]			3	95							3	95
A [A-fe]	1	6	12	565			18	309	1	36	32	916
A [A-pp]	8	276	10	598					1	327	19	1201
A [A-red]	86	1528	341	11,524	1	6	41	1624	60	2054	529	16,736
A [D]	9	252	8	610			3	168	6	220	26	1250
E	6	224	54	6880			4	419	16	945	80	8468
Q	7	290	61	3776	1	92	4	396	8	492	81	5046
QL			25	2107			1	29	2	60	28	2196
M									8	8	8	8
U			82	233							82	233
Post-Roman												
Mod							3	97			3	97
Concrete			1	257							1	257
Total	119	2657	597	26,645	2	98	74	3042	102	4142	894	36,584

Forms

Brick

Brick was classified on the same basis as described above for Langford Lane East. Most of the bricks were made in fabric Q, together with E and single examples in A-red, A-pp, A-fe and D. Most bricks had a smooth flat upper surface, a flat even rough or irregular lower surface and mostly rough edges with only one knife-trimmed. A few rougher bases also had evidence of knife or wire trimming. For most of the bricks the only complete dimension was thickness, which ranged from 24-53mm. These sizes are comparable to Langford Lane East and suggest a range of brick types and sizes are represented. In addition to the standard rectangular brick, a well preserved example of a semi-circular segmental brick (Fig. 3.24, no. 45) was found. This measured 60mm thick, 177mm wide and over 255mm long, and although missing both corners was estimated to be 300mm long in total based on the circumference. This is slightly under the average size recorded for such bricks by Brodribb (1987, 55) and is clearly based on the Roman foot. Although Brodribb suggests such bricks were made in a circular mould and cut in half, this example appears to have been made in a semi-circular mould from the character of the edges.

Flat tile

Flat tile formed a significant proportion of the assemblage (30% by weight, but half of all fragments) and occurs in all fabric types found on the site. Thickness ranged from 9-36mm with a peak

Fig. 3.24   Ceramic building material from Langford Lane South

between 20-25mm, indicating that much of the flat tile represents the central plain sections of tegulae, although all other major tile forms are almost certainly present within this group. One flat tile in Fabric A-fe had been roughly chipped to the form of a circular disc measuring 68 x 73mm and 18mm thick with edges bevelled top and bottom.

Tegulae

Tegulae surprisingly formed a smaller proportion of the assemblage than imbrices in both count (10%) and weight (23%). A minimum number of seven tiles is indicated by numbers of corners, whilst the total weight of tegulae is equivalent to a single complete tegula. Tile thickness ranged from 15 to 29mm, but no other dimensions were complete. The general character of tiles is similar to Langford Lane East with smooth flat tops, rough bases, occasionally knife- or wire-trimmed, and the edges were generally rough, occasionally with knife trimming along the lower part. The flange types encompass the same range as at Langford Lane East and are summarised in Table 3.40, with rounded type D forming the commonest category. The standard rectangular upper cutaway was found on thirteen tiles, but no complete lengths survived, the best preserved being over 55-61mm long. Some had been knife-trimmed following moulding, resulting on occasion in a bevelled flange end and in one case the end of the flange was thumb-pressed to create a bevel. Lower cutaways were identified on 12 tiles. They may all be of type C5, although some incomplete fragments could be type C4 or the earlier type B5. The few complete lengths range from 50 to 80mm and widths of the moulded rectangular recess measure 2-18mm and the lower cut wedge-shaped section 21-40mm. The cutaways all have a date range of mid-2nd to mid-3rd century based on the analysis by Warry (2006) and most were found in middle Roman contexts, apart from two from the lower fill of an early Roman ditch and some from post-Roman or undated contexts.

Imbrex

Imbrex accounted for a quarter of the assemblage by weight (12% by count). Imbrices were made in a range of fabrics, including all the group A fabrics, sandy fabrics Q and QL and fabric E, although fabric A-red was dominant. No complete examples survived, although width and height was estimated for a few examples where the tile apex and edge survived. These measured *c* 150-190mm wide and 75-90mm high. Thickness ranged from 10-28mm, usually thinnest at the apex and thickening towards the edges and corner. The maximum surviving length was 197mm. The outer surface was smooth and even, with only three having longitudinal shallow corrugations from shaping. The underside was even, rough-sanded or irregular, sometimes with rounded depressions left by clay pellets or lumps of moulding sand. Edges were a mix of rough and smooth, but both ends and sides were often concave. Side edges were often angled, especially in those with a more angular profile. Both angular and rounded profiles were present.

Flue tile

The flue tile formed a tiny proportion of the assemblage (less than 2%) and consisted mostly of box flue (*tubulus*) tile fragments, apart from a single example of scored wall tile (Fig. 3.24, no. 46). The latter was made in fabric Q and measured 31mm thick. The underside was deeply scored with a knife blade forming keying in a diamond pattern of thin lines 40 and 48mm apart. This type of flue tile was produced in the 1st-early 2nd century. It was found in middle Roman pit 2611, which also produced a piece of box flue. Box flue was identified on the basis of keying and form, and in one case the presence of a square-cut vent set 35mm from the corner angle. They were made in fabrics A and Q, with one in an unusual pale cream variety of fabric A. They measured 13-17mm thick and it is possible unidentifiable fragments occurred amongst the thinner flat tile. Combed

Table 3.40 Langford Lane South tegula flange types and sizes and associated features

Flange type	Number	Width mm	Height mm	Finger groove	Curved base angle	Angular base angle	Taper	Associated cutaway
A	2	25-28	46-52	-	2	-	-	-
A2	2	20-26	53	-	-	-	-	-
A3	4	22-38	42-55	1	2	1	2	B6, C5
A4	3	18-35	47-54	-	2	1	2	C5
A5	2	32-38	50-55	2	2	-	-	C4
A/D	5	23-33	44-47	1	2	1	1	-
D	14	22-31	47-60	2	8	-	-	B6, C5
D2	2	[17-20 at c/a]	>47	-	1	-	-	B6, C6
E	2	21-31+	49-54	-	-	-	-	C5
F	4	23-39	44-61	-	2	-	2	-
F2	4	23-28	42	1	1	-	-	C5
D/F	1	25	52	-	-	-	-	-
Total	45			7	22	3	7	

keying occurred on five fragments and took the form of straight bands, which on one ran alongside the edge and another parallel to the corner angle (Fig. 3.24, no. 47). Two complete comb widths measured 59 and 69mm wide, both with nine teeth. Combed box flue come into common use during the 2nd century and all were found in pits 2011 and 2047, both of middle Roman date, apart from one example from the topsoil.

Tesserae

A small number of tesserae were identified, largely based on shape and size, although some did appear to have a worn surface, but no mortar adhered to any. They were fairly coarse, measuring 20-40mm in size, though one was smaller at 13 x 17mm All were square or rectangular and occurred in a variety of fabrics (A, Q, E) and colours including red-orange, pink, grey, pinkish brown and salmon.

Markings

Apart from keying, markings occurred on only ten tiles. Two had imprints of fingertips from handling and a third imprint was uncertain, the depressions being rather larger for fingers and possibly being toes or part of an animal paw print. Signatures occurred on seven fragments of flat tile, most probably originating from tegula but one possibly from a brick, with fabrics A, Q, QL and E represented, including another example of the unusual cream coloured fabric A. Identifiable signatures comprised two forming arcs of type 1.2, one horseshoe-shaped of type 2.2 and very fragmentary examples of a possible loop of type 5 and circle of type 4.

South of Merton

A small quantity of Roman and later tile amounting to five fragments (251g) comprised Roman imbrex, brick and flat tile made in fabrics A, C, Q and E and a medieval/post-medieval flat roof tile made in Oxford tile fabric IV (Table 3.41).

Holts Farm Crossing

A small assemblage of tile was recovered from the site, amounting to 54 fragments (1601g), largely Roman in date but including a small quantity (10 fragments, 204g) of medieval, post-medieval and modern flat roof tile and peg tile and field drain, which were found in subsoil or furrow fills or in the upper silting of Roman ditches (Table 3.41). The roof tile was made in Oxford fabrics III and IV and whilst they may have been introduced as a result of manuring, none is particularly heavily abraded and it is possible they were used in the creation of early field drainage.

The Roman tile comprised predominantly flat tile and tegula together with an imbrex and possible brick made in fabrics A-red, A-pp, E, C, and Q. One tegula may be made in the pink grogged ware fabric (PNK GT) that is thought to derive from a source somewhere in the vicinity of Towcester-Milton Keynes. However, the identification is by no means certain and it is not typical in character, suggesting this may be one of the local E group fabrics. Only one tegula flange, of type D, was present and a separate tile had a lower cutaway of type C5 with bevelled end, which is dated by Warry to AD 160-260. Two small pieces of flat tile may have been deliberately shaped to form medium-sized tesserae: one is pink in colour and trapezoidal in shape and the other light orange and rectangular. The first measured 17-25 x 25mm and 23mm thick and the second 18 x 21mm and 15mm thick. Only three tiles had evidence of burning indicative of reuse in ovens or hearths.

Table 3.41 Quantification of the small ceramic building material assemblages by site and phase with a note of diagnostic forms

Site and phases	Nos	Wt (g)	Forms
Holts Farm Crossing total	54	1601	MFW: 30g
Phase 5: Early Roman (late 1st-early 2nd century)	5	296	Tegula, flat tile, tessera
Phase 6: Middle Roman (2nd century)	8	127	Flat tile, brick, tessera, peg tile, field drain
Phase 7: Late Roman (3rd-4th century)	27	639	Flat tile, tegula, imbrex
Phases 8 and 9: Post-Roman	6	169	Roof tile
Undated	8	370	Tegula, flat tile
South of Merton total	5	251	Mean fragment weight: 50g
Phase 6: Middle Roman (2nd century)	1	52	Brick
Undated	4	199	Flat tile, imbrex, roof tile
South of Oddington Crossing total	7	1004	Mean fragment weight: 143g
Phase 9: Modern	7	1004	Brick, refractory tile, pipe, ridge tile
North of Gallos Brook total	2	71	Mean fragment weight: 35g
Undated	2	71	Flat tile, brick
North of Oxford Parkway Station total	6	976	Mean fragment weight: 163g
Undated	6	976	Brick (RB), flat tile, tegula, roller-stamped flue tile

South of Oddington Crossing

Only a small quantity of ceramic building material was recovered, all of post-medieval date comprising a ridge tile, a refractory tile or hollow firebrick, a standard solid brick and a drainage or sewer pipe (Table 3.41). All are of 19th century date, except for the ridge tile which could be a little earlier.

North of Gallos Brook

A fragment of early post-medieval brick 51mm thick and made in fabric E, and an indeterminate scrap of undated tile, were recovered (Table 3.41).

North of Oxford Parkway Station

A small quantity of Roman tile amounting to six fragments weighing 976g was recovered from the site (Table 3.41). All was made in fabric E, a strongly laminated clay commonly containing cream marl pellets or red ferruginous clay pellets or haematite grits and occasional flint grit. The tile included tegula, flat tile, a brick and a roller-stamped flue tile. The tegula had a round flange of type F and a lower cutaway of Warry type C5, which Warry dates to AD 160-260. The flue tile came from the same context (3224) but has an earlier date range of AD 80-150. The roller-stamped keying on the surface is only very faintly visible and is in the pattern of Lowther's 'billet' design, Die 92 (Betts *et al.* 1997) (Fig. 3.25, no. 48). Other examples of Die 92 have been found at Lower Wanborough, Swindon, Littlecote Park, Hungerford, and Claydon Pike, Gloucestershire. It has been suggested that this die and fabric type was being produced at Minety. However, it is very clear from the similarity of fired clay fabrics on the

Fig. 3.25   Roller-stamped keying on box flue tile from North of Oxford Parkway Station

site with that of the tile that the tile could have been produced fairly locally.

Discussion

The assemblages from the individual sites vary considerably in size, date and character. Apart from the Langford Lane sites, the others are all relatively small with only Holts Farm Crossing and North of Oxford Parkway Station producing groups of any size. The others produced only a handful of fragments, each comprising a mix of Roman and post-medieval tile and brick. Holts Farm and North of Oxford Parkway Station are typical small rural assemblages, where a heterogeneous mix of tile was acquired in small quantities for reuse in structures such as hearths and ovens. Langford Lane East, by contrast, produced a very large uniform assemblage associated with three buildings fronting onto the road, while Langford Lane South contained a greater variety of fabrics and forms, which may represent a more typical range of the building material utilised in Alchester.

Production

The tile from the Langford Lane sites and other smaller sites has produced a range of fabrics, all of which are likely to be local or regional products. The Group A fabrics were found at most of the sites and is overwhelmingly dominant at Langford Lane East, where the assemblage may represent a single purchase of building material for the construction of one or more related buildings. At Langford Lane South the assemblage encompasses the same range of fabrics, although group A, whilst remaining dominant, forms a smaller proportion (Fig. 3.26). Roman tile production sites are poorly known in Oxfordshire, though suitable clay deposits are readily available, as is evident from the Roman Oxford pottery industry. The only tile production site in Oxfordshire has been identified some 15km south-west of Alchester near North Leigh, where tile-makers were probably exploiting the clay or mudstone of the Kellaways Clay Member and the Oxford Clay and West Walton formations (Brodribb *et al.* 1971, 10, note 1). This is well within the limits over which tile appears to have been marketed, which could be as much as 80km as suggested by the distribution of stamped tile from the Minety kilns (Warry 2006, 123). However, with suitable clay deposits available close to Alchester (deposits of Peterborough Member Mudstone and Oxford Clay and West Walton Formation outcrop in the neighbouring areas) it would be surprising if tile was transported in any quantity from further afield. Even in the 19th century, with improved transport, the cost of bricks doubled when transported by railway more than forty miles (Dobson 1850, 114) and the carriage of bricks a mere five miles could increase cost by 40% (Cox

1979, 31). Even if not strictly comparable, it is likely that transport costs would have added a significant element to the cost of tile in the Roman period and where suitable raw materials were available it is reasonable to start from the premise that production would be fairly local.

The similarities in character of the fired clay at North of Oxford Parkway Station to Fabric E suggests that relatively local production is a probability, whilst a mudstone nodule collected from the site as fired clay exhibited evidence of leaching and iron deposition in planes, similar to the effect found in fabric A-fe. The general uniformity of fabrics across the sites suggest relatively local production, although possibly supplied by two or three tileries exploiting slightly different clay sources. There is little evidence that tiles were obtained from more distant areas. One tile possibly in pink grogged ware from Holts Farm Crossing may suggest that tile was occasionally obtained from the Towcester-Milton Keynes area, but its identification as this fabric is uncertain and it may be a variant of Fabric E. The roller-stamped tile from North of Oxford Parkway Station may indicate that specialised tiles were sometimes acquired from the Minety kilns, although it is possible it was the tiler rather than the tiles that moved around.

The condition and quality of the tiles from Langford Lane East made in fabric group A are a further indicator that they were produced relatively close to the town. They range from overfired and vitrified (4%), with a few pieces even distorted and blown (some, but not all in fabric A-pp), through standard firing (fabrics A-pp, A-red, D) to underfired (fabric A-fe) with gradations between (eg A-pp/A-red, A-red/A-fe). A similar percentage of overfired tile was found at Langford Lane South, although underfiring was very rare. The relatively high proportion (24%) of underfired tile found at Langford Lane East may be accounted for by its unsuitability for recycling resulting in a greater quantity being discarded compared to the other types. The proportion of underfired tile suggests that production occurred sufficiently close to allow it to be brought to the construction site without serious breakage.

Dating

The majority of the Roman tile cannot be dated more closely than to the Roman period. Only the tegulae with lower cutaways surviving can provide an indication, which, based on Warry's (2006) analysis of tegula development, would indicate a broad date of mid-2nd to mid-3rd century. The absence of early forms of tegula cutaways or early types of flue tile suggests that ceramic building material was not generally in use at Alchester during the 1st-early 2nd centuries. The presence of a single early scored flue tile at Langford Lane South and the roller-stamped tile from North of Oxford Parkway Station are the only indicators of early tile use. Although a limited quantity of tile was recovered from features phased to the military and early Roman phases, the character of this tile is no different to the bulk of the assemblage for the middle Roman period and it is possible that much of the tile represents late infill (especially in the ditches) or debris trampled into earlier soil layers during construction activity. The date of the tile is consistent with the construction date of Building 7640 sometime during the mid-2nd century in Phase 6.

Langford Lane East

The characteristics of the Langford Lane assemblages are very similar in terms of all the major groups and deposits, especially in relation to the buildings located alongside the road. The quantities that can be directly related to the buildings stratigraphically is relatively small and much of the tile was found as demolition deposits encircling the

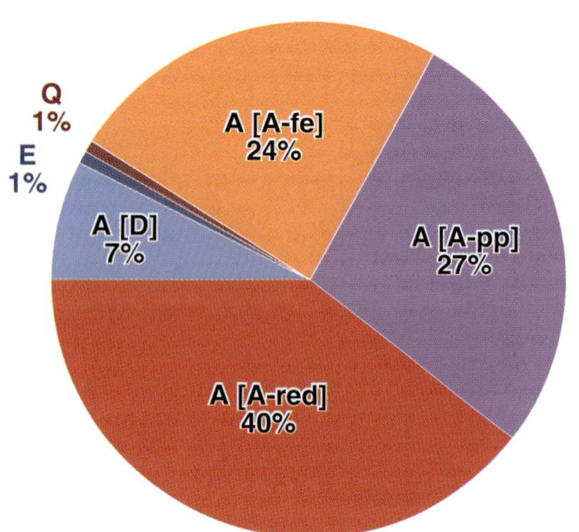

Langford Lane East

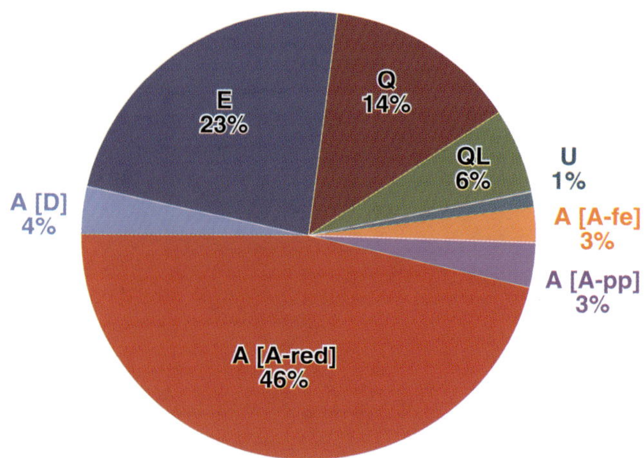

Langford Lane South

Fig. 3.26   Comparison of ceramic building material fabrics at Langford Lane East and Langford Lane South

northern side of Building 7640. Although these have been grouped with Building 7640, it is possible these deposits sealing the structures derive from all the buildings, representing dumps of broken waste debris following salvage of any usable material. The quantity of fragments comprising just the tegula flange suggests that much of the tile had been deliberately deflanged to be reused as brick. Although the quantity of tile appears to be large in terms of an excavated assemblage, the total weight of tegulae from Langford Lane East is equivalent to only 39 tiles, while numbers of corners indicate a minimum number of 91 tegula are represented, which would represent an area of c 9m^2 of roof. This implies much of the roof tile was salvaged for reuse elsewhere. The quantity of tegulae required for the buildings can be estimated based on a crude figure of 10 tegulae per m^2 (though with no complete tegula dimensions surviving for the site this must be regarded as very approximate), dependent on pitch and roof design. Building 7062 would have required at least 90 tegulae and Building 7222 at least 100, and although the total cannot be estimated for Building 7640, based on the exposed area, more than 220 tegulae would be required. The tile groups from each of the buildings and associated cobble surfaces is summarised below.

Building 7062

A modest quantity of tile (177 fragments, 9.7kg) was directly associated with the building (contexts 6550, 6826, 6829, 7602), comprising imbrex, tegula and flat tile. A small quantity of brick and a single fragment of flue tile also occurred in the overlying cleaning layer 6550.

Building 7222

The only layer producing CBM directly related to this building was the cleaning layer 6549 overlying the structure, which produced 347 fragments (13.9kg), comprising imbrex, tegula, flat tile, a small quantity of brick and a single tessera.

Building 7640

This building was only partly exposed and was either set back from the road or was a longer building compared to the other two. No internal contemporary layers survived within the excavation, but a layer of demolition debris (6548) overlying it contained the standard array of tegula/flat tile and imbrex, plus occasional brick (75 fragments, 3.7kg). Other demolition deposits surrounding the building to the north produced substantial quantities of CBM, of which the largest amount came from 6554 (1667 fragments, 90kg). Some of these deposits lay between buildings 7240 and 7222 and could represent demolition debris from all three buildings. These deposits comprised tegula, flat tile and imbrex together with a modest quantity of brick and a single small fragment of flue tile. Poorly fired tile (A-fe) was

predominantly tegula but included some imbrex and brick.

Cobbled surfaces

The cobbled surfaces associated with the buildings are predominantly assigned to the early Roman phase with one of middle Roman. The CBM comprised the typical mix of tegula and flat tile, with imbrex, brick and a couple of fragments of flue tile. A number of tegulae found in the deposits are likely to be of 2nd-mid 3rd century date, suggesting that the surfaces continued in use beyond the early Roman phase. It was observed that the surfaces included concentrations of CBM, which may represent later repairs and infilling of potholes and the continued use of the surfaces in the middle Roman phase.

The major use of the tile associated with these buildings was as roofing. The small quantity of brick associated with the buildings does not appear to have been used as flooring, which the excavated evidence indicates to have been cobbled or trampled earthen floors. The brick was presumably utilised in the walling, either as string courses, as door or window surrounds or for internal fixtures. The pattern of material from these structures is very uniform and suggests that the buildings may have been developed as a single enterprise, sourcing ceramic building material from a single supplier. The quality of tile was very variable and suggests that the standard of construction was not a priority.

The inclusion of what were in effect poor-quality seconds within the tile assemblage could be interpreted as indicating a high demand for tile at the time of construction of the buildings. An alternative interpretation is that the consignment reflects the financial status of the owner who, whilst wanting to give an impression of quality to the buildings, either did not have sufficient funds or was not willing to pay for top-quality materials. A third option is the integrity of the suppliers of the tile, who may have included a proportion of seconds, whilst passing on the full cost to the owner. If carefully positioned on areas of the roof not facing the prevailing weather, they may have survived for some years before serious deterioration set in. Without knowing the relationship between owner, builders and tilers it is impossible to deduce further the significance of the quantity of poor-quality tile within the assemblage. Whatever the circumstances, the assemblage from this group of buildings may provide an example of the full range of variation in tile quality from a single firing, suggesting that under normal circumstances the underfired tile was discarded by the producers, though as an overall percentage this is likely to have been a much smaller proportion than that of the abandoned demolition debris.

The uniformity of the tile assemblage implies that it represented a single consignment, which would in turn imply that all three buildings were roofed at the same time. The site phasing suggests buildings 7062 and 7124 were earlier constructions than 7640. The tegulae cutaways include a number classified as Warry's type B6, which he dates to *c* AD 100-180. However, the detailed archive record indicates all were incomplete and could be the lower sections of Warry's later type C5 dated to *c* AD 160-260, which was the variety that dominated the assemblage. There is therefore little evidence for two phases of roofing. An explanation is that the two earlier buildings were reroofed at the same time that building 7640 was constructed.

Langford Lane South

The assemblage from Langford Lane South cannot be related to any *in situ* structures and all of it occurs as discarded material, with the majority forming two particularly large dumps of debris in pits 2611 and 4047. The range of tile encountered in this area is greater in variety in terms of both fabric and form, suggesting that it is drawn from a number of different buildings and perhaps reflects the variety of tile in use across the town. It bears a greater similarity to the assemblage excavated in 1991 from the northern extramural settlement of Alchester (Atherton *et al.* 2001). Roofing forms a major component, together with bricks, whilst minor elements of flue tile and tesserae indicate the use of tile in specialised constructions. Some bricks may have been used as paving, but the tesserae provide firm evidence of flooring, probably tessellated pavements, based on the size groups of medium and coarse grades; the lack of small tesserae suggests that decorative mosaics are not represented. The flue tile is indicative of heated rooms or buildings incorporating hypocausts, and the semi-circular segmental brick should probably be seen in the same context. Although such bricks could be used to create columns or pilasters when plastered over, where they have been found *in situ* in Britain they are associated with baths, most commonly used as *pilae* in hypocausts such as those found in Room 9 of the villa at Gadebridge Park, Hertfordshire (Neal 1974, 15), whilst at Fishbourne they had been used to create seats in the period 3 plunge bath (Brodribb 1987, 55; Cunliffe 1971, 44).

Secondary use of the tile is more common at this site with a higher proportion having evidence of burning or heat discolouration of the surfaces indicative of reuse as hearth floors or in ovens. A quantity of tile had been incorporated as metalling into the surface of the Alchester to Dorchester-on-Thames road.

The tile assemblage in this site is a heterogeneous mix, no doubt originating from a variety of buildings elsewhere in the settlement and representing the reuse or disposal of disused building material in secondary contexts.

Catalogue of illustrated tile (Figs 3.20-3.25)

Langford Lane East

1. Flange type A and upper cutaway. Ctx 6554, demolition layer, Building 7640.
2. Flange type A and lower cutaway A3/C1. Ctx 6554, demolition layer, Building 7640.
3. Flange type A2 and upper cutaway. Ctx 7065, demolition layer, Building 7640.
4. Flange type A/A3. Ctx 6554, demolition layer, Building 7640.
5. Flange type A3 and lower cutway type A3/C1. Ctx 6947, ditch 7675.
6. Flange type A4. Ctx 6947, ditch 7675.
7. Flange type A4. Ctx 8006, road surface.
8. Flange type A4/D. Ctx 6554, demolition layer, Building 7640.
9. Flange type A5. Ctx 6716, demolition layer, Building 7640.
10. Flange type B. Ctx 6554, demolition layer, Building 7640.
11. Flange type B. Ctx 7065, demolition layer, Building 7640.
12. Flange type C. Ctx 6554, demolition layer, Building 7640.
13. Flange type C/F2. Ctx 6960, pit 6789.
14. Flange type D. Ctx 6554, demolition layer, Building 7640.
15. Flange type B/D. Ctx 6827, cobbled surface.
16. Flange type D. Ctx 6960, pit 6789.
17. Flange type D/F. Ctx 7046, cobbled surface.
18. Flange type D and lower cutaway type A3/C1. Ctx 7344, buried soil layer.
19. Flange type D. Ctx 7345, alluvial layer.
20. Flange type D2. Ctx 6723, cobbled surface.
21. Flange type D2/F2. Ctx 7078, demolition layer, Building 7640.
22. Flange type C/F. Ctx 7078, demolition layer, Building 7640.
23. Flange type E. Ctx 6716, demolition layer, Building 7640.
24. Flange type E. Ctx 6716, demolition layer, Building 7640.
25. Flange type E. Ctx 6826, Building 7062.
26. Flange type F. Ctx 6826, Building 7062.
27. Flange type F2/D2 and lower cutway type A3/C1. Ctx 6562, alluvial layer.
28. Flange type A3? Ctx 6559, ditch 8522.
29. Imbrex. Ctx 7233, gully 7238.
30. Imbrex. Three lines of finger prints are lightly impressed along the tile apex. Ctx 7588, pit 7582.
31. Combed keying. Ctx 7403, gully 7238.
32. Signature type 1.1. Very small variety; additional short thin arc may be hand accidentally marking clay. Ctx 7234, demolition layer, Building 7222.
33. Signature type 1.1b. Ctx 7539, demolition layer, Building 7640.
34. Signature type 1.2. Ctx 6832, hollow.
35. Signature type 1.3. Ctx 7078, demolition layer, Building 7640.
36. Signature type 1.4. Ctx 7065, demolition layer, Building 7640.
37. Signature type 2.1. Ctx 6554, demolition layer, Building 7640.
38. Signature type 4.1. Ctx 7220, Building 7222.
39. Signature type 5.1. Ctx 6554, demolition layer, Building 7640.

40. Signature type 5.1. Ctx 7065, demolition layer, Building 7640.
41. Signature type 5.1. Ctx 6716, demolition layer, Building 7640.
42. Signature type 5.1. Loop signature with additional finger marks (incomplete). Ctx 6934, pit 7689.
43. Footprint. Infant/young child footprint of right foot with all 5 toes and ball of foot clearly impressed, but not heel. Max width (across toes) 59mm, foot width 40mm, length from top of big toe to instep 53mm; big toe: 24mm long x 19mm wide. Age of child probably 18-30 months. Ctx 7063, demolition layer, Building 7640.
44. Footprints. Two partial overlapping footprints of toes of infant foot. Ctx 7116, demolition layer, Building 7640.

Langford Lane South

45. Segmental semi-circular brick. Ctx 2615, pit 2611, SF 2005.
46. Keying on wall tile. Scored keying in diamond pattern. Ctx 2615, pit 2611.
47. Box flue, combed keying. Ctx 2792, pit 4047.

North of Oxford Parkway Station

48. Box flue. Roller-stamped keying in 'billet pattern' Die 92. Ctx 3224, ditch 3078.

FIRED CLAY *by Cynthia Poole*

Introduction

Fired clay was recovered in small quantities from all eight excavations, amounting to a modest total of 1220 fragments weighing 6139g (Table 3.42). The material was found in a range of features, including ditches, gullies, pits and quarries, dating from the middle Iron Age to the late Roman period. A few pieces occurred in medieval or modern features, where it is likely to be residual from earlier periods.

The material is very fragmentary in all assemblages, frequently little more than small, amorphous scraps, and this is reflected in the low overall mean fragment weight of 5g. Fired clay is not intrinsically datable, except in the case of certain diagnostic forms. The majority of the site assemblages are indeterminate in character, except for that from South of Oddington Crossing, which was associated with metalworking. The few identifiable pieces are consistent with the overall Iron Age-Roman phasing of the sites.

Table 3.42 Quantification of fired clay by site and phase and presence of diagnostic forms

Site and phases	Nos	Wt (g)	Forms
Langford Lane East total	40	436	
Phase 3: Late Iron Age	20	258	Triangular perforated brick
Phase 4: Roman military phase	12	105	Oven furniture: disc, oven plate; oven structure
Phase 6: Middle Roman	2	24	
Phase 7: Late Roman	6	49	Oven ?furniture
Unphased	4	26	
Langford Lane South total	23	218	
Phase 5: Early Roman	1	4	
Phase 6: Middle Roman	21	204	Oven furniture: ?disc, ?pedestal
Phase 9: Modern	1	10	
Unphased	1	7	
South of Merton total	233	278	
Unphased	233	278	Oven wall, ?furniture
Holts Farm Crossing total	174	866	
Phase 2: Middle Iron Age	45	214	Oven/hearth floor, ?triangular perforated brick
Phase 3: Late Iron Age	12	29	
Phase 5: Early Roman	10	43	Oven structure?
Phase 6: Middle Roman	36	160	Oven furniture: ?disc, ?triangular perforated brick
Phase 7: Late Roman	51	266	Oven furniture: disc
Phase 8: Post-Roman	4	37	Oven structure? Furniture?
Unphased	16	117	?Triangular perforated brick
East of Oddington Grange total	8	55	
Unphased	8	55	
South of Oddington Crossing total	476	3323	
Phase 2: Middle Iron Age	266	1569	Furnace structure
Unphased	210	1754	Oven wall structure
North of Gallos Brook total	8	81	
Unphased	8	81	Furnace structure
North of Oxford Parkway Station total	254	1095	
Unphased	254	1095	Oven/hearth structure
Total	1216	6352	

Methodology

The assemblage has been fully recorded in accordance with guidelines set out by the Archaeological Ceramic Building Materials Group (ACBMG 2007), which whilst not specifically designed for fired clay provide appropriate guidance. The record includes quantification, fabric type, form, surface finish, organic impressions, dimensions and general description. Fabrics were characterised on macroscopic features and with the aid of x20 hand lens.

Fabrics

The fabrics were broadly similar across the sites, though exhibiting much minor variation. Two main categories were identified, comprising a fine smooth clay (fabric A) and a sandy clay fabric (Q), which contained varying quantities and grades of quartz sand and often utilised A as its base. Colour varied considerably, including a wide range of hues and shades in red, orange, brown, mauve, grey and black, with mottling and streaks of differing colours within individual pieces. Within these broad fabric groups there was also considerable variation of additional inclusions, with a scatter of red ferruginous grits, buff-cream grog or clay pellets, and small white inclusions which were sometimes identifiable as calcareous material or limestone grits, but also appeared to include white leached rounded mudstone grits and occasionally shell or flint. In some cases, the clay was strongly laminated with cream streaks often combined with marl and clay pellets, designated as fabric E where these characteristics were dominant. It is probable that the source of the raw material was local to each site; natural clay and alluvial deposits are recorded across the project area and there is no reason to believe that the raw material came from anywhere but the immediate vicinity of the sites in question. The inclusions were probably all naturally occurring within the clay and the variations observed merely reflect the natural variation within the clay deposits. Included with the fired clay were a number of natural burnt mudstone fragments, some of which were sandy and another was leached white with dark brown iron deposits in thin lenses within the clay in exactly the manner found in ceramic building material fabric A-fe. The only deliberately added material was found at Langford Lane East in a small number of objects from the Roman military phase that were made in a light red chaff-tempered fabric (V).

Langford Lane East

A small quantity of fired clay (including some burnt mudstone nodules) amounting to 44 fragments weighing 462g was recovered from late Iron Age and Roman deposits, including ditch and pit fills, a burial and demolition layers. Most was made in sandy clay (fabric Q) together with several pieces in fabric V. All the identifiable material was oven or hearth furniture. The corner of a triangular perforated brick was found in a late Iron Age pit (7306) together with some amorphous scraps that could be burnt natural or subsoil. The largest quantity came from the Roman military phase, mostly from ditch fills, and included fragments of thin flat discs or plates 10-18mm thick, all made in fabric V. Another piece with a flat edge and over 22mm thick could be a fragment of plate or a triangular brick. Only a few small indeterminate scraps in the sandy fabric were recovered from the middle and late Roman phases.

Langford Lane South

A small quantity of fired clay amounting to 23 fragments weighing 218g was recovered, almost exclusively from middle Roman pit and ditch fills with just a single indeterminate scrap from the early Roman phase and a couple of scraps from a modern field drain and undated context. Most was made in sandy clay fabric Q, whilst three fragments in fabric E contained clay pellets. Most pieces were indeterminate, either amorphous or with a single flat surface. One piece from pit 2611 appeared to form a slab 30mm thick and may have been part of an oven plate or disc, but its surfaces were very poorly preserved and identification is uncertain. Another fragment with a curving finger-smoothed surface may have been a fragment of pedestal or support, but is too fragmentary to identify with any degree of certainty.

South of Merton

A small quantity of fired clay was recovered, mostly from sieved samples, amounting to 233 fragments (278g). All was of indeterminate function, although hints of both oven structure and furniture were observed. Fragments were small, ranging in size from 8-42mm and with a very low MFW of 1g on account of the predominance of sieved material. All was made in a fine sandy fabric except for a few fragments in a shelly fabric with a smooth well finished surface, which may be an item of oven furniture. Most pieces were amorphous or had a single flat moulded surface. One small wattle impression 10mm in diameter was preserved, hinting at the presence of oven wall structure.

Holts Farm Crossing

A modest assemblage of fired clay amounting to 174 fragments (866g) was recovered from a range of features, including ditches, gullies, trackways, pits, a posthole and a cremation dating from the middle Iron Age to the Roman period and medieval furrow fills. Roughly equal quantities were recovered from middle Iron Age and late Roman contexts, with much reduced amounts in the intervening phases. Although this was one of the larger assemblages, the majority of the material recovered was small, indeterminate fragments, either amorphous or with a single moulded surface. A number of fragments of disc came from the backfill of late Roman pit 8617. These were made in fabric A and had a flat, smooth, even surface, generally well finished; some have fine organic impressions on the surface, though some are slightly rougher. One piece has two surfaces and a flat, straight edge with rounded arrises, and on three other pieces the surface is starting to curve to a rounded edge. All the characteristics suggest that these derived from one or more flat circular discs or rectangular plates. Two fragments of triangular perforated bricks included evidence of perforations 16-17mm in diameter. Triangular bricks originated in the Iron Age, but certainly continued in use in the early Roman period and probably later on some sites. The character of the surface finish suggested that a few other pieces probably derived from items of oven furniture, whilst a few pieces with finger depressions in the surfaces or wattle impressions suggest the presence of ovens or hearths. One fragment from middle Iron Age pit 8409 had a flat, even surface with a row of shallow fingernail marks, possibly representing deliberate decoration of a hearth surface.

East of Oddington Grange

This site produced only eight fragments of fired clay weighing 55g with a mean fragment weight of 7g. All was made in sandy clay of varying degrees of coarseness. All pieces were indeterminate in their function, being either amorphous or having a single moulded surface.

South of Oddington Crossing

This site produced the largest assemblage of fired clay, amounting to 476 fragments weighing 3323g. All was made in sandy fabric Q, except for three small scraps containing shell grits. The fired clay was recovered from a limited number of features comprising middle Iron Age ditch 153, where it was associated with metalworking waste, and five pits (102, 109, 119, 129, 130), all of which had fills containing burnt debris. Most of the pits were undated except for pit 109, which was also of middle Iron Age date.

The largest group came from ditch 153 (fills 14, 15) and consisted entirely of furnace structure. This included sizeable, fairly thin flat slabs with a flattish, undulating surface, heavily vitrified and cindered and black-grey in colour but sometimes with whitish veneer from a high density of semi-melted coarse quartz sand adhering. On one piece this graded to a less fired unvitrified, unsanded periphery. The blackened, cindered surface was *c* 8mm thick with a thin purplish band *c* 4mm thick and a sharp boundary to the bright orange-red core/back. The maximum surviving thickness for lining and wall structure was 39mm. It is probable that the complete wall would have been at least twice this, but would not have been fired through the complete thickness. No outer surface survives on any of these pieces but the back or underside is a worn, undulating interface either to unfired exterior wall structure or, if part of the floor, the underlying natural. Some pieces had deep, rounded hollows in the vitrified surface. Two pieces had part of a rounded edge that probably formed circular perforations, of which one measured *c* 25mm in diameter. A number of nodular vitrified lumps, probably broken bits of structure, were similar to fuel ash slag. One had a greenish sheen, which may be indicative of copper working. Two small fragments may be pieces of tuyère or bellows guard; one from the exterior has two flat surfaces at an obtuse angle and is 20mm thick. Another fragment may be the tip of a tubular object 30mm in diameter with a bore of 10mm diameter that had cindering around its end.

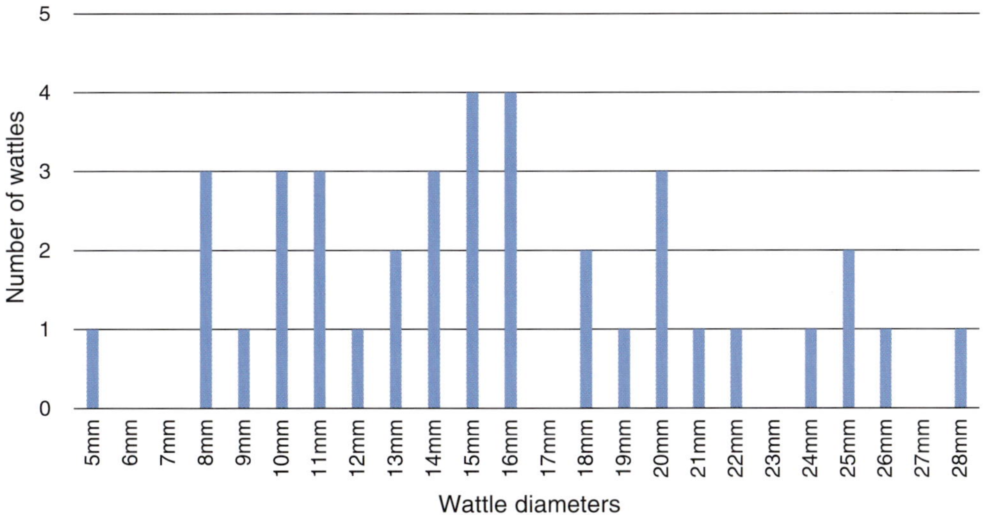

Fig. 3.27   Distribution of wattle sizes in fired clay from South of Oddington Crossing

The fired clay from the pits is different in character to the furnace structure and would appear to relate to a separate activity. The material from all the pits is very similar in character, suggesting that all may have originated from the same structure or very similar structures. The size and shape of the pits are consistent with the bases of small ovens or hearths. All the fired clay from these was made in a sandy clay containing sparse small flint grits fired to red, reddish/orange brown and black. Many fragments, especially those from samples or smaller pieces, were amorphous, but the larger, better preserved fragments had a flat or slightly curving, roughly moulded exterior surface and in most groups a few wattle impressions occurred on the back, usually only single impressions surviving, though one with two impressions indicates that the wattles were interwoven. The sizes range from 5-28mm in diameter and the sizes and quantities are illustrated in Figure 3.27 for the combined wattles from all pits. The sizes are typical of those usually found in oven structures and are likely to represent both horizontal rods and vertical sails. Only one of the pits has been dated to the middle Iron Age, but the similarity and consistency in character of the fired clay suggests that all features are likely to be broadly contemporary. Whether all or any served as oven or hearth bases is uncertain, since no *in situ* burning was noted. In most cases only charcoal (almost exclusively oak) was associated, probably representing the fuel used to fire the structures, but in the case of pit 109 abundant cereal grain was also present.

North of Gallos Brook

This site produced eight fragments of fired clay weighing 81g, half from a sieved sample. The four hand-collected fragments (context 203) were identified as furnace or smithing heath structure, possibly from the rim of the wall or kerb of a hearth. These comprised two refitting fragments and two others clearly part of the same structure, which formed part of a round edge/rim 31-37mm thick, heavily vitrified and vesicular fired purplish grey at the surface, grading through mauve and cerise to the orange core/exterior of the structure. This could form the rim of a metalworking hearth, although no other evidence for metalworking was found at this site.

North of Oxford Parkway Station

The modest assemblage of fired clay, amounting to 13 fragments (120g) of hand-collected material and 230 fragments (954g) of sieved material, comprised mostly indeterminate, poorly-fired fragments. These were made in a poorly mixed, sandy clay fabric, sometimes with a laminated swirly clay matrix of similar character to the tile fabric from the site.

The fired clay from oven 3047/3049 included pieces with a rough moulded flat surface, burnt black grading to dark maroon then bright red below,

all recovered from the sieved sample. The fragments were up to 20mm thick and were initially interpreted as hearth floor, although in view of their contextual setting this should clearly be reassigned as oven floor and lining. Those pieces without a blackened surface probably derive from the back of the oven or upper areas peripheral to the main firing area. An additional four amorphous pieces, slightly thicker and measuring 30mm thick, made in a more mottled clay coloured light brown, buff-yellow, pinkish red and grey, may represent a separate part of the structure, possibly areas of outer walling or superstructure. A further piece from the oven had a fairly even, flat moulded surface with a central depression, probably a finger or thumb mark pressed into the surface from the shaping, and formed a square corner with straight rough edges with a slight lip at the top, suggesting the clay has been inset against another structural element. This may have formed part of a suspended floor or oven plate inset against a kerb or upper walls, or possibly a resurfacing of the oven base. The surface was burnt or fired to dark red and grey, which also points to hearth or oven floor as its function.

A sieved sample from pit 3296 also produced oven wall lining, consisting of wedge-shaped pieces with a smooth moulded, curving surface; the wedge-shaped cross-section results from blocks of clay being smoothed out and thinned across preceding areas of structure. These were 22mm thick and some had gravel impressions on the back, suggesting that the structure had been inset into stony or gravelly subsoil or natural.

Discussion

The fired clay from most sites is poorly preserved with few diagnostic pieces surviving to suggest function and activity, although general characteristics, surface finish and degree of firing suggest that structural material and oven/hearth furniture are both represented. The few identifiable pieces of oven furniture, comprising triangular perforated bricks and circular discs or plates, are consistent with the phasing of the sites and features. The triangular bricks originated in the Iron Age and where they continued in use into the Roman period are no doubt indicative of the native population continuing tried and established practice. The circular discs or plates are a regular component of late Iron Age and early Roman fired clay assemblages in Oxfordshire and the east Midlands. Examples of circular discs have been previously found at Alchester (Booth 2001) from early Roman contexts, though in contrast to the present assemblage all were made in a shell-tempered fabric and on average were slightly thicker. Examples are also known from Watkins Farm (Allen 1990, 53), Farmoor (Lambrick and Robinson 1979, 53-4), Old Shifford (Barclay *et al.* 1995, 138), and South Parks Road, Oxford (Biddulph 2005b), where they are all associated with the Roman period.

Although there is little diagnostic material from most sites, it is probable that the fired clay broadly represents domestic oven or hearth structures and accessories used in everyday activities of cooking, crop processing and heating. The small oven base from North of Oxford Parkway Station is typical of Roman structures of this type, which were commonly used to dry or process agricultural produce, a function supported by the fairly abundant carbonised cereal grains found within the fill. It may not have had any significant super-structure as such, possibly a low kerb and a drying floor (possibly made of tile or stone slabs) accounting for the fairly sparse remains of fired clay recovered.

The only exception is the group of fired clay from South of Oddington Crossing, where the large quantity of fired clay from ditch 153 represents demolished furnace structure and was associated with large quantities of slag indicative of iron smithing and two crucibles used for copper alloy processing. It is probable that the fired clay was associated with both activities, though whether two different structures are represented or a single structure with multiple functions it is not possible to say. The fired clay from the five pits that lie some distance to the west of ditch 153 are unlikely to have any relationship to the metalworking and are more likely to represent some form of domestic or crop-processing activity. The wattle-supported structure could represent oven walls or a drying floor for crops.

WORKED STONE *by Ruth Shaffrey*

Langford Lane East

A total of three objects are identifiable to function. A quartzite pebble processor from Phase 4 layer 6641 has rubbed faces while one piece of sandstone from Building 7640, demolition layer 6554, has been extensively used as a hone. Half a single limestone spindle whorl of flat disc form was also found and this was the only spindle whorl from any of the sites.

A shelly limestone socket stone that was recovered from late Roman cobbled surface 6516 and a tooled limestone block (SF 6002, not illustrated) from the post-Roman palaeochannel are the only clearly worked structural stone, but other stones are likely to have been used structurally.

Langford Lane South

Two probable hones are the only stone objects from Langford Lane South. One has been reused as a hone but was probably originally a quern; it lacks any original edges or grinding surface but is of typical quern material (Millstone Grit). The other is a sandstone fragment that has been extensively used as a hone. Two slabs were probably used as building stone.

South of Merton

The only worked stone from this site is a group of 17 tiny worn fragments of lava quern. These are not directly dated but Roman lava querns are well known in the immediate vicinity, with examples from the northern extramural settlement area (Roe 2001, 248), as well as just to the north near Bicester (Chapman 2008, 143; Shaffrey 2014).

Catalogue of stone objects

Langford Lane East

Probable rotary quern. Very well sorted, medium-grained, feldspathic sandstone with occasional quartz grit, probably Millstone Grit. Part of one pecked roughly flat face. The other face is worn very smooth and concave but with slight ridges. Probably reused as a hone. No original edges survive, but it is very likely that this was originally part of a rotary quern. Measures 34mm thick. Weighs 376g. Ctx 2552, pit 4047, Phase 6, middle Roman period (2nd-early 3rd century). SF 2002.

Hone fragment. Fine-grained micaceous sandstone. Small fragment of flat stone with extensive wear on one face. Ctx 2034, ditch 2032, Phase 6, middle Roman period (2nd-early 3rd century).

Langford Lane South

Possible socket stone. Shelly limestone. Broken across the socket, which measures 55 x 48 x 60mm deep. Measures approximately 180 x 150 x 90mm. Weighs 4657g. Ctx 6516, cobbled surface, Phase 7, late Roman (mid 3rd-4th century). SF 6501.

Hone. Sandstone. Slab, extensively used on all faces and all edges. The edges are convex along the length and the faces are slightly convex. Measures 76 x 66 x 18mm. Weighs 126g. Ctx 6554, demolition layer, Building 7640.

Rubbed stone. Quartzite. Pebble, worn into slight facets. Measures 61 x 46 x 37mm. Ctx 6641, ditch 6642, Phase 4, Roman military phase (*c* AD 43-70).

Spindle whorl. Fine grained shelly limestone. Half a flat straight-sided 'disc'-shaped whorl with 8mm diameter perforation. Measures 41 x 9mm. Weighs 13g. Ctx 7053, unstratified.

South of Merton

Rotary quern fragments. Lava. Seventeen fragments, all rounded and worn. Weighs 71g. Ctx 213, ditch 214, undated.

Discussion

Very few worked stone objects were recovered. There is consequently little evidence for textile manufacture (only a single spindle whorl of any material was recovered) and comparably little indication for grain processing, evidenced only by two likely rotary quern fragments from Langford Lane East and South of Merton. Such an absence is particularly intriguing given the positive evidence for grain, particularly sprouted examples, amongst the charred plant remains. This would suggest that grains were soaked and heated here in order to turn them into malt for brewing, but that the subsequent process of crushing the grains took place elsewhere. This might have been in Alchester's northern extramural settlement area, which produced nine querns (Roe 2001) but otherwise only a few querns have been found in and immediately around the Roman town, with only two further examples from the town's defensive ditches (Young 1975). An alternative is that the malted grain was transported to a nearby mill, perhaps just to the north near Bicester, since two millstones indicating intensified levels of processing have been recovered near here, as well as quern fragments (Chapman 2008, 143).

Querns, hones, processors and spindle whorls are all finds that are typical of domestic activity and all the stone types could have been collected locally to the site, with the exception of the Millstone Grit and lava querns, which are typical imports of the period.

WORKED FLINT *by Michael Donnelly*

Introduction

A small assemblage of 33 flints was recovered from this project, with the flints occurring in varying amounts on seven of the sites. Only three of the seven sites had more than three flints (Table 3.43). Blades were quite common but later prehistoric flintwork is also represented and one post-medieval gunflint was recovered.

The assemblage

The assemblage contained a fairly high percentage of blades amongst its debitage, accounting for 36% of all blanks (flakes and blades). This clearly indicated a significant early prehistoric component. Flakes were more common but only two appeared to be typical of later prehistoric industries. The core and core rejuvenation flakes were also typical of Mesolithic or earlier Neolithic activity. The five tools recovered consisted of one post-medieval gunflint from Langford Lane South, one finely retouched and naturally backed knife of probable late Neolithic-early Bronze Age date from North of Gallos Brook, two scrapers from Langford Lane South, one of which is an undiagnostic end scraper, on a side trimming flake that has clearly been utilised and the other is either an example of an expedient Mesolithic form or perhaps even a slightly large early Bronze Age thumbnail. The final tool was the butt-end of a core tool from Holts Farm Crossing. It was quite large and thick and showed more careful and invasive retouch than is typical for Mesolithic picks or adzes and it is quite probable that this may have been a lower-middle Palaeolithic handaxe fragment.

Langford Lane East

This site contained eight flints in a very mixed state, usually in quite poor condition. The assemblage consisted of three flakes, two blades, a core rejuvenation flake and two scrapers. The flints were dispersed across seven contexts. Context 6944 yielded a squat hard-hammer flake of probably later prehistoric date alongside a quite long and early looking blade form. The two scrapers included one example (7556) with clear signs of use along its working edge, fashioned on a side trimming flake while the second (7239) was a slightly atypical thumbnail form. It was slightly larger than the norm

Table 3.43 The flint assemblage

Category type	Langford Lane East	Langford Lane South	South of Merton	Holts Farm Crossing
Flake	3			6
Blade	2	2	2	
Bladelet				
Blade-like				
Blade index	40% (2/5)	100% (2/2)	100% (2/2)	0%
Rejuvenation flake	1			
Core tablet				
Core single platform bladelets				1
Scraper end	1			
Scraper other	1			
Axe/pick				1
Knife backed				
Gunflint		1		
Total	8	3	2	8
No. burnt (%)	1/8 (12.5%)	0/3 (0%)	1/2 (50%)	0/8 (0%)
No. broken (exc. chips) (%)	2/8 (25.0%)	1/3 (33.3%)	2/2 (100%)	4/8 (50%)
No. retouched (exc. chips) (%)	2/8 (25.0%)	1/3 (33.3%)	0/2 (0%)	1/8 (12.5%)

and its edge consisted more of three angled edges rather than the one curved working edge that is more typical of early Bronze Age thumbnails.

Langford Lane South

Only three struck flints were recovered, two of which were blades while the third was a gunflint. The two blades include one very well made soft-hammer struck blade that was clearly early prehistoric in date and most likely belonged in the Mesolithic or early Neolithic. The post-medieval gunflint was small with clear signs of use and may have been from some form of pistol.

South of Merton

Two blades were recovered as residual finds. Neither was in particularly good condition but an early prehistoric date would be very likely.

Holts Farm Crossing

This site yielded eight pieces, consisting of six flakes, a blade core and the axe/pick fragment. The assemblage was in mixed condition with the largely undiagnostic flake debitage being freshest, alongside two pieces in much poorer condition that are far more interesting. The blade core was a single platform example with narrow bladelet removals that is typical of Mesolithic industries but could also date to the late Upper Palaeolithic or earlier Neolithic. The broken core tool butt may well be from a hand axe of lower-middle Palaeolithic date but could also be a preform of a Neolithic axe (Fig. 3.28). However, its thick triangular profile does not

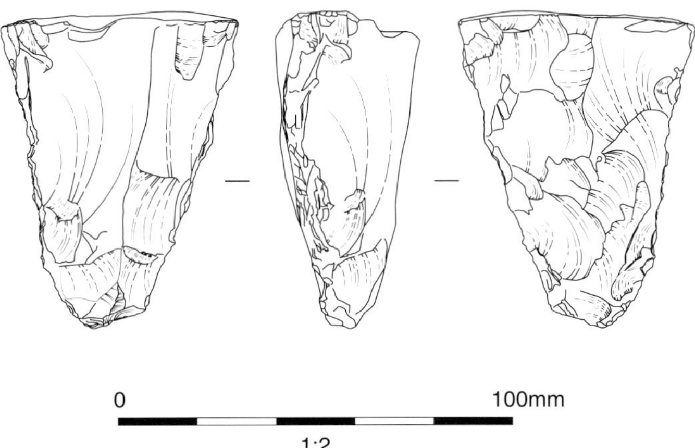

Fig. 3.28   Possible Palaeolithic axe from Holts Farm Crossing

quite fit the latter suggestion and it also displayed a heavy iron staining not found on any of the other pieces, all of which suggests the far earlier date. Its surface condition indicates that it was broken in antiquity as the iron staining extends across the break.

East of Oddington Grange

A single undiagnostic inner flake was recovered.

North of Gallos Brook

The sole find was a fine naturally backed knife with parallel invasive retouch along its cutting edge. This piece would date to the late Neolithic or early part of the Bronze Age and was clearly a residual find.

East of Oddington Grange	North of Gallos Brook	North of Oxford Parkway Station	Total
1		6	16
		2	8
		1	1
0%		33.3% (3/9)	36% (9/25)
			1
		1	1
			1
			1
			1
			1
	1		1
			1
1	1	10	33
1/1 (100%)	0/1 (0%)	0/10 (0%)	3/33 (9.09%)
0/1 (0%)	1/1 (100%)	2/10 (20%)	12/33 (36.36%)
0/1 (0%)	1/1 (100%)	0/10 (0%)	5/33 (15.15%)

North of Oxford Parkway Station

This site produced a small collection of fresh flints from a limited set of spatially close contexts and may have indicated some *in situ* flint-related activity. The site yielded five flakes, three blade forms and a core tablet. Context 3243 produced three flakes, a blade and the core rejuvenation tablet. Context 3285 had a flake and a blade while the remaining three contexts with flints contained single examples of flakes (3136 and 3252) and a bladelet (3298). Many of the flakes are thin and several of the pieces display soft-hammer bulbs usually associated with early prehistoric activity as would also be the case with the core tablet. The lack of diagnostic pieces renders any more accurate dating impossible.

Discussion

The assemblages indicate very limited prehistoric activity in this area. The flints suggest that most of the activity related to early prehistory, and while very small sites may have made up the bulk of any taskscape, the pieces identified here more closely resemble genuine stray finds or very low intensity activity away from any domestic focus. The broken axe butt may reflect another example of casual loss. Stray finds of Lower-Middle Palaeolithic material are known from the Thames Valley gravels (Morigi *et al.* 2011) and this may represent another example from the region.

Environmental evidence and radiocarbon dating

At all the sites animal bones were recovered by hand during excavation and bulk soil samples were routinely collected from deposits that had visual evidence for the presence of charred plant remains and charcoal. Charcoal was ubiquitous, although it generally occurred only in small quantities, and significant assemblages of charred plant remains were surprisingly rare, as a result of which only seven samples were progressed to full analysis. Smaller bulk samples of 10-20 litres were taken for waterlogged plant remains and insects at Langford Lane East, Langford Lane South and North of Oxford Parkway Station, and where samples originally collected for charred plant remains were identified as having potential for waterlogged remains subsamples were processed accordingly. Two samples from pit 8617 at Holts Farm Crossing were collected for waterlogged remains but no such material was present. Column samples were collected for pollen and incremental two-litre samples for molluscs. Analysis was targeted on features where a range of types of evidence was present, allowing the different information provided by each discipline to be considered together to produce a more complete picture of the Roman environment. These were focused on ditches 6715 and 7066, which flanked the road in Langford Lane East, ditch 2455, pit 2611 and roadside ditch 4158 at Langford Lane South and trackway ditch 3056 at North of Oxford Parkway Station.

ANIMAL BONES *by Lee G Broderick*

Introduction

All eight sites produced animal bone, but five of the assemblages were too small to support analysis (Table 4.1). Consequently, this report deals only with the material from Langford Lane East, Langford Lane South and Holts Farm Crossing. The excavations at Langford Lane South and Langford Lane East were adjacent to the Roman legionary fortress and small town at Alchester, which has been the focus of a previous study (Thomas 2008). Together with the assemblage from the rural settlement at Holts Farm Crossing, about 1km to the south-west, the sites give us an insight into the development of a local economy and environment as it reacted to the Roman military presence and the

subsequent urbanisation in the wake of the army's departure. Also uncovered were several ritual deposits, including cremated domestic fowl remains deposited inside ceramic vessels within the fills of ditches. These have not been found previously on Roman sites and their precise role and meaning is difficult to ascertain, but it is tentatively suggested here that they may be related to memorial activities.

Methodology

Recovery of material on site was principally through hand-collection. Environmental samples were also taken and these were sieved at 10mm, 4mm, 2mm and 0.5mm fractions. This material was recorded in the same way and is considered together below. Taxonomy follows Wilson and Reeder (2005) for mammals and Gill and Donsker (2013) for birds. The word 'caprine' is used when referring to an animal that may be a sheep (*Ovis aries*) or a goat (*Capra hircus*).

All specimens were identified with the aid of the OA reference collection. Bones were recorded using the diagnostic zones described by Serjeantson (1996) for mammal limb bones, Strid (2012) for mammal mandibles and Cohen and Serjeantson (1996) for birds.

The separation between sheep and goat was attempted on the following elements: mandible; dP3; dP4; M1; M2; M3; distal humerus; distal metapodials (both fused and unfused); distal tibia; astragalus and

Table 4.1 Summary of animal bone assemblages by site

Site	NISP	NISP+	NSP
Langford Lane East	600	2022	3299
Langford Lane South	263	1401	3825
South of Merton	39	68	144
Holts Farm Crossing	342	1401	5977
East of Oddington Grange	40	69	305
South of Oddington Crossing	20	33	140
North of Gallos Brook	34	80	165
North of Oxford Parkway Station	12	22	78

NISP = Number of Identified Specimens; NISP+ = NISP including specimens identified to categories such as 'large mammal' etc; NSP = Number of Specimens calcaneum, using the criteria described in Boessneck (1969), Payne (1985), Kratochvil (1969) and Halstead *et al*. (2002).

Tooth wear stages were recorded for P4, dP4, M1, M2, and M3 of domestic cattle (*Bos taurus taurus*), caprines and pig (*Scrofa domesticus*), both isolated and within mandibles, following Grant (1982). Horse (*Equus caballus*) incisor wear stages follow Levine (1982), withers height calculations follow May (1985) and separation between the various equid species was attempted on the molars, premolars, metapodials and astragali according to criteria laid out by Davis (1980).

A mammal bone epiphysis is described as 'fusing' once spicules of bone have formed across the epiphyseal plate, joining epiphysis to metaphysis, but while some gaps are still visible between the epiphysis and diaphysis. An epiphysis is described as fused once these gaps along the line of fusion have disappeared. Fusion stages follow Silver (1969). Only fused bones were measured, with measurements taken following the criteria laid out by von den Driesch (1976).

Bone condition was recorded following Lyman (1994).

Descriptions of the assemblages

Langford Lane East

A total of 2552 specimens were recovered by hand, of which 1790 (70.1%) were identifiable to at least a broad descriptive category such as 'large mammal' (cow/horse sized), including 530 (20.8% of NSP) to species. Most of this material came from Phase 4 (NISP=924), with Phases 3, 5 and 6 each also producing a NISP of more than 100 (Table 4.2).

The specimens were generally in moderate to poor condition, with the earliest phase on the site, Phase 3 (late Iron Age), being the worst preserved. Soil samples produced a further 747 specimens, with over half of them coming from Phases 3 and 4 (Table 4.2). For the most part, the samples reflected the composition of the hand-collected assemblage, with large and, particularly, medium mammals most abundant. They also contained specimens of frog (*Rana* sp.) and/or toad (*Bufo* sp.), reflecting a damp environment in roadside ditches 6715 and 7066, as well as several specimens of domestic fowl. A rabbit radius in ditch 7069 is likely to be intrusive.

Table 4.2   Quantification of animal bone by species from Langford Lane East

Phase	3	4	5	6	7	9	Undated
Domestic cattle	19 (2)	93 (3)	18	39	1 (1)		21 (1)
Domestic cattle?	2	3		2			2
Caprine	14 (5)	97 (5)	23	31 (2)	(2)	1	9 (1)
Caprine?	1	5		3			2
Sheep	3	11	4	2	(3)		2
Pig	1	10 (1)	(1)	4	1 (3)		
Pig?		1					1
Horse	2	41	13	13	1	1	12
Horse?		1					
Dog		11	1	5			1
Dog?			1				
Rabbit		1					
Micro mammal		(3)					
Small mammal	(3)	4 (3)		1			1
Medium mammal	11 (7)	105 (54)	36	51			12
Large mammal	77 (6)	540 (3)	126	177	22 (2)		89 (1)
Total mammal	**130 (23)**	**923 (72)**	**222 (1)**	**328 (2)**	**25 (11)**	**2**	**152 (3)**
Amphibian		(4)					
Frog/toad		(4)	(1)				
Total amphibian	**(0)**	**(8)**	**(1)**	**(0)**	**(0)**	**(0)**	**(0)**
Bird	1	(84)	1	(5)			
Domestic duck/mallard	5	1					
Domestic fowl		(15)		(1)			
Domestic fowl?		(6)					
Rook			1				
Total bird	**6**	**1 (105)**	**1**	**0 (6)**	**0**	**0**	**0**
Total NISP	136 (23)	924 (185)	223 (2)	328 (8)	25 (11)	2	152 (3)
Total NSP	150 (268)	1376 (267)	311 (10)	437 (59)	48 (132)	13	217 (11)

NISP = Number of Identified Specimens; NSP = Number of Specimens

Quantities from environmental samples in parenthesis (not included in main figure)

Domestic fowl specimens were completely absent from the hand-collected material, but a single bone was recovered from a sieved sample from Phase 6. Similar-sized duck specimens were identified among the hand-collected material from Phases 3 and 4 perhaps suggesting that this absence is not entirely down to sampling bias and perhaps reflects a genuine rarity of domestic fowl here. Notably, however, 21 bones from domestic fowl were identified from the fill of a vessel found in fill 7231 of roadside ditch 7453. The pot fill contained left- and right-sided elements of wing and leg elements of fowl (MNI=1), along with rib, vertebra and indeterminate bird specimens, all of which were calcined. No other faunal material was present (Table 4.3).

Generally throughout the history of this site there seems to have been a more or less equal distribution of medium and large mammals in the assemblage, with caprines and domestic cattle dominating. Sheep were definitely present among the caprines from each phase of the site, and horse gradually increased as a proportion of the overall assemblage by NISP from Phase 3 (late Iron Age) to Phase 5 (early Roman), before declining again in Phase 6 (middle Roman) (Fig. 4.2). This increase in horse bones comes primarily at the expense of domestic cattle. Although there were no pig specimens from Phase 5, pig does not seem to have been common in any period; their bones were less numerous than dog as well as horse in Phases 4-6. Significantly, a calcined pig tooth was recovered from cremation 6720, and calcined foetal or neonatal pig and bird (probably fowl) bones were recovered from cremation 417 (see McIntyre and Rose, Chapter 5).

Three horse specimens had been gnawed by canids – a tibia from Phase 4 and a calcaneum from Phase 5, as well as a metacarpal dated more loosely to the post-Roman period. It was possible to obtain several withers height estimates for horses from measurement of the metacarpals. These estimates were all from Phase 4 specimens and ranged between 1145.35mm (11.27 hands) and 1372.95mm (13.51 hands), the latter height estimate being obtained from a left and a right metacarpal in similar condition but recovered from different parts of the site. All these heights are within the known range for Romano-British horses (Johnstone 2004).

Table 4.3 Specimens recovered from the domestic fowl ABGs at Langford Lane East and Langford Lane South

Site	Context	Sample	Species	Quantity	Element	Side	Z1	Z2	Z3	Z4	Z5	Z6	Z7	Z8
Langford Lane East	7231	6037	Bird	53	indet.									
			Bird	12	vertebra									
			Bird	19	rib									
			Domestic fowl	1	pelvis	right			1					
			Domestic fowl	1	femur	right	1	1	1	1	1	1		1
			Domestic fowl	1	femur	left			1	1	1	1		
			Domestic fowl	1	tibiotarsus	right	1	1	1	1				
			Domestic fowl	1	tibiotarsus	left			1	1				
			Domestic fowl	1	tarsometatarsus	right							1	
			Domestic fowl	1	tarsometatarsus	left					1	1	1	1
			Domestic fowl?	6	phalanx									
			Domestic fowl	1	coracoid	right	1	1						
			Domestic fowl	1	coracoid	left							1	1
			Domestic fowl	1	scapula	right	1	1						
			Domestic fowl	1	humerus	right			1	1	1	1	1	1
			Domestic fowl	1	humerus	left	1							
			Domestic fowl	1	ulna	right	1							
			Domestic fowl	1	radius	right					1	1	1	1
			Domestic fowl	1	radius	left	1	1			1	1	1	1
Langford Lane South	137	20	Bird	142	indet.									
			Bird	4	vertebra									
			Bird	2	rib									
			Bird	5	phalanx									
			Domestic fowl	1	femur	right	1	1	1	1	1	1	1	1
			Domestic fowl	1	femur	left	1	1						
			Domestic fowl	1	coracoid	right					1	1	1	1
			Domestic fowl	1	ulna	right					1	1	1	
			Domestic fowl	1	tibiotarsus	left	1		1	1	1	1		
			Domestic fowl	1	tibiotarsus	right	1	1					1	1
			Domestic fowl	1	tarsometatarsus	tight	1	1					1	1

Z = diagnostic zone (following Cohen and Serjeantson 1996)

Fig. 4.1   Almost complete 'cooking pot type' jar and cremated domestic fowl remains from fill 7231 of roadside ditch 7453 at Langford Lane East

Butchery evidence from the site was sparse, with just 18 specimens in total exhibiting cuts or chops. These included one horse metacarpal from Phase 9 with a chop mark on the lateral side and, from Phase 3, a large mammal vertebra and a medium mammal rib that had been chopped through, along with a caprine pelvis with cut marks around the acetab-

ulum. Half of the butchered specimens were from Phase 4, and these included a caprine humerus with oblique cut marks on the lateral and medial sides of the shaft as well as eight butchered cattle bones. Most of these exhibited cut marks but the butchered ones also included a metacarpal chopped through the distal articulation and a mandible with a superficial chop mark on the buccal side of the ramus.

Langford Lane South

A total of 1986 specimens were recovered by hand, of which 1122 (56.5%) were identifiable to at least a broad descriptive category such as 'large mammal' (cow/horse sized) and just 225 (11.3%) to species. With the notable exception of a large number of caprine specimens, they almost all came from Phases 5 and 6 (Table 4.4). Those caprine specimens came from two adjoining undated pits (22 and 24). Pit 22 contained a probable associated bone group (ABG) consisting of a sheep of about 3½ years of age at death (both proximal humeri were in the process of fusing, whilst the right distal tibia, which fuses at around the same time, 3 to 3½ years, had already fused and tooth wear suggests an age of at least 3½ years). The smaller pit (24) contained two ABGs, both of which were foetal caprines which (assuming they are sheep, as the adult individual in the adjoining pit) were at around half-term in development (*c* 79 days, normal gestation being 147 days), based on measurements of various limb bones (Joubert 1956). Pit 24 also contained a femur, patella and tibia of an adult caprine, as well as a scapula, probably all from the same individual as in pit 22, as well as a single stray cattle tooth.

The material from Roman Phases 5 and 6 was generally in moderate to poor condition. The Phase 5 assemblage included specimens of caprine, domestic cattle, horse and dog (*Canis familiaris*). No body part pattern was observed for the bovids and although it was noted that the horse remains consisted of almost only head and foot elements (a possible horse scapula being the exception), no two

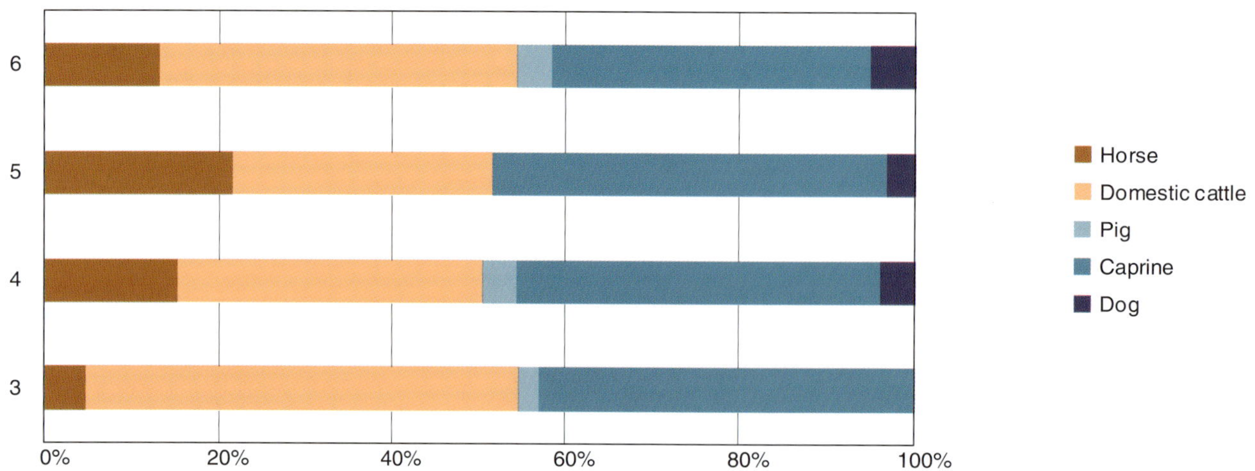

Fig. 4.2   Species proportions from Phases 3, 4, 5 and 6 at Langford Lane East

specimens came from the same context. A horse calcaneum had been gnawed by a canid, probably a dog, suggesting exposure prior to burial. It was possible to obtain withers height estimates from two of the horse bones, a metacarpal (1342mm/ 13.20 hands) and a metatarsal (1315mm/12.95 hands), providing heights that are close to the mean for Romano-British horses (Johnstone 2004).

The assemblage from Phase 6 was more than twice the size of that from Phase 5. Although all species present in the earlier phase saw an increase in NISP (except for dogs) and pig and domestic fowl (*Gallus gallus*) specimens were identified on the site for the first time, the big increase in NSP can largely be attributed to the greater number of domestic cattle recorded in the assemblage (Fig. 4.3). As in the earlier phase, no discernible body part distribution pattern was observed and most of the long bones were fused epiphyseally. The most notable exception to this was two of the six pig/possible pig specimens

– a 1st phalanx and a 4th metacarpal being unfused proximally, suggesting an age at death of under two years and before birth, respectively.

Canids, probably dogs, had gnawed at least eight specimens (five cattle and three caprine), two of which (a caprine humerus and a caprine tibia) also had butchery marks. The tibia had oblique cut-marks on the shaft, consistent with filleting, whilst the humerus had been chopped through obliquely, causing a helical fracture. Four cattle specimens, a pelvis, a mandible, a scapula and a horncore, also had chop-marks or had been chopped through.

Environmental samples were taken from both of these phases but samples from Phase 5 contained little mammal or bird bone (only a domestic cattle tooth and three large mammal specimens) whilst those from Phase 6 principally increased the numbers of medium and small animals recovered (Table 4.4). This is the trend that would be expected of sieved material and suggests that the number

Table 4.4 Quantification of animal bone by species from Langford Lane South

Phase	3	5	6	9	Undated
Domestic cattle		12 (1)	70 (6)		4
Domestic cattle?		1	6		
Caprine		7	16 (7)		57 (6)
Caprine?		1	2		1
Sheep			2		1 (1)
Pig			5 (7)		
Pig?			1		
Horse		9	18		4
Horse?		1	1		
Dog		2	1 (2)		
Small rodent			(3)		
Bank vole/field vole/common vole			(1)		
Small mammal		2	1		
Medium mammal		20	27 (3)		183 (73)
Large mammal		167 (3)	421 (13)	13	63
Total mammal	**0**	**222 (4)**	**571 (39)**	**13**	**313 (80)**
Domestic fowl			3 (7)		
Song thrush			(1)		
Total Bird	**0**	**0**	**3 (156)**	**0**	**0**
Total NISP	0	222 (4)	574 (195)	13	313 (80)
Total NSP	1	346 (4)	1092 (666)	14 (2)	533 (1167)

NISP = Number of Identified Specimens   NSP = Number of Specimens
Quantities from environmental samples in parenthisis (not included in main figure)

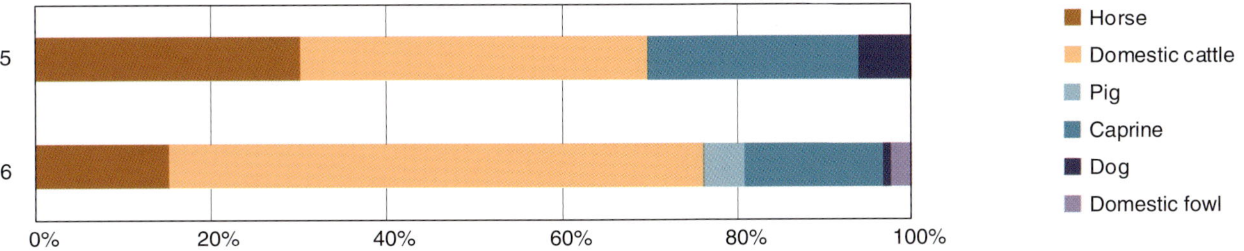

Fig. 4.3   Species proportions from Phases 5 and 6 at Langford Lane South

and proportion of these species may be adversely effected by hand-collection. The species represented were also increased through sieving – a song thrush (*Turdus philomelos*) ulna and a vole (*Myodes glareolus*/*Microtus* sp.) tooth being among the specimens recovered from pit 4047.

The fill of a ceramic vessel recovered from ditch 1063 contained 155 specimens of calcined bird bone. Among these it was possible to identify four vertebrae, two ribs and parts of seven domestic fowl wing and leg bones (from both the left and right sides), probably from a single bird (Table 4.3).

Holts Farm Crossing

A total of 1597 specimens were recovered by hand, of which 1082 (67.8%) were identifiable to at least a broad descriptive category such as 'large mammal' (cow/horse sized), including 260 (16.3% of NSP) to species. Four phases (2, 5, 6 and 7) had a NISP of more than 100 (Table 4.5). The condition of the specimens varied substantially between phases, with the bones from Phase 2 being the most poorly preserved and those from Phase 7 being the best. Soil samples produced a further 4380 specimens, with over half of them coming from Phases 2 or 5. The vast majority of this material was unidentifiable, however, and those few specimens that could be identified largely reflected the composition of the hand-collected assemblage, with large mammals most abundant. They also contained specimens of frog (*Rana* sp.)

and/or toad (*Bufo* sp.), reflecting a damp environment in and around undated pit 8004 and trackway ditch 8690, as well as a single specimen of the common shrew (*Sorex araneus*), also from ditch 8690.

The assemblage was generally in moderate condition, with the specimens from Phase 7 being in good condition. Large mammals, particularly domestic cattle, dominated the assemblage in every phase except Phase 7, which was skewed by the material collected from the fill of pit 8404. This was probably a sheep ABG, containing four of the six sheep specimens recovered from this phase as well as 45 of the 51 caprine specimens and 114 of the 115 medium mammal specimens, including ribs and vertebrae. All the long-bones of the individual were fused epiphyseally except the tibiae, which were unfused proximally, suggesting an age at death of between 3 and 3½ years. Other similarly late-fusing bones (distal femur and proximal humeri) were not recovered but it was possible to record a wear stage for the left and right mandibles, both Grant's (1982) wear stage 32, which suggest a broad range of possible age at death but a most likely date consistent with that provided by the epiphyseal fusion data. Lesions, consistent with osteochondrosis, were present on the proximal surface of both metacarpals and on the left astragalus. Oblique cut-marks were observed on the medial aspect of the distal end of both the right humerus and the right radius, suggesting that this limb, at least, was disarticulated before burial. According to criteria suggested for the astragalus by

Table 4.5 Quantification of animal bone by species from Holts Farm Crossing

Phase	1	2	3	5	6	7	8	Undated
Domestic cattle	2 (2)	29 (13)	16	14 (5)	19	17	7	1 (1)
Domestic cattle?	2 (2)	2 (1)	2	1 (6)	1			(3)
Caprine	2	15	6	7	6	51		
Caprine?		1 (3)		1 (3)		1		(3)
Sheep		1 (2)				6		
Pig		12 (10)	3	2 (2)	2	1		(9)
Horse		4	7	1	2	3	2	
Dog		1	1	(2)	5	1		
Dog?					2			
Common shrew				(1)				
Micro mammal		(6)		(2)				
Small mammal	(1)	2	2	(1)	2			
Medium mammal		37 (1)	5	31 (5)	35 (12)	115	1	(4)
Large mammal		220 (160)	55	62 (10)	97 (25)	88	64	6 (2)
Total mammal	**6 (5)**	**324 (196)**	**97**	**119 (37)**	**171 (37)**	**283**	**74**	**7 (22)**
Amphibian				(8)				
Frog/toad								(14)
Total amphibian				**(8)**				**(14)**
Swan					1			
Total bird	**0**	**0**	**0**	**0**	**1**	**0**	**0**	**0**
Total NISP	6 (5)	324 (196)	97	119 (45)	172 (37)	283	74	7 (36)
Total NSP	6 (19)	495 (1801)	215	172 (1028)	279 (665)	349	74	7 (867)

NISP = Number of Identified Specimens; NSP = Number of Specimens   Quantities from environmental samples in parenthesis (not included in main figure)

Boessneck (1969, 351) the individual was more likely to have been male than female but the reliability of this method is not absolute (Ruscillo 2003).

Specimens showing signs of having been gnawed by canids were recovered from every phase apart from Phase 8. These include specimens of horse from Phases 2, 3 and 7, domestic cattle from every phase, caprines from every phase except Phase 1, and a dog humerus from Phase 5. The last specimen was from the fill of trackway ditch 8696, along with a dog tooth (the only other dog specimen from this feature), domestic cattle bones and the amphibian and shrew specimens described above.

Apart from the sheep ABG already discussed, there was very little evidence for butchery on the site – a domestic cattle radius from Phase 5 had axial cut-marks on the cranial side of the shaft and a medium mammal lumbar vertebra from the same phase had been chopped through axially, through the centre of the bone. This suggests that the carcass had been hung up and spilt in half as a preliminary stage of butchery. This form of butchery is often thought to be a later Roman innovation and would have required considerable effort – often using pulleys for larger animals. As such this is quite significant, suggesting an earlier adoption of this technique in Britain than has been previously thought.

Discussion

Discussion of the various sites presented here must begin with reference to the report made of the animal bones excavated from the fort at Alchester (Thomas 2008). Not only did this describe a bone assemblage recovered from a site which is adjacent to the two Langford Lane sites analysed here, it also provided a summary review of contemporary sites in the region excavated up to the point of its publication. The principal result of that analysis was that whole animals were interpreted as being processed on the site, probably as a result of local trade as opposed to extensive military supply lines. The largest component of the Langford Lane East assemblage was contemporary with the fort, probably a civilian settlement associated with it, and so this is particularly relevant. As such, discussion will begin with this phase of activity before comparing it to the preceding Iron Age phases, which were small and best considered in comparison to the larger Roman assemblage.

As with Thomas's analysis, there was no noteworthy bias towards any particular element recorded from the Roman period on the site, suggesting that whole carcasses were being processed. This was also true of the later periods on the site and at nearby Langford Lane South. It is possible that households within these areas shared in the local supply enjoyed by the fort, eventually taking it over as a small town was formed. It is also possible, however, that the animals slaughtered both in the fort and the two sites studied here were reared on the surrounding land, owned by the people who lived in the settlements. Of course, the two possibilities are not mutually exclusive. Given that one reason for the settlement would have been the opportunities afforded by the garrison, it would seem odd given the pastoral nature of the landscape had the inhabitants not been engaged in rearing and supplying livestock.

Thomas also noted that sheep were the most common animal represented in the Alchester assemblage, a situation which is also true of the same phase at Langford Lane East, though barely. He also noted a higher proportion of pig than is typical of sites at this time, which is not true of the Langford Lane East assemblage. By contrast, domestic cattle were always the most common animal at Langford Lane South, as they also were in Phase 6 of Langford Lane East, the last phase with a NISP greater than 100. The rise in abundance of cattle to caprines has been suggested as a sign of Romanisation (King 1999) but it has also been argued that the Roman conquest saw the beginning of a market economy in Britain, which would see specialisation of production dependent upon what might be best produced in an environment (van der Veen and O'Connor 1998). As such, Alchester and the two Langford Lane sites become an interesting case-study.

The Alchester fort is one of the earliest in Britain, dated to within a few short years of the Roman arrival and occupied for a generation (Sauer 2000b). While noting that sheep were the most common species from the fortress assemblage (as with these sites, sheep were identified among the caprine remains and goats were not), Thomas stressed that domestic cattle would still have been the most important component of the inhabitants' diet when considering the amount of meat provided by the animals (Thomas 2008). That argument slightly misses the point, however, when it is held up to King's model, which was based on numbers of specimens and individuals, not on meat-weight (King 1999). We can also now see that the proportion of domestic cattle on the Langford Lane sites continues to increase relative to sheep throughout the Roman period. This could suggest that any shift towards a more Roman diet and away from a supposed earlier preference for sheep was far more gradual than King suggested. The suggestion that local environment might play a role in species proportions where whole animals are being processed on site (van der Veen and O'Connor 1998) seems like an important consideration though. Alchester is situated more or less midway between the Cotswold uplands and the Thames Valley gravel terraces; the former would favour the rearing of sheep and the latter cattle. Surrounded by rolling, low limestone hills, either could probably be herded with some success in the immediate vicinity.

It may be postulated then that local production changed between the earliest and later Roman phases on the site and that any slightly more distant supply changed from the Cotswold hills to the Oxford floodplains. The possibility of a switch to more cattle in the diet of later Roman Alchester is real but this change would appear to be a gradual shift in taste rather than an overnight shift to more fashionable cuisine. Evidence from the last decade or so increasingly points to a difference in the types of livestock that were a focus of production between the lowlands and relative uplands of the region (Strid 2018; forthcoming). In this light it is interesting to note the rise in the proportion of horse on both Langford Lane sites, reaching a peak in Phase 5.

A higher proportion of horse specimens has been noted at Roman rural and roadside settlements when compared to urban and military sites in the past and this has been interpreted as evidence for specialist horse ranching as part of a communications and transport infrastructure (eg Albarella 1997; Wright *et al*. forthcoming). It is notable, in this respect, that both Langford Lane sites have a much higher proportion of horse specimens than the decidedly more rural Holts Farm Crossing, which has a low proportion of horse throughout the Roman period. In this respect, a better point of comparison might be Roman Winchester, which saw a higher proportion of horse remains in the suburbs than in the centre (Maltby 2010) and the high presence here in the middle Roman period can perhaps be best understood when considered alongside more local evidence, which sees high proportions of horse on a number of Roman sites (Strid 2018; forthcoming). The Oxfordshire/Buckinghamshire region may well have seen a greater emphasis on horse rearing during the Roman period, amplifying the trends seen on rural sites elsewhere and reflected in the assemblage from the Langford Lane sites, on the edge of Alchester, by way of the local production/supply already outlined.

It must be acknowledged that this interpretation is based on relatively small assemblages, even though these are larger than the preceding Iron Age components, present at Langford Lane East and Holts Farm Crossing. The largest of these is the middle Iron Age (Phase 2) component from Holts Farm, comparable in size to the various Roman components already discussed here. With the caveats just outlined, it is interesting to note that this is the only assemblage from any of the sites discussed here to contain any significant quantity of pig. Although the assemblage is dominated by cattle, the unusually high (for the sites considered here) proportion of pig remains present might indicate a more wooded environment in the area at this time.

Unusual deposits

Given the relatively small size of the assemblages, the most notable aspects were the special deposits described above. Sheep ABGs were recovered from the late Roman phase at Holts Farm Crossing as well as from undated pits at Langford Lane South. All the bones from the pits at Langford Lane South were in

better condition than was typical of the site, and it seems likely that the three individuals represent the modern disposal of a ewe that died mid-pregnancy. The similarity of age with the individual from Holts Farm is interesting in that respect but probably no more than a coincidence. Although cause of death could not be determined, the animal was demonstrably butchered before disposal, so it seems reasonable to speculate that this represents more than mere dumping of deadstock. The lesions present on several of the bones of the individual were consistent with osteochondrosis but are unlikely to have visibly affected the animal during its life (Sewell 2010). Although caprines are the most common ABG recovered from late Roman rural sites in southern Britain (Morris 2011, 88), it is very rare for them to have pathologies. Less than 2% of ABGs from Britain have pathologies (Morris 2011, 144), suggesting that most are of animals free from long-term debilitating conditions. The fact that the lesions recorded here would have gone undetected by the people who buried the animal is, thus, significant in that it suggests that although the presence of them is uncommon it is not likely to have affected selection.

There has been a trend recently of assigning ritual interpretations to Romano-British ABGs (Morris 2011, 151), a trend which, it has been argued, may have little basis in the reality of the archaeological record (Wilson 1992; Broderick 2012). The presence of butchery marks in this case actually make a stronger argument for some kind of ritual activity than if the animal had been buried complete and unmarked (Broderick 2012). The precise nature of any ritual, of course, cannot be known but we can say with some certainty that if that is what it was, it was not the only ritual activity involving animals to be carried out at the site.

The two cremated domestic fowl, recovered from the fill of pots in ditches at Langford Lane East and Langford Lane South, are separated by a distance of *c* 1km. Given their geographical separation, it is surprising that the finds are so strikingly similar and are seemingly without exact precedent in the archaeological record of Roman Britain or elsewhere in the empire. Bird bones have been recovered from within the fill of pots on Roman sites in the Netherlands (Lauwerier 1993) but, unlike those studied here, they were unburned and thus interpreted as most likely representing food remains. Domestic fowl are one of the most common animals found in Roman graves and cremations in that region, along with pigs (Lauwerier 2004). A recent review in Britain has found that the same two animals are also the most common in Roman period cremations (although not in inhumations) (Allen forthcoming; cf. Worley 2008), with examples including Ebbsfleet (Grimm and Worley 2011) and Trentholme Drive in York (Fraser and Ryder 1968), the latter including two inhumation burials featuring calcined domestic fowl bones contained in pots.

The unusualness of the finds from the Langford Lane sites thus stems from the fact that they were not recovered from grave contexts. Expanding our search for comparanda, it has been suggested that domestic fowl are more likely to be found at temples than at rural shrines in Roman Britain (King 2005). The Mithraeum at Walbrook had an especially large assemblage of domestic fowl bones, almost all male where they could be sexed, with burned bones surrounding the apse and not being found elsewhere. It has been suggested that the sacrifice of domestic fowl to the Roman/Greek pantheon was relatively rare (Kadletz 1976), which would seem to fly in the face of the archaeological evidence, at least in Britain. Aphrodite, Ares, Artemis and Heracles/Hercules are all mentioned as appropriate deities to whom to sacrifice a domestic fowl (almost always a male bird). More generally, it has been suggested that the most common rituals are those that mark the beginning or end of something (Merrifield 1987) and the roadside, in particular, is an obvious place for beginnings and endings.

Perhaps, though, the best guide to interpretation for these finds are the pots of burned domestic fowl remains from Trentholme Drive. Cremation burials containing pig were found at Langford Lane East in Phase 5 (see above and McIntyre and Rose, Chapter 5). Given this background, we might entertain the possibility that the cremated domestic fowl remains represent a proxy burial for an individual where it was not possible to bury their body.

Conclusions

Although the three assemblages are relatively small they each, in their way, help us understand the economic and environmental development of the area through the Iron Age and Roman period. The two Langford Lane sites, in particular, help to flesh out the interpretations previously made of the Roman fort of Alchester. Together with the Iron Age inhabitation at Holts Farm Crossing we can begin to envision a region that was, at first, lightly wooded but which leant itself to the keeping of both domestic cattle and sheep. When the Roman military arrived a market was created for livestock and this was transported there whole, probably on foot, and some of it, at least, being raised in the immediate vicinity. Over time, after the fort was superseded by a town, demand changed to one which emphasised the supply of cattle, so making links to the Thames Valley arguably more important than those to the Cotswolds.

Perhaps most significantly, the faunal assemblage throws new light on Roman ritual activity. The sacrifice and burial of whole sheep is far from unknown at this time but the deliberate cremation and burial of domestic fowl in pots is something previously undocumented. As with any ritual activity, understanding it without direct textual or ethnographic analogues is difficult to impossible. It has tentatively been suggested here, though, that they may be related to memorial rites.

CHARRED PLANT REMAINS *by Julia Meen*

Introduction and methodology

A total of 92 bulk samples was taken during excavations at the eight sites, as well a further nine samples taken during earlier evaluation stages at four of the sites. Each sample was processed using a modified Siraf style flotation machine, with smaller samples (less than 5 litres in volume) floated by hand using the 'wash-over' technique. Flots were collected onto 250μm meshes and the heavy residues were sieved to 500μm, after which both flots and residues were dried in a heated room. The residues were sorted by eye for artefacts and ecofactual remains. Assessment of each of the flots was undertaken, on the basis of which only seven samples were selected for the full analysis of charred macrofossils owing to the frequently poor condition of the material: one sample from Langford Lane East, three samples from Langford Lane South, one sample from South of Oddington Crossing and two samples from North of Oxford Parkway Station. Full details of the assessed flots will be available in the site archive.

Each flot was sorted and identified using a LEICA EZ4D stereo microscope at x10-40 magnification, and with reference to published and online reference guides (including Cappers *et al.* 2006) and to the modern reference collection held at OA. Nomenclature follows Stace (2010). Detached coleoptiles were counted where the base was complete; numerous coleoptile fragments were present in several of the samples but these were not quantified. Cereal grains were mostly quantified using counts of embryo ends to avoid duplicate counting but in samples such as those from Langford Lane South, where many of the grains were missing the embryo ends, apical ends were counted instead.

The three samples from Langford Lane South were found to be encrusted with a mineral precipitate, which meant flotation was inefficient and that a large number of charred remains remained within the heavy residues. Therefore, the residues of each of these samples was refloated, producing highly rich secondary flots especially rich in cereal chaff. These 'refloats' were therefore riffled (cf. van der Veen and Fieller 1982) and a proportion sorted. For sample 2142 this proportion was 50% and for sample 2079 25%. For sample 2145 a 25% fraction of the refloat was found to still be extremely rich in cereal chaff and so following extraction of other remains (mostly detached coleoptiles and weed seeds) the flot was riffled further and 1/16 (6.3%) of the refloat sorted for cereal chaff. Quantities given in Table 4.6 therefore show numbers extracted from the 100% of the original flots, plus multiples of the counts from a proportion of the residue refloat in order to achieve as close as possible approximation of the true composition of the samples. However, owing to the presence of large numbers of unquantifiable chaff fragments and the fact that chaff tends to be dispro-

Table 4.6 Summary of charred plant remains

			Langford Lane East	Langford Lane South
		Sample no.	6034	2142
		Context no.	7018	2782
		Feature no.	Pit 7014	Pit 4047
		Phase	6	6
		Volume floated	40L	38L
		Proportion sorted	1/16 flot	100% flot
Cereal grain				
Triticum sp.	wheat	grain	20	81
Triticum sp.	wheat	germinated grain	16	40
Triticum sp.	wheat	tail grain		12
Triticum sp.	wheat	germinated tail grain		
cf. *Triticum* sp.	cf. wheat	grain		
Hordeum vulgare L.	barley	grain		1
Hordeum vulgare L.	barley	germinated grain		
cf. *Hordeum vulgare*	cf. barley	grain		
cf. *Secale cereale* L.	cf. rye	grain		
cf. *Secale cereale* L.	cf. rye	germinated grain		1
Cereal	indet.	grain	47	151
Cereal chaff				
Triticum spelta	spelt	glume base	687	183
Triticum spelta/dicoccum	spelt/emmer	glume base	1772	1393
Triticum spelta/dicoccum	spelt/emmer	spikelet fork	31	22
cf. *Triticum dicoccum* Schübl	emmer	glume base	1	
Triticum aestivum/durum/turgidum	free threshing wheat	rachis		
Hordeum vulgare L.	barley	rachis		1
Cereal		culm node	1	
Cereal		detached embryo	106	8
Cereal		detached coleoptile	141	53
Poaceae		culm node		
Weed seeds				
Papaver sp.	poppy	seed	1	
Ranunculus acris/repens/bulbosus	meadow/creeping/bulbous buttercup	seed		
Trifolium/Melilotus/Medicago	clover/melilot/medick	seed	3	
Vicia/Lathyrus	vetch/tare (2-3mm)	seed		1
Vicia/Lathyrus	vetch/tare (1-2mm)	seed	1	1
Indet. legume		seed		1
Urtica dioica L.	common nettle	seed		
Urtica urens L.	small nettle	seed		
Corylus avellana L.	hazel	nutshell fragment		
cf. *Linum usitatissimum* L.	flax	seed	1	
cf. *Linum catharticum* L.	fairy flax	seed		
Malva sp.	mallow	seed		1
Brassicaeae	cabbage family	seed		
Brassica sp.	cabbages	seed		
Raphanus raphanistrum L.	wild radish	fruit	1	1
Polygonaceae	knotweeds	seed	1	1
Persicaria sp.	knotweed	seed		
Polygonum aviculare L.	knotgrass	seed		
cf. *Fallopia convolvulus* (L.) A. Love	black-bindweed	seed		
Rumex sp.	dock	seed	21	9
Caryophyllaceae	pink family	seed		
Stellaria sp.	stitchwort	seed		
Agrostemma githago L.	corncockle	seed		
Silene sp.	campion	seed	2	
Chenopodium/Atriplex	goosefoot/orache	seed	55	

Langford Lane South					South of Oddington Crossing	North of Oxford Parkway Station	
2142	2145	2145	2079	2079	9	3001	3004
2782	2791	2791	2550	2550	108	3048	3109
Pit 4047	Pit 4047	Pit 4047	Pit 4047	Pit 4047	Pit 109	Oven/kiln 3047/3049	Pit 3114
6	6	6	6	6	2	6	6
38L	28L	28L	32L	32L	36L	40L	40L
50% residue refloat	100% flot	25% residue refloat (1/16 chaff)	100% flot	25% residue refloat	100% flot	100% flot	100% flot
	31	26	79	20	106	138	31
	20	7	58	8		5	
	5	8	7	1		5	
		2	2				
2							
			3	1	9	4	3
			1				
		2				5	3
							2
22	271	182	557	112	275	316	127
673	561	252 (1008)	1050	1169		5	
2486	1629	501 (2004)	1485	2498		79	1
49	41	15 (60)	35	42	2	37	2
1	1		1				
				1		8	
						2	
22	51	21	67	79		20	3
126	389	360	309	649		14	
						2	
		1					
		1	2				
				?		15	
1					1	13	2
						29	3
	2	2					
						22	
						4	
				1		4	
						1	
						1	
						18	
						4	44
	1		3	1		4	
				2		1	
						1	
2	3						
18	11	7	5	11	1	9	1
		1					
						1	
	1	1					
						2	
	4	2	3			6	2

Table 4.6 (continued)

			Langford Lane East	Langford Lane South
		Sample no.	*6034*	*2142*
		Context no.	*7018*	*2782*
		Feature no.	*Pit 7014*	*Pit 4047*
		Phase	*6*	*6*
		Volume floated	*40L*	*38L*
		Proportion sorted	*1/16 flot*	*100% flot*
Montia fontana L.	blinks	seed		
Galium sp.	bedstraw	seed		1
cf. *Solanum* sp.	nightshades	seed		2
Plantago minor/lanceolata	lesser/ribwort plantain	seed		
Asteraceae	daisies	seed	8	9
Cirsium/Caardus/Centaurea	thistle/knapweed	seed		
Cirsium cf *arvense* (L.) Scop.	creeping thistle	seed	1	
Centaurea cf *cyanus* L.	cornflower	seed		
Anthemis cotula L.	stinking chamomile	seed	38	
Tripleurospermum sp.	mayweed	seed	6	1
Tripleurospermum inodorum (L.) Sch. Bip.	scentless mayweed	seed	14	
Juncus sp.	rush	seed	1	1
Cyperaceae	sedges	seed		
Eleocharis sp.	spike-rush	seed		
Carex sp.	sedge	seed	1	
Poaceae (small)	small grass	seed	3	1
Poaceae (medium)	medium grass	seed	40	4
Poaceae (large)	large grass	seed	20 + 31F	7
Avena sp.	oat	caryopsis	2	5
Avena sp.	oat	germinated caryopsis	2	2
Avena sp.	oat (undiff)	caryopsis within floret		
Avena sp.	oat (non-cultivated)	caryopsis within floret		
Avena cf *sativa* L.	oat (cf. cultivated)	caryopsis within floret		
Avena sp.	oat (undiff.)	floret base		
Avena cf *fatua* L.	wild-oat	floret base	1	
Bromus sp.	brome	caryopsis	6	1
cf. *Bromus*	cf. brome	caryopsis		
Avena/Bromus	oat/brome	caryopsis	26	
indet.		seed	4	1
Other				
tree bud				

F=fragment; g=germinated

portionately destroyed during charring (Boardman and Jones 1990), the quantities of chaff should be seen as an underestimate. Sample 6034 from Langford Lane East was also extremely rich and was riffled. Figures given in Table 4.6 are unmultiplied totals from sorting 1/16 of the original flot.

Langford Lane East

The sample from Phase 6 pit 7014 is dominated by cereal chaff, with numerous weed seeds also present. The latter are predominately dock (*Rumex* sp.), goosefoot/orache (*Chenopodium/Atriplex*), oat/brome type caryopses (mostly too poorly preserved to differentiate), other grasses, and seeds of the daisy family, mostly stinking chamomile and scentless mayweeds

(*Anthemis cotula* and *Tripleurospermum inodorum*). Cereal grain was comparatively sparse, grains were often fragmentary, and tended to be poorly preserved, with a 'clinkered' appearance and often with a tarry substance at the apical ends (cf. Hubbard and al Azm 1990, distortion stage 6). Of the grains which could be identified as wheat (*Triticum* sp.), almost half showed one or more of the following characteristics indicative of germination: missing embryo or entire embryo end; sunken appearance; dorsal groove; attached coleoptile; hollow grain; leathery outer surface. A large number of detached coleoptiles and embryos were also present, in greater number than would be expected if they had fallen off the grains in the sample, suggesting they derive from grain processed in another episode of activity. Most of the coleoptiles

Langford Lane South					South of Oddington Crossing	North of Oxford Parkway Station	
2142	2145	2145	2079	2079	9	3001	3004
2782	2791	2791	2550	2550	108	3048	3109
Pit 4047	Pit 4047	Pit 4047	Pit 4047	Pit 4047	Pit 109	Oven/kiln 3047/3049	Pit 3114
6	6	6	6	6	2	6	6
38L	28L	28L	32L	32L	36L	40L	40L
50% residue refloat	100% flot	25% residue refloat (1/16 chaff)	100% flot	25% residue refloat	100% flot	100% flot	100% flot
							3
	1						
	1	1					
	6		2			13	3
	2						1
	1						
						7	
	6	7	8	1		16	4
						6	
						5	
1							
						1	
	4	1		1		29	
2	23	8	12	16		66	1
		6		2		2	
	2		9			18	
						2	
						1	1g
	1					1	
						3	
	1					1	
			5	2		7	
	4						1
	9	4	51	6		23	4
	3	3	3	3		13	5
1		1		1			

were broken, but two unbroken examples were 4.5 and 3.7mm in length respectively; most others had broken at between 2 and 3mm, whilst the embryos showed variable levels of sprouting.

Langford Lane South

The three samples from pit 4047 are all strongly dominated by glume wheat chaff, with abundant detached coleoptiles in all three examined assemblages and far fewer cereal grains. The better preserved glumes are almost all of spelt wheat (*Triticum spelta*) and it is likely that the majority if those identified as *T. spelta / dicoccum* are also spelt. It is notable that a high proportion of the cereal grains in all three samples show signs of germination and that high numbers of coleoptiles are present – at least as many detached coleoptiles as there are grains. Quantification of germinated grains includes only those which are definitely germinated, that is, with clear signs in the form of either sprouted embryo, attached coleoptile, or a groove on the dorsal side of grain where the coleoptile has become detached. This is almost certainly an underestimate of the true number; cereal grains in these samples are generally poorly preserved, which means that features that would be indicative of germination are obscured. Many have damaged or missing embryo ends; this is often regarded as a characteristic of germination, but as germination was not clearly seen these grains were not included in the germinated count, apart from those where the end of a dorsal groove could be seen extending beyond the break / damaged area. Many grains also had sunken surfaces, also indicative of germination, including many of the grains that were too poorly preserved to identify to genus. Therefore, although only around a third of the wheat grains are unequivocally germinated, the true number is almost certainly higher and it is likely that the majority of the grains are germinated. There is also a high proportion of indeterminate grain and grain fragments.

South of Oddington Crossing

The sample from middle Iron Age pit 109 was mostly composed of charred cereal grain, containing almost no chaff or weed seeds. The grain was often poorly preserved, with the outer surfaces often partly sunken or missing, while the grains that were recovered from the heavy residue appeared slightly mineralised. Owing to the distortion in the grains, the majority could not be identified to genus. The better-preserved examples were mostly wheat (*Triticum* sp.), although, due to distortion in grain morphology and the absence of cereal chaff to corroborate, it was not possible to differentiate which type of wheat was represented. A relatively small number of barley (*Hordeum vulgare*) grains were present, although distortion and poor preservation again made it impossible to determine if they included hulled or 6-row varieties and barley may form a larger proportion of the grain assemblage than indicated. It is likely that the deposit derives from a fully cleaned crop product, possibly charred during preparation for storage or consumption.

North of Oxford Parkway Station

The samples analysed from this site were both fills of 2nd-century pits. Both samples contain relatively little chaff, being dominated by cereal grain. The majority of the identifiable grain is wheat (*Triticum* sp.), with a small amount of barley (*Hordeum* sp.) also present. However, almost three quarters of the grain could not be identified to genus due to poor preservation and distortion; grains were often puffed and missing their outer surfaces, and many had sunken profiles. A small number of the wheat grains in sample 3001 could be seen to have germinated and it is probable that further germinated grain was present within the indeterminate grain. A small number of detached embryos and coleoptiles were also present in this sample.

Sample 3001 contained a high proportion of weed seeds, comprising over a third of all quantified items. These were dominated by grasses, particularly those which compare favourably to perennial rye-grass (*Lolium perenne*) and meadow-grass/cat's tail-sized caryopses (*Poa/Phleum*). *Avena*-sized caryopses were frequent; due to poor preservation these could often not be further differentiated, but better preserved examples showed that these caryopses were a mixture of brome grass (*Bromus* sp.) and *Avena*, with at least one example of a grain still held within a floret of cultivated type (*Avena* cf. *sativa*). Small legumes, including clover (*Trifolium*) type, members of the daisy family, particularly scentless mayweed (*Tripleurospermum inodorum*) and wetland taxa such as rush (*Juncus* spp.) and sedges (Cyperaceae), also frequently occurred in this assemblage.

Sample 3004, by contrast, was mostly notable by the presence of 44 fruits of wild radish (*Raphanus raphanistrum*). Wild radish is a common weed of arable crops but prefers non-calcareous habitats and may indicate the cultivation of sandy soils in the vicinity. This sample contained very little chaff and few other weed seeds, although cereal grain, mostly too poorly preserved to be identifiable to genus, was also present. It is likely that this assemblage represents the by-products of the final hand cleaning of processed grain to remove grain-sized and larger contaminants which would have escaped the fine sieving stages.

Discussion

Evidence for malting

A high proportion of the cereal grains in all three samples from pit 4047 at Langford Lane South show signs of germination and detached coleoptiles are present in great quantity. This strongly suggests that the pit contains waste from the malting of spelt grain. An increasing number of Romano-British sites have been found with assemblages consisting of high numbers of germinated grains, frequent detached coleoptiles and often highly abundant spelt chaff. This body of evidence demonstrates that spelt wheat was the principal cereal used for malting in this period, and that grains were apparently germinated still within their spikelets. Malting involves the deliberate, controlled germination of cereal grains in order to activate enzymes responsible for converting the starch held in the endosperm of the grain into sugar. Grains are first steeped in water to initiate this process. It is necessary to halt the germination process before the energy store of the grain can be used up in the production of the developing shoot, so that this sugar can ultimately be fermented to produce alcohol. The malting process involves gently heating the grain to a temperature that will kill the developing shoots without denaturing the enzymes. After drying the malt, the grains would be removed from the spikelets, along with the developing coleoptiles and roots, and the waste products most likely burnt as fuel.

The single sample from Langford Lane East may also be a waste product from the dehusking of malt. The coleoptiles are present in much greater number than grains in this sample, yet it would be expected that grain would be preferentially preserved over the much lighter fragments of coleoptile tissue; this indicates that the coleoptiles do not derive only from the grains in the pit but must have been removed from grain elsewhere before being discarded.

An assemblage similar in composition was recovered from a ditch forming part of the extramural settlement directly to the north-east of Alchester at Chesterton Lane (Pelling 2001). Although the feature was dated to the post-Roman period and argued to represent a continuity of Roman agricultural practice into the early Anglo-Saxon period, the material was not radiocarbon dated and has subsequently been suggested as likely to be Roman (Pelling 2011, 233). A high proportion of grains with characteristics of germination, frequent detached coleoptiles and abundant spelt glume bases were here suggested to be the dehusking waste of spelt malt, although numbers of coleoptiles were much lower than those identified at the Langford Lane sites. While Pelling suggested that cereal processing in the extramural settlement may have been relatively small in scale, evidence for large-scale malt production has been found less than a kilometre to the north along the Roman road from Alchester, at Whitelands Farm. Here, charred assemblages rich in chaff, germinated grain and coleoptiles were recovered from numerous contexts, including a corndryer, stone-lined tanks and a drainage ditch (Stevens 2011a). The stone tanks and drainage ditch would have been suitable for steeping the grain and disposing of waste water. As for the corndryer, it is increasingly accepted that these structures are likely to have been used to malt grain (see discussion in van der Veen 1989) and they have been shown experimentally to produce the gentle heat required to halt the germination process (Reynolds and Langley 1979). Although no corndryers were found at Langford Lane, the excavation areas revealed a relatively small slice of the settlement and such structures may well be present in the vicinity; a 3rd/4th century corndryer was discovered during the 1991 excavations in the northern extramural area (Booth *et al.* 2001).

The probable evidence for malting from both sites at Langford Lane, possible evidence from North of Oxford Parkway Station, and evidence from previously excavated sites in the vicinity, suggest that this activity was being routinely carried out in the environs of Alchester. Stevens (2011a) has suggested that the site at Whitelands Farm may have been producing malt, and probably ale, for sale in the town as well as to travellers, being at an important junction where Akeman Street crosses the Dorchester to Towcester road. Stevens has elsewhere noted a correlation between centres of malting and proximity to major roads (Stevens *et al.* 2011, 242). Although beer does not preserve well, malt is relatively stable and is likely to have been an important commodity for trade, and it would have been important to have ready access to markets. None of the evidence for malting at Langford Lane dates to earlier than the 2nd century and so provides no hint for whether malt was previously produced for consumption by the military. However, this is due to an absence of suitably dated material and work in the future may reveal whether the practice can be traced back to the earliest occupation of the site.

Evidence for stabling waste

Sample 3001 from North of Oxford Parkway Station was dominated by small and medium grasses, probably including meadow-grass/cat's tail and perennial rye-grass, as well as caryopses of oat/brome, small clover-type legumes, small daisies and frequent wetland taxa (rushes, sedges). A charred assemblage with many similarities was recovered from a late Roman pit at Whitelands Farm (Stevens 2011a). The Whitelands Farm sample contained frequent monocot stems and 'conglomerated' material in addition to a similar suite of wet grassland taxa and frequent charred cereal waste, and was suggested to derive from dung mixed with cereal processing waste. The North of Oxford Parkway Station assemblage includes four culm nodes, two of grass size and two of cereal size, which may indicate the presence of hay/straw. It is possible therefore the pit at North of Oxford Parkway Station similarly contained charred remains of stabling waste, presumably recycled as fuel. This would concur with the insect evidence which also indicates that stabling waste was being discarded into features at the site (Allison, this volume), and plant taxa of pasture and hay meadows were also identified in the waterlogged assemblages (Meen, below).

CHARCOAL *by Dana Challinor*

Introduction

Despite the large number of environmental samples taken during the excavations, preservation of material was generally poor. This limited the potential for analysis of the charcoal and dictated the methodology to gain the most informative dataset. Consequently, 40 samples were analysed (in varying degrees of detail) to provide a broad taxonomic list from which chronological comparisons and functional interpretations could be attempted.

Methodology

Given the poor quality of the material, a couple of necessary amendments to the methodology were made to avoid high numbers of indeterminate fragments and over-representation of oak, which can occur since this taxon is the most easily recognisable in poor material. Firstly, the selection of fragments for identification concentrated on the larger material (>4mm), which is easier to identify than the smaller fractions. Secondly, the number of fragments identified per sample was varied according to condition and diversity. If the material was very poor, identifications were stopped at 30 fragments (subject to availability), whereas up to 50 fragments were examined for higher diversity assemblages or special contexts. The consequences of this approach are that: 1) the indeterminate categories should not be taken as an accurate representation of unidentifiable fragments; and 2) the taxonomic composition of the samples is likely to be under-represented, that is, it is not unlikely that additional species would have been present.

Beyond these qualifications, standard identification procedures were followed; the charcoal was fractured and sorted into groups based on the anatomical features observed in transverse section at x7 to x45 magnifications. Representative fragments from each group were then selected for further examination using a Meiji incident-light microscope at up to x400 magnification. Identifications were made with reference to appropriate keys (Schweingruber 1990, Hather 2000) and modern reference material. Classification and nomenclature follow Stace (1997). Observations on maturity and character of the wood were recorded where visible, though this was frequently obscured. Comments on habitat preferences, wood properties and burning qualities are drawn from various sources including Stace (1997), Edlin (1949), Gale and Cutler (2000) and Warren (2006).

Notes on taxa

A total of 1400 fragments were examined for the analysis, from which 11 taxa were positively identified. All of these were consistent with native taxa, which is the most likely provenance for the material. It should be noted, however, that *Prunus domestica* (plum), which was a Roman introduction to Britain, is anatomically indistinguishable from the native *P. spinosa* (blackthorn) and where relevant the identification has been given as *P. spinosa/domestica* (albeit the native species is most probably represented).

ULMACEAE: *Ulmus* spp. (elm)
There is debate over the native status of some of the elm species, but all would have flourished on the alluvial and moist soils of the area. All are large trees and cannot be distinguished on anatomical grounds. The wood survives well in water and was often used for structures in permanently wet conditions. Its burning properties are poor, with a tendency to smoulder.

FAGACEAE: *Quercus* spp. (oak)
There are two oak species native to England, which are not distinguishable anatomically. Oak was ubiquitous in prehistory and commonly exploited for timber and fuelwood purposes. It coppices well and provides a good firewood with a high calorific heat, especially when well-seasoned. It also makes a good charcoal fuel, albeit with a tendency to fragment.

BETULACEAE: *Alnus glutinosa*, Gaertn. (alder)
Common alder is the sole species native to Britain and is a common tree on riversides and in wetland habitats. Alder woodland would have characterised localised wetland areas and along riversides. Alder is considered a poor fuelwood, slow to burn.

BETULACEAE: *Corylus avellana* L. (hazel)
Hazel commonly associates with oak woodland, often forming a shrubby understory. Like oak, it coppices well

and was important in woodland management practices. It makes a good fuel. Anatomically, hazel is very similar to alder and was difficult to distinguish in poorly-preserved charcoal.

SALICACEAE: *Populus* spp. (poplar) and/or *Salix* spp. (willow)
These two genera can occasionally be distinguished anatomically, but only in exceptionally well preserved material. *P. nigra* and the several native willow species favour wet soils and commonly grow in floodplains and near water sources. Neither were traditionally considered to make good firewood, although poplar was particularly ill-favoured.

ROSACEAE: *Prunus spinosa* L. (blackthorn), *Prunus avium* L. (wild cherry) and *P. padus* L. (bird cherry)
The differentiation between the three native Prunus species can be difficult and was generally not possible in the poorly-preserved material. However, wide rays consistent with the native *P. spinosa* or introduced *P. domestica* (plum) were recorded in some Roman samples. Blackthorn is a spiny shrub, while wild cherry tends to be a small to medium-sized tree. Both are light-demanding and commonly found in hedgerows, scrub or open woodland. Both provide good fuelwood with a pleasant smell.

ROSACEAE: Maloideae, subfamily, but including genera *Sorbus*, *Malus*, *Crataegus* and possibly *Pyrus* (referred to as hawthorn group)
There are many native species of the Maloideae family, which are rarely distinguishable by anatomical characteristics. They can be small trees or shrubs and are commonly associated with hedgerows and scrub. The wood of the Maloideae is generally dense and makes a good fuelwood, with some species producing a pleasant odour.

CORNACEAE: *Cornus sanguinea* L. (dogwood)
Dogwood is a shrub, growing in woodland margins or hedgerows especially on chalk or limestone. It can be coppiced and was commonly used for basketry. It was not particularly used for fuel, not least because it tends to produce thin, whippy stems.

AQUIFOLIACEAE: *Ilex aquifolium* L. (holly)
Holly is an evergreen tree or shrub, which can grow in the understory of oak woodland or in woodland margins and hedgerow or scrub and tolerates most conditions except very wet soils. It makes short-lived firewood, but can be burnt green.

ACERACEAE: *Acer campestre* L. (field maple)
Field maple is the only maple native to Britain and grows as a small tree in several habitats, including woods, hedgerow and scrub. It can grow on clay, but prefers well-drained soils. The wood is attractive and used for artefacts and turning; it also makes good firewood.

OLEACEAE: *Fraxinus excelsior* L. (ash)
There is only one species of ash native to Britain and, although it does occur in broadleaf woodland, it is light-demanding and commonly found as a pioneer species, colonizing open areas. Ash coppices well and makes superior firewood, which burns well green.

The sites

Langford Lane East

This multi-phase site yielded the most productive charcoal samples, albeit with poor preservation and difficulties in identifying the material. Much of the charred material from these samples (especially those from pit 6523/6533) failed to float during processing, leaving large, hard concretions of charcoal/sediment in the residues. Some of this material was still identifiable, although the possibility of over-representation of ring porous taxa must be emphasised. Iron and vivianite staining, which were observed in these samples, are commonly produced in charcoal as a result of deposition in waterlain conditions.

Cremation deposits

Several features dating to the early Roman period (Phase 5) produced cremated human remains (Table 4.7). The majority were dominated by oak, with lesser components of ash and field maple. A single fragment of elm was recorded in context 7407 of cremation burial 7408 and a possible fragment of Maloideae was identified in cremation burial 6720. Maturity data were limited by the poor preservation, but some oak heartwood, as well as sapwood and roundwood, were observed in the better preserved material.

Oak (and/or ash) was commonly used for cremation in late Iron Age/Roman period cemeteries, as it provides the high calorific heat necessary and makes a suitable bier support (Gale 1997; Challinor 2006; 2007). The trace presence of other taxa may represent kindling or pyre goods. Generally, the calcination of the bone indicated that cremation was efficient with pyre temperatures exceeding 600°, although there were some unusual patterns in the bone from burial 7408 (Chapter 5, below). Since these features were not pyre sites, it is possible that they include redeposited pyre debris from the edges of the pyre rather than the hottest part at the centre. In several samples the amount of charcoal was sparse and there was no charcoal recovered from at least one burial (6084). This suggests that the pits were indeed burials, with some accidental charcoal inclusions, or redeposited pyre debris with a high level of truncation.

A single cremation burial (417) from Trench 4 of the evaluation was uncovered and dated to the early-mid Roman period (AD 70-230). The sample produced a moderate charcoal assemblage, with predominantly small fragments and heavy infusion of sediment. Some fragments exhibited high levels of vitrification. All the identified charcoal was oak, with some fragments showing evidence for heartwood, sapwood and burrwood (Table 4.7). The remainder of the assemblage contained fragments which were highly comminuted, thin slivers, which is highly characteristic of the typical way that oak fragments along its rays.

Analysis of the human bone indicated an adult burial, although gender could not be ascertained (McIntyre and Rose, Chapter 5). Oak wood provides a high calorific fuel, suitable for efficient cremation, as testified by the calcination of the bone. The presence of heartwood, and especially burrwood, in the assemblage indicates the use of wood from a significantly mature tree.

Non-cremation deposits

Deposits of charcoal from a range of features of late Iron Age (Phase 3) to late Roman date (Phase 7) were examined for charcoal (Table 4.8). Oak was the most commonly identified taxon, in both abundance and frequency, with lesser components of alder, hazel, poplar/willow, blackthorn/cherry, Maloideae, field

Table 4.7 Charcoal from cremation burials at Langford Lane East

	Phase			5			5/6
	Description	Cremation burial 6711	Cremation burial 6720		Cremation burial 7408		Cremation burial 417
	Context	6712	6721	6722	7409	7407	418
	Sample no.	6020	6021	6022	6040	6041	400
Ulmus sp.	elm					1r	
Quercus sp.	oak	23	14 (hs)	17 (h)	22 (shr)	28 (srh)	50 (bhs)
Populus/Salix	poplar/willow						
Maloideae	hawthorn group		(1)				
Acer campestre L.	field maple		2				
Fraxinus excelsior L.	ash		2r	1	5 (r)	2	
Indeterminate	diffuse porous						
Indeterminate	ring porous	7				3	
Indeterminate			3	1			
Total		30	22	19	30	30	50

h=heartwood; s=sapwood; r=roundwood; b=bark

maple and ash. Notable assemblages included soil layer 7137 and context 6035 from pit 6523/6533, both of which were dominated by ash. Layer 7137 was beneath building 7222 and comprised mostly ash, although 20% of the identified assemblage was oak; there are regular, if low, levels of ash in domestic-type samples across the sites. However, it is an atypical assemblage, as is the one from pit 6523/6533, not least because sample 6035 contained a vast amount of large fragments of ash (preserved in concretions in the residue), while sample 6011, from the same context, was almost exclusively oak. Unfortunately, the condition of the charcoal in this feature precluded further analysis, but it seems likely that the context, which contained a layer of stones deposited into a pit, was unusual in itself.

An unusual deposit (7231) from Phase 4 was also examined; this comprised the contents of a pot from the eastern flanking ditch (7453) of the Roman road that contained the cremated remains of a chicken. If it represents a placed deposit or burnt offering, it is interesting that the charcoal assemblage differs from the human cremations, with no oak present, but mostly fragments of poplar or willow. Neither of these taxa are considered good fuelwood and their use elsewhere on the project was minimal.

Langford Lane South

Six samples from a range of pits and three ditches, all dating to the 2nd-early 3rd century AD (Phase 6), were analysed for charcoal (Table 4.9). Preservation was quite poor, but generally better than the material from Langford Lane East. Seven taxa were positively identified: oak, hazel, poplar or willow,

blackthorn/cherry, Maloideae, field maple and ash. The taxonomic list is comparable to that from Langford Lane East. Likewise, oak is the most abundant and frequent taxon, with typically minimal components of other taxa. Only one feature, ditch 4384, produced an assemblage with more ash than oak. The charcoal from this context was generally quite diverse (with a minimum of seven taxa), suggesting multiple origins for the material.

South of Merton

Two samples from the 2nd-early 3rd century AD (Phase 6) were analysed, from cremation burial 2522 and pit 2535 (Table 4.10). Preservation at this site was generally poor, with sparse material and small fragment size. The cremation assemblage was dominated by alder. Some fragments exhibited high levels of vitrification. The pit assemblage included oak, hazel and ash. Alder is traditionally considered a poor fuel wood (Edlin 1949) and its use in cremations is unusual, typically associated with a paucity of other, more suitable resources (eg Campbell 2004). The assemblage from pit 2535 would suggest that this was not the case at South of Merton, however, since other species, including oak, ash and hazel (all of which have good burning properties), were available, albeit these features were not necessarily contemporary. The calcination of the human bone in this deposit suggests uneven cremation to which the use of alder for fuel may have contributed. However, it should be noted that there are many factors in pyre technology/management which could have led to any inefficiency of cremation and well-seasoned alder should have performed adequately.

Table 4.8 Charcoal from non-cremation deposits at Langford Lane East

	Phase	3	3	4	4	4	5	6	6	7
	Description	Pit 6799	Pit 7306	Roadside ditch 6715	Soil layer	Pot content, roadside ditch 7453	Pit 6734	Pit 6523/ 6533		Pit 7047
	Context	6801	7307	6631	7137	7231	6735	6522	6522	7048
	Sample no.	6031	6038	6018	6039	6037	6023	6011	6035	6032
Quercus sp.	oak	4	22 (srh)	27 (hsr)	6 (r)		26	27 (rsh)	1r	30 (hsr)
Alnus glutinosa Gaertn.	alder			4						
Corylus avellana L.	hazel								1r	
Alnus/Corylus	alder/hazel								2r	
Populus/Salix	poplar/willow			1r		11				
Prunus sp.	cherry type	19r	2r	7r			1	2r	3r	
Maloideae	hawthorn group		2 (r)							
Acer campestre L.	field maple			3 (r)						
Fraxinus excelsior L.	ash			8 (r)	24 (r)	6r			41 (r)	
Indeterminate	bark							1		
Indeterminate	ring porous	7 (r)				5			2	
Indeterminate							3			
Total		30	26	50	30	22	30	30	50	30

h=heartwood; s=sapwood; r=roundwood

Table 4.9 Charcoal from Langford Lane South

					6		
Phase							
Description		Pit 4047	Pit 4047	Pit 4047	Ditch 2730	Ditch 4384	Ditch 4478
Context		2550	2782	2791	2708	2572	2643
Sample no.		2079	2142	2145	2149	2135	2113
Quercus sp.	oak	40 (hs)	24 (rh)	16 (rh)	21 (hsr)	4	17 (r)
Corylus avellana L.	hazel					1r	1r
Alnus/Corylus	alder/hazel	1r					
Populus/Salix	poplar/willow	(1)				(1)	
Prunus sp.	cherry type		1r		1r	1	
Maloideae	hawthorn group	3	(1)	1		(2r)	
Acer campestre L.	field maple					1r	
Fraxinus excelsior L.	ash	1		10 (r)	8 (r)	17r	8r
Indeterminate	diffuse	4 (r)	2	1			
Indeterminate	bark		1	1			
Indeterminate	ring porous			1r		3r	4 (r)
Total		50	29	30	30	30	30

h=heartwood; s=sapwood; r=roundwood

Table 4.10 Charcoal from South of Merton

		6	
Phase			
Description		Cremation 2522	Pit 2535
Context		2523	2537
Sample no.		2500	2501
Quercus sp.	oak		16 (r)
Alnus glutinosa Gaertn.	alder	34 (r)	
Corylus avellana L.	hazel		1r
Alnus/Corylus	alder/hazel	9 (r)	2r
Fraxinus excelsior L.	ash		1
Indeterminate		7 (r)	
Total		50	20

r=roundwood

Holts Farm Crossing

Five samples were examined from features associated with Phase 2 (middle Iron Age) to Phase 6 (2nd to early 3rd century AD), including one cremation burial (Table 4.11). The charcoal from this site was notably sparse, with some features (especially ditch 8681) containing material that was heavily stained with iron and vivianite. High levels of vitrification were also commonly observed. With the exception of the assemblage from ditch 8681, the charcoal assemblages were dominated by oak, with trace components of Maloideae, field maple and ash. This is especially interesting as the cremation burial (8547) appeared to be composed exclusively of oak. The predominantly white calcination of the bone (McIntyre and Rose, Chapter 5) is consistent with

Table 4.11 Charcoal from Holts Farm Crossing

		2	2	5	6	
Phase						
Description		Pit 8066	Penannular gully 8073	Pit 8224	Cremation 8547	Ditch 8681
Context		8065	8071	8225	8546	8673
Sample no.		8001	8005	8007	8010	8021
Quercus sp.	oak	20 (h)	20 (rhs)	46 (hsr)	40 (h)	9
Alnus/Corylus	alder/hazel					1r
Populus/Salix	poplar/willow					(1)
Prunus spinosa/domestica	blackthorn/plum					5r
Prunus sp.	cherry type					7r
Maloideae	hawthorn group		6	2		
Acer campestre L.	field maple			1		2 (r)
Fraxinus excelsior L.	ash			1		
Indeterminate	diffuse porous					5 (r)
Total		20	26	50	40	30

h=heartwood; s=sapwood; r=roundwood

the use of an efficient fuel and the use of oak for cremations was observed at South of Merton and Langford Lane East. It is interesting, therefore, that two earlier (middle Iron Age) deposits of burnt animal bone from pit 8066 and penannular gully 8073 were also fuelled by oak. These contexts were originally thought to be human cremation deposits, but contained only animal remains. Whether they were domestic debris or burnt offerings is unknown, but it is clear that oak was the primary fuel used. In contrast, the charcoal from ditch 8681 was notably more diverse, with a minimum of five taxa, including oak, alder or hazel, probable poplar or willow, blackthorn/plum and field maple. Gradual accumulation within the ditch fill may account for the diverse character of this sample or it may represent the use of a variety of taxa for domestic uses compared to specific ritual use.

East of Oddington Grange

Two samples were examined from Phase 2 (middle Iron Age) curvilinear ditch 29 and Phase 3 (late Iron Age) boundary ditch 44 (Table 4.12). Both produced similar assemblages, with a quantity of oak and a range of supplementary taxa, including hazel, blackthorn/cherry, Maloideae and ash. Also similar was the condition of the charcoal in both samples, which was heavily impregnated with orange (iron) inclusions, to the extent that the charcoal had failed to float and was recovered from the residues. Blue-green staining, characteristic of vivianite, was also visible. This indicates that the charcoal was deposited in a water-lain or seasonally waterlogged environment, which is consistent with the site's location adjacent to a tributary of the River Ray.

The charcoal assemblages were sufficiently abundant to indicate deliberate dumps of material, rather than purely wind-blown accumulation, although they may represent several events. The most likely origin is domestic waste, remnants of cooking fires, in which a range of locally available trees were used for fuel. It is likely that additional taxa may have been present, but the poor condition of the material limited the analysis and probably caused an over-representation of oak (since this taxon is the most easily recognisable, even in poor material).

South of Oddington Crossing

Ditch 153, possibly forming part of a rectilinear enclosure, contained evidence for metalworking, including ceramic crucibles used for casting copper alloy and ironworking slag. The charcoal assemblages from the main deposit (14) and the underlying layer (15) were analysed (Table 4.13). Both were dominated by oak, but layer 14 also contained a range of other taxa; hazel, blackthorn/cherry, Maloideae, field maple and ash. Although

Table 4.12 Charcoal from East of Oddington Grange

Phase		2	3
Description		*Ditch 29*	*Ditch 44*
Context		14	7
Sample no.		2	1
Quercus sp.	oak	37 (h)	36 (hr)
Corylus avellana L.	hazel		4r
Alnus/Corylus	alder/hazel		3
Prunus sp.	cherry type	3r	
Maloideae	hawthorn group	(1)	
Fraxinus excelsior L.	ash	4	4 (r)
Indeterminate	ring porous	3r	2 (r)
Indeterminate	diffuse porous	2	1
Total		50	50

h=heartwood; s=sapwood; r=roundwood

Table 4.13 Charcoal from South of Oddington Crossing

Phase			2	
Description		*Ditch 153*	*Ditch 153*	*Pit 109*
Context		14	15	108
Sample no.		1	2	9
Quercus sp.	oak	37 (hsr)	45 (shr)	38 (rs)
Corylus avellana L.	hazel	1		3r
Alnus/Corylus	alder/hazel	2		
Prunus sp.	cherry type	1r		
Maloideae	hawthorn group	5 (r)	3 (r)	2
Acer campestre L.	field maple	1r	2r	1r
Fraxinus excelsior L.	ash	1		6r
Indeterminate	diffuse porous	2r		
Total		50	50	50

h=heartwood; s=sapwood; r=roundwood

pit 109 contained no clear evidence to suggest it was associated with metalworking, the taxonomic composition of the charcoal assemblage was remarkably similar. This feature contained some charred cereal grains, and it is probable that the charcoal derived from wood fuel used for crop processing or cooking activities. The similarity in assemblages, therefore, probably relates to the utilisation of local woodland resources.

Both copper working and smithing would have used charcoal as fuel to provide the reducing atmosphere and high heat required (Cleere and Crossley 1985; Goffer 2007, 174; Paynter 2011, 2). Oak, especially heartwood, makes a good charcoal fuel and evidence from Iron Age and Roman metalworking sites shows that mature oak was commonly utilised in metalworking (eg Figueiral 1992; Challinor 2008). The presence of mixed industrial debris in context 14 may explain the range of other taxa in that sample, since the assemblage must represent more than one event or activity.

North of Gallos Brook

Two samples of Phase 2 (middle Iron Age) date were examined (Table 4.14). The first came from a ceramic pot (SF 1) in penannular gully 106. The charcoal from this pot was quite well preserved and composed exclusively of oak, with a significant quantity of heartwood observed. Many pieces were notably slow grown, with only the early-wood pores visible, no evidence for ring curvature, and ring counts of greater than 50 years' growth. This pattern of growth is not characteristic of coppicing and suggests that tree(s) of grand size and age had been felled; such wood is likely to have been considered valuable. The assemblage was very similar to a middle Iron Age

Table 4.14 Charcoal from North of Gallos Brook

		Phase	2	
		Description	Fill of pot (SF1), penannular gully 106	Ditch 265
		Context	10	220
		Sample no.	2	8
Quercus sp.	oak		30 (h)	15 (hr)
Corylus avellana L.	hazel			1r
Prunus sp.	cherry type			5r
Fraxinus excelsior L.	ash			4 (r)
Indeterminate	ring porous			2
Indeterminate	diffuse porous			3 (r)
Total			30	30

h=heartwood; s=sapwood; r=roundwood

deposit at Holts Farm Crossing (8066), which also contained burnt animal bone. At North of Gallos Brook, the charcoal assemblage strongly indicates that wood of significant age and size had been used for fuel (or off-cuts from such a tree), which supports the interpretation of the deposit as a special deposition, rather than just the remains of a cooking fire. It is also interesting that there is a strong contrast between the pot assemblage and the second sample analysed, from boundary ditch 265. The latter assemblage comprised oak, hazel, blackthorn/cherry and ash, including many roundwood fragments. Although the analysis of this charcoal was hampered by poor preservation (heavily concreted and impregnated material), the assemblage is more consistent with spent fuelwood from domestic refuse.

Table 4.15 Charcoal from North of Oxford Parkway Station

		Phase		6	
		Description	Oven/kiln 3047/3049		Pit 3114
		Context	3048	3050	3107
		Sample no.	3001	3000	3003
Ulmus sp.	elm	1			
Quercus sp.	oak	38 (rs)	9 (r)	47 (rsh)	
Corylus avellana L.	hazel		5r		
Alnus/Corylus	alder/hazel	5r	7 (r)		
Populus/Salix	poplar/willow		4		
Prunus spinosa/domestica	blackthorn/plum		11 (r)		
Maloideae	hawthorn group		5 (r)		
Cornus sanguinea L.	dogwood	(2)			
Ilex aquifolium L.	holly			3	
Acer campestre L.	field maple		1		
Fraxinus excelsior L.	ash	4	3		
Indeterminate	diffuse porous		4r		
Indeterminate	bark		1		
Total		50	50	50	

h=heartwood; s=sapwood; r=roundwood

North of Oxford Parkway Station

Three samples from features of middle Roman date (Phase 6) were examined (Table 4.15). Oven/kiln 3047/3049 produced two charcoal assemblages that were quite dissimilar, with a more mixed and diverse composition in the rake-out pit (3050), comprising oak, hazel, poplar/willow, blackthorn/plum, Maloideae, field maple and ash. The fill of the firing chamber (3048) included two rarer taxa; elm and probable dogwood. The diversity of taxa in the feature suggests that they represent domestic fuel sourced from local resources from multiple events. Asymmetric insect tunnels were observed in some of the alder/hazel fragments in 3050, which suggests that the wood had been seasoned prior to use, or came from deadwood gathered from the forest floor.

The later 2nd century pit 3107 produced an assemblage dominated by oak, with a few fragments of holly. Although there was no direct evidence for the function of this feature, there was enough debris (broken pottery, charred food remains) spread throughout the fills to suggest a domestic fuel origin for the remains. The dominance of a single taxon may indicate that fill 3107 represents a single deposit of material. In common with all of the samples from this site, the charcoal suffered from heavy encrustation, obscuring anatomical features and maturity data.

Summary

The charcoal analysis was hampered by poor preservation, mostly caused by waterlain or semi-waterlogged depositional conditions, evident in the strong iron and vivianite staining visible in the anatomical structure. Sites located close to rivers or tributaries were especially prone. However, the material was sufficiently productive to provide an insight into fuel use during a relatively short time span, from the middle Iron Age to the 2nd century AD. Even taking into account the possible over-representation of oak fragment counts in the analysis, it is apparent that oak dominates and remains dominant in the charcoal record (36/40 samples). Ash, which is a light-demanding taxa and colonises easily, is also well-represented, followed by scrub/hedgerow type taxa, such as blackthorn and hawthorn. This suggests that there was plenty of open, rather than closed canopy woodland. Despite the wet conditions indicated by the charcoal, and the proximity of rivers/streams to the sites, there is little use of wetland-type taxa, with relatively few identifications of alder (2/40) and willow or poplar (6/40). There is a consistent use of the same taxa throughout the phases, showing that resources remained stable.

Selection of fuel also appears to have remained fairly constant, with replication of resource use for different activities. All the cremation assemblages

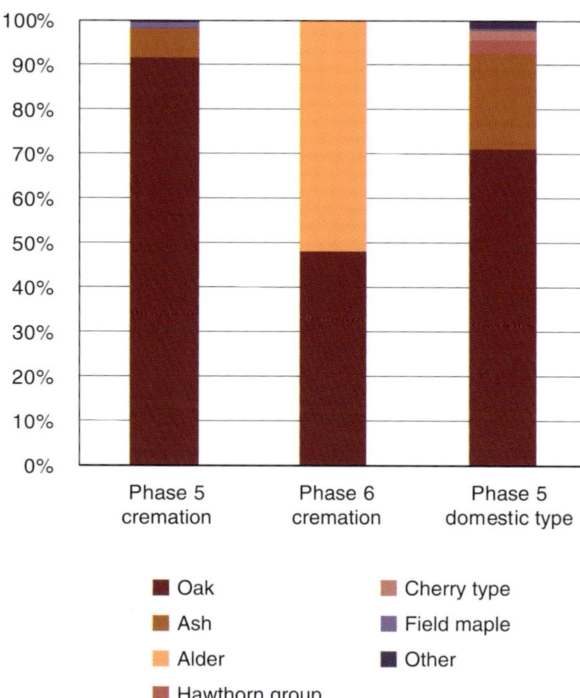

Fig. 4.4 Taxonomic composition of Phase 5 and 6 cremation and domestic type assemblages

from Phase 5 were dominated by oak (Fig. 4.4). There were only two Phase 6 cremation assemblages, of which one, from Holts Farm Crossing, was exclusively composed of oak, while the other was an unusual, alder-dominated deposit at South of Merton. The human bone analysis indicated that all were adult cremations and that, despite some variability in cremation efficiency, adequate temperature levels had generally been reached. It is interesting, however, that oak also dominated the assemblages from a number of other non-cremation context types, such as pits and ditches. There was greater diversity in these domestic-type assemblages, reflecting both the event type as well as fuel selection.

Analysis by phase of all the non-cremation samples also shows relative consistency in fuelwood selection (Fig. 4.5). It should be noted that while the majority of these samples derive from domestic-type waste, the figure includes the Phase 2 metalworking waste deposits from South of Oddington Crossing. The analysis illustrates several points:

- There is a broad replication of taxa throughout the phases, indicating stability in resources/management practices.

- Oak was the primary fuel for all purposes, not just cremation.

- There is a slight indication of a rise in the use of ash in Phases 5 and 6, which may suggest a change in fuelwood procurement, although this may have been due to specific function rather than resource.

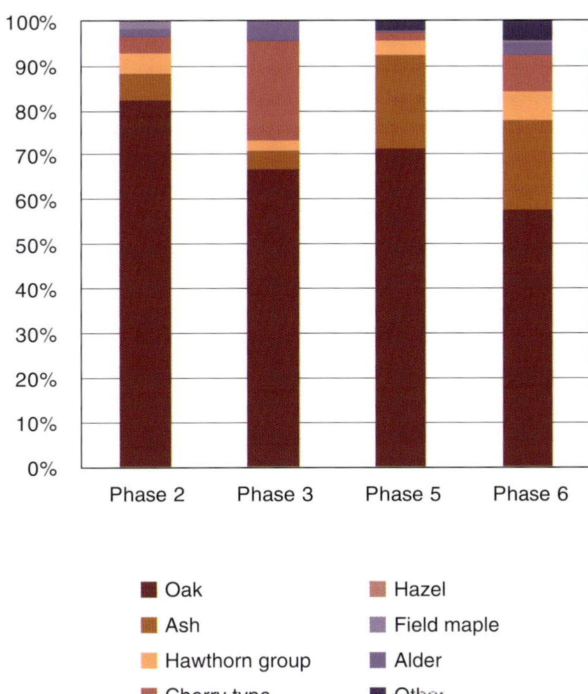

Fig. 4.5 Taxonomic composition of domestic and industrial type assemblages by phase

WATERLOGGED PLANT REMAINS
by Julia Meen

Introduction and methodology

The sites were situated in a low-lying clay vale and as such the water table lies close to the surface in some areas. Where an archaeological feature is permanently below the water table the resulting waterlogged, anoxic conditions may cause decay to be inhibited, which can potentially lead to a wider range of organic tissues, such as delicate plant parts and insect remains, being preserved. At Langford Lane East, Langford Lane South and North of Oxford Parkway Station samples were taken from features which extended below the water table when excavated and showed indications of being permanently waterlogged.

A total of 17 one-litre subsamples were processed from deposits thought to contain anaerobically preserved material. These were hand floated using the 'wash-over' technique, with flot and heavy residue from each sample collected separately onto 250µm meshes and stored damp in cool and dark conditions to prevent desiccation of organic remains. Assessment of each sample was made and on the basis of this, seven samples were selected for further analysis owing to the condition of the waterlogged material and their potential to enhance understanding of the environment and agricultural economy at and around the sites as part of a multi-proxy approach. All samples came from Roman (Phase 5 and 6) deposits.

Each of the seven selected flots was fully sorted for identifiable plant remains, which were then identified, quantified and tabulated (Table 4.16). Plant remains were particularly abundant in sample 6018 from Langford Lane East and samples 2165 and 4004 from Langford Lane South and consequently these samples were divided and either 50% or 25% sorted. Plant remains were identified using Cappers *et al.* (2006) and with reference to the modern reference collection held at Oxford Archaeology South and assistance provided by Ruth Pelling to identify several of the less common taxa. However, any errors in identification remain the author's. Nomenclature follows Stace (2010).

Langford Lane East

Roadside ditch 6715 (Phase 4, Roman military phase, c AD 43-70)

The assemblage has a strong aquatic component, with duckweed (*Lemna* sp.) and water-starworts (*Callitriche* sp.) probably growing within the ditch itself whilst frequent taxa of damp ground such as marshworts (*Apium* sp.), spike-rush (*Eleocharis* sp.), water-cress (*Nasturtium officinale*) and sedges (*Carex* spp.) may have colonised the ditch banks, alongside abundant nettle (*Urtica dioica*) and blackberry/raspberry (*Rubus* sp.). Open grassland or waste ground taxa, including greater plantain (*Plantago major*), prickly sowthistle (*Sonchus asper*), and redshank (*Persicaria maculosa/lapathifolia*) are also present, together with abundant grass caryopses (Poaceae). Together these indicate a ditch that contained standing or slowly flowing water running through damp, open grassland. A small number of fruit and nut stones (hawthorn, *Crataegus* sp. and hazel, *Corylus avellana*) provide some evidence for hedgerow or scrub along the banks of the ditch, a feature also identified in the pollen assemblage (Rutherford, below).

Langford Lane South

Ditch 2455 (Phase 5, late 1st-early 2nd century)

The ditch forms part of a series of enclosures set back from the main Alchester to Dorchester road. The assemblage is dominated by damp or wetland taxa, including crowfoots (*Ranunculus* subgenus *Batrachium*), gypsywort (*Lycopus europaeus*), water-plantain (*Alisma plantago-aquatica*), mint (probably water mint, *Mentha aquatica*) and abundant rushes (*Juncus* spp.). Although there are abundant seeds of nettle (*Urtica dioica*) and elder (*Sambucus nigra*), probably growing up to and overhanging the sides of the ditch, there is little other evidence for scrub or woodland taxa. Caryopses of grasses occur frequently, yet there are few other grassland taxa in the assemblage, so there is not the evidence for species-rich pasture or meadow seen from Phase 6 deposits at the site. There is also a lack of evidence for plants that unambiguously indicate arable cultivation. Overall, the assemblage shows relatively poor species diversity, with high numbers of rapid colonisers (elder, nettle) and ubiquitous wetland plants perhaps crowding out other plants. The enclosure which the ditch defined may have been too continuously wet to support a more diverse floristic habitat and this may have reduced its value as pasture land.

Pit 2611 (Phase 6, 2nd-early 3rd century)

Two samples were analysed from this deep pit. Sample 2122, from fill 2618, a black organic deposit, has two main components: abundant taxa of wet or damp ground, which may have been growing in or around the feature, and grassland species which could derive either from the adjacent enclosure or from material dumped into the feature. The damp ground taxa are mostly rushes (*Juncus* spp.) and spike-rushes (*Eleocharis* sp.), seeds of which are present in large numbers, as well as sedges (*Carex* spp.) and nettles (*Urtica dioica*). The grassland component includes meadowsweet (*Filipendula ulmaria*), fairy flax (*Linum catharticum*), selfheal (*Prunella vulgaris*), meadowrue (*Thalictrum flavum*) and buttercup (*Ranunculus* spp.), as well as frequent grass caryopses.

Sample 2165, from fill 2873, a dark bluish grey silty clay below 2618, which overlay the gravelly basal fill (2874), is characterised mostly by plants of open grassland. As well as abundant small grasses (*Poa/Phleum* type size), common chickweed (*Stellaria media*) occurs frequently, and there are smaller numbers of prickly sowthistle (*Sonchus asper*), greater plantain (*Plantago major*) and hemlock (*Conium maculatum*). Nettles are also extremely common, their abundance reflected in the presence of nettle-specific insects (Allison, below), which together with docks and sedges perhaps formed overgrown vegetation around the edges of the pit.

Roadside ditch 4158 (Phase 6, 2nd-early 3rd century)

This sample contained some evidence suggestive of arable cultivation in the vicinity, with seeds of stinking chamomile (*Anthemis cotula*), mayweed (*Tripleurospermum* sp.), poppy (*Papaver rhoas/dubium*) and chickweed (*Stellaria media*) being fairly common; all are plants of disturbed or cultivated ground. However, the presence of gypsywort (*Lycopus europaeus*), ragged robin (*Silene flos-cuculi*) and possible big stitchwort (*Stellaria alsine*) suggests areas of damper ground, while seeds of water-starwort (*Callitriche* sp.), water plantain (*Alisma plantago-aquatica*) and water crowfoot (*Ranunculus* subgenus *Batrachium*) indicate standing water within the ditch itself.

The grassland component was notably less prominent than in other samples from the site, but did include a small number of taxa found in pasture or hay meadow, namely selfheal (*Prunella vulgaris*), meadowsweet (*Filipendula ulmaria*) and possibly oxeye daisy (*Leucanthemum vulgare*). There was evidence for hedgerow close by; fruit stones of dogwood (*Cornus sanguinea*) and buckthorn (*Rhamnus cathartica*) were both recovered, as was the scrambling hedgerow plant bittersweet (*Solanum dulcamara*). A number of unidentified tree buds were also present.

North of Oxford Parkway Station

Trackway ditch 3056 (Phase 6, 2nd-early 3rd century)

The sample from fill 3303, at the base of the feature, and fill 3308, directly above (Fig. 2.61), include similar suites of plant remains, with evidence for standing, if not flowing water indicated by abundant seeds of water crowfoot (*Ranunculus* subgenus *Batrachium*), water-starwort (*Callitriche* sp.), duckweed (*Lemna* sp.), marshworts (*Apium* sp.) and water-cress (*Nasturtium officinale*). There is also a significant arable field component to the assemblages, including frequent seeds of stinking chamomile (*Anthemis cotula*). Although not unknown in the later Iron Age period (Jones 1991), stinking chamomile is more common from middle and late Roman assemblages and was recovered from 2nd-3rd century contexts during the 1991 excavations north of Alchester (Pelling 2001) and from a Phase 6 charred assemblage at Langford Lane East. Other arable weed taxa from the deposit include prickly poppy (*Papaver argemone*), common mallow (*Malva sylvestris*), parsley-piert (*Aphanes* sp.) and fairy flax (*Linum catharticum*). The last two taxa hint at the range of soil types that were being cultivated locally, parsley-piert preferring well-drained soils and fairy flax dry calcareous habitats, while stinking chamomile is usually associated with heavier clay soils. A seed of cultivated flax (*Linum usitatissimum*) was also present.

There is also evidence for both grassland and hedgerow/scrub vegetation nearby. Small to medium-sized grass caryopses occur frequently and taxa including hawkbit (*Leontodon* sp.), selfheal (*Prunella vulgaris*) and buttercup (*Ranunculus* sp.), would be consistent with damp grassland. A single seed of the climbing hedgerow plant, white bryony (*Bryonia dioica*), was recovered, alongside several fruit stones/nuts of hedgerow shrubs, including blackthorn/sloe (*Prunus spinosa*), hawthorn (*Crataegus* sp.) and a hazelnut (*Corylus avellana*).

Although fill 3308 contained a suite of arable weeds very similar in range and proportions of to that from the lower fill, it also included a higher proportion of nettle seeds as well as seeds of bramble (*Rubus* sp.), perhaps suggesting that conditions surrounding the ditch had become more overgrown. A greater number of grass caryopses were also counted and several stones of hawthorn (*Crataegus* sp.) were identified.

Although plants indicative of standing water were common in both samples, fill 3308 contained fewer seeds of water-starwort and greater numbers of duckweed seeds. However, despite these quantitative differences, the evidence from the plant remains suggests that both the upper and lower fills were laid down in very similar environments, with both samples consistent with a ditch that held standing water, probably with a hedgerow alongside.

Discussion

Previous excavations at Alchester have shown how the problems of waterlogging caused by the low-lying elevation of the town were tackled by constructing a series of drainage ditches and building up the ground surface to raise it above the level of the water table (Young 1975; Esmonde Cleary 1987). The presence of freshwater molluscs in many of the ditch fills from both Langford Lane sites (Stafford, below), the presence of aquatic plant taxa and, of course, the fact that organic preservation was so good in the samples analysed, all attest to continuing issues of waterlogged ground that would have created problems for the inhabitants of Alchester and influenced how they utilised the land directly surrounding the town.

The overall picture from the seven samples at Langford Lane and North of Oxford Parkway Station is one of open, wet grassland, with standing or slowly flowing water in several individual features and perhaps localised areas of overgrown vegetation. Taxa that recur in many of the samples include those of open, sometimes damp waste ground such as greater plantain, hemlock, common chickweed and prickly sowthistle. Taxa which may be found as arable weeds, such as stinking chamomile, were found to some level in all samples but were more frequent in the ditch samples from North of Oxford Parkway Station, suggesting the likelihood of some cereal cultivation nearby. This was also indicated by the pollen from the same feature, which included possible wheat and barley (Rutherford, below). Numbers of grass caryopses were generally high but it is taxa of damp or wet ground and aquatic plants that are consistently present in all samples.

Only sample 2165, from pit 2611 at Langford Lane South, is less dominated by wetland taxa, instead being characterised by plants of open, perhaps drier grassland; this is echoed in the insect fauna, which included fewer aquatic insects from this context, although some hinted at the presence of standing water (Allison, below). Since the insect fauna from sample 2122 also included a component likely to have been derived from organic waste within buildings, it is possible that the rushes and sedges within this sample came from a dump of roofing or flooring material.

Previous archaeobotanical studies of the environment around Alchester have also suggested a landscape of damp grass pasture or hay meadow,

with indicators of disturbed ground relating either to arable cultivation or to the town itself (Robinson 1975; 2011). At nearby Yarnton, wet grassland pasture was identified on the floodplain (Stevens 2011b), the marshy character of which was probably similar to that found in the low-lying fields around Alchester and North of Oxford Parkway Station. Several of the samples from the present sites contain taxa indicative of species-rich grassland; fills within pit 2611 at Langford Lane South included seeds from meadowsweet, fairy flax, selfheal, meadow rue and buttercup while ditch fill 4172, from the same site, also contained seeds from probable oxeye daisy. Each of these plants have been identified in modern-day hay meadows in the Upper Thames Valley (Robinson 2011). Although the taxa found in these samples include only some of the diverse range that might be expected from a species-rich hay meadow, a more limited suite of meadow plants might be expected if the remains instead came from dung or stabling waste. The insect assemblages from both of these contexts pointed strongly to their being used for the disposal of organic waste from a wooden building, which could include dung and straw cleaned out of stables. If derived from this source rather than coming direct from a hay meadow itself, it would be expected that the hay meadow flora might be more limited and diluted by seeds of plants growing in and around the feature. Evidence for the creation of hay meadows has come from elsewhere in the Upper Thames Valley at Claydon Pike (Miles *et al.* 2007), where it has been suggested that the hay meadows may have been developed to meet the needs of nearby Corinium, perhaps stimulated by the Roman state itself to provide fodder for the cavalry stationed there. Neither of the samples from Langford Lane East dates to earlier than the late 1st century and therefore no link can be made to the provision of hay to the military, but Alchester would still have had a great demand for hay as the civilian town developed, particularly as a stopping point for travellers at the junction of Akeman Street and the N-S road from Towcester to Silchester.

There is good evidence to indicate that a hedgerow would have run alongside roadside ditch 4158 at Langford Lane South, and further evidence for hedgerows alongside roadside ditch 6715 at Langford Lane East and trackway ditch 3056 at North of Oxford Parkway Station. It is difficult to conclusively determine where plant remains derive from a hedgerow, as the taxa commonly found in them also occur naturally in scrubby woodland (Robinson 1978), but Greig (1994) has identified an Iron Age hedgerow at Alcester, Warwickshire, based on comparable material to that found at Langford Lane. Greig points out that large fruit stones, such those found in ditch 4158, are heavy and unlikely to disperse far from the point where they fall, and where they are found in quantity it is more likely that they have fallen from vegetation overhanging the feature. Corroborating evidence for a hedgerow at Langford Lane East comes from the insect assem-

Table 4.16 Summary of waterlogged plant remains

		Langford Lane East	Langford Lane South	
	Sample	*6018*	*2068*	*2122*
	Context	*6631*	*2458*	*2618*
	Feature	*Roadside ditch 6715*	*Ditch 2455*	*Pit 2611*
	Phase	*5 Late 1st-early 2nd century*	*5 Late 1st-early 2nd century*	*6 2nd-early 3rd century*
Cultivated/waste ground				
Papaver argemone L.	prickly poppy	1		
Papaver rhoeas/dubium L.	common/long-headed poppy	2		
Potentilla anserina L.	silverweed	6		
Aphanes sp.	parsley-piert			
Urtica urens L.	small nettle			2
cf. *Euphorbia helioscopia* L.	sun spurge			
Linum usitatissimum L.	flax			
Malva cf. *sylvestris* L.	common mallow			
Lepidium coronopus (L.) Al-Shehbaz	swinecress			1
Thlaspi arvense L.	field penny-cress	1		
Persicaria maculosa/lapathifolia	redshank/pale persicaria	58	1	
Stellaria media (L.) Vill.	common chickweed	30	14	50
Hyoscyamus niger L.	henbane	3	1	
Plantago major L.	greater plantain	57	4	4
Sonchus asper (L.) Hill	prickly sowthistle	37	8	2
Anthemis cotula L.	stinking chamomile			
Tripleurospermum inodorum (L.) Sch. Bip	scentless mayweed	2		
Aethusa cynapium L.	fool's parsley			
Conium maculatum L.	hemlock		9	2
Dry calcareous				
Linum catharticum L.	fairy flax		1	2
Wet/damp				
Ranunculus sceleratus L.	celery-leaved buttercup		1	
Ranunculus subgenus Batrachium	crowfoot	1	38	2
Thalictrum flavum L.	common meadowrue			2
Filipendula ulmaria (L.) Maxim.	meadowsweet			23
Nasturtium officinale W T Aiton	water-cress	10	7	
Stellaria cf. *alsine* Grimm	bog stitchwort	3		
Silene flos-cuculi (L.) Clairv.	ragged robin			
Montia fontana L.	blinks			
Callitriche sp.	water-starwort	15		
Lycopus europaeus L.	gypsywort	1	43	5
Eupatorium cannabinum L.	hemp agrimony			
Apium type	marshworts	21	45	1
Lemna sp.	duckweed	28		
Alisma plantago-aquatica L.	water-plantain	1	53	1
Potamogeton sp.	pondweed	2		
Juncus spp.	rushes		++++	+++++
Eleocharis spp.	spike-rush	8	2	106
Isolepis setacea (L.) R. Br.	bristle club-rush			
Cyperaceae	sedge family			1
Carex spp.	sedges	4	6	79
Grassland				
Ranunculus cf *acris*	meadow buttercup	2		
Ranunculus acris/repens/bulbosus	meadow/creeping/bulbous buttercup	5 +F		21
Gentianella sp.	gentain	9		
Prunella vulgaris L.	selfheal	2		15
cf. *Prunella vulgaris* L.	selfheal			
Euphrasia/Odontites sp.	eyebright/bartsia	5		
Leontodon sp.	hawkbit	1		
cf. *Leucanthemum vulgare* Lam.	oxeye daisy			

Langford Lane South		North of Oxford Parkway Station	
2165	4004	3012	3013
2873	4170	3303	3308
Pit	Roadside	Trackway	Trackway
2611	ditch 4158	ditch 3056	ditch 3056
6	6	6	6
2nd-early 3rd century	2nd-early 3rd century	2nd century	2nd century
		1	
1	2		
			1
		5	4
2		3	
1			
		1	
		8	
		5	6
7	3		
189	44	48	37
1			1
9	3	20	7
8	4	5	4
	15	29	20
	1		1
8	1	2	7
	1		2
	53	163	130
	5	1	
		8 +2F	2
	2		
	2		
		2	
	21	34	5
1	2		1
	2		
1	3	118	177
		1	11
	38		
	+++	+++	+++
11	9	2	
	1		
46	10	10	6
3			
6	7	4	8 + 2F
3	1	3	2
			1
	1		
		3	
	1		

blage, which points to trees or shrubs located close to the ditch, while the pollen evidence shows evidence for hazel, hawthorn, elder and willow within a generally grassland-dominated landscape, suggesting that these shrubs occurred as isolated hedges within an otherwise cleared landscape. Such a hedgerow, containing both dogwood and buckthorn, is likely to be well established by this point, as both species are known to be slow colonisers and tend to be found in older, more species-diverse hedgerows. This may be evidence that the boundary that the ditch and its associated hedgerow were marking had some degree of longevity, and that the field system it is part of was not a new one at the time the deposit formed, during the 2nd-3rd century.

The presence of a single seed of cultivated flax from the lower fill of ditch 3056 at North of Oxford Parkway Station may be significant and could suggest that flax was grown, and perhaps also retted, locally. Flax retting involves the soaking of flax stems in water to break down the fibres so they can be extracted and worked into cloth and rope. Although retting is sometimes carried out in ponds or simply out in damp fields, the process produces foul by-products and soaking the stems in flowing water would have helped to reduce pollution. Evidence for Roman flax retting has been found at Old Shifford Farm, Standlake, where the recovery of flax seeds and capsules indicates that several pits were used for retting (Hey 1995). Remains of flax from a Roman well at Barton Court Farm, Abingdon, have been interpreted as flax-threshing debris (Miles 1986). However, a single seed provides only tentative evidence for retting or processing of flax.

POLLEN *by Mairead Rutherford*

Introduction

Two sequences were analysed for pollen, from the eastern roadside ditch (7066) at Langford Lane East and trackway ditch 3056 at North of Oxford Parkway Station. Ditch 7066 dated from Phases 4 and 5 (early Roman) and was a broad feature that was interpreted during excavation as having a stream channelled into it. Of the fourteen sub-samples processed from this feature, ten, from dominantly silty clays, contained sufficient pollen to analyse. The four sub-samples that proved largely barren of palynomorphs are from coarse sandy deposits. Ditch 3056 was a Phase 6 (middle Roman) recut of the northern ditch of a trackway that extended across the site on a WNW-ESE alignment, and at 15m wide, may have been intended as a route for droving livestock. All ten sub-samples processed from this feature proved positive for pollen.

Methodology

Volumetric samples (1ml) were taken from 24 sub-samples and processed using a standard chemical

Table 4.16 (continued)

		Langford Lane East	Langford Lane South	
	Sample	*6018*	*2068*	*2122*
	Context	*6631*	*2458*	*2618*
	Feature	*Roadside ditch 6715*	*Ditch 2455*	*Pit 2611*
	Phase	*5 Late 1st-early 2nd century*	*5 Late 1st-early 2nd century*	*6 2nd-early 3rd century*
Poaceae (small)	grasses	44	49	14
Poaceae (medium)	grasses	96	5	7
Poaceae (large)	grasses			
Woodland/hedgerow				
Prunus spinosa L.	blackthorn			
Crataegus sp.	hawthorn	1		
Rhamnus cathartica L.	buckthorn			
Corylus avellana L.	hazel	1		1
Bryonia dioica Jacq.	white bryony			
Cornus sanguinea L.	dogwood			
Solanum cf *dulcamara* L.	bittersweet			
Chaerophyllum temulum L.	rough chervil			
indet fruit stone				
Mixed habitat				
Ranunculus sp.	buttercup	1	5	6
Rubus spp.	blackberry / raspberry	49 + 28F	2	1
Potentilla sp.	cinquefoil			
cf. *Potentilla* sp.	cinquefoil	4		
Urtica dioica L.	common nettle	453	547	75
Viola sp.	violet			2
Hypericum spp.	St John's-worts	4	8	
Brassicaceae	cabbage family			
Polygonaceae	knotweed			7
Fallopia/Persicaria	knotweed			1
Polygonum aviculare L.	knotgrass	15	3	2
Rumex spp.	docks	7	12	3
Rumex spp. (fruit inside perinath)	docks	16	10	4
Rumex cf *acetosella* L.	sheep's sorrel	2		
Stellaria sp.	stichwort			3
cf. *Stellaria* sp.	stichwort			
Silene sp.	campion			
Chenopodium type	goosefoot / orache	13	1	117
Primula sp.	primroses			
cf. Boraginaceae	borage family			
Lamiaceae	dead-nettles		1	1
cf. *Stachys* sp.	woundwort			2
Ballota nigra L.	black horehound	4		
Mentha sp.	mint	1	75	8
Asteraceae	daisy family	2		2
Arctium lappa L.	greater burdock			1
Cirsium/Carduus spp.	thistles	5	4	2
Cirsium arvense (L.) Scop.	creeping thistle	2	12	
Tripleurospermum sp.	mayweed	2		
cf. *Senecio vulgaris*	groundsel		4	
Sambucus nigra L.	elder		120	1
Apiaceae	carrot family	1	35	
cf. *Torilis* sp.	hedge-parsley		7	
Indet seed				9
Tree thorn			3	
Tree bud		5		1
Moss fragments				

F = fragments; +++ = 25-49 items; ++++ = 50-99 items; +++++ = >100 items

Langford Lane South		North of Oxford Parkway Station	
2165 2873 Pit 2611 6 2nd-early 3rd century	4004 4170 Roadside ditch 4158 6 2nd-early 3rd century	3012 3303 Trackway ditch 3056 6 2nd century	3013 3308 Trackway ditch 3056 6 2nd century
110	7	33	37
3		7	92
2		7	
		1	
		1	6 + F
	2		
		2	
		1	
	2		
	3		
			3
		1	
	5		5 + 6F
	2		
2		1	
441	90	139	403
5	1		
1	3		1
		1	
	1		
2	8	11	3
44 + 33F	27	21	12 + 4F
49 + F	19	9	5
6		4	5
			1
	1		
27	15	39	28
	1		
		1	
3	7	3	1
	2		4
	6	12	7
3		3	
	3		
2			
3		1	
1	3		
2	1		
25	13		4
	4	4	7
	12	1	23
	4	2	

procedure (method B of Berglund and Ralska-Jasiewiczowa 1986). Pollen identification and nomenclature follows Moore *et al.* (1991) with reference to a small type-collection held by OA North. Plant nomenclature follows Stace (2010). Identification of non-pollen palynomorphs (NPP) follows van Geel (1978) and van Geel and Aptroot (2006). Non-pollen palynomorphs are prefixed by HdV, corresponding to their listing in the NPP catalogue in the Hugo de Vries laboratory, University of Amsterdam, The Netherlands.

Pollen counts of 300 grains (including trees and shrubs, herbs and fern spores) have been achieved for all but four of the sub-samples analysed. Four sub-samples proved too poor to achieve statistical counts and have been eliminated from the study. Pollen was counted from equally spaced traverses across whole slides at a magnification of x400 (x1000 for critical examinations). Pollen data are presented as percentage diagrams using the computer programs TILIA and TGView (Grimm 1991-2011). The percentage values are based on a total land pollen (TLP) sum that includes trees, shrubs, herbs and fern spores. Non-pollen palynomorphs and deteriorated grains are expressed as percentages of TLP plus the respective sum to which they belong. Rare pollen types (single occurrences of taxa) are marked on the diagrams using a symbol. Microscopic charcoal particles are expressed as percentages of TLP plus the respective sum to which they belong. Neither of the pollen diagrams is zoned, as there was insufficient difference within the various pollen assemblages to justify zoning. Context numbers are shown on the pollen diagrams.

Langford Lane East

Description of pollen assemblages

The pollen data reveal a relatively consistent picture through the contexts analysed (6743, 6744 and 6745, Fig. 2.7). The assemblages are dominated by pollen of grasses (Poaceae) and commonly occurring herbs inclusive of dandelion-type (*Taraxacum*-type), daisies (Asteraceae, a large group including taxa such as hawkbits, oxtongues and sow-thistles), carrot family (Apiaceae, including diverse plants such as cow parsley, pignuts and water-dropworts), buttercup-type (*Ranunculus*-type), ribwort plantain (*Plantago lanceolata*), sedges (Cyperaceae) and the pea family (Fabaceae, including vetches, clovers and peas). Pollen of herbs is particularly diverse and apart from the most commonly occurring taxa outlined above, there are also occurrences of pollen of the cabbage family (Brassicaceae, a large group including plants such as garlic mustard, mustards, cabbages and radishes), pinks (Caryophyllaceae), goosefoot family (Amaranthaceae, formerly Chenopodiaceae, including taxa such as good king henry, fat-hen and many-seeded goosefoot), common knapweed (*Centaurea nigra*), cornflower (*Centaurea cyanus*),

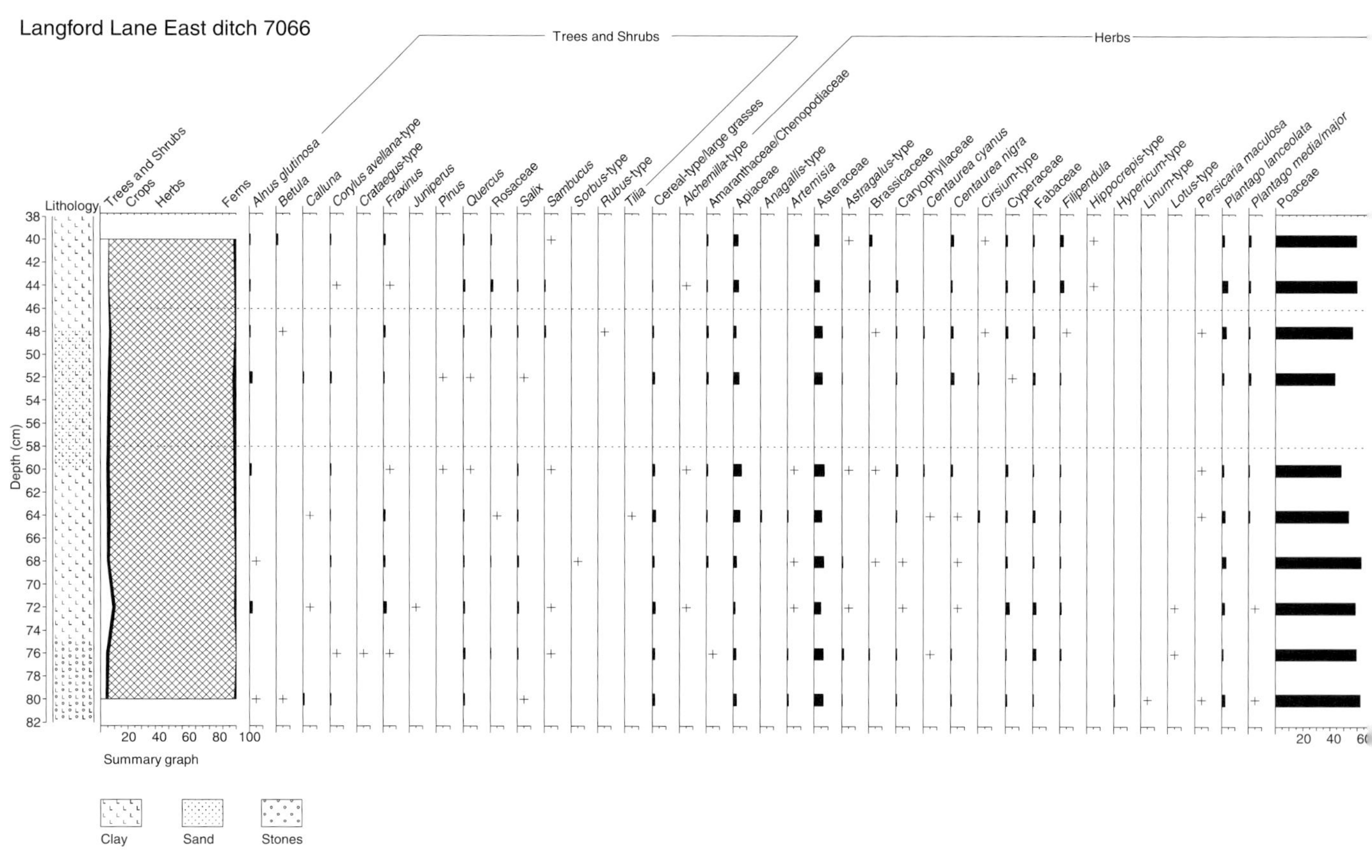
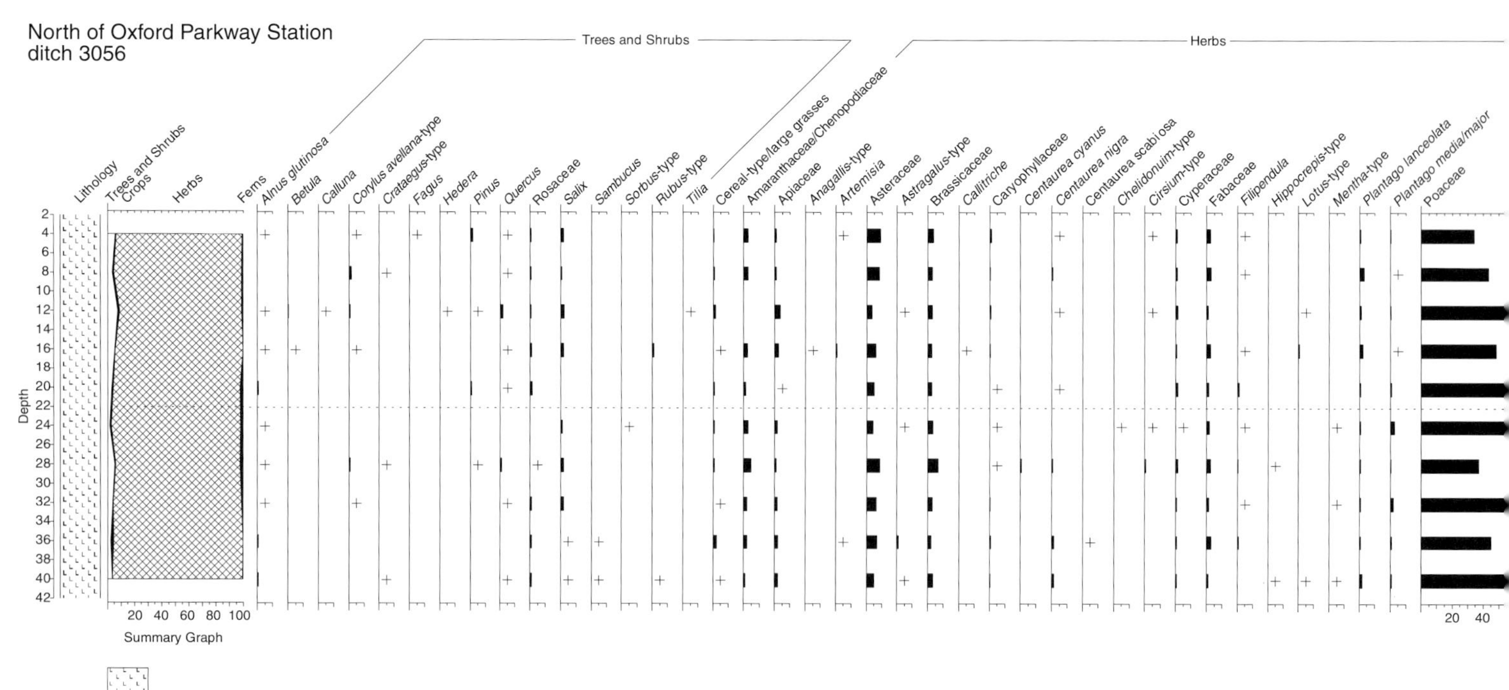

Fig. 4.6 Pollen diagrams for Langford Lane East ditch 7066 and North of Oxford Parkway Station ditch 3056

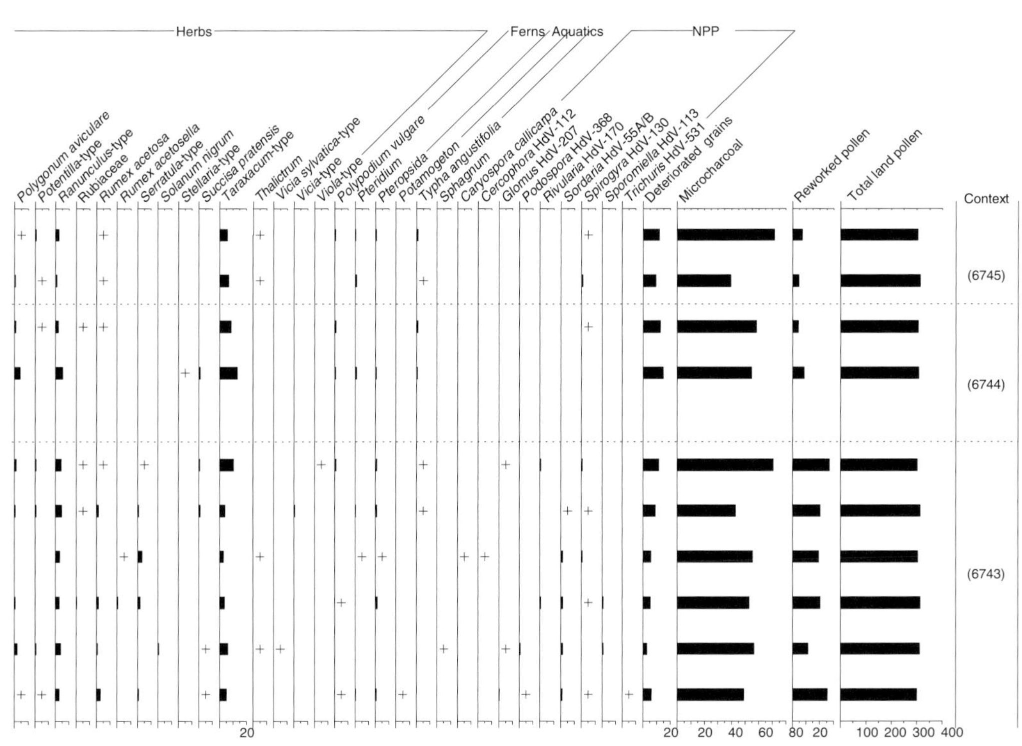

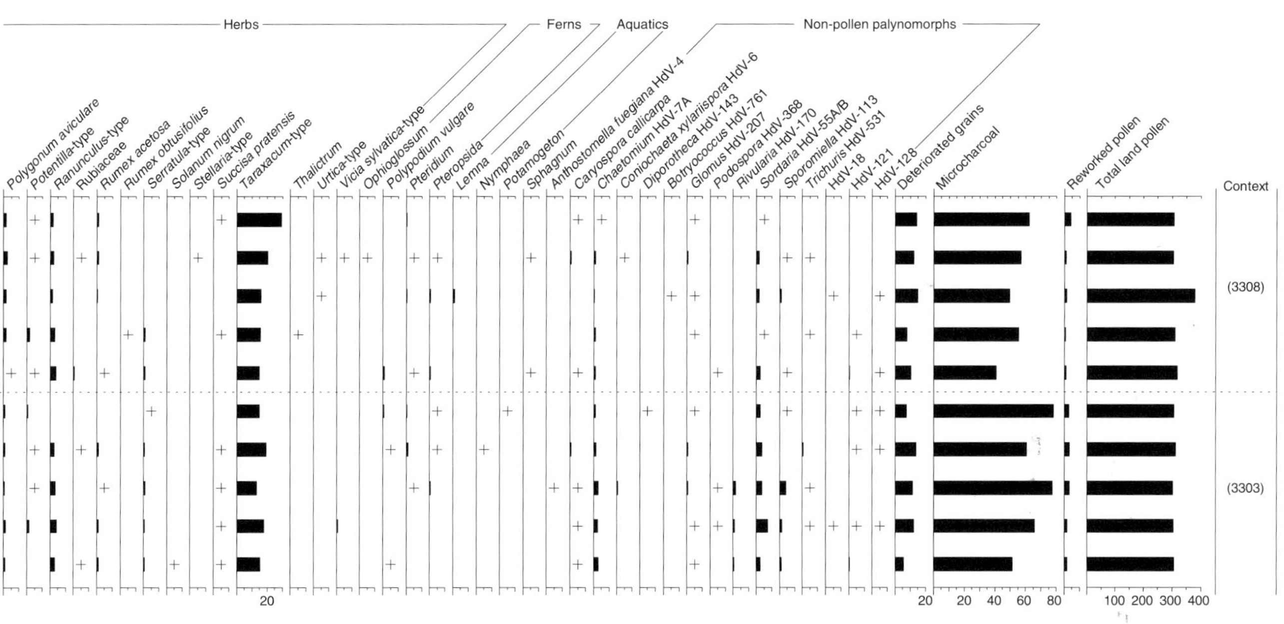

thistles (*Cirsium*-type), meadowsweets (*Filipendula*), hoary / greater plantain (*Plantago media / major*), knot grass (*Polygonum aviculare*), cinquefoils (*Potentilla*-type), bedstraws *(Rubiaceae)*, docks / sorrels *(Rumex-type)*, devil's bit scabious (*Succisa pratensis*), meadow-rues (*Thalictrum*) and of mugworts (*Artemisia*), the last limited to context 6743.

Cereal-type pollen or large grass pollen is recorded consistently through the section analysed. A diverse but weakly abundant range of tree pollen is recorded, including pollen of alder (*Alnus*), ash (*Fraxinus*), hazel-type (*Corylus avellana*-type), oak (*Quercus*), willow (*Salix*), wild roses (Rosaceae) and elder (*Sambucus*). Fern spores are also recorded in relatively consistent amounts and include common polypody (*Polypodium vulgare*), bracken (*Pteridium*) and monolete ferns (*Pteropsida*). Pollen of the aquatic plant lesser bulrush (*Typha angustifolia*) occurs more commonly towards the top of the section, in contexts 6744 and 6745. Non-pollen palynomorphs are represented mostly by fungal spores, in particular within the lower context 6743, in which *Sordaria* (HdV-55A/B) and *Sporomiella* (HdV-113) are recorded. The green algal type, *Spirogyra* (HdV-130) is present in low numbers throughout the section. A single record for the eggs of the intestinal parasite *Trichuris* (HdV-531) is present within the lowest context (6743). Microcharcoal is present in moderate amounts throughout the section. Pollen and dinoflagellate cysts reworked from the underlying geological formations (Oxford Clay) are more commonly recorded within the lower context (6743) than in the upper two contexts.

Interpretation of pollen assemblages

The pollen data suggest a dominantly open palaeoenvironment of grassland supporting a variety of herb flora, for example daisy-types, buttercups, thistles and pollen of the goosefoot family, typical of field edges and rough or waste ground. Ribwort plantain is present throughout; this taxon has been interpreted as an indicator of grazing pressure (Tipping 2002) and is commonly found in grassy areas (Stace 2010) and may be indicative of wet meadows / pastures (Behre 1981). Sedges and meadowsweets are also found in wet, damp areas (Stace 2010). Such damp, rich, grassy meadows would provide high-quality grazing areas. The abundance of grass may also have been used for making hay, for example, for overwintering animals (Wiltshire 2006). The presence of pollen of ruderal plants, for example pollen of the goosefoot family, greater plantain and common to abundant dandelion-types, may be suggestive of naturally trampled or deliberate trackways, perhaps for driving animals, separating fields or linking settlements (Behre 1981).

Cereal-type pollen grains, the dimensions of which include possible occurrences of barley (*Hordeum*-type) as well as wheat / oats (*Triticum /* *Avena*-type), occur with pollen of knotgrass and cornflowers, both plants associated with cereal cultivation, although knotgrass can also occur on fallow land and on footpaths and ruderal communities (Behre 1981). Cereal-type pollen may be indicative of arable agriculture in the vicinity or local cereal processing, or cereal-type pollen grains may have entered the ditch sequences along with straw or animal dung. The dimensions for cereal-type pollen overlap with those for wild grasses, but can be distinguished with careful identification and within the context of the overall pollen assemblage (Anderson 1979; Tweddle *et al.* 2005; Joly *et al.* 2007).

Stands of mixed woodland including birch, ash, oak and lime may have existed regionally on drier soils with alder occupying damper locations. If locally present, these trees would potentially have contributed much more pollen to the ditch record, suggesting that possibly regular pollarding and / or coppicing may have occurred to prevent flowering (Rackham 2003; Wiltshire 2006). An association of pollen of elder, willow, hazel-type, hawthorn-type and rosaceous shrubs including brambles (*Rubus*-type) may be indicative of development of hedgerows in the surrounding area (Stace 2010).

The fern spores comprise common polypody, bracken and monolete ferns. Bracken is known as an aggressive invader of open spaces (Wiltshire 2008), but is also known to grow preferentially in areas subject to burning (Innes 1999). Bracken may possibly have been used as bedding for people or litter for animals and may have been dumped in the ditch. Moderate to common counts for microcharcoal particles suggest burning episodes, which could have originated from domestic hearths or ovens. Among the fungal spores present, some are coprophilic forms (for example *Sporomiella* HdV-113 and *Sordaria* HdV-55A/B) and support the use of the land for grazing purposes. Interestingly, these spores occur within the lower context (6743) but are absent from the other contexts (6744 and 6745), which may suggest a greater emphasis on animal husbandry during the time period represented by the lower context. Specimens of the fungal spore *Caryospora callicarpa* (Currey) Nitschke, which is present within the lower context (6743), have previously been described from sites of Roman and medieval age from the UK (Hawkesworth *et al.* 2010) and an association with oak, elder and other deciduous woods is possible, although the ecological preferences remain obscure (ibid.).

The freshwater alga, *Spirogyra* (HdV-130) is present throughout the section analysed, suggesting that shallow, stagnant water was present in or adjacent to the ditch (van Geel 1978). There is a single record for the presence of eggs of the intestinal parasite whipworm *Trichuris* HdV-531 in the pollen assemblages from the lower context, suggesting the possibility that the ditch may have been used for human waste (although *Trichuris* species can infect other animals such as mice and pigs).

North of Oxford Parkway Station

Description of pollen assemblages

The palynomorph assemblages are very similar to those described above from Langford Lane East and reveal a fairly consistent picture through the contexts analysed (3303, 3308; Fig. 2.61). Pollen of herbs is both abundant and diverse, and includes primarily pollen of grasses, dandelion-type, daisies, carrot family, buttercup-type, ribwort plantain, sedges, pollen of the pea family, cabbage family and goosefoot family. Other commonly occurring herbs include the pollen of pinks, common knapweed, thistles, sawwort (*Serrtula*-type), meadowsweets, hoary/greater plantain, knotgrass, cinquefoils, bedstraws, docks/sorrels, devil's bit scabious and mugworts.

Cereal-type pollen, the dimensions for which suggest grains of both barley and wheat/oats, or large grass pollen, is present consistently through the section analysed. Low counts of tree and shrub pollen are recorded, and include alder, hazel-type, oak, willow, pine (*Pinus*) and wild roses, as well as sporadic occurrences of pollen of birch (*Betula*), lime (*Tilia*), hawthorn-type (*Crataegus*-type), elder, brambles and beech (*Fagus*). Fern spores are also recorded in relatively consistent but low amounts and include common polypody, bracken and monolete ferns. Pollen of aquatic plants is limited to isolated occurrences of duckweed (*Lemna*), pondweed (*Potamogeton*) and white water-lilies (*Nymphaea*); a single occurrence of the freshwater alga *Botryococcus* (HdV-761) is also recorded. Non-pollen palynomorphs are represented mostly by fungal spores, in particular within the lower context (3303), in which *Sordaria* (HdV-55A/B), *Sporomiella* (HdV-113) and *Chaetomium* (HdV-7A) are well represented. *Glomus* (HdV-207) occurs throughout in low numbers. Eggs of the intestinal parasite *Trichuris* (HdV-531) are present sporadically throughout the section. The fungal spore *Caryospora callicarpa* (Currey) Nitschke is also sporadically recorded. Microcharcoal is present in moderate amounts throughout the section. Small amounts of reworked palynomorphs are recorded.

Interpretation of pollen assemblages

As at Langford Lane East, the pollen evidence suggests an open palaeoenvironment supporting herb-rich grassland. The grasslands may have been used for grazing animals and this interpretation is supported by diverse and quite commonly recorded coprophilic fungal spores, including *Sporomiella* (HdV-113), particularly in context 3003. Many of the herb taxa in the assemblages are characteristic of grazed pasture, for example ribwort plantain, buttercup- and dandelion-types (Wiltshire 2006;

Tipping 2002). The presence of pollen of ruderal taxa such as goosefoot, mugwort and knotgrass that may suggest open, broken and possibly trampled soils is supported by the consistent recovery of the fungal spore *Glomus* (HdV-207), which is associated with eroded or disturbed soils (van Geel 1978).

The cereal-type pollen and plants associated with cereal cultivation, such as knotgrass and rare occurrence of pollen of cornflowers, may be indicative of arable agriculture in the vicinity or local cereal processing, unless the cereal-type pollen grains entered the ditch sequences along with straw or animal dung.

Pollen of trees such as oak, pine, hazel-type and rare beech is recorded, but generally in low quantities, suggesting possible distant woodlands. Smaller shrubs and trees such as willow, elder and rosaceous taxa such as hawthorn-type and brambles, may have grown in hedgerows.

The fern spores may indicate colonisation of the ditch and surrounding area or may represent the use of bracken as bedding for people or litter for animals that was subsequently discarded in the ditch. Moderate to common counts for microcharcoal particles suggest burning episodes.

Eggs of the intestinal parasite whipworm, *Trichuris* (HdV-531), are recorded in low numbers in both contexts analysed, suggesting the possibility that the ditch may have been used for human waste (although *Trichuris* species can infect other animals such as mice and pigs). Previous records of *Trichuris* HdV-531 from archaeological sites include for example, from the latrine of a Roman centurion (Kuijper and Turner 1992). *Chaetomium* (HdV-7A) fungal spores are also present throughout the section; these species are cellulose-decomposing fungi, occurring on plant remains, fibre and dung (van Geel and Aptroot 2006). Apart from occurrence in natural habitats, Chaetomium spores also appear to be linked to archaeological sites, where, for example, dung, damp straw and cloth may have been available as substrates (van Geel *et al.* 2003).

Discussion

Previous analysis of waterlogged remains (seeds, beetles and molluscs) from early Roman fort ditches at Alchester (Sauer 2000b) revealed that the ditches held stagnant water, that primarily the environmental conditions were open with evidence for disturbed ground, and that the grasslands were probably used as pasture for domestic animals. The occurrence of cereal bran was interpreted to suggest the presence of deposits of human sewage. Evidence for crop processing was interpreted from occurrences of glumes of spelt wheat. The similarity of this palaeoenvironmental evidence with that derived from the palynological analysis of the early Roman ditch 7066 at Langford Lane East is striking. Interestingly, palynological results from the middle Roman ditch 3056 at North of Oxford Parkway Station show very similar profiles to those interpreted from the earlier Langford Lane East site, suggesting that there was little change in agricultural practice between early and middle Roman periods at these locations.

Pollen from North of Oxford Parkway Station also shows similarity with several Roman settlements within the Upper Thames Valley (Lambrick, with Robinson 2009; Robinson 2011). These sites revealed an open agricultural landscape with both arable and pastoral farming (Booth *et al.* 2007). Although the grasslands of the floodplain areas in the Upper Thames Valley were utilised primarily for pasture, some may have been managed as seasonal hay meadow (Booth *et al.* 2007).

The palaeoenvironmental data from Langford Lane East and North of Oxford Parkway Station may be interpreted to suggest that agricultural practices varied little between the early and middle Roman periods. There is perhaps slightly stronger evidence to suggest phases of greater intensification of pastoral farming, based on continuous, robust counts of coprophilous fungal spores in association with pollen linked to grazing activity, for example, in context 3303 from North of Oxford Parkway Station. However, this may be a reflection of the specific on-site suitability for greater pastoral activity at this location, which appears to have been exposed to possibly less damp or wet conditions than at the Langford Lane East site.

In summary, the palynological data suggest:

- There is evidence at both sites for dominantly open, damp grasslands, probably used for pasturing animals.

- At both sites, arable agriculture or possible cereal processing may have occurred nearby, although the pollen could alternatively have entered the features in straw, animal dung or human faeces.

- The ditch at North of Oxford Parkway Station may have functioned as a repository for human as well as animal waste, based on near-continuous but low counts for *Trichuris* (HdV-531).

- At both sites, robust counts for pollen such as dandelion-type may be indicative of disturbed, cultivated or waste ground; records of greater plantain and pollen of the goosefoot family may be indicative of trackways.

- At both sites, possible development of hedgerows, comprising willow, hazel-type, elder, hawthorn-type and brambles, may be interpreted from the pollen record. Possible woodland stands may also have existed at some distance from the features, comprising ash, oak, birch, lime, or, if locally present, may have been subject to coppicing or pollarding.

- At both sites, commonly occurring microcharcoal suggests that some activity involving wood burning may have taken place.

INSECT REMAINS *by Enid Allison*

Introduction

Seven samples from Langford Lane East, Langford Lane South and North of Oxford Parkway Station were submitted for examination of insect remains. The samples were from the waterlogged fills of ditches and a pit dating to the Roman period.

Methods

Six of the samples had volumes of five litres, the seventh a volume of one litre. They were wet-sieved to 0.25mm and separated into a 'washover', consisting of the organic component, and a heavy residue predominantly made up of mineral material. Paraffin flotation was carried out on the washover fractions, since they had been so effective in separating the organic component. Methods followed Kenward *et al.* (1980) and recovery was on a 0.3mm mesh. The resulting paraffin flots were scanned in industrial methylated spirits, a petri dish-full at a time, using a low-power stereoscopic zoom microscope (x10 - x45). Abundances of insect taxa were estimated semi-quantitatively using a three-point scale: + 1-3 individuals, ++ 4-9, +++ 10-25. Some beetle and bug sclerites were picked out for closer identification to enhance interpretation. In these cases, identification was by comparison with modern insect material and reference to standard published works. Taxa were divided into broad ecological groups for interpretation following Kenward *et al.* (1986) and Kenward (1997). The abundance of other groups of invertebrates was recorded simply as present, common or abundant. Nomenclature follows Duff (2012) for Coleoptera and Bantock and Botting (2013) for Hemiptera: Heteroptera. Information on the food plants of phytophagous species used throughout this report has been obtained from Cox (2007), Harde (1984), Morris (1990-2012), Nau (2004), Southwood and Leston (1959) and the British Bugs website unless otherwise stated.

Results

Insect remains were abundant in all the samples. Fragmentation was relatively low, but a high proportion of sclerites in some samples showed moderate degrees of degradation in the form of thinning, loss of colour and 3-D structure, and surface modification.

The insect assemblages are described below. Host plants of plant-associated taxa are shown in Table 4.17 and lists of insects and other invertebrates noted during scanning each sample in Table 4.18.

Table 4.17 Habitat and food preferences of strongly plant-associated beetles and bugs

Species	Food and habitat preferences
Dolycoris baccarum	In flowery woodland margins and flowery grassland on diverse flowering plants
Podops inuncta	Dry litter under shrubs or in grassland (Nau 2004)
Coreus marginatus	Found in hedgerows, margins of cultivated fields, water meadows, wastelands and woodland edges. Nymphs develop on docks (*Rumex*) and other Polygonaceae. Found on diverse plants later in the year searching for seeds
Heterogaster urticae	Warm, sunny fields and non-acid wastelands, on nettles (*Urtica*)
Drymus ?sylvaticus	Common in grass, moss or litter on dry or dryish soils feeding on mosses and fungal hyphae and possibly other foods
Conomelus anceps	On rushes (*Juncus*)
Trioza urticae nymphs	On nettles (*Urtica*)
Phyllopertha horticola	Poor quality permanent grassland on light soils with a diversity of flowering plants and a high proportion of weeds. The larvae feed on turf roots
Dascillus cervinus	The larvae feed at the roots of short vegetation
Byrrhus sp.	Generally found in litter and moss or under stones, main habitats include heathland and moorland. Both adults and larvae are thought to feed on moss
Agrypnus murinus	The larvae feed at the roots of turf
Agriotes sp(p).	In soil below plants
Brachypterus sp.	On nettles (*Urtica*)
Meligethes spp.	Larvae feed on Brassiceae, adults feed on pollen of various flowers particularly yellow ones
Coccidula rufa	On reeds, rushes (*Juncus*) and reedmace (*Typha*) in wetlands. Occasionally found in grassland (Majerus 1994)
Bruchinae sp. (small)	Associated with leguminous plants, their larvae developing within the seeds
Donacia simplex	Usually found on bur-reeds (*Sparganium*). The adults eat the leaves and they are probably the larval food plant
Lema or *Oulema* spp.	Feeds on the leaves of grasses and cereals
Gastrophysa viridula	Usually associated with docks (*Rumex*)
Hydrothassa spp.	On Ranunculaceae
Prasocuris phellandrii	Adults and larvae feed on marsh marigold (*Caltha palustris*) and also other wetland Ranunculaceae. Adults can be found on leaves of other marginal plants
Phratora vulgatissima	Adults usually on willows, possibly on aspen, larvae usually on sallows and goat willow
Phyllotreta nemorum group	On wild and cultivated Brassicaceae
Phyllotreta nigripes	On wild and cultivated Brassicaceae
Phyllotreta spp.	Most species live on various Brassicaceae
Longitarsus spp.	Members of the genus are found on various herbaceous plants, especially Boraginaceae, Scrophulariaceae and Labiatae
Crepidodera spp.	On willows (*Salix*) and poplars (*Populus*), including aspen (*P. tremula*)
Chaetocnema concinna or *picipes*	Usually on members of the knotweed family (Polygonaceae) including *Polygonum* and docks (*Rumex*)
Ceratapion carduorum	On thistles (*Cirsium* and *Carduus*)
Taenapion urticarium	On nettles (*Urtica*)
Oxystoma spp.	Mainly on vetches (*Vicia* and *Lathyrus*)
Protapion spp.	Most species are associated with clovers (*Trifolium*), but some are found on other leguminous plants
Apionidae spp.	Most species are associated with herbaceous vegetation
Notaris acridulus	On semi-aquatic grasses. Reed sweet-grass (*Glyceria maxima*) is a common host in Continental Europe
Tanysphyrus lemnae	On duckweeds (*Lemna*)
Mecinus labilis	On ribwort plantain (*Plantago lanceolata*)
Mecinus pyraster	On ribwort plantain (*Plantago lanceolata*)
Isochnus foliorum	On willows and sallows (*Salix*)
Orchestes sp.	The genus is associated with various trees and shrubs
Tychius spp.	Associated with Fabaceae
Ceutorhynchus spp.	On various wild and cultivated Brassicaceae
Hadroplontus sp.	On thistles (Cirsium and Carduum)
Microplontus sp.	On chamomiles and allies (Asteraceae, Tribe Anthemideae)
Graptus triguttatus	Open and grassy places. Probably polyphagous, but shows a marked preference for ribwort plantain (*Plantago lanceolata*) in the British Isles
Sitona spp.	On Fabaceae
Hypera sp.	On herbaceous plants
Leiosoma cf *deflexum*	Often in damp or wet areas on wood anemone (*Anemone nemoralis*), *Ranunculus* spp. (especially *R. repens*), and marsh marigold (*Caltha palustris*) (Morris 2002)

Main sources: Bentock and Botting 2013; Cox 2007; Harde 1984; Nau 2004; Majerus 1994; Morris 1990-2012; Southwood and Leston 1959

Table 4.18 Insects and other invertebrates recorded by scanning

	Langford Lane East			Langford Lane South			North of Oxford Parkway Station
Feature	Roadside ditch 6715	Roadside ditch 7066	Pit 2611	Pit 2611	Ditch 2455	Roadside ditch 4158	Trackway ditch 3056
Context	6631	6743	2618	2873	2458	4170	3308
Sample no.	6018	6033	2122	2165	2068	4004	3013
Sample volume	1L	5L	5L	5L	5L	5L	5L
ANNELIDA							
Oligochaeta sp. (earthworm egg capsules)	P	C	C	-	-	-	-
CRUSTACEA							
Daphnia magna group (ephippia)	-	-	-	-	-	-	C
Daphnia sp. (ephippia)	P	P	P	C	C	-	A
Cladocera spp. (ephippia)	-	P	P	-	P	P	-
Ostracoda spp.	-	P	-	C	P	P	C
INSECTA							
DERMAPTERA (earwigs)							
Dermaptera sp. [u]	-	+	-	-	-	-	++
HEMIPTERA: HETEROPTERA (true bugs)							
Coreidae							
Coreus marginatus (Linnaeus) [oa-p]	-	+	-	+	+	-	-
Pentatomidae							
Dolycoris baccarum (Linnaeus) [oa-p]	-	+	-	-	+	-	-
Podops inuncta (Fabricius) [oa-p]	-	-	-	+	-	-	-
Pentatomoidea sp. [oa-p]	-	+	-	-	-	-	-
Anthocoridae							
Anthocoridae sp. and sp indet. [u]	-	+	-	-	-	-	-
Lygaeidae							
Drymus ?sylvaticus (Fabricius) [oa-p]	+	-	-	+	-	-	-
Heterogaster urticae (Fabricius) [oa-p]	-	+	-	-	-	-	+
Scolopostethus sp. [oa-p]	+	+	-	-	+	-	-
Lygaeidae spp. [oa-p]	-	+	+	+	-	-	+
Corixidae							
Corixidae spp. [oa-w]	-	-	-	-	+	+	-
Corixidae sp(p). nymphs [oa-w]	-	-	-	-	-	-	+
Hebridae							
Hebrus sp. [oa-p-d]	-	-	-	-	-	+	-
Saldidae							
Saldidae sp. [oa-d]	-	+	-	+	-	+	+
Heteroptera sp. (water bug) nymph [oa-w]	-	-	-	+	-	-	-
Heteroptera sp. [u]	-	-	-	-	-	-	+
HEMIPTERA: HOMOPTERA							
Aphrophoridae							
Aphrophora sp. [oa-p]	-	-	-	-	-	+	-
Cicadellidae							
Megophthalmus sp. [oa-p]	-	+	-	-	-	-	-
Anoscopus limicola Edwards [oa-p]	-	++	-	-	-	-	-
Delphacidae							
Conomelus anceps Germar [oa-p]	-	-	-	-	-	+	-
Delphacidae spp. [oa-p]	-	+	-	+	+	+	+
Auchenorhyncha spp. [oa-p]	-	++	+	+	++	++	++
Psylloidea (jumping plant lice)							
Trioza urticae (Linnaeus) nymph skins [oa-p]	+	-	-	+	+	+	+
Aphidoidea sp. (aphids)	+	-	-	-	-	-	+
Coccoidea (Diaspididae) sp. (scale insects)	-	-	-	-	-	+	+
TRICHOPTERA (caddis flies)							
Trichoptera sp. larval fragments	-	-	-	-	++	++	-
Trichoptera sp. larval case fragments	-	-	-	-	-	+	-

Table 4.18 (continued)

Feature	Langford Lane East			Langford Lane South			North of Oxford Parkway Station
	Roadside ditch 6715	*Roadside ditch 7066*	*Pit 2611*	*Pit 2611*	*Ditch 2455*	*Roadside ditch 4158*	*Trackway ditch 3056*
Context	6631	6743	2618	2873	2458	4170	3308
Sample no.	6018	6033	2122	2165	2068	4004	3013
Sample volume	1L	5L	5L	5L	5L	5L	5L
DIPTERA (flies)							
Bibionidae sp. leg spines	-	+	-	-	-	+	-
Diptera spp. adults	-	-	-	-	-	-	+
Diptera spp. puparia	+++	+++	++	+	-	+	+
HYMENOPTERA							
Formicidae spp. (ants)	-	-	-	-	-	+	+
Apoidea sp. (bee)	-	-	-	-	+	-	-
Hymenoptera Aculeata sp.	-	-	-	-	-	+	-
Hymenoptera Parasitica spp. (parasitic wasps)	+	+	+	-	+	+	++
COLEOPTERA (beetles)							
Gyrinidae (whirligig beetles)							
Gyrinus sp. [oa-w]	-	-	-	-	+	-	-
Haliplidae							
Haliplus lineatocollis (Marsham) [oa-w]	-	-	-	-	-	+	-
Haliplus sp. [oa-w]	-	+	-	-	+	+	+
Dytiscidae							
Agabus bipustulatus (Linnaeus) [oa-w]	-	++	-	+	+	+	+
Agabus sp. [oa-w]	-	-	-	-	-	-	+
Agabus or *Ilybius* spp. [oa-w]	-	-	-	-	+	+	-
Colymbetes fuscus (Linnaeus) [oa-w]	+	+	-	-	+	+	-
Hydroprus palustris (Linnaeus) [oa-w]	-	-	-	-	+	-	-
Hygrotus inaequalis (Fabricius) [oa-w]	-	+	-	-	-	+	-
Hydroporinae spp. [oa-w]	+	+	-	+	++	+	+
Dytiscidae spp. [oa-w]	+	+	-	-	-	+	+
Carabidae (ground beetles)							
Leistus sp. [oa]	-	+	-	-	-	-	-
Nebria sp. indet. [oa]	-	+	-	+	-	-	-
Notiophilus sp. [oa]	-	-	-	+	-	-	-
Clivina sp. [oa]	-	+	-	+	+	-	-
Dyschirius globosus (Herbst) [oa]	-	+	-	-	+	+	+
Trechus obtusus or *quadristriatus* [oa]	-	-	-	-	+	-	-
Trechus sp. indet. [oa]	+	-	-	+	-	+	-
Bembidion (*Metallina*) *properans* (Stephens) [oa]	+	-	-	-	-	-	-
Bembidion (*Metallina*) *lampros* or *properans* [oa]	-	-	-	-	+	-	+
Bembidion (*Phyla*) *obtusum* Audinet-Serville [oa]	-	-	-	-	+	-	-
Bembidion (*Philochthus*) *guttula* or *mannerheimi* [oa]	+	-	-	+	+	+	-
Bembidion (*Philochthus*) *lunulatum* (Geof. in Four.) [oa-d]	-	-	-	-	-	-	+++
Bembidion spp. [oa]	-	++	+	-	+	+	++
Poecilus sp. [oa]	-	-	-	+	+	-	-
Pterostichus niger (Schaller) [oa]	-	-	-	-	-	+	-
Pterostichus melanarius (Illiger) [ob]	+	+	-	-	+	-	+
Pterostichus anthracinus (Panzer) [oa-d]	-	+	-	-	-	-	-
Pterostichus ?anthracinus (Panzer) [oa-d]	-	+	-	-	-	-	-
Pterostichus vernalis (Panzer) [oa-d]	+	+	+	+	-	+	-
Pterostichus diligens or *strenuus* [oa]	-	+	-	-	-	-	-
Paranchus albipes (Fabricius) [oa-d]	-	-	-	-	-	-	+
Agonum sp(p). [oa]	-	+	-	+	-	+	-
Amara spp. [oa]	-	-	-	-	+	+	+
Harpalus rufipes (De Geer) [oa]	-	-	-	-	-	-	+
Harpalus ?rufipes (De Geer) [oa]	-	-	-	-	+	-	-

Table 4.18 (continued)

Feature	Langford Lane East			Langford Lane South			North of Oxford Parkway Station
	Roadside ditch 6715	Roadside ditch 7066	Pit 2611	Pit 2611	Ditch 2455	Roadside ditch 4158	Trackway ditch 3056
Context	6631	6743	2618	2873	2458	4170	3308
Sample no.	6018	6033	2122	2165	2068	4004	3013
Sample volume	1L	5L	5L	5L	5L	5L	5L
Ophonus sp. [oa]	-	-	+	-	+	-	-
Acupalpus sp. [oa-d]	-	-	-	-	+	+	-
Paradromius linearis (Olivier) [oa]	-	+	-	-	+	-	-
Syntomus sp. [oa]	-	-	-	-	-	-	+
Carabidae spp. and sp. indet. [ob]	+	-	-	++	-	+	++
Helophoridae							
Helophorus grandis Illiger [oa-w]	-	+	-	-	-	-	-
Helophorus aequalis or *grandis* [oa-w]	+	++	-	+	+	+	+
Helophorus spp. [oa-w]	+++	+++	++	+	++	+++	+++
Hydrophilidae							
Anacaena spp. [oa-w]	-	+	-	-	-	-	-
Chaetarthria sp. [oa-d]	-	+	-	-	-	+	-
Hydrobius fuscipes (Linnaeus) [oa-w]	+	++	-	-	-	+	+
Laccobius bipunctatus (Fabricius) [oa-w]	-	-	-	-	-	+	-
Laccobius sp. [oa-w]	+	+	-	-	-	-	-
Hydrophilinae spp. [oa-w]	-	+	+	-	+	+	-
Coelostoma orbiculare (Fabricius) [oa-w]	-	+	-	-	-	+	-
Cercyon ustulatus (Preyssler) [oa-d]	+	+	-	-	-	-	-
Cercyon convexiusculus group [oa-d]	+	++	-	+	+	++	+
Cercyon haemorrhoidalis (Fabricius) [rf-sf]	+	+	-	-	-	+	+
Cercyon impressus (Sturm) [rf-sf]	-	-	-	+	-	+	-
Cercyon nigriceps (Marsham) [rf-st]	-	+	-	-	-	-	-
Cercyon pygmaeus (Illiger) [rf-st]	-	-	-	-	-	+	-
Cercyon ?terminatus (Marsham) [rf-st]	+	-	-	-	-	-	-
Cercyon analis (Paykull) [rt-sf]	+	+	-	-	-	-	-
Cercyon spp. (decomposer group) [rt]	-	-	+	-	-	-	-
Cercyon spp. and sp. indet. [u]	+	-	+	-	-	-	++
Megasternum concinnum (Marsham) [rt]	+	+++	-	++	++	+	+
Cryptopleurum minutum (Fabricius) [rf-st]	-	+	+	-	-	-	-
Sphaeridium spp. [rf]	+	-	-	-	-	+	+
Histeridae							
Acritus nigricornis (Hoffman) [rt-st]	-	-	-	-	+	+	-
Onthophilus striatus (Forster) [rt-sf]	-	+	-	-	-	-	-
Atholus duodecimstriatus (Schrank) [rt-sf]	+	-	-	-	-	-	-
Histerinae sp. [rt]	-	-	-	-	+	-	-
Hydraenidae							
Hydraena testacea Curtis [oa-w]	-	+	-	+	+	++	+
Hydraena spp. [oa-w]	+	+	-	+	+	++	+
Limnebius spp. [oa-w]	-	++	-	-	+	++	+
Ochthebius dilatatus Stephens [oa-w]	-	+	-	-	-	+	-
Ochthebius (Asiobates) sp. [oa-w]	-	-	-	-	+	-	+
Ochthebius minimus (Fabricius) [oa-w]	-	+++	-	-	++	+++	+++
Ochthebius sp. indet. [oa-w]	+	-	+	-	-	-	-
Ptiliidae (featherwing beetles)							
Ptenidium sp. [rt]	-	-	+	+	-	-	-
Acrotrichis sp. [rt]	-	+	+	-	++	+	+
Leiodidae							
Cholevinae spp. [u]	-	-	-	+	-	+	-
Silphidae							
Silpha sp. [u]	-	-	-	-	+	-	-
Silphidae sp. [u]	-	+	+	-	-	-	-

Table 4.18 (continued)

Feature	Langford Lane East			Langford Lane South			North of Oxford Parkway Station
	Roadside ditch 6715	Roadside ditch 7066	Pit 2611	Pit 2611	Ditch 2455	Roadside ditch 4158	Trackway ditch 3056
Context	6631	6743	2618	2873	2458	4170	3308
Sample no.	6018	6033	2122	2165	2068	4004	3013
Sample volume	1L	5L	5L	5L	5L	5L	5L
Staphylinidae (rove beetles)							
Lesteva longoelytrata (Goeze) [oa-d]	++	+	+	+	+++	++	++
?*Lesteva* sp. [oa-d]	-	-	-	-	-	+	-
Omalium spp. [rt]	-	+	+	+	-	+	-
Xylodromus concinnus (Marsham) [rt-st-h]	+	-	+	+	-	-	-
Omaliinae spp. [u]	-	+	+	-	-	-	+
Metopsia clypeata (Müller) [rt]	-	-	-	+	+	-	-
Micropeplus fulvus Erichson [rt]	+	+	-	-	-	+	-
Micropeplus staphylinoides (Marsham) [rt]	-	+	+	++	+	-	-
Pselaphinae spp. [u]	-	+	-	+	+	+	+
Tachinus spp. [u]	+	+	-	+	+	+	-
Tachyporus spp. [u]	-	+	+	+	++	+	+
Cordalia obscura (Gravenhorst) [rt-sf]	-	-	+	-	-	-	+
Cordalia or *Falagria* sp. [rt-sf]	-	-	-	+	-	-	-
Falagria caesa or *sulcatula* (Gravenhorst) [rt-sf]	+	+	-	-	+	+	-
Cypha sp. [u]	-	-	-	+	+	+	-
Crataraea suturalis (Mannerheim) [rt-st-h]	-	-	+	-	-	-	-
Aleochariinae spp. [u]	++	++	++	+	++	++	+++
Anotylus nitidulus (Gravenhorst) [rt-d]	-	-	-	+	+	+	+
Anotylus rugosus (Fabricius) [rt]	+	++	++	+	+	++	+
Anotylus sculpturatus group [rt]	-	-	+	-	++	+	+
Oxytelus sculptus Gravenhorst [rt-st]	-	-	-	-	+	-	+
Platystethus cornutus group [oa-d]	++	+	-	-	-	-	++
Platystethus nitens (Sahlberg) [oa-d]	+	-	-	-	-	+	++
Platystethus nodifrons Mannerheim [oa-d]	-	-	-	++	+	+	-
Platystethus (*Craetopycrus*) sp. [oa-d]	-	+	-	-	-	-	-
Platystethus arenarius (Fourcroy) [rf]	+	-	-	-	-	+	+
Aploderus caelatus (Gravenhorst) [rt]	-	+	-	-	-	+	-
Carpelimus spp. [u]	-	+	++	-	++	+++	+++
Scydmaeninae spp. [u]	-	-	+	+	-	+	+
Stenus spp. [u]	+	+	+	+	+	+	-
Astenus sp. [rt]	-	-	+	-	-	-	-
Ochthephilum fracticorne (Paykull) [oa-d]	-	+	-	-	-	-	-
Lathrobium spp. [u]	-	+	-	+	-	-	-
Rugilus spp. [rt]	-	+	+	-	+	+	+
Othius sp. [rt]	-	-	-	-	-	+	-
Gabrius sp. [rt]	-	-	-	-	+	-	-
Quedius cinctus (Paykull) [rt]	-	+	-	-	-	-	-
Gyrohypnus angustatus Stephens [rt-st]	-	-	-	-	-	-	+
Gyrohypnus fracticornis (Müller) [rt-st]	-	++	-	-	-	+	-
Gyrohypnus sp. indet. [rt]	-	-	+	-	-	-	-
Xantholinus linearis (Olivier) [rt-sf]	-	-	-	-	-	+	-
Xantholinus gallicus/linearis/longiventris [rt-sf]	+	+	+	+	+	+	-
Xantholinini sp. [u]	-	-	-	-	+	-	+
Staphylininae spp. [u]	++	+++	-	-	++	++	++
Geotrupidae							
Geotrupinae sp. [oa-rf]	+	-	-	-	-	-	-
Scarabaeidae							
Aphodius rufipes (Linnaeus) [oa-rf]	-	-	-	-	+	-	-
Aphodius ater (De Geer) [oa-rf]	-	-	-	-	-	+	-
Aphodius fimetarius (Linnaeus) [ob-rf]	+	-	-	-	+	-	+

Table 4.18 (continued)

Feature	Langford Lane East			Langford Lane South			North of Oxford Parkway Station
	Roadside ditch 6715	Roadside ditch 7066	Pit 2611	Pit 2611	Ditch 2455	Roadside ditch 4158	Trackway ditch 3056
Context	6631	6743	2618	2873	2458	4170	3308
Sample no.	6018	6033	2122	2165	2068	4004	3013
Sample volume	1L	5L	5L	5L	5L	5L	5L
Aphodius granarius (Linnaeus) [ob-rf]	+++	+	-	-	-	-	++
Aphodius prodromus or *sphacelatus* [ob-rf]	++	+	-	+	+	+	+
Aphodius contaminatus (Herbst) [oa-rf]	-	+	-	-	+	+	+
Aphodius porcus (Fabricius) [oa-rf]	-	+	-	-	-	-	-
Aphodius sp. and sp. indet. [ob-rf]	-	+	+	-	-	+	-
Oxyomus sylvestris (Scopoli) [rt-sf]	-	++	-	-	-	-	+
Onthophagus sp. [oa-rf]	+	+	-	-	-	-	+
Phyllopertha horticola (Linnaeus) [oa-p]	+	-	-	-	-	+	-
Melolonthinae/Rutelinae/Cetoniinae (chafer) indet. [oa-p]	-	+	-	-	+	-	-
Scirtidae (marsh beetles)							
Cyphon sp. [oa-d]	-	+	-	-	-	-	++
Dascillidae							
Dascillus cervinus (Linnaeus) [oa-p]	+	-	-	-	-	-	-
Byrrhidae (pill beetles)							
Byrrhus sp. [oa]	-	+	+	-	-	+	-
Byrrhidae sp. [u]	-	-	-	-	+	-	-
Elmidae (riffle beetles)							
Oulimnius sp. [oa-w]	-	+	-	-	-	+++	-
Dryopidae							
Dryops sp. [oa-d]	-	+++	-	-	-	++	-
Heteroceridae							
Heterocerus sp. [oa-d]	-	-	-	-	-	-	+
Elateridae (click beetles)							
Agrypnus murinus (Linnaeus) [oa-p]	+	-	-	-	-	-	+
Agriotes sp. [oa-p]	-	+	-	+	+	+	+
Elateridae spp. [ob]	+	+	+	+	+	+	+
Cantharidae (soldier beetles)							
Cantharidae spp. [ob]	-	+	-	-	+	+	-
Ptinidae							
Tipnus unicolor (Piller and Mitterpacher) [rd-ss-h]	-	+	-	-	-	-	-
Ptinus fur (Linnaeus) [rd-sf-h]	-	+	++	-	-	-	-
Ptinus sp. indet. [rd-sf-h]	-	-	-	-	-	-	+
Stegobium paniceum (Linnaeus) [rd-st-h]	-	-	+	-	-	-	-
Anobium punctatum (De Geer) [l-sf]	-	+	+++	-	+	+	++
Kateretidae							
Brachypterus sp. [oa-p]	-	+	+	++	+	+	+
Nitidulidae							
Meligethes spp. [oa-p]	-	-	-	+	+	+	+
Monotomidae							
Monotoma picipes Herbst [rt-sf]	+	-	-	-	-	-	-
Monotoma sp. and sp. indet. [rt-sf]	-	+	-	-	-	-	+
Cryptophagidae							
?*Cryptophagus scutellatus* Newman [rd-st-h]	-	-	+	-	-	+	-
Cryptophagus spp. [rd-sf-h]	-	++	++	-	-	-	-
Atomaria spp. [rd-sf-h]	-	+	++	-	+	+	+
Ephistemus globulus (Paykull) [rd-sf-h]	-	+	+	-	-	-	-
Endomychidae							
Mycetaea subterranea (Fabricius) [rd-ss-h]	-	-	-	-	-	-	+
Coccinellidae (ladybirds)							
Coccidula rufa (Herbst) [oa]	-	+	-	-	-	-	-
Coccinellidae sp(p). and sp. indet. [oa]	-	+	-	-	+	-	+

Table 4.18 (continued)

Feature	Langford Lane East				Langford Lane South		North of Oxford Parkway Station
	Roadside ditch 6715	Roadside ditch 7066	Pit 2611	Pit 2611	Ditch 2455	Roadside ditch 4158	Trackway ditch 3056
Context	6631	6743	2618	2873	2458	4170	3308
Sample no.	6018	6033	2122	2165	2068	4004	3013
Sample volume	1L	5L	5L	5L	5L	5L	5L
Corylophidae							
Orthoperus sp. [rt]	-	-	+	-	+	-	-
Corylophidae sp(p). [rt]	-	+	-	+	+	-	+
Latridiidae							
Latridius minutus group [rd-st-h]	+	++	+++	+	+	+	++
Enicmus sp. [rd-sf-h]	+	+	+	+	++	+	++
Corticaria sp(p). [rt-sf]	-	-	++	+	-	-	+
Corticariinae spp. [rt]	-	-	++	+	+	++	+
Mycetophagidae (hairy fungus beetles)							
Typhaea stercorea (Linnaeus) [rd-ss-h]	-	+	-	-	-	-	-
Tenebrionidae (darkling beetles)							
?*Tenebrio obscurus* (unexpanded elytral fragment) [rt-ss-h]	-	-	+	-	-	-	-
Chrysomelidae (leaf beetles)							
Bruchinae sp. [u] (small species)	-	+	-	-	-	-	-
Donacia simplex Fabricius [oa-p-d]	-	+	-	-	-	-	-
Lema or *Oulema* sp. [oa-p]	-	-	-	-	-	+	-
Chrysolina sp. [oa-p]	-	-	-	-	+	-	-
Gastrophysa viridula (De Geer) [oa-p]	-	+	-	-	-	+	-
Phaedon sp. [oa-p]	+	+	-	-	-	-	-
Hydrothassa sp. [oa-p]	-	++	-	-	-	-	-
Prasocuris phellandrii (Linnaeus) [oa-p-d]	-	-	+	-	+	+	-
Phratora vulgatissima (Linnaeus) [oa-p]	-	-	-	+	+	-	-
Phyllotreta nemorum group [oa-p]	-	-	-	-	-	-	+
Phyllotreta nigripes (Fabricius) [oa-p]	-	-	-	-	-	+	-
Phyllotreta sp. [oa-p]	-	+	-	-	-	+	+
Longitarsus sp(p). [oa-p]	-	++	-	-	++	-	+
Crepidodera sp(p). [oa-p]	-	-	-	+	+	+	+
Chaetocnema concinna or *picipes* [oa-p]	-	-	-	+	+	+	+
Alticini sp. [oa-p]	-	-	-	-	+	-	-
Chrysomelidae spp. and sp. indet. [oa-p]	-	-	-	+	+	-	++
Rhynchitidae							
Rhynchitinae sp. [ao-p]	-	-	-	-	+	-	-
Apionidae							
Ceratapion carduorum Kirby [oa-p]	-	-	-	-	-	-	+
Taenapion urticarium (Herbst) [oa-p]	-	-	-	-	+	-	+
Oxystoma spp. [oa-p]	-	+	-	++	+	+	-
Apionidae spp. [oa-p]	-	++	+	++	++	++	+
Erirhinidae							
Notaris acridulus (Linnaeus) [oa-p-d]	-	++	+	-	-	+	+
Tanysphyrus lemnae (Paykull) [oa-p-w]	-	+	-	-	+	+	+++
Curculionidae							
Mecinus labilis (Herbst) [oa-p]	-	-	-	+	-	-	-
Mecinus pyraster (Herbst) [oa-p]	-	-	-	-	-	-	+
Isochnus foliorum (Müller) [oa-p]	-	-	-	-	-	+	-
Orchestes sp. [oa-p]	-	-	-	-	+	-	-
Tychius sp. [oa-p]	-	+	-	-	-	-	-
?*Tychius* sp. [oa-p]	-	-	-	-	-	+	-
Ceutorhynchus spp. [oa-p]	+	+	-	+	+	-	+
Hadroplontus sp. [oa-p]	-	-	-	-	+	-	-
Microplontus sp. [oa-p]	-	+	-	-	+	-	-

Table 4.18 (continued)

Feature	Langford Lane East			Langford Lane South			North of Oxford Parkway Station
	Roadside ditch 6715	*Roadside ditch 7066*	*Pit 2611*	*Pit 2611*	*Ditch 2455*	*Roadside ditch 4158*	*Trackway ditch 3056*
Context	6631	6743	2618	2873	2458	4170	3308
Sample no.	6018	6033	2122	2165	2068	4004	3013
Sample volume	1L	5L	5L	5L	5L	5L	5L
Ceutorhynchinae sp. [oa-p]	-	-	-	+	+	+	+
Graptus triguttatus (Fabricius) [oa-p]	-	+	-	-	-	-	-
Phyllobius sp. [oa-p]	-	-	-	-	-	-	+
Phyllobius or *Polydrusus* sp. [oa-p]	-	-	-	+	-	-	-
Sitona spp. [oa-p]	-	+	-	-	+	+	+
Hypera sp. [oa-p]	-	-	-	-	-	+	-
Leiosoma cf *deflexum* (Panzer)	-	-	-	+	-	-	-
Hylesinini spp. [l]	-	+	-	-	-	-	+
Curculionidae spp. [oa-p]	+	++	+	+	++	++	++
Coleoptera spp. [u]	-	-	+	-	-	+	-
Insecta spp. indet. larval fragments	++	-	++	-	-	+	-
ARACHNIDA							
Acarina spp. (mites)	C	A	C	-	A	C	-
Aranae sp. (spiders)	-	P	P	-	-	P	-
BRYOZOA							
Lophopus crystallinus (Pallas) (statoblasts)	-	-	-	-	-	P	-

Ecological codes shown in square brackets are: d - damp ground/waterside; h - house/building; l - wood/timber; oa - 'outdoor' taxa not usually found within buildings or accumulations of decomposing matter; ob - probably 'outdoor' taxa; p - plant-associated taxa; rd - dry decomposers; rf - foul decomposers; rt - eurytopic decomposers; sf - facultative synanthropes; ss - strong synanthropes; st - typical synanthropes; u - uncoded; w - aquatics
Abundance of beetles (Coleoptera) and bugs (Hemiptera) has been recorded semi-quantatively: + = 1-3 individuals; ++ = 4-9; +++ = 10-30
Other invertabrates have been recorded as: P = present; C = common; A = abundant

Langford Lane East

Western roadside ditch 6715 (Phase 4, Roman military phase, c AD 43-70)

This ditch was situated closer to the area of Roman settlement than any of the others from which insect remains have been examined. Despite the sample having a volume of only 1 litre, a good-sized assemblage of insect remains was recovered. Water flea ephippia (Cladocera: resting eggs) and a group of aquatic beetles indicated that the ditch had contained still to slowly-flowing water for at least some of the time, with taxa such as *Cercyon ustulatus*, *Anotylus rugosus*, *Platystethus cornutus* group and *Platystethus nitens* indicating wet and muddy conditions. The presence of nymphs of *Trioza urticae* indicated that nettles (*Urtica*) grew within or alongside the ditch. Land close to the ditch was probably drier and at least some of it may have been in agricultural use: the eurytopic ground beetle *Pterostichus melanarius* is especially found in agricultural fields, while *Bembidion properans* is found in open sunny situations on dry, open clay soils (Luff 2007 81, 113). *Agrypnus murinus*, *Dascillus cervinus* and *Phyllopertha horticola* all have turf-feeding larvae and are typical inhabitants of grassland. *P. horticola*, a small chafer, is particularly characteristic of permanent pasture land with a diversity of flowering plants and a high proportion of weeds (Raw 1951). Scarabaeoid dung beetles were relatively common, the most numerous of the five species identified being *Aphodius granarius* (at least 10 individuals). The abundance of this group may indicate grazing on adjacent land but might also relate in part to the use of the road as a droveway. *Aphodius granarius* is most commonly associated with cow dung, often when it is lying on paths or other thoroughfares (Jessop 1986, 24). Other beetles associated with dung and other foul organic matter included *Sphaeridium*, *Cercyon haemorrhoidalis*, and *Atholus duodecimstriatus*.

A small group of synanthropic insects suggested that limited amounts of occupation waste had contributed to the deposit. They included *Latridius minutus* group, *Xylodromus concinnus* and *Cercyon analis*, all typical of litter from within buildings (Hall and Kenward 1990; Kenward and Hall 1995; Carrott and Kenward 2001).

Eastern roadside ditch 7066 (Phase 5, late 1st-early 2nd century AD)

Insects were abundant but many of the remains were only moderately preserved. Erosion was evident in many sclerites, in some cases obscuring surface details, and some sclerites were folded or squashed, although fragmentation was relatively low. Aquatic insects were common, with taxa such as *Coelostoma orbiculare* and *Hygrotus inaequalis* indicative of well-vegetated still to slow-flowing water with moss or litter at the margins. *H. inaequalis* is usually found in permanent but often very shallow water (Foster and Friday 2011, 103). The presence of a riffle beetle (Elmidae: *Oulimnius*), however, suggested that there was a throughput of clean, clear, running water at least occasionally. Duckweed (*Lemna*) growing on the water surface was indicated by *Tanysphyrus lemnae* (an aquatic weevil). *Dryops* and several other taxa suggest that the water margins were quite muddy. Vegetation within or on the banks of the channel probably included tall plants such as reed sweet-grass (*Glyceria maxima*) and bur-reeds (*Sparganium*), the usual host plants of *Notaris acridulus* and *Donacia simplex* respectively. *Coccidula rufa* (a spotless ladybird) is usually associated with reeds (*Phragmites*), rushes (*Juncus*), and reedmace (*Typha*) (Majerus 1994, 142), and Hydrothassa occurs on Ranunculaceae. Ground beetles included *Pterostichus anthracinus*, found in damp, shaded habitats close to fresh water (Luff 1998, 84).

A range of insects found on nettles (*Heterogaster urticae*, *Brachypterus*, *Trioza urticae* nymphs) indicated that stands grew within or very close to the feature and *Gastrophysa viridula* occurs on docks (*Rumex*). Nymphs of the dock bug (*Coreus marginatus*) are found on docks and other Polygonaceae in sunny open sites (Nau 2004) but the adults, which were represented here, feed on seeds of various plants, especially in late summer when they can be common in hedgerows feeding on fruits such as blackberries (*Rubus fruticosa* agg.). An indication that trees or shrubs may have been present close to the channel was provided by bark beetles (Hylesinini, probably two species), but the remains were too poorly preserved to suggest particular hosts.

Ground outside the channel was probably drier. There were suggestions of disturbed, cultivated or waste ground from *Meligethes*, which is associated with Brassicaceae, and *Microplontus*, which is found on chamomiles (*Matricaria* and *Tripleurospermum*). Other taxa, including the plant-hoppers *Anoscopus limicola* and *Megophthalmus* and the hairy shield bug (*Dolycoris baccarum*), are indicative of grassy habitats. The weevil *Graptus triguttatus* occurs in open grassy places and shows a marked preference for ribwort plantain (*Plantago lanceolata*) in Britain.

At least seven species of scarabaeid dung beetles were recorded, which is certainly suggestive of grazing animals in the vicinity. They included *Aphodius porcus*, which often appears to be associated with dor beetle (*Geotrupes*) burrows (Chapman 1869), but is also found above ground in cow and horse dung. In the present day its occurrence appears to be dependent on dung availability and continuity of grazing to maintain open conditions (Hyman and Parsons 1992, 387).

There was a clear component indicating that occupation waste from within buildings had been incorporated into the deposit, most likely stable manure (*Tipnus unicolor*, *Ptinus fur*, *Latridius minutus* gp, *Typhaea stercorea*, *Cryptophagus* spp. *Ephistemus globulus*). A group of hydrophilid beetles associated with foul matter was probably associated with this group (*Cercyon haemorrhoidalis*, *C. nigriceps*, *C. analis*, *Cryptopleurum minutum*) and *Oxyomus sylvestris*, which is typical of decomposing vegetable matter such as stable straw and various types of dung (Harde 1984, 234), was well represented. Unexpanded (either unemerged or newly emerged) apionid weevils that often appear to be associated with cut vegetation such as hay were also noted; on archaeological sites these are often recorded in contexts where there is convincing evidence from plant and insect remains for the presence of hay and stable manure (Kenward and Hall 1997; Kenward 2009, 290). Woodworm beetles (*Anobium punctatum*) may also have been associated with the building fauna.

Langford Lane South

Ditch 2455 (Phase 5, late 1st-early 2nd century)

Water flea ephippia, caddis (*Trichoptera*) larval fragments and a group of aquatic beetles indicated that still to slowing water was present in the ditch for at least some of the time and that conditions within it were generally damp. Duckweed was indicated by *Tanysphyrus lemnae*, wetland Ranunculaceae by *Prasocuris phellandrii*, and nettles by *Trioza urticae* nymphs, *Brachypterus* and *Taenapion urticarium*. There were clear indications for the presence of trees or shrubs, possibly in the form of a hedgerow, from a rhynchitine weevil (possibly a species found on woody Rosaceae), *Orchestes*, *Crepidodera* and *Phratora vulgatissima*. The last of these is usually recorded from willow (*Salix*), the larvae usually occurring on sallows and goat willow (*Salix caprea*), while *Crepidodera* species are associated with willows and poplars (*Populus*).

The presence of ground beetles suggests that land outside the ditch was probably open and considerably drier, with a combination of disturbed or cultivated ground and grassy habitats; *Bembidion obtusum*, for example, occurs in open, dry situations especially on cultivated ground (Luff 1998, 68). A number of phytophages were indicative of particular groups of plants: *Meligethes* and *Ceutorhynchus* species are associated with wild and cultivated Brassicaceae, *Chaetocnema concinna/picipes* with Polygonaceae (especially *Polygonum*), *Oxystoma* with vetches (*Vicia* and *Lathyrus*), *Hadroplontus* with thistles (*Cirsium* and *Carduum*), and *Microplontus* with chamomiles (*Matricaria* and *Tripleurospermum*).

Four *Aphodius* species were recorded, hinting at the presence of grazing animals nearby. A small component of synanthropic beetles suggested that limited amounts of occupation waste had been incorporated into the deposit (*Latridius minutus* group, *Enicmus*, *Acritus nigricornis*).

Pit 2611, fill 2618 (Phase 6, 2nd-early 3rd century)

The main implication of the insect assemblage from this sample was for the disposal of organic waste from within buildings. Beetles characteristic of a building fauna included *Latridus minutus* group, *Ptinus fur*, *Stegobium paniceum*, *Ephistemus globulus*, *Xylodromus concinnus* and *Crataraea suturalis*. In addition, a small unexpanded elytral fragment was tentatively identified as being from a mealworm beetle (*Tenebrio obscurus*). Woodworm beetles (*Anobium punctatum*) were common, suggesting litter from within wooden buildings. There was a hint from a few taxa such as *Cryptopleurum minutum*, found in dung and other foul organic matter, and *Cratarea suturalis*, an aleocharine rove beetle that often occurs in mouldy straw (Harde 1984, 158), that the waste may have been stable manure.

Relatively few insects were indicative of natural conditions within the pit fill, but small numbers of water flea ephippia and a few aquatic beetles suggested that standing water may have been present for at least some of the time. *Notaris acridulus* was indicative of reed sweet-grass (*Glyceria maxima*), *Prasocuris phellandrii* of wetland Ranunculacae, and *Brachypterus* of nettles (*Urtica*). There was also a hint of grassland from *Pterostichus vernalis*.

Pit 2611, fill 2873, (Phase 6, 2nd-early 3rd century)

The insect assemblage from this fill was similar in implication to those from the ditches, although aquatic insects were less well represented. *Daphnia* ephippia and ostracod carapaces were common, however, indicating that the feature may have contained standing water for at least some of the time. Nettles (*Urtica*) were indicated by *Trioza urticae* nymphs and *Brachypterus*. Willow (*Salix*) growing close to the feature was suggested by the leaf beetles *Phratora vulgatissima* and *Crepidodera*. Other phytophages were typical of plants of disturbed/cultivated and grassy habitats; Brassicaceae were indicated by *Meligethes* and *Ceutorhynchus*, knotweed (*Polygonum*) by *Chaetocnema concinna/picipes*, vetches (*Vicia* and *Lathyrus*) by *Oxystoma* and ribwort plantain (*Plantago lanceolata*) by *Mecinus labile*. *Leiostoma deflexum*, a weevil found in damp places on wood anemone (*Anemone nemoralis*) or *Ranunculus* spp., and a knobbed shield bug (*Podops inuncta*), which occurs in dry litter under shrubs or in grassland, were also recorded.

Dung beetles were less common than in some of the other samples; remains of only two *Aphodius* were noted. Eurytopic decomposer beetles associated with accumulations of decaying organic matter were relatively well represented. A small group of insects suggested the deposition of litter from within buildings into the feature (*Xylodromus concinnus*, *Latridius minutus* group, *Enicmus*).

Roadside ditch 4158 (Phase 6, 2nd-early 3rd century)

The riffle beetle *Oulimnius* was common, indicating that the ditch contained clean, clear, running water. *Haliplus lineatocollis* is also typical of running water. Various other taxa, such as *Coelostoma orbiculare*, *Hygrotus inaequalis*, *Hydraena testacea* and *Laccobius bipunctatus*, suggest that the water flow may have been sluggish in places, however, and that there were areas of shallow, perhaps muddy water. Wet waterside mud was indicated by *Dryops*, duckweed (*Lemna*) by *Tanysphyrus lemnae*, and a number of beetles and bugs that would have lived in waterside moss and litter. Other vegetation within the ditch probably included reed sweet-grass (*Glyceria maxima*), rushes (*Juncus*) and Ranunculaceae, the host plants of *Notaris acridulus*, *Conomelus anceps* (a plant hopper), and *Prasocuris phellandrii* respectively. Nettles were indicated by *Trioza urticae* nymphs and *Brachypterus*, and docks (*Rumex*) by *Gastrophysa viridula*. There were a number of indications for the presence of trees or shrubs close to the ditch, and specifically for willows or perhaps poplars, from *Isochnus foliorum*, *Crepidodera* and scale insects (Coccoidea: Diaspididae).

A number of beetles suggested disturbed or cultivated ground where plants would have included Brassicaceae, knotweeds, and vetches (*Phyllotreta* spp., *Meligethes*, *Ceutorhynchus*, *Chaetocnema concinna/picipes*, *Oxystoma*), while grassland was suggested by ground beetles such as *Pterostichus niger* and *P. vernalis* and the weevils *Sitona* and *Hypera*. Four species of scarabaeid dung beetles were recorded which, together with the chafer *Phyllopertha horticola*, suggests pastureland in the vicinity.

There were hints from the presence of members of a typical 'building fauna' (*Latridus minutus* group, *Enicmus*, *Cryptophagus* ?*scutellatus*, *Atomaria*) that limited amounts of occupation waste from within buildings had been incorporated into the deposit. Beetles such as *Cercyon pygmaeus*, *C. haemorrhoidalis*, *Oxytelus sculptus*, *Acritus nigricornis* and woodworm beetle (*Anobium punctatum*) may have been associated with these, perhaps suggesting that this material was stable waste.

North of Oxford Parkway Station

Trackway ditch 3056 (Phase 6, 2nd century)

There was good evidence for aquatic deposition from abundant *Daphnia* ephippia and ostracod carapaces, and a range of beetles and bugs were suggestive of muddy shallow water and damp ground. *Tanysphyrus lemnae*, found on duckweed (*Lemna*), was common. Some beetles, including *Heterocerus* and the oxytelines *Platystethus cornutus* group, *P. nitens*, *Anotylus nitidulus* and *A. rugosus*, probably lived in organic-rich mud within the ditch. *Notaris acridulus* indicated that semi-aquatic plants growing in the ditch may have included reed sweet-grass (*Glyceria maxima*). Records of nettle ground bug (*Heterogaster urticae*), *Brachypterus*, *Taenapion urticarium* and *Trioza urticae* nymphs all indicated that nettles (*Urtica*) grew within or beside the ditch. Several taxa were suggestive of occasional trees and shrubs, or perhaps a hedgerow. The leaf beetle *Crepidodera* is found on willows or poplars, but a bark beetle (Scolytinae: Hylesinini) and scale insects found on trees and shrubs (Coccoidea: Diaspidae) were not closely identified.

Bembidion lunulatum, represented by at least 10 individuals and found on bare damp soils near water (Luff 2007, 102), was the most common ground beetle and its abundance might possibly relate to conditions on the trackway itself. Conditions outside the ditch were probably relatively dry. Other ground beetles indicated open grassland or disturbed or cultivated land on relatively dry soils and included eurytopic species such as *Pterostichus melanarius* and *Harpalus rufipes*. Plant-feeding insects indicating particular plants included *Chaetocnema concinna/picipes*, which is associated with Polygonaceae, especially knotweeds (*Polygonum*), *Phyllotreta nemorum* group, *Meligethes* and *Ceutorhynchus*, found on wild and cultivated Brassicaceae, *Mecinus pyraster*, found on ribwort plantain (*Plantago lanceolata*), and *Ceratapion carduorum*, which occurs on thistles (*Cirsium* and *Carduus*). Several species of click beetles (Elateridae) were represented, including *Agriotes* and *Agrypnus murinus*, which have turf-feeding larva. *Agriotes* species can become pests of root crops.

Dung beetles were relatively common, the most numerous species being *Aphodius granarius*. The other sample in which *Aphodius granarius* was notably common was from a Phase 4 roadside ditch at Langford Lane East (6715) and it was speculated that this may relate to use as a droveway, since the species is often associated with dung lying on bare ground, including trackways. (Jessop 1986, 24).

A group of synanthropic beetles typical of a 'building fauna' (*Latridius minutus* group, a spider beetle (*Ptinus*), *Atomaria*, *Mycetaea subterranea*), together with beetles such as *Oxytelus sculptus*, *Monotoma*, and *Corticaria*, which are associated with foul mouldering material, suggested the incorporation of waste from within buildings, perhaps stables.

Discussion

The insect remains from six of the seven samples produced a consistent picture of a generally open environment, much of it probably in agricultural use. Most samples contained insects suggesting that trees and/or shrubs may have formed hedgerows alongside the ditches and trackways. Willows (*Salix*) were specifically indicated in several samples.

Various insects in most samples were indicative of vegetation growing on disturbed, cultivated or waste ground and grassy areas, habitats that would be particularly typical of road- or trackside locations. Grassland and disturbed/cultivated

ground away from the features was suggested by various ground beetles.

The abundance and variety of scarabaeid dung beetles in four samples suggests that grazing animals were probably a common presence in the local environment. The abundance of these insects in samples from track- or roadside ditches may also relate to droving activity and the passage of animals used for transport. *Phyllopertha horticola*, a small chafer characteristic of permanent pasture land, was identified from two samples, and poorly preserved fragments of cuticle in a further two samples may be from the same species.

All the samples contained small or moderately-sized groups of beetles typical of a 'building fauna', clearly indicating that an element of waste from within buildings had contributed to the deposits. In some cases, it was possible to suggest that this might have consisted of stable manure but, since these components were relatively small, ideally the latter interpretation should be corroborated by evidence from plant remains. The term 'stable' in this context refers to any building that would have housed animals.

Insect remains from a single sample from a fill of pit 2611 consisted predominantly of taxa suggesting the disposal of organic occupation waste, but in the ditches the assemblages were dominated by insects from natural and semi-natural outdoor habitats. This suggests that waste disposal in these cases may only have been on a limited scale, at least in the sampled locations, and some material may simply have entered inciden-tally or in run-off from adjacent ground where manuring was taking place.

LAND AND FRESHWATER SNAILS
by Elizabeth Stafford

Introduction

A total of 47 samples were submitted for assessment of land and freshwater snails from Langford Lane East and Langford Lane South. The samples derived from incremental columns through a selection of ditch profiles across the sites, dated to the Roman period. The purpose of the assessment was to ascertain the presence/absence of identifiable shell, state of preservation, preliminary taxonomic content and to make recommendations for detailed analysis. Following on from this initial assessment, 19 samples were selected for further work, spanning occupation Phases 4, 5 and 6. This report presents the results of the detailed analysis of the samples from the following features:

Langford Lane East

- Trackway to the parade ground, eastern ditch 6091 (Phase 4-6)

- East Otmoor road, western ditch 6715 (Phase 4)

- East Otmoor road, eastern ditch 7066 (Phase 4-5)

Langford Lane South

- Boundary ditch 1063 (Phase 5)
- Boundary ditch 1068 (Phase 5)
- Enclosure ditch 2456 (Phase 6)
- Alchester-Dorchester road, western ditch 4479, 4481, 2835, 2887 (Phases 5 and 6)

Methodology

Between one and two litres of sediment was processed for each sample following standard methods (Evans 1972). The sediment was disaggregated in water and hand-floated onto a 0.5mm mesh. The fine residue was also retained to 0.5mm. Flots and residues were systematically sorted under

Table 4.19 Summary of molluscs

Feature	1063	1068	1068	1068	2456	2456	2456
Sample	9	12	14	16	2027	2030	2034
Context	147	12	13	15	2011	2192	2190
Volume processed (litres)	2	2	2	2	2	2	2
Taxa							
Bithynia tentaculata (Linnaeus 1758)	6	204	29	1	3		3
Valvata piscinalis (O. F. Müller 1774)				2			
Valvata cristata (O. F. Müller 1774)	3	267	15	21	4	4	3
Carychium minimum (O. F. Müller 1774)	3	73	9	8	23	4	11
Carychium tridentatum (Risso 1826)			2	2		2	
Carychium spp.		18	2	6			1
cf. *Clausilia bidentata bidentata* (Ström 1765)			1				
cf. *Cochlodina laminata* (Montagu 1803)		1	2	1			
Cochlicopa spp.		3	3	2	21	10	9
Discus rotundatus rotundatus (O. F. Müller 1774)			1			1	
Merdigera obscura (O. F. Müller 1774)							
Euconulus fulvus (O. F. Müller 1774)							
Cepaea/Arianta spp.	1		8	8	2	2	3
Candidula sp.	1						
Trochulus hispidus (Linnaeus 1758)	3	47	71	41	170	36	106
Galba truncatula (O. F .Müller 1774)		370	4	7	41	3	19
Lymnaea palustris (O. F. Müller 1774)		95		1			
Omphiscola glabra (O. F. Müller 1774)				1			
Radix balthica (Linnaeus 1758)				10	3	3	
Lymnaea spp.			2			2	2
Aegopinella nitidula (Draparnaud 1805)		21	2	4		2	20
Nesovitrea hammonis (Ström 1765)			1			1	
Oxychilus cellarius (Müller 1774)	1		1	1		1	
Aplexa hypnorum (Linnaeus 1758)		1		1			
Physa cf. *fontinalis* (Linnaeus 1758)							
Anisus leucostoma (Millet 1813)	4	437	92	126	21	4	7
Anisus vortex (Linnaeus 1758)							
Bathyomphalus contortus (Linnaeus 1758)	2		1	7	1		
Gyraulus crista (Linnaeus 1758)	1			3			
Gyraulus albus (Müller 1774)							1
Planorbis planorbis (Linnaeus 1758)	25	19	20	48	2	1	7
Vitrea sp.			1	2			
Punctum pygmaeum (Draparnaud 1801)		1		3		3	
Pupilla muscorum (Linnaeus 1758)		1		2	2	1	1
Succinea/Oxyloma spp.	2	155	12	16	62	5	7
Acanthinula aculeata (Müller 1774)							
Vallonia costata (Müller 1774)	1		2	5	1		
Vallonia excentrica (Sterki 1893)		11	2	3	13	1	2
Vallonia pulcella (Müller 1774)		18	1	5	12	8	7
Vallonia spp.	1	100	15	10	185	20	23
Vertigo antivertigo (Draparnaud 1801)	1	40	1	3	31	1	1
Vertigo pygmaea (Draparnaud 1801)		5	4	1	11	1	6
Vertigo angustior (Jeffreys 1830)							
Vitrina pellucida (Müller 1774)						5	
Total	55	1887	304	351	608	121	239

a binocular microscope at magnifications of up to x40. Whole shell and apical fragments were extracted, identified with the aid of a modern reference collection and counted. Nomenclature follows Anderson (2005) and habitat information follows Boycott (1936), Ellis (1926), Evans (1972), Kerney (1999) and Kerney and Cameron (1979). The results are presented in tabular format (Table 4.19) and as a percentage frequency histogram (Fig. 4.7).

For freshwater molluscs, groups habitat preferences consist of the following:

- Flowing water species: require a clean stream with a current

2887	2835	2835	4481	4479	4479	4479	6091	6091	6091	6715	7006
2180	2177	2179	2169	2172	2173	2174	6005	6007	6009	6014	6028
2836	2833	2834	2842	2837	2837	2889	6114	6115	6117	6629	6745
1	1.9	1.5	1.75	1.8	1.25	1.5	1.5	1.5	1.5	2	0.15
1	15	2		12	6	26	6	5	2		7
			2			1		2	10		24
15	38	21	41	44	16	49	11	12	69	4	10
35	33	28	3	45	21	9		12	6	3	2
35		12						1			
64	17	43		12	8	5	2	7			
1						1					
1		1									
10	44	40	6	33	24	11	3	3	3	2	
22	74	66		34				2			1
	3	7		1	2	1					
	2	1			2	1					
		1	1	3	4	5	1		1		
											1
11	28	39	26	48	24	37	8	44	17	8	4
2	5	8	10	34				4	2	3	1
1	4		2	2	2			2			2
			2			1					
				2		1		1	4	4	14
				4	4	4	3	2	3		
14	34	19		8	14	22	1	6	2	1	1
5			1	1				3			
8	39	33		17	7	4		2			
		3		2				2			1
											1
39	21	62	14	50	21	42	7	28	24	13	6
											29
1	5		34	5	6	7	3	1	27	8	8
				3				2	16	4	3
											1
	4	7		9	16	46	4	17	52	42	64
3	1										
		1	1	16	2	6		4	1		
	1		2					4	2		
3	17	8	17	20	4	14	2	21	2	2	6
1											
13	119	78		73	40	37	1	34	7		
						1	1	9	2	1	
		3	2	1		1	4	2	1		
	18	15	3	29	6	10	12	47	19	6	1
		8	2	1	1		1	1			
		2	2								
		1									
5	49	37	2	16	2	1					
290	571	535	180	526	233	341	67	282	274	102	186

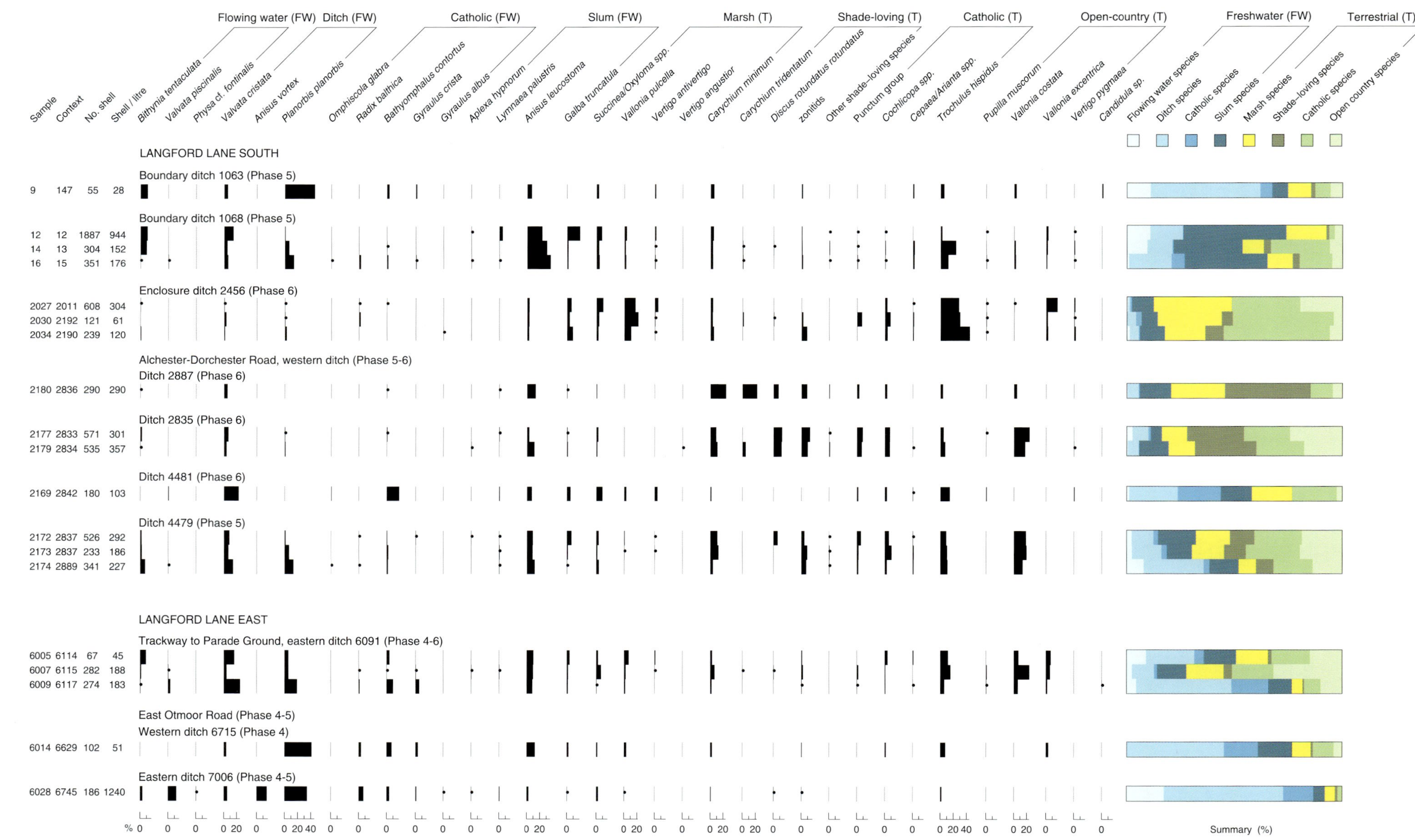

LANGFORD LANE SOUTH

Boundary ditch 1063 (Phase 5)

Sample	Context	No. shell	Shell / litre
9	147	55	28

Boundary ditch 1068 (Phase 5)

Sample	Context	No. shell	Shell / litre
12	12	1887	944
14	13	304	152
16	15	351	176

Enclosure ditch 2456 (Phase 6)

Sample	Context	No. shell	Shell / litre
2027	2011	608	304
2030	2192	121	61
2034	2190	239	120

Alchester-Dorchester Road, western ditch (Phase 5-6)
Ditch 2887 (Phase 6)

Sample	Context	No. shell	Shell / litre
2180	2836	290	290

Ditch 2835 (Phase 6)

Sample	Context	No. shell	Shell / litre
2177	2833	571	301
2179	2834	535	357

Ditch 4481 (Phase 6)

Sample	Context	No. shell	Shell / litre
2169	2842	180	103

Ditch 4479 (Phase 5)

Sample	Context	No. shell	Shell / litre
2172	2837	526	292
2173	2837	233	186
2174	2889	341	227

LANGFORD LANE EAST

Trackway to Parade Ground, eastern ditch 6091 (Phase 4-6)

Sample	Context	No. shell	Shell / litre
6005	6114	67	45
6007	6115	282	188
6009	6117	274	183

East Otmoor Road (Phase 4-5)
Western ditch 6715 (Phase 4)

Sample	Context	No. shell	Shell / litre
6014	6629	102	51

Eastern ditch 7006 (Phase 4-5)

Sample	Context	No. shell	Shell / litre
6028	6745	186	1240

Fig. 4.7   Summary of mollusc analysis

- Ditch species: require clean slowly moving water often with abundant aquatic plants

- Catholic species: tolerate a wide range of conditions except the worst slums

- Slum species: those able to live in water subject to stagnation, drying up and large temperature variations

For the terrestrial fauna, habitat preferences consist of:

- Open-country

- Shade-loving

- Catholic

- Marsh species

Results

Langford Lane East

Trackway to the parade ground, eastern ditch 6091 (Phase 4-6)

Three samples were examined from ditch 6091. Shell abundance was moderate in the lower two fills (6115 and 6117) at 274 and 282 individuals respectively (*c* 130 shells/litre). Preservation was poorer in the upper fill (6114) at 67 individuals (45 shells/litre). Initially, the lower fill (6117) produced an assemblage similar to the lower fill in ditch 4479 but with a higher proportion of freshwater ditch species (44%) including *Planorbis planorbis* and *Valvata cristata* and catholic species (17%). Overall freshwater taxa account for 76% of the total. The terrestrial taxa at 24% was varied but notable for the absence of shade-demanding species.

In the overlying fills the freshwater component is much reduced and terrestrial taxa become more abundant ranging from 72% in fill 6115 to 49% in fill 6114, although the numbers in the latter are considered unreliable due to low shell counts. The open country element (32%) in fill 6115 includes *Vallonia costata* and *Vallonia excentrica* with smaller numbers of *Pupilla muscoum*. Catholic species (19%) mainly comprise *Trochulus hispidus* (16%). There is a sizable marsh component at 17%, but shade-demanding taxa are limited to 4%.

Overall given the abundance of freshwater and ditch species in the lower fill, it is likely that the feature initially contained standing water, possibly with a slow flow but this dried up as the feature became silted. The assemblages in the overlying fills are probably more representative of the surrounding environment, which appears to have been quite open, probably grazed pasture with a short sward. There is no real indication of scrub or hedgerows. The limited range of terrestrial catholic taxa and general absence of shade-demanding taxa may suggest the edges of the ditch itself were being grazed.

East Otmoor road, western ditch 6715 (Phase 4) and eastern ditch 7066 (Phase 4-5)

Two samples were examined from ditches 6715 and 7066. Both samples contained high proportions of freshwater species at 76%, dominated by ditch species *Planorbis planorbis*. However, ditch 7066 had a greater range and abundance of flowing water and ditch species. This included *Bithynia tentaculata*, *Valvata piscinalis*, *Physa fontinalis* and *Valvata cristata* and *Anisus vortex*. This sample contained amounts of broken shell debris, along with large numbers of bivalve shells of *Pisidium* spp., including the greater European peaclam, *Pisiduim amnicum*.

In both samples catholic (16-14%) and slum species (16-5%) occurred at much lower proportions, along with terrestrial taxa (24%). Of the terrestrial taxa, this mostly comprised marsh and catholic species. Shade-demanding taxa were negligible and the open-country element was only present within ditch 6715 at 4% with *Vallonia excentrica*. Overall, the character of the assemblages suggests both ditches held water with some flow, but particularly 7066, which is consistent with deposition of flowing in-channel deposits or flood debris from a closely adjacent watercourse. There is little indication of the nature of the wider environment beyond the features.

Langford Lane South

Boundary ditches 1063 and 1068 (Phase 5)

One sample was examined from ditch 1063 and three from ditch 1068, all belonging to occupation Phase 5. Shell abundance was moderate to good in ditch 1068, with *c* 1800 individuals (944 shells/litre) counted in ditch fill 12. Preservation was poorer in the single sample examined from ditch 1063, fill 147, at 55 individuals (28 shells/litre). In ditch 1068 the assemblages are dominated by freshwater taxa. In fills 15 and 13, freshwater taxa account for 65% and 54% respectively. This rises to 74% in the uppermost fill 12. In all three samples the largest group within the freshwater component are slum species, mainly *Anisus leucostoma*, with smaller numbers of *Galba truncatula*, *Lymnaea palustris* and *Aplexa hypnorum*. Ditch species are also present such as *Planorbis planorbis* and *Valvata cristata*. The proportion of the flowing water group is notably higher in the middle and upper fills (13 and 12) as a result of increases in a single taxon, *Bithynia tentaculata*. This is accompanied by an increase in *V. cristata*. The terrestrial component of the assemblages account for 35% of the total in the lower fill (15), dominated by the catholic species *Trochulus hispidus* at 12%. Species that frequent marsh and damp ground are notable (12%), and include *Vertigo antivertigo*, *Succinea/Oxyloma* sp., *Carychium minimum* and *Vallonia pulchella*. Open country taxa that generally proliferate in drier conditions form a minor component of the assemblage (5%), although the latter include *Vallonia costata*, *Vallonia excentrica*, *Pupilla muscorum* and *Vertigo pygmaea*. Shade-demanding taxa (mainly the zonitids) account for only 3% of the total. There is little notable change in the composition of the terrestrial assemblages in the middle and upper fills.

Overall the dominance of the freshwater slum species, along with the range of marsh and catholic species, suggests quite mesic conditions. The feature was probably quite damp and probably held water seasonally, perhaps with a slow flow, drying in the summer months. This feature may have been located within an area of damp lightly grazed grassland that was very open; although longer grass and erect vegetation such as sedges may have grown within the ditch, there is no real evidence for areas of scrub or woodland in the vicinity. The increase in *Bithynia tentaculata* in the middle and upper fills may be a result of increased flooding in the locality as the ditch silted up.

Enclosure ditch 2456 (Phase 6)

Three samples were examined from enclosure ditch 2456. In contrast to ditch 1068, here the assemblages are dominated by terrestrial taxa, with the freshwater component accounting for only 12-18% of the totals, the majority of which are slum species, *Galba truncatula* and to a lesser extent *Anisus leucostoma*.

The terrestrial component of the assemblages account for 82-88% of the total, dominated by the catholic species *Trochulus hispidus* and marsh taxa such as *Succinea/Oxyloma* sp., *Vertigo antivertigo*, and *Vallonia pulchella*. Shade-demanding taxa (mainly the zonitids) account for up to 8% of the total but are absent from the uppermost fill. Open country taxa are a significant component of the assemblage in the upper fill at 20%, due to increases in the dry grassland snail *Vallonia excentrica*,

Overall the environment in the immediate vicinity of this feature was probably quite similar to boundary ditch 1068: lightly grazed, very open, damp grassland with an absence of scrub or woodland. There may have been longer vegetation growing within the feature, but it probably remained dry through much of the year. It may have occasionally held standing water but with no flow. There is no evidence of periods of flood during infilling.

Alchester to Dorchester-on-Thames road, western ditch 4479, 4481, 2835, 2887 (Phases 5 and 6)

Seven samples were examined from four intercutting ditches located on the western side of the Alchester to Dorchester-on-Thames road, spanning occupation Phases 5 and 6.

Three samples from the earliest sequence in ditch 4479 (Phase 5) produced moderate to good sized assemblages with up to 526 individuals counted in the upper fill (2837, sample 2172; 292 shells/litre).

The lowermost sample from fill 2889 produced quite a mixed assemblage of shell with almost equal proportions of freshwater and terrestrial taxa. The freshwater component included a high proportion of ditch species (28%), mainly *Planorbis planorbis* and *Valvata cristata*. Flowing water at 8% was mainly

attributed to *Bithynia tentaculata*. Catholic and slum species accounted for 16%, of which *Anisus leucostoma* was 12%. The terrestrial taxa were almost equally spread between groups, with the largest numbers of shell ascribed to the catholic snail *Trochulus hispidus* and the open country snail *Vallonia costata*. Marsh species include *Carychium minimum* and *Succinea/Oxyloma* sp. Shade-demanding taxa, mainly the zonitids account for 8% of the totals, although *Merdigera obscura* and *Clausilia bidentata bidentata* were also present.

In the upper two samples from fill 2837 the assemblages were similar but the overall terrestrial component increases to 70%. There is an increase in shade-demanding taxa up to 11% with the notable addition of *Discus rotundatus rotundatus* along with the slum species *Galba truncatula* and marsh species *Vertigo antivertigo* and *Vallonia pulchella*.

Generally, the mixed nature of the assemblages makes this sequence difficult to interpret and it is likely the shells, particularly in fill 2889, derive from a variety of environments both within and adjacent to the feature and possibly as a result of inputs by water flow. The predominance of freshwater ditch species in the lower fill indicates the feature did hold water at least seasonally, perhaps with a slow flow. The feature is likely to have been located in a grassland environment, although given the fact the open country component is mainly limited to *Vallonia costata* accompanied by a range of catholic species this may have been located away from grazed pasture. The presence of the shade-demanding taxa hints at an environment of long grass or scrub in the vicinity, perhaps a hedgerow, which becomes more prominent during later stages of infilling and the feature generally appears to become drier.

The single sample from ditch 4481 (Phase 6) produced a similar assemblage to the lower fill (2889) of ditch 4479 but with a much lower proportion of open-country taxa and no shade-demanding species. This would be consistent with a recut, effectively clearing away vegetation.

The two samples from ditches 2835 and the single sample from 2887 (Phase 6) were of similar character to fill 2837. However, here the terrestrial component rises to 85%, with the shade-demanding component prominent up to 39%. The latter includes *Carychium tridentatum* alongside *Discus rotundatus rotundatus*, *Clausilia bidentata bidentata* and *Cochlodina laminata*. Overall this strongly indicates the persistence of long grassland and scrub or an established hedgerow in the immediate vicinity. The open-country component continues to be dominated by *Vallonia costata* suggesting the feature was marginal to areas of open pasture.

Discussion

Overall, shell preservation and abundance was generally good in the samples selected for analysis and the distribution was well-spread across the range of features and periods. Superficially the assemblages appeared of similar character. The terrestrial component was for the most part of open country character and of low diversity, dominated by the Vallonidae grass snails and the catholic species *Trochulus hispidus*, which is typical of open floodplain grazed grassland. However, there was some variation, notably within the ditches associated with the Alchester to Dorchester-on-Thames road where a substantial part of the assemblages was of shade-demanding species (eg *Discus rotundatus*, various zonitids, *Merdigera obscura*, Clausiliidae, *Carychium tridentatum*). These species are not indicative of dense woodland but may suggest the close proximity of scrub or a hedgerow.

There was a very frequent freshwater component to many of the samples. This varied from assemblages dominated by flowing water and ditch species (eg *Bithynia tentaculata*, *Valvata piscinalis*, *Valvata cristata* and *Planorbis planorbis*), to more diverse assemblages which included catholic and slum species (eg. *Lymnaea* spp., *Bathyomphalus contortus* and *Anisus leucostoma*). It is possible the former may relate to flood episodes bringing in-channel debris across the floodplain, whereas a component of the more diverse assemblages may relate to communities living within the features. The proportions of these species relate to whether the feature was permanently damp or subject to seasonal drying. The presence of a range of marsh and catholic species such as *Vertigo antivertigo* and *Carychium minimum* is fairly typical of damp floodplain grassland, whereas *Succinea/Oxyloma* spp. are suggestive of vegetation such as tall reeds and grasses probably growing within or adjacent to features.

In summary, the earliest phases of activity occur at Langford Lane East. Ditch 6091 (Phases 4-6), on the eastern side of the trackway to the parade ground, is likely to have initially contained standing water, possibly with a slow flow but this dried up as the feature became silted. The environment appears to have been quite open, probably grazed pasture with a short sward. There is no real indication of scrub or hedgerows in the vicinity. There is some indication of wetter conditions and possible flood episodes in the upper fill but this is equivocal given the low shell count.

The ditches of the east Otmoor road (Phase 4) were dominated by freshwater species, indicating that they held water with some flow for part of the year at least. Notably, the assemblage from ditch 7066 is consistent with deposition of flowing in-channel deposits or flood debris from a closely adjacent watercourse. There is little indication of the nature of the wider environment beyond the features.

At Langford Lane South, boundary ditches 1063 and 1068 (Phase 5) appear to have been quite damp and probably held water seasonally, perhaps with a slow flow, drying in the summer months. The wider environment may have comprised lightly grazed grassland that was very open, although longer grass and erect vegetation such as sedges may have

grown within the ditch. There was some evidence for episodes of flooding in the upper fills.

Enclosure ditch 2456 (Phase 6) was probably located in a similar environment to the boundary ditches. There may have been longer vegetation growing within the feature but it probably remained dry through much of the year. It may have occasionally held standing water but with no flow. There is no evidence of periods of flood during infilling.

The molluscs for the sequence from the ditches associated with the Alchester to Dorchester-on-Thames road suggest initially the feature did hold water at least seasonally, perhaps with a slow flow. It appears to have been located away from grazed pasture in an environment of long grass or scrub which persisted through the phases of recutting, perhaps a hedge line, which becomes more prominent during later stages of infilling as the feature became drier.

MARINE SHELL *by Rebecca Nicholson*

Introduction

In total, approximately 1000 individual shells (13.5kg) were hand collected, in addition to which a relatively small number of shells (750g) were recovered from the residues of sieved soil samples. Almost all the shells are from the native oyster *Ostrea edulis* and for this assessment the left (lower) and right (upper) valves were counted separately for a selection of contexts with larger assemblages and the sieved material was rapidly scanned. Shell condition and any encrustation and/or parasite damage to the shells was noted (after Winder 1980).

Overview of the assemblage

Most contexts yielded single or small numbers of oyster valves of variable size and condition, but mostly large or very large and of the traditional round form of the common European flat oyster *Ostrea edulis*. Several contexts included over 20 valves, some of which are measurable (Table 4.20). There are similar numbers of left and right valves, indicating that the oysters were probably not served in the shell. While most valves are rounded, some are elongated or irregularly shaped, which, together with their variable but generally large size, suggests that the shellfish were collected from natural rather than cultivated beds, as well as indicating the likelihood of some crowding in the oyster bed. There are some examples of smaller oysters adhering to the valves of older individuals. In general, the oysters are in fair-poor condition, often with chalky deposits, possibly an indication of rapid changes in salinity and growth in estuarine conditions (Winder 2011). Some contexts included shells that were stained orange internally and/or externally, sometimes giving the interior of the shell a glossy appearance. While this orange staining may be due

Table 4.20 Contexts with more than twenty marine shells

Context	Feature	No. of shells	Wt (g)	Species	Oyster left valves	Oyster right valves
2004	Ditch 2012	29	610	Oyster	18	11
2049	Ditch 2012	21	305	Oyster, 1 Roman edible snail	9	11
2572	Ditch 4384	51	651	Oyster, mussel	22	27
2615	Pit 2611	61	1148	Oyster, 1 cockle	35	25
2808	Pit 2611	188	3986	Oyster, mussel	94	94
2809	Pit 2611	55	1023	Oyster, mussel, whelk	23	18

Table 4.21 Summary of radiocarbon dates

Lab. ID	Context	Feature	Material	δ13C (0/00)	Radiocarbon age (BP)	Calibrated date (95.4% confidence)
Langford Lane East						
SUERC-70884	418	Cremation burial 417	Human long bone	-18.6	1864 ± 29	Cal AD 70-230
SUERC-70885	6085	Cremation burial 6084	Human femoral shaft	-18.7	1998 ± 29	60 cal BC-cal AD 70
South of Oddington Crossing						
SUERC-70734	14	Metalworking debris in ditch 153	Charcoal: corylus/alnus	-26.2	2096 ± 30	200-40 cal BC

to mobilisation of iron in the soil, it may also be a product of heating or cooking.

Fewer than 5% of valves exhibit clear evidence for parasitic infestation or encrustation by other organisms, although internal blistering is frequent. Where present, most were tunnels consistent with those caused by the marine polychete worms *Polydora hoplura* Claparède and *Polydora ciliata* (Johnston). There were also several instances of holes, probably caused by predatory gastropod molluscs such as dogwhelks or sting winkles, and two examples of the pock-marked appearance typically caused by sponges, including *Cliona celata* Grant. Notches are evident on the posterior margin of a significant proportion of both left and right oyster valves resulting from opening the shellfish using a blade.

Shells other than oyster are rare. Occasional mussels (*Mytilus* cf *edulis*) were recovered, as well as single instances of whelk (*Buccinium undatum*) and cockle (*Cerastoderma* sp.).

In addition to the marine shells, a single example of the edible Roman snail, *Helix pomatia*, was recovered. Although now found widely on chalk soils of the south and west of England, these snails are thought to have been a Roman introduction into Britain and their presence in securely Roman deposits may indicate that these snails were imported to the site. Several other examples of land snails hand collected with the marine shell are unlikely to be of significance.

Conclusion

Oysters are known from most Roman sites in England. The assemblage does, however, demonstrate the regular movement of perishable items from the coast inland as far as Alchester in the Roman period, the consumption of oysters by the inhabitants and the likely exploitation of natural rather than cultivated beds.

RADIOCARBON DATING *by Andrew Simmonds*

Three samples were submitted to the Scottish Universities Environmental Research Centre (SUERC) AMS Facility, Glasgow, for radiocarbon dating (Table 4.21). The samples were carefully selected in order to address specific research questions. The first of these was to obtain a date for the burials alongside the trackway to the parade ground at East of Langford Lane in order to establish whether they were contemporary with the trackway or whether their proximity to it was coincidental. The second priority for radiocarbon dating was to establish a more precise date for the deposit of metalworking debris at South of Oddington Crossing than was possible from the ceramic evidence, and to this end a sample of charcoal from the deposit was submitted.

The results of the three samples are presented in Table 4.21. The radiocarbon ages are quoted in conventional years BP (before AD 1950) and as calibrated calendrical dates at 95.4% confidence. The error includes components from the counting statistics on the sample, modern reference standards, background standards and the random machine error. The calibrated age ranges were determined using the University of Oxford Radiocarbon Accelerator Unit calibration program OxCal 4.2 and the IntCal13 curve and have been rounded out to the nearest 10 years following Mook (1986). All radiocarbon date ranges cited in the text of this report are those for the 95% confidence level (2 sigma).

Chapter 5

Human remains

by Lauren McIntyre and Alice Rose

Introduction and methodology

The human remains comprised an inhumation burial (7124), some disarticulated unburnt bone (8066) and six cremation burials (417, 6084, 6711, 6720, 7272, 7408) at Langford Lane East, a cremation burial (2522) at South of Merton and an inhumation burial (8109) and a cremation burial (8547) at Holts Farm Crossing. All the remains were dated to the Roman period.

All human remains were examined in accordance with the recommendations set out by CIfA and BABAO (Brickley and McKinley 2004) and English Heritage guidelines (Mays 2004, 3-6). Deposits containing cremated bone were subjected to whole earth recovery and processed by wet sieving, to clean sort the burnt bone into >10mm, 10-4mm and 4-2mm fractions. The 2-0.5mm residues were also retained where possible from all deposits containing cremated bone. Where the 4-2mm or 2-0.5mm fractions weighed in excess of 30g, a sample (20g of 4-2mm; 10g of 2-0.5mm) was sorted and the total weight of cremated bone estimated.

Langford Lane East

Inhumation burial 7124

Skeleton 7125 was approximately 70% complete. Overall, the skeleton was in fair condition with bones that were highly fragmented and bone surfaces that had slight and patchy surface erosion (consistent with grade 1, after McKinley 2004a, 16). The skeleton was that of an older child, approximately 5-7 years of age. As the individual was a juvenile, biological sex could not be determined, since there are currently no standards for ascertaining juvenile sex using macroscopic osteological methods (Brickley, 2004, 23).

A total of 11 deciduous and 26 permanent teeth were present. Of the 26 permanent teeth, 15 were unerupted. Only one deciduous and one permanent socket were present. Dental caries were observed on three deciduous teeth. Development of dental caries results from the fermentation of food sugars in the diet, particularly sucrose, by bacteria that occur on teeth (Roberts and Manchester 1997, 45-6). Whilst diets high in sugar are a major factor in the forma-

tion of caries, poor dental hygiene is also a major component in the onset of the disease. Dental calculus was observed on five deciduous and two permanent teeth. Dental calculus is a mineralised plaque deposit that derives from a combination of plaque fluid, saliva, and micro-organisms associated with plaque deposits that may accumulate on tooth surfaces (Hillson 1996, 255).

No cranial or post-cranial non-metric traits were observed.

Increased porosity was observed in both orbits, consistent with a diagnosis of cribra orbitalia (Stuart-Macadam 1991). It has been suggested that cribra orbitalia may be indicative of iron deficiency anaemia or vitamin B12 deficiency (ibid.; Walker *et al.* 2009). When observed macroscopically, it is best utilised as a generic indicator of childhood stress (Steckel *et al.* 2006, 12-3).

Increased porosity indicative of elevated vascularity was observed in several bones of the cranium (right side of the pars basilaris, lateral side of the right occipital condyle, posterior to the zygomatic process of the left temporal bone, medial side of the ascending ramus of the left and right mandible, superior to the mandibular foramen and extending between the coronoid process and the head). Increased fine porosity was also observed in the supraspinous region of both the left and right scapulae, at the base of the supraspinous fossa. These lesions may be indicative of childhood scurvy (Brickley and Ives 2008, 56-7). Scurvy develops as a result of insufficient vitamin C uptake. In dry bone, diagnosis of scurvy relies upon identification of a characteristic pattern of skeletal involvement, which in archaeological skeletons can be difficult to find when skeletal elements are absent or abraded. Skeletal lesions frequently associated with the presence of scurvy are generally thought to be the result of localised haemorrhaging in the skin, subperiosteal regions, gums and joint spaces. Haemorrhaging causes inflammation of the periosteum, which can manifest skeletally as cortical porosity and periosteal new bone formation (most typically occurring in the orbits, mandible, temporal bones and the sphenoid). While the lesions observed in skeleton 7125 may be indicative of localised haemorrhaging linked to the presence of scurvy, it should also be noted that it was not possible to examine skeletal regions that are considered the most diagnostic of scurvy when affected (eg the greater wing of the sphenoid, the maxilla and palate; Brickley and Ives 2008, 56-7), as these elements were either incomplete, highly fragmented or absent. The diagnosis of scurvy is therefore tentative.

Periosteal new bone was observed in all six long bones of the lower limbs. This is formed as a response to inflammation of the overlying soft tissue, although its formation may also be a response to non-specific inflammation of overlying soft tissue as a result of trauma or pathological conditions including those of a metabolic (eg scurvy) neoplastic, or infectious disease (Resnick and Niyawama 1995; Roberts 2000, 148; Ortner 2003, 206). No evidence of traumatic injury was observed on any of the bones; the presence of diffuse, active periostitis in multiple anatomical locations may therefore indicate that this individual was suffering from a systemic condition. Possible causes can include treponemal disease, leprosy, tuberculosis, and soft tissue infection (Ortner 2003, 88), although it should be noted that no other evidence of specific infectious disease was observed in this individual. The presence of bilateral cribra orbitalia in conjunction with periosteal new bone formation may suggest that this individual was subject to general health stressors, for example unidentified/non-specific infectious disease or general poor health. Alternatively, both types of lesions may also be associated with the presence of scurvy.

Disarticulated bone

The nine fragments of human bone from context 8066 comprised one fragment of left inferior ilium/superior ischium and eight fragments of unsided femoral midshaft. The bone exhibited slight, patchy surface erosion consistent with McKinley's (2004a, 16) grade 1.

The fragments were all of a size and morphology that are consistent with one adult individual. No indicators of age at death, sex, stature, pathology or non-metric traits were present. Several small (*c* 3-6 x 0.2mm), straight, parallel striations were noted on the largest of the femoral shaft fragments. These are likely to be post-depositional, possibly from ploughing.

Cremation burials

Bone weight

Six cremation burials were recovered (Tables 5.1-5.6). Burials 6720 and 7408 were each recorded as having two fills but in both cases the distribution of bone suggested that only a single deposit was represented. The other burials each contained a single fill. Only four burials had bone weights of more than 100g (417: 667.6g; 6084: 238.9g; 6711: 140.0g; 6720: 334.8g). The remaining two had bone weights substantially less than 100g (7272: 0.7g; 7408: 53.6g). These bone weights are all substantially below the range of modern adult cremations (1000-2400g;

Table 5.1 Summary of cremation burial 417

Deposit	Skeletal region	>10mm	10-4mm	4-2mm	Colour, MNI, age, sex, pathology
418	Skull	20.1g (cranial vault, petrous, mandible)	36.3g (cranial vault, mandible, 15x tooth root fragments, 9x tooth enamel fragments)	-	*c* 80% buff-white, 10% blue/grey, 5% black
	Axial	1.3g (rib shaft fragments)	3.6g (vertebral and rib shaft fragments)	-	MNI = 1 Adult Unknown sex
	Upper limb	8.5g (humerus, left scapula, 1x right lunate)	4.0g (unsided radial head, left lunate, metacarpal, proximal and intermediate phalanges)	-	Periosteal new bone observed on 10x fragments – 8x tibial shaft, 1x unid. hand/foot (metacarpal/metatarsal?), 1x unid. Other
	Lower limb	10.2g (femur, tibia and fibula shaft, pelvis, 1x fragment cuboid)	24.0g (femur, tibia and fibula shaft, pelvis, proximal, intermediate and distal phalanges)	-	1x fragment vertebral body with marginal osteophytes and spondylolisthesis (spinal osteoarthritis)
	Unid. long bone	26.2g	64.7g	-	
	Unid. hand/foot	-	7.9g	-	
	Unid. joint surface	8.2g	16.3g	-	
	Unid. other	4.5g	205.1g	204.1g*	
	Unid. total	38.9g	294.0g	204.1g*	
	Total	79.0g	361.9g	204.1g*	645g*

Note: * denotes inclusion of estimated bone weight, based on a sorted 20g sample

McKinley 2000a, 26) and archaeologically recovered cremations (600-900g; McKinley 2013). As all six features were truncated, it is possible that large quantities of bone have been lost, and that the low observed bone weights are unlikely to be representative of the full amount of bone deposited in the features after cremation had taken place. The bone recovered from feature 7272 is so low that this may be residual rather than the result of deliberate deposition.

Fragmentation

Fragments ranged in size from 13.6mm (an unidentified fragment from pit 7272) to 49.2mm (a fragment of humerus shaft from burial 6084). Only one deposit had the largest proportional bone weight from the >10mm sieve fraction (6721, burial 6720: 136.9g, 44.5% of the total bone weight). However, a further 125.4g (40.7% of the total bone weight) was recovered from the 10-4mm fraction.

Table 5.2 Summary of cremation burial 6084

Deposit	Skeletal region	>10mm	10-4mm	4-2mm	Colour, MNI, age, sex, pathology
6085	Skull	6.5g (cranial vault)	26.8g (cranial vault, 1x zygomatic process, fragment of molar crown)	2.7g cranial vault)	*c* 50% buff-white, 20% blue/grey, 10% black, 20% brown
	Axial	2.6g (rib shaft fragments)	17.5g (vertebral and rib shaft fragments)	2.7g (rib shaft fragments)	MNI = 1
	Upper limb	13.4g (humerus, ulna and radius shaft)	0.4g (proximal, intermediate and distal hand phalanx fragments)		Adult Unknown sex
	Lower limb	20.6g (femur, tibia and fibula shaft, and calcaneus fragments)	4.6g (femur, tibia and fibula shaft, 2x metatarsal heads, proximal and distal phalanx fragments)	-	No pathology observed
	Unid. long bone	19.7g	51.4g	1.6g	
	Unid. hand/foot	0.3g	5.6g	0.6g	
	Unid. joint surface	-	7.8g	1.2g	
	Unid. other	-	14.3g	39.5g	
	Unid. total	20.0g	79.1g	42.9g	
	Total	63.1g	128.4g	48.3g	239.8g

Table 5.3 Summary of cremation burial 6711

Deposit	Skeletal region	>10mm	10-4mm	4-2mm	Colour, MNI, age, sex, pathology
6712	Skull	2.7g (cranial vault)	4.9g (cranial vault)	0.7g (cranial vault, molar crown)	*c* 70% buff-white, 20% blue/grey, 5% black, 5% brown
	Axial	-	11.4g (vertebral and rib shaft fragments)	1.4g (vertebral and rib shaft fragments)	MNI = 1
	Upper limb	2.2g (humerus shaft)	1.0g (proximal, intermediate and distal hand phalanx fragments)	-	Adult Unknown sex
	Lower limb	11.5g (tibia and fibula shaft, and pelvis fragments)	4.6g (fibula shaft, pelvis fragments, 1x metatarsal)	-	No pathology observed
	Unid. long bone	6.4g	18.1g	0.8g	
	Unid. hand/foot	-	3.9g	0.5g	
	Unid. joint surface	3.4g	5.9g	1.0g	
	Unid. other	1.7g	22.0g	34.7g	
	Unid. total	11.5g	49.9g	37.0g	
	Total	27.9g	71.8g	39.1g	138.8g

Table 5.4 Summary of cremation burial 6720

Deposit	Skeletal region	>10mm	10–4mm	4–2mm	Colour, MNI, age, sex, pathology
6721	Skull	53.1g (cranial vault, maxilla, mandible fragments and 2x tooth roots)	35.9g (cranial vault, maxilla, mandible fragments and 7x tooth roots and enamel)	2.0g (cranial vault, tooth root and enamel fragments)	*c* 70% buff-white, 10% blue/grey, 5% black, 10% orange, 5% brown
	Axial	12.8g (vertebral and rib shaft fragments)	27.3g (vertebral and rib shaft fragments, inc. 1x subadult/neonate rib fragment)	3.9g (rib shaft fragments)	MNI = 2 1x prime/middle adult Unknown sex 1x juvenile
	Upper limb	8.7g (humerus and ulna shaft fragments)	0.8g (radius shaft fragments and 1x metacarpal shaft)	-	No pathology observed
	Lower limb	46.8g (femur, tibia and fibula shaft, pelvis and navi–cular fragments)	5.0g (femur and fibula shaft fragments)	-	
	Unid. long bone	15.5g	23.1g	0.8g	
	Unid. hand/foot	-	4.3g	0.3g	
	Unid. joint surface	-	3.8g	0.3g	
	Unid. other	-	25.2g	39.1g	
	Unid. total	15.5g	56.4g	40.5g	
6722	Skull	5.9g (cranial vault, maxilla)	1.7g (cranial vault)	0.3g (cranial vault)	
	Axial	0.1g (rib shaft fragments)	2.5g (vertebral and rib shaft fragments)	0.2g (vertebral and rib shaft fragments)	
	Upper limb	3.9g (humerus shaft fragments)	0.2g (inter–mediate hand phalanx)	-	
	Lower limb	-	0.1g (intermediate phalanx)	-	
	Unid. long bone	1.6g	2.8g	-	
	Unid. hand/foot	-	0.4g	-	
	Unid. joint surface	0.3g	1.4g	0.1g	
	Unid. other	-	2.9g	2.7g	
	Unid. total	1.9g	7.5g	2.8g	
	Total	148.7g	137.4g	49.7g	335.8g

The largest proportion of bone came from the 10-4mm sieve fraction in all other deposits. This is unsurprising considering the low bone weights observed. Only small quantities of large (>10mm) bone fragments were observed.

Skeletal representation

Of the identified fragments, bone from the skull was the most frequently observed. The prevalence of skull fragments is a pattern often noted in crema-tion analysis reports because the skull vault is more easily identified than other bones, even within the smaller fractions. Axial skeleton elements (ribs and vertebrae) were also frequently identified.

Most of the recovered bone was unidentified. Smaller proportions of unidentified bone pertained to the upper and lower limbs and hands/feet, but most could not be assigned to any anatomical region. Proportions of unidentified bone ranged from 30.6% (417) to 85.7% (7272) of the total bone weight. As the total weight of bone recovered from burial 7272 was less than 1g, and all fragments measured less than 10mm, high proportions of unidentified bone may be expected. Larger propor-tions of unidentified bone may be expected where fragmentation is high, resulting in difficulty identi-fying the smaller bone fragments to a specific bone.

Efficiency of cremation

The majority of cremated bone from four of the burials were white in colour, with at least 65% of the fragments being white (417, 6711, 6720, 7272). This

Table 5.5 Summary of cremated bone from pit 7272

Deposit	Skeletal region	>10mm	10-4mm	4-2mm	Colour, MNI, age, sex, pathology
7273	Skull	-	-	-	*c* 65% buff-white,
	Axial	-	0.1g (rib shaft fragments)	-	30% blue/grey, 5% black
	Upper limb	-	-	-	MNI = 1
	Lower limb	-	-	-	Unknown age
	Unid. long bone	-	0.1g	-	Unknown sex
	Unid. hand/foot	-	-	-	
	Unid. joint surface	-	0.1g	-	No pathology
	Unid. other	-	0.4g	-	observed
	Unid. total	-	0.6g	-	
	Total	-	0.7g	-	0.7g

Table 5.6 Summary of cremation burial 7408

Deposit	Skeletal region	>10mm	10-4mm	4-2mm	Colour, MNI, age, sex, pathology
7407	Skull	-	2.5g (cranial vault)	1.2g (2x tooth roots, enamel fragment)	*c* 35% buff-white, 35% blue/grey, 10% black, 5% orange, 15% brown
	Axial	-	4.1g (vertebral and rib shaft fragments)	0.9g (rib shaft fragments)	
	Upper limb	-	1.2g (humerus shaft fragments)	-	MNI = 1 Adult Unknown sex
	Lower limb	-	-	-	
	Unid. long bone	1.6g	4.8g	0.1g	No pathology
	Unid. hand/foot	-	0.2g	0.1g	observed
	Unid. joint surface	-	0.1g	0.1g	
	Unid. other	-	0.3g	4.8g	
	Unid. total	1.6g	5.4g	5.1g	
7409	Skull	2.3g (cranial vault, zygomatic process)	2.4g (cranial vault, 1x tooth root)	0.2g (1x tooth roots, enamel fragment)	
	Axial	-	3.4g (vertebral and rib shaft fragments)	0.2g (rib shaft fragments)	
	Upper limb	2.8g (humeral head fragment)	-	-	
	Lower limb	-	0.4g (metatarsal, proximal and distal phalanx fragments)	-	
	Unid. long bone	5.6g	5.2g	-	
	Unid. hand/foot	-	0.3g	-	
	Unid. joint surface	2.9g	1.2g	0.1g	
	Unid. other	-	1.6g	3.0g	
	Unid. total	8.5g	8.3g	3.1g	
	Total	15.2g	27.7g	10.7g	53.6g

indicates a generally efficient cremation process with the majority of bones being burnt at a temperature in excess of 600°c. This is a common observation in most archaeological cremation burials (McKinley 2006, 84) and may indicate that most of the corpse was placed in a location on the pyre where maximum and consistent heat and oxygen supply were available (McKinley 2013, 158). However, this cannot be wholly confirmed as all the recovered bone weights were low and consequently a large proportion of each was absent and unavailable for examination. The remainder of the bone was coloured grey/blue, black, orange and brown, indicating that small proportions of bone were only charred or remained unaffected by heat.

Bone from the remaining burials (6084 and 7408) were much more mixed in terms of colour. Here, less than 50% of the bone was coloured white, with the remaining bone being coloured blue/grey, black, orange and brown. Fragments identified to skeletal region were a variety of colours, indicating that these deposits contained a mixture of totally calcined, charred, and unburnt bone. Notably, several cranial vault fragments from burial 7408 were white (calcined) on the ectocranial surface, but brown/orange on the endocranial surface. This is highly unusual, indicating that the outer surface of the skull had been exposed to high temperatures (over 600°), whilst the interior surface of the skull was barely affected by heat at all.

Prior to the use of modern crematoria, the efficiency of the cremation process would likely to be affected by an assortment of factors, including weather, fuel type and fuel availability. These and other factors may make it difficult to keep a consistently high temperature throughout the cremation pyre for the full duration of time (McKinley 2013, 158). Furthermore, the edges of the pyre may not reach the desired maximum temperature, so regions of the corpse located on the periphery of the pyre may be cremated unevenly (ibid.). Additionally, uncontrollable weather conditions, for example a sudden downpour of rain, may extinguish a pyre before cremation is complete. Experimental work pertaining to pyre technology has suggested that although the main pyre structure tends to burn down in approximately two hours (leaving much in the way of charred remains still retaining soft tissue), the bed of ashes may remain hot for around a further 6-7 hours, during which time the remainder of the soft and hard tissues become oxidised (ibid., 160). Interruption of this process may therefore result in a mixture of burnt, charred, and possibly unburnt remains.

Demography

A minimum number of six adults and one juvenile were identified, based upon the number of discrete deposits observable and identifiable skeletal elements. Osteological indicators of age were very limited, and indicators of biological sex were absent. Of the six adults, specific age could be estimated only for burial 6720, where one fragment of auricular surface of the pelvis was scored at Stage 3 to 4 (after Lovejoy *et al.* 1985), giving an approximate age at death of 30-40 years. Therefore, this adult was classified as a prime-middle aged adult. Several small fragments of juvenile bone were also recovered from this burial. The size and morphology of these fragments suggested a neonate (0-1 months),

although this classification remains tentative as the fragments were so small and few in number.

Non-metric traits and pathology

No evidence of non-metric traits was observed. Pathological evidence was only present in burial 417. Ten fragments of bone from this deposit exhibited evidence of active periosteal new bone formation, indicative of inflammation and/or infection of the periosteum (tissue directly overlaying the cortical surface of the bone; Ortner 2003, 206). Periosteal new bone (or periostitis) is formed as a response to non-specific inflammation of the overlying soft tissue as a result of trauma or other pathological conditions, for example metabolic conditions such as scurvy, neoplastic disease, or specific infectious disease (Resnick and Niyawama 1995; Roberts 2000, 148). In addition, one fragment of vertebral body exhibited marginal osteophytes and evidence of pitting and dense bone formation. The presence of both these indicators suggests the presence of spinal osteoarthritis (Rogers and Waldron 1995, 44).

Pyre/grave goods and pyre debris

Cremation burials occasionally include a number of fragmentary objects that have been burnt on the pyre and included in burial with the bone/ash deposit (Philpott 1991, 8). Burnt animal bone was found in burials 417, 6711 and 6720. Identified species included pig and chicken. Animals were sometimes placed on the funeral pyre as food offerings during the Iron Age and Roman periods and most commonly included pig, along with sheep or goat, ox and domestic fowl (Philpott 1991, 196). The faunal remains identified in the cremations therefore indicate the presence of pyre goods.

Additionally, three fragments of shell were present in burial 417. These comprised one fragment of burnt cockle, one unburnt, unidentified fragment, and one fragment of possible whelk, where it was unclear whether the fragment was burnt or just stained. Cockle shells (as well as oyster and mussel) are occasionally found in Roman cremation burials (ibid.). Other shell types are rarely found in this context.

Unburnt animal bone was also found in the same three burials. The presence of unburnt faunal remains may indicate the presence of grave goods, that is, unburnt items interred with the cremated bone in the grave or as a later deposition event (McKinley 2013, 151). However, the small and fragmentary nature of the unburnt bone, plus truncation of the features, may also indicate that these are residual or have entered the deposits during later periods of disturbance (eg ploughing).

Small charcoal fragments were found within the residues of five deposits from a total of four cremations (417, 6711, 6720 and 7408; Challinor, Chapter 4). This may be debris from the cremation pyre. Where charcoal was found, it was only present in relatively small quantities, in the smaller 4-2mm and 2-0.5mm

Table 5.7 Summary of cremation burial 2522

Deposit	Skeletal region	>10mm	10-4mm	4-2mm	Colour, MNI, age, sex, pathology
2523	Skull	23.7g (cranial vault)	53.9g (cranial vault, maxilla, tooth roots, hyoid)	7.8g (cranial vault)	*c* 80% buff white, 10% grey, 10% black
	Axial	-	11.6g (vertebral and rib shaft fragments)	3.8g (vertebral and rib shaft fragments)	MNI = 1 Adult Unknown sex
	Upper limb	23.1g (humerus, radius and ulna shaft fragments, possible metacarpal shaft fragments)	14.4g (humerus, radius and ulna shaft fragments)	-	Dental caries (small) observed on left maxillary I1, on the mesial aspect of the crown, at the CEJ
	Lower limb	4.6g (femur and tibia shaft fragments)	3.6g (femur, tibia and fibula shaft fragments, distal foot phalanx)	-	Possible periosteal new bone observed on 1x unidentified long
	Unid. long bone	6.3g	56.4g	1.6g	bone fragment
	Unid. hand/foot	-	1.9g	0.1g	
	Unid. joint surface	-	2.2g	0.8g	
	Unid. other	7.0g	110.5g	119.2g	
	Unid. total	13.3g	171.0g	121.7g	
	Total	64.7g	254.5g	133.3g	452.5g

Note: 890.6g of unsorted 2-0.5mm residue also retained. This was not added to the total cremation weight. A sorted 10g sample of this residue produced 0.9g of cremated bone and 0.1g of charcoal.

Table 5.8 Summary of cremation burial 8547

Deposit	Skeletal region	>10mm	10-4mm	4-2mm	2-0.5mm residue	Colour, MNI, age, sex, pathology
8546	Skull	15.1g (vault, temporal and maxillary fragments)	19.8g (vault and tooth root fragments)	0.3g (vault and tooth roots)	-	*c* 70% buff-white, 20% blue/grey, 5% black, 5% brown
	Axial	1.2g (rib and vertebral fragments – CV body)	14.1g (rib and vertebral arch fragments)	0.1g (rib fragments)	-	MNI = 1 Adult
	Upper limb	6.7g (scapula, radius and ulna shaft fragments, proximal phalanx)	3.1g (proximal and distal hand phalanges)	-	-	Unknown sex
	Lower limb	10.0g (femur, tibia and fibula shaft fragments, proximal phalanx)	0.8g (MT head, proximal and intermediate foot phalanges)	-	-	No pathology observed
	Unid. long bone	40.3g	19.2g	-	-	
	Unid. trabecular bone	-	6.2g	-	-	
	Unid. joint surface	3.7g	15.4g	0.2g	-	
	Unid. hand/foot	0g	2.7g	-	-	
	Unid. other	0.1g	138.1g	72.7g*	31.4g*	
	Unid. total	44.1g	181.6g	72.7g*	31.4g*	
	Total	77.1g	219.4g	73.1g*	31.4g*	401.0g*

Key: CV = cervical vertebra, MT = metatarsal Note: The level of fragmentation was high, and the majority of fragments were between 10-4mm in size. The largest fragment was a fragment of unidentified long bone shaft, measuring 44mm in length. * denotes inclusion of estimated bone weights, based on a sorted 20g (4-2mm fraction) or 10g (2-0.5mm fraction) sample sieve fractions. This may indicate that a deliberate attempt to exclude pyre debris was made prior to deposition.

South of Merton

A single cremation burial was found at this site (Table 5.7). The total weight of the cremated deposit was 452.5g. Fragments were predominantly a buff white colour, with lesser quantities of blue/grey and black fragments. Most fragments (85.7% of the total bone weight) were less than 10-4mm in size, the remaining fragments (64.7g, 14.3% of the total bone weight) were over 10mm in size. Fragments of skull (vault, maxilla, teeth and hyoid), axial skeleton (rib shafts and vertebrae), upper limb (humerus, radius, ulna and metacarpal) and lower limb (femur, tibia, fibula and distal phalanx) were identified and accounted for 32.4% of the cremated bone. The minimum number of individuals represented in the deposit was one, and the morphology (thickness) of the identified bone fragments was in keeping with that of an adult individual. It was not possible to estimate sex. One fragment of long bone shaft (either humerus or femur) was observed with periosteal new bone formation (periostitis) on the cortical surface. A single carious lesion was observed on the left maxillary first incisor.

Holts Farm Crossing

Inhumation burial 8109

Skeleton 8107 was less than 25% complete. Represented anatomical regions included the skull, axial skeleton, pelvis, lower limbs and feet, although the axial and pelvic regions were only represented by a few small fragments. Overall, the skeleton was in poor condition with bones that were highly fragmented and bone surfaces that were extensively eroded (consistent with grade 2 after (McKinley 2004a, 16). Specific age at death could not be assigned to the individual because of incompleteness and fragmentation. One fragment of femoral head was observed to be fully fused. This, coupled with the general morphology of the other fragments indicates that the individual is likely to be that of an adult aged over 18 years. Only two fragments of bone exhibited skeletal features that may be used to determine the sex of an individual. Both the supra-orbital ridges and slope of the frontal bone indicated that the individual is that of a possible male. It was not possible to calculate the living stature of the individual, or calculate skeletal indices. No dentition was observable. No cranial or post-cranial non-metric traits or pathology were observed.

Cremation burial 8547

One adult individual of indeterminate sex was represented, comprising fragments from all parts of the skeleton including the skull (cranium, maxilla and tooth roots), torso (ribs and vertebrae), upper and lower limbs, hands and feet (Table 5.8). The deposit weighed a total of 401.0g. Most of the bone fragments were white, with lesser quantities of blue/grey, black and brown fragments. No non-metric traits or pathology were observed.

Chapter 6

Discussion

Introduction

East West Rail Phase 1 followed the clay vale that extends NE-SW across north-east Oxfordshire and separates the limestone hills of the Cotswolds to the north-west from the chalk of the Chilterns to the south-east. This is an area that has seen only limited previous archaeological investigation, in stark contrast to the gravel terraces of the Upper Thames Valley a short distance to the south, which have dominated archaeological research in the Oxford-shire since the 1970s owing to the ongoing impacts of gravel extraction and housing developments (Booth *et al.* 2007; Lambrick with Robinson 2009). Most of the previous excavations in the vale have taken place in advance of residential development on the outskirts of Bicester, at the north-eastern end of the project, revealing elements of an Iron Age and Roman rural landscape (eg Cromarty *et al.* 1999; Ellis *et al.* 2000; Westgarth and Carlyle 2008). EWR Phase 1 afforded an opportunity to investigate part of the south-eastern extramural settlement of the Roman town at Alchester and several Iron Age and Roman rural settlements in the landscape to the south-west.

The investigations experienced the same advantages and disadvantages that characterise all such linear projects; whilst the transect provided by the route provided a random sample of the landscape, the alignment was not selected on archaeological grounds and the investigations were restricted to the footprint of the development. As a result of this, none of the settlements that were investigated were completely explored, as all extended beyond the limits of the development. The excavation areas at East of Oddington Grange, South of Oddington Crossing, North of Gallos Brook and North of Oxford Parkway Station were each limited to the width of the embankment widening, and clearly exposed only a narrow strip across more extensive settlements, and interpretation of the settlement at South of Merton was similarly affected by the exposure being restricted to the width of the new access track. Likewise, the excavations at Langford Lane were limited to the footprint of the road and bridge abutments, exposing a slice through the extramural settlement at Langford Lane East and part of the settlement at Langford Lane South and associated landscape. The excavation at Holts Farm Crossing was more extensive, since it comprised the area of a works compound, but archaeological features were recorded in evaluation trenches to the north and it was clear that the settlement continued further in this direction. In addition to these factors, many of the remains had been affected by trunca-tion by medieval and modern ploughing, as was attested by the evidence for ridge and furrow culti-vation that had been recorded at all the excavations except the Langford Lane sites and North of Oxford Parkway Station.

The character of the landscape, comprising low-lying, poorly-drained ground that is mostly situated on mudstone or alluvium, also provided issues, making excavation difficult in wet conditions, when the high water table resulted in ingress of ground-water into the excavated features. Gleying of feature fills was particularly extensive at Langford Lane East and made it difficult to define stratigraphic relation-ships, particularly in the complexes of shallow, inter-cutting late Iron Age and early Roman pits. The ground conditions may also have impacted on the survival and condition of some classes of artefactual and environmental evidence. Mechanical degrada-tion resulting from movement of the clay soil due to hot-cold and wet-dry cycles may be responsible for the poor preservation of charcoal noted by Challinor (Chapter 4) and for the abraded surfaces of the pottery sherds, to which Booth has attributed the scarcity of recorded instances of burnished decora-tion (Chapter 3). This effect may have been more widespread and perhaps explains the paucity of charred plant remains, since it is surprising that more of the 92 bulk soil samples that were taken over the course of the investigations did not produce signifi-cant assemblages. Perhaps the material had been comminuted to an extent that rendered it impossible to retrieve by sieving. The waterlogged conditions are certainly responsible for the mineral precipitate that encrusted the charred plant remains from Langford Lane South. The high water table had beneficial effects, however, in facilitating preserva-tion of plant and insect remains that would not other-wise have survived, at Langford Lane East, Langford Lane South and North of Oxford Parkway Station.

The high water table is likely to have become a significant factor in determining land use and settle-ment location in the vale during later prehistory, and was certainly important during the Roman period. There have been no studies of the palaeohydrology of the clay vale but it is likely to have followed a similar pattern to the Upper Thames Valley, where the appearance of preserved organic remains and gleyed fills in features dated to the middle Bronze Age indicate that this is when the water table began to rise, possibly as a result of extensive tree clearance (Robinson, with Lambrick 2009, 33). The earliest evidence comes from a pair of ceremonial ditches at Yarnton that contained organic remains that yielded radiocarbon dates ranging from 1630-1320 cal BC to 1420-1210 cal BC, while a very broad, shallow palaeochannel or low-lying area of floodplain at Oxford became submerged in 1010-400 cal BC and at Latton, Gloucestershire, the formation of organic sediments in a palaeochannel which had previously been dry has been dated by radiocarbon to 1376-929 cal BC (Robinson and Lambrick 2009, 29-30). By the middle Iron Age, seasonal inundation was occurring on the lower lying areas of the floodplain and began to deposit alluvium, deposits of which at Yarnton have been dated to 440-170 cal BC and 100 cal BC-cal AD 120, and at Farmoor, floodwater deposited molluscs of flowing water on the ground surface and in the ditches, dated to 229 cal BC-cal AD 80 (Lambrick and Robinson 1979, 111). The damp character of the environment in the clay vale during the Iron Age has been demonstrated by the identification beneath the Roman defences of Alchester of a marsh deposit that contained a few sherds of 'Belgic'-style pottery (Robinson 1975, 165-6). Robinson (ibid., 169) has suggested that the area was effectively drained during the 1st century, giving rise to the drier conditions that are indicated by the environmental evidence from the town's first defensive ditch. Nevertheless, it was found necessary to build up the ground level within the town to maintain it above flood level. Continued rise of the water table is indicated during the late Roman period, however, when a new ditch, which was no deeper than its predecessor, contained permanent water.

Environmental evidence from both ends of EWR Phase 1 clearly points to damp conditions during the Roman period. At the north-eastern end, the mollusc, plant and insect assemblages from the ditches flanking the road at Langford Lane East indicate that both features contained standing or slowly flowing water (Stafford, Meen and Allison, Chapter 4). The eastern ditch was a particularly broad feature, up to 5m wide, which may have been designed to channel the Langford Brook along the side of the road, and contained humic clay lower fills with molluscan and insect assemblages characteristic of clean, clear flowing water. The environment within both ditches is further indicated by the bones of frog/toad. Similar evidence for flowing water was recovered from the eastern ditch of the Alchester to Dorchester-on-Thames road at Langford Lane South. At the south-western end of EWR Phase 1, the plant and insect remains from trackway ditch 3056 at North of Oxford Parkway Station indicated that the feature contained muddy, shallow water.

Considered in the context of the regional pattern of a rising water table, this evidence suggests that the wet environment was one of the defining characteristics of the landscape of the clay vale during the Iron Age and Roman period. The large depth of many of the field ditches that were encountered in the various excavations may indicate that they were dug as much to drain the land as to enclose it, and the evidence from the 1st-century town ditch at Alchester suggests that the strategy was successful, if only temporarily. Such drainage schemes are likely to have been of only local significance, however, designed to ameliorate the environment in the vicinity of individual settlements, and although it has been suggested that Otmoor may have been drained during the Roman period (Robinson 1975, 169), there is no evidence for a large-scale engineering project comparable to that which drained the fens of East Anglia.

Early prehistoric activity

Activity before the middle Iron Age was represented only by a small collection of flint, mostly comprising flakes and other undiagnostic debitage that could only be ascribed to a broad period encompassing the Mesolithic, Neolithic and Bronze Age. The material was distributed thinly across the entire route of EWR Phase 1 and was found at every site except South of Oddington Crossing, although the largest group, from North of Oxford Parkway Station, comprised only 11 pieces. This is typical of the findings of other excavations within the clay vale, where larger assemblages of flint are very much the exception.

Of particular interest was a broken core tool from Holts Farm Crossing. It is probably the butt end of an axe but could date from the lower-middle Palaeolithic, Mesolithic or Neolithic periods, although the last is less likely. Its heavy iron staining, not seen on the other flints, may indicate an early date. A blade core of possible Mesolithic date was found at the same site. Evidence for early Mesolithic activity has previously been found at the north-eastern end of the Improvements, including an assemblage of more than 1000 flints at Slade Farm, Bicester, the composition of which has been interpreted as indicating a winter base camp (Bevan 2000). A smaller assemblage of similar date was recovered at Bicester Fields Farm, most of it from a feature of uncertain origin (Lamdin-Whymark 1999). These sites were located respectively on the limestone upland above the Langford Brook and on the floodplain, indicating that Mesolithic populations were exploiting a range of topographic environments in the area.

Most of the lithic material was recovered either from later features or from the topsoil, and the only instance of a feature that may have been contemporary with the flint it contained was pit 3296 at North of Oxford Parkway Station. This was a modest feature, comprising a bowl-shaped pit 0.6m in diameter and 0.12m deep filled with soil that included fired clay and charcoal flecks from which a single bladelet was recovered. The size and shape of the feature, however, are typical of a class of pits that form a characteristic feature type of the Neolithic period and early Bronze Age (Anderson-Whymark 2012; Lamdin-Whymark 2008). Such pits can occur in large groups, such as the 69 pits at Yarnton (Hey *et al.* 2016) or the group of 35 at Banbury Flood Alleviation Scheme (Simmonds 2013), but in this part of the country they are more commonly found in pairs or as isolated features (Anderson-Whymark 2012). The pits are often the only surviving evidence for occupation and it has been suggested that they were dug as part of a rite of abandonment, their fills comprising material scooped up from a midden or ground surface and buried in order to commemorate the end of a period of occupation or some other significant event in the life of the community. The fired clay and charcoal flecks within the fill of pit 3296 would be consistent with material derived from such a deposit. A closely similar pit was uncovered at Bicester Fields Farm and likewise contained only a single flint blade (Cromarty *et al.* 1999, 157-9).

No material was found that could definitely be dated to the Bronze Age, although an unusual thumbnail scraper from Langford Lane East may be of this date and a backed knife at North of Gallos Brook was attributed broadly to the late Neolithic or early Bronze Age. There is, however, evidence from the surrounding landscape that indicates that a population was present during this period. Cropmark evidence for ring ditches that probably represent plough-levelled barrows has been noted at several locations, including the curvilinear cropmark features at South of Oddington Crossing and at least two features within the complex at Water Eaton (Figs 1.6 and 2.58). The latter examples form part of a group that been recorded at the western end of EWR Phase 1, in the area between Islip, Gosford and Cutteslowe, and appear to represent the northern limit of a scatter of ring ditches that extends along the gravel and clay ridge between the Thames and Cherwell. The only ring ditches in the vicinity of EWR Phase 1 that have been investigated by excavation have been at the eastern end, where two ring ditches of differing sizes were recorded during the evaluation stage at Whitelands Farm (Martin 2011) and a pair of ring ditches excavated at Merton (Bradley *et al.* 1997). None of the ditches was associated with a central burial, but both ditches at Merton enclosed a scatter of cremation burials and the bottom fill of the larger ring ditch at Whitelands Farm comprised a charcoal-rich deposit, possibly from mortuary activity. Further funerary evidence, although not associated with ring ditches, is provided by a Beaker burial at Whitelands Farm (Martin 2011, 186), and a cremation interred in a Deverel-Rimbury vessel at Chesterton Lane (Booth *et al.* 2001, 423). A Food Vessel found near Oddington (Leeds 1939, 245 and plate viia), although not associated with human remains, may also have derived from a burial, but Beaker sherds at Chesterton Lane were from a domestic assemblage (Booth *et al.* 2001, 423).

The sparse scattering of early prehistoric flint-work from the sites suggests that the area experienced a very low level of activity spread over a long period of time. However, the very ubiquity of this material suggests that it should be given greater significance. It is generally accepted that such sparse distributions of material are characteristic of a mobile lifestyle during the early prehistoric period, comprising the hunter-gatherers of the Mesolithic and the pastoralists of the Neolithic and early Bronze Age. Such populations had only a limited archaeologically detectable impact on the environment; as Lambrick with Robinson (2009, 262-5) have argued in relation to some parts of the Upper Thames Valley, the absence of evidence for permanent settlement or clearly defined field systems in the clay vale may indicate that this lifestyle continued until the middle Iron Age, rather than representing an absence of population. The Bronze Age evidence is particularly important in this respect, since the presence of funerary monuments indicates that the area was inhabited despite the complete absence of evidence for settlements. It is possible therefore that the area was inhabited throughout the early prehistoric period by a population who were similarly elusive, who are only made apparent during the Bronze Age by their adoption of archaeologically visible funerary rites. This would mean that the communities living in this part of the landscape diverged significantly from their contemporaries in parts of the Thames Valley, who adopted permanent settlement and large-scale land management in the form of extensive field systems during the middle-late Bronze Age, but instead continued with their traditional low-intensity, residentially-mobile pastoralist traditions for several more centuries.

Middle Iron Age settlement

The absence of evidence for permanent settlement sites or agricultural activity from earlier periods may indicate that it was not until the middle Iron Age that the landscape through which EWR Phase 1 extended was settled by a sedentary population. However, the discovery of four middle Iron Age settlements within the narrow corridor of the project suggests that there may have been a considerable density of settlements at this time. Due to the limited confines of the excavation areas, it is likely that none of the exposed areas represents the entirety of the settlement area; in three instances this is certainly true, since only a very limited exposure was achieved, and although a larger area was opened up at Holts Farm Crossing, the recording of further middle Iron Age features in evaluation trenches to the north of the excavation area suggests that the settlement extended further in this direction. The range of features represented was limited, comprising penannular gullies, occasional shallow pits, and boundary ditches of uncertain significance, and the finds assemblages were similarly circumscribed, limited to small quantities of pottery and animal bone. The only exception to this was the dump of metalworking debris in a boundary ditch at South of Oddington Crossing. Environmental evidence was similarly scarce, the only significant assemblage of charred plant remains coming from a pit at South of Oddington Crossing, although charcoal was encountered more widely. The assemblage from South of Oddington Crossing indicated that wheat and barley were grown. The paucity of domestic refuse and crop processing waste from these sites may simply indicate that such material was being discarded in parts of the settlement that lay beyond the excavation areas, since none of the settlements was fully excavated, or in locations that left no archaeologically detectable evidence such as surface middens. However, remains of this type are rare regionally and it has been suggested that this may be evidence for a predominantly pastoral economy, with only limited cultivation of crops (Lambrick with Robinson 2009, 265).

The material culture from the sites provides very little evidence regarding the character of the settlements and their resident communities. The pottery was entirely handmade and there was no evidence that any of the sherds were not locally made. The material suggests a date range for the settlements of *c* 300 BC-1st century BC, and the radiocarbon date of 200-40 cal BC that was obtained for a sample of charcoal associated with the metalworking deposit at South of Oddington Crossing is consistent with this. The broad similarity of date does not, however, mean that the settlements necessarily had identical histories, and there was in fact clear evidence that they did not. Only at Holts Farm Crossing does the stratigraphic and artefactual evidence indicate continuity of occupation from the middle Iron Age into the Roman period, albeit that the settlement was significantly reorganised during this time. At East of Oddington Grange, it is unclear whether the coincidence of the middle Iron Age gully and the late Iron Age ditches is evidence for continuity between the periods or whether the earlier settlement had been abandoned for some time before the location was reused. The settlements at South of Oddington Crossing and North of Gallos Brook, on the other hand, certainly did not survive beyond the end of the middle Iron Age. Indeed, Booth (Chapter 3) has argued that the absence of grog-tempered fabrics at North of Gallos Brook may indicate that occupation ceased sometime before the end of the period, since such vessels are a characteristic component of other Iron Age assemblages in the Bicester area.

A discontinuity of occupation at the end of the middle Iron Age, as seen at South of Oddington Crossing and North of Gallos Brook, appears to be a common feature of settlements in the Bicester area. The settlement at Chesterton Lane that was initially investigated by Harden (1937) and subsequently partly exposed at Sites B and C of the dualling of the

A41 certainly does not appear to have continued beyond this date, since diagnostically late Iron Age pottery is almost entirely absent (Booth *et al.* 2001, 423-4). Similarly, the settlement at Slade Farm was abandoned and only the boundary ditch beside which it was situated continued in use, until sometime in the 1st century AD (Ellis *et al.* 2000, 265). The corollary of settlement abandonments at the end of the middle Iron Age is, of course, the inception of new settlements as part of the late Iron Age settlement pattern, although the sites may not be direct successors. This can be seen at the A41 dualling, where a settlement was established *de novo* during the late Iron Age at Site D, *c* 300m north of the middle Iron Age settlement, and at Oxford Road, Bicester, where occupation began at a similar date (Booth *et al.* 2001, 424; Mould 1996, 105-6). The recovery of residual middle Iron Age pottery from later features at Bicester Fields Farm is likely to indicate that activity of some sort began at the end of this period, but no features could be ascribed to this period and the main phase of occupation occurred during the late Iron Age (Cromarty *et al.* 1999, 224). Recent excavations at Graven Hill have uncovered a group of middle Iron Age enclosures, possibly of domestic character, and an area of late Iron Age settlement situated *c* 500m apart (OA 2016a; 2016b). The reason for this episode of settlement dislocation is unknown, and it is of course possible that it simply reflects the varied fortunes of the communities who inhabited them, although Lambrick (1992, 83) has identified this horizon as a period of settlement shift on the Thames gravels, which may hint at a more widespread phenomenon.

Two particular deposits, at North of Gallos Brook and Holts Farm Crossing, stand out as providing slight but nonetheless intriguing evidence for significant events within the settlement. The instance at North of Gallos Brook comprised the apparently deliberate placing of two vessels within penannular gully 106. One was burnished and may have been a globular bowl, while its companion was limestone-tempered and straight-walled. The upper parts of both vessels were missing, most likely as a result of plough-truncation of the gully, which survived to a depth of no more than 0.20m, but they may have been complete when deposited. The only associated finds were a single pig tooth and a few crumbs of unidentifiable animal bone, but the charcoal assemblage from within the limestone-tempered vessel was comprised entirely of oak and probably came from 'tree(s) of grand size and age' (Challinor, Chapter 4). A similar charcoal assemblage was recovered from pit 8066 at Holts Farm Crossing, a very shallow feature close to the centre of penannular gully 8701, and this deposit was likewise associated with pig remains, in this case represented by three lower limb bones and a large number of unidentifiable fragments from a soil sample. Only a single small sherd of pottery was present in this feature, but the broad similarity between the two deposits suggests that they may be the debris from similar or related events, perhaps involving the consumption of pig cooked on fires that were fuelled by wood that was selected from a presumably valuable source. These episodes could represent feasting in a ritualised context or more mundane consumption, but the association with the deliberately placed vessels at North of Gallos Brook may indicate that, in this instance at least, the former interpretation is more likely. The deposition of the material within the penannular gully suggests that this event may have occurred at the end of the feature's use, and may therefore have been associated with the abandonment of the structure.

Settlement forms

Although none of the settlements was completely exposed, and in three instances the excavations were limited to only a narrow trench, sufficient evidence was uncovered to draw some conclusion regarding their forms, complemented at East of Oddington Grange, South of Oddington Crossing and North of Gallos Brook by the evidence provided by cropmarks. The most obvious observation is that none of the settlement areas was surrounded by an enclosure ditch, although enclosures that lay beyond the excavation areas may have formed an element of the settlements. The contemporary settlements at Chesterton Lane and Slade Farm were likewise unenclosed, perhaps indicating a local preference for this arrangement in the Bicester area. Settlement forms during this period were quite variable, with both open forms and various types of enclosed settlement attested at numerous sites. The open form need not, however, imply that the settlements lacked spatial organisation, and the linear boundary ditch at Holts Farm Crossing may be evidence for a greater level of spatial division than is otherwise apparent from the surviving features. The settlement at North of Gallos Brook was also associated with a boundary ditch, although the ditch cut penannular gully 112 and may therefore have post-dated the occupation. In this instance the ditch may be associated with an extensive boundary that had previously been recorded from aerial photographic evidence, although the correspondence of its alignment with that of the cropmark as plotted is not exact (Fig. 2.54).

The most characteristic element of the settlements was represented by penannular gullies, which were recorded at three of the four sites. Such features are commonplace on settlements of the period and are likely to have defined the locations of roundhouses, although some may have served as animal pens. By this period the post-ring framework that characterised the construction of Bronze Age roundhouses had been replaced by structures that are typically represented by a penannular gully with few, if any, internal features. Such gullies are variously interpreted as either a trench that supported a wall of vertical timbers or a drainage feature intended to prevent surface water from gathering at the foot of the walls and to catch rainwater dripping from the eaves. The latter interpretation would suggest that the walls took a form that has left no archaeologically detectable evidence, such as some form of mass wall construction. The partial survival of gullies 1104 and 8701 at Holts Farm Crossing precludes detailed discussion, except to note that the latter had a segmented construction, as did the more complete gully 8563. Both 8701 and 8563 had a small number of internal postholes that support interpretation as the locations of roundhouses. Segmented construction of roundhouse gullies has been identified elsewhere, including Structure 4 at Slade Farm, which had two breaks on the north-west side and one on the south-east (Ellis *et al.* 2000, 227), and Structures 12 and 13 at Claydon Pike (Miles *et al.* 2007, 63 and fig. 3.11). All of these examples are similar to gully 8563 in that an excessively wide entrance appears to have been (subsequently?) mitigated by the insertion of a separate section of gully that was not joined to the rest of the circuit. The reason for this arrangement is uncertain, but in the case of gully 8563 no break was left that was wide enough to serve as an entrance into the building, suggesting that the gully was instead bridged by means of a plank or similar arrangement. Gully 8563 measured 11.8 x 10.7m and gully 8701 appears to have been rather large at *c* 16m in diameter. Both would therefore have comfortably accommodated a single roundhouse, which were typically up to 14m in diameter with an average of 8m (Pope 2008, 17). Four penannular gullies were uncovered at North of Gallos Brook, although none was completely exposed within the limits of the excavation area, and no internal postholes survived. Gullies 106, 107 and 110/111 were shallow but quite regular in plan and measured 8.5-10m in diameter and were interpreted as the locations of roundhouses. Gully 112, which did not intersect with the others, appeared to be slightly different, comprising a more substantial feature with a less regular shape that had relatively straight sides and curved corners hinting at a possible sub-rectangular or polygonal form. This variance in form may indicate a different function, perhaps as an animal pen, although it is alternatively possible that the larger size of the ditch was intended to emphasise the importance of the building within.

The arrangement of the gullies varied between sites and may indicate that the internal organisation of the settlements was similarly different. At Holts Farm Crossing, the structures were widely spaced, gully 8563 lying 55m east of gully 8701, with gully 1104 30m to the north, whereas the gullies at North of Gallos Brook were close together and three of them intersected. The latter arrangement demonstrated that the gullies were not contemporary but represented a sequence of structures, perhaps representing a single roundhouse that was rebuilt on two occasions on slightly different footprints. A similar situation was encountered north of Bicester, at Finmere Quarry, where a linear arrangement of eight penannular gullies, with some intercutting, was interpreted as a settlement of two or three buildings that were periodically rebuilt (Hart *et al.* 2010, 102-3). A little further afield, a clearer example of this phenomenon is provided by Claydon Pike, Gloucestershire, where three gravel islands separated by marshy ground were occupied sequentially; stratigraphic relationships demonstrated that only three or four of the seven or eight buildings on Island 3 could have been occupied at the same time, and two linear arrangements of penannular gullies on Island 2 appear to have similarly resulted from successive rebuilding of a smaller number of contemporary buildings (Miles *et al.* 2007, 59-60). The unsuitability of the surrounding land at Claydon Pike meant that only a restricted area was available for occupation, as a result of which the close proximity of the successive buildings was a necessity. It is possible that the repeated reuse of approximately the same location for the roundhouse at North of Gallos Brook could likewise be explained by some unidentified restriction on land availability. Indeed, the buildings at Finmere Quarry were arranged alongside a linear boundary ditch and, if the boundary at North of Gallos Brook later represented by ditch 265 existed in some form during the period when the settlement was occupied, it is possible that at both sites the buildings were situated beside a boundary to avoid impinging on the agricultural land beyond.

It is, of course, possible that the buildings at Holts Farm Crossing were similarly sequential, albeit built at distinctly different locations, but this is not capable of proof. If they were in contemporary use, their physical separation may indicate that they represent discrete social units within the community that occupied the settlement. Such an argument was made regarding the rather more densely-occupied settlement at Gravelly Guy, where the spatial arrangement of the features and the distribution of some categories of artefact were used to identify five or six possible domestic units (Lambrick and Allen 2004, 152-5). If the arrangement of the buildings at Holts Farm Crossing has similar significance regarding the organisation of the community, the same may apply at Slade Farm, where the spacing of the roundhouses is not dissimilar.

The significance of the apparently rectilinear arrangement of the ditches at South of Oddington Crossing is uncertain, although it seems reasonable to infer that they formed the corner of a rectilinear enclosure. Such a structure need not have enclosed an area of domestic occupation, since other functions are possible, although it is unlikely to have existed in isolation and was most likely associated with an area of occupation that lay somewhere nearby. The absence of evidence for buildings or of significant quantities of domestic refuse within the ditches may indicate that these features lay on the periphery of the postulated settlement.

The excavated evidence and the cropmark enclosures

Although the areas of occupation that were exposed within the excavations were not themselves enclosed, the sites at East of Oddington Grange, South of Oddington Crossing and North of Gallos Brook were each situated in proximity to cropmark evidence for enclosures that may have formed an element of the settlement. The most intriguing example was at North of Gallos Brook, where the excavated features were situated just 20-25m from the cropmark of an irregular enclosure with an annexe, with a D-shaped enclosure *c* 150m to the south (Figs 1.6 and 2.54). The enclosures have not been investigated by excavation and are therefore undated, but it would not be unreasonable to propose a middle Iron Age date based on the similarity of their size and shape to other enclosures in the region (eg Moore 2006, 45-57). If the enclosures are indeed contemporary with the excavated evidence, then the close proximity of the irregular enclosure to the penannular gullies would suggest a close relationship between them. This arrangement finds a close parallel at Silverstone Site 3, *c* 25km north-east of Bicester, where a group of roundhouses and ditched pens were situated adjacent to a larger ditched enclosure (Mudd 2007, 9-25). A little less than half the enclosure was excavated, uncovering a single roundhouse that had been rebuilt at least three times. This rebuilding clearly indicates some considerable longevity for the structure, which may therefore have been a significant building within the settlement, but there was otherwise no certain evidence to indicate whether occupation within the enclosure was of different status to that outside it (ibid., 167). The D-shaped enclosure at North of Gallos Brook was too far distant to be part of the same settlement, but may represent a neighbouring settlement. Indeed, the site at Silverstone 3 similarly lay only *c* 250m from a broadly contemporary enclosed settlement at Silverstone Site 2.

The excavation area at East of Oddington Grange lay on the north side of the existing railway embankment, with the cropmark of a possible banjo enclosure situated on the south side (Figs 1.5 and 2.50). The cropmark in fact appears to comprise two large, curvilinear enclosures with a ditched trackway running between them, but in the absence of excavation it is not possible to be certain of the relationship between these elements, or their respective dates. Identification as a banjo enclosure is therefore somewhat speculative, albeit this designation is recorded in the Oxfordshire Historic Environment Record (entry HER 15963). The cropmark of the enclosure closest to the railway is not complete, as it becomes indiscernible to the north, corresponding with a change in the underlying geology from alluvium to mudstone. The projected alignment, however, indicates that it should extend across the railway and encompass part of the excavated trench, but no evidence for it was found, unless it is represented by late Iron Age ditch 44. It is therefore uncertain whether the enclosure is potentially contemporary with the penannular gully recorded in the excavation, since the enclosure either does not extend as far as the excavation area or is of late Iron Age date.

Similar difficulties apply to the cropmark features at South of Oddington Crossing, which appear to represent part of two conjoined or intersecting curvilinear enclosures immediately north of the excavation area but for which no evidence was found within the trench. Neither cropmark preserves the entire circuit of the enclosure ditch, unless the enclosures were open to the south. The north-western enclosure, which is the more complete of the pair, measures *c* 35m wide, which is too large for a roundhouse drip-gully but may represent an animal pen or a small settlement enclosure, and a superficial resemblance to the category of 'pen and paddock' pastoral settlements that Lambrick has described, comprising conjoined enclosures and exemplified by the instances at Farmoor and Gill Mill, cannot be dismissed (Lambrick with Robinson 2009, 109-15). Since the features within the excavated area did not appear to represent an area of domestic occupation, it is possible that they comprised peripheral activity associated with a settlement that was focused on the cropmark enclosures, but this is entirely speculative. On the other hand, given that the date of the features has not been established, an alternative interpretation as Bronze Age ring ditches cannot be ruled out.

Metalworking at South of Oddington Crossing

The deposit of metalworking debris in ditch 153 adds to the corpus of sites in the region that have produced evidence for Iron Age copper or bronze working, in this instance dated by radiocarbon to 200-40 cal BC. At least two crucibles were present, the relatively shallow, triangular form of which is comparable to contemporary examples from Mingies Ditch (Salter 1993, fig. 36, no. 8) and Thrupp near Radley (Ainslie 1992, fig. 3). They were designed to hold a small charge of metal and were inserted into a hearth and heated from above (Bayley and Rehren 2007, 49). The rim shape provided three spouts to facilitate decanting the melted contents into a mould. The metals processed at South of Oddington Crossing were unleaded tin bronzes but the details of the process are uncertain. The slightly elevated iron content in the metal residue in crucible 2 may indicate that the vessel was used for alloying of copper by the addition of cassiterite, but there was insufficient evidence to confirm this and the iron may have derived from the burial environment, perhaps from the smithing debris within the deposit. It is equally possible (and in the case of crucible 1 perhaps more likely) that

disused bronze objects were being melted down to cast into new items.

Evidence for copper or bronze working has been recorded at a range of sites in the region, including Gravelly Guy (Lambrick and Allen 2004), Mingies Ditch (Salter 1993), Thrupp (Ainslie 1992) and Yarnton (Hey *et al.* 2011). The apparently widespread occurrence of bronze working at these sites, none of which is of especially high status, suggests that it was conducted within local communities and was not subject to any form of centralised control. Gravelly Guy is unusual for the quantity of evidence, but it is not clear whether this represents a greater concentration of production or whether it is a consequence of the unusual completeness of excavation. It is unclear, therefore, to what extent metalworking was a specialised activity, and the remains at South of Oddington and elsewhere could equally represent production by members of the individual settlements or the work of itinerant craftworkers. The association of bronze working debris with smithing slag that was evident at South of Oddington has also been noted elsewhere, including Mingies Ditch (Salter 1993) and Thrupp (Ainslie 1992, 63). It is uncertain whether this indicates that the two materials were being worked by the same craftworker, or perhaps as part of a single item, or whether it simply represents opportunistic use of the ditch as a convenient place to dispose of debris from separate activities. Certainly from the middle Iron Age onward composite artefacts combining bronze and iron (as well as enamel) were being created to produce items of particularly high prestige value such as scabbard chapes and horse gear.

Direct evidence for the precise location within the site where the metalworking was conducted is rare since, as at South of Oddington Crossing, the evidence typically comprises crucibles discarded in a secondary context. Previous studies have stressed the significance of the location of metalworking at the periphery of sites, which has been interpreted as being a suitably liminal location for such apparently magical transformative processes (Hingley 1997). A more recent analysis, based on a considerably larger number of sites, did not find such a pattern, however (Webley *et al.* forthcoming), and in some cases, at least, the apparent emphasis of metalworking residues on peripheral locations may be a product of excavation strategies that focus on the ditches enclosed the settlement.

Roman Alchester and its agricultural hinterland

The development of settlement on the southern outskirts of Alchester

Organisation of the landscape south of Alchester

The cropmark survey of the environs of Alchester that was undertaken by RCHME during the 1990s demonstrated that the landscape around the town was enclosed by a network of ditched boundaries of varying arrangement and complexity. The geophysical survey undertaken at Langford Lane produced disappointing results, which did not add significantly to the cropmark data, but the excavation of a transect across the area south of the town at Langford Lane has provided valuable detail that has contributed usefully to our understanding of the landscape and will be discussed here before moving onto a more detailed consideration of the part of the extramural settlement uncovered at Langford Lane East and the farmstead and landscape divisions at Langford Lane South. A great deal of effort appears to have been expended to create a managed landscape defined by the watercourses, roads and boundary ditches.

Watercourses

The fortress and later town at Alchester occupied most of the area of a narrow gravel terrace between the Langford Brook and a minor tributary, the Gagle Brook. It is inconceivable that its proximity to the two channels was coincidental and presumably the site was deliberately chosen in order to provide access to a ready supply of fresh water, and initially perhaps also to exploit the streams and their boggy floodplains for their defensive potential. It is unlikely that the Langford Brook was large enough to be navigable, but it is recorded that in 1764 a coal barge came as far up the River Ray as Arncott Bridge (Lobel 1957, 15). It would thus have been possible to use the waterways to bring provisions to within a few kilometres of Alchester before resorting to land for the final part of the journey, though there is no definite evidence for use of the river in the Roman period, and a wider regional review has suggested that even use of the upper Thames as a communication artery was probably quite limited (Booth *et al.* 2007, 313). The watercourses would, however, have provided the main impediment to the exploitation of the surrounding landscape and it was necessary to integrate them into the scheme of drainage channels and boundaries by which the countryside was brought under management.

The Langford Brook extends around the north side of Graven Hill then turns sharply southward, passing within less than 500m of Alchester. It flows alongside Langford Lane and is likely to have followed the road's Roman predecessor in a similar fashion. The section excavated across the road at Langford Lane East demonstrated that the eastern roadside ditch was a substantial channel up to 5m wide and 0.7m deep, completely different to the ditch on the west side, and indeed all the other roadside ditches excavated during the project, and was presumably created thus specifically to canalise the brook. The molluscan evidence from the ditch is unequivocal that it held flowing water. The channel has since migrated to the west of the Roman road and cuts obliquely across the cropmarks of the field system on an alignment that is clearly more recent

in origin, towards its ultimate confluence with the River Ray south of Merton.

Gagle Brook approaches Alchester from the north-west and flows along the line of the former town ditch on the west and south sides of the town toward its confluence with the Langford Brook. It is possible that Roman engineers deliberately channelled it into the ditch in order to provide a moat around the town, since environmental evidence from the 1975 excavation of the defences indicated that the late Roman ditch was permanently filled with water (Robinson 1975, 169). Thence it may have flowed along approximately its modern alignment (or perhaps along an east-west boundary indicated by a cropmark and corresponding to ditch 7069 at Langford Lane East) to a confluence with the Langford Brook east of the town.

An unnamed stream branches off the Gagle Brook south-east of Alchester and flows south-west across the field system south of the town before joining the Langford Brook north of Merton (Fig. 6.1). There is good reason to believe that the current arrangement is much as it was during the Roman period, and that parts are a direct result of engineering of the channels associated with the wider organisation of the landscape around Alchester. The stream proceeds south-westward for *c* 800m on an alignment that may be entirely natural and may have been its course when the Roman land divisions were laid out, since the enclosures on the north-west side appear to respect it. The stream then enters an area where it follows the alignment of boundaries that are demonstrably of Roman date, where it may have been canalised when the field system was constructed. The first element is a very straight north-south section that coincides with a cropmark boundary that extends from the south-eastern corner of the walled town, continuing the alignment of the east wall. The south end of this section turns west at a right angle into a channel that preserves part of the alignment of an east-west boundary that was recorded at Langford Lane South as ditch 2327 (Fig. 2.24). It is not clear how or where the stream crossed the Alchester-Dorchester road. Presumably there was a fording point, but it did not lie where the modern intersection is located, as the excavation demonstrated that the drainage ditches flanking the road were continuous at this point. The modern channel cuts obliquely across the road, after which it returns to alignments that are Roman in origin, following a series of right-angled turns that include the alignment of excavated ditch 2455 and two east-west boundaries that have been recorded as cropmarks. The final section before it rejoins the Langford Brook extends for a little under 800m on a north-south alignment that, although irregular in places, remains broadly parallel to the road and may therefore also represent a boundary that originally formed part of the field system. It is likely that this route through the boundaries of the field system represents only the surviving part of a more complex arrangement that originally was divided

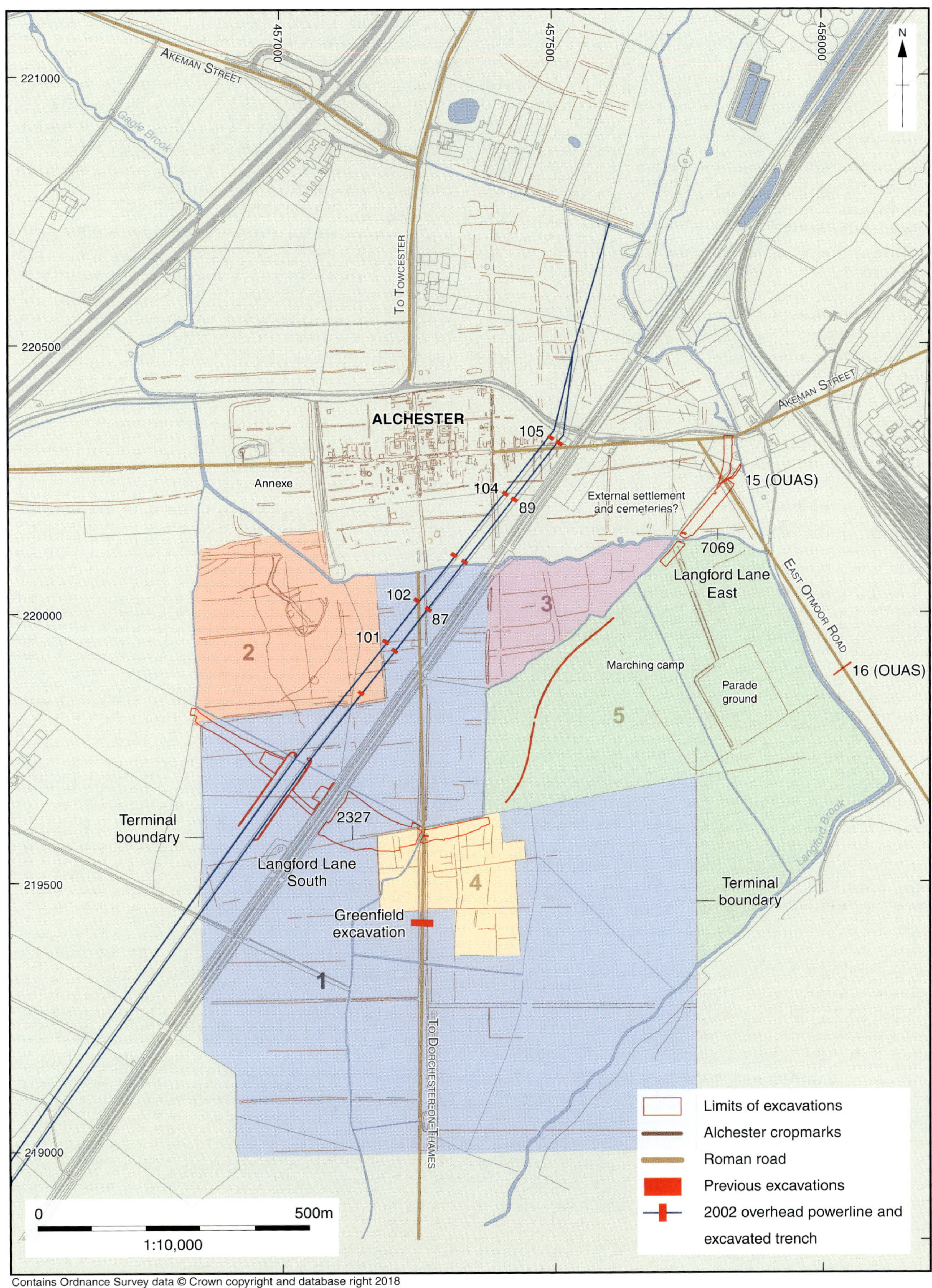

Contains Ordnance Survey data © Crown copyright and database right 2018

Fig. 6.1   Organisation of the landscape south of Alchester

247

and channelled through the network of drainage ditches, the other channels of which have silted up. The antiquity of the surviving channel is demonstrated, however, by its status as the boundary between the parishes of Wendlebury and Merton.

Akeman Street

As mentioned above, the principal route of Akeman Street passed to the north of the fortress and subsequent town at Alchester. The fact that there is no direct relationship between this road line and the fortress/town raises interesting questions of chronology. The road alignment is clearly laid out with a strategic purpose and is evidently early in date. It would typically be assumed that the siting of Alchester was a secondary element in the local settlement pattern, were it not for the dendrochronology date from the military annexe gate which suggests that the fortress was almost certainly the primary Roman feature in this landscape. The ideal course of Akeman Street must have been understood not to involve the specific location of the fortress, but to lie sufficiently close to it to allow ready access between the two, with the fortress and later town accessed by a road running round the north side of Graven Hill and then taking an east-west line, approximately mirrored by part of the line of Langford Lane, to enter an east gate (assuming that the locations of the later 2nd-century town gates reflected approximately those of the fortress, which seems likely). North of Alchester there can be little doubt that the line of Akeman Street is followed fairly closely by the modern Chesterton Lane, as shown by the 1991 excavations (at least from the line of north-south Wendlebury Lane (Alchester-Towcester road) westwards, eg Booth *et al.* 2001, fig. 5.2) and that there is a significant change of alignment in Chesterton itself, the northernmost point of the entire road, where Akeman Street assumes its principal course, slightly south of west, to head towards Cirencester. It is less clear, however, that this 'ideal' alignment was maintained east of the junction with Wendlebury Lane between this point and the position of the road on the northern slopes of Graven Hill. If it had been, it is likely that this alignment was not maintained in the long term. For example, the excavation at Faccenda Chicken Farm (Foreman and Rahtz 1984) provided no indication of the roadside settlement comparable to that seen less than 100m further west, although ditch alignments, and indeed a modern boundary, suggested some continuation in an ESE direction of the line notionally followed by the road. It is clear that the eastern approach to Alchester via (in part) Langford Lane was preferred in the long term, and it is just possible that this was the case from the very beginning, perhaps recognising the fact that part of the 'ideal' road alignment was not practicable because of the poorly-drained nature of some of the terrain that it had to cross.

In its developed form what may best be termed the Akeman Street diversion exited Alchester via the east gate and extended in a straight line as far as the Langford Brook, beyond which it took a slightly more north-easterly route to bypass the north side of Graven Hill. The route between Alchester eastwards to Wretchwick Farm was described in some detail by Hussey (1841, 22-3) before it became obscured by the construction of MOD Bicester on the lower slopes of the hill, and part of the road was recently sectioned on the north side of Graven Hill (OA 2016a; 2016b). Closer to Alchester, the road surface was exposed in a trench dug in 2002 at the location of one of the post settings for a new overhead powerline, a short distance outside the town's east gate (Wessex Archaeology 2002, 12). The watching brief conducted during stripping of the new road alignment through the area of the scheduled monument east of the town exposed part of the metalled surface beneath the southern edge of the carriageway of the modern Langford Lane. The road surface was a compacted layer of limestone pieces and survived only in a linear band no more than 1.45m wide, cut to the north by the construction cut for the modern road and to the south by the modern roadside drainage ditch. The road surface sloped down to the east, where there was presumably a ford across the Langford Brook, which lay only a few metres away.

The Alchester to Dorchester-on-Thames road

The roads excavated at Langford Lane East and Langford Lane South appear to represent two successive iterations of the route southward to Dorchester-on-Thames, the road at Langford Lane East having been constructed around the middle of the 1st century and the one at Langford Lane South at the end of the century. The earlier, eastern route was first noted by Hussey (1841, 25), branching off Akeman Street and extending to the south-east in the direction of Boarstall along the line of Langford Lane. He did not present any specific evidence for the Roman origin of the road, in contrast to his detailed descriptions of the visible remains of the other roads that he discussed, and it is likely that he had no direct evidence and inferred the date from the striking straightness of this part of the lane, which extends for some 2.5km as far as Astley Bridge Farm. A cropmark of the part of the road that ran alongside the modern Langford Lane was noted by Sauer (1999b, 62-3), who observed that a date during the military phase was suggested by its alignment, which differs from those of most of the Roman elements of the landscape and is shared only by the marching camp and parade ground. Under his direction, Oxford University Archaeological Society dug two trenches across the road in 1998 that confirmed its form and Roman origin (Trenches 15 and 16, Fig. 6.1). The excavation at Langford Lane East exposed a 22m-long stretch of the road, which comprised a metalled surface 9.5m wide of cobbles set in a sandy matrix, constructed directly on the gravel substrate with wheel ruts clearly visible and flanking ditches on either side.

The early date of the road was confirmed by a group of pottery from the lower part of the western ditch, which consisted mostly of 'Belgic'-type wares but also contained a substantial part of a South Gaulish samian ware bowl of form Ritterling 12, which is unlikely to date after the early Flavian period. The ditches were rather contrasting in character, the western ditch being a typical V-shaped feature but its eastern counterpart being a wide channel some 5m across. OUAS's excavation had encountered a similar disparity, leading Sauer (ibid.) to suggest that the engineers who designed the road may have deliberately channelled the adjacent branch of the Langford Brook along the side of the road. Confirmation of this interpretation was provided by the range and abundance of freshwater molluscs and by the insect assemblage, in which *Coelostoma orbiculare* and *Hygrotus inaequalis* suggest very shallow, still or slowly flowing water, with an occasional throughput of clean, clear, running water indicated by the riffle beetle *Oulimnius* (Stafford and Allison, chapter 4).

The destination of this road has not been demonstrated, but it may represent a part of the N-S route from Towcester to Silchester that bypassed Otmoor on its eastern side. Such a N-S connection would surely have been necessary from the outset to link the two E-W routes that extended along either side of the Thames Valley, represented by Akeman Street and the road from London to Bath, and the direct route across Otmoor does not appear to have been constructed until the end of the 1st century (below). Alchester and Dorchester represented neighbouring stations on this route, separated by a distance of *c* 25km, or one day's travel. The precise route that was taken around the east side of Otmoor is uncertain and may be irrevocably lost. It must have crossed the River Ray beyond Astley Bridge Farm, after which there is no definite trace, although a series of field boundaries that form the parish boundary between Fencot and Murcot and Arncot appear to continue the alignment as far as Boarstall Lane. Although the intervening course is lost, the alignment of the appositely named Straight Mile Road may indicate that it represents the southern part of the route, between Horton-cum-Studley and Woodperry, whence it curved southward to pass to the east of Oxford and thus on to Dorchester. There was no definite evidence from the excavation that the road was maintained after the 2nd century, although the latest recuttings of the roadside ditches lacked dating evidence and may have been later. The roadside occupation certainly did not continue long if at all after *c* 200, and Sauer (ibid., 63) suggested that the road may have been abandoned due to flooding, since it was buried beneath *c* 0.80m of alluvial sediment. It seems a reasonable supposition that the road may have been reduced in significance once the direct route across Otmoor was constructed, but its apparent partial survival as features in the historic landscape suggests that it survived beyond the Roman period

and perhaps continued in use until severed by the construction of Boarstall Lane. The suggestion that an early version of the north-south road ran west rather than east of Otmoor (Cheetham 1995, 422-35) is more speculative, though such a route could represent local alternatives to the easterly line indicated by the present evidence.

The direct route across Otmoor to Dorchester was excavated at Langford Lane South and South of Merton. Its route had previously been described in detail by Hussey (1841) and can be traced on Ordnance Survey maps, following a perfectly straight alignment from the south gate of Alchester and across Otmoor before climbing out of the clay vale at Beckley. It clearly represents a shorter journey than the putative eastern route and a date for its construction sometime shortly after AD 95 is provided by a dendrochronology date from a timber pile from a bridge that carried it across the River Ray at Murcott (Chambers 1986a). The road had previously been sectioned 140m south of Langford Lane South in 1967 by Ernest Greenfield (Chambers 1987), on the Corallian Ridge at Beckley in 1986 (ibid., 185) and east of Oxford at Open Magdalen Wood in 1958 (Linington 1959), as well as in investigations at the southern end near Dorchester (Chambers 1986b).

Hussey recorded the road at Alchester as an upstanding earthwork raised on an agger 2.5 feet (*c* 0.75m) high and described it as 'a high ridge, which is continued through the meadows to the south' (Hussey 1841, 5) and as being 'still plainly raised above the level of the ground on each side' as it crossed the central part of Otmoor between Fencott and Beckley (ibid, 7). However, the construction of the section from Alchester and across Otmoor is in fact more complex than this and appears to have been deliberately engineered to accommodate its situation on the floodplains of the Langford Brook and River Ray. The road was typically built on an upstanding agger, which created a low causeway that would have served to raise the level of the road and facilitate drainage of the surface, which may have been particularly important in the wetland environment of the clay vale. However, the causeway was interrupted by numerous breaks that are clearly visible on LiDAR survey, dividing the section between Alchester and the Ray into segments that vary in length from *c* 50-170m. South of the river, the construction of the road appears to continue in this vein, although it is obscured by medieval ridge and furrow earthworks. The parts of the road that were investigated at Langford Lane South and South of Merton both correspond with such breaks, which explains the absence of any evidence for an agger in the excavated sections. The metalled road surface at Langford Lane South was constructed directly on the surface of the gravel substrate and so the lack of a causeway here clearly represents the engineers' intention for this part of the road rather than resulting from a subsequent loss of material. The purpose of the breaks was presumably to allow floodwaters to pass, thus preventing the road from acting as a dam during periods of inundation and exacerbating flooding upstream. A similar situation was recorded at Irchester, where excavation in 1989 identified one end of a break in the agger of a road that approached the Roman town across the flood-plain of the River Nene, beyond which, as at Langford Lane South, the road was constructed directly on the surface of the valley gravels instead of on an upstanding causeway (Keevill and Williams 1995).

William Stukeley recorded the break in the causeway at Langford Lane South in his engraving (Fig. 1.3) and described the road in Wandlebury Meadow (*sic*), between Alchester and the Langford Brook, as being represented only by denudation of the grass over the metalled surface, with the agger not beginning until the road reached the pasture to the south of the brook (Stukeley 1776, 40). This segment of causeway was excavated by Greenfield, who recorded that it had been constructed on the surface of the contemporary topsoil using topsoil and subsoil cast up from the digging of the drainage ditches to create an earthwork that, in 1967, still survived to a height of 0.5-0.9m (Chambers 1987, 183). No metalling was identified at South of Merton, where the alignment of the road was defined only by the flanking drainage ditches, a situation that was also noted when part of the align-ment of the road immediately to the south was stripped during the construction of the M40 (Chambers 1992, 48). This was attributed at the time to the Roman engineers utilising the surface of the limestone brash geology that outcrops in this area as the road surface, with no need for further metalling, and such an explanation is still appropriate.

Landscape division south of Alchester

A substantial area south of Alchester was enclosed during the Roman period and divided into an organised agricultural landscape. It was defined by ditched boundaries whose arrangement has been recorded by cropmark evidence, and detail regarding the character of the boundaries is provided by the excavations at Langford Lane. The excavated boundary ditches were found to be substantial features, up to 0.85m deep, and they were probably designed to drain the land in addition to enclosing and dividing it. The bound-aries were aligned on the boundaries of the town and on the alignment of the road from Alchester to Dorchester-on-Thames. The inception of the scheme cannot therefore pre-date the construction of the road, which is attributed to sometime shortly after AD 95, and it is considered likely that the division of the landscape was undertaken at the same time or very shortly after. The pottery from the excavated ditches mostly dated from the 2nd century, with a small quantity of 3rd century material, presumably representing the period over which the ditches silted up. It is, of course, possible

that the boundaries continued in use after the ditches had silted, especially if the ditches were supplemented by hedgerows, as is indicated by the stones of dogwood and buckthorn in roadside ditch 4158 and the insect assemblage from ditch 2455 at Langford Lane South. The silting of the ditches would, however, have removed their utility for drainage and may have contributed to the wetter environment during the later part of the Roman period that was noted by Robinson (1975, 165-6). The arrangement of the boundaries strongly suggests that they were conceived as a single, integrated scheme and it appears to have remained substantially unaltered, with possible evidence for re-organisation limited to the area adjacent to the south-western corner of the town. There are, however, clear variations in the arrangement of different parts of the scheme, which have here been divided into five broad areas (Areas 1-5, Fig. 6.1).

The main axis of the boundaries was provided by the line of the road to Dorchester-on-Thames and the limits of the enclosed land were divided by two ditches, here termed the western and eastern terminal boundaries, which lay on parallel align-ments 390-400m to the west and 490-510m to the east of the road. The land between these limits was divided by a series of lateral boundary ditches that extended from the roadside ditches to the terminal boundary ditches (Area 1, Fig. 6.1). The western terminal boundary and a series of lateral boundaries were excavated at Langford Lane South. Some of the lateral boundaries branched off the road at right angles and lay on parallel E-W alignments, but others were on less regular alignments with the result that the areas they defined were neither regularly shaped nor equal in size. The most striking of these anomalous alignments was a ditch that extended across the middle of the field system and part of which was recorded at Langford Lane South as ditch 2327. It was clearly a significant boundary that also defined the northern limit of the farmstead in Area 4 (below). There is some evidence that the areas between the lateral boundaries were further subdivided by N-S boundaries, as indicated by cropmarks. However, these are few in number and the excavated transect provided by the excavation area at Langford Lane South found no additional instances, which would suggest that these extremely large areas were mostly undivided. The cropmark evidence suggests that lateral boundaries were less numerous east of the road, apart from a series of smaller enclosures that fronted onto it. This is unlikely to be explained by poor definition of cropmarks, since this area was situated on the gravel terrace so cropmark features should, if anything, be clearer here than elsewhere; indeed, the parade ground and marching camp lie in this area and were initially identified from cropmark evidence (Sauer 1998, 71). The paucity of cropmark boundaries may therefore represent a genuine lack of land division in this area, and it is possible that behind the roadside plots the enclosures contained only open ground.

The cropmark evidence south of the walled town does not contain any definite indication of extra-mural settlement, in contrast to the evidence for stone-founded buildings and areas of building rubble that have been recorded alongside Akeman Street outside the east gate. This need not imply that no settlement existed here, since the stone-founded buildings at Langford Lane East were not detected by cropmark evidence, and in any case buildings need not have been constructed in stone. Two of the trenches (87 and 102, Fig. 6.1) dug at the locations of post settings for the 2002 overhead powerline, a short distance outside the south gate, indicated that during the 2nd century the ground level had been deliberately raised and drainage gullies dug (Wessex Archaeology 2002), but whether this was associated with occupation could not be proven by such limited excavation. It is possible that a cropmark boundary that extends from the south-eastern corner of the walled town and defines the limit of the enclosures that fronted onto the east side of the road marked the rear boundary of an area of roadside settlement, but in the absence of structural evidence the enclosures could just as easily have been agricultural in function.

An area adjacent to the south-west corner of the walled town was enclosed on the south and east sides by an L-shaped boundary that appears from the cropmark evidence to have been defined by several closely-spaced ditches (Area 2, Fig. 6.1). The ditches may, of course, represent sequential itera-tions of the boundary, but the emphasis of this boundary surely indicates that it had some signifi-cance. The junction of this boundary with the western terminal boundary was investigated at the western limit of Langford Lane South, but insuffi-cient of the junction was exposed within the footprint of the proposed bridge abutment to allow the sequence of ditches to be fully understood. The pottery from the ditches mostly dated from the 2nd century but continued into the 3rd century. The sequence of lateral boundaries appears to continue across this area, suggesting that the L-shaped boundary may represent a separate phase of land division, but the evidence is insufficient to establish whether it pre-dated the main phase of boundaries or was superimposed on it. It is possible that the different treatment of this area is associated with the presence here of the cropmark of a banjo enclosure.

The lateral boundaries do not appear to have extended into the area at the south-eastern corner of the town, where there was instead a complex of conjoined enclosures of smaller size, the largest measuring *c* 100m across and the smallest *c* 45m (Area 3, Fig. 6.1). Some of the boundaries in between were defined by double-ditched trackways aligned north-south and east-west; a layout of comparable character is also seen north of the walled town on the east side of the Towcester road. The enclosures occupied a triangular area between the town and an existing stream, and the staggered boundary along their south-western side appeared

to respect the alignment of the watercourse, indicating that it followed a similar course to its current channel. They may have been delimited to the north by an E-W boundary defined by a cropmark and corresponding to the long-lived ditch 7069 at Langford Lane East.

In the middle of the surveyed area, and bounded to the north by the boundary excavated as ditch 2327, was a roughly L-shaped arrangement of enclosures (Area 4, Fig. 6.1) that was of distinctly different character to the boundaries that defined the surrounding landscape and has been inter-preted as a discrete farmstead. Although clearly set within the limits defined by the lateral boundaries, the intervening areas were different in being subdi-vided into a complex of much smaller enclosures. The excavation at Langford Lane South uncovered the northern limit of the complex and revealed enclosures, trackways and other features that may have been associated with management of livestock, as well as refuse that clearly came from domestic occupation somewhere nearby. The complex is discussed further below.

Much of the area east of the road appears to be lacking in evidence for landscape division (Area 5, Fig. 6.1). As discussed above, this is unlikely to be a consequence of poor definition of cropmarks, as the area lies predominantly on a gravel terrace, and it is therefore likely that the area was not incorporated into the enclosed landscape. Excavation of a long, sinuous trench that extended through this zone between Langford Lane East and Langford Lane South uncovered only natural features. This is a very large area, perhaps defined to the west by enclosures that fronted onto the Dorchester road, to the north by the boundary defined by ditch 7069 and to the east by the east Otmoor road, with a southern limit that has not been located. Why this area should be treated differently is uncertain, although it is possible that its previous use for the marching camp and parade ground suggests that it had a different history of ownership, perhaps remaining under military or municipal control.

Extramural settlement south-east of Alchester

The excavation at Langford Lane East exposed a slice through an area of occupation that it likely to represent part of the eastern extramural settlement of Alchester. Occupation outside the town's east gate had previously been identified by cropmark evidence for stone-founded buildings and areas of building rubble on either side of Akeman Street and the new evidence suggests that this settlement continued south along the east Otmoor route. This arrangement finds a ready parallel in the northern extramural area, which extended along both Akeman Street and the Towcester road. If the settle-ment extended unbroken from the east gate of Alchester, along Akeman Street and the east Otmoor route, it would comprise a substantial area of occupation that extended for a linear distance of *c* 500m. This is not unreasonable, however, as the corresponding distance to the part of the northern extramural area that was excavated at the A41 junction is *c* 700m.

The extramural settlement in this area was preceded by activity during the late Iron Age, although the precise relationship, if any, between the two phases remains uncertain. While there was no indication of any hiatus in occupation until the late 2nd/early 3rd century, when the area was finally abandoned, the character of the occupation changed completely. Interpretation of the late Iron Age features was in fact problematic, since much of the area comprised a spread of undifferentiated soil which, on excavation, was revealed to comprise both intercutting features and a soil layer, which presumably formed the ground surface during the late Iron Age and Roman periods. The soil layer and feature fills had been homogenised by the effect of gleying, indicating that the area had been subject to similar waterlogged condition to those identified by Robinson (1975) in contemporary deposits beneath the Roman defences at Alchester. The consequent similarity of the soil layer and feature fills made it difficult to define features in plan or to establish stratigraphic relationships. The features mostly comprised shallow, frequently intercutting pits, as well as part of a possible trapezoidal enclosure. The artefactual assemblage was very small and limited to pottery and animal bone, the only reasonably substantial groups coming from a single pit (7184). No buildings were identified and given the limited range of features and artefacts the activity was difficult to characterise. Domestic material was undoubtedly represented but whether the features related to occupation or off-site activity associated with settlement elsewhere in the vicinity is less certain.

The military phase at Alchester has been described in detail elsewhere and need only be sketched here insofar as is relevant to an understanding of the excavated features (eg Sauer 1999a; 2000b; 2006). The earliest feature is likely to be the marching camp south of the excavation area, which may date from the initial phase of the Roman conquest, although excavation by OUAS was unable to establish a precise date for its construction (Sauer 1999a; 1999b). Its coalignment with the road that was excavated at Langford Lane East may suggest that they were broadly contemporary and that the route to Dorchester around the east side of Otmoor was instituted very early, representing the first elements of a complete re-organisation of the landscape. The marching camp was very quickly superseded by construction of a permanent fortress, the gateposts of an annexe of which have been dated by dendrochronology to between October AD 44 and March AD 45 (Sauer 2006, 13). The discovery of a 1st-century tombstone commemorating a veteran of the 2nd Legion Augusta, reused as building material for the late 2nd century town wall, has led Sauer (2005b, 124-5) to argue that Alchester, rather than sites elsewhere in the south-west, was the main base of this legion perhaps up to about AD 60, being

succeeded by Exeter. The area of the marching camp was reused for the construction of a rectilinear enclosure that has been interpreted as a parade ground associated with the fortress (Sauer 1998; 1999a), accessed by means of a trackway that was exposed by the excavation at Langford Lane East. No metalling survived and unfortunately the pottery from the trackway's flanking ditches did not clarify the date of the feature, the small assemblage dating entirely from the 2nd century. Previous excavation of a series of trenches across the ditch that delimited the parade ground and within its interior were similarly inconclusive regarding its date, producing only a few sherds and none that were closely datable (Sauer 1998, 71-2). Presumably the 2nd-century sherds date from backfilling of the ditch at this time, since the association with the fortress demands a pre-Flavian construction date.

The area of late Iron Age activity was divided from the marching camp and parade ground by the construction of a boundary represented by ditch 7069. This was clearly a significant boundary, which was maintained into the late 3rd-4th century and may have divided the civilian settlement to the north from a military-controlled area to the south, into which domestic occupation evidently did not extend. The character of the activity north of this boundary remained difficult to define during the military period. Native, 'Belgic'-style pottery appears to have continued in use alongside Romanised wares, perhaps indicating continuity of population. Again, no buildings were uncovered, and many of the features of this phase were shallow pits that were similar to those of the preceding period. Ultimately, however, it must be accepted that the area exposed was insufficient to satisfactorily characterise the occupation. No evidence was found that could be associated with the military and it must therefore be assumed that the occupation was entirely civilian in nature. Although the pottery assemblage was generally typical of a rural settlement in the region at this time, it also included pre-Flavian samian ware and amphora sherds that are unusual in such a context. Access to these imported vessels may have been associated with an elevated social status, but it is equally possible that they were simply more readily available due to the proximity of the fortress, where such wares were presumably more common. A similarly precocious adoption of such wares was noted in contemporary deposits at the northern extramural area, although occupation had not really begun within the excavated area there at this time and the material was mostly recovered from boundary ditches (Evans 2001a, 383). The pottery is, however, the only indication for occupation of a possibly elevated status at Langford Lane East, the excavated features being otherwise prosaic in character.

The bulk of the evidence related to the civilian period at Alchester, and specifically to extramural occupation during the late 1st-early 3rd century. This phase produced a more coherent arrangement, comprising three stone-founded buildings (7062, 7222, 7640) and associated cobbled surfaces. Occupation appears to have been restricted to the western side of the road, the eastern side being the location of a wide ditch into which the eastern branch of the Langford Brook had been channelled. A wall extended alongside the edge of the western roadside ditch and hazelnuts and hawthorn stones preserved by waterlogging of the lower fills of the roadside ditch may have fallen from an associated hedgerow. It is not certain whether the buildings were contemporary; Building 7640 is described in Chapter 2 as being later than its neighbours but this is based entirely on its association with ditches 8520 and 8522, which define an enclosure around it and cut surfaces associated with the other buildings. However, it is equally possible that the buildings were contemporary and the enclosure a later addition, since there were no stratigraphic relationships to link them and little artefactual dating material. The only pottery that was directly associated with the construction of Building 7062 comprised a small sherd of South Gaulish samian from the floor level and a small fragment of Central Gaulish samian ware and a small piece of black-burnished ware from a possible occupation layer, which together suggest a date of at least AD 120, while the foundation of Building 7222 produced a small rim sherd from a South Gaulish samian dish of Dragendorff form 15/17, dated to AD 40-90. No artefactual evidence was found relating to the date of construction of Building 7640. The end dates for the buildings were similarly ambiguous. A coin of Victorinus dating from AD 268-70 that was recovered from a rubble layer above Building 7062 may provide a date for its demolition, but could be intrusive since the pottery from the demolition layers of this and Building 7222 suggested a date no later than the 2nd-early 3rd century. A much larger group of pottery was recovered from demolition layers associated with Building 7640, which included an Oxford white ware mortarium of Young type M14, dated AD 180-240. The ceramic roofing material from the buildings was sufficiently uniform in character to suggest that it represented a single production batch, but while this could imply that all three buildings were built at the same time it is alternatively possible that Buildings 7062 and 7222 were re-roofed when Building 7640 was built or that the smaller buildings did not have tiled roofs and all the material derives entirely from 7640. The most that can be concluded from the available dating evidence, therefore, is that Buildings 7062 and 7222 were probably constructed during the late 1st century, with Building 7640 being contemporary or slightly later, and that all three were probably in contemporary use during the 2nd century and probably demolished no earlier than *c* AD 180, and more likely not before *c* AD 200.

This chronology would make this part of the eastern extramural settlement a precocious development, broadly contemporary with the initial phase of construction of stone-founded buildings within the centre of the town, which Henig and Booth (2000, 56) have attributed to the late 1st century. This is very much earlier than equivalent developments in the northern extramural area, where, although the plots were laid out and the earliest buildings constructed during the middle of the 2nd century, the main phase of building did not start until the middle of the 3rd century (Booth *et al.* 2001, 428-32). Indeed, if the end of occupation at Langford Lane East can be extrapolated to indicate a contemporaneous decline in the rest of eastern extramural settlement, it is possible that the northern area developed as a direct replacement. It may be specious to attempt to derive a cause for the abandonment of this area from the small part that lay within the limits of the excavation, but it may have been associated with the decline in use of the road, which does not appear to have been maintained after the 2nd century if the absence of recutting of the roadside ditches after this time is any indication. The road may have become less important as a long-distance route to the south after the direct road across Otmoor was constructed and Sauer has suggested that it may have become increasingly affected by flooding until it could no longer be maintained, citing a depth of up to 0.8m of alluvium overlying it (Sauer 1999b, 62-3). Alternatively, the extramural settlement may have declined as a result of changes to the layout and functioning of the town after the town walls were constructed during the last quarter of the 2nd century (Henig and Booth 2000, 56), although it is not obvious why this should have had such an impact, since the town was presumably already enclosed by some form of earthwork inherited from the fortress within whose footprint it was constructed.

The buildings formed a somewhat dissimilar group, Buildings 7062 and 7222 being small square structures and Building 7640 probably a more typical strip-building. Buildings 7062 and 7222 were particularly unusual, comprising a pair of essentially identical single-cell buildings with stone-founded walls on three sides. Building 7222 measured 3.45 x 2.15m internally, with a pair of postholes representing an entrance on the north-eastern side, facing the road, and Building 7062 was probably of similar size, although the north-eastern side did not survive. There was little evidence regarding the form of their superstructures; a layer of small pieces of limestone rubble with occasional fragments of roof tile in Building 7062 may have been a rough floor surface but no evidence for a floor survived in Building 7222 and there was insufficient building material to be certain whether the walls were of stone or timber. Ceramic roof tile was recovered from demolition layers associated with both buildings but it was identical to the tile from the much larger spreads derived from Building 7640 and so it is possible that all the tile came from that building. The buildings were clearly too small to be domestic dwellings and an interpretation as storage structures may be more appropriate. Their situation on the road frontage may suggest a function as booths located to sell produce to passing travellers. The buildings are unlike the long, rectangular strip-buildings that typically lined the roads of Roman towns and served as shops, however, and in form their closest parallel is a three-sided structure at the temple complex at Marcham/Frilford that was interpreted as a shrine (Kamash *et al.* 2010, 113). This interpretation derived principally from the building's orientation, which was directed toward the amphitheatre, and a concentration of small finds in front of the structure, in particular personal items. The buildings at Langford Lane East were not obviously associated with such ritual deposition, unless a Hod Hill brooch and part of the bow of a large Colchester brooch from the cobbled surfaces adjacent to building 7062 were such. More speculatively, their symmetrical arrangement could be interpreted as representing opposite sides of a gatehouse that provided access from the road to the adjoining plot of land. Their location certainly coincided with a break in the wall that extended alongside the road. The cobbled surface that lay between the buildings and the road extended between them and into the area to the rear, but there was no indication of wheel ruts or other evidence that it was used as a road. If the structures did indeed form a gatehouse it would have been a monumental structure, measuring 9.4m across with towers flanking a carriageway 3.2m wide. Substantial gateway structures could certainly form an element of the extramural settlements, since a large timber gate, albeit of less monumental form than the putative structure at Langford Lane East, was constructed at the entrance to Plot N4b in the northern area, represented by six postholes that provided two carriageways each *c* 1.7m wide (Booth *et al.* 2001, 437). With the exception of the much larger structures associated with the entrances to walled towns or fortresses, monumental gateways comprising towers on either side of the carriageway are restricted to a small number of villas and religious sites. The villa complex at Winterton, Lincolnshire, for example, was entered via a metalled track that passed through a gatehouse comprising a pair of square, stone-founded towers *c* 3.65m apart (Stead 1976, 77) and the entrance to the *temenos* surrounding the main temple at Marcham/Frilford was flanked by two two-roomed structures that may have formed a gatehouse, which were associated with a pair of opposed stone plinths that could have supported an arch or columns (Kamash *et al.* 2010, 104-5). On a slightly less monumental scale, the farmstead at Claydon Pike was entered through a gateway that lacked towers but nonetheless had stone side-walls, with a central post against which closed a pair of gates, each *c* 1.2m wide. It is no surprise that such monumental entrances are typically associated with prestigious establishments such as villas and religious sites, designed to impress arriving visitors, but it is less clear why such a structure would be built at Langford Lane East,

where there does not appear to be any such complex, unless a building of some importance lies a short distance beyond the excavated area.

Building 7640 was only partly exposed at the edge of the excavation area, revealing a corner and parts of two external walls. Its location would be consistent with it being the rear corner of a rectangular building 17-18m long situated end-on to the road, representing a strip-building, a staple building-type in extramural settlements (Esmonde Cleary 1987, 182). Such buildings are typically interpreted as the homes and workshops of craftworkers, but in this instance insufficient of the building was exposed to provide any evidence as to its use. No floor levels survived and the relative absence of building stone suggests that the superstructure was probably of timber, although the foundations were substantial enough to have supported a stone structure. It was evidently roofed with ceramic tiles, since there was much such material among the demolition layers that formed an arc around the building. This material included three tiles that bore rare examples of human footprints, from a small child or toddler. Simple rectangular stone-founded buildings with differing configurations of (typically three) rooms were excavated in the north-eastern quarter of the walled town in the 1920s (eg Hawkes 1927, fig. 2; Iliffe 1932, fig. 1), though it is not certain that any of these examples represents a complete building plan. Similar rectangular buildings with foundations constructed primarily in stone were surprisingly rare in the excavated part of the northern extramural area, with only two examples, both 4th century in date (Buildings E and K; Booth *et al.* 2001, 435). Closer parallels, both in form and date, can be found in the small town at Asthall, where Buildings F and H had walls of similar size to Building 7640 and were similarly built during the 2nd century (Booth 1997, 154).

The settlement on the Alchester to Dorchester-on-Thames road

There is considerable uncertainty regarding the character of the area investigated at Langford Lane South, particularly as regards whether it represented part of the extramural occupation to the south of Alchester or a discrete settlement. It was situated *c* 470m from the south gate of Alchester on the road to Dorchester, and while this distance is perhaps at the upper end of the range for extramural settlement, the extramural occupation excavated to the north and east of the town at the A41 and Langford Lane East lay at a similar distance. The evidence for extensive settlement to the south of the town is ambiguous, however, since, although cropmark evidence clearly indicates the presence of enclosures on the road frontages, there is no indication as to their function. This contrasts with the clear evidence for stone-founded buildings and areas of building rubble representing extramural settlement outside the east gate, but it is uncertain how much significance should be placed on the lack of cropmark evidence since it had failed to detect the buildings that were uncovered at Langford Lane East. It is consequently uncertain whether the complex at Langford Lane South lay at the end of uninterrupted roadside occupation or was separated from the town by open fields. The preference here, however, is to see the complex as a discrete establishment, since the character of the cropmark enclosures was unequivocally different to the surrounding landscape divisions and it was located on the south side of a ditched trackway that can be traced as a cropmark that extends from east to west across the entire width of the landscape divisions south of the town and evidently represented a significant boundary, perhaps dividing land in different tenure. The excavation area encompassed only a very small area on the north side of the boundary, and the conclusions should therefore be treated cautiously, but no indication of occupation was found. Furthermore, although no structural remains were situated within the excavated area there was circumstantial evidence that the complex was distinguished by a building nearby, which may have been quite well appointed. The location of such a settlement so close to the town is unusual but can perhaps be paralleled at Dorchester-on-Thames, where intensive occupation at Meadside lies only *c* 500m south-east of the town walls but on the other side of the River Thame (Keevill 2010).

The cropmarks indicated that the complex encompassed both sides of the road and was roughly L-shaped in plan, with the smaller part lying on the west side of the carriageway. It comprised much smaller enclosures than were to be found in the surrounding areas, with substantially more subdivision, perhaps in order to facilitate management of livestock. The enclosures were clearly integrated into the wider scheme of landscape divisions and therefore cannot pre-date its presumed construction date shortly after AD 95, and the pottery indicates that it was occupied until the late 2nd/early 3rd century. The area that was exposed within the excavation areas was initially laid out as three adjoining enclosures, with entrances to allow access between them. It was reorganised during the 2nd century into a more complex arrangement of at least five smaller enclosures, at least two of which had entrances controlled by gates. This increase in the complexity of the enclosures represents an investment in the infrastructure of the establishment and may have been associated with a corresponding interest in the spatial separation of activities or the adoption of more complex husbandry practices. In both phases the entrances to the enclosures were situated on the west side, indicating that they were engaged in farming of the large enclosures that lay to the west.

Although no evidence was found for buildings *in situ*, domestic occupation was indicated by refuse that had been dumped into the excavated features,

particularly pits 2611 and 4047. The presence of buildings nearby, and some indication of their character, was indicated by the building material recovered from these features; bricks were incorporated into the walls or used as flooring and there were evidently glazed windows. The flue tile suggests that at least one building was provided with heated rooms or a hypocaust and semi-circular segmental bricks were found that are typically associated with baths. The small number of tesserae most likely come from tessellated floors, although the absence of smaller pieces indicates that decorative mosaics were not present. The waterlogged plant remains and insect assemblage from pit 2611 included a component likely to have been derived from organic waste within buildings, with rushes and sedges that may have been used either as roofing or flooring material. The insect remains were probably associated with organic waste from a wooden building, which could include dung and straw cleaned out of stables.

The artefactual assemblage corresponded with the structural material in suggesting that the occupants may have enjoyed a more comfortable lifestyle than their contemporaries at Langford Lane East or the other rural settlements. This is indicated by the diversity of the pottery assemblage, which included a large proportion of fine and specialist wares, with both samian ware and white-slipped wares being well represented; indeed, if taken as an index of status, this material places the settlement among the higher-ranked examples in the region at this time. An emphasis on dining is indicated by the quantity of table wares, in particular a strikingly large number of flagons.

The exposure of only a small area of the settlement within the footprint of the road realignment limits the ability of this investigation to provide a definitive interpretation of its character. However, it would appear to be a discrete farmstead of relatively high status engaged in farming the land on either side of the road to Dorchester, perhaps with an emphasis on husbandry rather than cultivation of crops. The proximity to Alchester is certainly no coincidence and was presumably intended to exploit the market provided by the town, or may indicate a tenurial relationship, perhaps as the residence of a member of the town's elite.

Rural settlement in the hinterland of Alchester

Rural settlements were encountered at Holts Farm Crossing, South of Merton, North of Gallos Brook and North of Oxford Parkway Station. All the sites lay within 10km of Alchester, which would therefore have been easily accessible in less than a day's travel and which they might reasonably be anticipated to have been engaged in supplying with food. They were nevertheless a diverse group, comprising a farmstead at Holts Farm Crossing, a settlement of uncertain character at South of Merton that may have been a higher-status farmstead or a roadside settlement, part of a field system at North of Gallos Brook and the periphery of a village-sized settlement at North of Oxford Parkway Station.

Holts Farm Crossing

The settlement at Holts Farm Crossing was the longest lived of the sites excavated during the project, with origins in the middle Iron Age and an apparently unbroken sequence of occupation that extended into the late Roman period. It may owe its longevity to its situation on a slight plateau that was raised 2-3m above the surrounding terrain, which would have been sufficient to keep it drier than most locations within the vale. This did not, however, enable the occupants to attain a higher status than their neighbours, as indicated by the proportions of fine and specialist wares in the pottery assemblage, which remained low compared to the other sites on the project and to other assemblages from the Upper Thames Valley region. Perhaps the material evidence combined with that for longevity of occupation in a topographically favourable location indicates the presence of a particularly conservative community.

During the late Iron Age, the open settlement of the middle Iron Age was replaced with one comprising a complex of conjoined rectilinear enclosures, the southern edge of which was uncovered within the excavation area. The continuation of the complex in the area north of the excavation area was demonstrated by features recorded in evaluation trenches, but this area was not ultimately subject to excavation because it was used for a construction compound with no intrusive groundworks. This arrangement formed the basis for developments during the Roman period, when a trackway was constructed along the southern edge of the Iron Age complex during the late 1st-early 2nd century and further enclosures were added adjoining the south side later in the 2nd century. There was no evidence for domestic occupation having been situated within the excavated area at any stage and it is therefore likely that the residential area lay in the northern part of the settlement. The only features south of the trackway were the field boundaries and so this area was clearly used only for agricultural purposes throughout the life of the settlement. The site is very similar to a settlement that has been excavated at Bicester Park, which likewise respected the alignment of an Iron Age boundary and developed during the late 1st-early 2nd century into a complex divided by a trackway, with occupation on one side and pens for livestock on the other (Westgarth and Carlyle 2008). Occupation at both sites appears to have petered out during the 3rd century, although the precise date of their abandonment is uncertain.

South of Merton

Of the eight excavations, South of Merton was the site whose interpretation was most disadvantaged by the limited width of the excavation area, and

even the broad character of the site in not entirely certain. The investigation comprised a single trench measuring 155m long and only 4m wide and the consequent limited exposure of the features rendered them difficult to fully understand. In addition to the exposure revealing insufficient of the settlement to allow its form to be seen, difficulty was encountered in characterising the features that were excavated, as many extended beyond the trench. This was particularly true in the roadside area, where intercutting features created a broad spread of deposits that were difficult to differentiate in plan. Excavation of a limited number of sondages through this material was only partly successful in resolving the features. The discovery of postholes that appear to be part of a substantial building further adds to the uncertainty regarding the character of the settlement.

The settlement was situated beside the road from Alchester to Dorchester-on-Thames, 1.7km south of Alchester, and had previously been recorded as an area of 'dark earth and Romano-British occupation debris' that was partly exposed during construction of the M40 in 1988-91 (Chambers 1992, 52). Within the excavated area, occupation was situated on the western frontage of the road, possibly bounded to the rear by a ditch (2515) set 25m back from the road, with further ditches that may have defined fields or other enclosures beyond this. A much smaller area was exposed on the east side of the road, interpretation of which should therefore be treated with caution, but the only feature uncovered was a boundary ditch that extended back from the road. It was uncertain whether this was the boundary of a plot that may have contained occupation similar to that on the west side of the road, or whether such occupation was absent from this side and the ditch defined a field boundary. The evidence for occupation included a shallow hollow on the road frontage with a complex of intercutting pits to the rear, none of which were particularly well understood, but the most significant element was a structure represented by substantial, stone-packed postholes. Three postholes were uncovered, each measuring 1.3-1.5m in diameter and more than 0.6-0.7m deep, forming an alignment parallel to the road and set back 3.5-4.0m from the edge of the roadside ditch. No other features were found that were certainly part of the structure, although a packed limestone feature at the edge of the trench may have been the edge of a wall or postpad. Other postholes were found but they were much smaller and their arrangement did not obviously relate to that of the main alignment, perhaps indicating that they represented ancillary structures, fencelines or a different phase of activity. If they did form part of the same structure, the contrast in construction technique might indicate that the side facing the road was deliberately built in a particularly imposing form. Such use of different construction techniques within a single structure is quite common, and can be seen in Buildings C, D and M in Alchester's northern extramural area (Booth *et al.* 2001, 188-94). The entrance to Building M utilised postholes of a similar size to those at South of Merton, the rest of the building comprising shallow stone footings, much of which had been removed by plough-truncation, and it is possible that the Merton postholes were similarly part of a building that had otherwise been truncated. It is alternatively possible that any return defining the south wall of the building may have been masked by a medieval furrow that extended across the trench on a perpendicular alignment a short distance south of the postholes. The almost complete absence of building material from the site indicates that the superstructure was entirely of timber, possibly with wattle and daub infill, and most likely with a roof of thatch or shingle.

The size of the postholes, however, clearly indicates that they formed a substantial structure. In the absence of evidence for returns or an opposite side, it may represent either a palisade beside the road or a rectangular building. Rectangular post-built buildings are not normally a feature of rural farmsteads in the region. Indeed, the scarcity of archaeologically detectable evidence for buildings on such settlements has been commented on and interpreted as indicating that construction more commonly used timber-framing or mass wall techniques (Booth *et al.* 2007, 35-6; Smith 2016, 51). Substantial post-built structures are more usually found on urban sites or higher-status rural sites, comprising the most common building form in the northern extramural area of Alchester, where the form was used throughout the Roman period (Booth *et al.* 2001, 437 and table 10.1), and also being widespread at the roadside settlement at Asthall (Booth 1997, 154). In a rural context, post-built buildings interpreted as barns have been excavated at the nucleated settlement at Gill Mill (Booth and Simmonds 2018) and the villa at Roughground Farm, Gloucestershire (Allen *et al.* 1993, 110). The postholes in these instances are not particularly deep, however, and the substantial pits at South of Merton are more akin to the postholes that supported the posts of aisled buildings, such as those at Neigh Bridge, Somerford Keynes, Gloucestershire (Smith 2007, 236-8), Claydon Pike (Miles *et al.* 2007, 160-1) and Kingshill South, Cirencester (Simmonds *et al.* 2018). This is not necessarily to suggest that the building was of aisled form, but the need for such substantial postholes implies that they were supporting a considerable weight. The associations of these buildings suggest that, if the postholes do indeed represent such a substantial building, then the settlement is likely to be more than a simple rural farmstead. The artefactual assemblage was small and provides no indication of the nature of the site, although the pottery indicates that occupation, at least within the excavated area, was restricted to the 2nd and early 3rd century, albeit with a small quantity of residual earlier material also present.

North of Oxford Parkway

The area excavated at North of Oxford Parkway Station formed part of an extensive agricultural landscape that has been recorded from cropmark evidence (Figs 1.4 and 2.58). The excavation area extended across the line of a trackway but appeared from the cropmark evidence to be situated in a rather peripheral location, well away from the main focus of settlement, which lay at a trackway junction 400-500m to the south-west. It was therefore surprising that the trench uncovered a moderately high density of features and provided evidence for the development of this part of the landscape over a period of several centuries. During the late 1st-early 2nd centuries the area was occupied by at least three discrete yet co-aligned rectilinear enclosures. No structures were identified and the artefactual assemblage from this phase was limited to a small quantity of pottery, as a consequence of which it is uncertain whether permanent occupation formed a part of the activities at this time or whether the use of the enclosures was entirely agricultural. A pair of stack rings situated within enclosure E1 indicates at least a partial agricultural function. The rings comprised annular gullies with diameters of 1.75m and 2.75m and are similar to features that have been interpreted elsewhere as fodder stands for the provision of livestock (Miles *et al.* 2007, 90).

The landscape was reorganised in the early 2nd century, when the trackway was constructed, flanked on either side by rectilinear enclosures, but the general alignment of the features was retained, suggesting that this represented controlled development of the landscape rather than a total break. In addition to their function as boundaries, the ditches that defined the trackway and enclosures may also have been intended to drain the surrounding land, since the trackway ditches were substantial features up to 0.90m deep and contained an assemblage of seeds indicative of standing or flowing water (Meen, Chapter 4). The enclosure ditches were shallower and may have been designed to drain into the trackway ditches, to which they were joined. Twigs, a thorn of blackthorn/hawthorn, fruit stones of blackthorn/sloe and hawthorn and a hazelnut preserved by waterlogging in the northern trackway ditch are likely to have fallen into the feature from overhanging plants forming a hedgerow. After the 2nd century the enclosures appear to have gone out of use, but a small quantity of late Roman pottery from the northern trackway ditch suggests that the trackway continued in use into the late 3rd century and possibly later. As in the earlier period, no buildings stood within the excavated area, although some of the material recovered from the features must have derived from domestic occupation somewhere nearby. The waterlogged deposits in the trackway ditch, for example, produced a group of synanthropic beetles typical of a 'building fauna', together with beetles which are associated with foul mouldering material, suggesting the incorporation of waste from within buildings, and the presence of eggs of the intestinal parasite whipworm *Trichuris* suggests that human waste was deposited in the feature. The pottery assemblage was fairly typical for a rural settlement, being dominated by reduced coarse wares, with *c* 10% of the total sherds comprising fine and specialist wares, most of which were white wares and a smaller quantity of samian ware. Interestingly, the coarse wares included a high proportion of vessels in fabrics assigned to the 'West Oxfordshire' industry, suggesting that some of it was sourced from a separate supply network to that available at Alchester.

The results of this excavation provide significant detailed information regarding the character of the landscape recorded from cropmark evidence. In particular, it represents part of the periphery of the settlement located at the nearby trackway junction. The junction is located *c* 250m south-west of Middle Farm and has the form of a triskelion, from which ditched trackways radiate in three directions: a straight branch extends southward, a dog-legged branch extends initially towards the east before turning northward and the third branch, which the excavation investigated, follows a more curved alignment to the north-west for a distance of *c* 500m before being truncated by the railway embankment. Conjoined rectilinear enclosures cluster on the west side of the junction and within the interstice between the dog-legged and curved branches, some containing smaller circular and rectilinear features that may be the locations of buildings, forming what appears to be a village-sized settlement. Settlements of this type, focused on trackway junctions, have been identified at several locations in the Upper Thames Valley and may have been a common element of the Roman landscape. The best known example was excavated in 1973 at Appleford Field, where occupation was arranged around a large triangular open area formed where a trackway from the south divides into two branches extending towards the north-west and north-east (Hinchliffe and Thomas 1980), and other sites identified from cropmark evidence are known at Standlake, at Cote, and near Lechlade, Gloucestershire (Henig and Booth 2000, figs 4.16 and 4.17; RCHME 1976, 73-4). The excavation uncovered an arrangement of roadside enclosures in an area where the cropmarks show no features other than the trackway, suggesting that more of the landscape was enclosed than is immediately apparent from the cropmark evidence. The evidence for possible occupation close to the excavated area suggests that either the settlement at the junction was considerably more extensive than it appears, or the excavation was situated close to a secondary focus of occupation that had not previously been identified. The substantial width of the trackway, which measured 15m, seems excessive for human traffic and may indicate that it was intended as a droveway for livestock, and this receives some support from the

recovery from the trackway ditch of the dung beetle *Aphodius granarius*, which is often associated with dung lying on bare ground. The trackway appears to have been flanked by hedgerows in addition to its drainage ditches, and it is quite possible that the boundaries of the surrounding fields were all defined in this way. Pollen of oak, pine, hazel-type and rare beech indicate that woodland also formed part of the environment, but probably at low levels and not close to the excavated area.

Economy

The extramural settlement

Esmonde Cleary (1987, 182-6) suggested that extra-mural areas of Roman towns were concerned largely with manufacture and commerce, but there was in fact comparatively little evidence for activities of this sort from the excavations at Langford Lane East, as was similarly noted in regard to Alchester's northern extramural area (Booth *et al.* 2001, 442). It might be assumed that the location of the extramural occupation, which appears to have been restricted to the road frontage, reflected a desire to attract passing trade, but the roadside setting here may simply have been a matter of convenient access for the residents. Tools that may have been used in manufacture or other crafts were very rare, represented only by an axe head and a possible punch, as well as a curved, socketed object of uncertain function. Two knives were found but these may have been household tools rather than industrial items. The only possible indication that any craft activity was undertaken came from a small number of cut marks on Phase 4 cattle metacarpals that may be associated with skinning, although there was no other evidence to indicate whether the skins were processed here or passed on to leather-workers working elsewhere. The complete absence of evidence for metalworking is particularly surprising, since smithing appears to have been carried out routinely at most settlements, if only on an occasional basis to repair broken tools, and it is generally believed that such artisans would have found a ready trade in towns of all sizes (Burnham 1988, 41). The two sets of slave shackles from pit 7014 serve as a reminder that slave labour was a ubiquitous element of the Roman economy, although there is no way of knowing whether the context of this particular find was some activity within the extramural settlement or agricultural work in the surrounding landscape. Given the probability that the town acted as the main market centre for the surrounding region, it is even possible that slaves were brought here to be traded.

Given the paucity of evidence for other activities, both at Langford Lane East and in the northern extramural settlement, it would appear that the town's suburbs may have been partly rural, engaged in farming the surrounding land. This suggestion is supported by the evidence of the pollen and insect remains from the roadside ditches, which indicate that the Phase 4 and 5 settlement lay in an open grassland environment (Rutherford and Allison, Chapter 4). This is hardly surprising given the low-lying and poorly-drained landscape, and an emphasis on pastoralism rather than crop growing would be consistent with Robinson's contention that by the Roman period soils in parts of the Upper Thames Valley may have become unsuitable for cultivation owing to waterlogging and overuse (Robinson 2011, 55). The south-west side of the road was built up, so the farmland presumably lay beyond this and on the north-east side of the road, where a few shallow ditches were recorded but no indication of settlement. Most of the material from the assemblages would be consistent with the use of the area for either pasture or hay production, which are difficult to distinguish from archaeological evidence as they produce a similar range of species (Hodgson *et al*. 1999; Robinson 2011). In practice, both uses may have coexisted over the course of the year, since Robinson (2011, 47) describes a typical Upper Thames Valley hay meadow as being grazed from August to February and shut up for hay during the spring and early summer. Hay would certainly have been required in large quantities by the fort and subsequent town for use as fodder and litter. However, the abundance and variety of scarabaeid dung beetles in both ditches suggests that at least part of the grassland was used for grazing animals, the most abundant specimen, *Aphodius granarius* being most commonly associated with cow dung. In addition to this, *Phyllopertha horticola*, a small chafer characteristic of permanent pasture, was recorded in ditch 6715, and pollen of ribwort plantain, a species that has been interpreted as an indicator of grazing pressure, appeared in ditch 7066. The animal bone assemblage provides evidence for the species that were consumed in the extramural settlement, although it is of course difficult to be certain how many of these animals represent livestock raised in the immediate vicinity and how many were brought to the town from afar; the food demands of the population would certainly have necessitated importation of meat and other foodstuffs from a large area and this is likely to have formed a major part of the economy of the surrounding region. The remains from the excavation indicate that cattle and sheep/goat were available in almost equal numbers, with the latter being slightly in the majority until the 2nd century, when they were overtaken. Butchery marks were quite rare and clearly represented routine processing at a household level for immediate consumption rather than the large-scale, industrialised processing by specialist butchers that has been identified elsewhere as a characteristic of urban centres (Maltby 2015, 181). The latter are characterised by high cattle percentages and by processing waste indicative of rapid, standardised division of the carcass, often with evidence that it was suspended for ease of access, none of which was evident here. There is no

evidence, therefore, that the part of the extramural settlement that was excavated was involved in large-scale processing of meat for supply to the fortress or town; equally, the evidence that whole animals were being butchered demonstrates that the animals were arriving intact, and presumably on the hoof, rather than as portions that had been butchered elsewhere. A similar pattern of generalised butchery was identified in the northern extramural area (Booth *et al*. 2001, 441) and is typical of most rural settlements of the period. The rarity of pig, which were common at Sauer's excavations within the fortress annexe, may indicate a difference in diet between the garrison and the population of the extramural area. In addition to livestock raised for food, horses may also have grazed in the areas around the settlement, as they comprised a small but significant proportion of the bone assemblage. None of the horse remains showed evidence for butchery and it is likely that they were reared for use as transport or draught animals rather than as a food resource.

In addition to pasture, the pollen evidence indicates that barley may have been grown locally, as well as wheat/oats. Little other evidence was recovered for the crops grown and/or consumed at the site, however, the only deposit with a significant assemblage of charred plant remains being a dump of wheat in Phase 6 pit 7014. The wheat could not be identified to species but included a high proportion of germinated grains and is therefore likely to be waste from malting. This process, part of the brewing of beer, comprises the deliberate partial germination of cereal grains – germination is halted by forced drying and deposits of charred, germinated grain are commonly found in corndrying ovens, which have been shown experimentally to produce the gentle heat required. No corndrying ovens were found at Langford Lane East, but since the excavation comprised only a small slice through the settlement such structures could easily lie close by; one example was present in the northern extramural settlement area (Booth *et al*. 2001, 147-52).

Evidence for the economic life of the settlement is also provided by the population's consumption of pottery and use of coinage. The pottery assemblage indicates that the population had access to an unusually large number of fine and specialist wares, particularly during the early part of the period when a similar pattern was evident in the northern extramural area. The prevalence of these types in both suburbs contrasts with the low values typical of rural farmsteads and places them alongside the early villas at Ditches, Gloucestershire and Combe, and the sites at Claydon Pike, Gloucestershire, and Didcot Great Western Park, which went on to become villas. Imports during the military phase included southern Spanish amphorae and samian ware from South Gaul, the latter being replaced during the early 2nd century by Central Gaulish samian ware. It is difficult to be certain, however, whether this correlates with a higher status for the extramural settlements or whether such exotica were simply more readily available here due to Alchester's nodal position in the road network and presumed function as a market centre for the redistribution of goods to the surrounding area. It should be stressed that despite this apparent difference from other contemporary settlements, most of the pottery from the phase of occupation contemporary with the fort consisted of 'Belgic'-style wares that would not have been out of place on any native settlement of the time and there was no material, ceramic or otherwise, that indicated an obvious link with the military. The material from Sauer's excavations within the fort has not yet been published and so it is difficult to draw comparisons between assemblages from the extramural area and a putative 'military assemblage' from the fort itself, but elsewhere in Britain the initial military occupation has been associated with pottery assemblages that consist overwhelmingly of non-native, 'Romanised' pottery, which are totally unlike the assemblage from Langford Lane East.

A further distinction between Langford Lane East and other sites in the region might be inferred from the coin assemblage. Although small, comprising a total of 21 pieces, it has an emphasis on the early Roman period that contrasts with the typical rarity of coins from this period from most settlements. One of the coins is a late Iron Age issue of Cunobelinus, albeit recovered from early Roman ditch 7069, and a denarius of Tiberius and a coin of Caligula could both have been imported as part of the early military coin pool. One definite and three possible coins of Nero are also likely to have been contemporary with military occupation at Alchester and although the issues of the late 1st and early 2nd century post-date military activity they are nevertheless unusually early. The precise significance of the pieces is uncertain but, whether they indicate that commerce in the settlement was undertaken on a monetised basis or merely that coins were kept for their value as bullion, coins were certainly used more here than in most contemporary settlements.

Langford Lane South

Although, as discussed above, there is reason to believe that the settlement at Langford Lane South may have been of higher status than the extramural settlement at Langford Lane East, the evidence for its economic basis was less certain. Given the proximity of the sites and their similar topographic setting, however, it would be surprising if the agricultural regimes were not very similar. Waterlogged plant remains from roadside ditch 4158 and pit 2611 indicated that the site was located close to open grassland, although a narrower range of species was represented. This may indicate that the grassland was of a different character to the rich, species-diverse meadow that was in evidence at Langford Lane East, but it is alternatively possible that the small number of samples do not represent the full range of species in the surrounding environ-

ment. Grazing is certainly indicated by the presence of dung beetles, and *Phyllopertha horticola* was again identified. It has been suggested above that the enclosures that characterised the settlement were designed to accommodate livestock, and the animal bone assemblage indicates that cattle predominated, particularly in the very large assemblage from Phase 6 (2nd to early 3rd century). This is entirely consistent with the increase in cattle at the expense of sheep/goat at Langford Lane East during this period. The appearance of small numbers of pig and domestic fowl in Phase 6 may indicate greater diversity of husbandry practices, if it is not simply an artefact of the larger assemblage. As at Langford Lane East, the evidence from charred plant remains comprises a dump of waste from malting. The wheat used for this was probably entirely spelt; it is uncertain whether it was grown in the immediate vicinity, although the ground beetles from ditch 2455 provided some evidence for disturbed or cultivated ground nearby.

The rural settlements

The rural settlements at South of Merton, Holts Farm Crossing and North of Oxford Parkway Station are likely to have had a purely agrarian focus, and their proximity to Alchester suggests that they could have been engaged in supply of food to the fort and subsequent town. Unfortunately, however, they produced only very limited evidence regarding their economic basis, limited to the animal bone assemblage from Holts Farm Crossing and assemblages of charred plant remains from two pits at North of Oxford Parkway Station, as well as waterlogged remains and insect and pollen assemblages from the latter. South of Merton produced no charred plant remains and only 144 fragments of animal bone, more than half of which could not be identified to species. The paucity of the assemblages may, of course, be a result of the limited excavation areas rather than indicating a genuine absence of material.

The evidence from North of Oxford Parkway Station provides the most rounded picture of the agricultural regime and suggests that a mixed strategy of cultivation and husbandry was practised. Although the landscape was similar to the countryside around Alchester, comprising low-lying, flat and generally wet ground, there was more evidence for arable production here. Arable weeds were identified in the trackway ditch from both the waterlogged plant remains and the pollen assemblage, and the latter also included barley and wheat/oats. Furthermore, the charred plant remains from pit 3114 appear to be a dump of waste from the final hand cleaning of processed grain. In addition to probable cereal crops, a single seed of cultivated flax recovered from ditch 3056 may be evidence that the plant was being grown nearby. Grazing animals were indicated by waterlogged remains consistent with the presence of damp grassland, dung beetles, and stabling waste reused as fuel in oven 3047/3049. The extremely small assemblage of animal bone from this site was insufficient to support any conclusions regarding the composition of the livestock, beyond noting that cattle, sheep and horse were all identified.

In the absence of plant remains or other environmental indicators from Holts Farm Crossing, it is not possible to comment on the balance between crops and husbandry, but the animal bone assemblage indicates that cattle comprised the majority of the livestock, followed by sheep/goats. Pig and horse were also present in small numbers. There was evidence for a butchery technique that is usually only found on urban sites. This came from a medium mammal lumbar vertebra that had been chopped through axially, through the centre of the bone, consistent with the animal having been hoisted up on a pulley and spilt in half as a preliminary stage of butchery. This technique is typically associated with specialist butchers who are rapidly processing large numbers of animals and is not usually encountered in a rural context (Allen 2016, 134-5). It is possible that an individual at Holts Farm Crossing had been trained in butchery techniques elsewhere, or that meat intended for the market at Alchester was being processed in a manner that would be consistent with the requirements of the population there. In the latter instance, however, it would be expected that animals destined for the tables of Alchester would be transported there on foot and slaughtered at their destination.

Burials and other ritual activity

Burials (by Lauren McIntyre and Andrew Simmonds)

The human remains comprised an inhumation burial, some disarticulated unburnt bone and six cremation burials at Langford Lane East, a cremation burial at South of Merton and an inhumation burial and a cremation burial at Holts Farm Crossing. The inhumation at Langford Lane East was an older child (5-7 years) and that at Holts Farm Crossing was an adult, possibly male. Cremation burial 6720 at Langford Lane East contained the remains of an adult of undetermined sex aged 30-40 years and a neonate. The other cremation burials each comprised the remains of a single adult individual, none of whom could be sexed.

Cremation burials 417 and 6085 were situated beside the trackway that led to the parade ground and if they were contemporary with the track they would be the earliest burials from the excavation, dating from Alchester's military phase and representing the remains of soldiers or their dependents. The radiocarbon date of 60 cal BC-cal AD 70 that was obtained for burial 6085 is consistent with this hypothesis, and although the burial was cut by one of the trackway ditches this could be explained by the ditches being a later addition to a route that was not originally thus defined or by the ditch having been recut. The radiocarbon date of cal AD 70-230 for burial 417 is a little more problematic and would

place it slightly after the abandonment of the fortress. Perhaps the burial is of an individual who was associated with the fortress but remained at Alchester after the garrison had moved on, or perhaps the date should be slightly earlier than indicated. This burial included an assemblage of 15 nails likely to represent the remains of a small box or casket that either held the cremated remains or was buried with them. Such an item would be outside the normal range of burial practices of the native population and emphasises the status of this individual as part of an intrusive group associated with the fortress.

The inhumation grave at Langford Lane East was placed close to the road frontage and three adult cremation burials were clustered at the rear, southwestern limit of the roadside occupation. A further possible cremation burial was located close by but was almost completely truncated and no bone was identified. Burial within areas of domestic occupation is not unknown during the Roman period but, with the exception of neonates, is typically a characteristic of rural settlements, since towns were usually provided with formal cemeteries (Esmonde Cleary 2000). Nothing is known of Alchester's municipal cemeteries, however, apart from a group of 28 graves outside the south-eastern corner of the walled area that were disturbed during the construction of the railway in 1848 (Harden 1939, 284). Two cremation burials were located within the northern extramural settlement and a small inhumation cemetery was identified, but the latter was interpreted as possibly belonging to the occupants of the adjacent settlement plot (Booth *et al.* 2001, 438-9). With the exception of one of the cremations, which was undated, the burials at the northern extramural area were, in any case, of considerably later date than the ones at Langford Lane East and it is possible that arrangements had changed during the intervening time. Interestingly, two late Roman cemeteries that have been identified at Dorchester-on-Thames are located at some distance from the town and are not situated on the roads leading into the settlement, as is usually the case (Harman *et al.* 1978), but a third fairly substantial cemetery is now known to have lain at the south-east corner of the walled settlement. It is possible that, being relatively minor towns, the two settlements did not develop formal cemeteries until rather late in their histories. At present, however, there is insufficient evidence to support any definitive statement on the matter.

The child at Langford Lane East had been buried in a crouched position and the burial at Holts Farm Crossing was in a supine posture. The latter had been decapitated, with the head placed by the lower legs. Unfortunately, the truncation of the upper part of the body and the high levels of fragmentation meant that it was not possible to observe the skeletal elements that commonly bear peri-mortem cut marks in cases of funerary decapitation, which usually occur on the mid-inferior bones of the cranium (eg mastoids, occipital and cranial base), mandible, cervical vertebrae of the neck, scapulae, and manubrium (Tucker 2012, 43). However, the location of the skull in the grave is consistent with instances of funerary decapitation elsewhere in Roman Britain (ibid., 83). Syntheses of decapitation burials have found that during this period the decapitated skull was most commonly placed by the lower legs or feet, particularly at rural sites (Harman *et al.* 1981, 165; Philpott 1991, 80; Tucker 2012, 84). The three burials in the northern extramural area that had been decapitated all had the head placed in this location (Boyle 2001, 386-7).

None of the cremation burials amounted to the weight that would be expected for a complete cremated adult. All had been exposed to truncation from ploughing, which may have resulted in the loss of some of the buried remains, but such low weights are common for burials of the period and may indicate that it was not considered necessary to collect all of the bone for burial. The very small quantity of bone in burials 7272 and 7408 at Langford Lane may indicate that they represent token deposits or cenotaph burials, where only a small quantity of cremated material was selected from the pyre for burial (Williams 2004, 418). In the case of 7272, the quantity is so small that it may have been incorporated incidentally into a feature that was not funerary in character. Small quantities of charcoal were found in cremated bone deposits from all three sites; this is likely to be pyre debris. Pyre debris is commonly found within cremation grave fills and features containing cremated bone (McKinley 2008, 171) and represents the remains of fuel used during the cremation process, typically surviving as charcoal, charred fragments of wood, or ash (McKinley 2013, 151). This is likely to have become mixed with the cremated bone during the cremation process, with bone and debris being collected together from the pyre site before being interred. The majority were dominated by oak, which provides the high calorific heat necessary and makes a suitable bier support. The absence of charcoal from the other burials indicates that some care was taken in picking out the bone from the pyre for subsequent burial.

Variation in the colour of cremated bone fragments may indicate that the degree of combustion was slightly variable in terms of temperature and heat distribution. Generally, cremated bone may range in colour from brownish-black (slightly charred) to white (fully calcined bone: McKinley 2000b, 405). These colour changes are determined by firing temperature, duration of exposure of the body to flames, and oxygen supply (McKinley 2000a, 66). While modern crematoria are able to maintain constant, optimal conditions (ie temperature, air circulation, fuel), these are more difficult to control when dealing with a pyre cremation (McKinley 2000b, 404). For example, the length of time that the pyre can burn and the attained temperature are often dependent on the quantity of fuel

utilised (McKinley 2000b, 269). Pyre technology, that is, the method and form of construction and degree of oxygen circulation, also influences the efficiency of cremation (ibid., 269). This may lead to less uniform combustion of the corpse, which is reflected in the colour variation of the remaining skeletal fragments. Thus, where variation in oxidation of bone was noted (most particularly in cremation burials 6084, 7408 and pit 7272, this is indicative of incomplete combustion. This may be evidence of either deliberate curtailment of the cremation process (eg where full oxidation of the remains was of no great concern), accidental interruption or conclusion of the cremation (eg weather-related), or poor cremation because of factors such as insufficient fuel (McKinley 2013, 84).

Cremation burial 6720 at Langford Lane East contained the remains of at least two individuals, comprising an adult and a juvenile. This occurs infrequently in Britain; it has been estimated that only around 5% of British archaeological cremation burials represent the remains of two or more individuals, and most frequently these comprise the remains of an adult and a child (McKinley 2013, 153). These may represent either the remains of two individuals cremated together on a single pyre, or ashes from two cremations interred in a single pit (McKinley 2006, 85).

The presence of burnt animal bone co-mingled with human bone in burials 417, 6711 and 6720 indicates that animal remains may have been placed on the cremation pyre with the cadaver. Unburnt bone fragments may represent the remains of grave goods, or may be incidental inclusions. Animals remains present (burnt or unburnt) in Romano-British cremation deposits may represent joints of meat, especially where domestic species are found (McKinley 2006, 83). The inclusion of small bird bones has also been suggested to represent the cremating of pets (ibid.).

Evidence for both dental calculus and dental caries was found in older child skeleton 7125 at Langford Lane East. The presence of dental calculus may be an indication of poor dental hygiene, although calculus severity in this individual was relatively low. Dental caries form when the enamel, dentine and cement of the tooth is destroyed as a result of contact with acid produced by the bacteria in dental plaque (Hillson 1996, 269). The condition may be exacerbated by increased consumption of sucrose, refined sugar and starch (ibid., 276-8), as well as other non-dietary factors such as dental wear and presence of other dental disease (Roberts and Manchester 1997, 47). Thus, the presence of caries may suggest that this individual was consuming cariogenic foods such as dried fruit, honey, or fermented grape juice, foods which are generally considered to be the main sources of dietary sugar in Roman Britain (Garnsey 1999, 118; Alcock 2001, 67 and 76; Sealey 2009, 28).

Observed pathological evidence in both the burnt and unburnt assemblage showed potential indicators of non-specific stress in the form of cribra orbitalia and periosteal new bone formation. This may be linked to observed porosity in several bones of the cranium and may also be indicative of the presence of scurvy. A moderately high prevalence of cribra orbitalia and scurvy in the juvenile population from the late Roman cemetery at Poundbury in Dorchester, Dorset, has been used to suggest that the community may have adopted child-rearing practices that involved fasting the newborn, a poor-quality weaning diet, and swaddling, leading to general malnutrition (Lewis 2010). The periosteal new bone formation observed in cremation burials at Langford Lane East and South of Merton could not be related to a specific disease or condition. Prevalence and severity of periosteal new bone formation in archaeological populations is generally regarded as being indicative of adaptation and/or maladaptation to environmental conditions, in particular poor sanitation, malnutrition and general health stressors (Roberts and Manchester 1997).

Possible priestly head-dress

A small, round copper alloy cap recovered from the road surface at Langford Lane East was probably a piece of priestly regalia, forming the central element of a chain head-dress. The cap, a disc 31mm in diameter with a central raised socket, would have sat at the top of the head, with chains hanging down, probably linked around the brow by further chains. The edge of the disc is pierced in two places by holes from which the chains would have been suspended and a probable third hole would have been located in a section of the object that was damaged in antiquity, the three holes being regularly spaced. One of the holes retains the first ring of its chain. The arrangement of three chains is unusual, most examples having four, and the regular spacing perhaps suggests that the chains hung at the temples and the back of the head. More complete examples have been found at the temples at Wanborough and Farley Heath, Surrey, and in a hoard of votive objects buried in an urn at Stony Stratford, Buckinghamshire (Bird 1994; 1996; 2007). Closer to Alchester, the remains of an incomplete headdress were represented by two copper alloy discs with pierced edges and two lengths of chain found at the temple at Woodeaton (Kirk 1949, 36). The details of the designs vary; three of the head-dresses at Wanborough are surmounted by wheels and one with a knob finial, while the example at Farley Heath has a double knob and the one from Stony Stratford is rather larger with a more cone-shaped profile. The socket in the piece from Langford Lane East may have allowed a decorative finial to be attached, as was probably the case with one of the examples at Wanborough.

In contrast to the examples mentioned above, which all appear to have been deliberately buried, the piece at Langford Lane East was evidently a casual loss. It nevertheless suggests the presence of a priest in the extramural settlement, whether perma-

nently or just passing through. While Roman temples would undoubtedly have required priests to lead religious ceremonies, in all but the largest establishments this is likely to have been an occasional role, and direct evidence for such individuals is in fact rare. A town the size of Alchester is likely to have possessed several temples and a number of possible buildings have been identified within the town from cropmark evidence. A large courtyard building beside the central crossroads may be either a temple or a market, while a more typical Romano-Celtic temple comprising a square structure within a perambulatory is located in the north-east quadrant, and a circular building in the south-west area may also be a temple (Foster 1989). Geophysical survey has identified a further probable temple in the western extramural settlement south of the bathhouse at 'The Castle' (Sauer 2000a, 74; Erwin and Sauer 2000, 77-8), and extramural temples have been identified at several towns in other parts of the country (Esmonde Cleary 1987, 178). The location of the temple at which the priest who wore the head-dress at Langford Lane East presided is therefore uncertain.

Special deposits

The excavations produced very few features or deposits that might have been associated with ritual activity. A pit on the north side of the trackway at Holts Farm Crossing contained the burial of a ewe, which may have represented the dedication of a sacrificed animal, although there was no definite evidence for this. Cut marks at the distal ends of the right radius and humerus indicated that the animal had been partly butchered before burial.

More intriguing were two instances of cremated domestic fowl, each of which had been inserted into a pot that was placed in a ditch. Both birds had been thoroughly cremated, discounting an interpretation as a cooking accident. Neither pot was burnt and the birds must therefore have been burnt elsewhere before being placed in the vessels for burial. One was found in a lower fill of the eastern flanking ditch of the road at Langford Lane East and the other in a ditch at the western extent of the landscape boundaries at Langford Lane South. They were therefore separated by a distance of *c* 1km, which makes their similarity all the more striking. Although the features were phased differently, the roadside ditch being associated with the initial construction of the road during Phase 4 and the boundary ditch being attributed to Phase 5, in practice both features silted up gradually over a long period of time and the deposits may therefore be broadly contemporary. The bird at Langford Lane East had been placed in a grey-ware cooking pot type jar that dated from the 2nd century and the fowl at Langford Lane South was deposited in a shell-tempered jar dated to the mid-2nd to early 3rd century. The latter was part of a deposit of more than 2.5kg of pottery that included a grey ware jar and at least two more shell-tempered jars, and was anomalous in such an apparently isolated location. No exact parallels could be found for these deposits, but domestic fowl are a common find in burials, particularly cremations, where they and pigs are the most frequently encountered species (Allen forthcoming; cf. Worley 2008). In such circumstances, the remains will, of course, be cremated if they have been placed on the pyre. Indeed, burnt remains of both domestic fowl and pig were recovered from cremation burial 417 at Langford Lane East. Other than birds that may have been cremated on a pyre, the closest parallels to the deposits at Langford Lane are calcined domestic fowl bones contained in pots that were interred with two inhumation burials at Trentholme Drive, York (Fraser and Ryder 1968). It is difficult to sex such remains due to fragmentation and incomplete representation of the bird, and it was not possible at Langford Lane, but the birds may be cockerels; these would be an appropriate offering in a funerary context since the cockerel was the totemic animal of Mercury, whose responsibilities included conducting souls to the underworld in his guise as Mercury Psychopompus (Barber and Bowsher 2000, 318). The cremated birds deposited at Langford Lane may therefore represent the remains of rituals that were associated in some way with funerary rites.

Alchester and its hinterland

The establishment of the fortress at Alchester must have had a significant impact on the population of the surrounding countryside, but the social, political and economic consequences for these communities are surprisingly difficult to identify archaeologically. Regionally, evidence for widespread settlement abandonment at the time of the conquest is absent and the pattern tends to be one of continuity. In the Alchester area, however, there are several settlements that were abandoned around this time. These include the enclosed settlement at Bicester Fields Farm (Cromarty *et al.* 1999, 231) and the poorly-understood settlement at Area D of the A41 excavations (Booth *et al.* 2001, 446), while the boundary ditch at Slade Farm appears to have finally silted at this time and was not recut (Ellis *et al.* 2000, 265). At Whitelands Farm the enclosed settlement in Area 1 was also abandoned, and occupation in Area 7 did not last long into the Roman period, although the excavator suggested that the latter may have been abandoned due to persistent flooding (Martin 2011, 179-81). It is uncertain whether the late Iron Age occupation at Langford Lane East adapted itself to the new situation and continued into the post-conquest phase or whether there was a replacement of population, but, as discussed above, there was certainly a major reorganisation of the landscape attendant on the arrival of the military. The available dating evidence is not precise enough to definitely attribute any of these abandonments to the effects of the Roman conquest. However, the coincidence of several abandonments in the vicinity of the fortress may suggest that they were associated with the imposition of Roman military control, which must have entailed large-scale seizure or re-allocation of land as well as less direct impacts on the local community. The garrison would have required a huge quantity of food and other resources, and while some of this material would have been acquired from elsewhere, it would have made sense to source as much as possible locally (Thomas 2008). Whether this was damaging to the local communities or whether care was taken to ensure the sustainability of supplies in uncertain. Certainly other native settlements appear to have continued unaffected by the arrival of Roman rule, including the farmstead at Holts Farm Crossing and the settlements at Oxford Road (Mould 1996, 106), Langford Park Farm (Pine and Mundin forthcoming) and an extensive area of settlement at Whitelands Farm Areas 14, 15, 16 and 18 that appears to have developed into a substantial farmstead during the 2nd century, albeit the main focus of occupation was located outside the excavation area (Martin 2011, 181-2). At several sites, significant new developments can be attributed to the early Roman period, although generally the dating evidence can only assign them broadly to the late 1st-early 2nd century and is not able to specify whether they were contemporary with the military phase at Alchester or with the subsequent civilian settlement. The farmstead at Holts Farm Crossing was reorganised with the addition of the trackway, and it was during this period that occupation at North of Oxford Parkway Station began, while the field system at South of Oddington Crossing may also have been initiated at this time. Similarly, the farmstead at Bicester Park was established during the late 1st century and settlement at Oxford Road was re-organised around AD 60-80, although the site appears to have subsequently been abandoned around AD 100/120 due to flooding (Mould 1996, 106). The immediate consequences of the establishment of the fort appear to have been quite varied, with disruption at some settlements but others continuing.

The impact that the arrival of the military had on the community at Langford Lane East is uncertain, with continuity or wholesale replacement of the pre-conquest population equally valid interpretations of the excavated evidence. It is clear, however, that the activity here during the military phase was entirely civilian in character, since items with military associations were completely absent. The character of the activity was ambiguous, since no structural evidence was identified, and the range of features was very limited, comprising shallow pits and gullies. The artefactual evidence, however, suggests that domestic occupation lay nearby, and the presence of pre-Flavian samian ware and amphora sherds in addition to the typical jar-dominated material indicates that it may have been of a distinctive character compared to contemporary rural settlements in the region.

The developmental history of the town is not understood in great detail, but it is likely to have commenced by the 80s/90s (Booth *et al.* 2001, 428) with the initial phase of construction encompassing the late 1st century and the early part of the 2nd (Henig and Booth 2000, 56). If this is correct, the part of the extramural settlement excavated at Langford Lane East would appear to be a precocious development that took place at the same time as the building of the main town rather than a later expansion or overspill. Occupation between this location and the town need not have been physically continuous at this stage, however, and could equally have comprised a separate settlement focus constructed around the junction of Akeman Street and the east Otmoor route. Such a subsidiary focus may have developed directly in this area from the pre-Roman occupation and the possible vicus, although the current evidence is insufficient to be certain. The relationship between the extramural settlement and the walled part of the town cannot be investigated with any confidence due to the lack of detailed evidence from the latter area, but the artefactual evidence from Langford Lane East, particularly the composition of the pottery assemblage, would not be out of place at a rural settlement and might suggest that the population here was more similar to its rural contemporaries than to fully urbanised areas. The structural evidence, on the other hand, was somewhat anomalous, with Buildings 7602 and 7222 being of unusual design and uncertain function, whether as booths, the towers of a gatehouse, or, less likely, a pair of shrines. Building 7640, on the other hand, is likely to be of more typical design for such a location, perhaps representing a typical craftworker's residence and shop. The decline and eventual abandonment of this area may have been associated with a decline in use of the east Otmoor route after it was superseded by the direct route to Dorchester across the middle of Otmoor, especially if its economy comprised a combination of agriculture and provision of service industries to the town and passing travellers.

The town was situated within a densely-populated landscape of rural settlements for which it must have been the principal market for food and other resources. Some of the needs of the urban community were met by farming of the immediately surrounding land from the town, as exemplified by the enclosed landscape to the south of the town and the evidence that both the eastern and northern extramural areas were engaged in agriculture, but this would not have been sufficient to satisfy the requirements of the population and sourcing of materials from the surrounding region would still have been necessary. Direct evidence for the undoubted economic and social links between Alchester and surrounding rural settlements nevertheless remains difficult to define. In this light the expansion of the area of enclosed fields at Holts Farm Crossing may perhaps be interpreted as a strategy to increase agricultural production, and the

replacement of the discrete enclosures at North of Oxford Parkway Station with a complex of conjoined enclosures during the 2nd century may represent the adoption of more intensive husbandry practices. The apparent adoption at Holts Farm Crossing of intensive butchery techniques that are more typically found at urban sites may have been intended to produce cuts that were to the tastes of the urban population. If this means that meat was being processed at rural sites before transport to the town it is likely that it would have required preserving, most likely by smoking or salting, although no direct evidence for this was found. The supply of large quantities of food and materials to the town would have required an efficient transport network, represented not only by the construction of the principal routes such as Akeman Street and the road to Dorchester but also by the trackways with which the settlements at Holts Farm Crossing, North of Oxford Parkway Station and Bicester Park were associated. These were typically wide thoroughfares that would have been appropriate for droving and were no doubt used for movement of livestock, delivered to the town on the hoof. The animal bone evidence from Langford Lane East demonstrated that entire animals were being butchered and some of these animals may have been delivered thus from farmsteads further afield, although it should be stressed that the community in the extramural settlement were processing carcasses for immediate domestic consumption and were not engaged in large-scale processing to supply the urban market.

Although there are currently insufficient data from the walled area of Alchester to investigate the issue of social inequality between the town and its rural hinterland, evidence from elsewhere in the province suggests that such inequalities should be expected (Smith *et al.*, 2016, 418). There is also considerable evidence for inequalities between rural settlements in the Alchester region, which may have resulted, at least in part, from their relationships with the town. The upper end of the spectrum is represented by the poorly-understood settlements at South Farm and Kings End Farm and at Middleton Stoney (Rahtz and Rowley 1984), all of which included stone-founded buildings (Chambers 1989; 1979), and by the villa overlooking the River Ray at Islip (Henig and Booth 2000, 83, 88-9; see also Cheetham 1995, 421). The indirect evidence for a well-appointed building at Langford Lane South, most likely with heated rooms and/or a bathhouse, may place this establishment in the same category and the prevalence of fine table wares in the pottery assemblage would also be appropriate. Conversely, the pottery assemblages from Langford Lane East and the rural settlements on EWR Phase 1, as well as the other sites in the area, place them among the ranks of farmsteads that were the homes of the bulk of the population, albeit only Holts Farm Crossing was at the lower end of the spectrum. Tenurial relationships between sites are difficult to establish, but it is possible that the economic effects of the town's relationship with the surrounding countryside were being mediated through the social system of rural communities and that the visible inequalities were maintained by the elite elements of the local community being enriched by their dealings with the town while such benefits were not passed on to those further down the social scale.

There is some evidence from the prevalence of 'West Oxfordshire' wares in the pottery assemblage at North of Oxford Parkway Station that the settlement here may have tapped into a slightly different exchange network to the other sites, perhaps indicating that it was not primarily associated with the town. Given the location of the settlement on the west side of the River Cherwell, it is possible that the river formed a significant economic or cultural barrier. It has been suggested that the river was the boundary between the Iron Age 'tribal' groups of the Dobunni and Catuvellauni (Allen 2000, 27-31) and was perpetuated during the Roman period as the boundary between civitates.

None of the rural settlements continued long into the 3rd century, the small quantities of pottery of late 3rd or 4th century date at Holts Farm Crossing and North of Oxford Parkway Station being associated with the trackways rather than the adjacent occupation areas. This is surprising, since settlement at Alchester does not appear to have been in decline. Although we know relatively little about the urban sequence, the coin list from the town indicates late occupation (Booth *et al*. 2001, 445). Furthermore, the most intensive phases of occupation within the northern extramural area occurred during this period and although there may have been some contraction of the occupied area during the second half of the 4th century the interpretation of this is far from straightforward (Booth *et al*. 2001, 432-3). The apparent conflict between evidence for depopulation in the countryside but continuity within the town is puzzling and may suggest that, in addition to a possible decline in the overall population (Smith *et al*. 2016, 416-7), there may have been substantial migration into the town from the surrounding countryside.

Bibliography

ACBMG, 2007 *Ceramic building material: minimum standards for recovery, curation, analysis and publication*, Archaeological Ceramic Building Materials Group

Ainslie, R, 1992 Excavations at Thrupp near Radley, Oxon., *South Midlands Archaeology* **22**, 63-6

Albarella, U, 1997 *Iron Age and Roman animal bones excavated in 1996 from Norman Cross, Tort Hill East, Tort Hill West and Vinegar Hill, Cambridgeshire*, English Heritage Res Rep 108/1997, http://research.historicengland.org.uk/Report.aspx?i=4944&ru=%2FResults.aspx%3Fp%3D301

Alcock, J P, 2001 *Food in Roman Britain*, Tempus, Stroud

Allen, M, 2016 The South, in A Smith, M Allen, T Brindle and M Fulford, *New visions of the countryside of Roman Britain. Vol. 1: the rural settlement of Roman Britain*, Britannia Monograph **29**, London, 75-140

Allen, M, forthcoming Animals in burials, in A Smith, M Allen, T Brindle, M Fulford, L Lodwick and A Rohnbognor, *New visions of the countryside of Roman Britain. Vol. 3: life and death in the countryside of Roman Britain*, Britannia Monograph Series

Allen, T G, 1990 *An Iron Age and Romano-British enclosed settlement at Watkins Farm, Northmoor, Oxon*, Thames Valley Landscapes: the Windrush Valley, vol. **1**, Oxford Univ. Committee for Archaeology, Oxford

Allen, T G, 2000 The Iron Age background, in Henig and Booth 2000, 1-33

Allen, T G, Darvill, T C, Green, L S, and Jones, M U, 1993 *Roughground Farm, Lechlade, Glos.: a prehistoric and Roman landscape*, Oxford University Committee for Archaeology, Thames Valley Landscapes: The Cotswold Water Park **1**, Oxford

Andersen, S Th, 1979 Identification of wild grass and cereal pollen, *Danmarks Geologiske Undersogelse*, 1978, 69-92

Anderson, R, 2005 An annotated list of the non-marine mollusca of Britian and Ireland, *Journal of Conchology* **38(6)**, 607-37

Anderson-Whymark, H, 2012 Neolithic to early Bronze Age pit deposition practices and the temporality of occupation in the Upper Thames Valley, in H Anderson-Whymark and J Thomas (eds) *Regional perspectives on Neolithic pit deposition: beyond the mundane*, Neolithic Studies Group Seminar Series **12**, Oxbow Books, Oxford, 187-199

Atherton, K, Booth, P, and Allen, L, 2001 Ceramic building material, in Booth *et al.* 2001, 253-61

Bantock, T, and Botting, J, 2013 *British bugs, an online identification guide to UK Hemiptera*, http://www.britishbugs.org.uk (consulted 30.7.2017)

Barber, B, and Bowsher, D, 2000 *The eastern cemetery of Roman London: excavations 1983-1990*, MOLAS Monograph **4**, London

Barclay, A, Glass, H, and Hey, G, 1995 Fired clay, in Hey 1995, 105-62

Bayley, J, and Rehren, T, 2007 Towards a functional and typological classification of crucibles, in S Niece, D Hook and P T Craddock (eds), *Metals and mines: studies in archaeometallurgy*, Archetype Publications, London, 46-55

Behre, K E, 1981 The interpretation of anthropogenic indicators in pollen diagrams, *Pollen et Spores* **23**, 225-245

Berglund, B E, and Ralska-Jasiewiczowa, M, 1986 Pollen analysis and pollen diagrams, in B E Bergland (ed.), *Handbook of Holocene palaeoecology and palaeohydrology*, Chichester, 455-484

Betts, I M, Black, E W, and Gower, J L, 1997 *A corpus of relief-patterned tiles in Roman Britain*, J Roman Pottery Studies **7**, Oxbow Books, Oxford

Bevan, L, 2000 The flint, in Ellis *et al.* 2000, 227-33

Biddulph, E, 2004 The Iron Age and Roman pottery, in R Heawood, Iron Age and Roman activity at Watchfield Triangle, *Oxoniensia* **69**, 298-309

Biddulph, E, 2005a Roman pottery, in Bradley *et al.* 2005, 155-167

Biddulph, E 2005b Fired clay, in Bradley *et al.* 2005, 167-169

Biddulph, E, 2008 Form and function: the experimental use of samian ware cups, *Oxford J Archaeol* **27(1)**, 91-100

Biddulph, E, 2010 Late Iron Age and Roman pottery, in Smith *et al.* 2010, 21-47

Bidwell, P, 1999 A survey of pottery production and supply at Colchester, in Symonds and Wade 1999, 488-499

Bird, J, 1994 Other finds, excluding pottery, in M O'Connell and J Bird, The Roman temple at Wanborough, excavation 1985-86, *Surrey Archaeological Collections* **82**, 93-132

Bird, J, 1996 A Romano-British priestly head-dress from Farley Heath, *Surrey Archaeological Collections* **83**, 81-89

Bird, J, 2005 Discussion of decorated samian from pit A [1066], in F Seeley and J Drummond-Murray, *Roman pottery production in the Walbrook valley: excavations at 20-28 Moorgate, City of London, 1998-2000*, MoLAS Monograph **25**, 32

Bird, J, 2007 Catalogue of Iron Age and Roman artefacts discovered before 1995, in R Poulton, Farley Heath Roman temple, *Surrey Archaeological Collections* **93**, 34-68

Boardman, S, and Jones, G, 1990 Experiments on the effects of charring on cereal plant components, *J Archaeol Sci* **17**, 1-11

Boessneck, J, 1969 Osteological differences between sheep (*Ovis aries Linné*) and goat (*Capra hircus Linné*), in Brothwell and Higgs 1969, 331-358

Booth, P, 1995 Roman pottery, in A Boyle, A Dodd, D Miles and A Mudd, *Two Oxfordshire Anglo-Saxon cemeteries: Berinsfield and Didcot*, Oxford Archaeological Unit Thames Valley Landscapes Monograph **8**, 16-26

Booth, P, 1996 Pottery and other ceramic finds, in C Mould, An archaeological excavation at Oxford Road, Bicester, Oxfordshire, *Oxoniensia* **61**, 75-89

Booth, P, 1997 *Asthall, Oxfordshire, excavations in a Roman 'small town', 1992*, Oxford Archaeological Unit Thames Valley Landscapes Monograph **9**, Oxford

Booth, P, 2000a Roman pottery, in P Booth and C Hayden, A Roman settlement at Mansfield College, Oxford, *Oxoniensia* **65**, 307-317

Booth, P, 2000b The Iron Age and Roman pottery, in R Bourn, Manorhouse Farm, Hatford, Oxfordshire, in R J Zeepvat (ed.) *Three Iron Age and Romano-British rural settlements on English gravels*, BAR Brit Ser **312**, 25-45

Booth, P, 2001 Fired clay in Booth *et al.* 2001, 260-261

Booth, P, 2004 Quantifying status: some pottery data from the Upper Thames Valley, *J Roman Pottery Studies* **11**, 39-52

Booth, P, 2007a Pottery, in A M Cromarty, M R Roberts and A Smith, Archaeological investigations at Stubbs Farm, Kempsford, Gloucestershire, 1991-1995, in Miles *et al.* 2007, 301-304

Booth, P, 2007b Cotswold Water Park Roman ceramic assemblages in their regional context, in Miles *et al.* 2007, 319-335

Booth, P, 2009 Late Iron Age and Roman pottery, in P Booth and A Simmonds, *Appleford's earliest farmers: archaeological work at Appleford Sidings, Oxfordshire, 1993-2000*, Oxford Archaeology Occ Paper **17**, Oxford, 64-85

Booth, P, 2010 Late Iron Age and Roman pottery [from Castle Hill], in T Allen, K Cramp, H Lamdin-Whymark and L Webley, *Castle Hill and its landscape: archaeological investigations at the Wittenhams, Oxfordshire*, Oxford Archaeology Monograph **9**, Oxford, 56-65

Booth, P, 2011a The Iron Age and Roman pottery, in G Hey, P Booth and J Timby, *Yarnton: Iron Age and Romano-British settlement and landscape:*

results of excavations 1990-98, Oxford Archaeology Thames Valley Landscapes Monograph **35**, 345-411

Booth, P, 2011b Iron-Age and Roman pottery, in A Simmonds, H Anderson-Whymark and A Norton, Excavations at Tubney Wood Quarry, Oxfordshire, 2001-2009, *Oxoniensia* **76**, 148-164

Booth, P, 2012a The occurrence and use of samian ware in rural settlements in the Upper Thames Valley, in D G Bird (ed.), *Dating and interpreting the past in the western Roman Empire: essays in honour of Brenda Dickinson*, Oxbow, Oxford, 254-265

Booth, P, 2012b The pottery, in G Speake, An early Romano-British villa at Combe East End, *Oxoniensia* **77**, 49-75

Booth, P, 2014 Late Iron Age and Roman pottery, in A Simmonds, *The archaeology of Banbury Flood Alleviation Scheme, Oxfordshire: Neolithic and Roman occupation in the Cherwell Valley*, Oxford Archaeology Monograph **21**, Oxford, 93-107

Booth, P, 2016 Oxford Archaeology Roman pottery recording system: an introduction, unpublished OA document, revised

Booth, P, 2017a Roman pottery from Horcott, in Hayden *et al.* 2017, 281-294

Booth, P, 2017b Pottery from Arkells Land, in Hayden *et al.* 2017, 451-477

Booth, P, 2018 Pottery, in Booth and Simmonds 2018, 259-395

Booth, P, forthcoming Late Iron Age and Roman pottery, in Hayden *et al.* forthcoming

Booth, P, and Green, S, 1989 The nature and distribution of certain pink, grog tempered vessels, *J Roman Pottery Studies* **2**, 77-84

Booth, P, Bingham, A-M, and Lawrence, S, 2008 *The Roman roadside settlement at Westhawk Farm, Ashford, Kent: excavations 1998-9*, Oxford Archaeology Monograph **2**, Oxford

Booth, P, Boyle, A, and Keevill, G D, 1993 A Romano-British kiln site at Lower Farm, Nuneham Courtenay, and other sites on the Didcot to Oxford and Wootton to Abingdon water mains, Oxfordshire, *Oxoniensia* **58**, 87-217

Booth, P, Dodd, A, Robinson, M, and Smith, A, 2007 *The Thames through time: the archaeology of the gravel terraces of the Upper and Middle Thames. The early historical period: AD 1-1000*, Oxford Archaeology Thames Valley Landscapes Monograph **29**, Oxford

Booth, P, Evans, J, and Hiller, J, 2001 *Excavations in the extramural settlement of Roman Alchester, Oxfordshire, 1991*, Oxford Archaeology Monograph **1**, Oxford

Booth, P, and Simmonds, A, 2018 *Later prehistoric landscape and a Roman nucleated settlement in the lower Windrush Valley at Gill Mill, near Witney, Oxfordshire*, Oxford Archaeology Thames Valley Landscapes Monograph **42**, Oxford

Boycott, A E, 1936 The habits of freshwater mollusca in Britain, *Journal of Animal Ecology* **144**, 129-30

Boyle, A, 2001 Human skeletal assemblage, in Booth *et al.* 2001, 385-94

Bradley, P, Charles, B, Hardy, A, and Poore, D, 2005 Prehistoric and Roman activity and a Civil War ditch: excavations at the Chemistry Research Laboratory, 2-4 South Parks Road, Oxford, *Oxoniensia* **70**, 141-202

Bradley, P, Parsons, M, and Tyler, R, 1997 The excavation of two barrows at Merton, Oxfordshire, *Oxoniensia* **62**, 51-86

Brickley, M, 2004 Determination of sex from archaeological skeletal material and assessment of parturition, in Brickley and McKinley (eds) 2004, 23-5

Brickley, M, and Ives, R, 2008 *The bioarchaeology of metabolic bone disease*, Academic Press, London

Brickley, M, and McKinley, J I (eds), 2004 *Guidelines to the standards for recording human remains*, IFA Paper No. **7**, British Association for Biological Anthropology and Osteoarchaeology

Broderick, L G, 2012 Ritualisation (or the four fully-articulated ungulates of The Apocalypse), in A Pluskowski (ed.), *The ritual killing and burial of animals: European perspectives*, Oxbow Books, Oxford, 22-32

Brodribb, A C C, Hands, A R, and Walker, D, 1971 *Excavations at Shakenoak Farm, near Wilcote, Oxfordshire Part II: Sites B and H*, privately published

Brodribb, G, 1987 *Roman brick and tile*, Alan Sutton, Gloucester

Brothwell, D R, and Higgs, E S (eds), 1969 *Science in archaeology: a survey of progress and research*, Thames and Hudson, London

Brown, K, 1999 The pottery, in Cromarty *et al.*, 182-195

Brown, K, 2003 Roman pottery, in D Miles, S Palmer, G Lock, C Gosden and A M Cromarty, *Uffington White Horse and its landscape: investigations at White Horse Hill, Uffington, 1989-95, and Tower Hill, Ashbury, 1993-4*, Oxford Archaeology Thames Valley Landscapes Monograph **18**, Oxford, 175-178

Brown, K, 2007a Pottery, in A Smith, Excavations at Neigh Bridge, Somerford Keynes, in Miles *et al.* 2007, 243-247

Brown, K, 2007b Pottery, in A Marshall, S Palmer and A Smith, Archaeological investigations at Whelford Bowmoor, Gloucestershire, 1983, 1985 and 1988, in Miles *et al.* 2007, 284-288

Brown, K M, 2011 Later prehistoric and Romano-British pottery, in J Martin, Prehistoric, Romano-British and Anglo-Saxon activity at Whitelands Farm, Bicester, *Oxoniensia* **76**, 201-210

Brown, L, 2010 Late Iron Age and Roman pottery, Digital Appendix 6 to G Lambrick, *Neolithic to Saxon social and environmental change at Mount Farm Berinsfield, Dorchester-on-Thames*, Oxford Archaeology Occasional Paper **19**, Oxford

Bryan, E, and Brown, K, 2004 Roman pottery (ceramic phase 3), in J Cook, E B A Guttman and A Mudd, Excavations of an Iron Age site

at Coxwell Road, Faringdon, *Oxoniensia* **69**, 229-231

Burnham, B C, 1988 A survey of building types in Romano-British 'small towns', *J Brit Arch Ass* **141**, 35-59

Camden, W, 1607 *Britannia*

Campbell, G, 2004 Charcoal and charred plant remains, in H E M Cool, *The Roman cemetery at Brougham, Cumbria: excavations 1966-67*, Britannia Monograph **21**, London, 267-271

Cappers, R T J, Bekker, R M, and Jans, J E A, 2006 *Digital seed atlas of the Netherlands*, Institute of Archaeology, Groningen

Carreras Monfort, C, 2004 Haltern 70: a review, *J Roman Pottery Studies* **10**, 85-91

Carrott, J, and Kenward, H, 2001 Species associations among insect remains from urban archaeological deposits and their significance in reconstructing the past human environment, *J Archaeol Sci* **28**, 887-905

Challinor, D, 2006 Wood charcoal from Pepper Hill, CTRL specialist report series, in CTRL digital archive, Archaeology Data Service, http://archaeologydataservice.ac.uk/archives/view/ctrl/envspr/downloads.cfm

Challinor, D, 2007 Wood charcoal, in J Timby, R Brown, A Hardy, S Leech, C Poole and L Webley, *Settlement on the Bedfordshire claylands; archaeology along the A421 Great Barford Bypass*, Bedfordshire Archaeology Monograph **8**, 382-8

Challinor, D, 2008 Wood charcoal, in Booth *et al.* 2008, 343-9

Chambers, R A, 1979 Bicester, Kings End Farm, *CBA Group 9 Newsletter* **9**, 123-5

Chambers, R A, 1986a A Roman timber bridge at Ivy Farm, Fencott with Murcott, Oxon., 1979, *Oxoniensia* **51**, 31-6

Chambers, R A, 1986b A section across the Roman road north of Dorchester-on-Thames, 1981, *Oxoniensia* **51**, 1934

Chambers, R A, 1987 Sections across the Roman road south of Alchester, *Oxoniensia* **52**, 181-4

Chambers, R A, 1989 Bicester: South Farm Development, *South Midlands Archaeology* **19**, 49-50

Chambers, R A, 1992 The archaeology of the M40 through Buckinghamshire, Northamptonshire and Oxfordshire, 1988-91, *Oxoniensia* **57**, 43-54

Chapman, A, 2008 The querns and millstones, in Westgarth and Carlyle 2008, 121-46

Chapman, T A, 1869 *Aphodius porcus*, a cuckoo parasite on *Geotrupes stercorarius*, *Entomologist's Monthly Magazine* **5**, 273-76

Cheetham, C J, 1995 Some Roman and pre-Roman settlements and roads by the confluences of the Cherwell and Ray near Otmoor, *Oxoniensia* **60**, 419-426

Cleere, H, and Crossley, D, 1985 *The iron industry of the Weald*, Leicester University Press, Leicester

Cohen, A, and Serjeantson, D, 1996 *A manual for the identification of bird bones from archaeological sites*, 2 edn, Archetype Publications, London

Cooper, N J, 1998 The supply of pottery to Roman Cirencester, in N Holbrook (ed.), *Cirencester: the Roman town defences, public buildings and shops*, Cirencester Excavations **5**, Cirencester, 324-350

Cooper, N J, 2000 Preliminary observations on the pottery from the excavations, in Sauer 2000b, 57-58

Cottam, E, de Jersey, P, Rudd, C, and Sills, J, 2010 *Ancient British coins*, Chris Rudd, Aylsham

Cox, A, 1979 *Brickmaking: a history and gazetteer. Survey of Bedfordshire*, Bedfordshire County Council

Cox, M L, 2007 *Atlas of the seed and leaf beetles of Britain and Ireland*, Pisces, Newbury

Cox, M, and Mays, S (eds), 2000 *Human osteology in archaeology and forensic science*, Greenwich Medical Media Ltd, London

Cromarty, A-M, Foreman, S, and Murray, P, 1999 The excavation of a late Iron Age enclosed settlement at Bicester Fields Farm, Bicester, Oxon., *Oxoniensia* **64**, 153-233

Cunliffe, B W, 1971 *Excavations at Fishbourne 1961-1969*, Rep Res Committee of the Soc of Antiquaries of London **26**

Darwish, D, 2001 Coins, in Booth *et al.* 1991, 216-221

Davies, B, Richardson, B, and Tomber, R, 1994 *A dated corpus of early Roman pottery from the City of London*, CBA Res Rep **98**, London

Davis, S J M, 1980 Late Pleistocene and Holocene equid remains from Israel, *Zoological Journal of the Linnean Society* **70(3)**, 289-312

Dobson, E, 1850 *A rudimentary treatise on the manufacture of bricks and tiles*, George Woodfall and Son, London

Duff, A (ed.), 2012 *Checklist of beetles of the British Isles*, Pemberley Books, Iver

Duvauchelle, A, 1990 Les outils en fer du Musée romain d'Avenches, *Bulletin de l'Association Pro Aventico* **32**, 5-118

Edlin, H L, 1949 *Woodland crafts in Britain: an account of the traditional uses of trees and timbers in the British countryside*, Batsford, London

Ellis, A E, 1926 *British snails: guide to the non-marine Gastropoda of Great Britain and Ireland, Pleistocene to recent*, Oxford University Press, Oxford

Ellis, P, Hughes, G, and Jones, L, 2000 An Iron Age boundary and settlement features at Slade Farm, Bicester, Oxfordshire: report on excavations, 1996, *Oxoniensia* **65**, 211-265

ERM, 2009a Evergreen 3 Project: The Chiltern Railways (Oxford to Bicester) Improvements: EIA Scoping Report, Environmental Resources Management

ERM, 2009b Evergreen 3 Project: The Chiltern Railways (Oxford to Bicester Improvements) Order Environmental Statement, Environmental Resources Management

Erwin, P, and Sauer, E, 2000 Wendlebury, the geophysical survey at Alchester (SP 570 203), *South Midlands Archaeology* **30**, 77-79

Esmonde Cleary, S, 1987 *Extra-mural areas of Romano-British towns*, BAR Brit Ser **169**, Oxford

Esmonde Cleary, S, 2000 Putting the dead in their place: burial location in Roman Britain, in J Pearce, M Millett and M Struck (eds), *Burial, society and context in the Roman world*, Oxbow, Oxford, 127-142

Evans, J, 2001a Iron Age, Roman and Anglo-Saxon pottery, in Booth *et al.* 2001, 263-383

Evans, J, 2001b Material approaches to the identification of different Romano-British site types, in S James and M Millett (eds), *Britons and Romans: advancing an archaeological agenda*, CBA Res Rep **125**, 26-35

Evans, J and Booth, P, 2001 Iron Age pottery, in Booth *et al.* 2001, 270-276

Evans, J G, 1972 *Land snails in archaeology*, Seminar Press, London and New York

Farci, C, Martinón-Torres, M, and González Álvarez, D, 2017 Bronze production in the Iron Age of the Iberian Peninsula: the case of El Castru, Vigaña (Asturias, NW Spain), *Journal of Archaeological Science Reports* **11**, 338-351

Figueiral, I, 1992 The charcoals, in M G Fulford and J R L Allen, Iron-making at the Chesters villa, Woolaston, Gloucestershire: survey and excavation 1987-91, *Britannia* **23**, 188-191

Foreman, M, and Rahtz, S, 1984 Excavations at Faccenda Chicken Farm, near Alchester, 1983, *Oxoniensia* **49**, 23-46

Foster, A M, 1989 Alchester, Oxon: a brief review and new aerial evidence, *Britannia* **20**, 141-7

Foster, G N, and Friday, L E, 2011 *Keys to adults of the water beetles of Britain and Ireland (Part 1)*, Handbooks for the identification of British insects **5(11)**, Shrewsbury

Fraser, F, and Ryder, M L, 1968 Animal bones, in L P Wenham (ed.) *The Romano-British cemetery at Trentholme Drive*, HMSO, London, 104-109

Frere, S S, and St Joseph, J K S, 1983 *Roman Britain from the air*, Cambridge University Press

Friendship-Taylor, R M, 1999 *Late La Tène pottery of the Nene and Welland valleys, Northamptonshire*, BAR Brit Ser **280**, Oxford

Gale, R, 1997 Charcoal, in A P Fitzpatrick, *Archaeological excavations on the route of the A27 Westhampnett Bypass, West Sussex, 1992*, Wessex Archaeology Report **12**, Salisbury, 253

Gale, R, and Cutler, D, 2000 *Plants in archaeology: identification manual of vegetative plant materials used in Europe and the southern Mediterranean to c 1500*, Westbury and Kew

Garnsey, P, 1999 *Food and society in classical antiquity*, Cambridge, Cambridge University Press

Gill, F B, and Donsker, D, 2015 *IOC World Bird List* (v 5.1), doi: 10.14344/IOC.ML.5.1

Goffer, Z, 2007 *Archaeological chemistry*, 2 edn, Wiley Interscience, New Jersey

Goodchild, R, and Kirk, J R, 1954 The Romano-

Celtic temple at Woodeaton, *Oxoniensia* **19**, 15-37

Grant, A, 1982 The use of tooth wear as a guide to the age of domestic ungulates, in Wilson *et al.* 1982, 91-108

Greig, J, 1994 A possible hedgerow flora of Iron Age date from Alcester, Warwickshire, *Circaea* **11**, 7-16

Green, L S, and Booth, P, 1993 The Roman pottery, in Allen *et al.* 1993, 113-142

Green, S, and Booth, P, 2007 Roman pottery, in Miles *et al.* 2007, CD ROM Section 3.2

Green, S, Booth, P, and Allen, T, 2004 Late Iron Age and Roman pottery, in G Lambrick and T Allen, *Gravelly Guy, Stanton Harcourt: the development of a prehistoric and Romano-British community*, Oxford Archaeology Thames Valley Landscapes Monograph **21**, Oxford, 303-334

Grimm, E C, 1991-2011 *Tilia, TiliaGraph and TG-View*, Illinois State Museum, Illinois, http://intra.museum.state.il.us/pub/grimm/tilia

Grimm, J M, and Worley, F L, 2011 Animal bone, in C Barnett, J I McKinley, E Stafford, J M Grimm and C J Stevens, *Settling the Ebbsfleet Valley: High Speed 1 excavations at Springhead and Northfleet, Kent: the late Iron Age, Roman, Saxon, and Medieval landscape. Vol. 3: late Iron Age to Roman human remains and environmental reports*, Oxford Wessex Archaeology, 15-52

Hall, A R, and Kenward, H K, 1990 *Environmental evidence from the Colonia: General Accident and Rougier Street*, The Archaeology of York **14(6)**, 289-434, London

Halstead, P L J, Collins, P, and Isaakidou, V, 2002 Sorting the sheep from the goats: morphological distinctions between the mandibles and mandibular teeth of adult Ovis and Capra, *J Archaeol Sci* **29(5)**, 545-553

Harde, K W, 1984 *A field guide in colour to beetles*, Octopus Books, London

Harden, D B, 1937 Excavations at Chesterton Lane, Alchester, 1937, *Oxfordshire Archaeol Soc Report* **83**, 23-39

Harden, D B, 1939 Romano-British remains: settlement sites, in Salzman 1939, 281-302

Harding, D W, 1987 *Excavations in Oxfordshire, 1964-6*, University of Edinburgh

Harman, M, Lambrick, G, Miles, D, and Rowley, T, 1978 Roman burials around Dorchester-on-Thames, *Oxoniensia* **43**, 1-16

Harman, M, Molleson, T I, and Price, J L, 1981 Burials, bodies and beheadings in Romano-British and Anglo-Saxon cemeteries, *Bulletin of the British Museum of Natural History (Geology)* **35(3)**, 145-188

Hart, J, Kenyon, D, and Mudd, A, 2010 Excavation of early Bronze Age cremations and a later Iron Age settlement at Finmere Quarry, north-east Oxfordshire, *Oxoniensia* **75**, 97-132

Hartley, B R, and Dickinson, B M, 2008 *Names on Terra Sigillata: vol. 3 (Certianus to Exsobano)*, Bulletin of the Institute of Classical Studies Supplement **102-03**, Institute of Classical Studies, University of London, London

Hartley, B R, and Dickinson, B M, 2010 *Names on Terra Sigillata: vol. 6 (Masclus i-Balbus to Oxitus)*, Bulletin of the Institute of Classical Studies Supplement **102-06**, Institute of Classical Studies, University of London, London

Hartley, B R and Dickinson, B M, 2012 *Names on Terra Sigillata: vol. 9 (T to Ximus)*, Bulletin of the Institute of Classical Studies Supplement **102-08**, Institute of Classical Studies, University of London, London

Hather, J G, 2000 *The identification of Northern European woods: a guide for archaeologists and conservators*, Archetype Publications, London

Hawkes, C F C, and Hull, M R, 1947 *Camulodunum: first report on the excavations at Colchester, 1930-1939*, Rep Res Comm Soc Antiq London **14**, Oxford

Hawkes, S C, 1927 Excavations at Alchester 1926, *Antiq J* **7**, 155-84

Hawksworth, D L, Webb, J A, and Wiltshire, P E, 2010 *Caryosora callicarpa*: found in archaeological and modern preparations but not collected since 1865, *Field Mycology* **11(2)**, 55-59

Hayden, C, Early, R, Biddulph, E, Booth, P, Dodd, A, Smith, A, Laws, G, and Welsh, K, 2017 *Horcott Quarry, Fairford and Arkell's Land, Kempsford: prehistoric, Roman and Anglo-Saxon settlement and burial in the Upper Thames Valley in Gloucestershire*, Oxford Archaeology Thames Valley Landscapes Monograph **40**, Oxford

Hayden, C, Simmonds, A, Lawrence, S, Masefield, R, and Wheaton, K, forthcoming *Great Western Park, Didcot, Oxon: excavations, 2010-2012*, Oxford Archaeology Thames Valley Landscapes Monograph, Oxford

Henig, M, and Booth, P, 2000 *Roman Oxfordshire*, Alan Sutton, Stroud

Hey, G, 1995 Iron Age and Roman settlement at Old Shifford Farm, Standlake, *Oxoniensia* **60**, 93-175

Hey, G, Booth, P, and Timby, J, 2011 *Yarnton: Iron Age and Romano-British settlement and landscape. Results of excavations 1990-98*, Oxford Archaeology Thames Valley Landscapes Monograph **35**, Oxford

Hey, G, Bell, C, Dennis, C and Robinson, M, 2016 *Yarnton: Neolithic and Bronze Age settlement and landscape: results of excavations 1990-98*, Oxford Archaeology Thames Valley Landscapes Monograph **39**, Oxford

Hillson, S, 1996 *Dental anthropology*, Cambridge University Press, Cambridge

Hinchliffe, J, and Thomas, R, 1980 Archaeological investigations at Appleford, *Oxoniensia* **45**, 9-111

Hingley, R, 1997 Iron, ironworking and regeneration: a study of the symbolic meaning of metalworking in Iron Age Britain, in A Gwilt and C Haselgrove (eds), *Reconstructing Iron Age societies: new approaches to the British Iron Age*, Oxbow Monograph **71**, Oxford, 9-18

Historic England, 2015 *Archaeometallurgy: Guidelines for best practice*, London, https://historicengland.org.uk/images-books/publications/archaeometallurgy-guidelines-best-practice/

Hobbs, R, 1996 *British Iron Age coins in the British Museum*, British Museum Press, London

Hodgson, J G, Halstead, P, Wilson, P J, and Davis, S, 1999 Functional interpretation of archaeobotanical data: making hay in the archaeological record, *Veget Hist Archaeobot* **8**, 261-71

Hubbard, R N L B, and al Azm, A, 1990 Quantifying preservation and distortion in carbonised seeds; and investigating the history of Friké production, *Journal of Archaeological Science* **17**, 103-106

Hughes, J, 1984 The pottery, in Foreman and Rahtz, 31-34

Hull, M R, 1963 *The Roman potters' kilns of Colchester*, Rep Res Comm Soc Antiqs London **21**

Hussey, R, 1841 *An account of the Roman road from Allchester to Dorchester*, The Ashmolean Society, Oxford

Hyman, P S, and Parsons, M S, 1992 *A review of the scarce and threatened Coleoptera of Great Britain, Part 1*, UK Conservation Series Report No. **3**, JNCC, Peterborough

Iliffe, J H, 1929 Excavations at Alchester 1927, *Antiq J* **9**, 105-36

Iliffe, J H, 1932 Excavations at Alchester 1928, *Antiq J* **12**, 35-67

Innes, J B, 1999 Regional vegetational history, in D R Bridgland, B P Horton and J B Innes, *The Quaternary of North-East England*, Quaternary Research Association Field Guide, 21-34

Jessop, L, 1986 *Dung beetles and chafers. Coleoptera: Scarabaeoidea*, Handbooks for the identification of British insects, **5(11)**, Royal Entomological Society, London

Johnstone, C, 2004 *A biometric study of equids in the Roman world*, University of York, http://www.york.ac.uk/depts/arch/pgstudents/Johnstone.html

Joly, C, Barille, L, Barreau, M, Mancheron A, and Visset, L, 2007 Grain and annulus diameter as criteria for distinguishing pollen grains of cereals from wild grasses, *Review of Palaeobotany and Palynology* **146**, 1-4

Jones, M, 1991 The development of crop husbandry, in M Jones and G Dimbleby (eds), *The environment of man: the Iron Age to the Anglo-Saxon period*, BAR Brit Ser **87**, 95-127

Joubert, D M, 1956 A study of pre-natal growth and development in the sheep, *Journal of Agricultural Science* **47(4)**, 382

Kadletz, E, 1976 Animal sacrifice in Greek and Roman religion, PhD thesis, University of Washington, Seattle

Kamash, Z, Gosden, C, and Lock, G, 2010 Continuity of religious practices in Roman Britain: the case of the rural religious complex at Marcham/Frilford, Oxfordshire, *Britannia* **41**, 95-125

Keevill, G, 2010 Archaeological impact assessment for PAGE of proposed gravel extraction in the Benson, Berinsfield, Berrick Salome, Drayton St Leonard, Dorchester, Newington, Stadhampton and Warborough area – RAS 13. Unpublished report submitted to Oxfordshire County Council

Keevill, G D, and Williams, R J, 1995 The excavation of a Roman road and a medieval causeway at Ditchford Pit, Wellingborough, Northamptonshire, *Northamptonshire Archaeology* **26**, 47-77

Kenward, H, 1997 Synanthropic decomposer insects and the size, remoteness and longevity of archaeological occupation sites: applying concepts from biogeography to past 'islands' of human occupation, in A C Ashworth, P C Buckland and J T Sadler (eds), *Studies in Quaternary entomology: an inordinate fondness for insects*, Quaternary Proceedings **5**, Wiley, Chichester, 135-152

Kenward, H, 2009 *Invertebrates in archaeology in the North of England*, Research Department Report Series **12-2009**, English Heritage

Kenward, H, and Hall, A, 1997 Enhancing bioarchaeological interpretation using indicator groups: stable manure as a paradigm, *J Archaeol Sci* **24**, 663-673

Kenward, H K, and Hall, A R, 1995 *Biological evidence from 16-22 Coppergate*, The Archaeology of York **14(7)**, York, 435-797

Kenward, H K, Hall, A R, and Jones, A K G, 1980 A tested set of techniques for the extraction of plant and animal macrofossils from waterlogged archaeological deposits, *Science and Archaeology* **22**, 3-15

Kenward, H K, Hall, A R, and Jones, A K G, 1986 *Environmental evidence from a Roman well and Anglian pits in the legionary fortress*, The Archaeology of York **14(5)**, York, 241-288

Kerney, M, 1999 *Atlas of land and freshwater molluscs of Britain and Ireland*, Harley Books, Colchester

Kerney, M P, and Cameron, R A D, 1979 *A field guide to the land snails of Britain and north-west Europe*, Collins, London

King, A, 1999 Diet in the Roman world: a regional inter-site comparison of the mammal bones, *Journal of Roman Archaeology* **12**, 168-202

King, A, 2005 Animal remains from temples in Roman Britain, *Britannia* **36**, 329-369

Kirk, J R, 1949 Bronzes from Woodeaton, Oxon., *Oxoniensia* **14**, 1-45

Kratochvil, Z, 1969 Species criteria on the distal section of the tibia in *Ovis ammon F. aries L.* and *Capra aegagrus F. hircus L.*, *Acta Veterinaria Brno*, **38**, 483-490

Kuijper, W J, and Turner, H, 1992 Diet of a Roman centurion at Alphen aan den Rijn, The Netherlands, in the first century AD, *Review of Palaobotany and Palynology* **73**, 187-204

Laidlaw, M, 2001 Pottery, in V Birbeck, Excavations at Watchfield, Shrivenham, Oxfordshire, 1998, *Oxoniensia* **66**, 250-265

Lambrick, G, 1992 The development of late prehistoric and Roman farming on the Thames gravels, in M Fulford and E Nichols (eds), *Developing landscapes of lowland Britain. The archaeology of the British gravels: a review*, Society of Antiq London Occ Papers vol. **14**, 78-105

Lambrick, G, and Allen, T, 2004 *Gravelly Guy, Stanton Harcourt, Oxfordshire: the development of a prehistoric and Romano-British community*, Oxford Archaeology Thames Valley Monograph No. **21**, Oxford

Lambrick, G, and Robinson, M, 1979 *Iron Age and Roman riverside settlements at Farmoor, Oxfordshire*, Oxford Archaeological Unit Report **2** and CBA Res Rep **32**, London

Lambrick, G, with Robinson, M, 2009 *The Thames through time: the archaeology of the gravel terraces of the Upper and Middle Thames. Vol. 3: the Thames Valley in late prehistory: 1500 BC-AD 50*, Oxford Archaeology Thames Valley Landscapes Monograph **29**, Oxford

Lamdin-Whymark, H, 1999 The struck flint, in Cromarty *et al.* 1999, 180-2

Lamdin-Whymark, H, 2008 *The residue of ritualised action: Neolithic deposition practices in the Middle Thames Valley*, BAR Brit Ser **466**, Oxford

Lauwerier, R C G M, 1993 Twenty-eight bird briskets in a pot: Roman preserved food from Nijmegen, *Archaeofauna* **2**, 15-19

Lauwerier, R C G M, 2004 The economic and non-economic animal: Roman depositions and offerings, in S J O'Day, W Van Neer and A Ervynck (eds), *Behaviour behind bones: the zooarchaeology of ritual, religion, status and identity*, Oxbow Books, Oxford, 66-72

Leeds, E T, 1939 Early man: the Bronze Age, in Salzman 1939, 241-251

Levine, M A, 1982 The use of crown height measurements and eruption-wear sequences to age horse teeth, in Wilson *et al.* 1982, 223-250

Lewis, M E, 2010 Life and death in a civitas capital: metabolic disease and trauma in the children from late Roman Dorchester, Dorset, *American Journal of Physical Anthropology* **142(3)**, 405-16

Linington, R E, 1959 A Roman road from Alchester to Dorchester, *Oxoniensia* **24**, 103-5

Lobel, M D (ed.), 1957 *A History of the County of Oxford, volume 5: Bullingdon Hundred*, Victoria History of the Counties of England, Oxford

Lovejoy, C O, Meindl, R S, Pryzbeck, T R, and Mensforth, R P, 1985 Chronological metamorphosis of the auricular surface of the ilium: a new method for the determination of adult skeletal age at death, *American Journal of Physical Anthropology* **68**, 15-28

Luff, M L, 1998 *Provisional atlas of the ground beetles (Coleoptera, Carabidae) of Britain*, Biological Records Centre, Monks Wood, Abbots Ripton

Luff, M L, 2007 *The Carabidae (ground beetles) of Britain and Ireland*, Handbooks for the identification of British insects **4(2)**, 2 edn, Shrewsbury

Lyman, R L 1994 *Vertebrate taphonomy*, Cambridge University Press, Cambridge

Majerus, M E N, 1994 *Ladybirds*, Harper Collins, London

Maltby, M, 2010 *Feeding a Roman town: environmental evidence from excavations in Winchester, 1972-1985*, Winchester Museums, Winchester

Maltby, M, 2015 Commercial archaeology, zooarchaeology and the study of Romano-British towns, in M Fulford and N Holbrook (eds), *The towns of Roman Britain: the contribution of commercial archaeology since 1990*, Britannia Monograph **27**, London, 175-193

Martin, J, 2011 Prehistoric, Romano-British and Anglo-Saxon activity at Whitelands Farm, Bicester, *Oxoniensia* **76**, 173-240

Martin-Kilcher, S, 2003 Fish-sauce amphorae from the Iberian peninsula: the forms and observations on trade with the north-western provinces, *J Roman Pottery Studies* **10**, 69-84

Martinón-Torres, M, and Rehren, T, 2014 Technical ceramics, in B W Roberts and C P Thornton (eds), *Archaeometallurgy in global perspective: methods and syntheses*, Springer, New York, 107-131

May, E, 1985 Widerristhöhe und Langknochen-maße bei Pferden – ein immer noch aktuelles Problem', *Zeitschrift für Säugetierkunde* **50**, 368-382

Mays, S, 2004 *Human bones from archaeological sites: guidelines for producing assessment documents and analytical reports*, English Heritage, Centre for Archaeology Guidelines

McKinley, J I, 2000a Cremation burials, in B Barber and D Bowsher, *The eastern cemetery of Roman London: excavations 1983-1990*, MoLAS Monograph **4**, 264-77

McKinley, J I, 2000b The analysis of cremated bone, in Cox and Mays 2000, 403-21

McKinley, J I, 2004a Compiling a skeletal inventory: disarticulated and co-mingled remains, in Brickley and McKinley (eds) 2004, 14-7

McKinley, J I, 2004b The human remains and aspects of pyre technology and cremation rituals, in H Cool, *The Roman cemetery at Brougham, Cumbria*, Britannia Monograph **2**, 283-310

McKinley, J I, 2006 Cremation...the cheap option?, in C Knüsel and R Gowland (eds), *The social archaeology of funerary remains*, Oxbow Books, Oxford, 81-8

McKinley, J I, 2008 In the heat of the pyre: efficiency of oxidation in Romano-British cremations – did it really matter?, in C W Schmidt and S A Symes (eds), *The analysis of burned human remains*, Elvesier, Amsterdam, 163-84

McKinley, J I, 2013 Cremation – excavation, analysis and interpretation of material from cremation related deposits, in S Tarlow and L N Stutz (eds), *The Oxford handbook of the archaeology of death and burial*, Oxford University Press, Oxford, 147-67

Merrifield, R, 1987 *The archaeology of ritual and magic*, B T Batsford, London

Miles, D, 1986 *Excavation at Barton Court Farm, Abingdon, Oxon.*, Oxford Archaeological Unit Report **3**, CBA Res Rep **50**, Oxford and London

Miles, D, Palmer, S, Smith, A, and Jones, G P, 2007 *Iron Age and Roman settlement in the Upper Thames Valley: excavations at Claydon Pike and other sites within the Cotswold Water Park*, Oxford Archaeology Thames Valley Landscapes Monograph **26**, Oxford

Millett, M, 1979 An approach to the functional interpretation of pottery, in M Millett (ed.) *Pottery and the archaeologist*, Univ London Institute of Archaeol Occ Pub No **4**, 35-48

Mook, W G, 1986 Business meeting: recommendations/resolutions adopted by the twelfth International Radiocarbon Conference, *Radiocarbon* **28**, 799

Moore, P D, Webb, J A, and Collinson, M E, 1991 *Pollen analysis*, 2 edn, Blackwell, Oxford

Moore, T, 2006 *Iron Age societies in the Severn-Cotswolds: developing narratives of social and landscape change*, BAR Brit Ser **421**, Oxford

Morigi, A, Schreeve, D, and White, M, 2011 *The Thames through time: the archaeology of the gravel terraces of the Upper and Middle Thames, early prehistory to 1500BC*, Oxford Archaeology Thames Valley Landscapes Monograph No **32**, Oxford

Morris, J T, 2011 *Investigating animal burials: ritual, mundane and beyond*, BAR Brit Ser **535**, Oxford

Morris, M G, 1990 *Orthocerous weevils, Coleoptera Curculionoidea*, Handbooks for the identification of British insects **5(16)**, London

Morris, M G, 1997 *Broad-nosed weevils. Coleoptera Curculionidae (Entiminae)*, Handbooks for the identification of British insects **5(17a)**, London

Morris, M G, 2002 *True weevils (Part 1), Coleoptera Curculionoidea (Subfamilies Raymondionyminae to Smicronychinae)*, Handbooks for the identification of British insects **5(17b)**, London

Morris, M G, 2008 *True weevils (Part 2), (Coleoptera: Curculionidae Ceutorhynchinae)*, Handbooks for the identification of British insects **5(17c)**, Shrewsbury

Morris, M G, 2012 *True weevils (Part 3) (Coleoptera: Curculioninae, Baridinae, Orobitinae)*, Handbooks for the identification of British insects **5(17d)**, Shrewsbury

Mould, C, 1996 An archaeological excavation at Oxford Road, Bicester, Oxfordshire, *Oxoniensia* **61**, 65-108

Mudd, A, 2007 *Iron Age and Roman settlement on the Northamptonshire uplands: archaeological work on the A43 Towcester to M40 road improvement scheme in Northamptonshire and Oxfordshire*, Northamptonshire Archaeology Monograph **1**, Northampton

Nau, B, 2004 *Guide to shield bugs of the British Isles*, Field Studies Council, Shrewsbury

Neal, D S, 1974 *The Roman villa in Gadebridge Park, Hemel Hempstead*, London Soc Antiq Res Rep **31**, London

OA, 2013 The Chilterns Railways (Bicester to Oxford Improvements) Order 2012: Written Scheme of Investigation for archaeological works, Oxford Archaeology unpublished client report

OA, 2014a Power cable burial and pole replacement within Alchester Scheduled Monument, Langford Lane diversion, Wendlebury, Oxfordshire: Written Scheme of Investigation for archaeological monitoring, excavation and recording, Oxford Archaeology unpublished document

OA, 2014b The Chiltern Railways (Bicester to Oxford Improvements) Order 2012: Written Scheme of Investigation for archaeological excavations at Langford Lane overbridge, Wendlebury, Oxfordshire, Oxford Archaeology unpublished document

OA, 2014c The Chiltern Railways (Bicester to Oxford Improvements) Order 2012: Written Scheme of Investigation for archaeological excavation and preservation *in situ* monitoring at Langford Lane diversion and overbridge, Wendlebury, Oxfordshire, Oxford Archaeology unpublished document

OA, 2014d Langford Lane road diversion within Alchester Scheduled Monument, Wendlebury, Oxfordshire: Written Scheme of Investigation for an archaeological trial trench evaluation and geotechnical soils investigation, Oxford Archaeology unpublished document

OA, 2015a College Farm barn access track, Merton, Oxfordshire: Written Scheme of Investigation for ground bearing testing and archaeological excavation and preservation *in situ*, Oxford Archaeology unpublished client report

OA, 2015b The Chiltern Railways (Bicester to Oxford Improvements) Order 2012: Written Scheme of Investigation for an archaeological excavation at Langford Lane diversion Site 31d, Wendlebury, Oxfordshire, Oxford Archaeology unpublished document

OA, 2015c Langford Lane road diversion within Alchester Scheduled Monument, Wendlebury, Oxfordshire: Written Scheme of Investigation for archaeological recording and monitoring during construction activities, Oxford Archaeology unpublished document

OA, 2015d Langford Lane level crossing turning head within Alchester Scheduled Monument, Wendlebury, Oxfordshire: Written Scheme of Investigation for archaeological recording and monitoring during construction activities, Oxford Archaeology unpublished document

OA, 2016a Bicester MOD, Graven Hill, Bicester, Oxfordshire: evaluation report, Oxford Archaeology unpublished client report

OA, 2016b Bicester MOD, Graven Hill, Bicester,

Oxfordshire: archaeological watching brief and evaluation report, Oxford Archaeology unpublished client report

Ortner, D, 2003 *Identification of pathological conditions in human skeletal remains*, Academic Press, London

Oswald, F, 1936-37 *Index of figure-types on terra sigillata*, Annals of Archaeology and Anthropology 23-4, Liverpool

Payne, S, 1985 Morphological distinctions between the mandibular teeth of young sheep, Ovis, and goats, Capra, *J Archaeol Sci* **12**, 139-147

Paynter, S, 2011 *Pre-industrial ironworks*, Introductions to Heritage Assets, English Heritage

PCRG, SGRP and MPRG, 2016 *A standard for pottery studies in archaeology*, Prehistoric Ceramic Research Group, Study Group for Roman Pottery and Medieval Pottery Research Group

Peacock, D P S, and Williams, D F, 1986 *Amphorae and the Roman economy*, Longman, London

Pelling, R, 2001 Charred plant remains, in Booth *et al.* 2001, 418-422

Pelling, R, 2011 Charcoal, in Martin 2011, 233-4

Philpott, R, 1991 *Burial practices in Roman Britain: a survey of grave treatment and furnishing AD 43-410*, BAR Brit Ser **219**, Oxford

Pine, J, and Mundin, A, forthcoming Early Roman and late Anglo-Saxon occupation at Langford Park Farm, London Road, Bicester, *Oxoniensia*

Poole, C, 2010 Ceramic building material in Smith *et al.* 2010

Pope, R, 2008 Roundhouses: 3000 years of prehistoric design, *Current Archaeology* **222**, 14-21

Rackham, O, 2003 *Ancient woodland: its history, vegetation and uses in England*, Castlepoint Press, Kirkcudbrightshire

Rademakers, F, and Farci, C, 2018 Reconstructing bronze production technology from ancient crucible slag: experimental perspectives on tin oxide identification, *Journal of Archaeological Science Reports* **18**, 343-355

Rademakers, F W, Rehren, Th, Pusch, E B, 2018 Bronze production in Pi-Ramesse: alloying technology and material use, in E Ben-Yosef (ed.), *Mining for copper: essays in honor of Professor Beno Rothenberg*, Institute of Archaeology of Tel Aviv, Tel Aviv, 503–525

Rahtz, S, and Rowley, T, 1984 *Middleton Stoney: excavation and survey in a North Oxfordshire parish, 1970-1982*, Oxford

Raw, F, 1951 The ecology of the garden chafer *Phyllopertha horticola* (L.) with preliminary observations on control measures, *Bulletin of Entomological Research* **42**, 605-46

RCHME, 1976 *Ancient and historical monuments in the County of Gloucester. Vol. 1: Iron Age and Romano-British monuments in the Cotswolds*, Royal Commission on Historical Monuments England, London

Resnick, D, and Niyawama, G, 1995 Enostosis, hyperostosis and periostitis, in D Resnick (ed.), *Diagnosis of bone and joint disorders*, Saunders, Philadelphia, 4396-466

Reynolds, P J, and Langley, J K, 1979 Romano-British corn-drying oven: an experiment, *Archaeol J* **136**, 27-42

Roberts, C A, 2000 Infectious disease in biocultural perspective: past, present and future work in Britain, in Cox and Mays 2000, 145-62

Roberts, C, and Manchester, K, 1997 *The archaeology of disease*, Sutton Publishing, Stroud

Robinson, M, 1975 The environment of the Roman defences at Alchester and its implications, in Young 1975, 161-170

Robinson, M, 1978 The problem of hedges enclosing Roman and earlier fields, in H C Bowen and P J Fowler (eds), *Early land allotment*, BAR Brit Ser **48**, 155-158

Robinson, M, 2011 The paleoecology of alluvial hay meadows in the Upper Thames Valley, *Fritillary* **5**, 47-57

Robinson, M, and Lambrick, G, 2009 Setting the scene: the natural environment and the geography of settlement, in Lambrick with Robinson 2009, 17-51

Roe, F, 2001 Worked stone, in Booth *et al.* 1991, 248-255

Rogers, G B, 1974 *Poteries sigillées de la Gaule centrale, I, les motifs non figurés*, Supplément 28, Gallia, Paris

Rogers, G B, 1999 *Poteries sigillées de la Gaule centrale, II, les potiers*, Revue archéologique sites, Hors Série **40**, Lezoux

Rogers, J, and Waldron, T, 1995 *A field guide to joint disease in archaeology*, John Wiley and Sons, London

Romeuf, A-M, 2001 *Le quartier artisanal Gallo-Romain des Martres-de-Veyre (Puy-de-Dôme).* Revue archéologique sites, Hors Série **41**, Lezoux

Rowley, R T, 1975 The Roman towns of Oxfordshire, in W Rodwell and T Rowley (eds), *The 'small towns' of Roman Britain*, BAR Brit Ser **15**, Oxford

Rowley, T, and Brown, L, 1981 Excavations at Beech House Hotel, Dorchester-on-Thames 1972, *Oxoniensia* **46**, 1-55

Ruscillo, D, 2003 Alternative methods for identifying sex from archaeological animal bone, *British School at Athens Studies* **9**, 37-44

Salter, C, 1993 Metalworking, in T G Allen and M A Robinson, *The prehistoric landscape and Iron Age enclosed settlement at Mingies Ditch, Hardwick-with-Yelford, Oxon.*, Oxford Archaeological Unit Thames Valley Landscapes: the Windrush Valley vol. **2**, Oxford, 77

Salzman, L F (ed.), 1939 *A History of the County of Oxford, volume I*, Victoria History of the Counties of England, Oxford

Sauer, E, 1998 Merton/Wendlebury, the Roman military base at Alchester, *South Midlands Archaeology* **28**, 70-3

Sauer, E, 1999a The military origins of the Roman town of Alchester, Oxfordshire, *Britannia* **30**, 289-297

Sauer, E, 1999b Merton/Wendlebury, the Roman army at Alchester, *South Midlands Archaeology* **29**, 61-5

Sauer, E, 2000a Wendlebury, the Claudian fort at Alchester, *South Midlands Archaeology* **30**, 72-9

Sauer, E, 2000b Alchester, a Claudian 'Vexillation Fortress' near the western boundary of the Catuvellauni: new light on the Roman invasion of Britain, *Archaeol J* **157**, 1-78

Sauer, E, 2001 Wendlebury (Alchester), a vexillation fortress of the year AD 44, *South Midlands Archaeology* **31**, 72-6

Sauer, E, 2002 Wendlebury (Alchester), an annexe of AD 44 and the earlier(?) main fortress, *South Midlands Archaeology* **32**, 84-94

Sauer, E, 2003 Wendlebury (Alchester fortress): headquarters, granary and timber bridge, *South Midlands Archaeology* **33**, 92-105

Sauer, E, 2004 Wendlebury (Alchester fortress): the 2003 season, *South Midlands Archaeology* **34**, 78-84

Sauer, E, 2005a Wendlebury (Alchester fortress): two tombstones, the first known life story of a pre-medieval inhabitant of Oxfordshire and a geophysical survey south of the town, *South Midlands Archaeology* **35**, 89-94

Sauer, E W, 2005b Inscriptions from Alchester: Vespasian's base of the Second Augustan Legion(?), *Britannia* **36**, 101-133

Sauer, E W, 2006 Alchester: origins and destiny of Oxfordshire's earliest Roman site (The Tom Hassall Lecture for 2005), *Oxoniensia* **71**, 1-29

Schweingruber, F H, 1990 *Microscopic wood anatomy*, 3 edn, Swiss Federal Institute for Forest, Snow and Landscape Research

Seager Smith, R, Marter Brown, K, Mills, J M, and Biddulph, E, 2011 Late Iron Age and Roman pottery, in E Biddulph, R Seager Smith and J Schuster, *Settling the Ebbsfleet Valley: High Speed 1 excavations at Springhead and Northfleet, Kent. The late Iron Age, Roman, Saxon and medieval landscape. Vol. 2: late Iron Age to Roman finds reports*, Oxford Wessex Archaeology, 1-157

Sealey, P R, 2009 New light on the wine trade with Julio-Claudian Britain, *Britannia* **40**, 1-40

Sealey, P R, and Tyers, P A, 1989 Olives from Roman Spain: a unique find in British waters, *Antiq J* **69**, 53-72

Serjeantson, D, 1996 Animal bone, in S Needham and T Spence (eds), *Runnymede bridge research excavations. Vol. 2: refuse and disposal at Area 16 East, Runnymede*, British Museum Press, London, 194-223

Sewell, L, 2010 *Osteochondrosis in sheep and cattle: differential diagnosis and estimating prevalence*, University of York, York

Shaffrey, R, 2014 Stone, in Oxford Archaeology, Bicester Eco Development, Bicester, Oxfordshire, unpublished client report

Silver, I A, 1969 The ageing of domestic animals, in Brothwell and Higgs 1969, 283-302

Simmonds, A, 2013 *The archaeology of Banbury Flood Alleviation Scheme, Oxfordshire*, Oxford Archaeology Monograph **21**, Oxford

Simmonds, A, Biddulph, E, and Welsh, K, 2018 *In the shadow of Corinium: prehistoric and Roman occupation at Kingshill South, Cirencester, Gloucestershire*, Oxford Archaeology Thames Valley Landscapes Monograph **41**, Oxford

Simpson, G, 1957 Metallic black slip vases from central Gaul with applied and moulded decoration, *Antiq J* **37**, 29-42

Smith, A, 2007 Excavations at Neigh Bridge, Somerford Keynes, in Miles *et al.* 2007, 229-273

Smith, A, 2016 Buildings in the countryside, in Smith *et al.* 2016, 44-74

Smith, A, Allen, M, Brindle, T, and Fulford, M, 2016 *New visions of the countryside in Roman Britain. Vol. 1: the rural settlement of Roman Britain*, Britannia Monograph **29**, London

Smith, A, Powell, K, and Booth, P (eds), 2010 *Evolution of a farming community in the Upper Thames Valley. Excavation of a prehistoric, Roman and post-Roman landscape at Cotswold Community, Gloucestershire and Wiltshire. Vol. 2: the finds and environmental reports*, Oxford Archaeology Thames Valley Landscapes Monograph **31**, Oxford

Southwood, T R E, and Leston, D, 1959 *Land and water bugs of the British Isles*, Warne, London

Stace, C, 1997 *New flora of the British Isles*, 2 edn, Cambridge University Press, Cambridge

Stace, C, 2010 New flora of the British Isles, 3 edn, Cambridge University Press, Cambridge

Stanfield, J A, and Simpson, G, 1990 *Les potiers de la Gaule Centrale*, Revue archéologique, Hors Série **37**, Recherches sur les ateliers de potiers de la Gaule Centrale, Tome V, Lezoux

Stansbie, D, 2009 The late Iron Age and Roman pottery, in K Powell, G Laws and L Brown, *A late Neolithic/Early Bronze Age enclosure and Iron Age and Romano-British settlement at Latton Lands, Wiltshire*, Wiltshire Archaeol Mag **102**, 69-75

Stead, I M, 1976 *Excavations at Winterton Roman villa and other sites in North Lincolnshire*, Dept of Environment Archaeol Rep **9**, London

Steckel, R H, Larsen, C S, Sciulli, P W, and Walker, P L, 2006, *Data collection codebook: the Global History of Health Project*, Ohio State University, Ohio

Stevens, C, 2011a Charred plant remains, in Martin 2011, 226-233

Stevens, C, 2011b, Crop husbandry as seen from the charred botanical samples from Yarnton, in Hey *et al.*, 534-568

Stevens, C, Grimm, JM, and Worley, F, 2011 Agriculture, food and drink, in P Andrews, E Biddulph, A Hardy and R Brown, *Settling the Ebbsfleet Valley: High Speed 1 excavations at Springhead and Northfleet, Kent. The late Iron Age, Roman, Saxon and medieval landscape. Vol. 1: the sites*, Oxford Wessex Monograph, 236-24

Strid, L, 2012 Specialist report 15: animal bone, in E Biddulph, S Foreman, E Stafford, D Stansbie and R Nicholson, *London gateway: Iron Age and Roman salt making in the Thames Estuary, excavation at Stanford Wharf Nature Reserve, Essex*, https://library.thehumanjourney.net/909/102/15.Animal bone.pdf

Strid, L, 2018 Animal remains, in Booth and Simmonds 2018, 559-91

Strid, L, forthcoming Animal bones, in Hayden *et al.* forthcoming

Stuart-Macadam, P, 1991 Anaemia in Roman Britain, in H Bush and M Zvelebil (eds), *Health in past societies – biocultural interpretation of human skeletal remains in archaeological contexts*, BAR Int Ser **567**, Oxford, 101-13

Stukeley, W, 1776 *Itinerarium curiosum: or an account of the antiquities and remarkable curiosities in nature or art observed in travels through Great Britain*

Symonds, R P, and Wade, S, 1999 *Roman pottery from excavations at Colchester, 1971-86*, Colchester Archaeol Rep **10**, Colchester

Thomas, R M, 2008 Supply-chain networks and the Roman invasion of Britain: a case study from Alchester, Oxfordshire, in S Stallibrass and R M Thomas (eds), *Feeding the Roman army: the archaeology of production and supply in NW Europe*, Oxbow Books, Oxford, 31-41

Thompson, H, 1993 Iron Age and Roman Slave-Shackles, *Archaeol J* **150**, 57-168

Thompson, I, 1982 *Grog-tempered 'Belgic' pottery of south-eastern England*, BAR Brit Ser **108**, Oxford

Timby, J R, 1995 Pottery, in Hey 1995, 124-136

Timby, J, 1996 The pottery, in N Holbrook and A Thomas, The Roman and early Anglo-Saxon settlement at Wantage, Oxfordshire, Excavations at Mill Street, 1993-4, *Oxoniensia* **61**, 131-147

Timby, J, 1999 Roman pottery from Birdlip Quarry, Cowley, in A Mudd, R J Williams and A Lupton, *Excavations alongside Roman Ermin Street, Gloucestershire and Wiltshire: The archaeology of the A419/A417 Swindon to Gloucester Road Scheme, vol. 2*, Oxford Archaeological Unit, 339-365

Timby, J, 2001 Pottery, in A Barber and N Holbrook, A Romano-British settlement to the rear of Denchworth Road, Wantage, Oxford-shire: evaluation and excavation in 1996 and 1998, *Oxoniensia* **66**, 306-315

Timby, J, 2004 The pottery, in D Jennings, J Muir, S Palmer and A Smith, *Thornhill Farm, Fairford, Gloucestershire: an Iron Age and Roman pastoral site in the Upper Thames Valley*, Oxford Archaeology Thames Valley Landscapes Monograph **23**, Oxford, 90-108

Timby, J, 2008 The Roman pottery, in Westgarth and Carlyle 2008, 136-141

Timby, J, 2015 Pottery, in J Pine and S Preston, *An Iron Age round house and Roman villa at Chilton Fields, Oxfordshire*, Thames Valley Archaeological Services Monograph **21**, Reading, 39-45

Timby, J, and Harrison, E, 2004 Pottery, in J Pine and S Preston, *Iron Age and Roman settlement and landscape at Totterdown Lane, Horcott near Fairford, Gloucestershire*, Thames Valley Archaeol Services Mono **6**, Reading, 55-67

Tipping, R, 2002 Climatic variability and 'marginal' settlement in upland British landscapes: a re-evaluation, *Landscapes* **19**, 333-348

Tomber, R, and Dore, J, 1998 *The national Roman fabric reference collection: a handbook*, MoLAS Monograph No **2**

Trow, S, James, S, and Moore, T, 2009 *Becoming Roman, being Gallic, staying British. Research and excavations at Ditches 'hillfort' and villa 1984-2006*, Oxbow Books, Oxford

Tucker, K, 2012 'Whence this severance of the head': the osteology and archaeology of human decapitation in Britain, unpublished PhD thesis, University of Winchester

Tweddle, J C, Edwards, K J, and Fieller, N R J, 2005 Multivariate statistical and other approaches for the separation of cereal from wild Poaceae using a large Holocene dataset, *Vegetation History and Archaeobotany* **14**, 15-30

Tylecote, R F, 1962 *Metallurgy in archaeology: a prehistory of metallurgy in the British Isles*, E Arnold, London

van der Veen, M, 1989 Charred grain assemblages from Roman-period corn driers in Britain, *Archaeol J* **146**, 302-319

van der Veen, M, and Fieller, N, 1982 Sampling seeds, *J Archaeol Sci* **9**, 287-298

van der Veen, M, and O'Connor, T P, 1998 The expansion of agricultural production in late Iron Age and Roman Britain', in J Bayley (ed.), *Science in archaeology: an agenda for the future*, English Heritage, London, 127-143

van Geel, B, 1978 A palaeoecological study of Holocene peat bog sections in Germany and the Netherlands, *Review of Palaeobotany and Palynology* **25**, 1-120

van Geel, B, and Aptroot, A, 2006 Fossil ascomycetes in Quaternary deposits, *Nova Hedwigia* **82**, 313-329

van Geel, B, Buurman, J, Brinkkemper, O, Schlevis, J, Aptroot, A, van Reenen, G B A, and Hakbijl, T, 2003 Environmental reconstruction of a Roman period settlement site in Uitgeest (The Netherlands), with special reference to coprophilous fungi, *J Archaeol Sci* **30**, 873-883

von den Driesch, A , 1976 *A guide to the measurement of animal bones from archaeological sites*, Peabody Museum Press, Cambridge, Massachussets

Walker, P L, Bathurst, R R, Richman, R, Gjerdrum, T, and Andrushko, V A, 2009 The causes of porotic hyperostosis and cribra orbitalia: a reappraisal of the iron-deficiency-anemia hypothesis, *American Journal of Physical Anthropology* **139(2)**, 109-25

Warren, P, 2006 *British native trees: their past and*

present uses, including a guide to burning wood in the home, Wildeye, Norwich

Warry, P, 2006 *Tegulae: manufacture, typology and use in Roman Britain*, BAR Brit Ser **417**, Oxford

Webley, L, Brück, J, and Adams, S, forthcoming The social context of technology: non-ferrous metalworking in prehistoric Britain and Ireland, Prehistoric Society Monograph

Webster, G (ed.), 1976 *Romano-British coarse pottery: a student's guide*, CBA Res Rep **6**, London

Wessex Archaeology, 2002 Southern Electric 33Kv refurbishment Headington to Bicester overhead line, Oxfordshire: archaeological watching brief and excavation, unpublished client report

Westgarth, A, and Carlyle, S, 2008 A Roman settlement at Bicester Park, Bicester, Oxford, *Oxoniensia* **73**, 121-145

Wilkinson, D (ed.), 1992 Oxford Archaeological Unit field manual, unpublished

Williams, H, 2004 Potted histories – cremation, ceramics and social history in early Roman Britain, *Oxford J Archaeol* **23(4)**, 417-27

Wilson, B, 1992 Considerations for the identification of ritual deposits of animal bones in Iron Age pits, *Int J Osteoarchaeol* **2(4)**, 341-349

Wilson, D E, and Reeder, D M, 2005 *Mammal species of the world: a taxonomic and geographic reference*, 3 edn, Johns Hopkins University Press, Baltimore

Wiltshire, P E J, 2006 Palynological analysis and evaluation of vegetation and landscape from Mesolithic to Romano-British times, in J Lewis, *Landscape evolution in the middle Thames Valley: Heathrow Terminal 5 excavations. Vol. 1, Perry Oaks*, Framework Archaeology Monograph **1**, CD-ROM

Wiltshire, P E J, 2008 Palynological analysis of sediment from Roman waterholes, in Booth *et al.* 2008, 337-343

Winder, J, 1980 The marine Mollusca, in P Holdworth (ed.), *Excavations at Melbourne Street, Southampton, 1971-76*, Southampton Archaeological Research Committee Report **1**/CBA Res Rep **3**, London, 121-127

Winder, J M, 2011 *Oyster shells from archaeological sites: a brief illustrated guide to basic processing* http://oystersetcetera.files.wordpress.com/2011/03/oystershellmethodsmanualversion11.pdf

Woodward, A, and Marley, J, 2000 The Iron Age pottery, in P Ellis, G Hughes and L Jones, An Iron Age boundary and settlement features at Slade Farm, Bicester, Oxfordshire: a report on excavations, 1996, *Oxoniensia* **65**, 233-248

Worley, F L, 2008 Taken to the grave: an archaeozoological approach to assessing the role of animals as crematory offerings in first millennium AD Britain, unpublished PhD Thesis, University of Bradford, https://bradscholars.brad.ac.uk/handle/10454/4282

Wright, E, Tecce, S, and Albarella, U, forthcoming The animal bone, in *Allen and Hanbury Roman Roadside Settlement (Ware, Hertfordshire, UK)*, KDK Archaeology Monograph

Young, C J, 1975 The defences of Roman Alchester, *Oxoniensia* **40**, 136-170

Young, C J, 1977 *The Roman pottery industry of the Oxford region*, BAR Brit Ser **43**, Oxford

Index